Without Prejudice: Women in the Law

Gill Gatfield

Brooker's

LEGAL INFORMATION

Published by
Brooker's Ltd
Level 1 Telecom Networks House
68–86 Jervois Quay
PO Box 43
Wellington
New Zealand

ISBN 0-86472-231-1

Publishing Editor: Belinda Hill
Cover illustration by Debe Mansfield

Typeset by Brooker's Ltd, Wellington, New Zealand
Printed by Hutcheson, Bowman & Stewart, Wellington, New Zealand

For Mark

Be just and fear not

Inscription on the New Zealand Law Society's Coat of Arms

Contents

Illustrations

Tables

Tables

In June 1992, when research on this project commenced, three objectives were set:

1. To document the history of women in the law;

2. To explore the nature and extent of sex discrimination and gender bias in the 1990s legal profession; and

3. To provide ideas on future strategies to achieve gender equality.[1]

The breadth of the project demanded a range of primary and secondary research and analysis over three and a half years.

Sex discrimination and gender bias

Throughout the research for and the writing of this book the identification of sex discrimination as defined by law was a primary focus. Unlawful sex discrimination occurs in a work context where one person (or group of persons) has less favourable terms, conditions, opportunities and rewards than another person (or group of persons) by reason of the first person's (or groups') sex. This may occur as a result of explicit prejudice or it may occur inadvertently. The legal concept of discrimination seemed the most appropriate first point of inquiry for this research, for the simple reason that discrimination is prohibited by New Zealand law. How the legal profession and the judiciary measure up against this minimum standard gives a clear indication of how the legal actors are likely to interpret and administer justice.

The second level of research and analysis involved exploring the extent to which gender bias occurs in the legal profession. 'Gender bias' refers to individual instances of sex discrimination which conform to a consistent and clear-cut pattern. 'Gender' refers to the natures of men and women, their roles within families, workplaces and society, and the assumptions and stereotypes about men and women in those roles. Gender bias results where the assumptions and stereotypes, which may appear neutral or even positive, consistently carry an underlying negative meaning or produce a negative outcome for one sex and not the other. For example, the assumption that women are good at dealing with emotional issues appears positive but in practice it has been used to justify the unrelated assumption that women are not equipped to handle difficult business matters. Although men are subjected to the corresponding negative assumption that they are ill-equipped to deal with emotions, this rarely limits the work opportunities or benefits available to them.

Whether relating to intellectual, psychological, physical or social capacity, gendered assumptions and stereotypes have been examined to determine whether they operate to women's detriment in the legal professional workplace.

Gender-biased behaviour and attitudes are rarely explicit. They are often almost invisible, ingrained in the culture and systems which create and support family, work and social arrangements. In effect, gender bias is cultural and systemic discrimination against women.

Throughout this book the phrase 'the gender problem' is used because the problem is about gender and therefore affects men and women. Sex discrimination and gender bias are not, as many in the legal profession believe, 'women's problems' nor are the issues solely 'women's issues'. These problems ultimately belong to the profession.

A national survey

The first major research task was a national survey of women and men lawyers designed to identify the nature and extent of sex discrimination in the legal profession of the 1990s. Research by the Auckland District Law Society in 1981 and 1987 and by the Wellington District Law Society in 1982 demonstrated a pattern of discrimination which was confirmed by more recent anecdotal evidence. However, it was doubted that this would be enough. Too many key decision makers were of the view that in the 'politically correct' 1990s there was no problem with discrimination or, according to a minority, that it happened only in the large law firms in the metropolitan areas. It was also feasible that among the large numbers of women who had entered the profession since 1987 there could be those who might be faring better than their counterparts of the early 1980s.

With the assistance of Alison Gray, the support of the women lawyers' associations, and financial sponsorship from the New Zealand Law Society (NZLS), the Wellington law society, and the Auckland law society, the 1992 national survey 'Women Lawyers in New Zealand' was organised.[2]

The survey was designed to identify how women were faring in the legal profession and to compare their position and experiences on national and regional bases with the position and experiences of men in the profession. In addition, the survey was specifically designed to update two of the three earlier regional studies—the 1982 Wellington law society survey and the 1987 Auckland law society survey. Comparison with those earlier surveys would allow an accurate assessment of whether there had been changes in the position of women and men in the previous five and ten year periods.

In September 1992, questionnaires were sent to all women lawyers in New Zealand who held practising certificates and to 1,386 men lawyers, making a total sample of 2,767. The men lawyers were randomly selected from the practitioner lists of each law society district, in equal numbers to women in that region.

In all, 1,469 lawyers in an even spread across the country voluntarily completed questionnaires, giving a national response rate of 53 percent. Those lawyers represented 24 percent of the total practising profession. This response rate exceeded that obtained by the Auckland law society in its 1987 survey and was considered good by local and international standards.[3]

The national survey provided a wealth of information, including many valuable comments. Although a snapshot of these comments was included in the survey report, several hundred more were collated for this book with Sue Brown's assistance.

Consultation

Following the national survey, a series of consultation meetings was held to discuss gender issues. In some cases my role was as a presenter; on other occasions I attended as an observer.

Of particular value were two large forums held in 1993, one during the New Zealand Law Conference and the other during the inaugural Women's Law Conference. Although both meetings were held in Wellington they were attended by many women from around the country who were working in or otherwise involved with the legal profession. At both meetings the overriding theme was the need to redress gender bias and discrimination in the profession so that women lawyers could get on with the business of being lawyers. For many, freedom from personal discrimination was the precursor to enabling them to advance women's general position at law more effectively.

Other valuable meetings were hosted by the Auckland Women Lawyers Association (AWLA), the Wellington Women Lawyers' Association (WWLA), the Canterbury Women's Legal Association, and the Otago Women Lawyers' Society. At these meetings I was able to hear directly from members of those groups about their concerns regarding women in the law in their district, and their concerns for the future. For cost reasons, meetings with women lawyers outside the main centres were not feasible. Instead, personal contact was made with a range of women lawyers in provincial cities and towns, often with the assistance of the local law society. Also, I was able to attend a meeting of women lawyers' representatives from the fourteen districts hosted by the NZLS in September 1993 to discuss the need for a national coordinating group to address gender issues.

Other professional associations representing particular groups of lawyers in New Zealand were invited to provide information and ideas on any problems or issues faced by their women members. The four Bar associations were consulted (the New Zealand Bar Association, the Criminal Bar Association of New Zealand, the Wellington Criminal Bar Association and the Canterbury Criminal Bar Association), as was the Corporate Lawyers' Association. In each case, their responses were helpful, although they largely followed the theme that there was little concrete evidence about issues of special concern to their women members.

Other organisations representing specific groups of lawyers which were also consulted included: Te Hunga Roia Maori o Aotearoa (the Maori Lawyers' Society), Nga Wahine Ma Roopu (the Maori women lawyers' subgroup), and the Auckland Lesbian and Gay Lawyers' Group.

With regard to Maori women in the law, it was proposed that input be sought from individual Maori women lawyers across the country. In June 1993, Te Hunga Roia Maori o Aotearoa was approached for assistance and guidance.

By October 1993, in discussions with Gina Rudland, then president of Te Hunga Roia Maori o Aotearoa, it was apparent that the position of Maori women lawyers could not be addressed outside the context of Maori-controlled research. Our efforts to meet concerns regarding Maori autonomy over the research and the reporting of findings were unsuccessful. As a result, with real regret, this story is largely monocultural. Initial research uncovered evidence that Maori women lawyers' position and prospects were being impeded by race and sex discrimination.[4] I subsequently heard several strong pleas by individual women that Maori women's position in the legal profession be included in the research, but I was not prepared to do so without the endorsement of Te Hunga Roia Maori o Aotearoa.

With the assistance of Dame Silvia Cartwright (then Chief District Court Judge Cartwright) and in consultation with the women judges, the views of women judges were obtained by way of an anonymous survey in September 1993. Ten of the then eleven women District Court judges conveyed their personal experiences and perceptions of sex discrimination in the legal profession and the courtroom, and their views on the role of women in the judiciary.[5]

Interviews

In addition to consulting with groups representing lawyers, it was important to meet with key members of the profession and with women lawyers in particular.

Throughout 1993 and 1994, I interviewed approximately one hundred people from across the country, in person or by written correspondence or by telephone.

Interviews fell into two categories—those with women lawyers and law students who worked in the legal profession before the 1960s, and those who were representative of a particular group in the 1990s, namely: women lawyers on maternity leave, partners in law firms, women lawyers from ethnic minority groups, women barristers and sole practitioners, law society staff and council members, law lecturers and tutors, women law students and recent graduates, women lawyers working in government, and non-law professionals.

Interviews and exchanges of correspondence with early women lawyers canvassed a range of personal and career issues, including experiences at law school and during legal careers, experience of combining childcare responsibilities with careers, and involvement in women's rights and professional associations. The interviews with the '1990s group' likewise covered personal and career issues, but also invited professional observations and opinions about gender issues and prospects for women in the law.

In one quarter of the interviews, some degree of anonymity was requested and this has been respected. The comment of one recent graduate was typical; asking that her identity be protected she said: 'I have nothing to hide but much to fear.' As a result there are numerous unattributed quotes and comments throughout *Without Prejudice*. This is also the case for respondents to the 1992 national survey and the other surveys, although the relevant survey is identified in each case.

In addition to these formal interviews, I had countless informal discussions with women and men lawyers about the issues raised in this book. Once it became known that this research was under way many colleagues and others with interests in the profession contacted me with their thoughts and experiences. Others answered my questions and provided the information I sought.

Statistics
Meaningful statistics on and about the New Zealand legal profession are rare and what is available is of variable quality.

In putting together the sample for the 1992 national survey, I had already discovered that methods of data collection and collation were inconsistent across the fourteen district law societies. Some of the smaller law societies held only very basic information on practitioners, while others had more sophisticated computerised databases. For some districts, a request to provide a statistical breakdown of the status of women practitioners meant manually identifying each woman, firm by firm. For other districts, the answer involved several cross-tabulations from a print-out of names.

Because the national survey canvassed only those holding practising certificates, it was necessary to undertake further studies to obtain information on the status of women lawyers outside private practice. The State Services Commission was unable to provide information on legally qualified women working in the public sector, and the diverse range of job descriptions and job types meant that official census data would be less than reliable. Eventually, at Margaret Wilson's suggestion, core data on women lawyers working in government was obtained by surveying six government agencies that were known to employ large numbers of legally qualified staff.

Again, while the bar associations provided some helpful data, there was no way of knowing with any certainty how frequently women lawyers were appearing in the courts and at what levels. To provide an insight into the pattern of women lawyers' court appearances, Sue Brown ascertained the gender breakdown of counsel appearing in the Wellington High Court by painstakingly reviewing nearly 250 judgments issued by that court over the period January to August 1993. Wellington was the obvious choice because, unlike other High Courts, it has a policy that women counsel be identified in judgments by their full names.

Other data gathered included the numbers of women and men holding positions on courts, tribunals, commissions, authorities, boards and committees in 1983 and 1993; and the numbers of women and men lawyers holding positions on law society councils from 1993 to 1996.

The primary sources of historical national statistics on the numbers of women and men in the legal profession were the five-yearly censuses of the population. Censuses from 1851 to 1991 were checked for information about women working in the legal profession and about the profession in general. Statistics New Zealand was able to extract more specific information on the age, ethnicity and income of women and men in the profession from the 1981, 1986 and 1991 censuses.

The gender pattern in law student enrolments and law graduate numbers from 1874 to 1992 was obtained from a combination of data in the census, the *Appendices to the Journals of the House of Representatives* (AJHR) and *Education Statistics New Zealand*. Information on law graduate employment and unemployment was obtained from data collected by the New Zealand Vice Chancellors' Committee, the Institute of Professional Legal Studies and the Victoria University of Wellington Careers Advisory Service. This information was updated in 1994 by Joanna Lawrence who also assisted in compiling the bibliography.

Statistics on the numbers of women and men holding practising certificates from 1977 to 1995 and admissions of women and men to the New Zealand Bar from 1979 to 1995 were obtained from the annual reports of the fourteen district law societies to the NZLS. From 1991, information was collected on the numbers of women and men principals, employees, and barristers, giving a more detailed snapshot of the profession.

Sage Consultants Ltd was contracted to help collate these statistics, and in particular to assess whether the drop-out rate of women and men lawyers could be calculated. Using the law societies' admissions and practising certificate data from 1979 to 1993, a mathematical model was developed and estimates of the gender drop-out rate were able to be made.

Other historical records

In addition to the collation of statistics, substantial research was needed to compile the histories of women in the law and to determine the professional environment which early women lawyers encountered.

Official records checked included: Auckland, Wellington, Otago and Canterbury district law society papers, minute books and annual reports; Parliamentary debates on the legal profession from the late 1870s to 1896; archived parliamentary and ministerial papers; major daily newspapers from 1881 to 1897; the High Court Rolls of Admission; and old minutes and other papers of the Women and the Law Research Foundation, AWLA and WWLA.

Other sources referred to included published sources, such as colonial and American law journals; reports of royal commissions on education in 1879 and 1925; back copies of the *New Zealand Law Journal* (NZLJ) and law society newsletters (*LawTalk, Counsel Brief, Canterbury Tales* and *Northern Law News* or their predecessors), and women lawyers' associations' newsletters and pamphlets; university, law school and law firm histories; and all relevant honours papers and theses including published and unpublished biographies on early women lawyers. Of particular value was Angela Beagley's 1993 Otago University history thesis, 'Ladies at law', which included detailed biographies of four early Otago women lawyers.

Biographies

Although Ethel Benjamin, Stella Henderson and Ellen Melville are reasonably well known, other early women lawyers and law graduates have slipped into obscurity. Even finding the names of early women lawyers proved elusive. Fortunately, from admission records and information provided by twelve of the fourteen district law societies, I was able to compile a list of women who were admitted and practised in New Zealand from 1897 to 1959. There are possible omissions from or inaccuracies in this list. The Wanganui and Westland district law societies did not respond to the request for information and a number of the district law societies that did respond pointed out that their records were possibly incomplete.

Using a range of sources, including the women themselves or their family members and colleagues, detailed biographies were completed on most of the women known to have embarked on a legal career between 1897 and 1959. Spanning just over sixty years, those biographies shed considerable light on the experiences of women lawyers and on the profession they entered.

From a sample of forty-three of those early women it was possible to identify and compare their qualifications, connections in the profession, career paths, and marital and family status. The resulting information, compiled with Sue Brown's assistance, enabled the research to move beyond individual stories to more conclusive findings about the careers and lives of our early women lawyers.[6]

Biographical research was also completed on the men lawyers and non-lawyers who, in their capacity as employers or their involvement in the law societies, Parliament and universities, influenced the entry into and participation of women in the profession. In stark contrast with the early women lawyers, these men were readily identifiable and information about their careers, political involvement and even their family lives was more available.

Specific biographical research was undertaken on New Zealand's High Court judges, who in 1993, with one exception, were all men. Again using official sources, but also assisted in some cases by the judges themselves, a statistical profile of High Court judges was compiled. That profile shed considerable light on the personal and professional qualities expected of those who are appointed to the Bench.[7]

Comparative research

With invaluable assistance from Jenny Gibson, research and reports on women lawyers and judges in comparable overseas legal professions were obtained and analysed against the New Zealand findings. Research on the position of women in the legal profession is a burgeoning field internationally. Contact was made with academics and independent researchers as well as those within organisations such as the Canadian Bar Association, the American Bar Association, the New South Wales Law Society, the Law Society of Western Australia, the Australian Law Reform

Commission, the United Kingdom Bar Association, the United Kingdom Law Society and the Lord Chancellor's Office.

Correspondence with these organisations and individuals added greater depth to the official reports and studies. In addition, I was able to interview several women lawyers from Australia, the United States and England when they were visiting New Zealand.

Although the New Zealand legal profession is directly comparable with overseas legal professions, it also shares much in common with other male-dominated New Zealand professions and occupations. Where available, published information on the accountancy, engineering and medical professions, the police force and the corporate sector was obtained and analysed.

Limitations

The breadth of the book's content has meant that inevitably some sources remain unexplored. The history of women in the law generally, and of the lives and careers of individual women, warrants many more years of research. It is a past we have overlooked and are in great danger of losing.

The concerns of lawyers with disabilities or who are Maori, lesbian, gay or members of another ethnic or cultural minority group in the profession, are not the subject of detailed coverage in this book. I chose to concentrate on the larger problems of sex discrimination and gender bias in the hope that the discussion and solutions will benefit all minority groups who suffer discrimination in the legal profession. The position, aspirations and experiences of each of these groups, particularly Maori lawyers, needs comprehensive research and analysis, and I hope that this will be undertaken in the near future.

Future strategies

To a large extent the gender problem revealed in the broader research has dictated the solutions needed. Because the sex discrimination and gender bias evident in the legal profession so clearly occurs within a broad legal, economic, social and political context, the solutions proposed involved addressing that framework. As appropriate, interdisciplinary ideas have been used in developing the overall strategy of change needed to achieve gender equality.

To ensure that my suggestions for the future would meet the problems as understood by those in the profession, I invited ideas and thoughts about future strategies in all the surveys, interviews, meetings and consultations. The many considered responses from people within the profession have been used as a guideline to what is considered appropriate across the range of professional contexts.

The options which have been employed by the law societies, law firms and judiciary to date were examined with a view to identifying what has made them succeed or fail. Different sized law firms and differing resources have been considered, so that the solutions offered are both feasible and constructive.

The strategies proposed, I hope, will be the subject of debate by members of the profession, the judiciary and others with interests in the legal system. I do not purport to know the right way for all law firms, for all law societies and for all decision makers to eliminate sex discrimination and gender bias. However, what I do suggest is a range of ideas which the profession may apply or adapt in a constructive and proactive manner.

I have no doubt that in the next century the legal profession and those in it will face many changes. The aim of this book is to ensure that gender is included in the profession's agenda for change—not as an afterthought, but as a central and fundamental part of that agenda.

Acknowledgements

My thanks go to all those who have contributed to this work over the past four years. In particular, I wish to acknowledge the very able research assistance given at various stages of the project by then law graduates Tanya Thomson, Sue Brown and Joanna Lawrence, all of whom tackled the work with enthusiasm; and by Janice Donaldson who delved through historical material in Christchurch and Lisa Hansen who located material for me in Dunedin. Many others provided information, including Moira Henderson who provided valuable papers and background information on Stella Henderson and Janet Wills who chased material on her grandfather, William Izard. Countless members of the profession and judiciary, law societies and other professional associations also assisted by making time available to meet with me, by providing information, articles and papers, or by completing my questionnaires. I thank you all and hope that this work fairly reflects your input.

My task in locating mostly non-indexed historical material was made that much easier by the helpful advice of librarians and archivists at the Alexander Turnbull Library, Auckland Institute and Museum Library, Hocken Library, Canterbury Museum Library, and the National Archives. Other references were also located by Bethli Wainwright, law librarian at Simpson Grierson, Frances Austin at the Ministry of Women's Affairs, Linda Clark at the Sound Archives, New Zealand Public Radio and by the law librarians at the Victoria University of Wellington law library and the Wellington, Canterbury and Otago High Court libraries. Thanks also to the organisations and people who helped locate illustrative material, often at short notice.

I am most grateful to the New Zealand Law Foundation (NZLF) for the research grant that enabled me to research the history of women lawyers, obtain some research assistance and to concentrate on the writing of the book. The patient confidence in and support for this project shown by the NZLF trustees and by Peter Connor (NZLF President), Judith Potter (NZLF Trustee) and Rae Mazengarb (NZLF Director) in particular, was greatly appreciated.

Thanks also to the Auckland Women Lawyers Association and the Wellington Women Lawyers' Association for their assistance and support.

My heartfelt thanks goes to a group of especially generous and talented colleagues and friends who discussed ideas with me, read and commented on numerous draft papers, checked references or simply took me out for much needed coffee breaks. This group included Jenny Gibson,

Jenny Rouse, Elizabeth Gunn, Mark Jeffries, Christine O'Brien, Sue Brown, Greg Drumm, Ann Else, Margaret Wilson, Hannah Sargisson, Anne Hinton and Marie Koreman. Despite this invaluable input, none of these people can be held responsible for the final content.

While every effort has been made to double check all information within the text, the range of material has meant this has not always been possible.

The staff at Brooker's, particularly the principal editor Belinda Hill, did an excellent and efficient job in producing this book in time for the centenary in 1996.

Last but by no means least, the greatest thanks goes to my family who supported me throughout this project; to my law school buddy, Jenny Gibson and to my partner, Mark Jeffries. Without their support this work could never have been undertaken or completed.

By its very nature, the legal profession is not open to everyone. Professions regulate the criteria for and the process of entry. To enter the legal profession, a prospective member must have a law degree, be at least 21-years-old, have completed a thirteen-week professional studies course, and be approved by a local law society for admission to the Bar. Educational opportunities, career aspirations, access to universities and the costs involved determine who joins the legal profession. Still, law in the 1990s is one of the more popular courses of study in New Zealand.

Law opens doors. A career in law seems to promise opportunities and rewards which would be unimaginable in most other arts-related occupations. The potential income is impressive—with some law firm partners and senior barristers earning more than $500,000 per annum. For those with political aspirations, the law offers practical skills and even a potential route to Parliament. For the community-minded, legal knowledge and training enables practical assistance to be given to people in need. For those with commercial inclinations, law may open the way to appointments on boards, quangos, and commissions. For those seeking to sit in judgment on others, law is the only formal qualification required.

Since the mid-1970s, large numbers of women have joined the men seeking the opportunities and benefits offered by the law. In the mid-1980s women comprised half the students studying law in New Zealand universities, and by the early 1990s women made up half of those gaining admission to the profession. Yet, despite these facts, women law students and lawyers are widely believed to be experiencing fewer opportunities and fewer benefits than their male colleagues. Is the legal profession less 'open' to women than it is to men? If so, why? What, if anything, could be done to change this situation? This book aims to answer these questions.

The past, the present and the future

There are three parts to this book—the past, the present and the future. This reflects the way in which the research was undertaken and, more importantly, it provides a valuable framework for assessing changes in women's status in the legal profession and changes in the profession itself. These developments give a clear indication of where the profession and the women within it are heading.

Part one: the past

Women lawyers have had a largely silent past. With the exception of Ethel Benjamin, the first woman admitted to the Bar, the careers and lives of our early women lawyers are relatively unknown. Official law society and law firm histories make little, if any, reference to the women in the profession. Before the early 1970s, women remained almost invisible in the law journals and law society newsletters.

This history of women in the law demonstrates how women's position and progress in the legal profession has been dictated and shaped by legal, social, economic and political factors predominantly outside women's control.

It is ironic that the first and foremost barrier to women's entry into the legal profession was the law itself. As chapter one explains, from the time of New Zealand's colonisation, the status of women under British common law prevented their participation in public life generally. A career in the legal profession was inconceivable. However, as the colony grew, economic and social changes necessitated the expansion of women's legal rights. Piece by piece the legal limitations on women's opportunities were eroded. Developments in Britain and the United States suggested it would be inevitable that women would seek entry into the New Zealand legal profession. But in 1881, without warning, the New Zealand Parliament changed the law to confirm that there was still a ban on women lawyers.

Chapter two documents the seven attempts made between 1883 and 1896 to change the law to allow women into the legal profession. Unlike debates in other Commonwealth countries, where women lawyers and law students openly fought the law societies and Bar associations in the courts, the New Zealand debates were conducted in Parliament and in the council rooms of the law societies. By the end of 1896 there were two laws enabling women to enter the legal profession.

Few women were expected to take up the new opportunity to enter the law and, as chapter three demonstrates, this prophecy was fulfilled. From 1896 to 1970 women provided a predominantly cheap and expendable labour force for law firms and legal offices. Backed by economic, government and social policies, employers in the profession profited from the low status positions held by women lawyers and law clerks.

While economic policies and other external influences determined women's access to the profession, women also had to contend with the 'old boys' network'. Chapter four describes how women's prospects in the law were enhanced or constrained by their connections in the profession or by the patronage of men lawyers. However, no amount of patronage could alter the fact that these were women in a men's profession. They were socially and morally out of place.

As chapter five describes, from 1896 to at least the late 1970s, assumptions about women's abilities and proper roles were used to limit the terms on which women would be employed, the type of work they would be offered, and the status they would be allowed to have. While this was the prescribed position for women in the profession, many women did not accept that it was just or reasonable. They fought for the expansion of women's rights and, within various women's organisations, they demonstrated their true abilities as lawyers and advocates for justice.

From the early 1960s, as a result of legal, economic and social changes outside its control, the legal profession was unexpectedly inundated with women. Chapter six documents how this change in the gender balance initially resulted in confusion and then in conflict. The previously well-defined and limited career path for women lawyers was challenged as discriminatory and unjust. Sexual harassment was named and defined. Lawyers and judges, law societies and employers took sides. Only a minority of those in the profession advocated change.

Part two: the present

By the mid 1990s, a distinct gender gap in the legal profession remained. As shown in chapter seven, the score card was overwhelmingly in favour of men in the law. Despite the large numbers of women entering the legal profession, women's position overall remained less favourable than men's. The uneven representation of women lawyers and women judges throughout the legal system, the comparatively limited opportunities and poor prospects enjoyed by women lawyers, and the evidence of discrimination, paint a bleak picture of the quality of justice in New Zealand.

Chapters eight, nine and ten explore the three primary explanations for women's position in the legal profession in the 1990s: that merit determines success; that women lawyers are incompatible with men lawyers and men clients; and that women lawyers will ultimately prefer their family responsibilities over their careers. In each case, these explanations bear little resemblance to the reality for most women and for an increasing number of men in the profession. Instead, they have become self-fulfilling prophecies which have stymied the profession's ability to examine and tackle the gender problem.

The majority of employers in the legal profession believe that merit is objectively and fairly determined; as such, it is unquestionably 'gender-free'. Although few employers are willing to state it, the clear implication of this explanation of women lawyers' low status in the profession is that women do not have what it takes to 'make it' in the law. However, as chapter eight demonstrates, in a profession-wide equal employment opportunities (EEO) audit, 'merit' in legal professional decision making is far from being a gender-free concept. On the contrary, direct and indirect sex discrimination influence the decision-making criteria and processes, limiting women lawyers' opportunities in all aspects of the profession: recruitment; work allocation; promotion; pay; partnership; and judicial appointment.

Chapter nine examines the second key factor influencing decision making: 'compatibility'. Instead of being a gender-neutral criterion as claimed, 'compatibility' is revealed as the 1990s mechanism for sustaining the 'old boys' network'. Women lawyers remain professional and social misfits in the predominantly male profession.

Chapter ten explores the myths about women lawyers' choices: that they 'choose' family commitments over their careers and that they 'choose' to leave private practice. Over the past decade, women lawyers have repeatedly expressed their desire to remain within the mainstream profession but have ultimately been left with little choice but to go outside the firms. Their 'choices' to establish their own firms or to work in government or corporates or as sole practitioners and barristers, are often made within the context of private sector career constraints or, in some cases, out of a desire to create 'women-centred', family-friendly ways of practising law.

Chapter eleven examines the ongoing problem of sexual harassment and its effects on women lawyers and their careers. Women lawyers' experiences of sexual harassment are compared with the views of men lawyers—that sexual harassment is exaggerated, that some women like the attention, and that some women just can't take a joke. The nature of the responses from law firms and other employers raises serious questions about when this problem will stop.

The contemporary debate on the need to appoint more women to the judiciary is explored in chapter twelve. Arguments for and against more women judges are examined, as is the process of getting to the Bench. Although many believe that an insufficient number of women with the right experience explains why there are so few women judges, the judicial criteria and appointment practices are shown to play a large part in limiting the numbers of eligible women.

Chapters thirteen and fourteen examine the responses in the 1990s to the problems of sex discrimination and gender bias. As demonstrated in chapter thirteen, law societies and law firms, in general, have had a lot to say about the position and prospects for women in the profession, but have done very little. Women lawyers continue to be the primary protagonists and the primary initiators of change. Chapter fourteen explains how this impasse has come about. Philosophical and practical differences continue to fuel the problem, as has the predominant reactive, ad hoc approach to implementing change. This chapter looks at why more time and more women entering the law schools and the profession will not solve the gender problem.

Part three: the future

The legal profession, and legal businesses in particular, have two choices as to how to respond to the gender problem—continue with the present haphazard approach or solve it and survive.

Chapter fifteen outlines the inevitable outcome of the 'head-in-the-sand' approach—law firms and other employers of lawyers will face increased exposure to discrimination law suits. Women lawyers and law students who experience discrimination have a range of individual and class remedies available to them. In future, they may be more inclined to exercise their rights and enforce these laws on equality.

While legal action may prompt the profession to initiate change, chapter sixteen describes other compelling business and professional arguments in support of eliminating discrimination. Law firms and other employers in the profession need to adapt to meet the needs of changing and increasingly diverse social and work environments. A new business culture is required if the profession is to meet the requirements of clients and serve the needs of a changing workforce. Discrimination and bias are incompatible with these goals. Developments in business management and human resources theories offer more constructive and innovative paths forward and see diversity as a bonus rather than a problem.

Chapter seventeen outlines the practical tools needed to eliminate sex discrimination and to harness the benefits of diversity. Existing policies and practices within law firms and law societies need to be reviewed and a new equity-based approach developed. Equal employment opportunities programmes, harassment procedures, and family-friendly practices are described in this chapter. The law societies, it is argued, have an appropriate role in coordinating, directing, and monitoring the process of change.

How to achieve equal opportunity appointments to the New Zealand Bench is addressed in chapter eighteen. The criteria and the practices of such appointments need to be reassessed. Inadvertent gender bias within the processes for selection and appointment should be eliminated. Likewise, the job itself requires restructuring to ensure all eligible candidates are included in the pool of potential appointees.

Chapter nineteen argues that political scrutiny of the legal profession's response to discrimination and gender bias is long overdue. The government has facilitated and then ignored the private sector's poor compliance with human rights laws and half-hearted attempts to implement EEO programmes. Policy inconsistencies between public and private sector standards on and support for EEO initiatives are examined in this chapter, as are some policies on childcare costs. Proposals for law change are suggested. The objective is not to compromise efficiency or justice, but to give life to those ideals.

Part One

The Past

Chapter One

The Law Against Women Lawyers
1840–1882

I t is ironic that the first and foremost barrier to women's entry into the legal profession in New Zealand was the law itself. As the colony grew, economic and social changes necessitated the expansion of women's legal rights, and piece by piece the legal limitations on women's opportunities were eroded. Just as it appeared that New Zealand women, like their counterparts in Britain and the United States, would seek entry to the legal profession, the New Zealand Parliament changed the law to keep them out.

English common law

A law against women lawyers

The place of women lawyers in New Zealand's legal profession was predefined; they had no place. Among the British exports to New Zealand in the early 1800s was a law which prohibited women from practising law.

The source of this prohibition was the English common law. This law, based on the customs of England, was exported to all the colonies. It eventually formed a uniform legal backbone throughout the English speaking world. It was the task of the judges to discern the common law, and in the case of the law against women lawyers, the accepted authority was a sixteenth century statement from the highest authority—the Chief Justice of England, Lord Edward Coke. He said simply and without elaboration, 'Fems ne poient estre attorneyes' (women cannot be attorneys).[1]

Although Lord Coke referred only to attorneys (the predecessors of solicitors) and not to barristers (who practise in the courts), there was no need for him to elaborate or to explain why the prohibition existed. His statement was simply accepted (as it would be for hundreds of years) as authority for the wholesale exclusion of women from the legal profession. As recently as the late nineteenth century the prohibition on women lawyers was merely one in a range of legal disabilities preventing women from participating in economic and public life.

Women's legal disabilities

The prevailing belief was that women were disabled simply because of their sex. Underpinning this were the legal and economic concepts of marriage.

According to Sir William Blackstone, the eighteenth century English judge and highly regarded academic:

> The husband and wife are one person in law: that is, the very being or existence of the woman is suspended during the marriage, or at least is incorporated and consolidated into that of the husband: under whose wing, protection, and *cover*, she performs every thing.[2]

A woman's legal condition during marriage was therefore described in Law French as her *coverture*. She was known as a *feme-covert*, while her husband was her *baron*, or lord.

The legal consequences of marriage dictated the allocation of roles and functions between men and women in all civil, public and social affairs. As Blackstone pointed out, 'almost all the legal rights, duties, and disabilities' stemmed from the principle of the 'union of person in husband and wife'.[3]

Married women: in legal limbo

This 'union of person' through marriage, carried severe consequences for women. Immediately following the marriage, a husband acquired sole control of any land and personal property owned or leased by his wife, which he could then choose to sell or mortgage, taking all profits.[4] He became liable for all of his wife's debts, including those secured over her property before the marriage. He was required to provide her with the 'necessaries' of life.[5] The only property which a married woman retained was her *'paraphernalia'*, the 'apparel and ornaments suitable to her rank and degree'.[6]

The rights and obligations obtained by men through marriage went beyond the economic sphere. A husband acquired the right to give 'moderate correction' to a disobedient wife. The degree of correction was determined by the severity of the misdemeanour. As Blackstone explained, 'the law thought it reasonable to intrust him with this power of restraining her, by domestic chastisement' because, at law, the husband had to 'answer for her misbehaviour'.[7]

In practical terms, a married woman at the turn of the twentieth century was in a form of legal limbo. She was unable to vote or to stand for public office or Parliament. She was considered 'incompetent' to make a will, incapable of contracting, and generally unable to do any other act which would bind herself or her husband unless her husband consented. If she did try to enter into a contract, it would be void at law.[8]

At common law, a married woman could not be a juror or a judge. She was unable to take court proceedings in her own name without her husband's consent, though where he was unable to appear in court she could do so as his attorney because that implied 'no separation from, but . . . rather a representation of, her lord'.[9]

The laws prescribing women's disabilities were so well entrenched that, when the Pacific was being colonised in the early nineteenth century, British women simply did not expect to have any formal role in the machinery of justice.

On a practical front, even if women had wished to practise law, their legal disabilities directly removed their eligibility to do so. For example, the inability to contract effectively barred women from obtaining legal training. In nineteenth century New Zealand, the primary method of learning the law was by working as a law clerk or a barrister's pupil with a qualified solicitor or barrister for up to five years. This apprenticeship system, known as 'articling', was cemented by a contract between the law clerk and the lawyer—a contract outside the contemplation of a married woman. Making binding contracts on behalf of clients was also an essential part of the lawyer's job, but one that married women were unable to perform.

In essence, at common law married women's legal status equalled that of lunatics, idiots, outlaws, and children.[10] Even companies had greater legal rights and protection than women. From the sixteenth century, companies in England had acquired a separate legal status,[11] a status not enjoyed by a married woman in New Zealand until the end of the nineteenth century.[12]

Unmarried women: more able

Technically, the common law applied only to married women, so theoretically unmarried women were free of the legal disabilities. An unmarried woman, or *feme sole*, could sue and be sued at common law.[13] She could also enter into contracts, own property, and manage her own affairs but, like a married woman, she could not vote.

The reality in colonial New Zealand, though, was that most European women did marry. Single women were in such short supply that new immigrants were urged to bring wives.[14]

Maori women: disabled by stealth

Maori women were not automatically subject to the common law disabilities. Under Maori customary law, women were entitled to own property, to lead their tribes and to participate in decision-making. In theory, Maori customary law survived conquest, discovery or cession, and was to be upheld at common law.[15] For this reason, at least in the early years of colonisation, Maori women were able to retain their own legal status, enjoying greater rights than British women. So, for example, when Queen Victoria's representatives traversed the country obtaining signatories to the 1840 Treaty of Waitangi, the common law restriction on women signing deeds and contracts was overlooked in some cases. At least nine Maori women signed the Treaty on behalf of their people, an act which in itself confirmed the customary legal status and mana of Maori women, but one which presented difficulties for the Queen's representatives.[16]

Maori women also conducted cases before the Native Land Court, taking the roles of advocates on behalf of their tribes. From the mid to late 1870s, and continuing for over thirty years, one such woman, Airini Tonore, appeared in the Native Land Court for Ngati Kahungungu of Hawke's Bay. She was widely known to have a detailed working knowledge of the law and legal procedures.[17] In 1894, Hone Heke, the member of Parliament for the Northern Maori electorate, reported in Parliament that he had known several Maori women who had conducted cases before the Native Land Court. In his view: 'that was a very difficult thing to do; and several had been very successful, and were very able.'[18]

While Maori women appearing in the Native Land Court may have been tolerated by British lawyers, they constituted no threat to the legal profession. For one thing, they represented their people, not the fee-paying government agents and settlers. In the unlikely event that the Maori women advocates tried to seek formal admission to the colonial legal profession they, like their English counterparts, would have been prevented by the common law disability. Under the law, it was sex, not race, that determined entry to the legal profession.

In a piecemeal and inconsistent manner, English law eventually supplanted Maori customary law and many of the common law disabilities were applied to Maori women.[19] In 1881, Wellington politician George Waterhouse pointed out in Parliament that the common law restrictions on women's property-owning rights were discouraging Maori women from marrying. In fact, he said: 'In Hawke's Bay ... large numbers of Maori women absolutely refused to enter into the marriage state, because by doing so the land, which was under Crown grant, became subject to European law, and they were deprived of it.'[20]

Seven years later, in 1888, the Chief Justice of New Zealand, Justice Prendergast, ruled that all marriages, including those between 'natives', were governed by the common law and had been since the first Marriage Ordinance in 1842.[21] By the late nineteenth century, Maori women in the eyes of the British law were no better off than their European counterparts.

Inroads into the common law

Equity softens the law

Inevitably, those with substantial property interests sought to bypass the common law disabilities. Concerned fathers made arrangements for their daughters' property to be held in trust.[22] It was common for the would-be husband of a propertied woman to enter a settlement contract agreeing to pay his wife a life-time income.[23]

Marriage settlements cut across the intentions of the common law and were sometimes unpopular with men who regarded their wives' wealth as theirs to control. In some cases, where a marriage broke down, the husband would seek to enforce the common law, asking the courts to set aside the contract.[24] For women in this position, the solution was found in a strand of law known as equity.

Originally administered in the English Courts of Chancery, equity was developed by the judges specifically 'to abate the rigour of the common law'.[25] From its establishment in 1860, the New Zealand Supreme Court had jurisdiction to apply equity and, although very few cases were reported, it was accepted that the rules of equity provided an exception to women's legal incapacities.

Thanks to equity, by the middle of the nineteenth century, married women from the propertied classes, in certain circumstances, could retain title to their separate estates and sell or mortgage property at their pleasure.[26] However, equity would not always intervene in the injustice produced by the common law,[27] nor would it help working-class women who had limited access to legal advice and were left to fare as best they could.

Social and economic necessity: desertion as a plus!

As the colony expanded, the common law position on women and property became hard to justify. Women who emigrated to New Zealand were expected to be useful and active in the business of colonisation.[28] Even middle-class women had greater responsibilities in the home—domestic servants being in short supply—and in the community, setting up and running schools, fundraising for charities and helping in their husbands' businesses. By 1878, there were more than one thousand women teachers and nearly five thousand women working in industrial occupations.[29]

Meanwhile, married men were failing to keep their side of the common law bargain. Instead of providing the 'necessaries of life', some colonial husbands were deserting their wives. Lured by goldfields, adventure, and the promise of a quick fortune, men would leave their wives and children unsupported.[30] Adding insult to injury, they could reappear, penniless, months or even years later, and resume control of the matrimonial property. Even worse, if the husbands did not return, creditors could claim repayment of their debts from money earned by their deserted wives.

While the churches and fledgling charities tried to pick up the pieces, the State was faced with an ever increasing number of destitute women and children.[31] Not only were married women denied the security of their income or property post-desertion, they were limited in their ability to borrow money. Women were regarded as bad risks for moneylenders and businesses because they were unable to enter into binding contracts. The law was proving to be a thorn in the side of the young colony's progress.

By 1860, the New Zealand Parliament was moved to legislate. Following England's lead, New Zealand passed the Married Women's Property Protection Act, the first legislative erosion of the common law disabilities. The Act gave to a married woman, during the period of desertion, the rights and obligations of an unmarried woman, or *feme sole*. A deserted wife was specifically empowered to take court action against her husband for the return of property, to enter contracts, and to sue and be sued.[32] Thus, the Act gave protection to a woman against her husband, and it enabled her to contract with vendors and moneylenders.

But the new law was little used. Desertion carried a social stigma which kept many eligible women from pursuing their rights.[33] In the meantime, the conditions giving rise to married women's economic strife continued to escalate. By 1870, Parliament again considered it 'expedient' to review the law on married women's property, this time expanding the grounds of relief to circumstances beyond legal desertion.[34]

Certainly Parliament was not intending to liberate married women by making major inroads into the common law disabilities. William Fox, then Premier of New Zealand, described the 1870 extension of *feme sole* rights as providing only a 'small measure of protection, in extreme cases', something of 'great importance and utility' for the country.[35] Women themselves, it was conceded, had claimed much greater rights. Parliament was not yet inclined to heed them.[36]

International inroads: 1867–1881

New Zealand was not the only country reflecting on women's legal status in the latter part of the nineteenth century. In England and the United States women's position at law was also under scrutiny. Developments in those countries would prove to be influential in the New Zealand context. In many cases, it was the right to vote which attracted most attention.

Looking back, some of the ensuing parliamentary debates and court decisions seem ridiculous. Often the legal arguments and sleights of hand were unjust and remarkably shallow. In other cases, the logic of the lawyers and judges seems absurd or humorous. Inevitably, many women had doors of opportunity slammed shut in their faces during the next half century of pantomime.

England: are women men?

The English Parliament first debated in 1867 whether propertied women should be entitled to vote. Pro-suffrage campaigner and politician John Stuart Mill proposed that, by replacing the word 'man' in the voting laws with the word 'person', propertied women be granted the vote.[37] Mill's proposal failed and the law was passed with the word 'man' intact. However, another pro-suffrage politician pointed out that the law did not need to be changed—the Interpretation Act said that in the laws made by Parliament the word 'man included all females' and so women already had the vote.[38]

A year later, the question came before the English judges in the case of *Chorlton v Lings*.[39] Mary Abbott, an unmarried woman, had claimed the right to vote in the Manchester Borough elections on the ground that the electoral law passed in 1867 applied to every 'man' and, as a result of the Interpretation Act, 'man' included 'woman'.[40] The outcome of her case would determine the legal rights of over five thousand women who had tried to register for the vote.

Counsel for the women voters argued that, 'If the legislature had intended to exclude women from the new franchise, they might have used the words "male person" ', as was done in an earlier, extant electoral Act.[41] In other words, he claimed that the word 'man' was defined to include women and by using it Parliament did not mean to exclude women.

The judges would have no bar of this argument. The Chief Justice thought it 'perfectly clear' that women were not entitled to the vote, citing legislation enacted earlier that same year which did apply to women, as demonstrated by the express use of the words 'women' and 'females'. The judges relied on the definition of 'man' in the Interpretation Act which included woman *'unless the contrary is expressly provided'*. By reading the two electoral Acts together, all four judges found that Parliament had 'expressly' intended that only men could vote.[42] As the Chief Justice saw it: 'If so important an alteration of the personal qualification was intended to be made as to extend the franchise to women . . . I can hardly suppose that the legislature would have made it by using the term "man".'[43]

In any case, according to the judges, Mary Abbot and the other women were handicapped by the lack of a legal precedent showing women voting or any court decision in favour of a woman's right to vote. At the end of the day, despite what the legislation said, the judges confirmed that what had been the law raised a strong presumption of what the law was.[44]

New Zealand: is a woman a man, a person, or neither?

The arguments put by John Stuart Mill in the English Parliament and by counsel for the women voters in *Chorlton v Lings* had implications in New Zealand. Previous erosion of women's common law disabilities in New Zealand had been in equity or through economic and social necessity. Now, a new focus was placed on the meaning of the words in laws passed by Parliament. The New Zealand Interpretation Act would be the first target.

The 1858 New Zealand Interpretation Act definition of 'man' differed in one vital respect from the definition in the English law. It simply said: 'Words importing the masculine gender only shall include females.' There was no safety net proviso.[45] If the British pro-suffrage arguments were applied it would mean that where Parliament had made laws using only the word 'man', those laws would apply to women.

There was, however, no opportunity for this challenge to be made in New Zealand. In 1868, just days before the English court gave its decision in *Chorlton v Lings*, the New Zealand Parliament passed a new Interpretation Act which contained the critical proviso that 'man' would include woman *'unless the contrary . . . is expressly provided'*.[46] By bringing the New Zealand law in line with that of England, the colonial Parliament ensured that the reasoning used by the judges in *Chorlton v Lings* would apply here, should the question arise.[47]

Ten years passed before the New Zealand Parliament had to decide whether, at law, women were people. Throughout the 1878 and 1879 debates on electoral bills, pro-suffrage politicians tried to extend the vote to women by simply having the word 'person' substituted for the word 'man'. At least seven times during 1879 the words 'person' and 'man' yo-yoed in and out of the relevant bill.[48]

A new attempt at women's suffrage began in 1880,[49] followed by various measures aimed at improving women's position at law.[50] Most important among these was another Married Women's Property Protection Bill, introduced—and promptly discarded—in 1874, which proposed to grant to all married women the rights of a *feme sole* in relation to property and income.

By the early 1880s, New Zealand women had not advanced very far in their legal standing. Women were 'men' in some cases but they were not men in relation to voting and other important rights. They were fortunate in that they were arguably 'persons', but only men had legal rights. Needless to say, the vote stayed outside women's reach, as did the legal rights to control their economic wellbeing.

The more specific issue of women practising law started to gain some momentum around this time. Many of the early initiatives occurred overseas.

United States: can women be lawyers?

On the other side of the Pacific Ocean, there was sustained agitation by American women for the vote, for the end to the common law disabilities and for the right to practise law. Suffragists, like Susan B Anthony who was arrested for the crime of voting, took to soapboxes across the country, passionately decrying women's common law disabilities.[51]

In America, lawyers were trained predominantly by the universities and women had gained access to some law schools, particularly in the mid-West.[52] Having obtained law degrees, however, they still had to apply to the local Bar association for admission to the profession. Myra Bradwell and Lavinia Goodell went to court to contest their exclusion from the legal profession.[53] New Zealand lawyers leafing through the *Albany Law Journal* in 1875 would also have read that Carrie Burnham had sued the Pennsylvania Bar, seeking US$200,000 damages for their exclusion of her from the law admission examinations.[54]

Some American women successfully gained access to the legal profession at local levels, but when they applied for licences to practise in the state Supreme Courts, the higher courts ruled that women could not be lawyers on the basis of women's common law disabilities. In 1872, the Supreme Court of Illinois relied on a married woman's contractual inability as the ground for refusing to grant a licence to Mrs Myra Bradwell, one of the first American women to apply to practise law. The decision was confirmed by the highest appeal court, the United States Supreme Court.[55]

Women thought they had countered this problem when Lavinia Goodell, a single woman, applied for admission to the Bar of the Wisconsin Supreme Court. The Chief Justice of that court recognised that '[t]he cruel chances of life' meant that some women might need employment. But, he said, 'it is public policy to provide for the sex, not for its superfluous members'.[56] Unmarried women, according to one Supreme Court judge, were 'exceptions to the general rule'. His view, shared by many at the time, was that:

> The paramount destiny and mission of women are to fulfil the noble and benign offices of wife and mother. This is the law of the Creator. And the rules of civil society must be adapted to the general constitution of things, and cannot be based upon exceptional cases.[57]

Lavinia Goodell's application failed.

But the women's campaign could not be stopped by resistance from the Bar associations and the higher courts. Their opposition served only to fuel women's indignation and to increase male support for their cause.[58] Frustrated by the lack of progress through the courts, women began to agitate for legislative action, promoting bills allowing women to practise law. They were successful in many states, even though some courts questioned the legislation, preferring to have full control over admission themselves, 'as a necessary and inherent part of their powers'.[59] By February 1879, the United States Senate passed 'An Act to Relieve Certain Legal Disabilities of Women' and allowed women to be admitted to practise law at federal court level.[60]

England: can women be lawyers?

At the same time, in England, women's exclusion from the legal profession was hitting the headlines. The *Solicitors' Journal*, popular among colonial lawyers, reported:

> Almost simultaneously with the request by a young lady to be examined at the preliminary examination for solicitors, an application in writing from another lady has been received at one of the Inns of Court with reference to the preliminaries for call to the bar.

The Law Society and the Inns of Court dealt with both in the same manner—they disallowed women.[61]

These rulings were not wholeheartedly embraced. According to the *Solicitors' Journal*, the Law Society's action was that of an 'ungallant body',[62] while another article in the journal, 'The lady candidate', warned that the law society's decision would stand only 'until it shall be thought advisable, by those interested in seeing women enabled to take part in any suitable branch of the legal profession, to test the question by taking steps to obtain judicial opinion'. It was further noted by the same correspondent that an association had been formed recently to promote legal education for women and secure their access to the profession.[63]

By April 1880, a debate organised by the United Law Students' Society on the decisions of the law society and the Inns of Court to exclude women from legal practice 'excited the keenest interest'. The team arguing against the decisions won by two votes.[64] The professional associations, however, remained unmoved.

New Zealand: 1880–1882

Changing laws on women

For women aspiring to a legal career, the 'radical' proposals of the Married Women's Property Protection Bill 1881 (which proposed to grant to all married women the rights of a *feme sole* in relation to property and income) were a major leap forward.[65] In addition to declaring married women 'capable of entering into . . . any contract', the bill allowed a married woman to carry on a trade or business separately from her husband. She would be entitled to keep 'any wages, earnings, money, and property gained or acquired by her in any employment, trade, or occupation' she engaged in or conducted.[66]

By 1881, the idea of the law encouraging women to pursue careers, while not warmly received by conservatives, was no longer perceived as absurd.[67] In 1881, 25 percent of people working in professional occupations were women.[68] Three women had graduated from the University of New Zealand with BAs.[69] These degrees satisfied half the academic requirements for entry into the legal profession.[70] As in England, it would take only one woman seeking a position as a law clerk or applying to sit the professional examinations to bring the issue to the fore.

Women can be persons but not lawyers

On 10 August 1881, the prospect of women lawyers was raised for the first time in the New Zealand House of Representatives. The Law Practitioners Bill, introduced by Sir George Grey, provided that 'every person' over the age of 21 years, of good character, and who passed the required examinations, would be entitled to be admitted as a barrister and solicitor.[71]

Grey had no intention of including women in his proposal but William Downie Stewart, the member of Parliament for Otago and a highly regarded lawyer, stated what had by then become obvious—that 'person' might include 'women': 'As the Bill was drafted it would appear that under it women would be entitled to be admitted to the Bar.' As a result, he supposed the profession would be 'deluged with young and old lady practitioners'.[72] Without elaborating, Stewart proposed that the bill be amended, 'limiting the provisions to male persons only'.[73]

As Stewart was possibly aware, there was nothing new in the words 'every person' in the bill. That phrase was simply copied from the 1861 law governing admission to the profession.[74] But, by 1881, there was more than a shadow of legal doubt that a law referring to 'persons' would be enough to exclude women. To be on the safe side, a clear statement was needed to demonstrate that Parliament did in fact intend that there still be a law against women being lawyers.

The law societies: gatekeeping for the profession

William Downie Stewart's 1881 proposal to change the law and ensure that only men could be lawyers was made on behalf of the profession's official representatives—the Auckland, Wellington, Canterbury, and Otago district law societies. Alerted to the Law Practitioners Bill by telegrams from the Wellington District Law Society, the Canterbury, Otago, and Auckland societies called urgent meetings.[75] Although the minutes contained no reference to discussion on the question of women lawyers, the law societies' spokesperson, Stewart, had told Parliament that the societies had given the Law Practitioners Bill 'very full consideration' and that they were 'unanimous in their disapproval of it'.[76]

The submission by the New Zealand law societies in 1881 dispensed with only one of many problems confronting the profession. The 1881 Law Practitioners Bill was part of a string of measures sponsored by Sir George Grey, a backbencher who had earlier been colonial Governor and then Premier of New Zealand.[77] A declared liberal, Grey had many hobby-horses, including 'throwing open' the New Zealand legal profession.[78] He firmly believed the law and the profession had been formed to suit the interests of a few privileged men rather than the colony as a whole. In his view, New Zealand would do better to take the less regulated American profession as its model.[79]

Grey had called the 1881 Law Practitioners Bill a 'charter of intellectual freedom'. If the bill were passed, he envisaged 'hundreds of young men' taking up legal study. The objective was not that they would all succeed and go on to practise the law, his motive was broader—he sought to 'create a field for the talent of every man, and in that way to raise up a race of young men who would be superior to what was to be seen in most countries'.[80]

Grey proposed to liberalise entry by abolishing three of the basic entry criteria: the requirement for law clerks to serve a period of articles, the general knowledge exam sat by law clerks, and the £40 fee paid on admission to the Bar. Aspiring lawyers would need only to pass an exam in law and meet the test of 'good character'.[81]

Maintaining status by restricting entry

For the colony's infant legal profession, the bill signalled disaster. The criteria for entry, including the standard of education required, were integral to the status, and hence the wealth, of the profession. Elimination of the general knowledge exam, set and marked by the then Supreme Court judges, was antithetical to the law being 'a learned profession'. These examinations meant that candidates had to be conversant in Latin and Greek, subjects taught largely to the privileged classes.[82] Only a century earlier, the English legal profession had struggled to free itself from an inferior reputation, to climb the social ladder and acquire the status of a respected occupation.[83] The New Zealand profession aspired to the same heights. Grey's bill was wildly inconsistent with that aim.

Quite apart from the question of women lawyers, the New Zealand legal profession was highly sensitive to competition. It was overcrowding and unemployment in the English profession which had induced many lawyers, along with other middle-class professionals, to emigrate to the colonies in the first place.[84] The colonies had opened 'an ever widening field of employment' and, even better, 'a way to speedy success' for the lawyer with the 'right stuff'.[85]

Ensuring the continued wealth of the young profession was of foremost concern. Inroads into the lawyers' monopoly over conveyancing, in particular, were promptly blocked by the district law societies which had been formed, in part, for that purpose.[86] But by 1881 when the prospect of women contenders was raised, the prosperity of the legal profession seemed less than assured. Having more than doubled in size since 1871, the profession was facing an influx of law students graduating from the new university law courses.[87] Compounding the problems were Grey's incessant attempts to ease the entry criteria. New Zealand lawyers faced the prospect of being relatively underqualified and ineligible to practise elsewhere.

They need not have worried. Parliament in the early 1880s was too conservative to consider revolutionising the legal profession seriously. New Zealand's trade and debt links with Britain required compatibility in laws and legal processes—an American-type profession was inconceivable. In addition, the legal profession was considered among the 'civilising influences' in the still raw colony.[88] Civilisation meant colonial success.

Politics in this period revolved around land values and personal allegiances. Politicians were a homogeneous group—mostly wealthy landowners, merchants, and professional men.[89] Lawyers, unlike women, were well placed in the political arena. The profession had its own political 'head' and 'representative' in government—the Attorney-General. In 1876, the Attorney-General became a member of Cabinet, enabling him to advance the profession's interests directly. This innovation, and the presence of nine or ten lawyers in the House, prompted the editor of the *New Zealand Jurist* to hope there was now 'at least a prospect of the legal profession "coming to the front" '.[90]

The profession did indeed retain its influence in Parliament. There was little option. Being among the few educated men, lawyers were clear contenders for political office, often taking top posts.[91] By 1891, the annual conference of the law societies was held in Wellington during the parliamentary session because 'such a large number of the profession are members of the House of Representatives'.[92]

Parliament agrees: women cannot be lawyers

The parliamentary debate on women lawyers on 10 August 1881 lasted no more than ten minutes. Dr Wallis, the strident pro-suffrage campaigner, advocated opening all the professions to women.[93] But Sir George Grey typified the general response when he declared that he had 'no hope' of giving effect to the notion of women lawyers: 'In order to gratify the wish of what he believed to be a majority of the members of the House, he would, in Committee, introduce the word "male" before the word "person".'[94]

The motion was passed, but by a margin of only one vote.[95] After the vote was taken, Frederick Whitaker, a lawyer and the son of the Attorney-General, moved that the change to the words 'male person' be reconsidered. Unlike the first vote, this motion was lost by a clear majority—several of those who had voted in favour of women lawyers had left the House.[96]

After the vote was lost, Frederick Whitaker sounded a warning which the New Zealand Parliament ignored at its peril:

> Considering the number of motions and bills they had had on the Order Paper to give voting power to women, it was an important question also whether they should not, as in America and other places, admit women to practise at the Bar.[97]

By 1881, through legislation or court decision, women had been admitted to the Bars of fourteen American states.[98]

The 1881 New Zealand bill was not passed—for reasons unrelated to the exclusion of women—but the words 'male person' resurfaced in subsequent bills.[99] Finally, on 15 September 1882, a new Law Practitioners Act required that a solicitor or a barrister of the Supreme Court of New Zealand be a male person only.

In the hundreds of years since Lord Coke's proclamation, women's legal progress and opportunities had been stifled. Opportunities were denied through perceived legal or moral disabilities, legal trickery dressed up as 'statutory interpretation', and vested interests of the law societies and Parliament. In New Zealand, women, for legal purposes, were sometimes men and sometimes persons, but never were they lawyers.

Chapter Two

The Law Allowing Women Lawyers
1883–1896

In New Zealand, unlike in England and the United States, the decision to confirm women's exclusion from the legal profession apparently passed unnoticed. There was no media coverage, no articles in the law journals, and no letters of support or complaint to the law societies. By all accounts, it was a non-event—except for the women it would eventually affect.

The passage of a law allowing women access to the legal profession would eventually be won, but the battle was protracted and confused. The politicians involved in the debates expended much time and energy arguing about the *process* for including women's right to practise law within the statutes, rather than debating the substance of the matter. The struggle involved seven Bills and was not to be won for another fifteen years.

Lady lawyers: a joke

In this era before party politics, politicians had free reign to voice their views on women's rights. At best this translated into banter, and, at worst, contempt. The idea of the 'lady lawyer', when raised in Parliament, was a useful example of how bad things might get in the profession if Sir George Grey's reforms were implemented.

On two occasions in the early 1880s, senior politicians proposed that reforms affecting entry to the profession be extended to include women.[1] Neither politician was serious, and both were using the prospect of women lawyers as an argument against the Bill under discussion. During the debates on one of these proposals, another member of the House interjected, 'We have already too many women lawyers'—a comment aimed at the profession.[2]

Politicians were not oblivious to women's legal and civil rights, but the initial emphasis was firmly on the franchise. The connection between the franchise and women's wider common law disabilities had not yet been made. For this reason, politicians such as Sir William Fox and Sir George

Grey who advocated women's suffrage voted quite happily against women lawyers. This hypocrisy did not go unnoticed. In 1884, Colonel Trimble, a politician from Taranaki, criticised one of Grey's law practitioners Bills for benefiting 'male persons' only. He was 'quite astonished' that Grey, an avid supporter of women's suffrage, aimed to open 'the whole career of the Bar' while at the same time shutting out 'half the human race'.[3] Trimble's disquiet, however, did not motivate him, or any other politician, to propose that the words be changed.

By 1885, New Zealand had entered what would become known as the Long Depression. For the next ten years, the legal profession could ill afford an influx of new admissions, regardless of sex. The depression brought unprecedented hardship to the young colony with business stagnation and high unemployment.[4] Law firms inevitably suffered the effects.[5] Although there was plenty of legal work, there was little money to pay for it.[6] Astute lawyers converted their practices from conveyancing to debt recovery and bankruptcies.[7] Many others found themselves unable to make a living.[8]

From the beginning of the depression it seemed that the professions, more than other occupations, were opposing women on the grounds of competition. At the 1885 Otago University graduation ceremony, Dr John Mainwaring Brown LLM, barrister and professor at Otago University and an advocate of higher education for women, said:

> [opposition to professional women was coming] from those who dread their competition where competition is already keen enough ... There are many industrial occupations open to [women], but following the example of the learned, the artisan objects to a woman competing with him. Woman has to encounter the same difficulty in nearly every direction.[9]

If women invaded the legal profession, they would be expected to compete for law clerk positions and in doing so would deny promising young men the opportunity to take articles—the main route to professional qualification at that time. Even worse, perhaps, it was widely believed that women's employment in the professions would lower the overall rate of remuneration.[10] Despite the efforts of women suffragists,[11] women law clerks could be employed to do the same work as male clerks but for lower rates of pay.[12] Employers looking to cut costs would have an easy choice—employ women or pay men less.

Although the Women's Christian Temperance Union, founded in 1895, sought to advance women's suffrage, there was no parallel campaign to increase women's opportunities within the professions. Many in the Women's Christian Temperance Union were motivated by a determination to achieve 'social purity', not sexual equality.[13] They, and others campaigning for women's franchise, saw the vote as enabling women to safeguard 'the morality of the colony and the sanctity of the family', not to invade the legal profession.[14]

A new political climate for women's rights

In 1890, the election of a Liberal Government heralded a new political climate. For the first time in New Zealand a discernible political party with a clear reformist agenda was in government. Outwardly, the Liberal Government professed support for women's suffrage.[15] It also appeared more inclined to take the prospect of women lawyers seriously.

First challenge to women's exclusion from the profession: 1891

On 20 August 1891, only a year after the election, the first attack on women's exclusion from the legal profession took place. Appropriately, the focus of the attack was another of Sir George Grey's law practitioners Bills, which still aimed to throw open the legal profession to more 'male persons'.

Robert Thompson, the member of Parliament for the Marsden electorate and a strong supporter of women's suffrage, proposed that the word 'male' be struck out.[16] He argued that Parliament was likely to 'confer the franchise on the ladies'—a direct reference to the heated debates over the previous two months on Bills giving women the vote.[17] Thompson said there was 'no reason' why women should be kept out of the legal profession and, therefore, there could be 'no desire' on the part of Grey to exclude them.[18] Richard Taylor, a Christchurch politician, endorsed Thompson's proposal. He was 'astounded' that politicians 'who would give the ladies the franchise would debar them from exercising their privileges when they got a vote'.[19]

Connecting women's access to the legal profession with women's suffrage was a timely move. In August 1891, politicians were under scrutiny from a growing number of articulate and well-connected women. The *Otago Daily Times* reported that women, although banned from the Public Gallery, were crowding the Ladies Gallery in Parliament 'to excess'.[20] From this vantage point, women were observing the proceedings and sending notes to erring politicians. On one occasion, sixty-eight occupants of the Ladies Gallery advised that they 'utterly repudiated' one politician's view that women regarded the suffrage 'with indifference'.[21] Even members of the House of Representatives who were averse to women's suffrage were hedging their bets. Few members were game to oppose women's suffrage openly in case the reform succeeded and they faced women voters at the polls.

Predictably, no one was brave enough to speak against the motion to include women lawyers in the Bill. Without a vote, the word 'male' was dropped.[22] Sensitivities were running high. William Buckland, an Auckland politician, hastened to add for the record, that in voting against the Bill in its entirety he had not voted out of any objection to the inclusion of women. He said, if the Bill became law, he 'would be very glad that the door to the profession should be open to women as well as to men'.[23]

At the very moment that the 1891 Law Practitioners Bill was passed by the House of Representatives, Parliament Buildings was jolted by one of the severest earthquakes felt in Wellington for years. Buckland commented that it was 'an omen of the enormity of the Bill they were passing'.[24]

For the first time, the question of women lawyers was the subject of press coverage. The *Otago Daily Times* and the *Press*, in identical articles announced, that a Bill allowing women to practise in the courts of law had passed the Lower House.[25] The *New Zealand Herald*, in a column entitled 'Women as barristers', reported that Thompson, the main advocate of the amendment, had been thanked personally by one of the lawyers in the House, who considered the proposal 'a very wise and beneficial one'.[26]

Rumours abounded, however, that the whole thing was a joke. Sir George Grey was reported to have accepted the inclusion of women lawyers in the Bill 'with a light heart'.[27] Even Thompson was said to be joking. But the *Otago Daily Times* informed its readers that Thompson was serious.[28] Likewise, the *New Zealand Herald* reported that, contrary to the 'ungallant' claims of some members, 'Mr Thompson says he was in real earnest, and repudiates any thought of joking'.[29]

Throughout the fuss, the law societies remained conspicuously silent. The Auckland, Canterbury, Wellington and Otago district law societies' minute books contain no records of discussions on the clause relating to women lawyers. As it had previously, the Otago law society objected to the broader changes proposed by the Bill, this time asking William Downie Stewart to obtain a compromise when the Bill went before the Legislative Council.[30]

For the Bill to become law, it needed the concurrence of the Legislative Council (also known as the Upper House), whose accepted role was to revise legislation, usually in accordance with the government's direction.[31] Some had predicted that the inclusion of women lawyers would 'imperil the Bill' in the Legislative Council.[32] An unattributed article in the *Press* urged the Legislative Council to use its ultimate weapon and reject the Bill. The author claimed that the wider reforms in the Bill were 'calculated to lower the status of the legal profession', including a 'ridiculous' measure allowing women to be lawyers.[33]

As it happened, the 1891 Law Practitioners Bill started out on the wrong foot in the Legislative Council. It was the usual practice for a member of the House of Representatives to arrange for a member of the Upper House to sponsor the Bill—not an easy task for an unpopular private member's Bill such as this. When the Law Practitioners Bill was called for its first reading, the Speaker asked who was in charge of the

Bill. The reply, it was reported, was 'a slight titter which ran round the Council Chamber and was followed by an ominous silence'.[34] The *New Zealand Herald* speculated that Sir George Grey 'either forgot to ask some Councillor to take charge of his pet measures or else deliberately abstained from doing so'.[35]

On 10 September 1891, a sponsor was found. John Wilson, from Hawke's Bay, agreed to present the Bill to the Legislative Council, but without the clause admitting women. Keen to dissociate himself from that proposal, he told the council he had 'no intention—in fact, [he] could not dream at the present time—of asking the Council for one moment to admit women to practise in the Courts'. The proposal was, to his mind, 'quite impossible'.[36] With no further comment, the clause which would allow women into the legal profession was dropped.

The defeated women lawyers clause was in good company. That same day, the Legislative Council also threw out the Female Suffrage Bill. The council, unlike the House of Representatives, viewed the strengthening political position of women with indifference. These men, with their life appointments to the Legislative Council, held the safest political seats in the country.[37] They would never face women at the polls.

Second challenge to women's exclusion from the profession: 1894

Over the next two years women's exclusion from the legal profession took a back seat in Parliament. All efforts by women's supporters were aimed at obtaining the franchise for women. In September 1893 an Act allowing female suffrage was passed—despite an eleventh-hour campaign to strangle the measure.[38] But only ten months after women's franchise was secured, the question of women lawyers was back on the political agenda, again piggy-backed on another Law Practitioners Bill.[39] For the first time, however, the Bill, when introduced, already contained a specific clause allowing women lawyers. This was achieved by deleting the word 'male' from the phrase 'male person'.[40]

On 14 August 1894, the Canterbury law society council held a meeting on the Bill. Without recording any discussion or reasons, the council resolved that it 'disapproved' of the clause omitting the word 'male' from the Act.[41]

The Canterbury law society was keen to see this and other aspects of the Bill defeated. It resolved to send its list of objections to John Joyce, the member of Parliament for the Lyttelton electorate, requesting 'his help as a member of this society in giving effect to the Council's views'.[42] But it was too late. The next day, in Grey's absence, his colleague George Hutchison, a practising lawyer, sponsored the second reading of the Bill in the House.

The admission of women, according to Hutchison, was 'in keeping with the genius of the age'.[43] Six members of the House spoke in favour of women lawyers, including Wellington lawyer F H D Bell, one-time Wellington law society president. As was the case in 1891, no one spoke against the admission of women. On 15 August 1894, without a vote on the specific clause concerning gender, the Bill passed its second reading.

Five days later, the Canterbury law society wrote to Joyce. It acknowledged that it had 'lost the opportunity of being heard upon the principle' of the Bill, and asked him if he could, in Committee, 'do something in the direction of the Council's views'.[44] Whether Joyce succeeded is unknown. The Bill, originally scheduled for a third reading on 5 September, simply 'lapsed' and disappeared from the Order Paper.[45]

The Canterbury law society council was not unanimous in its opposition to women lawyers. One council member, William Izard, a local law lecturer,[46] had already openly demonstrated his support for women entering the profession. By 1894, Izard was teaching Stella Henderson in his law classes and employing her as a law clerk, although he knew she was barred from practice.[47] He had not attended the critical meeting of the Canterbury law society council held on 14 August 1894, but in a town the size of Christchurch it was highly likely that the law society and Izard were well aware of their opposing positions on the question of women lawyers.

Unbeknown to Henderson and Izard, there was another woman studying law at a New Zealand university. In Dunedin, Ethel Benjamin had already successfully completed the first year of her law degree.[48]

The Otago law society certainly knew of Benjamin's presence in the law classes but offered no comment on the 1894 Law Practitioners Bill. In comparison with the law society, her male classmates followed the Bill with interest. The Legal Club adjudged the Bill 'altogether objectionable, except in one important particular—namely, its provision for the admission of women to the Bar'. Benjamin's male classmates registered their 'unanimous approval' of that clause.[49]

Despite the law society's opposition, Izard would take the initiative to achieve the necessary law change. According to Henderson, he used his influence 'quietly' in both Houses of Parliament to allow women into the profession.[50] One of his contacts was the local member of Parliament, George Russell.[51] Russell had already signalled his support for women lawyers in the debates on the 1894 Law Practitioners Bill. His was a pragmatic, education-based argument. He thought there was little logic in the State providing higher education for women but debarring them from using their knowledge.[52]

Call to undo the disabilities: 1895–1896

From 1894, the debate about the entry of women into the legal profession ceased to revolve around the words 'male persons' in Acts of Parliament. Over the next years George Russell, as the women lawyers' champion in the House of Representatives, promoted four Bills which sought to open the profession to women—two aimed specifically at the legal profession and two aimed at the wholesale removal of women's legal disabilities. The opening of the legal profession to women would eventuate as a by-product of the latter Bills.

The Female Law Practitioners Bill 1895

On 12 July 1895, Russell introduced the first of those four Bills, the Female Law Practitioners Bill. The preamble to the single page Bill stated: 'Whereas women are now prevented by statute from exercising their talents in the study and practice of the law, and it is desirable that such disabilities shall no longer continue.' The Bill was ordered to be read a second time in the House on 7 August.[53]

The reference to women being prevented by statute from *studying* law is curious. As early as 1885, it had been announced publicly in New Zealand that degrees in law were 'open to the ladies'.[54] Ethel Benjamin and Stella Henderson openly attended the law schools at Otago and Canterbury universities. The law societies may, however, have taken a different view of the legality of women studying law. In April 1895, the Otago District Law Society had tip-toed around the issue when faced with a request from Ethel Benjamin to use the law library. The council, then chaired by William Downie Stewart, resolved that, although she was in her third year of study, 'a special permit be accorded to Miss Ethel Benjamin to read in the Judge's Chamber Room there being no rule applicable to her case'.[55]

The Removal of Women's Disabilities Bill: 1895

George Russell, at the same time as introducing the Female Law Practitioners Bill, promoted a broader measure. The Removal of Women's Disabilities Bill, if enacted, would enable women to be nominated, appointed, or elected to any public office or position to which men could be appointed or elected. The preamble to that Bill declared: 'Whereas women are now possessed of equal voting powers with men, and it is desirable that equal opportunity should be given to them to serve the country in offices which they are competent to fill.'

Technically, legal practice was not a public office, but judicial appointment was. Women required access to the profession if they were to be eligible for judicial office.

Although the Canterbury law society had warned in its 1894–1895 annual report that it would 'probably be necessary for the incoming Council to renew the protests made . . . or to take such further action as may be possible to guard the interests of the profession',[56] the new council did not respond to Russell's 1895 Bills officially. Nor, true to form, did any of the other law societies. In any case, on 2 October, without explanation, both Bills were withdrawn.[57]

Figure 1

Removal of Women's Disabilities Bill 1896

Mr. G. W. Russell

REMOVAL OF WOMEN'S DISABILITIES.

ANALYSIS.

Title.	1. Short Title.
Preamble.	2. Women eligible to any office or position.

A BILL INTITULED

An Act to remove the Disabilities of Women.   Title.

WHEREAS women are now possessed of equal voting powers with   Preamble.
men, and it is desirable that equal opportunity should be given to
5 them to serve the country in offices which they are competent to fill:
    Be it therefore enacted by the General Assembly of New
Zealand in Parliament assembled, and by the authority of the same,
as follows :—
    1. The Short Title of this Act is " The Removal of Women's   Short Title.
10 Disabilities Act, 1896."
    2. From and after the passing of this Act a woman may be   Women eligible
nominated, appointed, or elected to any public office or position to   to any office or
which a man may be appointed or elected, any law or statute to the   position.
contrary notwithstanding.

By Authority: John Mackay, Government Printer, Wellington.—1896.

No. 22—1.

Election year: 1896

While politicians may have been disinterested in women's legal status in 1895, the mood had certainly changed by the next year, an election year. For the second time, women would vote in national elections. The *Evening Post* described women's forthcoming vote as having 'a most salutary effect upon the interest taken by members in the welfare of the weaker sex'.[58]

Women's organisations made the most of the pre-election politicking. The Canterbury Women's Institute, typical of many organisations, wrote to politicians such as George Russell, thanking them for their efforts to remove women's legal disabilities.[59] The Women's Political League asked prospective members of Parliament: 'Will you persistently endeavour to secure to women by legislation, equal rights and privileges with those now possessed by men?'[60] In monthly reports the *White Ribbon*, a widely read women's newspaper published by the Christian Women's Temperance Union, monitored the progress of all legislation affecting women.

In June 1896, Russell reintroduced the Female Law Practitioners Bill and the wholesale measure, the Removal of Women's Disabilities Bill (Figure 1). Speaking to the latter, Russell placed women's exclusion from the legal profession at the top of his list of legal disabilities. The 'male persons' restriction, he said, meant that women were 'unable to occupy the position of Judges of either the District or Supreme Courts, or any other position in the Civil Service for which a prior qualification is that they shall be members of the legal profession'.[61]

Russell called the wholesale Bill, 'The Charter of the Independence of Women', which in one page would sweep away all women's legal disabilities. The 'sex distinction', he claimed, had been 'exploded by the granting of the franchise'.[62]

Opposition to the Removal of Women's Disabilities Bill proved widespread. As a result of the seemingly never-ending depression, concerns about competition for jobs were heightened. 'Liberal policies' such as the removal of women's disabilities were thought to be leading to increased competition among men. Whether women should be added to the problem was, according to politician James Allen, 'a question of expediency'. In his view, removing women's disabilities would double the competition: 'not a very encouraging prospect to look forward to for some of our boys and men.'[63]

Even politicians who supported the employment of women lawyers agreed that Parliament needed to address the effects that women's entry would have on the employment of men. Dr Newman said the issue was 'worse than a Chinese invasion',[64] an expression which meant that women would monopolise legal employment perhaps to a greater degree than the

Chinese were believed to have monopolised local industries with their 'cheap and docile labour'.[65]

Of all the occupations women were yet to enter, law was one of the most lucrative and least accessible. William Bolt, a firm supporter of women lawyers, pointed out: 'With the exception of law, nearly every profession had been invaded by women; but the law seemed to be a Tom Tiddler's ground that women were not to be allowed to enter upon at all.'[66]

These arguments proved to be compelling. The *Evening Post* reported: 'after amusing themselves with the measure for half an hour, members killed it by 23 votes to 17.'[67] The 'In Parliament' column in the *White Ribbon* noted: '[the] prospect of a woman possessing the same right to shape her life as a man has, was too awful a thing for a majority of our [members of the House of Representatives].'[68]

On that same day, 2 July 1896, the Female Law Practitioners Bill was scheduled for its second reading. George Russell came straight to the point. This Bill, he said was 'a short one, and required no discussion'. He pointed out, as he had done on previous occasions, that women were able to obtain higher education and there were, at present, 'one or two ladies who were fully qualified to practise' if the 'sex-disability' was removed. Not only were they ready to practise, they were also doing very well. Russell was 'very pleased' to report that Ethel Benjamin had scored the highest mark in the Roman law examination in the entire colony and had also passed the second part of her LLB examinations.[69]

Russell was blunt. He told the House that it 'should recognise its responsibility to the ladies' for the existence of the disability. It should not now stand in the way of those women who wished to join the profession.[70] Without debate, the Bill was passed. This time, the media seemed uninterested—only the *Evening Post* published a short notice.[71]

The Legislative Council: 1896

The 1896 Female Law Practitioners Bill had yet to survive the scrutiny of the Legislative Council. William Bolt moved the second reading, saying that the Bill would appeal 'equally to the chivalry, to the common-sense, and to the sense of justice of the honourable members'.[72] He could not see how there could be any argument against women entering the legal profession. Women were lawyers in America and doctors in New Zealand; they did not ask for any special rights, they simply asked that when they had the necessary qualifications they should be allowed to practise equally with men.

The only other speaker in the council, Samuel Shrimski, was not so generous. He suggested they postpone the proposal until females had entered Parliament and 'could plead their own cause in the Council'.[73] Given the fervent opposition to the Admission of Women to Parliament Bill, this was not a serious proposition.[74] Shrimski moved that the debate be adjourned because the government had referred another Bill 'of a similar nature' to the council. He thought it would be better to have 'the two debates on the one Bill'.[75]

The government's agenda

Samuel Shrimski's suggestion won the day. A government Bill allowing women into the legal profession was certainly noteworthy and not to be treated lightly by the pro-government Legislative Council. So far, all the attempts to undo women's legal disabilities, including gaining access to the legal profession, had been instigated by private members. The Liberal Government, coming into an election, was under intense criticism from women's organisations for failing to advance, and in some cases deliberately obstructing, women's progress.

The Liberal Premier, Richard John Seddon, came in for special criticism. His two-faced politicking on women's suffrage had earned him the reputation of being women's 'worst enemy in the Cabinet'.[76] An article in the *Press* asked: 'Has any politician ever fooled the women as he has done?'[77] Nor did the Legislative Council escape scrutiny. Women's organisations held public meetings and passed resolutions protesting against its attitude to women's legal rights.[78] The *White Ribbon* lambasted the council for its 'steady policy of obstruction' and called for its abolition.[79]

In this climate, the issue of women lawyers took on a new meaning. It was increasingly evident that the government needed to take credit for a reform which would increase women's rights. Allowing women to practise law was infinitely more palatable than the alternatives. A wholesale 'Charter of Independence', in the form of the Removal of Women's Disabilities Bill, was too radical. Letting women be jurors or judges would devastate the entire justice system. The prospect of women in Parliament had attracted frenzied opposition and for the politicians was too close to home for comfort. Measures to allow women lawyers was an initiative the Liberal Government could advance with less opposition.

The difficulty facing the government was that already there had been numerous measures aimed at admitting women to the legal profession, none of which it had sponsored or supported.[80] A vehicle for the reform and a possible godsend turned up in the form of a Bill promoted by the law societies.

The law societies' agenda

As desperately as the government needed to appease women voters, the district law societies needed help with the organisation and discipline of the profession. A national body, the New Zealand Law Society, had been established for that purpose in 1869,[81] a move that proved premature.[82] The editor of the *New Zealand Jurist* described the national society as:

> [an] unfortunate body [which] renders us aware of its existence only by an occasional exhibition of impotence; and for any practical services it renders the profession, it might as well resolve itself at once into a Society for the Protection of Animals.[83]

The onus of policing the profession fell on the district law societies. By the 1890s, with ever-increasing numbers and a rash of negligent and criminal acts by members, the district law societies were struggling. Senior politicians said:

> [it was] a scandal to the colony that the Law Societies did not in the smallest degree correct the mistakes of the profession . . . Hardly one prosecution of any consequence had been instituted by the Law Society against members of the profession.[84]

The problem came to a head in Canterbury in 1893 when the firm of Harper and Co was declared bankrupt, losing £182,830 of client investments.[85] The Canterbury law society struggled for over two years with the expense of disciplinary proceedings and the public relations aftermath. In 1895, a conference of delegates of the district law societies decided it was time to revive the moribund New Zealand Law Society. Its primary role would be disciplinary.

The task of drafting a new New Zealand Law Society Bill was left to the Wellington District Law Society.[86] Its president was directed to confer with Sir Robert Stout and Francis Bell, 'as to the introduction of the Bill'.[87] Stout, an influential politician and lawyer,[88] was a well-known 'suffragist' and a close acquaintance of Stella Henderson.[89] It was rumoured that Francis Bell,[90] brother of Wellington law society council member Ernest Bell, had been elected in 1893 on the women's vote.[91]

The 1896 Law Practitioners and New Zealand Law Society Bill

No records survive of the meeting between the Wellington president, Bell and Stout, but the events that followed indicate that the law societies and the government did a deal—the pay off being to allow women to practise as lawyers. As a condition of its sponsoring the Bill, the government apparently inserted a clause enabling women to be lawyers. The benefit to the beleaguered law societies was simple: the revival of the New Zealand Law Society would ultimately enhance the status and influence of the profession.[92] However, this was likely to attract opposition in the Liberal-dominated House of Representatives, making the passage of the Bill through the Lower House less than certain. Introducing the Bill as a government-sponsored measure directly into the Legislative Council, including the piggy-back clause allowing women into the profession, would increase its chance of success. This was the seventh challenge to women's exclusion from the legal profession.

What the law societies had not reckoned on was that the government would add clauses amending the Law Practitioners Act 1882. If passed, these clauses, like Sir George Grey's reforms, would reduce the criteria for admission to the profession to a bare minimum. Incensed, the Wellington District Law Society promptly prepared a submission, advising that: 'this Council disapproves of that portion of the Bill intended to amend the Law Practitioners Act 1882.'[93] The law society cited each offending clause with one notable exception—the clause relating to women.

Competing Bills in the Legislative Council

On 14 August 1896, as Samuel Shrimski had requested, the Law Practitioners and New Zealand Law Society Bill and the Female Law Practitioners Bill appeared on the Order Paper of the Legislative Council. Both Bills would be short-lived. That same day, for a myriad of reasons, the council voted against both Bills.

The Law Practitioners and New Zealand Law Society Bill, addressing as it did a range of contentious matters, was doomed to failure.[94] While the Female Law Practitioners Bill was more straightforward, its opponents regarded it as an electioneering Bill which on 'calm reflection' was not in the interests of the colony.[95]

However, one week later on 20 August, the council did an about-face on the Law Practitioners and New Zealand Law Society Bill. Despite intense objections, the Bill was reintroduced. The Minister of Education William Walker, said it was 'not fair' that those who objected to the clause allowing women into the profession had voted against the whole Bill.[96] He advocated that the council refer the Bill to the Statutes Revision Committee for its opinion. Advocates of women lawyers supported that move, the Statutes Revision Committee being 'the proper Court to judge' the Bill.[97]

But the supporters of women lawyers had another agenda. The next day, William Bolt moved that the Female Law Practitioners Bill also be reinstated. Although it had failed the week before, he said, it was apparent that 'in one or two cases votes were given under a misapprehension'.[98]

George McLean, an opponent, suggested they wait until they heard what the Statutes Revision Committee had to say on the equivalent clause in the law society Bill.[99] Others objected to the attempt to reintroduce a Bill already dismissed by the council.[100] On a close vote it was agreed that the Female Law Practitioners Bill would be reinstated. This was possibly influenced by Bolt's comment that it had 'a better chance of becoming law' than the government-sponsored law society Bill.[101]

Bolt's suspicion proved well-founded. When the Statutes Revision Committee reported back on the Law Practitioners and New Zealand Law Society Bill, all the clauses relating to admission to the profession were deleted—including that relating to women lawyers.

Thomas Kelly, a firm proponent of women lawyers, complained that the committee had exceeded its mandate. Its task 'was not to instruct the Council in matters of policy, but to instruct the Council as regards arranging, modifying, and amending the clauses'. He thought it 'very peculiar' that the four lawyers on the Statutes Revision Committee had 'voted in a solid block' against the clauses. They did not, in his view, give 'fair consideration to the Bill'. [102]

Charles Bowen disagreed. He replied that the arguments of the 'legal gentlemen' on the committee 'were sound'.[103] In his view, it was the duty of the committee to revise the Bills submitted and to 'put their objections and suggestions in a concrete shape'. If that meant deleting clauses, then so be it. In any case, Bowen noted, the clauses dealing with the New Zealand Law Society had been passed by the committee and he did not think there was any more to be said about it.[104]

But Bowen was in the minority. By a clear majority, the council voted to reinstate the clause on women lawyers to the law society Bill. The next day, however, when the Female Law Practitioners Bill came up for its second reading, William Bolt reminded the council that the law society Bill had yet to pass the Lower House, which had already passed the 1896 Female Law Practitioners Bill. If the council voted in favour of the Female Law Practitioners Bill, it could become law at once.[105]

McLean thought it 'very bad practice' that the council should be asked to pass two Bills allowing women to practise law.[106] His objection was overridden. Walker declared he would vote for the Female Law Practitioners Bill even though the other measure was a government Bill. That Bill, he said, 'had still to take its chance' in the House of Representatives and there was no certainty it would become law.[107] Without further ado, the Female Law Practitioners Bill passed its second reading.

Two laws allowing women lawyers

On 4 September 1896, both Bills were again before the Legislative Council—this time for their third and final readings. Complaints were made about these 'double-barrelled Bills', bringing the council 'into discredit'.[108] But, in the face of government support, the opponents were quick to add that they did not object to the principle of women lawyers but to the process.[109] Thomas Kelly suggested that the procedural problems could be resolved at the next stage. He supposed 'the Government would move to strike out the clause giving women the right to practise' from the law society Bill.[110] This proposal was endorsed by Walker.[111] With this assurance, the council finally conceded and passed the Female Law Practitioners Bill and the Law Practitioners and New Zealand Law Society Bill, with the women lawyers clause intact.

On 11 September 1896, when the Female Law Practitioners Act received the Royal assent, there was no longer a law against women lawyers in New Zealand (Figure 2). But the law change did not end the political wrangle.

On 25 September, Richard John Seddon claimed centre stage in the House of Representatives. Personally moving the second reading of the government-backed Law Practitioners and New Zealand Law Society Bill, Seddon announced that 'the only matter of importance' in the Bill was the clause giving 'a right to the other sex to become members of the legal profession'. Women's great academic achievements and their 'high qualities' meant he 'had no hesitation' in granting women the privileges they sought.[112] Despite the government's promise to the Legislative Council, it clearly had no intention of deleting the women lawyers clause from the law society Bill.

So, on 12 October 1896, the Law Practitioners and New Zealand Law Society Bill joined the Female Law Practitioners Bill on the statute books. (Figure 3)

Seddon's efforts to grab the limelight seemed to have failed. The passing of the two laws admitting women to the legal profession provoked little interest. Only the *Press* reported, in two short sentences, the enactment of the Female Law Practitioners Act.[113]

Nor were the law society councils moved to discuss this innovation. Only the Wellington law society pointedly recorded in its annual report, that all the parts of the law society Bill objected to by the council had been struck out, 'except one, which was not objected to, namely, a clause permitting women to practise'.[114] In October 1896, the Otago law society council wrote to Ethel Benjamin in response to her request for renewal of her six-month library permit and advised her that: 'the Society recognize[s] her as a student and consequently [she is] entitled to use of the Library.'[115] After a long and protracted struggle through both Houses of Parliament, the law now permitted her to do more than study law—she and other women could practise it.

The *White Ribbon*, in a brief report on the passage of the Female Law Practitioners Bill, proclaimed with pride: 'Our New Zealand Portias have now a clear field for their powers.'[116]

Figure 2

Female Law Practitioners Act 1896

New Zealand.

ANALYSIS.

Title.
Preamble.
1. Short Title.

2. Women may become barristers and solicitors.

1896, No. 11.

AN ACT to enable Women to practise the Profession of the Law. Title.
[*11th September, 1896.*

WHEREAS women are now prevented by statute from exercising Preamble.
their talents in the study and practice of the law, and it is desirable
that such disabilities shall no longer continue :

BE IT THEREFORE ENACTED by the General Assembly of New
Zealand in Parliament assembled, and by the authority of the same,
as follows :—

1. The Short Title of this Act is " The Female Law Practitioners Short Title.
Act, 1896."

2. Notwithstanding anything to the contrary contained in " The Women may
Law Practitioners Act, 1882," and the Acts amending the same, any become barristers
woman of the age of twenty-one years and upwards may be enrolled and solicitors.
as a barrister or solicitor on passing the examinations required to be
passed by males, and on payment of the fees and compliance with the
law in that behalf.

WELLINGTON : Printed under authority of the New Zealand Government,
by JOHN MACKAY, Government Printer.—1896.

Figure 3

Law Practitioners and New Zealand Law Society Acts Amendment Act 1896

New Zealand.

ANALYSIS.

Title.
1. Short Title.
2. Candidates of either sex.

AS TO THE NEW ZEALAND LAW SOCIETY.

3. Constitution of Council modified.
4. First election of members.

5. Term of office.
6. Re-election.
7. Meetings of Council.
8. Meetings of Law Society.

GENERAL.

9. Acts and rules modified or repealed.

1896, No. 22.

Title.   AN ACT to amend the Law relating to Law Practitioners and the New Zealand Law Society.   [*12th October, 1896.*

BE IT ENACTED by the General Assembly of New Zealand in Parliament assembled, and by the authority of the same, as follows :—

Short Title.   1. The Short Title of this Act is " The Law Practitioners and New Zealand Law Society Acts Amendment Act, 1896."

Candidates of either sex.   2. Candidates for admission as barristers or solicitors may be of either sex.

AS TO THE NEW ZEALAND LAW SOCIETY.

Constitution of Council modified.   3. The constitution of the Council of the New Zealand Law Society is hereby modified in manner following, that is to say,—

(1.) Each of the respective District Law Societies for the Northern District, the Wellington District, the Canterbury District, and the Otago and Southland District shall elect two members of the Council ; and

(2.) Each of the respective District Law Societies for the other districts throughout the colony shall elect one member of the Council.

First election of members.   4. The first election of members of the Council under this Act shall be held on a day to be appointed by the Governor, and on that day the members then in office shall cease to hold office.

Term of office.   5. The member elected by each District Law Society at the first election under this Act shall hold office until the date of the first ensuing annual meeting of such society, on which date, and annually thereafter, a successor shall be elected :

Provided that if such society at any time fails to duly elect a member the District Council of such society may do so in its stead,

Figure 3—*continued*

*Law Practitioners and New Zealand Law Society Acts Amendment Act
1896—continued*

and the fact that such District Council so elects shall be sufficient
evidence of its authority so to do.

6. Every retiring member shall be eligible for re-election.   Re-election.

7. The Council may hold meetings at such time and place as Meetings of Council
it thinks fit, but shall hold a meeting in Wellington on a date to be
fixed by the President, being within fourteen days after the date
appointed for the commencement of each half-yearly sitting of the
Court of Appeal.

8. The Council may convene meetings of the New Zealand Meetings of Law
Law Society, and fix the time and place of meeting thereof.   Society.

GENERAL.

9. "The Law Practitioners Act, 1882," "The New Zealand Acts and rules
Law Society's Act, 1869," and all other Acts and the respective rules modified or repealed.
thereunder that are in any way in conflict with this Act are hereby
modified or repealed in so far as such conflict exists, but not further
or otherwise.

WELLINGTON : Printed under authority of the New Zealand Government,
by JOHN MACKAY, Government Printer.—1896.

Chapter Three

Training and Employment of Women in the Profession: 1896–1977

Removal of the legal barriers to women entering the legal profession was only the beginning. It was widely thought that the majority of women would accept that they were unsuited for the profession of law; practising lawyers were unlikely to employ them and clients were unlikely to instruct them.

The politicians, including William Downie Stewart, had reassured themselves that if the legal barrier were removed, few women would flock to the profession.[1] During the parliamentary debates, the Minister of Education William Walker, had noted: 'It was absurd to say that a large number of women must be lawyers ... That was not likely to occur. It would not be the rule, but the exception, that women would become lawyers.'[2]

As predicted, women lawyers were to be the exception. Regardless of their personal ambitions and skills, the employment playing field was consistently tilted against them. Examining women's employment in the legal profession through the twentieth century's two world wars and several economic recessions and booms, two patterns emerge. First, women would be used by the legal profession as an expendable labour force, when and as required. Secondly, women would be under-employed in the profession.

Qualified women would be employed as permanent clerks and unqualified women would also perform legal work, both groups on low rates of pay. Backed by government policies and laws, these employment patterns ensured that women's labour in the legal profession was undervalued and underpaid, into the 1990s.

Women legal typists and law clerks: 1896–1914

In 1896, the year that women were allowed to apply for entry into the legal profession, there were fourteen women working as law clerks in New Zealand law offices. Only one of those women, Stella Henderson

(Figure 4), was working toward her professional qualifications, studying part time at Canterbury University College. The other women were 'para-legals', clerks who prepared conveyancing documents, deeds and accounts, and provided administrative support to their employers.

Ethel Benjamin was in her last year of law studies at Otago University, but unlike her male contemporaries she did not work as a law clerk with a practising lawyer or barrister. Instead, immediately following her admission to the Bar in 1897, she struck out on her own as a barrister sole in Dunedin. (Figure 5)

As clerical work became one of a very few respectable occupations for single women, this early trickle of women into New Zealand law offices soon became a flood. From the end of the nineteenth century, women entered the profession en masse—not with degrees, but with clerical skills. As in England, the influx of women into legal offices followed closely on the introduction of a new machine, the typewriter.[3] First appearing around 1893 in the more modern law offices, the typewriter soon replaced the old practice of engrossing legal documents by hand on fine quality bond paper. Performed by male scriveners, this work, an exacting art, had involved long hours and little remuneration.[4]

Initially, typing in New Zealand legal offices was a male domain, to the extent that the male clerk who operated the machine was for some years called 'the typewriter'.[5] By 1901, ten men but only one woman were employed in the new census category of 'legal typists'.

The male typists' head start, however, was short-lived. As predicted, women law clerks and legal typists could be employed to do the same work as men but for lower rates of pay. There was nothing illegal about this. On the contrary, unequal pay was sanctioned by the Arbitration Court in its first award in 1903.[6]

Within a decade, the proportions had reversed—fifty-seven of the legal typists in 1911 were women and four were men. Five years later, there were 616 women typists and no men.[7] The influx of women did not mean that the men found themselves without jobs. Instead, the number of men employed as non-articled law clerks from 1901 to 1911 continued to increase.[8] It is possible that the employment of women typists allowed the now senior male clerks to be 'more profitably employed' within the law offices, as had occurred in England.[9]

Wellington's first woman legal typist, and probably the first woman to work in a Wellington legal firm, was Miss Barnicoat from Nelson who was employed by Bell Gully and Izard.[10] In 1906, she was joined at the firm, by then renamed Bell Gully Bell and Myers, by Alice May Carter who was also the firm's librarian for more than thirty years and, in 1913, by Miss Gordon.[11] Jackson Russell, an Auckland firm, employed its first woman typist in 1907.[12]

Figure 4

Stella May Henderson

Photograph reproduced with the permission of the Pictorial Department, Canterbury Museum, Christchurch, New Zealand, ref 12945.

At the same time as women were entering law offices in large numbers as typists, they were also finding employment as law clerks. Geraldine Hemus, the first woman articled clerk in Auckland, was employed by sole practitioner C J Parr in 1898.[13] He took her on in the knowledge that he would assume full responsibility for her early legal education, there being no law classes available at that time.[14] The following year, the respected Auckland firm Devore and Cooper (later Devore and Martin) employed eighteen-year-old Ellen Melville as an articled clerk.[15]

Although the number of women law clerks soared from 29 in 1901 to 202 ten years later,[16] this influx did not result in the profession being flooded with women lawyers. Few, if any, of the women clerks were taking articles—still the predominant method of obtaining professional qualifications. Of the 29 women law clerks in 1901, only one was articled. By comparison, 14 percent of the 766 men clerks were articled. In 1911, of the 202 women clerks, still only one was articled.[17]

In the same period (1901 to 1911) the number of women law students wavered between nil and one.[18] Ethel Benjamin and Stella Henderson in the south were followed by Ellen Melville and Geraldine Hemus, who completed their law degrees at Auckland University College and were admitted to the Bar in 1906 and 1907 respectively. The next woman law student, also at Auckland university, was Annie Lee Rees, daughter of prominent lawyer and politician William Lee Rees. Annie Lee Rees had already qualified with an MA(Hons) and had an established career as a teacher and school principal when she enrolled to study law. On completion of her law degree she was admitted to the Bar in a special ceremony in Gisborne in 1910.[19]

Even though women completed their professional qualifications they would still be aligned within the profession with the women law clerks rather than the men lawyers. Despite Annie Lee Rees' impressive qualifications, she did not ever practise in her own right. According to family history, she was no more than an assistant to her father.[20] When he died in 1912, she returned to her first career of teaching.[21] Harriet Vine, the first New Zealand woman to obtain an LLM, was also employed as a 'qualified clerk'. She held this position in the Wanganui law firm Treadwell and Gordon for over forty years, even though she was admitted to the Bar in 1915, about two years after joining the firm. Her title was specifically chosen to recognise her qualifications and distinguish her from the other women clerks working in accounts, deeds, and registrations at Treadwell and Gordon. It also neatly set her apart from the qualified men. Consistent with her position, Harriet Vine typed all her own letters, although according to Gordon Swan, currently a partner in the firm and a grandson of one of the founding partners, the typists could have done them if she had asked.[22]

Figure 5

Ethel Rebecca Benjamin

Photograph reproduced with the permission of the Hocken Library, Dunedin, New Zealand.

World War I: exceptions in times of need

In August 1914, when war with Germany was declared, the legal profession, along with the rest of the country, responded with patriotic fervour.[23] Large numbers of men lawyers and law clerks entered active service, but their absence did not provide openings for qualified women. Instead, older men lawyers delayed, or came out of, retirement and women continued to join law firms in non-professional capacities.[24] By 1916, two years into World War I, the number of women law clerks had more than doubled from the pre-war level.[25] A total of 1,104 women were employed in law offices, making up 37 percent of those working in the profession. Of those 1,104 women, only three were lawyers and none were articled clerks.[26]

A similar scenario was taking place in the law schools. Over the war years, the number of men law students decreased sharply.[27] But their seats in the law lecture rooms were not filled by women. The number of women law students increased only marginally, from one in 1914 to seven in 1919.[28] One of those women was Rebecca Pallot (née Macky) who, having moved to Napier and married Walter Pallot in 1915, was 'determined to study law by correspondence'.[29] Unlike most of her contemporaries, Rebecca Pallot completed her law degree. By comparison, women flocked to Otago Medical School, optimistic that the projected shortage of trained doctors needed in the war effort would ensure their later employment.[30] Women law graduates had no such hopes.

1920s: social and economic restraints

After the war it was thought that opportunities for women would expand. Auckland's first woman lawyer, Ellen Melville (Figure 6) described the war in a 1919 public lecture as having given women 'a stronger sense of the value of common effort'. It was, she thought, an experience which 'removed their sense of inferiority to men'.[31] Similar sentiments were expressed by Rose Henderson, younger sister of Stella Henderson:

> Less than a century ago ... woman had entered only seven occupations. To-day she is competing successfully against men in all industries, save six or seven such as killing animals, hanging men, driving locomotives, chimney sweeping, and climbing poles.[32]

However, women would not be competing with men in any way in the legal profession. By the end of the war, the number of women lawyers had barely increased—from three in 1911 to four in 1921.[33] Nor did women flock to the law schools. In 1920, no women were enrolled in university law classes.[34]

Figure 6
Eliza Ellen Melville

Photograph reproduced with the permission of Auckland City Libraries (NZ).

By comparison, immediately following the end of the war, the number of male law students doubled.[35] Returned servicemen took advantage of government-sponsored rehabilitation schemes giving them provisional admission to university, lower pass levels and financial assistance.[36] One wartime pilot, later a partner at Russell McVeagh, acquired a law degree in two years using the concession system.[37]

The profession was keen to ensure that those who did return were not disadvantaged. The Otago law society lobbied for a law change to ensure the period of military service would not count against solicitors seeking to qualify as barristers.[38] At that time, solicitors could apply for a barrister's certificate as a matter of course after five years in practice.

In that era of user-pays university education, the concessions for returned servicemen disadvantaged civilian students, including women— not that they complained. The general consensus of opinion was that the concession scheme was less than generous and that a great deal more should have been done to enhance the welfare of returned servicemen.[39]

For several years after the war, recovery for the legal profession was slow. The part-time training system meant the new law students did not qualify until around 1923—the same time that the economy boomed.[40] There was plenty of legal work and many young lawyers 'launched out into practice on their own account'.[41] Others, encouraged by the promise of prosperous careers, took up legal studies.

Women's response to the economic boom brought the number of women law students to an all-time high of thirteen in 1926.[42] Certainly, schoolgirls showed an interest in pursuing legal studies, but few made it to the doors of the universities. In 1925, eight girls from St Dominic's College in Dunedin passed the Solicitors' General Knowledge Examination, but only one, Mary Hussey, went on to study law.[43] Women's participation in legal employment was mostly in non-professional work. Between 1916 and 1921, over 200 women joined the profession as non-articled law clerks.

New government policies aimed at encouraging an increase in family sizes directly countered the economic incentives to enter law. Among these policies were a family allowance and tax exemptions for families with dependents.[44] In 1921, the government stopped employing female cadets in the government service and hired women clerks as temporary workers only.[45] There was little support for increasing women's work opportunities outside the domestic sphere. According to the Leader of the Legislative Council, doing so would 'interfere in a very great measure with our social and home life'.[46]

These policies and attitudes reinforced the idea that women should not pursue legal careers. Exceptions were few and far between. Rachael Zister, a Maori woman with tribal connections to the ariki lines (lines of chieftancy) of Ngati Kahungungu, Te Aitanga-a-Mahaki, Ngati Porou and to the Kahuiariki of Waikato, entered the office of Kirk, Neumegan, Nolan and Haron in 1917 as a legal adviser. Although her formal qualifications are unknown, she was a respected adviser on the Maori Land Court and Maori law. In 1920 she joined the Public Trust Office in Wellington as an adviser on Maori law and three years later was appointed to assist Judge Rawson with Maori legal matters.[47]

In 1925, Lyra Taylor was reported to be practising as a partner in a Wellington law firm, making her possibly the first woman partner in New Zealand.[48] The only other women lawyers in practice at the time were Ellen Melville, Geraldine Hemus, Harriet Vine and Esther Ongley. None of them were married and none had children. In any case, even single women were not generally expected to seek partnerships. As Gordon Swan pointed out, Harriet Vine did not aspire to partnership at Treadwell and Gordon. He explained: 'She was a pretty retiring kind of woman. She never married but she would not have been offered a partnership anyway. There were no ladies in partnership then.'[49]

Added to the disincentives faced by women wishing to enter into or advance within the legal profession in the 1920s was the fact that the profession was again overcrowded. The 1925 Royal Commission on University Education was perturbed to find there were 1,200 practising lawyers and 586 law students. Even allowing for the law graduates who would enter commerce and industry, the Royal Commission concluded: 'We cannot conceive that New Zealand requires such an output of lawyers.'[50]

The low pay received by women clerks was another disincentive to women taking up law classes at university. Studying law was not cheap—most students had to work to cover the costs of fees and books. The Royal Commission found that men students who studied in the evenings and worked as clerks by day were nearly twice as likely as their women counterparts to be earning over £4 per week. Women students were much more likely to be earning under £2 per week. Law students employed in the public service were much better off than those in private practice. In 1925, they received on average a salary 100 percent higher than that of their peers in law firms.[51]

It is not known whether any of the law students employed as clerks in the public service in 1925 were women but, if they were, it is unlikely they would have received the same salaries as their male counterparts. Equal pay was not implemented in the public service until the early 1960s.

Despite the obstacles, a few women persevered with their plans to study law. Marion Thomson decided to study law while working as a junior typist in the Dunedin law firm of Sievwright James and Nichol in 1927. Inspired by a photograph of practitioners taken at the opening of the

Dunedin High Court in 1902, with Ethel Benjamin featured centre stage in wig and gown (Figure 7), Marion Thomson attended night classes to complete her secondary education and found her own tutor for Latin. In 1932, she enrolled in law classes at Otago University.[52]

Margaret Mackay also studied law while working as the junior typist for her uncle's Oamaru law firm, Grave and Grave. Being outside a university town, Mackay studied for the Solicitor's Examination by correspondence. In 1929, having completed the examinations, she was admitted to the Bar and in recognition of her qualifications she was promoted to the position of managing clerk.[53]

Figure 7

Ethel Benjamin and the Otago legal profession, 1902

Photograph reproduced with the permission of the Otago District Law Society.

1930s: depression policies

By the early 1930s, at exactly the time when the flood of new graduates entered the profession, New Zealand was in the midst of the Great Depression.[54] Legal employees, like everyone else, took salary cuts and, in some cases, redundancy.[55] As in the 1890s, there was a rush for legal advice to stave off the effects of the depression on businesses, mortgages, and investments, but few were able to pay for such advice.[56]

In 1932, poor employment prospects prompted Otago University to warn students not to enrol in law.[57] Nationally, law student numbers plummeted. Between 1932 and 1939, the number of men law students dropped by 13 percent (from 412 to 359), while the number of women law students fell by 55 percent (from 22 to 10).[58]

When Elisabeth Urquhart began studying law in 1935 she was not alone. Other women law students at that time included Nancy Noy (later Nairn) who did third year law but did not qualify, marrying instead; Jocelyn Miller (later Gregory) from Kawakawa who qualified and practised for a couple of years (her father was also a lawyer); Valerie Anderson who held a practising certificate from 1940 to 1945, married a lawyer and went to the United States, practising there; and Miss Pabst who studied law while working in the office at Auckland University.[59] She was perhaps the first female 'mature student' when she qualified in 1935, then 36 years old. However, she did not practise law, instead joining a convent in 1939.[60]

During the depression, women law graduates needed to be doubly resourceful to find work. Dorothy Raymond, the first woman law graduate from Canterbury University College, recalls that when she finished her law degree in 1931 jobs were nearly impossible to find. Her particular disadvantage was a lack of typing skills. She explained: 'In those days a woman couldn't get a job in a law firm unless she could do shorthand and typing.' To equip herself, she enrolled in a crash course in typing and shorthand and on 1 September 1934 started as a shorthand typist in her uncle's firm, Raymond Raymond and Tweedy in Timaru. Only several years later would she be allowed to do legal work.[61]

For eighteen months, during her third and fourth years at law school, Elisabeth Urquhart also worked as a legal typist in the office of her father's Auckland agents. She knew of no men law students who were employed in that capacity. They were employed as law clerks. On one occasion, when Urquhart had applied for a law clerk position, the law firm did not even acknowledge her letter. In 1939, she joined her father's law firm in Rotorua.[62]

Overall, employment policies during the depression reinforced women's dependence on men by favouring male employment. For example, women were ineligible for unemployment benefits being expected to rely on their husbands or fathers for financial support.[63] Large employers such as the Auckland City Council resolved in 1933 not to employ married women who had husbands in permanent employment, defeating Ellen Melville's petition against the policy.[64] The next year, Otago University followed suit and decided not to employ married women.[65] On a national basis, the secondary status of women's work was confirmed by the Arbitration Court's decision in 1936 to fix a minimum wage for women at 47 percent of the male rate. At the same time, legislation provided for a basic male wage which would allow a man to maintain a wife and three children to 'a fair and reasonable standard of comfort'.[66] The legislation was hailed as progressive—women were to be assured security as wives and mothers.[67]

Predictably, women lawyers left their jobs on marriage, as did other employed women. When Marion Thomson became engaged in 1937, soon after graduating LLB, she resigned from her position as senior typist in the firm, prompting a newspaper to report: 'The profession has nothing to fear from her, however, as she has decided that law and order can be established even more successfully through the medium of matrimony with Mr Jack G Thomson.'[68]

World War II: a problem of womanpower

At the outbreak of World War II in September 1939 there were only twenty-four women in the country with law degrees and at most fourteen women in practice—too few to fill the gaps left by the men lawyers who enlisted. In the first year of the war, the rush of men lawyers and law clerks to join the armed forces produced difficulties in many law offices.[69] Despite the submissions of the New Zealand Law Society, the legal profession was denied 'essential industry' status.[70] As a result, male solicitors, barristers and law clerks were eligible for conscription.

Firms such as Bell Gully in Wellington and Adams Bros in Dunedin were 'torn apart' by the loss of staff.[71] The Auckland law society responded by keeping a register of solicitors and clerks.[72] The Otago law society reinstated the World War I arrangement of relying on older practitioners to protect the practices of those who enlisted. Ex-employees, particularly married women and war widows, were called back to work. While the rate of enlistment was sufficiently high to lead to a manpower shortage for the legal profession, it was 'a problem of womanpower which brought the crisis to a head'; the government had decided in 1942 to enrol women compulsorily for service.[73]

The Otago law society responded to the crisis by surveying firms about their staffing requirements. They found that many offices were heavily reliant on women non-professional staff, women clerks now outnumbering men clerks by two to one.[74] In addition, law firms found themselves competing for women staff, some of whom were lured by other more glamorous or lucrative war-time occupations, while others were 'man-powered' to work in factories.[75] Turnover was high. When Bea Rostance, a solo mother, started work in the accounts section at Bell Gully in July 1943, a staff member said to her: 'Oh, you're the new cost clerk. We've had six in the last three months.'[76]

In the erratic war-time environment, women clerks and lawyers assumed new responsibilities. For periods, women clerks were left in charge of practices.[77] The Wellington firm of Bell Gully, for example, according to one observer, was left in the care of 'old men and a whole pack of women'.[78] Women lawyers also enjoyed greater opportunities. Betty Thorpe (née Webster), an Auckland graduate, described the war years as 'exceptional'—women received the same treatment as their male colleagues. Her employer, she recalled, was 'virtually forced' to give her court appearances 'because there was no one else'. It was, at the time, 'very unusual' for women lawyers to appear in court.[79]

For some the opportunities extended to partnerships. Marjorie Feist (née Taylor) was made a partner in the Lower Hutt firm of Haldane and Haldane in 1941.[80] At her uncle's insistence, Margaret Mackay became a partner in Lee, Grave and Zimmerman in 1946, seventeen years after her admission to the Bar. Even then, opposition from one of the partners to her admission into the partnership was so fierce that her name would not be added to the partnership list until he retired in 1961.[81] Others were even more unlucky. For Dorothy Raymond it would be twenty-four years after the war before she was offered a partnership.[82] Betty Thorpe also found at the end of the war that her father, while keen to support her legal education, gave preference to her brother when it came to partnership.[83] Elisabeth Urquhart side-stepped the issue of partnership. In November 1944, she became the first woman in the Hamilton district to open a law practice on her own account. She practised in conveyancing, estates and Maori Land Court work.[84]

Post-World War II: a preference for men again

New Zealand women's participation in the paid workforce skyrocketed during the 1940s as a result of World War II.[85] But the liberating effect of the war was temporary and, as far as the legal profession was concerned, barely noticeable. By the end of the war in 1945 there were only fifteen women law students and nineteen women lawyers. In the two years following the war, the number of men law students more than doubled.[86]

Post-war government policies were designed to ensure that returned service personnel were re-integrated into New Zealand society. Although women who served during the war were also eligible for assistance, returned servicemen were overwhelmingly the beneficiaries. Employers in the legal profession, along with all other employers, were required by legislation to reinstate employees at the end of their military service.[87] In addition, government subsidies boosted the salaries paid to some returned servicemen lawyers.[88]

New Zealand post-war policies resulted in women leaving their employment in law offices. As temporary employees, they were legally required to relinquish their positions and expected to retire gracefully.[89] As a result, the net increase in women law clerks between 1936 and 1945 was a mere fifteen.[90] Again, this was not the cause of complaint. Returning lawyers and law clerks who had served overseas were welcomed by the profession as national heroes.[91]

Many 'rehabs', as returned servicemen were known, enrolled in university law classes under a generous rehabilitation scheme.[92] Financial assistance included service bursaries and text book allowances, making full-time study possible. Academic concessions for law students included exemptions from up to four subjects, special examinations, concession passes, and a general easing of degree requirements.[93] By 1946, 'rehabs' made up 69 of the 185 law graduates at Auckland University.[94]

The universities' 'rehab' policies had a mixed effect on women's access to the profession. For the first time, training for professional occupations was widely accessible to working-class men. Government assistance enabled ex-servicemen with long service records to embark on professional studies that in pre-war days they had 'hankered after but lacked the means to attempt'.[95]

By flooding the law schools and ultimately the profession, 'rehabs' filled places that might otherwise have attracted and been taken by women. No formal limits were placed on student numbers but the availability of jobs inevitably affected the inclinations of women to take up legal study. On the other hand, rehabilitation policies resulted in at least one woman enrolling in law. Difficulties getting into medical school at the end of the war prompted Fay Matson (later Wellwood) to take up her second choice of law instead.[96]

Qualified women still stayed out of the limelight. Mary Hussey became a highly qualified and permanent law clerk for almost thirty years following her admission to the Bar in 1947. She had a string of qualifications that few men lawyers could match—masters degrees in arts and law as well as formal qualifications and experience as a librarian. Despite her undoubted talent, Mary Hussey was employed as the chief law clerk at Adams Bros, the Crown Solicitors in Dunedin, for approximately twenty-eight years. As with Harriet Vine and other early women lawyers, Hussey's male employers and colleagues were quick to point out that Mary Hussey herself did not seek any greater status or recognition.[97]

Any hope that women's post-war status might generally be improving was quashed by the 1947 Arbitration Court decision to continue unequal pay. The court declined to decrease the margin between women's and men's rates of pay because the 'grave social and economic consequences' made this a decision for the legislature and not the courts.[98] Parliament too was far from convinced that this step was necessary.

1950s: mixed messages

The post-war period was characterised by mixed messages for women. Full employment had unexpectedly followed the end of the war and the few women graduates, in Auckland at least, had no difficulty finding work. By 1951 there was again a 'chronic shortage of junior clerks' and the Auckland District Law Society had to undertake a concerted recruitment campaign targeting secondary schools.[99] Alison Quentin-Baxter (née Souter), who worked as a law clerk at Hanna and Coates until 1951, recalled that on her admission in 1952 there were 'plenty of jobs' and good opportunities for both sexes. She was offered a position as a solicitor at a well-known Auckland firm with a view to partnership in a year or two, but did not take up the opportunity, having already decided on a career in the foreign service.[100]

However, at this time, qualified and unqualified women still left legal work on marriage. Sheila Macdonald, who completed her LLB during the war, having already declined an offer of partnership from Dunedin firm Gallaway and Mowat, gave up her job at the Public Trust Office when her fiancee returned from service and had instead 'a busy married life'.[101] Fay Matson, the only one of four women in her university law classes to graduate, married soon after admission and did not practise.[102] After the war, Betty Thorpe retired from practice, five months' pregnant. It was, she reflects, difficult to combine family and career: 'Society seemed to regard the business and professional worlds as being for men.'[103]

In effect, the post-war baby boom and the enhanced social status of motherhood kept women out of the law schools and away from employment in the legal profession. The number of women law students in the early 1950s remained less than thirty.[104] Nationwide, the number of women law clerks decreased.[105] By 1956, the Minister of Social Welfare, Dame Hilda Ross, was announcing that in these prosperous times there was 'no necessity' for women to seek independent incomes. Instead, she said: 'Married women with 'children should wake up to their responsibilities in the home and stay at home.'[106] A link between 'maternal deprivation' and moral decay in the youth of New Zealand had already been made by the 1954 Special Committee on Moral Delinquency chaired by Dr Mazengarb QC. These images of neglectful mothers helped sow the seeds of guilt in women who wanted careers in addition to childrearing or who sought childcare alternatives.[107]

For single women, careers were still acceptable—within certain limits. In the early 1950s, Paddy Steele (née West-Walker) became interested in taking up the law while working as a shorthand typist for her lawyer father, A J West-Walker. However, when she travelled overseas after her admission to the Bar in 1955 it was her typing skills and not her legal qualifications which secured her a job in an English law firm. She worked as a shorthand typist for five months, filling in for the secretaries during the summer holidays.[108]

Other women lawyers avoided being restricted to administrative work by not obtaining clerical skills. When Shirley Parr was studying law at Victoria University in the early 1950s she recalled 'one good piece of advice' she received from one of her professors: 'If you want to be a lawyer, don't learn to type or they'll get you to do your own typing.'[109]

Women with incomplete law qualifications were also sought-after as law clerks by law firms and government departments. The three women in Fay Matson's law classes in the late 1940s and early 1950s who did not finish their law degrees were all employed in some law-related capacity. Isobel Tocken (née McKay) worked in the Land Transfer Office, Marion MacBeth (née Wood) worked in Duncan Cotterill as a law clerk, and Joan Thacker found employment as a law clerk in Christchurch.[110]

1960s: a new era

A new era dawned for women in the 1960s with the contraceptive pill and the Women's Liberation Movement. At the same time, the government introduced policies aimed at encouraging women to return to the workforce. Trained women teachers and nurses with grown children were needed to meet the demands on social services resulting from the baby boom.[111] In 1962 a new, more favourable tax regime was introduced—for the first time since 1939, a married woman's income was to be treated as her own.

Encouraged by this new climate of acceptability towards women in paid work, women lawyers who had qualified many years before returned to or finally entered the legal profession. In 1960, twenty-three years after graduating in law, Marion Thomson was finally employed as a lawyer with Rutherford, McKinnon and Neil. She practised in family law, estate work, and conveyancing with the firm for the next eighteen years, but did not seek partnership. Her salary increases paralleled those of the younger practitioners in the firm.[112] In 1963, Sheila Macdonald, who qualified in 1942, returned to law clerking.[113] Fay Wellwood (née Matson) joined Hallet O'Dowd and Co in Hastings as a part-time solicitor in 1964, her first legal job since her admission in 1952.[114]

In 1961, the first New Zealand 'all-women' law partnership was formed when Elisabeth Urquhart invited Hamilton lawyer Patricia Lee to join her in Rotorua. Pat Lee had been admitted to the Bar in Auckland on 23 September 1960, more than twenty years after Elisabeth Urquhart's admission. Even so, Pat Lee was still only the twentieth woman to be registered on the Auckland High Court Roll of Solicitors.[115] Urquhart and Lee remained in partnership until 1966.[116]

Legal education changes

Although shifts in economic policy and social thinking had profound effects on women already in the profession, it was changes to legal education during the 1960s which irrevocably changed women's profile in the legal profession. Initially, the largest group to benefit were non-professional women, an unplanned result of the shift from part-time to full-time university study.

Part-time study ceased to be an option from 1960 when the law schools started to eliminate lectures outside working hours.[117] In a replay of the debates of the 1880s and 1890s, the profession protested vigorously— enforcing full-time study would mean the elimination of law clerks as a source of cheap labour.[118] But the universities were adamant, and by the mid-1960s the profession faced an acute shortage of legal clerical staff.

Women again filled the gap. Even firms which, up to this point, had remained exclusively male, finally capitulated and employed women as law clerks.[119] The New Zealand Law Society was forced to negotiate with the technical institutes for the establishment of courses for non-graduate clerks who would train to become 'legal executives'.[120] Given the history of women's employment in the profession, it was no surprise that the majority of these para-professionals would be women. Like their non-articled predecessors, legal executives would fulfil an important economic function in the profession, being fee producers without any realistic aspirations to a seat at the partnership table.[121]

In 1968, Auckland law school introduced new entry criteria that would turn the tide for women seeking professional careers. The new system heralded the start of a national policy of restricted entry based on academic grades.[122] Inadvertently, the new criteria advantaged women over men. An Auckland study showed that women consistently obtained higher grades than their male colleagues in all law subjects from 1973 to 1977.[123] A similar pattern emerged in Wellington.[124] At a national level, women law students obtained a greater proportion of honours degrees for the next five years.[125]

Once the universities took control of legal training there was no going back—for women or the legal profession. From 1967 to 1977, the proportion of women law students shot up from a barely noticeable 6 percent to a remarkable 30 percent of the national law student body.[126] The influx of women into the law schools was not matched in any other professional discipline.[127]

The number of women lawyers also increased. From 31 women in practice in 1966, there were 142 in 1976.[128] For the first time, in 1977, the Auckland and New Zealand law societies began to count the number of women taking out practising certificates.[129] The experiment was over—the exception was becoming the rule.

Chapter Four

The Old Boys' Network: 1896–1970s

While economic policies and other external factors determined the ebb and flow of women in and out of the legal profession, each individual woman lawyer's success or failure rested in the hands of the men in the legal profession. Through the allocation of jobs and the extension of professional and social contact, men lawyers retained ultimate control over women's access to and advancement within the profession.

Women lawyers needed to break into a profession which operated essentially as a closed network of colleagues, relatives and business acquaintances. The obstacles created by this 'old boys' network' played a significant part in defining and restricting women's role in the profession.

Getting into the profession

Family connections

While the first women who entered the profession were unusual by virtue of their sex, their profile as a social group was not unlike that of their male colleagues. They came from middle-class and upper-class backgrounds and most had connections in the profession. Of the women lawyers admitted to the Bar from 1897 to 1959 whose family occupations were known, approximately 70 percent had a male lawyer in the family.[1] Some, like Ellen Melville and Rebecca Pallot, had only one or two male cousins, but the vast majority had lawyer fathers or uncles. Several came from well-known legal families.[2]

Over the same period, men lawyers were also likely to be well connected in the law. Michael Cullen's study of the Otago profession found that on average 20 to 25 percent of the predominantly male profession had lawyer fathers.[3] If that study was extended to include other male relatives, the proportion could well match more closely that of the women lawyers.

For women entering the profession, family support was essential. Legal training was a lengthy and expensive undertaking, more so for women who worked as law clerks at rates of pay less than half that of men clerks.[4] Most of the early women lawyers enjoyed family support—financial and moral—for their ambitions of qualifying and practising. Their parents placed a high value on the education of their daughters and encouraged their decisions to take up the profession. For many, as Dorothy Raymond explained: 'Law was after all in the blood.'[5]

Connections in the profession could make or break an aspirant's legal career. In certain periods, or in rural areas where university law classes were not available, legal training rested exclusively with the practising profession.[6] Several of the early women lawyers studied by correspondence but by far the majority worked as law clerks while studying. The quality of that training was certainly not guaranteed, and largely depended on whether the clerk happened to be 'in the office of some person who [took] an interest in them'.[7]

The family firm

The way to ensure that a qualified practitioner took an interest in the training of a prospective member of the profession was for the prospective member to enter the family firm. A significant number of the early women lawyers followed the traditional pattern and began their legal careers in the offices of family members. Of the women studied who were admitted between 1897 and 1959, an estimated one-third worked in family practices at some time during their legal careers.[8]

New Zealand's first 'legal daughter' and fourth woman lawyer, Annie Lee Rees, joined her father's practice after finishing her law degree in 1910. Her admission to the Bar exemplified the familial and collegial traditions of the profession. The ceremony, according to the *Gisborne Herald*, was held in open court in 'compliment to her father's leading position among members of the Bar'.[9] This important occasion in the provincial town of Gisborne was attended by 'a large number of ladies and prominent business men'.[10] The admission itself was conducted by Judge Chapman, whose father had admitted Rees' father to the Bar in 1866.[11]

Rees' father was not only a prominent lawyer. As a member of Parliament, William Lee Rees had supported the 1891 attempt to open the profession to women, calling the proposal 'a very wise and beneficial one'.[12] That public display of support came several years before the idea attracted political appeal, making William Lee Rees unique not only among politicians but among his legal colleagues.

The *Gisborne Herald* commented, some years after Rees returned to teaching on the death of her father, that 'prejudices against woman's participation in professional careers' had prevented her from being 'a brilliant success' in the law.[13] Teaching, by comparison, was a wholly acceptable occupation for a woman.[14]

Following Rees, many other early women lawyers joined their male relatives in practice. Julia Dunn joined her father's firm, as did Esther Ongley, Elisabeth Urquhart, Patricia Webb, and Paddy Steele.[15] Margaret Mackay worked in her uncle's law firm,[16] Dorothy Raymond joined the family firm in Timaru,[17] and Betty Thorpe worked at various times on a part-time basis with her father, her brother, and later, her son.

Obtaining work in the family firm meant that a significant number of early women lawyers did not test the attitudes of the wider profession, at least when it came to employment. A Wellington graduate of the 1940s observed that she had 'no problem' obtaining a job as she simply joined her father's practice.[18] Similarly, Rebecca Pallot, according to family history, could have joined her cousins in practice, had she and her husband moved back to Auckland.[19] As it was, there were no legal openings for her in the small provincial town of Napier.

At the end of the day, legal fathers and uncles preferred the admission of male relatives to the family firm. The traditional 'right of family succession' meant, in some cases, that specific provision was made in partnership deeds for a partner's son to join the firm as a law clerk or a partner.[20] This practice prevailed even where there was a highly competent daughter who openly aspired to a legal career.[21] Law was after all a career for a man, a profession. Sons, brothers, or nephews would stay in the practice, ensuring it would survive up to four generations still bearing the family name.[22] For women, it was assumed that marriage would still take precedence—any careers would be hobbies.

Patronage outside the family

Patronage did extend beyond the immediate family—but again the sons of colleagues, clients, and friends were preferred. Commercial city firms such as Bell Gully, for example, had a recruitment policy that tended to 'favour sons from old families, well-to-do merchants and up-country squattocracy, many of whom were educated at private schools'.[23] Employing these young men served the useful purpose of cementing client loyalty and business contacts—benefits which could more than repay the costs of employing and training law clerks.

If any of the early women lawyers brought valuable family business or contacts to the practices, those benefits arguably were outweighed by the risks involved. Women lawyers were more likely to attract curiosity or disapproval from members of the public and the legal profession than a certain client base. There was no guarantee that other employees would accept women as law clerks or lawyers, and certainly no guarantee they would be accepted in the profession as a whole. As Dorothy Thompson (née Simes) recalled, when a friend of her father offered her a job in 1939 he had 'decided to take a chance and employ a female'.[24]

Men lawyers with a sense of justice

Those men, whether related or unrelated to the woman in question, who did 'take a chance' by employing and supporting a woman law clerk's or lawyer's career ambitions, were a select and special breed. They were often popular and highly regarded members of the profession, holding law society office, academic positions, or public office at some point in their careers. Talented young men law clerks and lawyers would have jumped at the opportunity of their patronage. Instead, these pioneer men lawyers participated in a social experiment by employing or supporting women.

William Izard and H H Loughnan, the first lawyers known to employ a woman law clerk, shunned current professional thinking when they employed Stella Henderson in 1894—the same year the Canterbury law society was openly opposing women's entry to the profession. As a member of the Canterbury law society council, Izard not only ignored its opposition to the entry of women by teaching and employing Henderson, he actively defied the society by lobbying for the law change so that she could practise.[25]

Although initially Henderson's position in the firm of Izard and Loughnan was a temporary one, any hesitation on the part of the partners was soon dissolved by her ability. Her temporary position was transferred into a salaried 'regular place', an offer Izard had assured her was based solely on her merits.[26]

Both men were credited by Henderson as having played an important part in her all too brief legal career. She described Loughnan as being 'as generous and as broadminded as Mr Izard'. They had all shared the hope that she would achieve 'a successful legal career', an ambition which, Henderson reflected, was made impossible by 'circumstances'.[27]

C J Parr employed Geraldine Hemus as Auckland's first woman law clerk in 1898, assuming full responsibility for her early legal education, there being no law classes available at that time.[28] When the respected Auckland firm Devore and Cooper (later Devore and Martin) employed Ellen Melville as a law clerk the following year, Albert Devore and James C Martin not only encouraged her to qualify in law but supported and promoted her entry into local government politics—another exclusively male domain.[29]

Of the early women lawyers whose career paths can be traced, Ethel Benjamin is the only one who did not start her legal career as a law clerk. Whether she could not find a position or, buoyed by her outstanding academic success, she chose not to, she instead set up as a barrister sole straight after graduation. She was not without friends in the Dunedin legal fraternity, however, among them two influential lawyers— J M Gallaway, a member of the Otago law society council, and Saul Solomon, a prominent lawyer with whom Benjamin shared an interest in divorce cases.[30]

Several judges also publicly supported these pioneer women. In 1903, Mr Justice Edwards appointed his daughter as his associate, apparently against the wishes of the other employees. As Hubert Ostler (later Mr Justice Ostler) later recalled: 'We male associates considered [her appointment] as hitting below the belt.'[31] Mr Justice Chapman, at Annie Lee Rees' admission in 1910, offered her his public congratulations, commenting on 'the advance made since his boyhood days when angry comments were made upon the aspirations of women obtaining University degrees'.[32]

The example set by these pioneer men lawyers was followed in later years. E W R Haldane employed school-leaver Marjorie Taylor (later Feist) as a law clerk in the 1930s and, on her admission as a barrister in 1942, offered her a partnership.[33] Sievwright, James & Nichol supported the ambition of Marion Thomson, a junior typist in the firm, to study law.[34] J P Ward, a lecturer at Otago University, went 'against the grain of social opinion' in the late 1930s by offering Marion Thomson a position in his practice when she was newly engaged.[35] Garth Gallaway (son of Ethel Benjamin's supporter J M Gallaway) and his partner J C Mowat employed Sheila Macdonald as a junior law clerk in 1937, offering her a partnership in their firm when she graduated in 1942.[36]

The early women lawyers were dependent on these and other men in the profession to give them opportunities for work, supervision and training. Unfortunately for women, those men lawyers who were prepared to do so represented only a small minority of the profession. What characterised the experience of women law students, law clerks and graduates more than anything else was professional isolation and professional exclusion. Women, by virtue of their sex, could not fit the prescribed professional model.

Professional exclusion

A question of morality

From the time of colonisation, men and women were ascribed distinct social roles—men were believed to be inclined to immorality and vice, such as drinking and gambling, while women, particularly those of the middle and upper classes, tended to high morals and innocence. This neat division of morals worked well. While men tested the boundaries of social life, women were expected to temper men's excesses.[37]

To maintain this balance, it was critically important that women's morality was protected—a task which fell to men, and to gentlemen in particular. So, when called on to explain the legal disabilities of women, New Zealand politicians and lawyers, like their American and English counterparts, hastened to point out that the source of the disability was the law. They upheld the law without malice or disrespect to the intelligence or high regard in which women were held. They talked in terms of women being 'excluded, or rather excused, by the common law'.[38] As Charles Button, president of the Auckland District Law Society and member of Parliament, said: 'I do not regard these disabilities as being a reproach at all, but rather [women's] glory or pride.'[39]

Protection of women was a consistent theme throughout the common law, equity and legislation. The common law disabilities of a married woman were described as being 'for the most part intended for her protection and benefit: so great a favourite is the female sex of the laws of England'.[40] Equity was spurred by 'parental solicitude' toward married women; to 'guard the interests, and succour the weakness of those who are left without any other protectors'.[41] Parliament, whether in legislation relating to women's employment in factories, prostitution or matrimonial property, claimed to be motivated by the need to protect women. All these laws, of course, were made by men—in women's interests.

These men were also acting in the greater interests of society. As one American judge said when declining to allow a woman to practise law: 'It is public policy . . . not to tempt women from the proper duties of their sex by opening to them duties peculiar to ours.' Women's involvement in legal affairs would 'tend to relax the public sense of decency and propriety'.[42]

Consistent with these beliefs, social conventions required that the sexes be kept apart.[43] If women and men mixed freely in education or in social interaction, the delicate moral balance could be easily upset. Women would become tainted and men would lose their respect for women. Sexual impropriety, moral decline, and all manner of social ills would inevitably result.

Legal education

From the early 1900s to the 1950s, most women who studied law had attended single-sex schools. For these women, enrolling in university law classes or seeking to attend law student debates was a direct confrontation of the convention that females and males received separate educations. Entering the male learning environment was no superficial or easy obstacle to overcome. Geraldine Hemus and Ellen Melville, for example, unbeknown to each other, both delayed the moment when they had to enter the all-male law school environment. Although keen to attend the 1904 classes so they could qualify for practice, both women were hesitant and shy about attending alone. Hemus tried to find another woman student to go with her, but without success. Finally, after missing the first week, she 'plucked up courage' to go alone. At the second lecture, she was met at the door by Melville who asked: 'Are you the girl who is attending the law lectures? I wanted to come to them but did not like to go alone.'[44]

From that point on, Melville and Hemus attended the lectures together, but their experience was unusual. Until the 1950s, most women law students attended classes alone. Dorothy Raymond, the sole woman law student at Canterbury University College for the greater part of her studies from 1927 to 1931, 'sat alone on a long bench' at most lectures. She 'felt isolated at lectures', commenting that '[a]part from a couple of students whom I knew socially, no others made any attempt to be friendly'.[45] Isobel Matson (née Wright), who studied at Canterbury in the late 1930s, did not recall any particular difficulty at law school 'apart from having to sit down at the front of the tiered lecture hall'.[46]

Segregation of the sexes was not limited to the formal learning environment. The Otago law society council complied with convention when it allowed Ethel Benjamin to use the Supreme Court law library—if separated from the men. Restricting her to the Judge's Chamber Room would apparently save the male lawyers 'from unnecessary and distressing contact with a woman'.[47] Over thirty years later, probably for the same reason, a Christchurch male lawyer told recent graduate Dorothy Thompson (née Simes) to leave the Canterbury Supreme Court library.[48]

Other women students received a mixture of support and opposition to their attendance at lectures or their use of law libraries. When Dorothy Raymond went with her father to meet the chancellor of Canterbury University College in 1926 to discuss her intention to enrol in law, he 'raised no opposition' and was 'welcoming'. Likewise, the dean of the law faculty, Thomas Rowe, a sole practitioner, was friendly towards the solitary woman student in the law school, but Raymond would find that half the lecturers 'actively discouraged' women law students and the rest were 'not encouraging'.[49] Not long after Raymond completed her degree in 1932, the environment for women at Canterbury University College changed for the worse. Rowe was replaced by a new dean who, Raymond said, 'openly discouraged women'. She recalled that 'some years passed before [women] had the courage to reappear'.[50]

Marion Thomson, studying law at Otago University in the mid-1930s, recalled that her lecturers and fellow students were courteous.[51] Isobel Matson had a similar experience when she enrolled in law at Canterbury University College in the late 1930s, although in hindsight she wondered whether the other students and lecturers, who were mostly local practitioners, were courteous towards her because they were 'mindful' of her father's senior position in the local profession.[52]

By the late 1950s, with the appointment of Professor Hamish Gray as the first full-time dean of the Canterbury university law faculty, the environment for women had improved markedly. Ann McAloon (née Barcham) who studied during this period recalled that Professor Gray was 'very encouraging and supportive' to her throughout her student years. She directly attributed her 'easy acceptance' by students and staff to the influence of Professor Gray.[53]

Being the only woman among a large group of men ensured the popularity of some early women lawyers. Sheila Macdonald, an Otago graduate in the early 1940s, was said by a fellow student to have 'played her full part in faculty affairs' being 'much in demand as a partner at the Law Ball'.[54] Alison Quentin-Baxter (née Souter), who enjoyed student life at Victoria University College in the late 1940s, recalled that she and her female colleagues were made 'rather a fuss of, both by our fellow students and our teachers'.[55] Paddy Steele (née West-Walker), who in the mid-1950s was the only woman in her class of twenty or so students at Victoria University College, was friendly with many of the men students, most of whom she had already met while working in her father's law office. She joined in social activities and received help with her legal studies: 'It was no problem at all. I didn't feel I was different. I was treated as one of them.'[56]

Other women were reminded that they were unusual among their classmates. An Auckland woman law student in the 1950s recalled 'no obvious distinction' between the treatment received by women students and that received by the men, although, she added, they 'probably thought we were a bit odd'.[57] Shirley Parr, who attended Victoria law school with the tail-end of the World War II 'rehabs', recalled loneliness and isolation. Although she would sometimes have afternoon tea with a group of men students, most were unfriendly. At one point she was so desperate to have the company of another woman, she rang a friend and said, 'Talk!'[58]

Sex-related lectures

Education on the laws pertaining to sex-related topics most directly confronted the social conventions regarding women's modesty. Among the reasons given by the Chief Justice of the Wisconsin Supreme Court in 1875 when declining a woman's application to practice law was that the profession of law involved 'all that is selfish and malicious, knavish and criminal, coarse and brutal, repulsive and obscene in human life'. Lawyers, the Chief Justice said, had to deal with 'unclean issues' such as 'sodomy, incest, rape, seduction, fornication, adultery, pregnancy, bastardy, illegitimacy, prostitution, lascivious cohabitation, abortion, infanticide, obscene publications, libel and slander of sex, impotence, divorce'. These issues were 'bad enough for men'. Women were 'moulded for gentler and better things'.[59]

These sentiments were echoed by Charles Button, president of the Auckland District Law Society and member of Parliament, when in 1896 he opposed the wholesale removal of women's disabilities and the consequent entry of women into the law. Button, like many of his contemporaries, believed women's 'delightful quality of modesty will vanish, or, at all events, be very much marred, if we bring women into close intercourse with those rough affairs with which the other sex have to contend'. He compared women with flowers, asking: 'Who would expect the violet and the lily to withstand the rough storms of the mountain-tops?'[60]

Men were vested with the responsibility of protecting women; failing to do so meant failing to respect women—not the mark of a gentleman. The male law lecturers teaching at universities around the country responded either by excluding women students from the lectures that touched on sex-related laws or by omitting those parts of the lectures. These practices continued at least until the 1960s.

For many of the early women lawyers, the lecturers' reactions to their attendance at these classes was quite memorable. Dorothy Raymond recalls the point in a criminal law lecture at Canterbury University College in the late 1920s when the students came to the chapter headed 'Rape': 'The lecturer, a practising solicitor, took one look at me and said, "Now we'll turn to page so and so" . . . Of course we never went back.'[61] The lecturer at Otago University avoided the problem when it came to Marion Thomson's criminal law class in 1935. He asked her father to ask her to refrain from attending the lectures on rape and incest.[62] The reason, as she understood it, was that the lecturer was apparently too embarrassed to discuss those topics in the presence of a woman. A private lecture on those aspects of criminal law was arranged for her instead.[63] Fay Wellwood recalled that her lecturer at Canterbury University College in the early 1950s was 'very careful not to offend' when it came to the 'details of the Crimes Act'.[64]

Reticence to discuss sex in the presence of women law students extended beyond the criminal law sphere.[65] Shirley Parr recalls being told by a professor in the early 1950s not to attend a jurisprudence lecture on divorce and sexual assault because, he said, 'she would be embarrassed'.[66] By 1952, when Shirley Smith enrolled at Wellington law school, women students were 'warned about . . . Professor McGechan's customary exclusion of women from one of his lectures'. The practice ended, not with Shirley Smith's planned challenge, but with Professor McGechan's unexpected death.[67]

Even into the 1960s, law lecturers remained uncomfortable with mixed-sex legal education on 'sensitive' matters. When Silvia Cartwright, (later Justice Cartwright) attended Otago University, the lecturer skipped the entire section on sexual crimes. The reason, she was told, was that the content may have been embarrassing to her, although she suspected it was more embarrassing to the lecturer.[68] Likewise, Cecile Fleming (later Rushton and a District Court judge), was excluded from law lectures on the Crimes Act during the early 1960s at Canterbury University. The lecturer made an announcement in class that he would 'be pleased if the ladies in the class' would refrain from attending. Cecile Fleming was the only woman law student.[69]

In general, women students accepted their exclusion from these lectures.[70] Judge Rushton pointed out that the lectures women could not attend 'dealt with sex, unnatural acts with animals and little boys and all those nasty things which nice young ladies are not meant to know about, let alone discuss'.[71] Ironically, the subject-matter considered most unfit for women law students—rape, incest, sexual assault and divorce—concerned events in which women played central parts and laws which had the most fundamental impacts on women's lives. The distinction was justified on the basis that, unlike the women law students, the women who would be involved in these events were presumed not to be 'ladies'.

Professional and social isolation

The few women who managed to complete their legal qualifications, find jobs and stay in the profession were geographically and professionally isolated. Until the mid-1950s each was usually the only woman in her law class and the only woman professional at her workplace. Even into the early 1970s, a women lawyer remained a novelty, unusual, an oddity.[72]

The low numbers and geographical isolation of women lawyers made social and professional interaction with their male colleagues both unavoidable and essential. As is still the case, the business of law necessitated working with and against other lawyers on transactions and cases as much as it involved working with clients. In addition, the common 'learning by doing' method of legal training inevitably required mixing with those in the profession who were already proficient in the law and legal procedure.

Women lawyers, however, were confronted by a policy of exclusion which limited their opportunities for professional contact and access to legal information. The similar socio-economic and family backgrounds of women and men lawyers mitigated that exclusion in some cases, but this was no guarantee that all women would be accepted as professional equals. The problem for women lawyers was that, despite their personal characteristics, they remained female in a profession which, until the early 1960s, was almost exclusively male with identifiably male social rituals.

Women lawyers' family connections, patronage, or social and economic class could only go so far toward alleviating their social displacement.

According to the official view, prejudice against women lawyers was simply not an issue. As late as 1967, the Council of Legal Education and the New Zealand Law Society declared:

> the small percentage of ladies-in-law is due less to prejudice against women by male practitioners and by clients, than to the fact that the majority of women graduates find that marriage and the upbringing of children prevent their pursuing an exacting professional career. It is a matter of regret that more of our women graduates, many of whom had high academic attainments, do not remain in the law.[73]

Bar dinners and other social interaction

Men only

Consistent with the belief that 'lady' law students and lawyers should remain untainted by the 'unclean' aspects of law, they were excluded from professional social occasions involving alcohol and the prospect of coarse humour. Whether hosted by the law students or the law societies, Bar dinners and social functions were regularly closed to women law students and women lawyers.

The relationship between women and alcohol was particularly vexed. Dating back to the suffrage movement, women's early political efforts were closely aligned to the temperance movement. 'New women', like law student Stella Henderson, made public comments such as, 'Drinking leads to degradation and crime' and 'Wrong social conditions and criminal neglect lead to drinking'.[74] Ethel Benjamin was exceptional, being openly in support of the liquor industry as a shareholder and manager of at least five Otago and Southland hotels. Publicans were among Benjamin's major clients. From 1902 to 1905, she acted on behalf of the local liquor trade, aiming to defeat the polls to introduce dry areas and lobbying for licensing law reforms.[75]

The consumption of alcohol by women carried a heavy social stigma. Although women had brewed beer and made wine in colonial days, abstinence was a mark of 'the good woman'.[76] Only 'bad women'—whores and criminals—were seen to drink publicly in hotels with men. These social taboos lessened during World War II as women's opportunities expanded, but legislation passed in 1948 formally restricted women's access to hotel public bars.[77] Even in the 1950s, when beer drinking became a national pastime, women's use of alcohol remained stigmatised.

By comparison, men lawyers gathered openly and regularly in clubs and bars for social drinks, meals and chats. In the nineteenth century, Auckland lawyers regularly lunched together at the Northern Club and, to a lesser extent, at the Auckland Club.[78] In Wellington, they frequented the Wellesley Club. As with all the gentlemen's clubs around the country until the late 1980s or early 1990s, women were not eligible to be members.

On more formal occasions, following the English tradition, Bar dinners were held—often at the men's clubs or in hotels. At these events, lawyers and law students met to socialise during conferences, to celebrate official local milestones, such as the appointment of a judge or the opening of a new courthouse, or simply to celebrate the end of a university year. Bar dinners customarily involved the consumption of alcohol, often to excess, and speeches alluding to 'unclean' matters—known by women lawyers in the 1950s as 'blue jokes'.

Within some firms the social mixing of women and men lawyers was difficult. In 1948, Buddle, Richmond & Buddle held its first Christmas party attended by partners and women and men staff. Segregated morning and afternoon teas for professional and non-professional staff were common in firms (a situation still common in some firms in the 1990s). When women joined the professional staff they presented a problem—should they take tea with the women typists or try to mix with the men who were inclined to talk 'about nothing but cricket, rugby and race horses'?[79] The problem presented by morning tea apparently influenced one Auckland firm in the 1970s not to employ a woman lawyer.[80]

Professional networking

Although at face value the purpose of legal functions and gatherings was social, there were other more important professional reasons for attending. By meeting at social functions, lawyers could move beyond the usual adversarial stances they assumed when acting for opposing clients. Here, among friends, legal information and anecdotes could be exchanged and contacts made or reaffirmed. For new entrants to the profession, the networking opportunities were vital in advancing their careers. For existing members of the profession, information about unreported cases or a judge's latest pronouncement could be invaluable to their work and their clients.

Women law students may have accepted their exclusion from sex-related law lectures (even though this subsequently may have prejudiced their clients), but they and women lawyers were not as ready to be denied the social and professional interaction of Bar dinners. The women excluded from Bar dinners were much more inclined to voice their objections.

Women challenge their exclusion

In 1899, Ethel Benjamin wrote an uncompromising letter of complaint to the secretary of the Otago law society:

> I wish to ask you why I was not notified of the Bar Dinner recently held under the auspices of the Law Society. I am exempted from none of the obligations imposed on members of the Profession, and I consider all privileges extended to them as such, should also be extended to me.[81]

Benjamin had in fact been excluded from the Bar dinner the previous year, despite having indicated her intention to attend. Her name—included, in brackets, in the original seating plan—was struck off the final invitation list.[82] She was concerned by the precedent created by her exclusion. In her 1899 letter, she wrote:

> It may be of course, that the omission of my name was an oversight, but, if purposely omitted on account of my sex, I have to enter a protest against such treatment ... Moreover, I do not think that without protest I should allow a precedent to be established that may affect the rights of other members of my sex who will follow in my footsteps.[83]

Her prescient protest was not heard—Ethel Benjamin was not invited to the next Bar dinner held in 1902.

The dinners of the Auckland Law Students' Society were opened to women in the early 1940s when Betty Thorpe became the society's secretary, perhaps the first woman to hold an office in a law student body. Until then, women had not been invited to social occasions.[84]

In 1951, Shirley Parr decided to protest her exclusion from the Victoria law faculty dinners by organising a women's dinner. She found five women in the whole law faculty—Paddy West-Walker, Shirley Sunley, Lady Amelia Reedell, and two other women students. In a bold act of defiance, these women held their own dinner at the same venue and on the same night as the men.[85]

In the late 1950s and early 1960s, Shirley Smith challenged the Wellington District Law Society on several occasions about its policy of men-only Bar dinners.[86] In 1961, Cecile Rushton, 'led the assault' against the decision of the Canterbury Law Students' Committee to exclude the fourteen women law students from the annual law student dinner.[87] Around the same time, Judith Mayhew and other Otago women lawyers protested against their exclusion from the Otago District Law Society Bar dinners.[88]

Women lawyers' challenges to the men-only policies, where successful, often had the support of men students or lawyers. Their first official invitation to the Victoria Law Faculty Club's annual dinner in 1952 came only after the intervention of a law professor who thought it was not right that women were excluded.[89] When the club reneged the next year, Shirley Smith enlisted the support of men law students, having them propose and speak to a motion requiring the dinner to be open to all students. Likewise, she sought senior male practitioners' support when tackling the Wellington law society's exclusion of women.[90]

On occasions the break with the men-only tradition was short-lived. The Victoria Law Faculty Club, for example, changed its policy on women three times in less than a decade.[91] The Wellington law society also wavered in its resolve to include women, effectively changing the policy back to men-only in 1961.[92] Even where the official policy of allowing women remained in place, some men lawyers in the 1970s, as in Otago, continued to bristle openly at the thought of socialising with women practitioners.[93]

The price of attending: being 'one of the boys'

Some women lawyers stayed away in deference to the convention that the potentially bawdy drunken atmosphere of a Bar dinner was no place for ladies. Others who insisted on attending took the risk they would not be treated like ladies. It seemed that winning the right to attend professional social functions involved losing the right to be accorded the common social courtesies displayed when 'ladies' were present. Women lawyers had a clearly defined choice—stay away or be 'one of the boys'.

For some of these women, the offensive language and ribald humour was unforgettable. Shirley Smith, when describing the 1952 Wellington Law Faculty Club dinner, said: 'The air was blue and the behaviour drunken. One senior practitioner gave tongue to a degree of lewdness that delighted the male students and led me to swear to myself, "Never again".'[94] Shirley Parr, as a committee member at that dinner, was isolated from the other women, having to sit up on the dais. She recalled a particular lecturer at her table who had 'too much to drink' and told 'too many blue jokes'.[95] That was the first and only dinner she ever went to.

Women were often the butt of legal jokes and anecdotes. 'Rape jokes' were popular, often being told in a spirit of male camaraderie.[96] Bar dinner speeches would also play on stereotypes about women.

'[F]eminis, in one shape or another' was, for example, the topic chosen by the after-dinner speaker at the 1954 Law Conference, Thaddeus McCarthy (later Sir Thaddeus and president of the Court of Appeal). He said he knew little about the subject and so his speech relayed the advice he claimed to have received from his 'seniors in the law'. He began:

> I turned to an old family friend, now a member of the Judiciary, and put my case to him. 'What can I say?' I asked, 'And what is your opinion of marriage and women generally?' 'Marriage has many pains,' he said, 'and, as for women, they are not to be trusted. They poke the fire from the top, and so they are not to be trusted. But there are exceptions, and my wife, of course is an angel.' 'In what way?' I asked. 'She is usually up in the air, is always harping on something, and she has not got a damned thing to wear', he explained.[97]

McCarthy also claimed to have consulted practitioners, whose comments he reported, ranged from, 'Women? . . . They are intolerable; that is their only fault' to 'For a man to pretend to know all about women is bad manners, and for a man really to know all about them is bad morals!' McCarthy concluded his speech by extolling the virtues of lawyers' wives, and proposing a toast: 'Once again . . . our wives have placed our wants before their own. They were to be here [at the dinner]; but knowing that we needed this place, they went elsewhere.'[98]

Women lawyers were expected to display the same selfless virtue admired in men lawyers' wives by staying away from 'the men's functions'. Augusta Wallace, a student at Auckland University law school in the early 1950s and later New Zealand's first woman judge, recalled that she 'used a certain amount of discretion' in deciding which social activities to attend. She happily attended law dinners but would not go to the stein evenings because: '[f]or one thing I didn't drink beer and for another I accepted that it was the young men's night. I instinctively knew that to go there could have caused embarrassment.'[99]

Women lawyers in court

For the same reasons that the law lecturers excluded women from classes on sex-related laws and the law societies resisted women's inclusion at professional social occasions, women lawyers were discouraged from attending court. It was here, in the courts, that vice and violence were openly paraded for public and judicial scrutiny. Women who took an interest in these matters were certainly not ladies. One English judge even banned women from the public gallery in his divorce court. According to a legal text, the judge remarked at the close of a case:

> I have observed with the greatest pain that the public gallery has never been empty of two or three women—I shall not call them ladies—listening to the filthy details day after day which have been laid before the Court. I think it is a great pity such things are allowed'.[100]

The text's author warned that those women would 'carry their curse about with them—a diseased and blackened mind'.[101]

A correspondent to the *Solicitors' Journal* in 1896 suggested that the judges might discourage women from litigating in person. He wrote:

> If women choose to usurp the functions of men, they ought to expect to receive the same treatment as men. It is not necessary to be rude to them, but a little salutary firmness and curtness of speech would go a long way to reduce their number.[102]

Some men feared that women barristers, by their very physical presence in the courtroom, might subvert the course of justice. In 1881, Sir William Fox, formerly Premier of New Zealand, relayed to the House of Representatives this story about a case conducted by an American woman lawyer:

The Judge was under the powerful influence of her beauty, the exquisite good taste of her costume—only one beautiful rose was in her bosom; and a verdict was obtained in favour of a murderer who had committed a horrible crime, though the facts were dead against him. The jury—the Judge—they were all taken in, and a verdict brought in in favour of one of the most notorious, bloodthirsty criminals who ever lived on the face of the earth.[103]

Women lawyers were expected to have particularly strong powers of persuasion—linked not to their legal talents but to their seductive charms. While wishing Ethel Benjamin every success as a barrister, an *Otago Daily Times* columnist expressed the hope that 'her predatory raids may be mitigated by feminine compassion, and her pleadings mindful of the susceptibilities of juries, who are only human after all'.[104] Three months later, a male law student reported:

The seductive charms of a lady pleader have long been a source of premonitory consternation to judicial circles, but as yet, Miss Benjamin has fluttered the heart of no jury, nor even made to tremble the judicial equilibrity of a justice of the peace.[105]

Prescribing women barristers' court attire

One way of controlling women barristers' assumed seductive influences was by regulating their court attire. Ladies' fashions were perceived as more frivolous than those of professional men and the profession made it a high priority to place restrictions on what women lawyers could wear in court. The concern was not so much for consistency with male court attire, but to obscure women's sexuality.

In 1896, the Ontario Law Society set the precedent which would be followed in New Zealand. Following Clara Brett Martin's successful appeal against its decision refusing to admit her to the profession, the society published rules on women barristers' court attire. A lady barrister, according to the Ontario Law Society, should be 'attired in a black dress under a black gown, with white collar and cuffs, and bareheaded'. The editors of the English *Solicitors' Journal* were unimpressed. Why stipulate that the dress would be worn under the gown? It was not practicable, they pointed out, to put the dress over the gown. There was no mention of the material from which the dress should be made nor the trimmings, and finally, they asked, why were the 'all-important' barrister's bands overlooked?[106]

A further and equally notable omission from the court dress prescribed for women by the Ontario Law Society was the absence of the barrister's wig. Not only would this differentiate women barristers from men barristers, it also offended social convention—no self-respecting nineteenth century lady would appear bareheaded in a public forum such as the courtroom.[107] Even women offenders appearing in the court wore cloth caps. In directing that women barristers be bareheaded, the Ontario Law Society was overriding convention and placing women at a distinct disadvantage.

In New Zealand, the task of prescribing court attire fell to the Otago District Law Society. On the admission of Ethel Benjamin to the Dunedin Bar in 1897, the Otago society council passed this resolution:

> In view of the fact that women are now admitted to the privileges of the Bar it is desirable that some dress should be prescribed, and it is suggested that the Judges should make a regulation and this Council submits that the regulation should be as prescribed by the Ontario Law Society.[108]

No doubt aware of the shortcomings of the Ontario rules, John McRae Gallaway, a council member and supporter of Ethel Benjamin, dissented from the resolution. The resolution was sent to Justice Williams who had admitted Benjamin to the Bar. He declined jurisdiction and, several meetings later, the matter was dropped.

In 1907, a cartoon of Ethel Benjamin getting ready for court was published in the *Exhibition Sketcher*. Depicted in full court dress and preening before a mirror, she asks her maid, 'Does my jupon show below my gown?' A visible petticoat at that time was a matter of some excitement and certainly inappropriate for a lady barrister. (Figure 8)

The question of women barristers' court dress prompted no further public comment until the admission of Ann Barcham and Angela Satterthwaite in Christchurch in 1961. Justice Macarthur agreed to a request from the *Press* for a photograph of him with the newly-admitted women barristers, 'subject to their being properly dressed in accordance with the rules of the profession'. According to the *New Zealand Law Journal*, this condition 'caused some little stir'—no one in Christchurch was sure how a woman barrister should be dressed. Research by Justice Macarthur and the court registrar, however, uncovered rules prepared by a committee of Canadian judges and barristers. Those rules, published in the *New Zealand Law Journal*, provided that a woman lawyer should wear the ordinary barrister's wig which should 'completely cover and conceal the hair', an ordinary barrister's gown, barrister's bands and a plain black or dark coloured dress 'high to the neck with long sleeves, and not shorter than the gown'.[109] The prescribed attire would ensure that women's sexuality remained well and truly under wraps in the courtroom.

Changing and other facilities

That women barristers were usurping ground where they were not wanted is nowhere better illustrated than in the continuous struggle to acquire separate changing facilities for women in New Zealand's courthouses and law libraries, commonly situated in the court buildings.

Figure 8
'A Cherry Barrister'

A Cherry Barrister.

Look after my clients, and give them lots of cream and heaps of cake.
I'm counsel for the defence in the divorce case Smith *v.* Smith,
and intend giving old Smith taffy!   Oh heavens, where are my
wig pins!   Now my brief.   Does my jupon show below my gown?
Right now for the court!

W A Bowring cartoon from the 'Exhibition Sketcher', 2 February 1907. Reproduced with the permission of the Canterbury Museum, Christchurch, New Zealand, ref 8126.

In 1918, the Otago law society opposed a proposal that toilets near the law library should be taken over for use by women. Without the society's knowledge, a card had been nailed to the door of the lavatory with 'Ladies Only' printed on it in large letters. Incensed, the law society condemned the move in a letter to the Minister of Justice, which, according to Michael Cullen, the society's historian, was one of the longest letters the society had ever written.[110]

The Otago profession's opposition to the intrusion of women into its domain was not directed at any particular women barristers. At that time the local profession was entirely male—Ethel Benjamin had left for Wellington eleven years before and Margaret Mackay was not admitted to the Bar in Otago until 1929. What the 1918 objection meant, however, was that the profession certainly did not take seriously the prospect that there could be women needing facilities in future. There were none at the time and that was the way it should remain.

This reaction was echoed more than forty years later by the Gisborne profession. During the planning of a new courthouse in the early 1960s, local practitioners 'expressed surprise at the intention of the Ministry of Works to make provision for women barristers'.[111] In doing so, they forgot not only that Annie Lee Rees had been admitted to the Bar in 1910 but that there was a woman lawyer actually in practice in town at the time. Ellen Evans was admitted in Gisborne in 1939 and practised there until about 1978.[112]

Women lawyers persistently battled with a lack of changing facilities. Shirley Parr encountered problems when she went to court in the late 1950s and early 1960s, as there were no changing rooms or toilets for women. At a social gathering in New Plymouth in the early 1960s she tackled the then Chief Justice about facilities for women barristers. She recalled: 'They were talking of the need for women's toilets in courthouses because of the recent acceptance of women on juries, so I said 'What about women barristers' toilets?' I got no answer.'[113]

Even as more women were admitted to the Bar and were seeking to appear in the courts, the facilities remained inadequate. Margaret Wilson (later Professor Wilson and Dean of Waikato Law School) recalled that being in the changing room for women lawyers at the Auckland Supreme Court in the 1970s was 'like being in a broom cupboard'. Women barristers were not expressly excluded from the robing room but, as Auckland lawyer Prue Kapua observed, to change into court garb along with the men was for many women 'a challenge to their modesty'.[114]

When five women were to be admitted to the Bar in Christchurch in 1976, they were not allowed to use the robing room. In the end, the registrar gallantly gave up his office so that that they could change.[115] Likewise, in Dunedin there were no separate facilities. Silvia Cartwright (later a High Court judge) changed in the witnesses' toilet in the Dunedin courthouse until just before her appointment to the District Court in 1981.[116]

The denial of separate changing facilities exemplified the message that if women insisted on invading a male domain by practising law, they would have to do so on male terms. No concessions would be made to protect women's modesty—they were either excluded entirely or subjected to embarrassing and offensive behaviour. Even women lawyers with family connections in the profession found that they were excluded when it came to wider professional and social contact. While a minority of men in the profession would provide opportunities to women lawyers, the reaction of the majority up to the early 1970s confirmed that women lawyers were simply not welcome. They lacked one essential qualification —they were not men.

Chapter Five

Proving Ability: Women Lawyers 1896–1970s

Professional and social exclusion were not the only obstacles facing women lawyers. From the mid-nineteenth century, medical and scientific theories asserted a wide range of supposedly immutable intellectual and physical differences between women and men. These differences were relied on to prove male superiority, particularly in relation to education and employment. From the outset, women lawyers believed they could disprove these theories by demonstrating their ability to succeed in legal education and in the practice of the law. But this was no easy task. No matter how often the early women lawyers disproved the theories, they would resurface and repeatedly be used to justify where and how women could work in the profession.

The terms of inclusion

No concessions

Law changes in 1896 which allowed women into the legal profession did not give women new abilities—they simply removed a legal disability. Women themselves had not asked for any concessions, and none were offered.[1] The law merely gave to those women who proved they possessed the necessary qualifications and could pass the examinations, the 'privilege', not the 'right', to practise law.[2]

But there was considerable scepticism among others that women who aspired to 'legal fame and prosperity' would succeed.[3] According to the public, the media and the male profession, the pioneer women lawyers were on trial. Publicity about Ethel Benjamin's admission to the Bar extended even to English newspapers.[4] Her first court appearances, although of little legal merit, were covered in detail by the local papers.[5] Speculation about Stella Henderson's intentions to practise fuelled articles in one Wellington newspaper over three years.[6] The women who followed faced similar public scrutiny.

This was a social experiment. The pioneers' success, or lack of it, would affect the ambitions of all women who would follow in their tentative footsteps.[7] Other women, like Australia's first woman lawyer, G Flos Greig, argued against assessing women's success or failure 'from a few isolated cases'. Instead, she said:

> A sound induction can only be made from the examination of innumerable instances. And one must remember that there are brilliant, mediocre and inferior men in every trade and profession, and the same will apply to women.[8]

In New Zealand it would prove impossible to assess women lawyers' success based on 'innumerable instances'. As predicted, admissions of women were few and far between. In addition, mediocre or even average women were not encouraged to apply.

Exceptional women only

For those who supported the entry of women into the profession, it was critically important that women were seen to succeed. The surest way to achieve this was to encourage only exceptional women to apply. In 1897, Ethel Benjamin wrote in the *Press*: 'If women are determined to succeed, if they are diligent and "pushing", if they make the most of every opportunity that presents itself, sooner or later success will crown their efforts.'[9] The editor of the *Commonwealth Law Review* agreed. In his view, a woman entering the legal profession, more so than any other profession, needed exceptional qualities. She required 'not only courage and persistence, but a more than ordinary careful professional preparation, and a resolve to win through'.[10]

The pioneer women lawyers knew that for 'many years to come' women lawyers would face an uphill battle. Benjamin wrote: 'The advance of the pioneer is always difficult and slow; at times so great will appear the barriers which block the way, that progress will seem impossible.'[11] But, she remained optimistic, believing that, sooner or later, circumstances would yield to the woman with a 'will of iron'. On this basis, she advised: 'The average woman with average ability had, I think, better leave law to her more gifted brothers and sisters.'[12]

Academic ability

Women's smaller brains

The first 'ability' hurdle which women lawyers had to overcome was their presumed lesser intelligence. Nineteenth century scientists had claimed, and it was fairly well accepted, that women had smaller brains and therefore inferior mental ability to men.[13] It followed that women's powers of reason were also impaired.

The *Canadian Legal Scrap Book* put it bluntly: 'A woman does not, as a rule, arrive at a conclusion by logical reasoning, but rather by a species of instinct, which, no matter how unerring, cannot assist others to arrive at the same conclusion.'[14] These enhanced intuitive powers, of all women's qualities, were most incompatible with the dispassionate logic required for the law. How could women be lawyers when they had difficulty distinguishing between truth and fiction? Even as witnesses women were unreliable.[15] In 1928, O T J Alpers, a Supreme Court judge, compared women witnesses with child witnesses and concluded: 'Women are simpler; when they lie deliberately they do it from some indirect motive— envy, jealously, sheer malice, and evil-mindedness.'[16]

Equally disturbing was the idea that women's thought processes gave greater scope for creativity which would wreak havoc with the law, especially given its reliance on precedents which should always be followed unless there was good reason to do otherwise. No wonder, then, that Sir George Whitmore, a fervent opponent of women lawyers, argued that letting women practise law would 'lead to an enormous quantity of unnecessary litigation'.[17]

Education

The critical question toward the end of the nineteenth century was whether women's inferiority could be corrected by education. Some theorists, like Charles Darwin, were sceptical, suggesting that the only way women could reach the same intellectual standard as men was by inheritance.[18]

Local teachers and politicians were more optimistic, including those who thought there might be some substance to the concerns about women's abilities.[19] They suspected that education was the key to women's advancement. How could women dismantle the self-fulfilling prophecy of their inferior intellect without the opportunity to test it?

Since the Education Act 1877, a new attitude to education was evolving. Girls' high schools were being established in provincial towns and cities;[20] public schools which for the first time offered girls a real academic curriculum.[21] For women aiming at a legal career the secondary school curriculum was critical. Latin, one of the compulsory subjects in the law professionals examinations, was included in the new girls' curriculum and, although opposed by the Education Department, many teachers taught it with vigour at Auckland Girls' School, Christchurch Girls' High School and elsewhere.[22]

But girls did not necessarily receive the same quality of education as boys. Where financial sacrifice was involved, parents favoured their sons' education, and the inferior resources of girls' schools made it harder for girls to compete for the few university scholarships. Education

Department officers continued to object to teaching girls Latin,[23] which was believed to 'train the mind in [the] habits of logic',[24] a capacity few women were thought to possess.

Study will unsex women

Objections to teaching academic subjects to girls were supported by medical theories about the effects of intellectual exertion on women. Medical experts cautioned that women embarking on professional studies such as law risked severe mental strain.[25] As the theories on women's smaller brains lost ground, gynaecological theories took over.[26] The results of intellectual exertion could be disastrous. Women taking up academic study after the onset of puberty could suffer menstrual irregularity and, ultimately, 'nervous collapse and sterility'.[27]

The medical scare that women would be 'unsexed' by intellectual exertion became another reason for keeping women out of the legal profession. As Dr Truby King, founder of the Plunket Society, often declared, this was not in the interests of women, the family, or ultimately, the nation. In the Legislative Council, Sir George Whitmore objected to allowing women into the legal profession on the grounds that 'it would have the effect of inducing a number of females to quite unsex themselves and to neglect the ordinary female duties',[28] while Henry Scotland said it would not only encourage women to unsex themselves, it would 'make the colony ridiculous in the eyes of the world'.[29]

The fertility scare of the 1900s

From 1900 to 1914, university enrolments of women steadily increased across all disciplines except law. The low enrolment of women law students over this period coincided directly with a fertility scare. Rapidly falling population growth had raised fears that urbanisation was undermining male virility and, more significantly, had rekindled past concerns that academic pursuits were affecting female fertility.[30] Concerned for the future 'vitality of the race', medical experts, including Dr Batchelor and Dr Truby King, publicly opposed women undertaking university study, entering professions and obtaining clerkships.[31] King announced that educating women for the learned professions involved excessive mental, physical and nervous strain and was 'absolutely indefensible'.[32] There were no guarantees that women embarking on professional study would succeed.

But there was no documented evidence of the adverse physical effects of academic exertion on women. On the contrary, Stella Henderson and Ethel Benjamin had both emphatically denied any impairment to their health.[33] It seems the women themselves knew the argument was spurious. Dr Emily Siedeberg, the first woman to graduate from Otago

University Medical School, challenged Batchelor to name one woman who had 'broken down' as a result of academic work.[34]

As it transpired, the real issue, according to King and others, was not so much higher education for women; it was the type of education. Professional studies were believed to distract women from their main purpose—the acquisition of domestic skills in preparation for motherhood. The advocates of this view, including William Downie Stewart, pushed for the teaching of home science in the universities in an open attempt to divert women from taking professional courses.[35] The campaign was successful. In 1913, nine women were enrolled in medicine, one in law, and forty-one in the new bachelor of home science degree.[36]

The reality: academic excellence

Those few women who did study and graduate in law persistently achieved academic excellence. There was no evidence that Ellen Melville and Geraldine Hemus, who studied at night and qualified by way of the professionals course, had any difficulty. Ethel Benjamin, Stella Henderson and Annie Lee Rees, the only women known to study law at university in Batchelor and King's time, all demonstrated superior academic abilities.

Benjamin was a brilliant scholar. By the time she had completed her LLB she had gained first place in the colony in at least one examination each year.[37] In 1895, an article in the *Otago University Review* reminded the men law students of their scholarly inferiority. The *Review* admonished: 'Let the weaker sex—the men of course—look to it, they are not eclipsed, as happened last session, by the other representatives.'[38] There was only one 'other representative': Ethel Benjamin.

Benjamin was not the only woman to outclass her male counterparts. The following year, women's academic success prompted the Otago male students to 'prove' the early suspicions about women's inferior intellect. A survey of examination results was conducted to dispel claims that the women were surpassing the men. Men were found to have 'a clear and not inconsiderable excess of ability'.[39] No disrespect toward 'our lady students' was intended. The men conceded: 'They are our superiors in the faculty of feeling and our equals in that of willing [but] surely they will not strive to prove their total superiority to us, by claiming equality in the faculty of cognition.'[40]

Stella Henderson, with a BA(Hons) in political science and an MA with first class honours in Latin and English, was one of the first women to enrol to study law.[41] According to one of her employers, Christchurch lawyer H H Loughnan, she had enjoyed 'distinguished success' in her law examinations. Dr McMillan Brown, a leading academic at Canterbury College, referred to her as 'one of [Canterbury College's] most distinguished graduates'.[42]

Annie Lee Rees, New Zealand's fourth woman lawyer, also had a 'distinguished career as a student', graduating with a BA in Latin, English, jurisprudence and constitutional history, an MA and an LLB.[43] Harriet Vine, Rebecca Pallot, Isobel Wright (later Matson), Betty Thorpe (née Webster) and Mary Hussey, among other early women law students, were recognised for their exceptional scholastic ability. Approximately 50 percent of the women who studied law before 1959 obtained commercial or academic qualifications in addition to LLBs or passes in legal professionals courses. Second degrees were common—six of the early women lawyers held BAs or MAs and another three held LLMs.[44]

Several early women students were awarded scholarships. Isobel Wright was awarded the Winter Williams Women's Law Scholarship after her admission to the Bar in 1938 and undertook further study in law at Oxford University.[45] Betty Thorpe also won a scholarship—the New Zealand University senior scholarship in law, being in 1943 'the only Auckland girl to have done so'.[46] However, she was unable to take it up as she married and had children shortly afterwards.[47]

Type of work and work ability

As women gradually began to enter the profession, even with superior academic qualifications, most were encouraged or restricted to doing only certain types of work while a general presumption of women's unsuitability for legal work prevailed; exceptions would be made where work involved matters compatible with women's gentler 'disposition'.

Competition v sympathy

Legal work invariably involved competition and conflict. Women, being generally unaccustomed to public conflict, were considered incapable of holding their own in debate. Men, on the other hand, were believed to be naturally inclined to rivalry. According to Charles Darwin, from the days when men fought for wives, they had learnt the art of and delighted in competition.[48] Legal work required 'the benefit of those energies and responsibilities, and that decision and firmness which are presumed to predominate in the sterner sex'.[49]

The problem with women, at least with regard to their ability to perform legal work, was their inclination to 'tenderness and less selfishness'. These 'maternal instincts' would extend to the way a woman dealt with her 'fellow creatures' making her non-competitive.[50] Women, the theorists explained, had an innate feminine capacity to empathise with the weak.[51] How could they act on behalf of a client against the interests of the weak?

John Stuart Mill, on the other hand, claimed that women's sensitivity was not necessarily a weakness. Women were competent, he said, at 'dealing with things as individuals rather than in groups'. This ability, coupled with their 'more lively interest in the present feelings of persons', enabled women to ascertain the impact of an action on the people affected.[52] Women's thoughts, he suggested, could be 'as useful in giving reality to those of thinking men, as men's thoughts in giving width and largeness to those of women'.[53]

For their opponents, the propensity of women lawyers to 'feelings' was the final straw. In 1896, James Allen, a member of the House of Representatives, had spoken against allowing women into the New Zealand profession because women would then be eligible to be appointed as judges. What was needed 'more than anything else in a Judge . . . is a mind that is cool, and calm, and reasonable, and actuated only by reason and argument'.[54] Women, Allen pointed out, had none of these qualities. In this, he was in the majority. Even the most avid supporters of women lawyers in the House of Representatives agreed: 'Women are affected by their sympathies more than by their judgement.'[55]

Family law: women lawyers' speciality

Fortuitously for women lawyers, at the same time as their entry into the profession was under discussion a new area of law was being developed—family law—which women were considered most suited for (although presumably with the exception of those areas which related to sex or violence).

Before the 1880s there had been little or no legal regulation of family affairs, but by 1896, when women were allowed into the profession, there was a mass of legislation on marriage, divorce, wife beating, matrimonial property, incest, adoption and child maintenance. The women's movement had played a large part in bringing into effect these new laws. Predictably, its emphasis on the legal position of women translated into the expectation that the first women lawyers would work in family law.

As early as 1881, Dr Wallis, a supporter of women entering the profession, had pointed out in the House of Representatives that: 'no one was better adapted to draw up a marriage settlement than a woman.'[56] Women lawyers, said Sir George Grey, would be 'the cherished advisers of widows and other females'.[57] By 1896, some politicians were justifying the removal of women's disabilities, including the right to practise law, so that women would be able to 'deal with all cases in which women are concerned'.[58] They would, said George Russell, 'direct the attention of the country . . . to questions that are of special importance and interest to women'.[59] Ethel Benjamin gave her public support to this proposal when she wrote in the *Press* in 1897 that women lawyers might usefully make 'a speciality of those branches of the law which especially affect their own sex'.[60]

Quite simply, women lawyers were expected to fulfil a professional role which was entirely consistent with their domestic, nurturing functions within the family. Women doctors were accepted on a similar basis, that their primary function was to care for the health and welfare of women and children.[61] Women entering the police force were also expected to deal mainly with women and children, with a particular emphasis on catching shoplifters and finding lost children.[62] By confining their professional work to the laws affecting the welfare of women and children, women lawyers complied with the notion that they were primarily driven by sympathy. Just as important, their concentration on family law would keep women lawyers out of the market for other, more lucrative work.

Commercial law: more lucrative work

Although the 1890s depression came to an end around the time that women were allowed into the legal profession, the profession remained overcrowded and fiercely competitive for clients. Among those who could most afford legal fees were banks, insurance companies, land speculators and others in business. Family law was much less commercially attractive, much of it being done through charities or government-sponsored schemes. Assigning women lawyers to work in this area ensured that they did not add to the competition for the more lucrative commercial work; they would be too busy working for women clients—very few of whom had independent financial means—and for charitable causes.

From the point of view of early women lawyers it was not a lack of ability that kept them from commercial work. Ethel Benjamin argued that women lawyers were capable of practising in any area of legal work. She wrote:

> As with men, the branches of the profession in which women will be most successful depend on the bent of their individual ability. There is no department of legal work in which I could not conceive women successful. Of course the average woman would be hopelessly at sea in intricate mercantile suits, and involved equity cases of every description, but so I take it, would be the average man.[63]

Australia's first woman lawyer, C Flos Greig, went one step further. She pointed out in the *Commonwealth Law Journal* that women had already demonstrated the qualities needed to succeed in business—'sound commonsense, shrewdness and tact'—the exact qualities needed to succeed in law. In response to the argument that women lacked commercial sense, she explained that some business took less time, less patience and no more brain power than patchwork quilting. The mystique surrounding business, she suggested, was not without good reason. Had women known that commercial matters were no more complex or exacting than patchworking, 'how would your hero from behind the mercer's counter have degenerated in your eyes?'[64]

Benjamin, Grieg and others in fact did prove their abilities to handle all kinds of legal work—and to run their own businesses. Benjamin totally defied expectation and managed her own busy practice in litigation and commercial work, ran her own small business, and even managed hotels and entered into property speculation. She also had a reasonable number of women clients who sought her advice on their investments in property and shares.[65]

Ellen Melville also ran her own practice. She undertook commercial work for women's organisations such as incorporation of societies, commercial conveyancing, and advising on rent contracts and leases.[66] Geraldine Hemus followed suit and ran her own practice, although nothing is known of the type of work she did. Harriet Vine, the fifth woman lawyer in New Zealand, had an exclusively commercial practice. But few of the other early women lawyers were known for their involvement in commercial law.

Firms' reluctance to employ women to undertake commercial work was explained as being due to client preferences. In the late 1950s, for example, a woman law graduate being interviewed for a job by a senior practitioner was told: 'A business client would not be prepared to discuss the reorganisation of his company with a woman solicitor.' She pointed out that at that time such an attitude was reasonable.[67]

Conveyancing and research

In the 'back room'

Women lawyers were considered particularly well suited to undertake conveyancing or research. According to the *Canada Law Journal*:

> As conveyancers or as compilers of text-books, there may be no reason why some women should not succeed as well as some men: but to refuse to allow them to embark upon the rough and troubled sea of actual legal practice, is, as it appears to us, being cruel only to be kind.[68].

Conveyancing was exacting work, requiring attention to detail. Women were considered ably equipped to perform this work—under the supervision of a qualified male lawyer. The *Canadian Law Times* observed in 1892 that women lawyers would be 'suitably qualified' uneducated, unlicensed conveyancers.[69] Mistakes by these people provided a steady flow of work, especially litigation, for the qualified profession. Women conveyancers, according to the sceptics, might increase the flow of this fruitful source of work to the male profession.

Several women lawyers were successful in conveyancing, however. Marjorie Taylor (later Feist) set up her own conveyancing practice while other early women lawyers did conveyancing within the firms.[70]

A significant number of early women lawyers did as the *Canada Law Journal* and some individuals suggested and concentrated on research as employees within firms. Dunedin lawyer Mary Hussey, for example, was renowned for her legal research and court document drafting. Bill Wright, who worked with her at Adams Bros, recalled how she could turn totally disorganised files 'into immaculate proceedings which often drew favourable comment from the Bench'. Royden Somerville also remembered Mary Hussey as 'totally dedicated to ... the training of the younger members of the practice' including giving her time freely to law clerks involved in the university mooting tournaments.[71]

According to Murray Cochrane, who worked as a law clerk in Adams Bros, Mary Hussey was the 'power behind the throne'. Many of the men lawyers whom she assisted or worked for would become well known in the profession, a good number being made Queen's Counsel or appointed to the Bench.[72] After twenty-eight years with Adams Bros, Mary Hussey left the firm in 1975 and set up as a barrister sole, but only on the understanding that she would do research and draft pleadings, not appear in court.

Academic positions

Other early women law graduates sought teaching positions within university law schools. Stella Henderson was the first woman to seek a position as a law lecturer within a New Zealand university. In January 1900, with a string of degrees and four impressive testimonials to her credit, she applied for the position of law lecturer at Victoria University College law school. William Izard, H H Loughnan, Sam Saunders and Dr McMillan Brown attested to her scholarship, her work ability and excellent personal qualities. Dr McMillan Brown adjudged Stella Henderson 'admirably fitted to fill a lectureship in a University College'.[73]

Despite her glowing references and undisputed academic ability, Henderson did not get the job. Whether her sex was the obstacle is unknown. William Izard had certainly attempted to allay any concerns on that count when he added in his letter to the Victoria college board: 'Whilst in my office I found no difficulties arose in consequence of her sex—on the contrary her business relations with my clerks and with my clients were eminently satisfactory.' If there were doubts about a woman controlling the all-male law classes, Dr McMillan Brown had advised that Henderson would 'manage with ease any position of authority in a College'.[74] However, Victoria University College would not employ a woman law lecturer until more than fifty years later.

Shirley Smith was probably the first woman to lecture in law at Victoria University. A mature graduate in 1957, she had not been working long in the Wellington firm Duncan, Matthews and Taylor when she was invited to join the staff at Victoria law school. She lectured in Roman law and then constitutional law and was the first editor of the *Victoria University Law Review*. Her stay at the university was short as she decided to 'forsake the hill for the town'.[75] Later, Alison Quentin-Baxter (née Souter) worked as a tutor in law at Wellington Polytechnic from 1965 to 1966 before joining the Victoria University law faculty in 1967 where she lectured for three years.

Canterbury University College also employed its first woman law lecturer about this time. Isobel Matson (née Wright) worked as a temporary lecturer in 1967 and 1968, lectured in family law and legal history throughout the 1970s, and was a part-time tutor from 1980 to 1983.[76]

Court work

Women lawyers were least expected to undertake court work. It was thought that women's tendency to emotion and their inability to reason would ill-equip and overwhelm women lawyers in the adversarial court environment. Women were also considered ill suited to public oratory as they would have difficulty being heard in a public forum, such as the court room, without raising their voices in an unpleasant shrill tone.[77]

As late as the 1970s, women lawyers were believed to be ill-equipped for the rigours of courtroom battle. Glanville Williams noted in his 1973 guide to would-be barristers: 'An advocate's task is essentially combative, whereas women are not generally prepared to give battle unless they are annoyed. A woman's voice, also, does not carry as well as a man's.'[78]

Being briefed

For women wishing to make careers at the Bar, success or failure depended on the referral of work from a predominantly male profession. When Ethel Benjamin said she particularly wanted to practise as a barrister, an *Otago Daily Times* columnist wished her success in her ambition and hoped 'that briefs will come as thick as autumnal leaves'.[79] Benjamin hoped one day 'to make [her] mark at the Bar'. But she did not overlook the fact that referrals of work would determine her ability to reach that goal, saying: 'Of course, at present, I will not refuse any law work.'[80]

Benjamin's hopes of being able to practise solely at the Bar were short-lived because she could not earn enough. When claiming her right to advertise her services in Wellington in 1907, she told the Wellington law society:

> I know from experience that no business will be put my way by other Solicitors, and I must look to the Public for support. If the Law Society is prepared to guarantee me a practice producing say £2,000 per annum (I have not extravagant

ideas), I am willing to sit still and wait for clients! If not I intend to push my business all I know.[81]

Following Ethel Benjamin, few women lawyers enrolled as barristers. Stella Henderson regularly attended the Wellington courts in 1902 and 1902 in preparation for her dream of admission to the Bar, but she attended only in the public gallery. In 1910, Annie Lee Rees became the second woman to be admitted as a barrister, although it is unlikely she appeared in court other than for her admission ceremony. Similarly, Lyra Taylor, the first woman to be admitted to the Bar in Wellington, enrolled as a barrister and solicitor in 1918 and Esther Ongley followed suit in 1921, but there is no evidence that either appeared in court as an advocate. Alison Carey was admitted to the Bar in Christchurch in 1938. Dorothy Simes (later Thompson), who was admitted to the same Bar the following year, observed that women 'were not welcome in the High Court and were deemed capable of appearing only on judgment summonses in the District Court'.[82]

A woman barrister was specifically sought out by Sir Francis H D Bell in 1926 when he prepared the New Zealand Government's arguments for a case to be heard by the highest appellate court, the Privy Council. Sir Francis, wrote from London to the Attorney-General:

> I told [William Downie] Stewart before I left that I meant to have as one of the Juniors a young lady lawyer because of the enormous mass of evidence and the necessity of getting somebody at a reasonable cost to master (or mistress) it for the Conferences of Counsel. And I have, after conference with the Government solicitors in London, sent preliminary papers, including the evidence, to Miss Clarkson who is a grand-daughter of Sir John Gorst and a daughter of a lady born in New Zealand. She will not, of course be heard in the [Privy Council], but she is already doing what I want in absolutely mastering the evidence.[83]

While she might not formally appear at the hearing, the attendance of Miss Clarkson, an English barrister, was certainly required. In a similar letter to the Solicitor-General, Sir Francis observed that, 'she [would] be able to supply the answer' if any questions of fact arose at any conference of counsel or at the Privy Council hearing itself. He lamented: 'The solicitors will never do it and since Northcote's death we have never been able to get a Junior to master the fact when the evidence is voluminous.'[84]

Several decades later, some women lawyers were lucky enough to work with men lawyers who gave them briefs *and* encouraged them to appear in court. Olive Smuts-Kennedy, who worked on her own account 'devilling' for practitioners before her admission in 1955, was greatly helped by Auckland barrister 'Scotty' King.[85] Along with others, King gave Smuts-Kennedy the occasional brief, enabling her to appear in court on routine matters.[86] Fay Matson (later Wellwood), who was admitted in 1952, did 'all kinds of work' when employed with Hastings firm Hallet O'Dowd in the mid- to late 1960s, debt collecting and appearing in the Police Court and the Maori Land Court.[87]

Shirley Smith, after her admission in 1957, continued working for the Wellington firm Duncan, Matthews and Taylor and for the next two years appeared in the Magistrate's Court, once or twice junioring in the Supreme Court. Her appearances were mostly confined to obtaining adjournments, an interlocutory process which at that time involved 'endless hours . . . wasted in lengthy battles'.[88]

Some women lawyers undertaking litigation found that other colleagues acting as counsel objected to their involvement. Judith Potter, who did personal injury cases in the Magistrate's Court after qualifying in 1965, found in one case that counsel for the opposition unexpectedly sought to settle. She had overheard him say: 'If it's that girl Potter appearing we're going to settle because I lost to her last week and I'm not losing to a bloody woman again.'[89]

Novelty: increasing the pressure

The very novelty of women lawyers appearing in court added to the pressure women experienced when they appeared as advocates. Betty Webster (later Thorp) was only given court work by her employers during World War II because there were no men to do the job. She recalled feeling very self-conscious in court. She was, she said 'a fish out of water'.[90] When Cecile Rushton first appeared in court in Taumarunui after her admission in 1968, she described 'sitting between two very senior men. My knees were knocking, I was so petrified'.[91] Another woman who would later be appointed to the Bench, Carolyn Henwood, recalled that when doing court work for law firm Olphert and Bornholdt in 1970: 'It was very daunting being one of the few women lawyers in court.'[92]

Women lawyers' court appearances frequently attracted publicity in local newspapers. The admission of women as barristers certainly attracted the attention of the profession and the media, much more so than their admission as solicitors. In 1933, the *New Zealand Law Journal* reported that Mr Justice Herdman had admitted Auckland's first woman barrister, Marion van Beeresteyn Hollway (later Kirk), a law clerk in the firm of Thorne, Thorne, White and Clark-Walker.[93] Whether Hollway actually practised in court is unknown. She took out a practising certificate for the next three years but appears to have ceased practising on her marriage.[94] Two years later the *New Zealand Law Journal* described the presence of Isobel Wright (later Matson) as 'an interesting feature' at the laying of the foundation stone of the new Christchurch Court. Wright, daughter of A F Wright, a 'well known member of the firm of Messrs Duncan, Cotterill, and Co', had been recently admitted and was 'Christchurch's first lady barrister'.[95]

In the mid-1950s, a 'notable appearance' for Shirley Smith which resulted when neither of her employers were able to appear in court, earned her a report, with photographs, in a local tabloid newspaper.[96]

Attention came not only from the media. Some women also came under the additional scrutiny of judges. Soon after her admission in 1975, Patricia Costigan (later Judge Costigan) had 'the law laid down to her' when she appeared a second time in the Christchurch Magistrate's Court to defend a man on charges involving assault of a woman. The magistrate, who had also heard the first case, called her into Chambers where she recalls being told that: 'The criminal court was no place for a woman . . . and I had better think about what I was doing. Why couldn't I be satisfied with doing family work which was more suitable for a woman?'[97]

Even in 1982, when Anne Gaskell (later Judge Gaskell) was employed by Wellington Crown Prosecutor Jim Larsen, she made the local head-lines. An *Evening Post* journalist asked the inevitable questions about how the 'Capital's first lady prosecutor' was going to handle the prosecution of a rape trial. She replied that she thought she would handle rape trials the same as any other type of trial although it was 'one type of trial on which I would be very happy to be on the prosecuting side, rather than the defence side'.[98]

Few, if any, young men barristers received the same degree of public attention that the women did. While women's advancement in the profession was, and is, no doubt of public interest, for a shy and inexperienced woman lawyer, the prospect of public scrutiny may have been yet another reason to stay away from the limelight that court work (and success in general) brought.

Judging: out of the question

Inevitably, women lawyers' limited access to the courts and the assumptions about their abilities as litigators seriously affected their chances of becoming judges.

The prospect of women judges had stirred strong feelings during the 1890s debate about allowing women into the New Zealand legal profession. These concerns were articulated again in the 1920s, during the debates about allowing women to be appointed justices of the peace. Sir William Fraser, leader of the Legislative Council, warned that if the council allowed women to become justices: 'there will be a demand that they be allowed to be appointed Magistrates, and from Magistrates to Judges'. He personally was not prepared to 'take the responsibility of opening the flood-gates.'[99]

Some women lawyers agreed that women did not belong on the Bench. In 1942, one of New Zealand's few women lawyers was asked why there were no women judges. Her reply was:

> As for women being judges, I don't think we're particularly suited to it. Law is after all a machine, and one that I don't think woman is geared to. Being a judge is largely a matter of seeing that the workings of the machine are correctly applied. I can't help feeling that in giving judgment the average woman would tend to go

by her intuition rather than the evidence, and intuition, as yet, has no place in a court of law.[100]

Fighting for women's rights

Although they might have limited roles within the profession, the early New Zealand women lawyers took to heart their prescribed roles as advocates for women's rights. Many unquestionably accepted their obligation to apply their skills not singularly toward their own advancement but to the cause of women's equality in general. They tirelessly applied their skills, knowledge, and personal understanding to legal problems which were otherwise being ignored or advanced in directions that cemented injustice for women. In this, 'the women's sphere', their abilities were unquestioned and appreciated.

These women lawyers were not oblivious to their own plight but perhaps implicitly understood that they could not grapple with the problems faced by women in the legal profession until there was a wider framework for equality. This would be needed to allow more women to enter the profession and to succeed without having to be exceptional.

Women lawyers were rarely remunerated for their skills in this area. Compared with the rewards received by men lawyers for their 'civic contributions', women lawyers' work went largely unrecognised in official and professional circles. Sometimes it was the subject of criticism. Yet despite the disincentives, they persistently made their talents and abilities available to women's organisations and women's causes.

Ethel Benjamin declared in 1897 that she was 'deeply interested in the "Women's Rights" movement'. It was, she said, one of her 'pet ambitions . . . to be useful to [her] own sex'. On her admission, she immediately set about putting her convictions into action, writing articles encouraging women to study the law and enter the profession, presenting conference papers on women's legal inequalities, and supporting the formation of a Dunedin branch of the Society for the Protection of Women and Children in 1899,[101] and volunteering her services as an honorary solicitor.[102]

Stella Henderson, like Ethel Benjamin, openly declared her intention to use her legal knowledge to advance women's rights. In 1898, she told a *White Ribbon* interviewer:

> When admitted I do not intend devoting my time to any one special branch of the profession . . . wherever my work may lie, I shall always hope to help forward the social movements of the day, and want especially to be of service in helping to remove the unjust restrictions which the law imposes on our sex.[103]

Although unable to practise law, Henderson was true to her promise. She 'fought . . . vigorously with her pen' for women's right to sit in the Press Gallery of the House of Representatives with the male journalists.[104] She campaigned for women's equality at law, for equal pay in particular, as active in the National Council of Women and was vice-president of the

Christchurch branch of the Society for the Protection of Women and Children.[105] According to her obituary in the *Press*, Henderson had 'devoted herself to the service of women'.[106]

Many women lawyers, with other women professionals, played active and often overtly political roles within women's organisations for sixty years or more from the turn of the century. Ellen Melville, admitted to the Bar in 1906, became an acclaimed leader of the women's movement in Auckland. She wrote and presented papers arguing for women's full participation in the workforce, for equal conditions and equal pay, and for women's rights as citizens.[107] She gave a series of lectures on women's position under New Zealand law at the Grafton Library on Saturday evenings.[108] Like Benjamin and Henderson, she was also involved in the Society for the Protection of Women and Children, as a member from 1915 to 1934, providing free legal advice to women in her capacity as an honorary solicitor, and eventually becoming vice-president of the Auckland branch.[109]

Melville undertook 'an enormous amount of free legal work' for women's organisations. She founded the Auckland Women's Club (later the Lyceum Club) and was the force behind the establishment in 1918 of the Auckland branch of the National Council of Women, becoming its first president. The National Council of Women was one of various organisations in which Geraldine Hemus worked with Ellen Melville for many years.[110]

As a member of the Auckland City Council, Melville did much to advance women's interests, often playing the role of intermediary in the discussions between the council and women's groups.[111] She campaigned actively for women to enter Parliament, to serve as jurors, and be appointed as justices of the peace.[112]

According to Rosemary Rees, Annie Lee Rees' sister, Annie 'was always public spirited'.[113] Over the years 1924 to 1925 she lectured for the conservative patriotic organisation the Victoria League and became president of its Gisborne branch in 1927. She received a Coronation Medal in recognition of her devotion to social work and the community. According to the *Gisborne Herald*, Annie Lee Rees' 'standing among members of her sex was truly national'.[114]

While Harriet Vine was not known for having a role in women's groups in Wanganui where she practised law for approximately forty years, she was very actively involved in the St John's Ambulance Association, being at various times secretary and treasurer.[115]

Another woman lawyer prominent in the National Council of Women was Lyra Taylor. In 1925 she was a New Zealand delegate to an International Council of Women conference in Washington, attending meetings of the Committee on Lay and Legal Status of Women as proxy for Ellen Melville.[116]

Rebecca Pallot (née Macky), the next woman law graduate, worked full time as secretary to the Young Women's Christian Association in Wellington. She believed deeply that women should have equal opportunities to develop their talents, but also that 'as men and women are fundamentally different they should seek complementary rather than competing roles'.[117]

Marjorie Taylor (later Feist), admitted in 1936, was a foundation member of Soroptimist International of Lower Hutt and honorary solicitor to that body and to the New Zealand branch.[118] She was also a member of the New Zealand Federation of University Women.

The New Zealand Business and Professional Women's Clubs were the focus of Timaru lawyer Dorothy Raymond's community involvement throughout her career. She attended international conferences of that organisation in Montreal (1956) and in London (1968) and was elected the national president in 1971. Raymond was also involved in the Federation of University Women which, with the National Council of Women and the New Zealand Business and Professional Women's Clubs, worked toward the introduction and passage of the Equal Pay Act 1972. She says she was, 'always interested in improving the conditions and wages of working women'. She also appeared regularly in newspapers around the country— always encouraging women to study and practise law.[119]

Elisabeth Urquhart had extensive involvement in women's groups and, like Ellen Melville, also in local government. She was a founding member of the Rotorua branch of the Federation of University Women in 1959, belonged to the National Council of Women and the Altrusa Club among other clubs, and was on the advisory board of the Plunket Society for twenty years. In 1962, she was elected to the Rotorua City Council, topping the poll, and in 1965, following in her father's footsteps, was elected deputy mayor. In recognition of her standing as a lawyer and as a trailblazer for women lawyers in Rotorua, she was nominated patron of the Rotorua Legal Association in 1993.[120]

Audrey Gale, admitted in 1939, was president of the Taranaki branch of the New Zealand Federation of University Women by 1968 and became women's vice-president of the National Party in 1953.[121]

Patricia Webb, admitted in 1941, was involved in the International Federation of University Women which had consultative status at the United Nations. She was president of the New Zealand branch for three years at the time it was encouraging women to volunteer for jury service. Her work as a legal officer in the Department of Justice frequently involved questions of women's rights and she was an early member of the Equal Pay Committee. In 1962, she attended a United Nations seminar in

Tokyo as New Zealand's representative to discuss the status of women in family law.[122]

Sheila Macdonald (later Williams), who in 1942 had been admitted as the first woman lawyer in Southland, joined the Canterbury Federation of University Women in 1960 and was involved in committees of that organisation until her death in 1986.[123]

Olive Smuts-Kennedy, admitted in 1955, was not interested in women's rights at first, feeling that she had 'experienced no disadvantage' in her personal life. However, within several years of practice she changed her views. She disagreed with those who allocated legal work on the basis of the sex of the worker and with those who said: 'women who take up a profession are selfishly "fulfilling" themselves rather than performing a useful service for family and community.' Smuts-Kennedy chaired the Council for Equal Pay and Opportunities from 1959 to 1961 and acted as an honorary solicitor for the National Council of Women from 1958 to 1968. She observes that there was no benefit for her career in holding these positions, but that the time spent on this work would otherwise have been spent on her own affairs or advancement.[124]

Early women lawyers also applied their skills to other forms of unpaid work. Many of those who were not practising while they had children, like Betty Webster, were involved in kindergarten committees, playcentre groups and primary and secondary school parent teacher associations. At times when it was unacceptable or impossible for them to be in the paid workforce, the early women lawyers were nevertheless working unpaid for their families and communities. Through this work they proved their abilities as lawyers beyond doubt and, in many cases, their abilities as community leaders.

Chapter Six

Liberation and Discrimination
1970–1989

The period from 1970 to 1989 was characterised by direct conflict between women and men in the legal profession. In less than two decades, the legal concept of sex discrimination was named, defined and stigmatised. Across the country change was advocated, but the majority of people were disinclined to respond. It was apparent that the problem of discrimination would be largely left to women to address and resolve.

Women's liberation and discrimination

In the early 1970s, women and men in the legal profession, with the rest of New Zealand society, were confronted with two new concepts—'women's liberation' and 'discrimination'.[1] Whereas previously there had been no name and no convincing explanation for the different treatment accorded women lawyers, there was now a notion that they were disadvantaged solely by reason of their sex.

As in the 1890s, the law was again a major focus for achieving women's equality, and New Zealand women were prepared to act on a wide scale. Women's liberation groups called for new laws on equal pay, maternity leave, abortion, rape, matrimonial property and state-funded child care. In 1971, the Commission of Inquiry into Equal Pay recommended the removal of discrimination in rates of pay in the private sector to match the public service. The following year, despite employer concerns that the economy would collapse, the Equal Pay Act was passed.[2] Pay rate differences based on sex for work requiring the same or similar skills were to be eliminated by 1977.

Employment discrimination on a wider scale was also identified. At the first United Women's Convention in 1973, Margaret Wilson (later president of the Labour Party and dean of University of Waikato Law School) stated that discrimination 'operates when a woman may wish to enter a particular type of employment that had previously been considered "men's work". It operates when a woman seeks promotion or advancement in her employment'.[3] Discrimination was not illegal but it was plainly unjust. The question inevitably had to be asked—was sex discrimination an issue in the legal profession?

Sex discrimination in the legal profession

The first opportunity to collate information on women in the legal profession occurred in the context of the second United Women's Convention held in 1975, International Women's Year. In preparation for the convention, Carolyn Henwood (later Judge Henwood) entered into correspondence with 'as many women lawyers as possible' who were practising across the country. The results of her research were unequivocal.

Henwood reported to the convention that the main areas of difficulty facing women lawyers related to obtaining partnerships, the lack of flexible working hours, the cost of child care, and the pigeon-holing of women into a limited range of legal work. Men in the profession, Henwood said, 'must encourage women whenever possible', 'must be prepared to give women their chance', and women, for their part, 'must come to grips with the fact that they are lawyers and not allow themselves to slip into the role of a skilled clerk'.[4]

Henwood reminded women lawyers that they were in a 'privileged position in society'. She urged her colleagues to make themselves available to women's organisations striving to improve women's status, to provide advice on legal matters to those organisations, and to promote their ideas. Women lawyers, she advised, should 'make a special point of researching the areas of law that are most inconsistent between men and women' and should present submissions on those issues to the law society and the government.[5]

Like their predecessors, women lawyers were well equipped to take up the challenge. At the 1975 United Women's Convention, Rosemary Tomlinson, Cordelia Thomas, Gloria Drury, Meredith Ross, Pauline Vaver (née Tapp), Shirley Smith, Ann Wilson and Jane Lovell-Smith presented papers on a range of legal topics, including: women and their financial position; child maintenance; matrimonial property; women as victims of crime; and women as criminals.[6] That same year two books explaining women's legal rights were published, one by Kaye Turner and Pauline Vaver (née Tapp), the other by Pauline Tapp and Margaret Wilson.[7] These were among the first books by lawyers aimed at informing the public about the law in simple, lay terms. They were also notable for being books written by women for women.[8] At about the same time, women academics introduced feminist analysis into their courses and set up new courses specifically on women and the law.[9]

Of course, not everyone was convinced that women lawyers faced unique obstacles in their careers or even that the campaign against discrimination was a good thing. Some saw the movement as being led by militant women who were unable to succeed in the profession by ability and hard work. Some believed the concept of discrimination was anathema to the ideal that women could do anything and be anything regardless of the barriers. Still others feared that the excessive emphasis on gender problems and the requests for concessions based on sex would only exacerbate the problem.

In May 1975, Auckland barrister Anne Gambrill (later Master Anne Gambrill) drew attention in the Auckland District Law Society newsletter to the fact that no women had been invited to comment on a right to life paper at the recent national law conference. This gave women an opportunity to criticise the profession for being discriminatory. She said: 'I say this because I have not felt any discrimination exists in this Society.'[10] Ted Thomas, a partner at Russell McVeagh and a member of the Auckland law society council, was not so sure. Although on sabbatical in Boston, in a three page memorandum to the council he wrote:

> Ms Gambrill is quoted as saying that she has not felt that any discrimination exists in the Society. Because of Ms Gambrill's many worthwhile personal qualities, this may be so in her case but I am not satisfied it is universally true.

He pointed to the large numbers of women law graduates and asked:

> How many will readily obtain partnerships or even how many will be employed in jobs involving allegedly more satisfying kinds of legal work? How many women barristers are there? How many women are there on the Council? Do newly qualified women solicitors find it difficult to get jobs? How do rates paid to female solicitors compare with rates paid to their male counterparts? ... These and other similar questions require honest answers.[11]

Thomas proposed that the Auckland law society council appoint a committee to 'conduct a discreet inquiry' and report back to the council with recommendations. 'Needless to say,' he wrote, 'a woman, or even women (including Ms Gambrill), should be co-opted onto the committee'. In his view, a report was needed to document, among other things, women lawyers' abilities and to promote confidence on the part of the public—thereby overcoming client reluctance to using women solicitors. The overall objective was to ensure that 'the lot of our "sister-in-law" may become more fair and equitable'.[12]

The council agreed to refer the suggestion to a committee of the law society for its deliberation. However, there would be no tangible action by the law society for another six years.

In the meantime, the view that women lawyers suffered no problems continued to be aired. For example when Augusta Wallace, a South Auckland sole practitioner, was appointed New Zealand's first woman judge in September 1975, she publicly supported the view that the 'rather noisy business about women's rights' was 'doing women a disservice'.[13] Despite the history of women in the law and the fact that 1975 was designated International Women's Year, the new judge commented that there was 'nothing remarkable in being appointed New Zealand's first woman magistrate'. Instead, she viewed her appointment 'as encouragement, believing that if anyone put the appropriate hard work and endeavour into their field of work there should be no reason why they should not succeed'.[14] Judge Wallace, along with many others, considered that merit, hard work, and 'good sense' were paramount—and sufficient.

Other women lawyers, however, were confronted by events which could not be explained by any lack of common sense, ability, or hard work on their part. The legal 'fraternity' remained fraught with unwritten codes which materially affected success. Professional social occasions were still resulting in conflict between men and women lawyers, resolved by the latter staying away.

Professional exclusion

With the increasing numbers of women law students and graduates entering the profession, women's attendance at professional events was becoming more of an issue. When Judith Medlicott went to an Otago law society Bar dinner in 1973, a senior practitioner advised her that she 'had no business to be there, it was the boys' night out'. He told her that because she was married to a professional man she 'should be playing golf, having coffee mornings and not clogging up the law school'.[15] Carolyn Henwood observed two years later at the United Women's Convention that over the years many women had 'opted out' from attending law society functions, dinners and seminars because they had 'found the whole minority situation overwhelming'.[16]

By the mid-1970s, a direct link was being made between women lawyers' 'choice' to stay away from professional functions and their poor position in the profession. Henwood told the convention that this opting out was 'detrimental'. In her view, it was essential women attended professional occasions 'to make the acquaintance of other lawyers ... Only in this way and by practising to a high standard can a woman be accepted as a full member of the profession.'[17]

Her view was confirmed by the Parliamentary Select Committee on Women's Rights in 1975. Noting the absence of women from the judiciary, the committee reported to Parliament that 'nominees for appointments very often arise out of the so-called "old boys'" network which is strengthened by the association of professional men with one another in clubs, over business luncheons, and so on.'[18] Women lawyers were simply not in the club.

More significantly, however, the 1975 Parliamentary Select Committee on Women's Rights had collected extensive evidence on employers' attitudes toward women at work. One study showed that employers were using 'prejudiced arguments' with no scientific basis to avoid employing women.[19] Generalisations about women's physical and intellectual abilities and their childbearing functions were said by the committee to discriminate against women in employment.[20] The committee recommended the enactment of a statute prohibiting discrimination on the ground of sex.

Human Rights Commission Act 1977

In 1977, after continued pressure by women's lobby groups, the National Government introduced the Human Rights Commission Bill. Modelled on similar laws in the United Kingdom, South Australia, Ontario, and British Columbia, the bill would make it unlawful, for the first time, for an employer to deny women access to employment opportunities simply on the ground of sex.[21]

Profession objects to inclusion of partnerships

According to common practice, the New Zealand Law Society, on behalf of the legal profession, made a submission on the bill to Parliament. The society generally supported the principles of the bill, calling it 'an important step forward in protecting human rights and attaining equality under the law for all citizens'.[22] But on one specific clause, the law society showed its hand—it objected to the inclusion of partnerships in the bill.

If the bill was passed it would be unlawful for partnerships of six or more persons to decline the admission of a person to the partnership by reason of that person's race, colour, ethnic or national origins, marital status, religious or ethical belief, or sex.[23] According to the New Zealand Law Society, the clause overlooked 'the very personal nature of a partnership which is quite outside the concept of employer-employee'. Among its members, the view was 'strongly held that it is quite unnecessary and indeed wrong to take away the right of existing partners to decline to admit a new partner because of eg his ethical belief'.[24]

The law society did not ask that an exemption be provided on account of ethical belief or any other ground. Instead, it proposed that partnership admissions be taken outside the ambit of the law against discrimination. In effect, the law society claimed the right for law firm partners to decide not to admit a new partner solely by reason of that person's sex, race, ethnicity, marital status or any other prohibited ground. In other words, the profession was claiming the right to discriminate for reasons that were about to be prohibited in most other areas of social and business life.

Nor did the law society stop there. In the alternative it suggested that, if Parliament sought to keep partnerships within the law, the size of the partnerships affected should be increased to twenty-five or, as 'a second best' option, to fifteen or more.[25] This alternative proposal, if successful, would have effectively defeated the protection offered by the bill. In 1977 very few law firms had partnerships of this size.

In making this submission, the New Zealand Law Society went out on a limb. The accountancy profession, which also relied heavily on the partnership , did not object to the partnership provision in the bill.[26] In fact, the Department of Justice reported to the parliamentary select committee examining the bill that the inclusion of partnerships had 'struck a sympathetic chord among the great majority', the New Zealand Law Society being a 'notable exception'. Instead of arguing to limit the coverage of partnerships, the majority of other organisations and individuals commenting on the bill supported no limit on the size of partnerships affected.[27] As Margaret Wilson pointed out in her submission, the effect of the provision as drafted was 'to legalise discrimination for partnerships of less than six members'.[28]

The Department of Justice warned that deletion of the partnership clause would attract 'adverse public reaction, particularly among those groups concerned with the elimination of discrimination against women'. It recommended that the clause be retained with the number of partners either reduced or left at six.[29]

Two weeks later, support for the law society's stand came from the Government Research Unit. In a paper to the Minister of Justice and the select committee, the unit followed the law society line, that partnerships should fall outside the ambit of the bill on the ground that they involved 'personal and intimate relationship[s]'. Placing constraints on the choice of partners was considered 'quite contradictory' to the partnership concept which was based on the 'principle of free association'. The external imposition of anti-discriminatory rules would be 'a gross invasion of [the] privacy, and individual liberty' of the partners concerned.[30]

The law society was ultimately unsuccessful in its efforts to exclude partnership admissions from the Human Rights Commission Bill, but so were the many organisations and people who had argued for no limitation on partnership size. On 21 November 1977, the Human Rights Commission Bill was passed with the cap of six partners intact. Law firms and other employers in the profession, however, were wholly accountable for all other types of discrimination. The new Act made it unlawful for an employer to fail to employ a suitably qualified woman simply because she was a woman, or to fail to give a woman the same terms of employment, conditions of work, benefits and opportunities for training and promotion given to a man with the same or substantially similar qualifications.[31]

Women lawyers' reaction

During the mid to late 1970s the number of women lawyers, particularly in Auckland, had swelled sufficiently for women lawyers to contemplate seriously forming their own organisation. In light of the intense legislative activity around the Human Rights Commission Act 1977, it was appropriate that the women's focus should be law reform. In 1977 the first women's organisation dealing specifically with the law itself, the Women and the Law Research Foundation, was formed.

The guiding force behind the organisation (and its first president) was Margaret Wilson, then a lecturer at Auckland law school.[32] Membership comprised lawyers, judges and law academics, including several men. The foundation aimed to keep women informed of laws that affected them, to assist women to make sure their voices were heard in the law reform process, to assist women to fully utilise their rights under the Human Rights Commission Act, and to provide a central information and resource centre for women.[33]

Profession's response

While women lawyers were determined to inform women about the new law, the professional bodies did little to educate lawyers. Despite the direct significance of the new Act to the legal profession, little notice was taken of it. When the bill was being debated in 1977, only the Auckland District Law Society ran an article on the bill in its local newsletter.[34] The New Zealand Law Society merely reported that a submission had been made but not what the substance of the submission was.[35] The following year, when the new law was in force, a small notice informed the profession that the Department of Justice had published a pamphlet and that copies were available from the department at no charge.[36] Apart from a Sunday evening lecture in Auckland by Dr Elkind from the law school, no education on the new law was offered to the practising profession.[37]

In 1978, the first year of the Act's operation, the legal profession was 94 percent male. There were very few women lawyers appointed to statutory boards or government quangos, and only one woman judge. However, in a New Zealand Law Society survey of lawyers, more than 80 percent of practitioners surveyed claimed to have welcomed the increasing number of women in the profession.[38] Women lawyers, according to the survey, were seen by their colleagues as being committed to their careers, suitable to hold positions of authority over men, and as suited as men to all aspects of legal practice.[39] At the same time, 71 percent did not favour 'employer concessions' to enable women to combine family responsibilities with their careers.[40]

But the stated 'welcome' of the men lawyers was not easily translated into practice. From the early 1980s, studies on the status of women in the law, whether commissioned by law societies or conducted independently, documented an entirely different story.

Mounting evidence of sex discrimination

Committee on Women: 1980

The first official inquiry into the position of women in the legal profession was undertaken in 1980 by the Committee on Women, an official advisory body to the National Government. The committee was to identify the status of women lawyers in Wellington law firms. From the evidence collected, the committee hoped to assess the viability of compiling a register of the names of women lawyers which could be used when judicial and other public appointments were considered.[41]

The committee found that more than half of the forty-three Wellington law firms surveyed had never employed woman lawyers.[42] Several had never received job applications from women, causing the committee to query where women graduates were being employed, if not in legal firms.[43]

The committee noted that of the many comments made by respondents, not one referred to the existence of discrimination in the legal profession or in society generally. It was as if the problem did not exist. Instead, there was a degree of hostility in some firms' responses, causing the committee to remark: 'As lawyers are only too aware of the implications of the questionnaire, answers were often evasive or snide.' The committee concluded that: 'Lawyers are fully conversant with the Human Rights Commission Act and therefore are knowledgeable in how to deal with [or] avoid such questions with expertise.'[44]

The report of the Committee on Women was sent to the national and district law societies, to the Minister of Justice and to the Human Rights Commission. Aside from publishing the report (including the critical comments) in *LawTalk*, the national law society took no action.[45] The Wellington law society council replied formally to the Committee on Women, stating that:

> The appointment of properly qualified suitable women lawyers to the Bench or to Statutory Boards should be encouraged; but . . . care should be taken to ensure that, whilst encouraging the appointment of women, it must not be overlooked that the prime responsibility is for the appointees to be properly qualified lawyers, irrespective of their sex.

The council disagreed with the idea of establishing a register of women lawyers, saying: 'If this were done there would, to be consistent, need to be a similar register for lawyers who happened to be men.' The law society, for its part, continued to encourage women lawyers to play the fullest part in law society activities and committees.[46]

Auckland District Law Society's first working party: 1981

While the first study on women lawyers was undertaken by a government advisory committee, it was the Auckland District Law Society which took the initiative. This first piece of law society research provided a more detailed and compelling insight into the problems being encountered by women lawyers in Auckland and raised questions about the situation in other regions.

In 1981, then president of the Auckland District Law Society Ted Thomas (later Justice Thomas of the Court of Appeal), revived his 1975 proposal for an in-depth study by the law society. Aware that a standing committee of the law society was not the right structure for advancing the issue, Thomas appointed a special committee—the Auckland District Law Society Working Party on Women in the Legal Profession. He made a conscious decision to appoint a male convener, Rod Hansen, concerned that the findings would otherwise be challenged as biased.[47] The working party membership comprised five women and five men.[48] The terms of reference directed the working party to identify any evidence of prejudice or discrimination.

Nationwide, this was a time of high unemployment and the few vacancies for new law graduates were attracting dozens of eager applicants, of whom approximately one-third were women. In Auckland, recently admitted women lawyers were finding their progress impeded for no reason other than their sex, while women law graduates suspected that their employment prospects were less favourable than those of their male colleagues.

The 1981 working party found evidence of discrimination in nearly every facet of women's experiences in the profession—employment, salary, areas of work and partnership. The majority of women surveyed considered that their male colleagues did not accept women as professionals, and did not consider that the 'fellowship of the profession' was unreservedly extended to women.[49] The Auckland law society was openly criticised for patronising clubs and other organisations which excluded women from membership.[50]

The 1981 working party was advised by both women and men that 'some employers had unequivocally stated that they will not employ a woman solicitor'. The preference for men was confirmed in a survey of law professional students undertaken by the Auckland law school— 45 percent of women law students seeking employment in the profession were unemployed compared with 34 percent of the men students.[51]

The working party also found that sex-related harassment was widespread. More than 40 percent of the women lawyers surveyed reported that they had been subjected to discrimination in the form of 'belittling or embarrassing talk or conduct'.[52]

The working party cited the 'instrumental cause' of discrimination as 'the attitudes of men'. The arguments most often put forward to 'explain or excuse' discrimination were: women were less intelligent, less capable and less suited to legal careers because of their manner and psychology; women were less acceptable to clients; women chose their families over their careers; and, lastly, that women did have equal opportunities but they failed to take advantage of them.[53]

One by one the working party discounted each argument, setting out the arguments and evidence to the contrary.[54] Women's supposed lesser intelligence was not borne out by University of Auckland records showing that women law students' academic results from 1973 to 1977 had far exceeded those of the men students. Despite the statistics, that same group of men, by then in the profession, had an inflated view of their own intelligence—80 percent of the men surveyed claimed to have been in the top 50 percent of their law school class.[55]

In response to the argument that women lawyers, as a matter of course, would choose family responsibilities over their careers, the working party pointed out that this assumption failed 'to treat women as individuals'.[56] Less than a quarter of women lawyers in practice in Auckland had children and of those who did, nearly half had taken up law when their children reached school age. Women who did take maternity leave took no more than the usual sabbatical period of three months. The working party concluded that the fears of disruption associated with childbearing and childrearing 'seemed greatly exaggerated'. In fact, there was little difference in the 'drop-out rate' of men and women admitted in the mid-1970s and both women and men who changed jobs did so for a variety of reasons.[57]

The working party emphasised that discrimination in the legal profession was unlawful, unprofessional, unfair to women, contrary to the public interest and contrary to the interests of the profession. In setting out a list of seventeen specific recommendations, the working party urged the Auckland District Law Society to 'spare no effort to eliminate discrimination against women in all its forms'.[58]

That 'no effort be spared' to eliminate sex discrimination in the profession was supported by the then Minister of Justice, Jim McLay. In his view, '[t]he concern must be to ensure that members of the profession have equal opportunity to progress', an ambition he believed was made more possible by the working party's study.[59] Likewise, Auckland District Law Society President Ted Thomas QC, praised the report, calling it 'well-reasoned, balanced and constructive'. He believed the council would 'fully consider the report and recommendations'.[60]

Of the seventeen working party recommendations, the council referred six to a committee which had 'a limited period of activity',[61] acted on six, and resolved to take no action on five. Some members of the profession privately regarded the report as 'flawed' which may explain the council's hesitancy when it came to acting on the recommendations.[62]

Although the council was willing to endorse the principle that discrimination was 'totally unacceptable', it shied away from the recommendations relating specifically to the legal and disciplinary consequences of discrimination—aspects most directly within the law societies' ambit of responsibility. The council declined to adopt the recommendation that it 'stress to the profession that in some respects discrimination on the ground of sex is unlawful' or to 're-affirm that discrimination on the ground of sex is unprofessional conduct and may, in appropriate circumstances, be the subject of disciplinary proceedings'. In the same vein, the council resolved to take no action on the recommendation that it 'express its concern' to the New Zealand Law Society in respect of the submission made on the partnership clause in the Human Rights Commission Act; nor would it recommend that the national society seek an amendment making the provision 'applicable to partnerships of all sizes'.[63]

Hannah Sargisson's study: 1982

Partly motivated by the doubts about the 1981 working party's findings, Hannah Sargisson, a staff solicitor at Russell McVeagh McKenzie Bartleet & Co in Auckland, embarked on a more detailed study for her LLB honours dissertation the following year. She re-ran the working party's survey, examined overseas studies on women in the profession, and explored in more detail the explanations for women lawyers' lower status. In every area, the working party's findings of discrimination were confirmed.[64]

In addition, Sargisson gathered anecdotal evidence from men and women that employers were shying away from recruiting women in favour of recruiting men. One senior partner confided that his firm 'would not have a woman [as] long as he was a principal in the firm'. That example was 'one of many similar cases'.[65]

Sargisson concluded in 1982 that the 'single most important reason' for women's comparatively slow progress in the profession was 'the attitudes of male lawyers and employers'. She doubted that the sheer increase in numbers of women with experience would assure women entry into the higher echelons of the profession, such as the judiciary, 'unless and until attitudes change'.[66]

Education, affirmative action or discipline?

It was on the question of how to change attitudes that the opinions of law society office holders and those who researched the problem differed. Sargisson, relying on successful strategies used in the United States, argued that affirmative action programmes were needed to counter negative attitudes. Those programmes would redress the effects of past discriminatory policies and practices and ensure discrimination did not continue.[67] The law societies, however, took a different view.

One of the major recommendations of the 1981 working party which was taken up by the Implementation Committee of the Auckland law society related to an ethical rule on discrimination. The ethical rules which, if breached, could attract disciplinary action by the law societies already required that a 'lawyer shall treat his [sic] professional colleagues with the utmost courtesy and fairness'.[68] But the Implementation Committee wanted a specific provision to the effect that: 'discrimination in the profession on the grounds of sex relating to employment opportunities, allocation of work, remuneration, partnership prospects, and relations between practitioners, is totally unacceptable.'[69]

There was considerable debate about the legal and professional implications of an ethical rule on sex discrimination. The New Zealand Law Society Ethics Committee thought the Auckland suggestion was formulated 'on what was essentially a "trade union" basis'. The Ethics Committee did not believe that the provision should be restricted solely to the ground of sex. It was also 'mindful' of the contentious partnership provision in the Human Rights Commission Act 1977. In light of these factors, the Ethics Committee 'did not support a rule expressed in a negative manner', as had been suggested by the Auckland society. Instead, the committee thought that 'some sort of positive statement in the Code would have a very strong persuasive effect on members of the profession'.[70]

Members of the Auckland Implementation Committee met with National President Bruce Slane (later appointed Privacy Commissioner), to discuss why the ethical rules needed 'specific reference to discrimination against women members'. The committee did not seek to elevate sex discrimination over other forms of discrimination but, at the same time, was 'most anxious that the reference to women [was] not lost in a rolled-up rehash of the provisions of the Human Rights Commission Act'. Sian Elias (later Justice Elias), on behalf of the Auckland law society committee, argued that it was 'timely and entirely responsible for the New Zealand Law Society to affirm that women have an equal place with men in the profession'.[71]

Although a specific explanatory note would have opened the way for professional disciplinary action by district and national law societies, that dimension was downplayed. Instead, the Auckland Implementation Committee highlighted the 'educational impact' of an explanatory note which 'could significantly assist in reducing the time during which this particular problem will cause the profession concern'.[72] After further meetings and discussion, it was agreed that a new general rule against all forms of discrimination and an accompanying statement relating to women lawyers would meet all concerns.

On 26 November 1982, the New Zealand Law Society Council considered the proposed new rule. The draft provided that practitioners 'shall not discriminate against nor treat unfairly any practitioner by reason of the colour, race, ethnic or national origins, sex, marital status, or religious or ethical belief of that practitioner', and was followed by an explanatory statement:

> The position of women within the profession is at present of special concern to the Council. It is acknowledged by the Council that women practitioners, who are entering the profession in increasing numbers, are experiencing particular difficulties within the profession.
>
> Discrimination against or other unfair treatment of women practitioners in respect of employment opportunities, remuneration, allocation of work, admission to partnership or any other matter is not only unfair but is harmful to the profession's standing and ability to serve the community's needs.
>
> Any such act of discrimination or unfair treatment is a breach of Rule 3 and may lead to disciplinary proceedings.[73]

At the special invitation of the New Zealand Law Society, Hannah Sargisson and Sian Elias attended the meeting—probably the first women lawyers to be present at a national law society council meeting. They argued for the new rule on the basis of the problems uncovered in Auckland. But the rule would have national effect, and so, for a part of the meeting, the discussion turned to evidence of sex discrimination outside Auckland.

Problems outside Auckland?

In preparation for the November 1982 law society council meeting, Bruce Robertson, president of the Otago law society (later a High Court judge), consulted with women practitioners in Dunedin about the problem of discrimination. As a result, he reported to the national council, that he was 'convinced that similar problems existed' in the Otago region.[74] The Wellington representatives, however, said they 'were not convinced that this was the prevailing situation in Wellington'. As a result, they proposed an amendment to the explanatory statement—deletion of the sentence acknowledging that women practitioners were experiencing particular difficulties within the profession.[75] Their motion was defeated and the new rule and explanatory statement were adopted unchanged.[76]

Less than a year before the national council meeting, research by Megan Richardson on women in the law had been published in *Council Brief*, the Wellington law society newsletter. National statistics on women law graduates and lawyers had revealed that at the recruitment stage women law graduates, who, on the whole, were more academically successful than men, were more likely to find work in government departments, as judges' clerks or in law schools. Women graduates were least represented in the practising profession.[77]

Richardson discovered that while women law students did not 'drop out' or fail university at any greater rate than men, the position in practice was quite different. Nationally, women lawyers were leaving their jobs at a much higher rate than men lawyers—a rate that was noticeably increasing. Placed alongside the finding that the women who stayed in the profession did not succeed to the same extent as their male counterparts, Richardson concluded: 'This too must be a reason for the high dropout rate of women lawyers.'[78]

Wellington District Law Society's working party: 1983

Despite Richardson's research and the findings of the 1980 Committee on Women, the Wellington law society wanted to await the results of a study by its own working party before accepting that discrimination was a problem in the profession in Wellington. The Wellington District Law Society's Working Party on Women in the Legal Profession was established as a result of a heated debate that took place at the March 1982 annual general meeting of the Wellington District Law Society.

The outgoing president of the Wellington law society, Don Inglis QC (later a Family Court judge), had made a number of remarks in the society's annual report relating to discrimination and women lawyers. One comment referred to the 'mindless generalities' which came out of the Human Rights Commission, while another implied that 'women lacked the professional dedication necessary to justify partnership status'.[79]

Local lawyer Helen Cull addressed the meeting, pointing out that in light of the Auckland working party report, subjective assessments of the kind in the outgoing president's report were inappropriate. She proposed that the Wellington law society set up a working party so that it could 'view the matter in more detail before we record attitudes'. Other women lawyers, including Ruth Charters, Carolyn Henwood and Shirley Smith, supported the motion to establish a Wellington working party, with Carolyn Henwood pointedly recalling a decision by Wellington women lawyers in 1976 not to form a separate women's group, believing then that women should progress as part of the law society. 'Six years later,' she said, 'it just hasn't happened'.[80]

Des Deacon agreed that the remarks in Inglis' report were 'throw away lines' and neither the council nor the outgoing president objected to the motion to amend the report. John Upton (later appointed Queen's Counsel) did point out that many lawyers would endorse the statements that:

> it would be a sad day for the profession if we ever allowed ourselves to consider a prospective employee or partner on anything other than merit [and] the biological fact of being a woman or man has nothing to do with professional aptitude or suitability to practise one's chosen profession.[81]

The proposal to establish the working party was carried by a large majority. According to Inglis: 'A study of this kind could do a great deal of good, and if it turns out there is unfair discrimination, then clearly the society must act.'[82]

The Wellington working party was convened by Chris Pottinger and its men members (including Pottinger) outnumbered the women by five to three.[83] The working party adopted the same terms of reference as those used by the Auckland working party two years earlier.

The findings of discrimination in the Wellington working party's study were striking. A vast majority of all the Wellington lawyers surveyed thought there was discrimination against women—91 percent of women and 76 percent of men. Women experienced difficulties gaining entry into commercial areas of practice, were paid less than men with the same years of experience, and had difficulties with male colleagues who were patronising and refused to accept women as professional equals.[84]

Employment opportunities were also denied women on the basis of their sex. Women lawyers surveyed were twice as likely as the men to have made four or more job applications. Employers, according to the women, were 'overconcerned' about their plans to marry and have children.[85]

Again, employers made direct references to predetermined policies not to hire or promote women. One firm had told a prospective woman employee that 'they had two women lawyers and didn't want any more'. Another fifteen women were specifically told that they had no partnership prospects on account of their sex. The reason given to one woman was that there were 'too many women coming up in the firm, therefore numbers would be unbalanced'.[86]

Men who supported the employment of women lawyers also referred to opposition from their male colleagues. One firm which was said to have had 'three unfortunate experiences' with women lawyers had to be convinced 'that maybe it is the fourth time lucky'. After much effort by one of the partners that firm decided to employ a female undergraduate on a part-time basis.[87]

According to men lawyers, 'feminist women lawyers' had 'elitist attitudes', 'negative attitudes', or simply 'lack[ed] a sense of humour'.[88] Women lawyers described being in a no win situation. An unemployed woman said:

> If you complain, you are labelled a hysterical, neurotic women's libber, all said contemptuously. If we don't complain, how will the message ever get through? It is difficult to explain my present unemployment—I left because of harassment—and get understanding . . . What do I say to future employers?[89]

As with the 1980 Committee on Women study, there were signs of hostility surrounding the issue of discrimination. One woman referred to the profession's resentment of the Human Rights Commission Act, while another described 'the awareness and liberalism of many practitioners, young and old' as being 'only skin deep . . . When you really touch a nerve, the Doctor Jekyll disappears, and the Mr Hyde comes snarling out of the shadow'.[90]

Social interaction remained a problem. As suggested by Carolyn Henwood in 1975, women lawyers had increased their attendance at law society functions and seminars. While the men tended to go to functions for social reasons, women, when they attended, were more inclined to do so for professional reasons. However, the events themselves were still geared for men. Most of the women surveyed in 1983 said they had felt uncomfortable for reasons relating to the 'excessive consumption of alcohol' and the 'night out with the boys' feel of the functions. Even at a law society 'Devil's Own' Golf Tournament, the women entrants had been made to feel 'less than welcome'.[91] When a group of women lawyers attended a Bar dinner in 1982 the *New Zealand Woman's Weekly* reported that they were asked whether they were 'lawyers or groupies'.[92]

Overall, 70 percent of the women surveyed had been subjected to 'belittling talk or derogatory remarks directed at women in general'. Colleagues were said to be the primary offenders.[93]

The Wellington working party concluded that the 'recent development' of women entering the profession had 'perhaps caught some a little off balance'. It said, although 'a growing number of us now accept them [women] as normal' there was 'still, however, a distinct measure of prejudice against women practitioners'.[94]

Recommendations for change

The working party recommended that 'positive moves' be made to 'anticipate and to forestall prejudice rather than to react to its presence'; that the public be made aware that 'women and men are of equal value as lawyers'; that there be equal pay for equal work; that advertising and communication be conducted on the basis that lawyers were both women and men; and lastly, that women be recognised as 'an indispensable and inseparable part of the profession as a whole'.[95]

The working party considered that the problem and its resolution rested with 'each and every lawyer' in the Wellington region. No responsibility for action rested specifically with the law society, employers or male practitioners. Nor did the working party propose how the changes it recommended could be implemented nor how progress would be measured. Discrimination was clearly an individual's problem.

It seems that the working party considered the matter well in hand. Its recommendations were tempered by the fact that the national law society had implemented the new ethical guideline and the belief that two other law societies had set up committees on discrimination.[96] Perhaps more importantly, however, the working party observed that the number of women lawyers had increased and, in their view, would continue to do so. It believed there was 'a growing awareness not only concerning the problems faced by women in the law but also the need for *individual* members of the legal profession to take positive action to mitigate those problems' (emphasis added).[97]

Publicity about the survey downplayed the findings of sex discrimination. On Radio New Zealand's *Morning Report*, a member of the Wellington working party, Linda Howes, attributed the results to the relatively recent entry of women to the profession, their lack of family connections, and, 'to a large degree', youth, not gender. Discrimination was 'apparent' or 'perceived', and resulted 'in many instances from the youth of the respondents rather than from purely the fact that they are women'.[98]

In distinct contrast, Chris Pottinger, the working party's convener, defended the research findings. A rural practitioner had complained that the working party's report was full of emotive, unsubstantiated and subjective complaints instead of real evidence of prejudice and discrimination.[99] Pottinger replied that under the law of evidence the responses to the survey were 'the best evidence'. In his view: 'The facts in the report are found in the percentages quoted which have been precisely calculated ... I believe the statistics produced cannot be ignored.'[100]

But ignoring the findings was precisely how the Wellington law society council responded. It debated neither the report's findings nor whether action was required, and made no formal resolutions with regard to the report. Instead, like the Auckland law society, the council formed a Women in Law Committee which was to have responsibility for the survey. It appeared that the issue which stimulated most interest at council was the circulation and distribution of the full report to practitioners, and particularly the photocopying costs.[101]

Neither did the national law society council consider the report. The only national coverage it attracted was an article in *LawTalk*.[102]

Education, not enforcement

The Wellington working party, like the Auckland working party, placed considerable reliance on the 1982 ethical guideline as an answer to the problem of discrimination in the profession. In effect, the law societies saw the 1982 ethical rule and explanatory statement as 'a confirmation of the place of women . . . and, as such [it] would be of considerable support to them'.[103]

Despite the New Zealand Law Society's explanatory statement, there was no intention on the part of the law societies that a breach of the rule against discrimination would lead to disciplinary proceedings. On the contrary, the national president, Bruce Slane, told the 1983 Conference of Law Societies in Surfers Paradise that the new ethical guideline was 'not suggested with the aim of fostering formal complaints'. Discrimination, he said, was widely believed to be 'notoriously difficult to establish'. In addition, there was a 'natural reluctance' on the part of those who experienced it to publicise the fact.[104] No consideration was given to a complaints procedure or enforcement mechanisms that might overcome that 'natural reluctance' or ensure that discrimination was fairly established—the ethical guideline had a purely educational purpose.

Even Bruce Slane had some doubts that men lawyers would change their ways. At the Surfers Paradise conference he observed:

> there may be many male practitioners who now feel that as members of the Law Society they have made their token gesture towards women and that things will carry on very much as before. It would do for both sexes to think a little further.[105]

Alan Ritchie, a legal officer at the New Zealand Law Society (later the executive director), commented in *LawTalk*: 'One thing is for sure, it is not now appropriate for practitioners of either sex to be complacent or to think that the job is done.' He noted that women lawyers were forming an organisation and asked the pertinent question: 'What are the men doing?'[106]

Women lawyers take initiative

From 1983 to 1987, women lawyers took the initiative in addressing sex discrimination. No one else was going to do so. In Auckland, Wellington, Hamilton and Dunedin, women lawyers met to discuss discrimination and to identify ways of tackling it. Although the Auckland and Wellington law societies formed women lawyers' committees, women lawyers in those centres and elsewhere grouped themselves into independent, women-only organisations outside the law society structure. Regardless of the organisational status of these groups, women lawyers accepted that they had to provide the impetus for change. They could not wait or rely on the law societies or their male colleagues to voluntarily bring about sex equality.

Auckland women lawyers: 1984

After several years in operation, the Women and the Law Research Foundation had lapsed, partly due to excessive pressures on the time of too few women lawyers. However, informal meetings of women lawyers continued and in early 1984, Sian Elias, Nancy Dolan, Rowena Lewis, Hannah Sargisson and Margaret Wilson (Figure 9) among others, met to discuss the need for a formal support network in the form of an association. Initially they canvassed the possibility of a national association but the impetus was clearly in Auckland, where 45 percent of the women lawyers in the country were in practice.[107]

Figure 9

Margaret Wilson, 1995

On 16 April 1984, the inaugural meeting of the Auckland Women Lawyers Association (AWLA) was held. Margaret Wilson, in an introductory speech, spoke of the need for an association 'where women could socially support each other and use their skills as lawyers, not only to help themselves but also other women in the community'. The timing was obviously right. Within a month, the new association had received forty-two applications for membership and by May 1987, 268 of the 329 women in practice in the Auckland region had joined.[108]

From the outset the women behind the new organisation suggested the association should adopt a 'friendly foreign policy'. But the 'women only' membership criterion raised questions at the inaugural meeting. On behalf of the organisers, Margaret Wilson suggested that men could be invited to cooperate on projects and to speak at functions, 'but not be members—the control must remain with women, always'.[109]

There were suspicions that this new women's group would specifically target the law society. However, at the first committee meeting chaired by the first president, Helen Melrose, it was resolved that the association was not 'set up in competition or reaction to the law society'. It would 'simply have a different perspective, and focus on the particular concerns of women lawyers'.[110] As Hannah Sargisson observed, the law society's women's committee had:

> steered away from the politically sensitive questions of change and focused on social events. Women lawyers needed an independent group outside the law

society which could both support women lawyers and be a driving force for change. That did not mean the law society was under attack.[111]

Despite the group's intentions, the *National Business Review* reported that: 'Women lawyers in Auckland, demanding greater voice and support, have incorporated an association as a "counter measure" to the male-dominated Auckland District Law Society.'[112] New Zealand Law Society President Bruce Slane, however, described the new women's association as an 'excellent idea'. In his view, the association would give women lawyers 'an opportunity to communicate with each other on matters that concern them. The law society can't cope with every aspect related to women in law.'[113] Apart from passing the ethical rule, the national law society had not in fact taken any steps to address the problems being faced by women lawyers.

By comparison, the AWLA tackled the problem of discrimination with vigour. Within two months of the inaugural meeting, the association had published a newsletter, organised a seminar and a social function, liaised with the law society, made contact with women lawyers in Wellington, set up a database of women lawyers, compiled a resource list for appointments, and made a 'formal complaint' to the Management Committee of the University of Auckland law faculty regarding the timetabling of 'so called "heavy subjects" ' before 9 am and after 3 pm. The association considered this to be 'unfavourable to women who have children'.[114]

By August 1984, the association was looking at a proposal that the law society adopt the Australian 'uncle' committee system, assessing Australian research on students leaving law school, supporting local barrister Lowell Goddard's election to the law society council, and monitoring the appointment of women partners in firms and the employment of women law students through the University Interviewing Programme. The AWLA executive, aware of the task ahead, established five subcommittees to look into: liaison with schools; in vitro fertilisation; child care; suburban practitioners; and tax and insurance.[115]

Making women visible

Increasing women's visibility in the profession and the law was high on the agenda of many women lawyers' groups. In particular, the AWLA's early emphasis on sexist language and assertiveness training had a far-reaching impact on interaction between women and men in the profession.

The first seminar organised by the association was on assertiveness training. Entitled, 'Strategies for equal opportunities for women' it was run by Dr Sharon Lord, a well-known American feminist. The response to the seminar was 'overwhelming', with 'women flying from Wellington and driving from as far as Gisborne and Hamilton'.[116]

Dr Lord advised women lawyers to 'utilise for their own advantage the gestures and props which men use to make them feel at ease', such as shaking hands when greeting a client. 'Women,' she said, 'must give clear cues as to who they are and how they want to be treated.' In her view, women who failed to do so were 'less justified in complaining of ill treatment and discrimination'.[117]

At the same time, Shayne Mathieson, then a mediation officer at the Human Rights Commission, encouraged women lawyers to combat sex stereotypes in legal documents. For example, in conveyancing documents, it was 'very common for the husband to be named first and his occupation ... specified, while his wife is simply referred to as "his wife" or "married woman"'. Mathieson suggested that lawyers should 'make a point' of asking clients how they would like to be described in documents.[118]

The Auckland law society's women's subcommittee was also trying to tackle visible forms of sexism. In 1985, the subcommittee addressed sexist language in legal documents, forms of addressing women, professional advertising, names of law society committees, and general everyday language. Of particular concern was the law firm tradition of addressing correspondence 'Dear Sirs' and the resistance on the part of '[m]any Judges and practitioners' to addressing women by their chosen title—particularly where they preferred 'Ms'.[119]

Compliance with gender-neutral language was closely monitored. The AWLA awarded bouquets to firms who adopted gender-neutral forms of address on their letters and brickbats to those who did not.[120] Some law firm drafting manuals pointed out that documents and letters should avoid gender specific pronouns, and articles informing practitioners about 'sex-neutral' language appeared in professional newsletters.[121]

In a similar vein, women lawyers, particularly those appearing in court, asserted their presence by insisting that their full names or honorifics be used on judgments and in case reporting. Men counsel were commonly described only by their surnames and initials although occasionally 'Messrs' was used. Rather than be included in the invisible ranks of the initialled, women lawyers asked to be clearly identified.

This preference on the part of women litigators was so marked that in Wellington in 1985 the Chief Justice prepared a policy on the naming of counsel in judgments of the High Court. The convention would be for women counsel to be described by their first names and surnames. The titles 'Miss', 'Mrs' or 'Ms' were not to be used. Male counsel would be described by their initials and surnames only. 'Mr' and their first names were not to be used. The policy concluded with the statement that: 'In case you think this is sexist, it is at the specific request of the ladies.'[122]

Wellington women lawyers: 1984

Following the 1983 Wellington working party report, the Wellington law society council formed a Women in Law Committee.[123] But that committee had no formal objectives and, understandably, had difficulty ascertaining its mandate.[124] In 1984, the convener, Sandra Moran, reported that the committee had decided: 'if it was to make any decisions regarding issues affecting women then it would only want to do so if it had the approval of the majority of the women practising in the profession.'[125] Accordingly, in October 1984, the first meeting of Wellington women practitioners was held.

At the request of the women lawyers, the Women in Law Committee placed an early emphasis on providing a forum where women lawyers could socialise and exchange ideas. The meetings rarely attracted fewer than seventy lawyers, some of whom were not in practice and therefore did not belong to the law society. At one meeting, in early 1985, it was agreed that a separate association be formed to include all women lawyers and law students, and to enable the group to address concerns faced by women in the community in general.[126] Sandra Moran reported: 'There may be occasions when we want to make submissions that are in conflict with those put forward by the Wellington District Law Society and we want to be able to do that without embarrassing the law society.'[127]

In November that year, forty-two women attended the inaugural meeting of the Wellington Women Lawyers Association (WWLA) and elected Margaret Lee (later Judge Lee) as its first convener. The new association aimed to facilitate social contact among members, to work for the equal opportunity and advancement of women studying or practising law, and to work for law reform of social policies affecting all women.[128]

Hamilton women lawyers: 1984

Around the same time, a group of women lawyers based in Hamilton had been meeting informally. They arranged an unofficial luncheon for women lawyers attending the 1984 Easter Law Conference and thereafter continued to meet to network, to support each other and to socialise.[129]

Otago women lawyers: 1986

On 1 August 1986, the informal social group of Otago women lawyers which had been meeting for several years was formalised as the Otago Women Lawyers' Society. The society, or OWLS as it soon became known, was established, as 1992 secretary Claire Elder recalled, because: 'The increasing numbers of women working in the profession at that time highlighted the inadequacy of the District Law Society in responding to and fulfilling the needs of the women practitioners.'

Women lawyers in the male dominated Dunedin profession needed support.[130] The OWLS constitution was virtually identical to that of the Wellington women lawyers' group, with references to social and political objectives.[131]

Heightened sensitivity: mid-1980s

By the mid-1980s, there was a heightened level of sensitivity surrounding the subject of discrimination in the profession. The new women's groups had caused some unease. Some feared the new associations could make matters worse, while others were more concerned about challenges to the law societies and the firms.

The terms of the partnerships being offered by firms to women were the subject of some negative comment. Colin Pidgeon, incoming president of the Auckland District Law Society, expressed concerns of tokenism at the 1985 annual general meeting of the society. He was concerned at the imbalance between the large number of women law students and the ten or so women in partnerships. In his 1985 presidential report, he said: 'This imbalance must be corrected and the admission of women to partnerships must be on full and equal status with their male counterparts, and not just as token gestures.'[132] A month later, the AWLA formed a Partnership Support Group for prospective women partners.[133]

During the 1985 Auckland law school graduate recruitment programme, city law firms were believed by women graduates to be 'on the defensive', bending over backwards to appear non-discriminatory. They avoided blatant sexism but were thought to be touting their 'token' women partners or employees as 'evidence of equality'. By comparison, the less sophisticated provincial firms still resorted to questions like 'Is there a fella in your life?' and 'Are you in love yet?' to ascertain women graduates' marriage prospects and hence their presumed likelihood of dropping out.[134]

The following year, concerns about pre-interview screening by employers prompted the removal of references to sex, age and marital status from the recruitment scheme forms.[135] At the interviews, several large city firms were said to have resorted to stereotyped or 'chauvinistic' comments about women lawyers,[136] but again most firms were keen to emphasise there was no discrimination against women entering partnerships, an assertion certainly not borne out in the law society surveys.[137]

In comparison with the firms, the law societies were becoming more openly sensitive to women's issues, demonstrated by their approach to the programming of conferences and seminars. In 1986, the committee organising the Waitangi Law Conference endeavoured to ensure that the programme would appeal to women as well as to men practitioners.[138]

Likewise, the Otago law society when planning the 1987 national conference set up a Women Practitioners' Committee to consult with women lawyers and ensure that their interests were included in the programme.[139]

At this time, the Wellington law society Women in Law Committee, under Barbara Buckett's convenorship, kicked back into action. The committee conducted a survey on the need for childcare services for lawyers, ran a seminar on equal pay, and met with the WWLA and representatives from the Ministry of Women's Affairs.[140] Colleen Singleton, then executive director of the law society, reflected that the law firms' response to the childcare survey was poor and the law society's response was not much better. The proposal for a childcare centre came at a bad time economically for the profession. There were also stringent regulations limiting where the centre could be situated. In addition, Singleton pointed out, the women were equivocal—while they needed help with child care they did not want their employers to view their needs as problems.[141]

A hardcore structural problem

By now it was obvious that discrimination in the profession was a widespread problem. Research by Georgina Murray at the University of Auckland during the mid to late 1980s confirmed the existence of 'hardcore discrimination' in the profession affecting ethnic minorities and those from non-elite class backgrounds as well as women.[142] It was now widely apparent that the problem was not simply the attitudes of men lawyers nor the wider social context of discrimination.

Mary O'Regan, then chief executive of the newly established Ministry of Women's Affairs, explained at the 1986 Waitangi Law Conference that the problems for women were twofold—attitudinal and structural. She spoke of the need to examine law firm practices to see how they discriminated against women, and advocated affirmative action to redress the imbalance caused by discrimination. Firms needed to resolve issues of flexible working hours, maternity and parental leave, and child care. O'Regan challenged firms and partners to 'stick their necks out, take a lead—open things up'.[143]

Further evidence of discrimination

National survey 1987

O'Regan's challenge went unheeded. In 1987, a New Zealand Law Society national survey of, among other things, the profession's attitude toward women lawyers, uncovered a bleak picture. '[D]ifficulties faced by women in making progress in the profession' was considered a problem by over

50 percent of the respondents but, in the context of other issues, it was not thought to be greatly significant.[144] However, analysing the findings by gender showed that the majority of women lawyers surveyed ranked women's difficulties in the profession as the number one issue facing the profession. For the majority of the men (who made up 85 percent of the respondents), it was an issue of little or no consequence.[145]

The same divergence of views between women and men lawyers was apparent on nearly every point: 46 percent of women lawyers said they experienced difficulty working with male colleagues, only 24 percent of men agreed; 66 percent of women believed that women were not given the same opportunities to do challenging and prestigious work, only 19 percent of men agreed; 60 percent of women considered that women were less well paid relative to their male colleagues, only 13 percent of men agreed.[146] The only issue on which the men and women surveyed nearly agreed was that women lawyers were less likely than their male colleagues to become partners or senior management executives.[147]

In addition, the 1987 survey revealed that men lawyers had exaggerated ideas of the actual number of women in the profession. Men lawyers said that, on average, 22 percent of the lawyers they worked with were women,[148] whereas in fact women made up only 15 percent of all lawyers in the country.

The New Zealand Law Society survey report concluded that the 'question of women in the profession must be addressed, especially the gap which exists between the perceptions of women about their role in the profession and the perceptions of male lawyers about women's roles in the profession'.[149] Aside from a law society press release highlighting the problems facing women in the profession, the society took no action on the survey findings.[150] At the 1987 National Law Conference, O'Regan stressed: 'The good intentions behind the working parties, the surveys and the reports must be translated into action to facilitate equality of outcome.'[151]

Appointments of women

Over this period, the focus was turning to the appointment of women lawyers to positions within the profession and the legal system. In 1984, Hannah Sargisson was appointed chair of the Equal Opportunities Tribunal for a five-year term. In 1987, the new Labour Government appointed four women District Court judges bringing the total number of women judges to seven. In 1988, Judith Potter became the first woman president of a district law society and Lowell Goddard and Sian Elias were appointed the first women Queen's Counsel (Figure 10).[152] In that same year, Judge Silvia Cartwright was appointed Chief District Court Judge.

Figure 10

Sian Elias QC, President of the Auckland District Law Society Judith Potter and Lowell Goddard QC

Photograph taken at the Auckland High Court after the call to the inner Bar of the first two women QCs. Photograph by Terry Winn reproduced with the permission of Terry Winn and Associates, Auckland, New Zealand.

Senior members of the profession, such as Pat Downey, editor of the *New Zealand Law Journal* and previously a Human Rights Commissioner, suggested the profession should prepare itself for change. He pointed to the significant and increasing number of women studying law and seeking admission to the Bar and remarked:

> The implications of these figures are sometimes overlooked. It means that there will be over the next few years or so a marked change in the legal profession. Those who imagine that the principle of equality means that the profession will simply continue as before are going to get a few surprises. Despite the pretence of some of the more foolish feminists equality does not mean sameness. Women are not men in dresses—not even when they are wearing slacks![153]

Auckland District Law Society's second working party: 1989

The 'tensions and misunderstandings' predicted by Downey were confirmed only months later when the Auckland District Law Society released a second report on women in the profession.

When the second Auckland working party was established in 1986 by the then Auckland law society president, Simon Lockhart QC, women lawyers, for the first time, objected openly to the law society's choice of a male convener. The law society's argument was that a man would be seen to be more impartial—thereby giving the study and its conclusions more credibility; while the women lawyers argued that it was more appropriate that a woman lead a committee concerned with women's position in the profession.[154] After meeting a deputation, the law society capitulated and appointed Elizabeth Minogue co-convener with Norman Shieff. Two members of the working party, Anne Hinton and Dale Green (later Judge Green) resigned as a result of the society's decision. As with the 1981 working party, the 1989 working party was comprised of five women and five men.[155]

The second Auckland working party discovered that little had changed since the first Auckland study in 1981. Over half the women lawyers surveyed believed their progress was impeded, particularly by negative attitudes toward women.[156] Women were found to take longer to reach partnership than men, to be paid less than male colleagues in equivalent positions, and to be working in areas of law offering low prospects for advancement.[157] At employment interviews, men were more likely to discuss advancement potential and career aspirations while women were asked about their reasons for leaving their previous job, their marital status and the possibility of motherhood.[158]

Social interaction between the sexes was still largely on male terms. Men gathered in clubs or bars where women either could not or did not wish to attend. Social talk was considered 'exclusionary', centring on 'stereotypically male pursuits' such as rugby and cricket and involving coarse, sexist jokes. Women remained outside the social circle 'unless they participated as "one of the boys" '.[159]

A similar conclusion was reached by Stephanie Knight in her research on the use of alcohol by Auckland women lawyers. She found that the women were cautious drinkers, constantly having to maintain a balance between being accepted as 'one of the boys' and maintaining respect. Women had little scope for letting their guard down, particularly when drinking with colleagues.[160]

The 1989 working party recognised that the nature of sex discrimination had shifted: 'It became clear that much of the discrimination experienced by women within the profession is of a covert, rather than overt, nature.'[161]

The structural discrimination pointed out by Mary O'Regan was also in evidence. Firms were failing to incorporate the needs of women with respect to the provision of flexible maternity leave and childcare facilities. The working party noted that this 'can result in an apparently equal, neutral system operating in a discriminatory way'.[162]

Concerned that there had been 'a negative concentration on discrimination', some members of the Auckland working party wanted to shift the focus to 'a positive confidence in the future'. Recommendations were made to enable women to 'take advantage of all the opportunities available to them'.[163] They cited assistance with child care, tax deductibility for childcare expenses, parental leave, flexible employment options, partnership, elimination of sexist language and sexist behaviour, and recourse for problems of sexual harassment.[164] The second working party, unlike the 1983 Wellington study, directed its recommendations specifically at the Auckland law society and employers.

A mixed response

On release of the report, the AWLA, according to the *New Zealand Herald*, called for a 'get-tough approach to discrimination'. The association was reported to tell its members: 'It is time to take off the kid gloves and for the profession to act.'[165] The *Dominion*, in a fiery editorial, likened discrimination in the legal profession to guerrilla warfare. The 'enemy' had gone 'underground'—no one could predict 'where the next skirmish would take place'. Women lawyers, it claimed, were taking a stand. The problem could 'no longer be dealt with nicely'.[166]

This time, the Auckland law society council was prepared to take a lead. It unanimously endorsed the working party report and set up an Implementation Committee to start working on the recommendations.[167] Copies of the 104-page report were sent to every practitioner in the Auckland region. Law firms were asked by the then president, Colin Nicholson QC, to invite a council member to a partners' meeting for the purpose of discussing the report's findings.

The request for meetings became 'a sensitive exercise'.[168] Although some firms gave a 'very positive response', others did not react kindly to the suggestion that the law society sought to meddle in their in-house affairs. Jeannine Cockayne, the law society's public relations director, observed that:

> in some quarters the purpose of the talks has been misconstrued. Mr Nicholson's letter went to all law firms and already some have replied declaring the meetings unnecessary. They have assumed that the report ... does not apply to them because they don't discriminate against women, are sole practitioners, already have women partners and subscribe to all the working party's recommendations anyway.

Cockayne noted that the 'needless flutter' had come particularly from the smaller firms. None of the larger firms had declined to cooperate.[169]

The larger Auckland firms may not have declined to meet with council members but that did not mean they wholeheartedly supported the initiative or even that they were prepared to take it seriously. Judith Potter, then an Auckland council member, recalled one meeting with the partners of one of the largest firms. One partner explained to her 'very clearly' that while they were glad to have her along and that they liked her very much, she needed to understand that 'their clients were not at all interested in seeing women and so it was not appropriate for them to take women into their firm'.[170] A partner present at another large firm meeting with a law society council member recalls the partners being polite during the meeting, but making light of the discussion afterwards in the partners' lounge.[171]

The final word: silence

Following the 1989 second working party, the Auckland law society developed a concerted plan of action to tackle the problem of sex discrimination. Outside Auckland, however, the response of the official representatives of the profession was largely silent. The Canterbury law society noted the existence of the various studies but did not come to any particular view on their findings. The reports were made available for perusal in the High Court Library but, according to Cushla McGillivray, executive director of the Canterbury law society until 1994, there was no great level of interest in them.[172]

The Otago law society did not consider the reports. Like the Canterbury law society it also made them available to members in the library. On matters relating to women, the Otago law society consulted with OWLS through its long-serving secretary and executive director, Katherine Dolby.[173] According to women lawyers in the smaller provincial districts, the question of discrimination in the profession, as far as they knew, did not feature at law society council meetings. It remained a non-issue.

The New Zealand Law Society, at the request of the Auckland law society, endorsed a submission prepared by the Women in Law Subcommittee that the government consider tax deductibility for childcare expenses. Apart from that, the 1989 study and its recommendations went unnoticed at the national level.[174]

Only the women lawyers' groups, individual women lawyers and a select group of supportive men kept the issue alive and on the profession's agenda. In March 1989, Court of Appeal judge and chair of the Council of Legal Education, Sir Ivor Richardson, compiled a shortlist of crucial issues relevant to New Zealand lawyers and their education for the twenty-first century. Included in the list was the issue of 'recognising and rectifying discrimination against women and minorities in the marketplace and the corridors of power'.[175]

The women lawyers' groups and those men and women on the various working parties were genuinely motivated to do something and see it take effect in the profession, but for a number of reasons they were unable to achieve significant change. First, they lacked the resources to make it happen—the time, skills, knowledge and status to implement and enforce their own recommendations. Secondly, the law society councils found themselves relatively powerless to promote change within the profession and—in the face of opposition—were unwilling to force change. The law societies were unconvinced that the problem of discrimination was theirs to solve.

In general within the legal profession, there was a relatively unsophisticated level of understanding of gender discrimination and how it could be eliminated. There was little theory or documented practice for the working parties to draw on. Research on career discrimination in the professions was in its infancy and the working parties were delving into what was still a largely unexplored and undocumented area of social and work life. Despite their limitations, the law society studies were, in the private sector at least, leading the challenge to change

By 1989 the problem of sex discrimination in the legal profession was clearly out in the open. As a result, many in the profession thought it had been fully addressed and solved. But, as the profession entered the 1990s, it was found that the 'change' was more apparent than real.

Chapter Seven

Status of Women in Law: 1990s

The position of women in the legal profession in the early 1990s was a disconcerting mix of good and bad news. On one hand, women seemed to be doing well. They were qualifying from the law schools with higher average grades than their male colleagues, and were entering the profession in equal numbers with men. In 1989, for the first time, the same number of women as men had graduated in law. Law societies, law firms and other organisations had established committees and working groups to look at gender issues. Women lawyers and judges were visible, audible and clearly going places.

In 1992, a national survey of a quarter of the lawyers in practice gathered information on the status of women within the profession. Of the lawyers surveyed who had been in practice for more than ten years, 99 percent were of the view that women lawyers' opportunities had improved significantly in the past decade.[1] Women District Court judges, surveyed in 1993, agreed.[2]

However, at the same time, bad news kept surfacing. The 1992 survey found that sex discrimination was widespread: 82 percent of women lawyers said sex discrimination existed in the legal profession and 54 percent of men lawyers agreed.[3] Nine of the ten women District Court judges surveyed in 1993 also agreed that sex discrimination was a problem in the profession.[4]

The evidence demonstrated that women lawyers were not enjoying the same work opportunities as their male colleagues. Sexual harassment was on the increase, pay inequity continued, and partnerships for women were still few and far between. The number of women lawyers in private practice did not reflect the high number of women graduates. Women barristers were finding it hard to get good work and, despite one or two appointments, women judges remained very much a minority.

The higher in the legal profession one looked, the fewer the number of the women. The closer one looked, the more complex the problem.

Demographic profile

Ethnicity

The cultural and racial composition of women in the profession has changed. From there being one Maori woman lawyer in 1971, Georgina Te Heuheu of Ngati Tuwharetoa, there were fifty-two Maori women in the profession in 1991 and another twenty-five Maori women employed outside the profession as 'other legal professionals'.[5]

Pacific Islands women lawyers have also increased in numbers. In 1982, Mary Tuilotolava, a lawyer in South Auckland, was the only Tongan woman lawyer in Auckland, a city which had the largest Tongan population in New Zealand.[6] By 1991, the census counted twenty-eight Pacific Islands women lawyers and seven Pacific Islands women working as 'other legal professionals'.

In addition to Maori and Pacific Islands women lawyers, 5 percent of women lawyers in 1991 were of non-European lawyers ethnicity.

Age

The age profile of women lawyers has changed noticeably since 1981 when 65 percent of women lawyers were aged under 30 years. By 1986, this had dropped to 54 percent and by 1991 it had dropped to 44 percent. In 1991, more than half the women lawyers surveyed were aged 30 to 49 years. (Table 1)

Table 1

Age distribution of women lawyers, 1981–1991

Age group	Number			Distribution		
	1981	1986	1991	1981 %	1986 %	1991 %
15–24 years	105	138	222	27.6	17.3	16.1
25–29 years	144	294	384	37.8	36.8	27.9
30–39 years	90	276	525	23.6	34.6	38.1
40–49 years	21	66	192	5.5	8.3	13.9
50–54 years	9	12	33	2.4	2.0	2.4
55–59 years	12	6	12	3.1	0.8	0.9
60 years and over	3	6	12	0.8	0.8	0.9
Total	381	798	1,377	100.0	100.0	100.0

Source: Department of Statistics. *New Zealand Census of Population and Dwellings,* 1981–1991. Wellington: Department of Statistics, 1982–1992.

However, generally women lawyers are much younger than men lawyers. In the 1991 census, women made up only 3 percent of the lawyers (barristers and solicitors) aged 60 years and over. At the opposite end of the age spectrum, women comprised 55 percent of those aged between 21 and 24 years. (Although the census category is 15 to 24 years, in practical terms, this can be taken as being 21 to 24 years because lawyers must be at least 21 years old prior to admission to the Bar.) (Table 2)

Table 2

Age distribution of lawyers, 1991

Age group	Number			Women %
	Total	Women	Men	
15–24 years	405	222	183	54.8
25–29 years	900	384	516	42.6
30–39 years	2,040	1,525	1,515	25.7
40–49 years	1,548	192	1,356	12.4
50–54 years	345	33	312	9.5
55–59 years	210	12	198	5.7
60 years and over	348	12	336	3.4
Total	5,790	1,377	4,413	23.7

Source: Department of Statistics. *1991 New Zealand Census of Population and Dwellings.* Wellington: Department of Statistics, 1992.

Where are all the women lawyers?

Private practice

In 1995, women made up 28 percent of lawyers holding practising certificates. Women lawyers' representation in private practice had increased noticeably from 1990, with the proportion of women rising from 22 percent to 28 percent. Over the years 1990 to 1995, the number of women lawyers in private practice increased by 58 percent.[7] (Table 3)

Employees

The majority of women lawyers in private practice are employees. In 1995, more than three-quarters of women practitioners worked as employees rather than principals (partners or sole practitioners) or barristers. By comparison, over half the men lawyers in private practice were principals and only 39 percent were employees. (Table 4)

Table 3

Private practice lawyers, 1990–1995

	Number		Women
Year	Total	Women	%
1990	5,704	1,225	21.5
1991	6,069	1,345	22.2
1992	6,243	1,383	22.2
1993	6,450	1,548	24.0
1994	6,745	1,686	25.0
1995	6,995	1,940	27.7

Source: New Zealand Law Society annual practising certificate data.

Table 4

Positions held by legal practitioners, 1993–1995

	1993		1994		1995	
Position	Women %	Men %	Women %	Men %	Women %	Men %
Employee	76.5	38.9	75.9	39.4	75.7	38.5
Barrister	6.5	8.3	6.5	7.6	7.0	9.3
Principal[a]	17.0	52.8	17.6	53.0	17.3	52.2
Total	100.0	100.0	100.0	100.0	100.0	100.0

[a] The position of principal includes partners and sole practitioners.

Source: New Zealand Law Society annual practising certificate data.

Of the total employee lawyers holding practising certificates in 1995, 43 percent were women. (Table 5)

Employee lawyers work in private practice law firms, government departments and state-owned enterprises, local government, tertiary education institutions, trade associations and commercial entities. The vast majority are in private practice. New Zealand Law Society (NZLS) statistics for 1995 indicate that 77 percent (2,621) of all employed lawyers work in private practice; of these, 43 percent are women. (Table 5)

Employment situation

Although there are no statistics on the numbers of employees in each firm, practice management surveys provide some indication of the likely employment situation of women lawyers.

Table 5

Employee lawyers, 1993–1994

	Number[a]			Distribution	
Year	Total	Women	Men	Women %	Men %
1993	3,092	1,183	1,909	38.3	61.7
1994	3,270	1,279	1,991	39.1	60.9
1995	3,413	1,468	1,945	43.0	57.0

[a] The number of employees was calculated by subtracting the numbers of principals and barristers from the total number of lawyers who held practising certificates.

Source: New Zealand Law Society annual practising certificate data.

According to Doug Arcus, member of the NZLS Practice Management Committee and organiser of the Waikato University annual law firm practice management surveys, the employment practices in law firms vary depending on the location and type of firm. New Zealand law firms generally fall into four location types: central city; suburban; provincial city; and rural. The ratio of principals to fee earning staff ('leverage') ranges from 1:3 to 1:2 in larger firms (usually central city and suburban), to 1:1 or less for provincial city and rural firms.

There are no statistics breaking down the distribution of women staff by size of law firm. It is generally understood that women lawyers are well represented as staff solicitors within the larger law firms. Small and medium sized firms, particularly outside the main centres, are believed to employ smaller proportions of women practitioners.

In December 1994, there were an estimated eighty-seven medium sized firms (six to fourteen partners), but by far the majority of firms were small law firms (two to five partners)—405 firms were in this latter category. There were an estimated twelve larger firms in New Zealand (fifteen or more partners).[8] Larger law firms commonly have offices in more than one location and tend to have between six and thirty-seven partners in any one office.

Of the larger firms in January 1996, ten had more than twenty partners. These firms, known nationally as the 'big firms', were: Bell Gully Buddle Weir; Brookfields; Buddle Findlay; Chapman Tripp Sheffield Young; Hesketh Henry; Kensington Swan; Phillips Fox; Rudd Watts & Stone; Russell McVeagh McKenzie Bartleet & Co; and Simpson Grierson.

Legal executives

In the 1990s, as in the 1970s, the majority of legal executives are women. In 1992, 80 percent of the 400 members of the New Zealand Institute of Legal Executives were women.[9]

It is also likely that the proportion of legal executives who are women will increase. In 1994, 90 percent of the legal executive trainees on the Wellington Polytechnic course were women.

Support staff

Support staff are employed by law firms, sole practitioners and barristers in a range of administrative roles as secretaries, librarians, receptionists, telephonists, word processors, filing clerks, search clerks, mail room staff and kitchen staff.

Although there are no statistics on the number of women support staff working in the legal profession, it is uncommon for men to be employed in this capacity. Within the New Zealand workforce in 1991, 46 percent of employed women worked as clerical, service or sales workers compared with 13 percent of men.[10]

The ratio of support staff to fee-earners (partners, staff solicitors and legal executives) is 1:1 in most firms. Larger firms have a slightly lower ratio of 1:1.3.[11] Technology plays a significant role in the number of support staff employed. The general rule, as explained by Doug Arcus, is 'the less technology, the greater the number of support staff'.

Based on an estimated seven thousand fee-earners in the profession (legal executives and practising lawyers), there are approximately another seven thousand people employed in the New Zealand legal profession— most of whom will be women.

Principals

The proportion of principals (partners and sole practitioners) who were women over 1991 to 1993 remained stable at just over 9 percent. This proportion increased slightly in 1994 and by 1995 had reached 11 percent. (Table 6)

The number of these women who are actually partners in law firms (as opposed to being sole practitioners) is unknown. New Zealand Law Society statistics do not differentiate between sole practitioners and partners—both are in practice on their own account.

Regional statistics, however, indicate regional variations between the numbers of women in practice as sole practitioners and those practising as partners in law firms. In Auckland in July 1995, for example, just over 15 percent of sole practitioners were women, and 10 percent of partners were women. In Wellington in February 1996, women made up 12 percent of sole practitioners and 12 percent of partners.[12] In the smaller district law society regions, most women principals are believed to be sole practitioners not partners.

Table 6

Principals in private practice, 1991–1995

| Year | Number[a] | | | Distribution | |
	Total	Women	Men	Women %	Men %
1991	2,789	261	2,528	9.4	90.6
1992	2,859	265	2,594	9.3	90.7
1993	2,853	264	2,589	9.3	90.7
1994	2,979	298	2,681	10.0	90.0
1995	2,976	336	2,640	11.3	88.7

[a] The position of principal includes partners and sole practitioners.

Source: New Zealand Law Society annual practising certificate data, 1991–1995.

Barristers sole

In 1993, the NZLS published statistics on women practising as barristers sole for the first time. In 1995, 22 percent of barristers sole were women. (Table 7)

Table 7

Barristers sole, 1993–1995

| Year | Number | | | Distribution | |
	Total	Women	Men	Women %	Men %
1993	505	101	404	20.0	80.0
1994	496	109	387	22.0	78.0
1995	606	136	470	22.4	77.6

Source: New Zealand Law Society annual practising certificate data, 1993–1995.

From the early 1990s, there has been a discernible trend of lawyers going out on their own as barristers. In 1991, there were 331 barristers sole while in 1993 there were 505 (an increase of 53 percent). This trend was caused probably in part by partners leaving law firms to avoid the Solicitors' Fidelity Fund levies imposed as a result of Renshaw Edwards and others defalcations.[13] Although the total number of barristers dropped from 1993 to 1994 (by 2 percent), the number of women practising as barristers sole increased (by 8 percent). In 1995, the number of barristers sole rose by 22 percent, with another 110 lawyers commencing this type of practice. (Table 7)

The large number of women barristers sole may not accurately reflect the number actually practising at the 'independent Bar'. In some district law societies, the category of 'barrister' includes those barristers working in government agencies, state-owned enterprises, community law centres, unions, corporations and tertiary education institutions. While barristers working in these organisations may be appearing before the courts, their income is unlikely to depend solely on solicitors in practice instructing them with briefs. For that reason, they are not, in the traditional sense, practising as barristers sole.

There are also likely to be regional variations in the numbers of women barristers. In Wellington in 1993, 18 percent of barristers sole were women.[14] In the same year in Otago, 25 percent of barristers sole were women,[15] and in Auckland in 1995, 28 percent were women.[16] Anecdotal evidence suggests that even fewer women practise at the independent Bar in the smaller regions.

Queen's Counsel

Women are particularly under-represented as Queen's Counsel (QCs). In 1994, of the fifty-seven QCs, only two were women: Sian Elias and Lowell Goddard. A third woman QC, Judith Ablett-Kerr, was appointed in 1995. Later that same year, Sian Elias and Lowell Goddard were appointed to the High Court Bench, leaving Judith Ablett-Kerr as the only woman practising as a QC in New Zealand.

In January 1996, out of the fifty-five QCs, there was still only this one woman,[17] but in June 1996 Denese Bates' admission to the 'inner Bar' brought the number of women to two.

Outside private practice

Women lawyers and law graduates continue to work in large numbers outside private practice. In the 1986 census women made up 75 percent of the 'other legal professionals' category, and in the 1991 census the proportion of women legal professionals had reached 81 percent. As non-practising legal professionals, women outnumbered men by four to one—exactly the inverse of their position in private practice. (Table 8)

According to the 1991 census, 'other legal professionals' are university graduates who perform legal tasks other than those performed by barristers, solicitors or judges. As such, they need not take out annual practising certificates although their work has a high legal component, for example drafting new laws and legal codes, advising on legislation, conducting legal research, writing comparative legal analyses, advising organisations on legal matters, or studying jurisprudence.[18]

Table 8

Other legal professionals, 1981-1991

	Number			Distribution	
Year	Total	Women	Men	Women %	Men %
1981	15	6	9	40.0	60.0
1986	612	456	156	74.5	25.5
1991	1,044	843	201	80.7	19.3

Source: Department of Statistics, *New Zealand Census of Population and Dwellings*, 1981–1991. Wellington: Department of Statistics, 1982–1992.

However, some of these legally qualified professionals will still hold practising certificates and will, therefore, belong to district law societies. Of the total law society membership in 1995, 13 percent were working outside private practice in government, corporate, academic or other employment. Most of these lawyers worked in Wellington, the centre of central government.

According to 1995 district law society records 30 percent of Wellington practitioners worked outside private practice. Auckland had the second highest proportion of government, corporate and academic lawyers (10 percent) while Otago had the lowest (6 percent).[19]

Public sector

The majority of women 'other legal professionals' work in the public sector. Traditionally, this sector consisted of the core state services (government bureaucracies, health, education, social welfare and public utilities), the public sector now comprises a mix of state sector agencies (government departments and ministries) and state-owned enterprises. Overall, an estimated 24 percent of the workforce is employed in the state sector.

In 1982, Hannah Sargisson reported that women made up 19 percent of legally qualified people working in the public service. At that time, women made up only 7 percent of the practising profession.[20] In the 1992 survey, 69 percent of lawyers holding practising certificates and working in government departments were women.[21]

A closer examination of five government agencies known to employ a significant number of legally trained people confirmed high numbers of women lawyers in the public sector. Of the 160 lawyers employed in 1993 by the Department of Justice, the Ministry of Foreign Affairs and Trade, the Inland Revenue Department, the Department of Labour, and the Treasury, 47 percent were women. Sixty-eight percent of the women were employed as solicitors or legal advisers, with the second largest group being policy analysts (27 percent). Overall, the largest group, of solicitors/legal advisers, was 55 percent female. (Table 9)

Table 9

Legally qualified employees in five government departments, 1993

	Number			Distribution	
Position	*Total*	*Women*	*Men*	*Women* %	*Men* %
Senior manager	4	1	3	25.0	75.0
Solicitor/legal adviser	93	51	42	55.0	45.0
District land registrar	5	1	4	20.0	80.0
Policy analyst	55	20	35	36.4	63.6
Legal clerk	3	2	1	66.7	33.3
Total	16.0	75	85	46.9	53.1

Source: 'Lawyers in government: statistics on legally qualified women and men employed in government departments, 1993.' Research undertaken by Equity Works Ltd in 1993.

Likewise, women lawyers were better represented in the Crown Law Office than in private practice. Of the legally qualified staff in the Crown Law Office in 1993, 46 percent were women. (Table 10)

Corporate lawyers

No official data is available on the numbers of women lawyers working in corporates as in-house counsel or legal advisers, but it appears that the percentage of women lawyers working in this sector is slightly higher than that of women in private practice. Of the 210 paid up members of the Corporate Lawyers' Association in 1993, which included lawyers working in education, government and corporates, 28 percent were women.[22]

Likewise, in 1995 in Auckland the percentage of women lawyers working in corporates exceeded that of women in private practice. Of the 130 corporate lawyers, 30 percent were women.[23]

Table 10

Lawyers employed in the Crown Law Office, 1993

Position	Number			Distribution	
	Women	Men	Total	Women %	Men %
Solicitor-General	0	1	1	0.0	100.0
Deputy Solicitor-General	1	0	1	100.0	0.0
Crown counsel team leader	4	3	7	57.1	42.9
Crown counsel	7	14	21	33.3	66.7
Assistant Crown counsel	6	3	9	66.7	33.3
Total	18	21	39	46.2	53.8

Source: 'Lawyers in government: statistics on legally qualified women and men employed in government departments, 1993.' Research undertaken by Equity Works Ltd in 1993.

Academia

Women are better represented among the staff in the five law schools than in private practice. By the commencement of the 1995 academic year, women comprised 28 percent of the legally qualified staff members. This relatively positive picture was tempered by the generally low status of the positions held by women law lecturers: 68 percent of the women were lecturers or part-time/associate/honorary lecturers while almost the same proportion of the men (67 percent) held senior lecturer or more senior positions. (Table 11)

Status of work/work types

Despite the entry of women lawyers into areas of work which were traditionally 'closed' to women, a gender division is still evident. Studies since 1982 have demonstrated that women lawyers have been proportionately well represented in all areas of legal work, except commercial (where they are under-represented) and family (where they are over-represented).[24] The 1990s are no different.

Litigation

By 1992, an estimated 40 percent of women lawyers regularly appeared in the courts. This rate of appearance may be even greater than that of their male colleagues. Of the lawyers surveyed in 1992, the number of women lawyers who were currently working in litigation in the High Court, District Courts and tribunals exceeded the numbers of men.[25]

Women lawyers are also taking up the practice of alternative dispute resolution. In 1995, an estimated 33 percent of the members of Lawyers Engaged in Alternative Dispute Resolution (LEADR) were women, a proportion which Executive Officer Carol Powell predicts will increase.

Table 11

Academic positions held by women in law schools, 1995

Position	Number		Women
	Total	Women	%
Law school dean	5	1	20.0
Professor	20	2	10.0
Associate professor	14	3	21.4
Senior lecturer	51	8	15.6
Lecturer	49	26	53.0
Part-time/ associate/ honorary lecturer	18	4	22.2
Total	157	44	28.0

Source: Calendars for the law schools of Waikato University, the University of Auckland, University of Otago, University of Canterbury and Victoria University of Wellington for the 1995 academic year.

This high representation of women litigators is a clear indication that women lawyers and law graduates have acted on the understanding that if they want to progress in the profession they must obtain experience at the Bar. Lawyers of both sexes have consistently been of the view that litigation, particularly in the High Court, offers excellent prospects for advancement, experience second only to corporate and banking law experience.[26] Experience in the courts, more so than any other form of legal work, opens the door to the higher positions in the profession, especially to the judiciary.

Although women lawyers are probably at least as likely as men lawyers to appear in court, their work is concentrated in the lower courts and in interlocutory and non-trial appearances in the High Court. A survey of unreported 1993 Wellington High Court judgments showed that women lawyers made up only 16 percent of the 636 lawyers who appeared as counsel.[27] This level of representation was probably indicative of other regions as the judgments surveyed included those of Wellington circuit judges sitting in Napier, Wanganui, Palmerston North, Masterton, Blenheim, Christchurch, Greymouth, Dunedin and Invercargill. (Table 12)

Of the few women who featured in the High Court judgment study, the majority were junior counsel rather than senior counsel. Women made up 31 percent of those junioring in cases in the Wellington High Court study but only 10 percent of those appearing as senior counsel. In comparison, men more frequently appeared alone and were by far the majority of senior counsel in cases. (Table 12)

Table 12

Women counsel in the Wellington High Court, 1993

	Number		*Women*
Position	*Total*	*Women*	*%*
Appearing alone	447	64	14.3
Senior counsel	94	9	9.6
Junior counsel	95	29	30.5
Total counsel	636	102	16.0

Source: A 1993 survey by Sue Brown for Equity Works Ltd of unreported judgments issued by the Wellington High Court January–August 1993.

By 1993, women litigators had still failed to make much of an impression. When the new Wellington High Court was opened in 1993, women lawyers were surprised to find there was no separate women's robing room. A local barrister, Kristy McDonald, expressed the sentiments of many when she wrote to the local lawyers' newspaper: 'But this is 1993 and the number of women practitioners continues to increase. How could the planners not have foreseen the need for separate facilities?'[28]

At the Hamilton High Court, the women's robing room, described as an 'extended toilet', was one-fifth of the size of the men's robing room. The Waikato Women Lawyers' Consultative Group were about to make a formal complaint when the decision to dispense with wigs and gowns forced them to reconsider.[29]

According to women lawyers, the opportunities offered by specialisation in litigation accrue to men lawyers and not women lawyers. One-fifth of women lawyers surveyed in 1992 believed they faced difficulties not experienced by men when appearing in the District Court and before tribunals. Women lawyers' views of their experiences in the High Court, however, was even more acute. A disturbing 49 percent of the women lawyers surveyed in 1992 said that it was easier for men to practise and to progress in High Court litigation than it was for women; 28 percent of men lawyers agreed.[30]

Commercial law

Commercial law is another 'good prospect' area of law which women lawyers have entered en masse since the 1970s. In 1992, an estimated 37 percent of women lawyers were practising in commercial law, whereas in the early 1980s a smaller proportion practised in that field. As with court work however, women lawyers are believed to have more difficulty practising and fewer chances to progress in that area compared with their male colleagues. The prognosis is even worse for women in banking law: 61 percent of women lawyers considered banking and finance were areas where men were more likely to practise and progress than women; 33 percent of men lawyers agreed.[31]

Criminal law

Another area of legal work where women have poor prospects compared with men is criminal law. Unlike commercial law, women lawyers are more likely than men lawyers to practise in the criminal law field: 27 percent of women did so in the 1992 national survey compared with 21 percent of men. Criminal law work is generally low paid, legally aided work and, according to lawyers of both sexes, offers the poorest prospects for advancement; prospects which are less favourable again if the lawyer is a woman.[32] Male partners, in particular, rate criminal law as a low prospect area.[33]

Family law

Women lawyers are still more likely to practise in family law than in any other area of law. In 1992, 45 percent of women in the national survey were working in family law. Another 9 percent wanted to move into that area. In addition to this being the most common area of practice for women lawyers, they also significantly outnumbered: 61 percent of the lawyers practising family law were women and 39 percent were men.[34]

Only in family law do women lawyers enjoy good prospects for advancement. According to the lawyers in the 1992 survey, the prospects for women lawyers in that area far exceeded those of their male colleagues: 53 percent of women lawyers and 43 percent of men lawyers said that it was easier for women to practise and progress in family law.[35] Overall however, when compared with other areas of legal work, family law does not rate as an area offering great prospects for advancement, especially from the point of view of those who most practise it: only 35 percent of women lawyers thought the advancement prospects in family law were good while another 22 percent considered them poor.[36]

Conveyancing

Another traditional area of legal work where a high number of women lawyers still practise is domestic conveyancing. Here, as with family law, women lawyers are said to enjoy better prospects than men. Consistent with the traditional domestic/commercial gender division, the conveyancing performed by men lawyers is commercial conveyancing; an area offering very good prospects for advancement, especially for men.[37]

As in the past, a large amount of conveyancing is performed at a cheaper rate by para-professionals—the majority of whom are women. In 1994, Kevin Morris, a lay observer on the Wellington Law Practitioners' Disciplinary Tribunal, pointed out that in the cost-conscious 1990s, conveyancing and matrimonial work were increasingly being handled by legal executives or in some case by secretaries.[38] The lower rates of pay received by these women makes the premium higher for firms. Understandably legal executives are preferred employees in many law firms.[39]

Lower status jobs and fewer prospects

In the legal profession of the 1990s, there remains a chasm between the status of women and the status of men. The majority of women lawyers are employees rather than employers. In fact, women lawyers in private practice are more than twice as likely as their male colleagues to be employees: 75 percent of women lawyers in practice in 1995 were employees compared with 38 percent of men lawyers.

Men lawyers in private practice, by comparison, are three times more likely than women lawyers to be either a partner or a sole practitioner: 52 percent of men in practice in 1995 were principals compared with 17 percent of women.

In the 1990s, as in the 1980s, women lawyers are widely believed to have poor prospects of progressing in their organisation, and even poorer prospects of being offered partnerships. Less than a quarter of the lawyers surveyed in 1992 said that women had the same opportunities to achieve partnership as men.[40] Women lawyers were much less optimistic than their male colleagues—an assessment which matched that of women lawyers in Wellington ten years earlier.[41]

Women lawyers' pessimism is borne out by other findings. Men are more favoured than their women colleagues in relation to receiving information about the firm's criteria for partnership and their prospects of meeting that criteria.[42] Men also obtained partnerships in a much shorter time than women. Most men became partners in firms within one to four years of admission to the Bar while most women became partners after five to ten years' post-admission experience.[43]

Instead of becoming partners in law firms, it appears that women lawyers become permanent associate partners. Comparing the length of time spent as associates, women noticeably out-distance men. They are twice as likely as men to have spent in excess of three years as associate partners, indicating that associate status is a stopping point for women but a route to partnership for men.[44] This would explain why women associates are more likely than any other group to doubt that women's position in the profession has improved over the past ten years.[45]

Even where women lawyers do make partnership, they do not suddenly acquire control over decision making in the workplace, especially in a large or medium sized partnership. Newly admitted partners, regardless of sex, usually enter at the lowest levels of a hierarchy, where they hold little or no sway. As Auckland lawyer Josephine Budge (later Judge Bouchier) observed in 1985, 'the power structure in large firms was weighted towards the senior partners ... junior partners may just as well have been employees for all the say they had in running the partnership'.[46] In the 1990s, many law firms have endeavoured to move toward more democratic partnership decision making but, despite these efforts, there remains a hierarchy of authority in many firms.[47]

In the early 1990s, women lawyers were still being offered 'second-class partnerships'. Some women lawyers have found that their promotion to full partnership was in fact a fictional partnership as firms use the concepts of salaried partners or fixed junior partnerships. In several instances, the women who had been offered these partnership deals were expected to assume unlimited liability and full partnership responsibilities with the men partners but with limited access to profit sharing and reduced roles in decision making.

Nationwide, women partners are rarely found on the executive and main decision-making committees within firms.[48] In the larger firms, these committees or management boards make the majority of decisions relating to recruitment, promotions, employment policies and partnership policies in general. Women partners are also infrequently found on the firms' 'money' committees in the same way that women lawyers are less likely to be found in the banking law department.[49]

As in the past, women lawyers still obtain partnerships in family firms, now mostly in provincial areas. Alternatively, some women lawyers who make partnership do so in newly established 'women-only firms'. In November 1994, it was estimated that there were eight 'women-only firms' in New Zealand and in these firms, there were approximately seventeen women partners.[50]

Employers in the public sector, as in the private sector, are predominantly men. Although women made up 52 percent of those employed in the public service in 1993, they were only 18 percent of the senior managers.[51] Of the legally qualified people in the larger government agencies men were more likely than women to hold senior management or senior analyst positions. Judging by pay rates alone, women lawyers in government agencies are most likely to be 'junior employees' and as such will not be primary decision makers in the public sector workplace.

Lower pay

Despite the 1972 legislative requirement for equal pay, women have remained, in general, cheaper employees for the legal profession.

In 1991, women legal professionals, judges, and lawyers were paid between 70 percent and 80 percent of the amount paid to men in the same occupational groups. These statistics are only indicative of the overall pay gap as they do not take into account differences in positions held within each occupational category. (Table 13)

Table 13

Average incomes of legal professionals, 1991

Occupation	Average income		Women's average income as a proportion of men's average income %
	Women %	Men $	
Judge	54,636	68,309	79.9
Barrister/solicitor	41,086	55,571	73.9
Other legal professional	30,651	43,350	70.7

Source: Department of Statistics. *1991 New Zealand Census of Population and Dwellings.* Wellington: Department of Statistics, 1992.

In the 1992 national survey, women lawyers were two and a half times more likely than men lawyers to earn less than $40,000 per year: 45 percent of women did so compared with 18 percent of men. At the opposite end of the income scale, men were four times as likely as women to earn $95,000 or more per annum: 38 percent of men lawyers did so compared with 9 percent of women.[52]

The 1992 survey revealed that the gender income disparity occurred across all sectors of legal employment. Women lawyers employed in the corporate sector were three times as likely as men lawyers employed in that sector to earn under $40,000. Corporate men lawyers were nearly three times as likely to earn in excess of $95,000 per annum. Women sole practitioners earned less than men sole practitioners, as did women lawyers employed in government departments. Of the lawyers employed in the public sector, women were nearly five times as likely as the men to be earning under $40,000 per annum.[53]

A more detailed survey of legally qualified employees in five large government agencies confirmed the gender pay gap.[54] Over three-quarters of the women in that study were paid a salary of $50,000 or less per annum compared with 57 percent of the men. Again, men employees dominated the higher income brackets with 43 percent earning in excess of $50,000 compared with 22 percent of women. (Table 14)

Table 14

Salary ranges of legally qualified government employees, 1993

Salary range $	Number			Distribution	
	Total	Women	Men	Women %	Men %
20,001–30,000	12	7	5	9.7	6.4
30,001–40,000	26	12	14	16.7	17.7
40,001–50,000	63	37	26	51.4	32.9
50,001–60,000	29	12	17	16.7	21.5
60,001 and over	21	4	17	5.5	21.5
Total	151	72	79	100.0	100.0

Source: 'Lawyers in government: statistics on legally qualified women and men employed in government departments, 1993.' Research undertaken by Equity Works Ltd in 1993.

In response to claims of pay inequity, many point out that women lawyers cannot expect to be paid as much as men lawyers because women lawyers are usually younger, are less experienced and are less likely to have senior positions in firms or other organisations. However, this explanation holds little water in light of the evidence of a distinct gender pay gap between lawyers with the same years' experience in the same positions.

After two years' post-admission legal experience, 87 percent of women lawyers in the 1992 survey were earning under $40,000 compared with 67 percent of men lawyers. At the five-year post-admission mark, the earnings gap closed, but at the ten-year mark the gap increased again. Over half the men lawyers with more than fifteen years' experience were earning $95,000 or more per annum while only 14 percent of women with that length of experience were in that income bracket. Instead, an estimated one-third of women lawyers with over fifteen years' experience were earning under $40,000 compared with only 7 percent of men lawyers with this length of experience.[55] As very few of these women were working part-time,[56] it can be concluded that women lawyers in general have lower paying jobs.

Even women lawyers who break with tradition and practise in the highly regarded areas of legal work can still expect to be paid less than men working in those fields. In the 1992 survey, for example, 17 percent of men lawyers with between five and ten years' experience practising in commercial law earned $95,000 a year or more compared with 8 percent of women in that category. Women lawyers were better off if they stayed with family law but even then they did not get paid as well as men practising family law: 20 percent of men lawyers practising in family law with between five and ten years' experience earned $95,000 per year or more compared with 15 percent of women.[57]

On average women partners also earn less than men partners. In 1987 in Auckland for example, the pay gap between women and men partners or principals was significant: 56 percent of the men earned $80,000 or more per year while only 13 percent of the women were in that income bracket. This pay disparity remained when the salary packages of men and women who had been with their current organisation for the same length of time were compared.[58] Again in 1992, 8 percent of women and only 2 percent of men partners had incomes under $40,000 per year. By comparison, 57 percent of men partners earned over $95,000 while only 37 percent of women lawyers in partnership were in that income bracket.[59]

Partnerships, of course, vary in terms of profitability, which is reflected in the income received. But even taking the most conservative view, these findings demonstrate that women lawyers enter partnerships on less favourable terms than their male colleagues who entered partnerships at the same time and/or that women lawyers are more likely to obtain partnerships in less profitable firms.

Where salary rates are fixed there is no gender gap. Judges, for example, are paid according to the position they hold, not according to their sex. In 1994, the Chief Justice received an annual salary of $191,500, High Court judges were paid $166,500, and District Court judges were paid $133,000.[60] Likewise there is no gender disparity in the benefits received by law society presidents. The national law society president is paid half the salary of a High Court judge plus expenses (a total of $123,000 in 1994). The president of the Auckland law society receives a third of the salary of a High Court Judge, and from 1992, the Wellington law society president was paid an annual salary based on 20 percent of the salary paid to a High Court judge.[61]

Participation in professional associations

As in the late nineteenth century, the law societies and other professional associations continue to perform an important role in New Zealand society. Although principally concerned with managing and disciplining the profession, the fourteen district law societies and other professional associations also play key roles in the law reform process and in the appointment of judges.

Law societies

Women lawyers have historically been under-represented on the major decision-making law society committees and councils. In 1993 women lawyers made up 16 percent of the members of the fourteen district law society councils and 7 percent of those on the national law society council and board.[62] The participation of women in the Auckland district far exceeded the participation of women in any other district; one-third of Auckland council members were women. In Wellington, the second largest law society region, women's representation on the council was only 18 percent.

Women lawyers' representation among the office holders in 1993 was even lower. Of the 48 district law society office holders in 1993, only 8 percent were women. Of the six national law society office holders, there was one woman—Judith Potter. In 1993, she was also the only woman law society president. Three women were district vice-presidents and one was secretary/treasurer. (Table 15)

In 1994, the number of women elected to three of the provincial law society councils increased. The Marlborough law society had two women council members (Blenheim lawyers Pauline Shoemack and Alison Loach) and Jeannie Warnock joined Sheryle Proctor on the Wanganui law society council. The Manawatu law society increased its women council members from one in 1993 to four in 1994. In the same year, Levin lawyer Rosemary Rutherford made history by becoming the first woman president of the Manawatu law society.

Despite these significant gains in 1994, women lawyers overall still made up only 18 percent of the total members of district law society councils. The gender make-up of the Auckland council remained unchanged while the number of women councillors in each of Wellington and Otago dropped from three to two. Rosemary Rutherford's elevation to the Manawatu presidency coincided with Judith Potter finishing her term as the national president. No other women lawyers held a district law society presidency. (Table 15)

Once Judith Potter had completed her term at the national law society, only two of the three women nominated were elected for one of the eight ordinary places on the national law society board—the group delegated the majority of decision making. Voting for the board was by the full council of the law society as voting by all practitioner members was turned down in 1992. In 1994, the representation of women on the national law society council and board showed little improvement. Only two of the thirteen-member board and three of the twenty-nine member council were women. None were office holders. (Table 15)

Table 15

Women's participation in law society councils, 1993–1995

Office held[a]	Number						Women %		
	Total			Women					
	1993	1994	1995	1993	1994	1995	1993	1994	1995
DLS council	167	167	157[b]	27	30	36	16.2	18	22.9
DLS office	48		39[b]	4	-	6	8.3	-	15.4
NZLS council	29	29	29	2	3	6	6.9	10.3	20.1
NZLS office	6	6	6	1	0	0	16.7	0.0	0.0
NZLS board	13	13	13	1	2	2	7.7	15.4	15.4

[a] DLS means district law society and NZLS means New Zealand Law Society.

[b] Excludes Westland District Law Society.

Source: New Zealand Law Society data.

In 1995, the number of women on the national law society and district law societies councils increased. Three women were elected district law society presidents: Christine Grice (Waikato/Bay of Plenty); Rosemary Rutherford (Manawatu); and Judith Flett (Southland).

Despite the notable increase in 1995, women were still under-represented on the councils when compared with their numbers in the profession, and likewise, remained under-represented on the main decision-making bodies. Women comprised 15 percent of the NZLS board, none of the NZLS council office holders, and 15 percent of district law society council office holders. (Table 15)

Women lawyers generally are better represented on 'special' law society committees than they are on the main decision-making bodies. District law society family law committees, for example, usually now have at least 50 percent women members. The women in law committees of the Wellington and Auckland law societies have been comprised almost exclusively of women. The newly-established NZLS Women's Consultative Group (WCG) consists of eight women lawyers selected by women's groups across the country. Excluding the consultative group, women made up 30 percent of the members of the national law society's special and ad hoc committees in 1994.[63]

Two years later, women made up 29 percent of the 128 NZLS special committee members. With the exception of the Taxation Committee, where three of the seven members were women, women lawyers were under-represented on the 'good prospect' committees: the Commercial and Business Law Committee had no women members; the Property and General Practice Committee had no women members; and the Civil Litigation and Tribunals Committee had one woman member. Another core committee with no women members in 1996 was the all-important Publicity Review Committee which oversees public relations on behalf of the profession. The Legal Education Committee, the Management-Solicitors' Fidelity Guarantee Fund Committee, and the Ethics Committee also each had only one woman member.

While the NZLS may rightly assert that its special committee membership comprises the expertise known and available to it, the gendered division of roles within NZLS committees certainly does not reflect who is doing the particular types of legal work within the profession. As previously explained, women lawyers are as likely, if not more likely, than their male colleagues to be practising as litigators. They also commonly work in commercial law and conveyancing. Their absence from the related committees which deliberate and advise on these areas of law calls into question the representativeness of the law societies and, as a consequence, the nature of their input to the law-making process.

Other professional associations

The 1993 Suffrage Centennial Year was certainly the year of women leading lawyers' organisations. Te Hunga Roia Maori o Aotearoa (the Maori Law Society) determined at its 1993 hui to take 'positive steps' and ensure that women had leading positions in the organisation. As a result, Wellington lawyer Gina Rudland was elected as the first woman president and Marama Henare was appointed secretary of the society.[64]

In 1993, for the first time in its nine year history, a woman barrister, Marie Dyhrberg, became president of the Criminal Bar Association. Ten of the forty-one members were women. In that same year, Sonja Clapham, another Auckland barrister, was elected secretary of the New Zealand Bar Association—the first woman to hold office in that organisation.

Judges

In January 1996 there were 157 judges in New Zealand, of whom nineteen (12 percent) were women. Of those women judges, all but three sat at the District Court level, the lowest level in the hierarchy. (Table 16)

Table 16

Women judges, 1996

| Position | Number | | Women |
	Total	Women	%
District Court judge	106	16	15.1
High Court judge[a]	34	3	8.9
Court of Appeal judge	7	0	0.0
Total	157	19	12.1

[a] Includes permanent, acting and temporary High Court judges.

Source: Chief District Court Judges' Office statistics as at 26 January 1996 and Chief Justices' Office statistics as at 29 January 1996.

Of the District Court judges, women were more likely to hold Family Court warrants than Youth Court or jury warrants. (Table 17)

None of the ten judges sitting on the Maori Land Court in 1991 were women.

Table 17

Warrants held by women District Court judges, 1996

| Position[a] | Number | | Women |
	Total	Women	%
District Court judge	106	16	15.1
District Court judge (jury warrants)	62	8	12.9
District Court judge (Family Court warrants)	30	5	16.6
District Court judge (Youth Court warrants)	42	4	9.5
Planning Tribunal judge	4	1	25.0

[a] Some judges hold more than one warrant.

Source: Chief District Court Judges' Office statistics as at 26 January 1996 and Chief Justices' Office statistics as at 29 January 1996.

In accordance with common practice, the two women appointed to the High Court Bench in 1995 were appointed as temporary judges. This is to allow appointment pending an opening in the number of permanent positions. The statutory limit on the number of permanent appointments to the High Court is thirty. (Table 18)

Table 18

Positions held by women in the High Court, 1996

	Number		Women
Position	Total	Women	%
Permanent	30	1	3.3
Acting	1	0	0.0
Temporary	3	2	66.6
Commercial List	2	0	0.0
Lay members	3	1	33.3
Masters	4	1	25.0

Source: Chief Justices' Office statistics as at 29 January 1996..

Justices of the peace

Justices of the peace (JPs) also perform judicial duties. Justices of the peace who have completed Open Polytechnic courses are able to go on the District Court registrar's list for court duties. These duties can include remanding arrested people, hearing minor traffic cases and hearing evidence to determine if a trial should be held. Although there were an estimated nine thousand JPs in New Zealand in 1994, only about five hundred were involved in court duties.[65]

There are no national statistics on the number of women JPs performing judicial duties.[66] In February 1996, the Auckland Justices of the Peace Association advised that of the fifty-three JPs sitting in the Auckland area, twelve were women (23 percent), and of the 1,684 JPs within the Auckland area, 467 were women (28 percent).

It is likely that the proportion of women JPs nationwide will increase. In 1996, the Minister of Justice reported in Parliament that of the 273 JPs appointed in the first nine months of 1995, 97 were women (36 percent).

What about the new women lawyers?

By the mid-1990s, the number of women enrolled in New Zealand law schools exceeded the number of men. In 1995, 52 percent of students at the University of Auckland law school were women. Of intermediate law students seeking to enter Auckland law school in 1996, 55 percent were women.[67] At the Waikato University law school, 58 percent of students enrolled in 1995 were women. Of the first intake to graduate from Waikato law school in 1995 54 percent were women.[68]

New admissions

Before 1990, new admissions of women to the Bar had been steadily increasing. Women made up 48 percent of all new admissions in 1989. The next year, the proportion of admissions by women law graduates dropped by 2.4 percentage points and during 1991 and 1992 the proportion of women levelled off at 47 percent.[69]

The pattern changed in 1993, when, for the first time, admissions of women outnumbered those of men: 266 women compared with 249 men. For the next two years women outnumbered men but the gap closed in 1995, when the proportion of admissions of women dropped to 51 percent. (Table 19)

Table 19

New admissions of barristers and solicitors, 1990–1995

| Year | Number | | Women |
	Total	Women	%
1990	491	225	45.8
1991	520	245	47.1
1992	559	263	47.0
1993	515	266	51.6
1994	624	347	54.0
1995	710	361	50.8

Source: New Zealand Law Society annual new admissions statistics, 1990–1995.

Graduate employment

While the number of students graduating from law schools has continued to increase during the 1990s, the number of unemployed law graduates has also increased. In 1993, 54 percent of graduates found employment, while in 1994, only 48 percent of graduates did so.[70]

The number of unemployed women law graduates is unknown, as no statistics are gathered on the basis of sex.[71]

Data on graduate employment does suggest, however, that women law graduates do not have the same employment prospects as their male colleagues. In 1992 and 1994, the proportion of women law graduates who found employment was less than their proportion in the total graduating law student group. The result in 1994 was that there were fewer men law graduates but men graduates were more likely to find work. Although more women found jobs than men in 1993, the percentage of women employed that year was no different to their proportion of the student body. (Table 20)

Table 20

Employed law graduates, 1992–1994

| | Number | | Women |
Year	Total	Women	%
1992	271	128	47.0
1993	326	168	52.0
1994	356	175	49.0

Source: New Zealand Vice-Chancellors' Committee, *Graduate Employment in New Zealand: A Summary of the Destinations of University Graduates, 1992–1994.* Wellington: New Zealand Vice-Chancellors' Committee, 1993–1995.

The differences in male and female graduate employment in 1992 and 1994 are not readily explained by the different preferences of women and men regarding entering the workforce. In both years, very similar proportions of women and men graduates said they were going overseas, undertaking further study or were not available for employment.[72]

In addition, women graduates were not obtaining employment in law firms as readily as men. From 1992 to 1994 women law graduates were more likely than men law graduates to take jobs outside the business and financial services category (which includes the profession itself). In 1992, one-third of women law graduates took jobs in other sectors compared with 22 percent of men. Again, in 1993 nearly 30 percent of women went outside the profession for jobs, compared with one-quarter of the men.[73] The New Zealand Vice-Chancellor's Committee, noting the slight increase in the proportion of law graduates finding employment in 1993, has suggested this reflects, in part, graduates' willingness to apply for a variety of jobs outside law firms.[74] The 'willingness' in this case seems more on the part of women law graduates than men graduates.

This pattern continued in 1994 with 34 percent of women law graduates finding employment outside the private sector. A significant number (22 percent) found work in the community, social, and personal services sector.

Professional legal studies' students and employment

A gender discrepancy in the proportions of men and women employed is confirmed by data from the professional legal studies courses across the country.[75] In 1993, during the first intake when unemployment is usually high, a straw poll of students on the law professionals course in Wellington found that 60 percent of those with jobs were men and 40 percent were women. Those proportions were the inverse of the gender make-up of the students in that intake.[76] At Otago, the pattern was similar. Over the four student intakes from 1993 to 1994, women made up 42 percent of the students on the courses but only 37 percent of those with jobs.[77] Alison Fulcher, the branch director of the Otago Institute of Professional Legal Studies (IPLS), collated the statistics and was surprised that 63 percent of those with jobs were men. Her impression had been that more women had jobs, although she noted in hindsight that it may have seemed that way because more women than men applied for jobs during the course. On the Canterbury IPLS course, men law graduates were also more likely to have jobs than their women classmates.[78]

The one exception to this pattern occurred in Auckland. Mark Mason, the branch director of the Auckland IPLS, said there was no noticeable gender difference in the large numbers of unemployed students in the first intakes of 1993 and 1994. In the 1993 second intake, however, he recalled that there did appear to be slightly more employed men.[79]

University recruitment programmes

Large law firms which participated in the universities' careers advisory service law graduate recruitment programmes appeared to employ equal numbers of women and men during the early 1990s. The programme is used by the larger law firms to recruit temporary summer clerks and permanent law clerks, who on admission to the Bar stay on with the firm as solicitors.

Data from the 1993 and 1994 Victoria University programmes reveals, however, that men law students had greater chances of success than their female classmates when it came to gaining an interview or obtaining a job. In 1993, for example, 82 percent of the men interviewed for permanent positions were successful. Of the women interviewed, only 52 percent were offered jobs.

In the 1994 programme, more women law students than men sought interviews but men students had a higher chance of successfully obtaining an interview with a recruiting firm. Of the 160 women students who sought interviews, fifty-eight (36 percent) were granted interviews. Of the 103 men students seeking interviews, forty (39 percent) successfully obtained interviews.

Although equal numbers of women and men obtained permanent positions in 1994, men students were more successful at winning summer clerk jobs. Of the forty-four women students interviewed, twenty (45 percent) were successful; of the twenty-seven men students, twenty (74 percent) were successful.[80]

Employment of lawyers

Employment difficulties do not end at the recruitment stage. Women lawyers currently in employment consider that women face obstacles when it comes to finding jobs within the profession. Close to half of the women lawyers surveyed in 1992 said that women did not have the same opportunities as men when applying for jobs. These numbers show disturbingly little change from earlier surveys.[81]

The views of employers in the profession depends on their gender. While the majority of men partners in 1992 thought women had the same opportunities as men when it came to getting jobs, about one-third of women partners agreed that women lawyers had less than equal opportunities when it came to job-hunting.[82] Given the likely involvement of women partners in the recruitment process, their assessment is compelling.

High exit rates

Statistics based on new admissions and numbers already in the profession indicate that women lawyers exit the profession at a much higher rate than men. (Table 21)

From 1980 to 1992, qualified women lawyers left the profession at nearly three times the rate of men lawyers. Over that period, on average, 10 percent of women lawyers dropped out each year compared with only 4 percent of the men lawyers. While retirement after a long career in the law would account for the majority of men who have left, it does not explain the high exit rate for women. In the 1991 census only twenty-four women lawyers were 55 years or older compared with 534 men lawyers. (Table 2)

Conclusion

Despite the increasing numbers of women who have entered the legal profession since the 1970s, the opportunities, rewards and prospects of women lawyers in the 1990s remain equivocal.

Overall, women lawyers are under-represented in private practice, making up only 27 percent of the profession. Of those who do work in private practice, the majority are employees rather than employers. Although women lawyers are comparatively well represented in public sector, corporate and academic positions, they are more likely to hold lower status positions with lower pay. In general, legally qualified women can expect to be paid less than their male colleagues even where they have similar qualifications and experience, and are performing similar work.

Table 21

Lawyer drop-out rates, 1980–1992

Year	Drop-out rate[a]	
	Men	Women
1980	3.47	18.26
1981	1.10	13.98
1982	6.71	(2.63)
1983	4.29	17.21
1984	4.32	11.18
1985	(0.39)	12.04
1986	6.23	6.04
1987	2.24	2.82
1988	3.12	0.00
1989	7.94	11.20
1990	5.30	18.85
1991	0.47	8.57
1992	2.94	15.39

[a] These figures represent the average drop-out rates per 100 practising certificates held over the relevant years for men and women.

Source: Drop-out rate estimated by Sage Consultants Ltd for Equity Works Ltd and based on New Zealand Law Society annual practising certificate data and annual admissions data.

Women lawyers still tend to work in the areas of law considered appropriate for women. In general, these areas of legal practice are not considered to offer good prospects for advancement. Even where women lawyers practise in high prospect areas, their chances of enjoying the benefits are smaller than those of their male colleagues.

The experiences of recent women graduates offer little hope that the prospects for women lawyers will change in the near future. They have more difficulty obtaining jobs in private practice, and so, like many other women lawyers before them, seek employment outside the firms.

Despite the confident assessment by lawyers with ten or more years' experience that women's opportunities in the legal profession have improved, equality of the sexes in the 1990s is far from being the reality. Explanations for this situation are many and varied. Most people surveyed have considered that discrimination is at least a factor in the equation but other explanations are commonly used to downplay the role of discrimination in limiting women's opportunities.

Chapter Eight

The Merit Myth

Many decision makers in the profession, the judiciary and government assert that decision making in these areas is fair and neutral. Opportunities and rewards are not provided to anyone for reasons which cannot be explained and justified. The criteria and the process apply across the board—sex is irrelevant. Women lawyers, like men lawyers, are said to have the opportunities to succeed on their abilities. Merit is the true determinant of success.

These views provide a short answer to any concerns about discrimination. According to a majority of men lawyers, women lawyers will do as well as their male colleagues in any area of legal work as long as they have the ability.[1] As one law firm partner with twenty-five years' experience in the law explained: 'personality and ability are paramount and outweigh gender.'[2] Therefore, if women do not make the grade or cannot manipulate the system to their advantage they have only themselves to blame.

This argument has conveniently been used throughout the past century of women's involvement in the legal profession as a way of distancing the profession from the problem. The problem is perceived fairly and squarely as a women's problem.

How is ability tested in the 1990s legal profession? How neutral are the criteria and the processes used in recruitment, work allocation, performance and pay reviews, training, supervision, promotion, admission to partnerships and briefing barristers? Does sex make a difference, and if so, how is that difference valued?

Decision makers

Training

Few of the people charged with selecting staff or undertaking performance reviews are actually trained in these tasks. Sole practitioners and barristers usually do their own recruitment without external help. Law firms, keen to reduce overheads, commonly delegate recruitment and staffing matters to 'staff partners'. Larger firms use the services of employment consultants but mostly where they are looking for a lawyer with particular expertise or experience and not when recruiting law graduates.

Some administrators in law firms may also have roles in selection, recruitment and performance reviews but these functions are fitted around the many other tasks and responsibilities involved in running the firm. Outside the largest law firms, specially trained human resources personnel are rare. For firms with human resource managers, few are trained in employment equity or know how to identify and eliminate systemic bias. Even if they have the necessary skills and training, they may face other, seemingly more pressing, priorities, or they may be reluctant to highlight issues of gender equity where partners are sceptical of the business benefits.

Decision-maker discretion

When it comes to decision making which affects a particular employee lawyer, there is a large amount of supervising partner discretion. If, in a ten partner firm, the supervising partner decides that a staff solicitor 'does not have what it takes', there are few mechanisms which allow a more objective check of that assessment. In even smaller firms, junior lawyers' careers and reputations can rest almost solely in the hands of one person who conceivably may have an ulterior motive for distorting a review or assessment process. A poor review or a delayed review is likely to result in no pay increase—an outcome which financially benefits the employer.

In law firms, decisions taken by partners regarding staff are final. Partner accountability within the firm is often limited. They may work in isolation from other partners for long periods. The law firm hierarchy often works in such a manner that an aggrieved staff member has no opportunity for review of a decision within the organisation. Partners will defend other partners' decisions or, at least, are perceived to be obliged to do so. Managers, other than dedicated human resource managers, usually have little influence over working relationships between partners and their staff.

The lack of procedures for review or even for the raising of employment related issues works largely in favour of employers. They do not have to hear the gripes of disgruntled employees and can be fairly confident that few will seek external advice. Only the very well resourced and extremely confident will engage in legal battle with a law firm.

An individual partner's discretion is also relevant when it comes to selecting new partners. Most partnership deeds provide that the decision must be unanimous. It therefore takes only the objection of one partner who does not want a woman lawyer on the partnership.

The nature of the decision-making process in law firms can result in inconsistent information and advice being given by different partners. Helen Melrose experienced this when seeking a partnership in a large Auckland firm in the early 1980s:

> I did everything right in my job. I got clients, I produced high fees and at one time was earning the highest fees in the firm. I made a point of fitting in ... I consciously lobbied ... But when my name was formally put up for a partnership in April 1982, they turned me down. They said, maybe next year.

Her mentor was astonished and suggested that the reason might have been because of how she dressed.[3] While this may not have been the reason for the partnership decision, poor communication and inconsistent advice between partners left the decision open to this interpretation.

Deficiencies in the decision-making processes in the legal profession impact on all who work within it. But, as seen in the following analysis of recruitment, career advancement and assessments of expertise and ability, it has a particularly detrimental effect on the careers of women in the profession.

Recruitment

Academic achievements

Without question, women lawyers have risen to the challenge laid down during the early part of the nineteenth century that they had to prove they possessed the intellectual capacity to cope with the complexities of the law. Women law students over the past two decades have consistently scored higher grade averages than their male classmates.

Between 1973 and 1977, women law students at the University of Auckland obtained higher overall degree pass rates than their male classmates and were more likely to achieve A and B grades in all compulsory subjects.[4] In 1995, with the exception of the public law paper, the average grades achieved by women law students continued to exceed those of men students. In papers on legal systems, contract law, commercial law and family law women's average grades were higher than men's average grades.

Again, in 1995, women law students were more likely than their male classmates to achieve high grades. In the compulsory first year legal systems paper, 34 percent of women students got A grades compared with 29 percent of men students who were more likely to obtain C grades: 32 percent did so compared with 18 percent of women. Similarly, more women students than men obtained As in the commercial law paper: 26 percent did so compared with 14 percent of men; and in the family law paper: 39 percent of women obtained A grades compared with 26 percent of men.

Although more men than women obtained A grades in the contract and public law papers, they were only slightly more likely to do so: 15 percent of men students scored As in contract compared with 13 percent of women and 12 percent of men students scored As in public law compared with 11 percent of women.[5]

Although these statistics relate to students at the University of Auckland law school, there is no reason to believe the results from other law schools would be dissimilar. Across New Zealand, men and women lawyers, especially those involved in recruitment, have frequently observed that women students' academic achievements exceed those of their male counterparts. This view is certainly supported by the data from the University of Auckland and by a study of student grades at the Victoria University of Wellington.[6]

Academic performance is an important consideration when it comes to law graduate recruitment. Although only 17 percent of employers in John Caldwell's 1990 law graduate recruitment study ranked academic grades first in importance, the majority of employers ranked them second. Most employers required that applicants had B grade degrees with the better grades being in 'core subjects' (for example, contract, land or torts) and not in optional subjects. Academic performance, however, was then overshadowed. As Caldwell found: 'although an applicant's grades provided the initial basis of interview selection, the personal attributes of the applicant then became more important.'[7]

The reversal of emphasis from academic performance to personality in the recruitment process is significant for women law graduates. Data on the 1993 and 1994 Victoria University law recruitment programmes shows that more women students than men were offered interviews but men students had a greater or at least equal strike rate in getting the jobs.[8] If the emphasis remained on grades, women students would be expected to fare better.

There is no suggestion that the top women graduates are overlooked by the profession. To the contrary, they readily find employment, often in the larger law firms. It is in what Canterbury University senior law lecturer Michele Slatter calls the 'miscellaneous group'—the non-conjoint degree, non-honours student bracket—that women students miss out. Slatter points out, women honours students get top marks and have no problem getting jobs while women in the miscellaneous group are less likely than their male classmates to get summer clerk or permanent clerk positions.[9]

Interviewing processes

According to women law students and women lawyers, the interviewing processes used by law firms in the 1990s in part are designed to screen women out. These concerns are not new—there has been a consistent history of law firms using interviewing methods that discriminate against women.

In the 1982 Wellington survey, many women lawyers referred to difficulties in interviews. One woman recounted an experience shared by many: 'Employers seemed to lose interest when they learnt I had no family connections in the law. I was also asked at interviews about personal relationships and whether I intended marrying in the near future.' Three other women referred to being told by firms that they 'had two women lawyers and didn't want any more'. One woman at a law firm interview said that she wanted to be a criminal lawyer but was told by the interviewer that she 'would never make it because [she] had to look like a criminal and [she] was just too pretty!'[10]

In 1987, Auckland lawyers were asked what topics were discussed at their job interviews. Men were more likely to have discussed their potential for advancement, hobbies and interests, career aspirations and travel possibilities. Women interviewees were more likely to have discussed why they left their previous job, their marriage, spouse or boyfriend, and the possibility of motherhood.[11]

Since the mid-1980s some New Zealand law firms have made efforts to include women lawyers on their interview panels. Small and even medium sized firms do not have this option—few having women on their professional staff. However, including women lawyers in the interview process does not necessarily eliminate discrimination. Some women interviewers have felt pressured to bend over backwards to avoid charges that they favoured women. To the surprise of the prospective women employees, these interviewers have taken more hostile approaches than the men. Some even persisted with the questions which the men had been criticised for asking previously.

In the 1990s, questions relating to contraception, parenting and marriage intentions are still being asked of prospective women employees and are not being asked of male interviewees. In their choice of interview style or by using a venue where women may feel uncomfortable, law firms continue to convey to women that they are not welcome in the firm. In these cases the interview process becomes a sham. Even if a job is offered, the women candidates are unlikely to accept.

Students on the Victoria University law recruitment programme in the early 1990s, raised concerns about interviews by some law firms. Elizabeth Medford, head of the Careers Advisory Service, noted that they received more complaints about law firm interviews than about interviews by any other type of employer. While that might point to law graduates being more prone to complain, the substance of their complaints suggests they have cause for concern. In recent years, women law students have reported that interviewers asked gender biased questions such as when do they expect to have a family and what kind of family planning do they use. Other firms have used less direct tactics to elicit the same information, in some cases using what amounts to subtle bullying about career plans. Recently, after being grilled about her family plans, one woman graduate left an interview in tears.[12]

The number of complaints relating to two firms in particular were so high that those firms were not invited to participate in the Victoria University recruitment programme in 1994. Medford noted that if the same questions were being put to men law graduates they did not cause any concern. However, men graduates have complained about other recruitment tactics used by firms, some of which have been distinctly sexist. In 1992, for example, the recruiters from a small Wellington firm took their prospective employees (all male) to a strip-tease club as part of their recruitment interview. In doing so, the firm conveyed the clear message that interviewing while women were removing their clothes for the pleasure of the (predominantly male) audience was an appropriate test for prospective lawyers. There could be little question that this was an indication of the firm's culture.

Needless to say, very few women would probably agree to being interviewed in a strip-tease joint which may be why there were no women selected for interviews. However, the firm made the mistake of assuming that none of the men would object. The choice of venue so affronted one of the men being interviewed that he left and complained to the Careers Advisory Service. For fear of repercussions he asked that no action be taken. Perhaps aware that the firm had overstepped the mark, it did not seek to participate in the recruitment programme the following year.

On the positive side, other law firms, having shortlisted their prospective employees make efforts to schedule meetings at times that allow people to attend easily. Functions for prospective employees to meet other staff at some law firms, for example, are held between 5.30 pm and 7.30 pm so that parents can attend when the other parent or caregiver can look after children. However, this attempt to accommodate family needs is exceptional. Most firms expect that prospective staff members will fit in with the firm's timetable.

Gender-balancing policies

In his 1990 law graduate recruitment study, Caldwell asked law firms whether gender was a relevant consideration in their employment decisions. He found: 'Not surprisingly, it is apparent that gender now plays no real part in employment decisions—though *many* firms do strive to avoid significant imbalances between the sexes.'[13] (Emphasis added.)

Only one Christchurch firm in Caldwell's survey openly expressed a 'very slight' preference for male graduates.

National statistics on law graduate recruitment indicate that gender is still a relevant factor in employment decision making. The interview experiences of women law graduates also indicate gender considerations are still apparent in the process. Likewise, gender is also raised as a factor when employing women lawyers who already have work experience.

In some instances employment consultants are being used to screen out 'wrong gender' applicants. In the 1992 survey, a woman lawyer with six years' experience reported that during a recent job hunting exercise she was informed by an employment consultant, 'off the record', that 'there was no point' recommending her to an employer because 'he had specified he wanted a male solicitor'.

Consultants confirm that some law firms have expressed an 'off the record' preference for male job applicants. According to one Auckland consultant, the employment preference for male lawyers emanates mostly from the big firms. He explained that some of these firms feel they are being 'overwhelmed by women' where, for example, they have a whole department staffed by women or 'too many women' at the staff solicitor or senior associate level. A Wellington-based employment consultant, agreed that some law firms have expressed preferences for male lawyers because they have 'a whole team of women'. The focus seems to be on achieving a balance between the sexes although, she added, merit followed by personality and 'cultural fit' will determine who is the successful applicant.

Statistically, as women lawyers make up less than one quarter of the lawyers in New Zealand, there could be only a small minority of law firms where there is a gender imbalance. In the majority of firms, women lawyers are in the minority. It may be that the 'imbalance' is not in fact one of professional staff but one of staff in general. Given that the number of women support staff and women legal executives in many firms will often equal the number of men lawyers, the entry of women lawyers would tip the total gender balance.

This stated gender preference by some firms places employment consultants in a difficult position. The employer is commonly the client who pays the consultant's fee so there is little point putting forward a candidate that does not meet the specified gender criterion. Some consultants are aware that gender screening is illegal but for the majority of consultants' business survival dictates that they follow instructions. One consultant, who had 'been in the business long enough' said he would 'point out a really exceptional candidate even if they do not meet the specified criteria'. In other words, the gender disqualification could be overcome if the woman concerned was 'really exceptional'. Apart from exceptional women, law firms' preferences for women, according to some consultants, are evident consistently in relation to family law positions.

In distinct contrast to the private sector, government departments apparently operate a reverse gender balance policy. According to employment consultants and women lawyers, the operation of employment equity policies in the public sector has resulted in a trend in favour of employing women lawyers. The recruitment practices largely eliminate entry level discrimination against women. The statistics confirm this.[14]

Reasons for the gender balance recruitment policies can be tracked back to employers' perceptions about the appropriate roles for women lawyers. They will not be committed to their careers (they will as a matter of course leave and have children). They are not wanted by clients and they will not be made partners; so why employ them? John Laurent, while secretary of the Institute of Personnel Management, expressed some sympathy with the employer's position. Making an analogy with machines that break down, a woman who fulfils '[her] childbearing function' can be 'a bad investment'. In a competitive legal market, he points out, there is 'no luxury of taking risks'.[15]

This concept of gender balance is effectively discrimination in a different guise. In a backdoor and apparently legitimate way, gender imbalance is used as a reason for not recruiting, appointing or promoting women. The openness of the policies demonstrate that few people realise that the practice is illegal.[16] Ironically, most of those applying this test are motivated by notions of sex equality—at least in the sense of equality in numbers. In the case of women lawyers, gender balance policies are being used to prevent equal numbers being achieved.

Age and maturity

Age discrimination affects women's and men's opportunities in the profession but it has a greater impact on women. In terms of personal experience, the occurrence of age discrimination was second only to sex discrimination for women lawyers in the 1992 survey: 34 percent of women lawyers had personal experience of age discrimination—more than three times the number of men.[17]

There is no consensus about whether mature women graduates experience more difficulty getting jobs than other graduates. Some employment consultants believe it is easier for mature women law graduates to get jobs than for other graduates. Women who study law later in life apparently do better because of their maturity.[18] Alison Fulcher, the director of the Otago Institute of Professional Legal Studies (IPLS), has observed that most of the older women law students taking the Otago professionals course seem to get jobs, while Anna Tutton from the Canterbury IPLS branch has commented that mature women students seem to find it harder to get employment (although, she added, it is difficult to assess as there are more mature women students than mature men on the IPLS course).[19]

Certain firms, however, have conveyed publicly their aversion to mature graduates. One woman lawyer, recently admitted but with 10 years' experience as a secretary, reported: 'Some law firms seem to have a conscious policy of not employing "mature" graduates. Indeed, this was more or less admitted at a law firm talk at Victoria University.'

Head of the Victoria University Careers Advisory Service, Elizabeth Medford, believes it is more difficult for mature women law graduates to find employment, although, she says, law firms insist that is not the case. She cited the example of a woman graduate in her mid-thirties with a straight-A LLB(Hons) degree, another bachelors degree and good work experience. Overall 'a brilliant student' but, to Medford's surprise, the graduate was not offered even one interview with a firm. On behalf of the graduate, Medford contacted the firms to inquire why they had not offered her an interview. The reasons they gave ranged from 'she did not include her school grades in her curriculum vitae' and 'there were too many other good students' to 'her curriculum vitae was not well presented'. In Medford's view, school grades, in this student's case, were largely irrelevant; her qualifications placed her ahead of the rest and her curriculum vitae was as professional as the others. She could only conclude that the applicant's age was seen as a problem.[20]

Employer's attitudes toward mature women graduates seem to vary according to firm size. Medford points out that smaller firms seem to prefer mature graduates on the basis that they are perceived to have more mature outlooks. Larger firms, however, have expressed concerns about how mature graduates will fit in with their younger graduates. But as Medford observes: 'Mature graduates have fitted in just fine over the past four or five years at law school. Why should it be an issue now?'

The reluctance on the part of some employers to take on mature women law graduates adds another dimension to sex discrimination. Employers may find it easier to overlook a younger woman lawyer when it comes to work opportunities than a woman lawyer of their own age group. If the more mature woman has a grown-up family or is beyond childbearing age, the firm would find it difficult to apply the subconscious rule that her career will be of secondary importance. Where an employer has any qualms about how a woman will fit into the workplace, one who is mature and probably less malleable may pose more of a threat.

With regard to obtaining jobs, it is certain that whether a woman graduate's age is seen as a bonus or as a disadvantage depends on the discretion of the recruiting employer. What is also clear, from the perspective of women lawyers at least, is that their age is more likely to be a detrimental factor than it is for men.

Employment history

Women law graduates and lawyers are more likely than their male colleagues to have what appears to be 'problematic' work histories. Their limited job prospects mean they are more likely to have worked in less prestigious or less reputable law firms, where competition for jobs is not so fierce. In addition, women lawyers more so than men lawyers may have resigned from their previous jobs as a solution to discrimination or sexual harassment (especially where the discrimination or harassment was by a more senior person in the firm).[21] In these circumstances, they are unlikely to obtain references or even use referees from that job. It is likely that their work productivity and work relationships suffered, and their confidence may have been impaired also.

Discrimination in the recruitment process can also leave an unearned question mark on a woman's curriculum vitae. Wellington IPLS Branch Director Robin Fuller relayed the recent experience of a 'very bright, A grade law student with a second degree who did very well on the professionals course' but could not get a job. In later interviews, she found that prospective employers assumed that there was something she had to hide. It seemed to them otherwise inconceivable that someone so bright and apparently competent was unemployed.

Career advancement

Career progression in the legal profession is largely informal. While in the past, some women lawyers were permanently employed as law clerks, today progression from the status of 'law clerk' to 'staff solicitor' occurs automatically on admission to the Bar. From that point, however, there is no certainty about career progression. Promotion does not automatically follow increasing years of experience. Each staff solicitor's prospects are monitored and measured—in varying degrees of sophistication, depending on the firm's management system and size.

It is relatively common for lawyers to change firms or sectors. Firms regularly recruit beyond the law clerk level to fill gaps in expertise or experience resulting from staff solicitor or partner departures. Lawyers swap between private practice and the corporate and public sectors, again depending on their areas of expertise and their perceived prospects in other sectors. Others leave firms to become sole practitioners or barristers sole, or to set up their own firms. These and other major career decisions are influenced by the availability of strategic information, advice from mentors, the training and supervision received and feedback through formal performance reviews. In each case, women law graduates and lawyers do not enjoy equal opportunities with men.

Access to strategic information

Lawyers and law graduates have limited access to information about criteria for decision making. At the recruitment stage, for example, many prospective lawyers are unsure about the criteria for the job. In 1990, Caldwell found that Canterbury University law students 'significantly underestimated' the importance attached to personal attributes. Only 34 percent ranked them as most important compared with 77 percent of the employing law firms.[22]

The information gap is known to continue in practice. Often lawyers are not well informed about the standards expected for performance of their job in general. One woman lawyer in a small firm found out at her performance review that she was expected to generate income by bringing in clients although she had not yet completed one year in practice. Another recently admitted woman solicitor knew that her performance would be linked to her budget but did not know what her budget was.[23] In many cases, lawyers remain unaware of their hourly rates and firm billing policies, indicating a lack of business management competence on the part of some partners or legal employers who are perhaps more preoccupied with the professional or legal aspects of their businesses than with staff management.

Criteria for promotion to associate partner, which in some larger firms is again tiered, usually bears a close resemblance to the criteria for partnership—with adjustments for fee-earning and client base. Associate partners are looked on by clients and other staff as 'junior partners'; prospective partners, without the concomitant liability. Few firms, except some of the largest, provide any detailed information for staff about how and when associate partnership or full partnership might be sought.

For many firms, partnership information is strategic business information which must be jealously guarded. As few employees will ever make partner, there is no point widely advertising the partnership criteria. At the same time however firms quite openly use partnership prospects as a recruiting device or as an entitlement to keep top fee producers in the firm. Advertisements for lawyers in law society newsletters frequently end with comments that 'partnership may be available to a promising candidate' or 'the right candidate will be considered for partnership.' In addition, partnership prospects are a common topic at recruitment interviews and few interviewees are given a definitive 'no'. Firms, it seems, carefully control who receives this information, and provide it according to gender.

Equal numbers of women and men lawyers aspire to partnership, but women lawyers are less likely to be given information about their chances.[24] In the 1992 national survey, advice on the firm's criteria for partnership had been given to just under one-third of the lawyers employed in law firms. Men employees were more likely to be favoured with that information than women: 43 percent of men had received that advice compared with 34 percent of women. As to the particular individual's partnership prospects, again men lawyers were more likely than their women colleagues to have been offered this advice: 35 percent had received this information compared with 27 percent of women.[25] Assuming that this information oils the path to partnership, women lawyers are less likely to know how to get there.

Role models

Compared with one hundred years ago, or even twenty years ago, there is now a comparative abundance of women who are role models in the legal profession. When Judith Potter was making career decisions in the late 1960s, there were so few women in senior positions of the profession that she knew no women to go to for advice and was in fact uncertain whether women could be partners in law firms. Now, women in the profession have a wide range of women role models to look to—in government, corporates, sole practice, partnerships, at the Bar and on the Bench.

Mentoring

Mentoring for new entrants into the legal profession is vital. While law studies equip a student for the academic aspects of law, it is widely accepted that much of legal practice is learnt on the job. Even the thirteen-week professional studies course introduced in 1988 gives students only a taste of how to handle the many complex practical and ethical issues that will arise over the course of their careers. The time and experience required before a lawyer can 'go it alone' is reflected in the statutory requirement of three years' experience in practice before becoming a partner or setting up as a sole practitioner.

Contrary to common belief, women lawyers in New Zealand are more likely to have mentors than men lawyers. In the 1992 national survey, 50 percent of women lawyers said they presently had or at some time had had a mentor at their place of work; only 37 percent of men lawyers said this.[26]

By far the majority of mentors—of women and men lawyers—are men, but senior men are more likely to mentor men than women: 90 percent of men lawyers had male mentors compared with 76 percent of women lawyers. Senior women, by virtue of their smaller numbers, are much less likely to have the experience or position to be mentoring others but, where they do take on mentoring roles they are much more likely to mentor women lawyers than men lawyers. Women lawyers are three times more likely to mentor women than men.[27]

Senior women lawyers generally may be more inclined to look after the interests of women in their workplace judging by the amount of time spent supervising support staff, an almost exclusively female group. Women partners are more likely than men partners to spend non-fee-earning time supervising support staff and helping them with work-related problems. Men partners, by comparison, spend more time supervising professional staff.[28] New Zealand men lawyers have not been known to refuse to mentor women lawyers unlike Australian male university staff who have refused to mentor young women postgraduates because 'discrimination is an easier charge to defend, than alleged sexual harassment'.[29]

The divergence of perceptions and the notion of incompatibility between the sexes in the profession provide ready explanations as to why women tend to mentor women and men tend to mentor men. In an ideal world this would be of no consequence but, at present, this same-gender mentoring preference is problematic—particularly for women lawyers. Men who are mentors are approximately nine times more likely to be partners or employers than women mentors. Accordingly, they have more knowledge about the profession and arguably more influence over their proteges' prospects. Because this influence and knowledge is what counts, men lawyers with men mentors will generally be better off than women lawyers with women mentors.

Training and supervision

All new staff below partner or principal level theoretically receive supervision and training on the job—the amount required decreasing with seniority. Through the supervising partner mechanism, firms control quality and cost-efficiency. Having more junior staff doing the work under the supervision of a partner, in theory, ensures that the client gets a good job for a fair price. It also maximises the profit to the firm.

In supervising junior professional staff, partners and employers assume significant educational roles, yet few have any experience or formal training in this area. In recognition of this some of the larger firms have started to appoint training managers recently, but even then the majority of training occurs in an unstructured way on a daily basis through file interaction or crisis control. Both men and women lawyers complain about partner non-availability, poor supervision and last-minute assistance when the job is nearly finished. There is also concern that the supervision system works less favourably for women.

The fact is that the people vested with the responsibility for training and supervising staff are the people with the most pressures on their time. Partners and other employers of lawyers tend to be the busiest people in offices. The demands on their time are immense. Most are multi-functional—they are 'rainmakers' (job winners), producers (actual workers on the files), managers (of other people's work and of the businesses) and executive decision makers (determining policies and strategies on recruitment, marketing, financial planning, business goals, partnership organisation and so on). Given this range of roles, it is no wonder that law firm partners work more hours per week than anyone else in the firm.[30] By default, the task of supervising often falls to the next senior staff member or does not occur at all.

When faced with competing pressures, training and supervision of women lawyers appears to be where cuts are made. Fewer than half the women lawyers surveyed in 1992 said that women lawyers have equal access to 'good' training and supervision. They pointed out they get less partner time, less coaching and less file supervision. Women partners were less likely to agree and men partners had a totally different view on the matter—90 percent saying that women and men lawyers had identical opportunities for training and supervision.[31]

Supervision usually means ensuring that the work delegated to a lawyer matches their level of experience and knowledge; and is good fee-earning work. The delegation of work by partners is one of the most critical factors in allowing lawyers to gain experience, confidence and expertise. In addition, it provides lawyers with valuable opportunities to earn fees, make 'client contact' and 'build their practice'.

Women lawyers strongly believed they did not have equal opportunities with men to get 'good' work. Only one-third of women lawyers in the 1992 national survey believed that women lawyers got the same quality work as men lawyers in comparable positions. Many women partners agreed—over half being of the view that women did not have the same opportunities for good work as men in the profession.[32]

Time-recording can be a disincentive to good on-the-job supervision. In the usual business set-up, partners and other senior staff members record their time on files where they give assistance to more junior staff members. This can act as a disincentive to junior staff members as it inflates the cost to the client of what is often routine work and, as significantly, it usually means their time spent on the files will be discounted—for the reason that they are learning by doing, they are yet to become proficient, and the partners' or senior staff members' time is more valuable. Seeking help can then directly affect their own fee performance—the main criteria for advancement.

Outside this fee-earning type of supervision, law firm partners spend a surprisingly small amount of time supervising legal staff. While an estimated 60 percent of partners oversee the work of legal staff, very few spent more than five hours per week of non-billable time on this task.[33]

The type of law practised by women lawyers may also have an influence on the quality of training and supervision they receive. For example, family law, an area in which women predominate, is said to be an area where supervision is neglected. An interdisciplinary committee reported to the Principal Family Court Judge in 1993 that:

> There is a perception that many senior practitioners and partners regard family law work as unimportant work which warrants Family Court appearances being entrusted to junior staff members. [In some firms those junior practitioners were] inadequately trained and supervised.

Even where they tried to obtain guidance from employers, it was not forthcoming.[34]

Even women who use recommended tactics like making fixed appointments to see their supervising partners found this did not work. As one woman lawyer observed, she would literally stand outside the partner's office for over an hour past the appointed time waiting for him to come free and when he finally did, he would apologise but say he urgently needed to speak to another member of the team about another matter first. Part of the problem relates to the disorganisation of some partners and managers but also it relates to the fact that women lawyers predominantly occupy junior positions and do lower status work. As a result, their work is of less strategic value to the firm and so, when time pressures are high, supervising them is accorded a lower priority.

Also, there is likely to be some connection between the attitude that women are not serious about their careers and the amount of time given to them. If the supervising partner thinks, as many partners do, that a particular woman, like most women, will inevitably leave the firm that view may influence, consciously or subconsciously, how much investment is made in that woman. Why direct valuable time and energy to a resource that is likely to move on? This becomes a self-fulfilling prophecy in many firms, since to deny women lawyers of decent work, good supervision and training is a sure-fire way to send them out the door in search of equal opportunities.

Performance reviews

Performance appraisal systems vary widely across firms.[35] In the larger national law firms, six-monthly formal performance appraisals are usually scheduled for each professional staff member. However, small and medium sized firms often have no formal systems.

In the larger law firms, the employee lawyer and the supervising partner usually complete performance review forms. At the review meeting, they exchange feedback about the employee's performance and the employer's supervising skills. In practice, however, many staff solicitors say they are less than frank when it comes to giving feedback about their supervisor or about difficulties in the firm. Women lawyers in particular comment that they hesitate to use this opportunity to raise gender related concerns because their supervising partners, who are usually present, are in many cases at least a part of the problem.

Women lawyers are more likely than their male colleagues to highlight the importance of being assertive in their performance reviews. One woman recent graduate pointed out that while she was able to be forthright, she knew that other women were inhibited by the performance interview process.

Outside the larger law firms, performance reviews occur in informal and, some say, haphazard ways. Reviews are not conducted at set intervals for every employee and are often postponed or cancelled at short notice due to supervising partners or managers not being available. Women lawyers taking maternity leave from small or medium sized firms may miss the opportunity for performance appraisals. In some firms, performance review meetings are held with all the partners—increasing women lawyers reluctance to raise gender-related concerns.

On the positive side, lawyers employed outside the big firms can enjoy more regular feedback about their work because it is not saved up for the six-monthly review. But satisfaction with the informal systems varies widely depending on how well liked the employee perceives himself or herself to be. As men lawyers generally have greater access to information, well-informed mentors and better prospects for advancement, informal review processes can be expected to benefit them more than they benefit women.

Legal expertise and experience

Do women lawyers practise in desirable areas of the law? Do they have the right expertise and experiences? How do their expertise and experiences affect their prospects?

Expertise and type of law

Expertise in law is ranked consistently among the top three criteria for partnership. The complexity of the law means that most lawyers acquire expertise in one or at most two types of legal practice. This experience is their most marketable commodity.

Not just any expertise is good expertise. Technical know-how and legal brilliance are only valuable, particularly to a law firm, if they are in a 'hot' area of law. The desirability of certain legal expertise changes considerably as market demands change or new legislation is enacted. For example, commercial conveyancing offered the best prospects for advancement in 1987 but in the post-crash 1990s, that type of work was no longer such a safe bet. Environmental and planning law went from having equivocal prospects in the mid-1980s to better prospects in the more environmentally conscious 1990s.[36]

However, two areas of work have consistently offered good prospects: High Court litigation and commercial law. Two-thirds of men partners and just over half the women partners in the 1992 survey said commercial law offered good prospects for advancement, followed by banking and finance law. A similar ranking was given to High Court work.[37]

Since the mid-1980s, women lawyers have made efforts to move into these desirable areas of practice. For example, in the 1987 Auckland survey, 26 percent of the women surveyed practised in 'company law'.[38] By 1992, the proportion of women working in 'commercial law' had increased to 37 percent. At the same time the proportion of men lawyers practising in that field also increased—from 40 percent in 1987 to 59 percent in 1992. Likewise, women lawyers moved into High Court litigation. In 1987, 24 percent of Auckland women lawyers appeared in the High Court on civil litigation matters. In 1992, an estimated 33 percent of women lawyers did that type of work—the same proportion as men.[39]

Women lawyers mobility into desirable areas of practice does not mean necessarily that they will enjoy the same prospects for advancement as their male counterparts. In the 1992 national survey, men and women lawyers agreed there was a significant gender difference when it came to expertise and prospects. The majority of both sexes said it was easier for men to practise and progress in the areas of law which offered the best prospects for advancement: banking and finance, commercial law, commercial conveyancing, tax and High Court litigation. Thirty-nine percent of lawyers surveyed said that it was easier for men lawyers to practise and to progress in High Court litigation. Only one percent believed it was easier for women lawyers.[40] In other words, despite having desirable expertise in a desirable area of practice, women lawyers still failed to make the grade.

No one suggests openly that women lawyers lack the level of expertise required for advancement. To the contrary they are 'held out' as being at the forefront of most areas of law and as being competent to teach other lawyers. The 1995 New Zealand Law Society continuing legal education seminar programme, for example, involved women presenters in most seminars. Overall their involvement in the programme reflected their representation in the profession: 26 percent of the presenters were women. Likewise, women were represented fairly in family law seminars: 35 percent of the presenters being women.

So how do women lawyers fare in the areas of law where they predominate? Expertise in family law is no sure bet for advancement but, for women, it offers better chances than any other area of practice. Overall, lawyers rate family law expertise as offering middle of the range prospects for advancement compared with all other areas of law. Partners of both sexes were more confident than the overall sample that prospects in that area were good.[41] But when looking at women lawyers prospects in particular, most agreed that family law offered women the best opportunities for advancement in the profession. Over half of the women lawyers surveyed in 1992 selected family law as the one area of law where women had greater chances to practise and progress. Over 40 percent of men lawyers agreed.[42]

Family law expertise certainly does not offer good prospects for women when it comes to Queen's Counsel (QC) appointments. Dr John Priestley (appointed QC in 1994) was the second family law specialist admitted to the 'inner Bar' in recent history. Although an area of practice involving litigation, most family law work is conducted in the Family Court—a division of the District Court. Queen's Counsel are expected to have broad experience in the appellate courts, the High Court and the Court of Appeal where very few family law cases are heard. In addition, family lawyers are under a statutory duty to encourage reconciliation between the parties and failing that to promote conciliation before applying for a hearing in the court.[43] Litigation alternatives such as mediation are required and out-of-court settlements are common. While beneficial for the clients, this type of legal work is not good for women who aspire to higher positions in the profession.

Expertise in criminal law, another area of practice where women predominate,[44] is more likely to jeopardise rather than to advance women's partnership prospects. Criminal law is considered by both sexes to offer the poorest prospects for advancement. Men partners are even more firmly of this view than employed lawyers.[45]

Women lawyers are also more likely than men to practise in the District Court: 43 percent of women surveyed in 1992 did so compared with 35 percent of men.[46] Overall, lawyers rate District Court work as offering good prospects for advancement with a high number of partners being of this view. Although the majority thought that women and men had equal opportunities to practise and progress in District Court litigation, one-fifth of the women surveyed believed that men had better chances.

Another area of expertise predominantly held by women lawyers is what could broadly be described as 'women's law'.[47] Traversing a wide range of legal topics, the common theme in this area of work is the feminist analysis of the law and the legal system. Within the profession this perspective is sometimes rejected outright.[48] Outside a few government agencies and small private sector firms this expertise is not highly valued.

Stereotyped skills

Women are widely believed to bring to legal practice skills which differ from the skills of men lawyers. Skills relating to handling emotions, communication and problem solving are commonly attributed to women lawyers. However, instead of having a positive or at least neutral value these skills have been used to justify decisions limiting women lawyers' opportunities.

Women lawyers' skills (or lack thereof) have influenced the decisions about where women should work and for whom they should work. In 1987, for example, 10 percent of Auckland men lawyers surveyed said that women, by nature, were ill-suited to commercial and litigation work. In their view, their women colleagues were too emotional, not tough enough, not as competent and had softer voices.[49] The logical conclusion was that women were well suited to family law work.

This tendency to stereotype women as 'naturally suited' to particular types of legal work remains in the 1990s. Over 30 percent of women lawyers in the 1992 national survey believed that assumptions about their abilities and personalities played a central role in where they were employed and what work they were given.[50] Nor are men lawyers oblivious to the tendency for employers to steer women down the family law track. One male associate partner observed: 'I have noticed many young female staff solicitors are urged into areas of family law where the work is mundane and repetitive ie nonmolestation.' Another partner commented: 'The areas of law which deal with "emotions" tend to be areas women are expected to work in and clients/practitioners accept women in those areas.'

Predictably, when placing or moving staff within firms or organisations, employers tend to make decisions which support gender stereotypes. Women lawyers have made requests to move into commercial areas or into High Court litigation but been bypassed in favour of male employees.[51] One woman eventually left her firm to obtain experience in commercial law. She had asked to be transferred to the commercial division when a position was available but was told she was 'too people-oriented' and it would be 'a waste' for her to do anything other than family law.

Even where women do manage to obtain commercial law positions, they find that partners assume they will still handle family law work. Countering this expectation can bring women lawyers into conflict with partners, who understandably believe they can refer files where and to whom they wish. One woman partner in a medium sized firm referred with exasperation to her role 'fighting against the constant referral' of family law work to the women lawyers in her firm.

The assumption that certain work is 'women's work' can also override the fact that the work would be more cost-effectively done by others. A woman associate partner was often told to 'see the little old lady clients or do the house calls to get documents signed even though there were more junior males who could have done it'.

The stereotypes also apply to women barristers as Sonja Clapham, then secretary of the New Zealand Bar Association, pointed out: 'There is a suspicion that women at the separate bar do not get the good quality work—whatever the field. There is a tendency to pigeon-hole women barristers into the Family Court or criminal jurisdictions.' She adds, however, that there are 'some more senior women barristers' who now feel they are gradually getting a flow of better commercial work.[52]

Traditional job evaluation systems have tended to measure only the mental and physical aspects of a job. New job evaluation schemes, such as that designed by Janice Burns and Martha Coleman, have taken a broader approach by including the human relations and emotional aspects of jobs as criteria in their own right. Emotional demands were recognised by the scheme's authors as 'an important but invisible aspect of work traditionally done by women.'[53]

Burns and Coleman emphasise that the emotional demands of a job can be measured. Emotional demands, they say, occur in two ways:

> Firstly, they occur through dealing directly with the needs of people who require care, attention, instruction or assistance ... The second way emotional demands occur is through inherently stressful and frustrating situations such as conflicting work demands ... dealing with angry, upset or difficult people, time pressure and deadlines.[54]

Men lawyers will be quick to claim that they too deal with difficult people who need care and attention. All lawyers, regardless of the type of legal work, operate under time pressures. But, for those in family and criminal law work, the emotional component is much more likely to be at a consistently high level. It is arguable that family lawyers and criminal lawyers require an extra set of skills to handle the emotional component of this work—if they are to be successful at it.

How skills are described (and are commonly perceived) has a profound influence on the value placed on those skills. Women lawyers' work, particularly where dealing with women, children and families, is seen by many as a natural extension of their work in the home. So, a woman lawyer's competence in dealing with a child custody dispute or a sexual abuse case is somehow natural while a man lawyer's competence in a commercial matter is technical brilliance. Likewise, handling the emotional demands of criminal law work, also work performed predominantly by women lawyers, is typically defined as a natural skill.

Describing a lawyer's skills as 'natural' entirely ignores the fact they are acquired through training and experience—either in the formal environment of legal practice or in the informal and unpaid environment of the home and community. Training in the latter environment is not remunerated and in general carries little or no value in the formal assessment of a lawyer's ability. So, the 'natural' connection most importantly means that those skills can be devalued and excluded from consideration where promotion or pay is concerned.[55]

There is, in terms of functions and skills, very little difference between the work of a family lawyer and the work of a commercial lawyer. Each area requires technical expertise in law, procedure and document preparation; each requires communication and client management skills; and each requires strategic planning to produce the best outcome for the client. There is no tangible reason for the prospects of lawyers practising in either of these areas to differ—except for the fact that a higher economic value is placed on business matters than is placed on family and personal matters.

Women in authority

Women lawyers in the 1990s still refer to the need to be exceptional before being considered for the same work or the same positions as men lawyers, particularly where those positions or work involve status or authority. As it is mostly men who allocate work and delegate or share authority, why are women overlooked or expected to meet a standard different to that required of men?

Research shows that some men experience difficulty relating to women in positions of authority. Women with authority, particularly in a traditionally male dominated area such as law, are considered a direct threat by some of the men who work under them. Where women control rather than comply they are thought to be assuming male authority or, even worse, are converting 'men's work' into 'women's work'. Either way, the masculinity of the men under their control and the status of the occupation or profession in general, may be perceived as being under threat.[56]

Single-sex schooling may also have a negative impact on male attitudes towards professional women. An estimated one-third of both women and men lawyers, have received private secondary schooling, most of which will have been at single-sex schools.[57]

Men who have attended boys' schools have less healthy attitudes towards girls and women than men who have attended coeducational schools.[58] English research in the early 1970s found that men educated at all-boys' schools were less likely to believe in the equality of the sexes than coeducated men.

Twenty-seven percent of men from boys' schools thought working under a woman was difficult compared with only 15 percent of men from coeducational schools. Men from boys' schools said women bosses were 'inferior, had no natural authority, were petty, domineering and emotional, and not impartial'. Women who had attended girls' schools did not experience these same difficulties in working under or with men in their adult working relationships.[59]

Men who attended law school from the late 1970s (when women made up at least 30 percent of the student body) have had more opportunities to counter any negative attitudes towards women which were formed during their childhoods and at high school. However, the extent to which this redresses formative impressions depends on the individual's receptiveness to the idea of treating women as equals.[60]

Whatever the reasons, the career experiences of women lawyers confirms that there remains a different, higher standard required of women before they are offered status and authority.

Seniority takes longer

The time taken to achieve partnership is one example of the extra mile women lawyers are required to go. Although lawyers place very little weight on years of experience as a partnership criterion there is a distinct gender difference in how long it takes to reach partnership.[61] In Auckland in 1987, over half of the men partners but only 17 percent of the women partners had obtained partnership within three years of admission to the Bar. In 1992, that gap had closed slightly but men were still twice as likely as women to have obtained a partnership within three years.[62]

The time taken to achieve partnership status varies significantly depending on the health of the economy and the structure of the particular firm. From the late 1970s to the mid-1980s when the profession was undergoing a period of growth, firms readily appointed new partners and other lawyers left established firms and set up new practices. In the late 1980s new partnership appointments slowed down and only in the early 1990s did they start to pick up again. The 1990s increase in the numbers of barristers sole also created gaps in some firms with partners leaving to go to the Bar.

External influences on partnership opportunities, however, should not disproportionately affect women. The fact that the discrepancy in time taken to reach partnership remained across the last decade—a period where women had aspired to partnership in at least equal numbers to men—is a firm indication that the playing field is not level. In many cases, men it seems, need only meet the statutory minimum of three years' experience while women lawyers have more to prove before being admitted to partnerships.

Women barristers also believe there is a different and higher standard being required of them before they are considered eligible for good work. Barristers, unlike solicitors, do not receive instructions directly from clients, rather, they receive their briefs from solicitors (either in firms or from sole practitioners). Sonja Clapham, the secretary of the New Zealand Bar Association, pointed out in 1993: 'It seems to take women barristers far longer than their male peers to attract good quality work and to establish profitable practices. Solicitors ... are suspected of being reluctant to brief women barristers.'[63]

President of the Criminal Bar Association Marie Dyhrberg agreed. In her view, the difficulties experienced by women barristers in Britain in obtaining substantial briefs are also common in New Zealand.[64]

It not only takes women barristers longer to get good quality work, they must also be exceptional. As Clapham explained:

> Generally the feeling is that women have to be much better than their male colleagues before they can progress up the ladder of establishing a reputation of being someone of professional standing who is worth briefing and someone worth paying a higher level of remuneration.[65]

The connection between prestigious work and high levels of remuneration is significant. Barristers fees are not paid directly by clients but by the instructing solicitors, many of whom are familiar with women lawyers performing cheaper legal work for lower rates of pay. Women barristers who charge the same rates for their labour men barristers are outside the norm so it is assumed they must possess some special qualities.

Seniority and status have direct effects on the value placed on the work done. Where an emphasis is placed on seniority or years of experience rather than on competency in the job it is likely that gender bias will result in salary levels and pay increases. Research in the United Kingdom has shown that those in lower positions in an organisation receive lower percentage pay increases than those at higher levels—regardless of the performance assessments.[66] Seniority creates what is called an 'expectancy bias'—the employer expects that senior staff members have crossed the minimum performance threshold and can only go up in a career sense.[67] In a highly gender-stratified profession such as the law, this means men lawyers are well placed for larger pay increases than more junior women employees.

The 'expectancy bias' arguably affects all levels of the legal hierarchy. Seniority is the key to many of the doors in the profession and the judiciary. Queen's Counsel, for example, need proven 'eminence' at the Bar which, according to a contributor to the *New Zealand Law Journal*, means they 'should be engaged reasonably frequently in important litigation'.[68]

This poses real problems for women litigators because they will be involved infrequently senior counsel in 'important litigation' so their perceived 'eminence' will be much lower than that of their male colleagues. Add to this the disinclination of solicitors to brief out important cases to women barristers and the perception that women litigators should do only limited types of work and the prognosis is not good.

Even where women lawyers have succeeded in obtaining 'senior' work, men lawyers and judges can be taken aback or even doubtful that this can be the case. In November 1995, for example, when for the first time all of the counsel appearing before the Privy Council in a New Zealand case were women lawyers, a male barrister passing through the court looked around at the robed women lawyers and asked 'Who's appearing in this case?' According to Auckland barrister Denese Bates (one of the counsel appearing), the judges were also initially a bit surprised to see an all female line-up, especially as none were QCs.[69]

Productivity

Another apparently neutral criterion affecting career advancement is productivity. Typically measured by reference to fees performance, productivity is also affected by client base, hourly rates and hours worked. In each case, women lawyers are less likely to measure up.

Fees performance

In the past decade, fees performance has remained in the top three criteria used to assess a candidate's eligibility for partnership. Although lawyers of both sexes have clearly got the message that fees are a significant partnership consideration, this criterion weighs more heavily on women lawyers than on men lawyers. In 1987, women lawyers placed greater emphasis on fees performance than did men lawyers: 66 percent of women employed solicitors emphasised fees performance compared with 56 percent of their male counterparts.[70] Again, in 1992, women lawyers stressed fees performance more than men lawyers: 43 percent of women lawyers ranked fees performance first compared with 28 percent of men. According to the women, fees were the number one criterion for partnership.[71]

While women lawyers are placing more weight on the importance of fees performance, partners are moving away from it as a preferred partnership criterion. In 1987, fees were ranked third by women and men partners, while in 1992, fees did not even rate in the top three preferred criteria by partners of either sex. Instead, law firm partners preferred that more emphasis was placed on expertise, an ability to bring in clients and compatibility with existing partners.[72] This new ranking demotes fees performance which of all the criteria was the one tangible, measurable criterion which women lawyers were striving to meet.

In any event, women in the profession are more likely to struggle to meet fee targets because fees are dependant on the type of client base, hourly rates charged and the hours worked.

Client base

For most legal firms, revenue is generated from existing clients. This makes opportunities for 'client contact' particularly important to lawyers who are below partner level and who aspire to partnership. In most cases the chance to forge working relationships with the firm's existing clients requires introductions, usually provided by other senior lawyers in the firm. Where introduction opportunities are denied to women lawyers, whether through omission, preference, perception or direct discrimination, the resulting loss to career advancement can be immense.

A lawyer's client base has a direct impact on their fees performance. As a group, women lawyers' practices will largely involve individuals— reflecting the kind of work that many women perform (criminal law clients, family law clients and domestic conveyancing clients). With the possible exception of criminal clients, most of these clients do not bring a regular amount of repeat business to the firm. Once the transaction is completed or the dispute is resolved, there is no further contact with the client unless another dispute arises or conveyance is needed.

By comparison, the clients serviced mostly by male lawyers have regular contact with their lawyers. Commercial and banking clients, faced with increasingly complex business and tax laws, need frequent legal advice. Larger corporate clients often budget an annual sum for legal fees in advance. Assuming the client is happy with the work, these fees provide a relatively high level of certainty that the lawyer will meet budget.

Hourly rates

While business clients effectively save 33 percent in legal fees by deducting that expense in their tax returns, individual clients bear the whole cost. For this reason, some lawyers are more inclined to discount the bill or reduce their normal hourly rate when billing individuals. Women lawyers' client base makes this more an issue for them than for their male colleagues.

Likewise, many criminal law clients and family law clients are legally aided. The rates paid to lawyers who do legal aid work are low by comparison with the rates non-legally aided clients will pay for the same work. Again, this disparity will have a greater impact on women lawyers productivity.

Hours worked

Although the number of hours spent in paid work is said to no longer rate as an important criterion when it comes to employers' consideration of promotion and partnership prospects,[73] hours matter when a demonstrated commitment to the job is required. Women lawyers, more so than men lawyers, find they need to prove their commitment by putting in the hours because partners and employers doubt that women put their careers first.

Most women and men lawyers work more than 40 hours per week. Over 50 percent of women lawyers in the 1992 national survey said they worked between 40 and 49 hours per week as did 44 percent of their male colleagues. However, men certainly put in the longest hours, with another 41 percent saying they worked in excess of 50 hours per week. Most of those in this category were partners.[74]

Working long hours poses more of a problem to women lawyers than to men lawyers. Of the estimated one-third of women in the profession who have children, just over 50 percent have the primary responsibility for the care of those children. During usual business hours, these children are at school or are being cared for by paid childminders or other persons, but after-school care still falls principally to their mothers.[75]

Women partners often refer to the importance of being seen on the job rather than leaving to 'go home to the family'. Cathy Quinn, a partner in national firm Rudd Watts and Stone, explains that achieving partnership in a large commercial firm requires a 'major commitment of time and energy'. As Quinn points out:

> if it is known that you must leave the office at 5 pm on a regular basis, I suspect it is highly unlikely that you would be considered to work on a major (and probably highly billable) project over a period of months which will undoubtedly involve long hours.[76]

Jane Meares, a partner at Bell Gully Buddle Weir, agrees that to be 'a typical success story' in a large firm, a lawyer needs to 'be in the firm, putting in the hours'. She elaborates that this does not necessarily mean hours in the office itself but it does mean being available to clients and partners and 'being visible where necessary'.[77]

'Hours worked' is effectively an expression of compatibility with the ideal of what makes a good lawyer and a potential star. The message is simply that if women lawyers are to make the grade, they need to model themselves on men lawyers. This mostly requires hours 'at the office', with little regard to the efficiency of work habits while there.

Conclusion

Contrary to commonly-held beliefs, 'merit' in legal profession decision making is not an objectively determined and applied concept. It is a misnomer. What is little appreciated is that for women, 'ability' is being defined and tested to a different standard than that applied to men. Whether in relation to recruitment, promotion, partnership or pay, decision making is influenced negatively by gender. Women's 'inability' to succeed in the 1990s is reminiscent of women's 'disabilities' in the

1890s. In both cases women's presumed limitations have been proved to be unfounded yet have continued to be relied on to limit women's opportunities. The outcome not only disadvantages women but disadvantages law firms and by implication the clients they advise.

Women lawyers in the 1990s are well aware that the standard against which they are measured is higher than that faced by their male colleagues. They must meet criteria which are based on negative gender stereotypes and which reduce their opportunities and benefits within the profession. Also they must be assessed by processes supposedly designed to assist advancement but which achieve the opposite for women. These gender-skewed outcomes repeatedly point to discrimination: prohibited behaviour and acts for which employers are legally culpable.

In relying on an irrelevant criterion such as gender, law firms may be typical of New Zealand businesses. A 1989 study of managerial decision models found that job irrelevant factors were used extensively in selection decisions. Race and sex, in particular, had significant effects on favourability ratings. According to university lecturers, Stephen Dakin and Mike Smith, this study 'emphasises that equity in human resource management demands that personnel decisions should not be the responsibility of a single individual, and that any group making personnel decisions should be carefully constructed'.[78] In the legal profession this is certainly not the case—the decision maker's discretion is paramount and group decision-making techniques leave a lot to be desired.

Despite the evidence, many employers and partners defend the idea that the system is neutral and that ability is objectively and fairly determined. The degree of self-interest in these arguments cannot be overlooked. Today's decision makers in the legal hierarchy were promoted under a system which valued their skills, accepted their culture and assumed their abilities. Questioning the legitimacy of this system is tantamount to questioning the legitimacy of their own successes.

A ccording to the men and women in the profession, many of the problems faced by women lawyers can be traced to their incompatibility with men. So, when explaining why women have poor chances, the majority of men and women in the 1992 national survey pointed to entrenched attitudes, the 'old boys' network' and the prevailing perception that women were 'less compatible' with colleagues and clients.[1]

Compatibility ranks highly as a factor in decisions about the right person for particular work or a particular position. Cultural, personal and professional fit are in many instances the paramount considerations. Is the notion of compatibility itself a problem? How does it manifest itself? How neutral is this criterion? Is it being used (knowingly or otherwise) to screen out women and to advance men? How compatible are today's women lawyers with men lawyers and men clients?

Socio-economic status

Since the 1970s, the mass entry of women into the New Zealand legal profession certainly did not alter the overall socio-economic profile of the legal profession. Consistent with a worldwide trend, the women who entered the profession, like their predecessors in the first half of the twentieth century, were still from backgrounds that matched those of the men lawyers. If anything, women lawyers in New Zealand were more likely to come from higher socio-economic brackets than their male counterparts.[2]

In the same way, women and men lawyers have continued to be well connected in the profession. In the mid-1980s, an estimated 30 percent of lawyers had at least one relative in the law while in the early 1990s, approximately 25 percent had a family member in the profession.[3]

Old boys' network

Despite the social and economic similarities with men lawyers, women lawyers in the 1990s remain outside the inner circle. Even family connections, while lessening in importance, are still assisting men obtain jobs and partnerships more so than women. Women's continued exclusion from the social and professional male networks throughout the country has been said to be a major impediment to women lawyers' progress in the profession. The 'old boys' network', according to lawyers of both sexes, was alive and well in the law and working to women lawyers' detriment.[4]

Being outside the old boys' network is of particular concern to women practising in commercial law and women at the Bar. One woman barrister (who had left a firm as a result of discrimination) had to overcome problems with obtaining work because she was not 'part of the male networks'. Now a judge, she clearly succeeded.[5] Marie Dyhrberg notes, however, that those reluctant to brief women need not be men: '[F]emale solicitors are often reluctant to brief serious work to female barristers. The old boy network may not in fact be the greatest obstacle—do we, as women, have enough faith in ourselves—or in each other?'[6]

While some women solicitors may perpetuate women's exclusion it is doubtful that their contribution to the problem equals that of men solicitors. As only a quarter of the total profession and an even smaller proportion of those senior enough to influence which barristers get briefed, women solicitors have a marginal impact at best. Women barristers themselves certainly support other women at the Bar. Of the nine women who appeared as senior counsel in the Wellington High Court between January and September 1993, six appeared with a woman as junior counsel. The network, given the much larger numbers of men in business and men in law, is still predominantly male.

The early 1990s saw much trumpeting over the opening of several men's clubs to women.[7] The Wellington Club had to specifically revise its policy on the appointment of the first woman, Dame Silvia Cartwright, to the High Court in 1993. High Court judges, until that point, had automatically become members on their appointment.[8] When the Wellesley Club voted to open its doors to women in December 1993, women lawyers were personally invited to join in a letter sent to every woman holding a practising certificate co-signed by then Wellington law society Executive Director Colleen Singleton.[9] Several women lawyers publicly joined, commenting that they knew other members, their family had been members and that it was beneficial to belong to such clubs.[10] Privately, most saw the initiative as a public relations exercise primarily aimed at increasing the number of members which was known to have been falling.[11]

However, 'men's clubs' are only one manifestation of the old boys' network and the 'opening' of these clubs to women is unlikely to alter the outcomes for women. The network has always been informally sustained through the shared interests and involvement of men whether in relation to particular sports, business activities, political affiliations, ethnic or cultural backgrounds or their extended families. While Lions and Rotary clubs, business lunches, golf courses and 'men's clubs' may provide locations for the exchange of information and the cementing of network ties, the opportunities for networking are boundless.

Although women are no longer denied membership of or access to these clubs, they are still denied the benefits of belonging. Women's entry into the business scene since the 1980s has not in any way prompted a reallocation of alliances or patronage. In general, women do not share men's interests, involvement or perceptions, so opportunities for informal business relationship building between women and men remain limited. In addition, it is argued, men may continue to be attracted to the company of men because they benefit from the power and resources which men hold. Women, by comparison, have less to offer.[12]

For many women lawyers the cumulative result of these factors has been that clients have kept doing business with their male lawyers or their male dominated law partnership. As one woman partner in a large national firm explained, women lawyers have real difficulties 'pulling' clients into the firm because 'the old boys' network has consumed all the commercial clients'.

However, the problem remains with new clients and new businesses. Women lawyers, it is said, are basically less compatible with commercial clients—who happen to be predominantly men.

Client compatibility

Nearly one hundred years after women's entry into the legal profession, lawyers are still saying that compatibility with clients is a major factor in determining women lawyers' opportunities in the profession. Commercial clients, who are predominantly men, are said to prefer men lawyers and family law clients, especially women, have a preference for women lawyers. Some commercial male clients not only prefer to work with male lawyers—they are said to openly oppose working with women lawyers.

Opposing women

How widespread is client resistance to women lawyers? When elaborating on who discriminated, 36 percent of women lawyers in the 1992 national survey referred to clients. Men lawyers were four times less likely to point to clients as the source of discrimination: only 9 percent did so.[13] For women lawyers, clients discriminated by objecting to leaving 'important matters' to women, by not taking women lawyers seriously, by being condescending towards them or simply by assuming that women lawyers were secretaries or clerks and not lawyers.[14] Still others have observed that client opposition is expressed in very subtle, almost undetectable mannerisms and comments.

When it comes to the type of client who discriminates, many women lawyers singled out the banking and finance industry. Banking, according to women lawyers, is a very male dominated area of law and bankers prefer to work with men. Women lawyers point out that bankers accept only men as having knowledge of things commercial. Women cannot be trusted with their business. For similar reasons, women lawyers say that other finance sector commercial clients, insurance companies and certain off-shore investors have a predilection for men lawyers.[15]

In some international commercial transactions, cultural differences may require the involvement of men lawyers and not women lawyers. An American author observed in the early 1980s that: 'Firms doing business with foreign corporations (for example, Japanese corporations) . . . are extremely sensitive to cultural innuendos, and some attorneys have confided that women are excluded in such cases.'[16] More recently, a partner in an Auckland firm observed that 'in banking and commercial areas some overseas attitudes to women may be a disadvantage to women practising in those areas of law'. The cultural misfit can also backfire on women lawyers from minority ethnic groups as was found by one Asian woman graduate when she was turned down for a job in Wellington. In addition to being doubtful that she could deal with his male clients, the employer told her, he was 'not sure' she would 'fit into the New Zealand corporate culture'.[17]

Client preferences for men have also influenced recruitment decisions by provincial law firms. In 1994, for example, a Wellington based employment consultant recounted: 'Occasionally, firms in provincial centres will prefer a man over a woman because a male lawyer suits their client base.' This preference has lead some firms to instruct consultants to find a male for the job for the reason that the clients have indicated that they have a 'comfort zone' with men lawyers.

Client resistance to women lawyers was first identified in the 1987 national public poll by the New Zealand Law Society (NZLS). Although a significant majority of respondents (67 percent) had no preference for a male or female lawyer, 21 percent preferred a man lawyer and 9 percent preferred a woman lawyer. People who had never consulted a lawyer expressed a greater preference to see a woman lawyer than those who had used a lawyer's services in the past: 15 percent compared with 9 percent overall. Women were three and a half times more likely to prefer a woman lawyer than men (14 percent compared with 4 percent) and 'home-makers', a predominantly female group, had the greatest preference overall to see a female lawyer (19 percent compared with 9 percent overall).[18]

Men and women in Napier, Hastings and the South Island were less likely to prefer women lawyers than respondents in other regions.[19]

The preference for women lawyers was greatest in regard to matrimonial cases 'and other personal matters' but, even then, this preference was outweighed by the preference for men: 21 percent of clients preferred men for matrimonial work and 14 percent preferred women. Predictably, client preference for women was lowest in regard to advice on 'business matters concerned with property, borrowing and investment'.[20]

Overcoming client opposition

When examining the experiences of women lawyers it is apparent that client resistance has been of a predominantly minor nature. Of the early women lawyers, for example, Ethel Benjamin, Ellen Melville and Harriet Vine, all of whom practised in commercial areas, none had difficulties with clients. In an employment reference, H H Loughnan specifically emphasised that Stella Henderson had no trouble dealing with clients when working for him.

Again, in the 1970s there was little evidence of women lawyers facing opposition from clients. To the contrary, Carolyn Henwood reported to the 1975 United Women's Convention:

> I have gathered from my own experience and from the correspondence and discussions with other women lawyers that few have experienced any difficulty with their clients because of their sex. A prospective client wishes to consult a competent lawyer who will provide a prompt and efficient service. If this service is provided the client is not concerned whether the lawyer is male or female.[21]

In the 1981 Auckland survey, although over half of the women lawyers surveyed had experienced resistance from clients which they perceived to be on the grounds of their sex, that resistance was, for the vast majority, infrequent.[22] In Hannah Sargisson's study the following year, client opposition to women lawyers was said to be minor, taking the form mostly of 'initial surprise on the part of a client who had not anticipated seeing a woman'.[23] Again in Wellington in 1983, difficulties with clients, male and female, experienced by women lawyers were predominantly rare or short-lived. In the main, the problems were similar to those experienced by women in the 1992 national survey: not being taken seriously and being mistaken for a secretary or assistant to a partner or having advice questioned.[24] In all surveys where client opposition had occurred it was more often from men.[25]

Repeatedly, women lawyers have shown that client resistance on the occasions it has occurred has been resolved easily. Women lawyers interviewed in 1981 said that clients quickly adjusted 'to the idea of a woman doing a "man's job"'. By the end of the first client interview, the majority of women lawyers considered they had won their clients' confidence.[26] In 1982, it was found that in nearly every case, client resistance to women lawyers was easily overcome by the women.[27]

Social incompatibility

Whether women lawyers had problems with clients seemed to depend largely on how the supervising partner responded to the clients' objections. The 1981 Auckland working party pointed out:

> The likelihood of resistance is increased if a defensive or apologetic attitude is adopted by practitioners when introducing clients to female solicitors. This will exacerbate the misgivings of clients or create misgivings where none existed before.[28]

The working party concluded that: 'the fears of practitioners ... are greatly exaggerated. In part they are caused by the practitioners own reservations which he has assumed are shared by his client.'[29]

Stories by women lawyers confirm that the supervising partners' reactions usually made all the difference. When working at MacAlister's, Shirley Parr's single encounter of opposition from a male client in forty years of practice was 'straightened out' by the then senior partner. The client, a man, had been 'a little taken aback to be given a woman lawyer' but after the senior partner's intervention, Shirley Parr acted for him without any problem. Judith Potter likewise recalled that client opposition was avoided when she first worked at Wallace McLean by the partners meeting the client with her in the first instance. The client was given the message that a woman lawyer was 'normal, competent and able to do the job'.

When the scope of inquiry has been widened it has become evident that men lawyers also experience some client resistance—but for reasons unrelated to gender. Sargisson discovered in 1982, that male lawyers frequently experienced resistance from clients for reasons including age, inexperience and personality. In addition, she found that the men surveyed were less able to overcome client resistance than the women had been. Unlike the women lawyers, the men lawyers interviewed 'accepted philosophically that they were going to lose clients occasionally for whatever reason'. The findings demonstrated that: 'it cannot be concluded that women are any less acceptable to clients than men ... If anything, men encounter more resistance.'[30]

When the issue of client compatibility is closely examined it becomes apparent that a women lawyer's incompatibility relates more to social incompatibility than to professional skill. Fitting into the corporate culture, according to women lawyers, means more than being well informed on business matters. Commercial work means working hard and playing hard.

It is in the social environment that women lawyers find they are considered most incompatible. All the old problems about male and female social interaction, alcohol and the 'boys' night out' resurface when commercial lawyers entertain with commercial clients. Women lawyers can find, as Teresa Shreves did, that their social interaction with male clients is met with 'smirking suspicion' that the relationship is more than purely professional.[31] Some women lawyers find that while they might be allowed to do commercial work, they are excluded from the play. One woman solicitor working in commercial law in a large city firm, found herself left out when it came to socialising with clients. The reason she was given by her supervising partner was that women 'are perceived as being less socially compatible with contacts in large commercial clients'.

Partner opposition

Partners and employers feature regularly in stories about client opposition to women lawyers or women's incompatibility with clients. The fact remains that while clients may oppose women lawyers doing commercial work, men lawyers themselves have long expressed a preference for women doing non-commercial law work. In the 1978 NZLS practitioner survey, 28 percent of the predominantly male respondents considered women lawyers were more suited to matrimonial and conveyancing work than to other work. In 1982, although client attitudes were cited as the main reason for women's difficulties when practising in commercial or criminal law, some Wellington women lawyers pointed out that employer attitudes were also a source of difficulty. Employers were, according to one woman, 'less willing to give women a chance'.[32]

Men partners have been more sensitive to the real or perceived client opposition to women lawyers than any other group of lawyers. In the 1987 Auckland study, prejudice or discrimination by clients towards women lawyers was perceived by equal proportions of men and women lawyers but was cited by male partners in particular.[33]

By 1987, women lawyers gave equal weight to the bias of partners and clients in relation to difficulties experienced in commercial areas of practice. Eighteen percent of women thought clients were more comfortable with or preferred male solicitors for commercial work. The same percentage said that partners discriminated against women lawyers when allocating commercial work or simply assumed that women were not interested.[34]

Throughout the surveys and studies on women and men in the legal profession there is a discernible shift in the source of discrimination. While men clients topped the list up to the mid-1980s, men lawyers, and men partners in particular, are now the primary perpetrators of discrimination. In the 1990s, it is clear that in some instances, clients and their perceived preferences have become a scapegoat for what is in fact the preferences of men lawyers.

Compatibility in practice

'Compatibility' influences a range of decision making in the legal profession. Recruitment, promotion to partnership, and even appointment as Queen's Counsel (QCs) are influenced by perceptions of compatibility. It is usually measured with reference to personality, confidence, school background, sporting ability and compliance with the rules or ethical fit. For a number of reasons women lawyers are more likely to be unable to make the compatibility grade.

Personality

Personality (or personal attributes) is a factor in most professional decision making. In recruitment of law graduates, according to the 1990 nationwide survey by John Caldwell, the number one recruitment criterion was 'personality'.[35] A candidate's personal attributes over-shadowed all other criteria including academic performance, subjects taken in the law degree and work experience.

So, how is personality measured? The legal profession, unlike the commercial sector, has not adopted psychological testing as a mainstream form of ascertaining a person's aptitude for a particular job.[36] Instead, according to law firm partners, personality is the impression gained from observing and assessing a candidate's confidence, integrity and personal style during an interview.

When elaborating on what comprised 'personal attributes', Caldwell reported that firms commented, almost uniformly, that they sought 'positive, motivated, well-balanced individuals who will relate well to both staff and clients'. The list of attributes given by one Wellington firm reflected that of the majority. The list comprised: 'communication skills, demeanour, selfconfidence (but not too much), strong outside interests, proven integrity, a willingness to work hard and start at the bottom, and an ability to think laterally.'[37] These 'attributes' would ultimately form the primary basis of a firm's decision to employ one candidate over another.

Personality plays a part across a range of decision making. Personal style, for example, is also an often mentioned criterion when it comes to allocating files to certain solicitors or briefing barristers for particular work. A connection is made between the type of legal work and the type of person believed to be most suited to perform the work. In relation to the appointment of QCs, the official criteria include 'personal qualities' although there is no elaboration of what that involves.[38] 'Compatibility', it seems, is the partnership equivalent of the recruitment criterion 'personal attributes'.

Compatibility with partners

Of all the factors that influence a person's prospects for partnership, compatibility with existing partners carries the greatest weight. Men partners ranked compatibility with partners as the most important partnership criterion in the 1987 Auckland survey and again in the 1992 national survey. Even if these partners were to revise their partnership criteria, compatibility would remain at the top of the list, ranking number one in 1992 ahead of expertise, ability to bring in clients and fees performance. There is very little difference between women and men partners when it comes to the importance of compatibility. In both surveys, women partners included compatibility in the top three criteria, although in the more recent study, women partners gave a higher rating to expertise.[39]

So what is this all-important criterion 'compatibility'? When asked to define it, partners most often talk about a candidate's personality, attitudes and ambitions. Reference is made to professional integrity, ethics, competence and business nous. In some firms compatibility means that a person will maintain excellent professional standards of work while in another it means a person will aim to balance their work and lifestyle.

In effect, compatibility is a measure of how the existing partners perceive themselves or would like to be perceived by others. Psychologists observe that we are all inclined to see excellence in our own image. For this reason, people tend to associate with, befriend, mentor and promote those who bear some resemblance to themselves—politically, culturally, socially or intellectually. As has been demonstrated in relation to women lawyers and the old boys' network and clients, many women do not make the grade.

Although the personality or compatibility component underlying recruitment and partnership decision making may appear gender-free, this is not the case. As explained below, seemingly neutral criteria like confidence and ethical fit are actually gendered preferences for characteristics commonly expected to be displayed by men.

Confidence and modesty

The requirement for self-confidence can be a no-win criterion for women lawyers. Some women lawyers have taken to heart the message that to get on in a commercial world, they have to be tough and uncompromising. In some cases, adopting this style in the workplace has brought censure or sideways glances. An Auckland woman partner said that women who do not give up and go elsewhere (electing to 'fight on') are likely to be seen as 'too aggressive' and will not get anywhere anyway. It is, she says, 'a catch 22' situation, or as the president of the Criminal Bar Association, Marie Dyhrberg, commented in 1994: 'Women barristers, particularly in criminal cases, are paradoxically chided for being either too much of a girl or too aggressive—too much like a man . . . Serious criminal work is also definitely for the boys.'[40]

Research has consistently shown that women who are confident are seen as overly assertive and risk being penalised for being 'pushy', or 'arrogant'. Conversely, men displaying the same amount of self-confidence are perceived as 'competent' or 'authoritative'.[41] The reason for the gendered perception of confidence goes back to the subconscious expectation that women will be submissive in the company of men and an equally hidden distrust or fear of apparently dominant women. Robin Fuller, the director of the Wellington Institute of Professional Legal Studies (IPLS) has said that this explains why 'very bright women law graduates with strong personalities are threatening to some men interviewers'. Modesty is still a quality admired in women.

Women graduates and women lawyers applying for jobs have good reason to be underconfident. They expect to be presented with more hurdles such as questions at interviews which test their commitment to their careers. Many women would be forgiven for confidence lapses on realising that their chances may be adversely affected by their sex, their age (particularly if in their potential childbearing years), their family responsibilities or their lack of contacts. The fact is, as Michele Slatter, a lecturer at Canterbury University law school, observed: 'Women students are less confident about their prospects than men students.'

School background and socio-economic status

Secondary school background is, according to lawyers, relevant to their job prospects. The emphasis placed by employers on the school attended by the prospective employee is seen by many as symptomatic of socio-economic discrimination—a type of discrimination mentioned by 33 percent of women and 22 percent of men lawyers surveyed in 1992.

Schooling in New Zealand is very much an indication of a person's 'class'. Private schools, for example, are generally believed by those in higher socio-economic groups to provide a better education. These schools are usually fee-paying single-sex schools with long traditions. Entry can involve waiting lists, parent interviews and fees outside the reach of most New Zealand families.

The number of lawyers attending private schools may be on the decline. In Georgina Murray's 1984 study of Auckland lawyers, 52 percent had attended 'elite private schools' which were defined as schools reputed to be 'good' schools because students achieved top grades, usually with a price tag to match. Extending the elite category to highly regarded public schools, like Auckland Boys' Grammar School, the proportion of lawyers who had attended elite schools soared to 75 percent.[42]

In 1992, over one-third of lawyers had had private secondary schooling—with no difference between the women and men. Another 5 percent of lawyers were educated overseas, possibly also in elite schools. While the proportions may be declining compared with the earlier survey, the rates of private schooling are still very high when compared with the population in general. Attendance at private schools by lawyers is more than twice the national average: 34 percent compared with 13 percent.[43]

Women's school background, judging by lawyers' comments, is as relevant as men's school background. Many of the women judges and senior women in the profession have attended single-sex schools. For example, in 1994, both the then women QCs and a recently appointed woman judge, Jane Lovell-Smith had been in the same year and the same class at a private Auckland girls' school, Diocesan School for Girls.

Both women and men lawyers mentioned that the school attended made a difference. One woman after five years' experience in practice said: 'In a job interview situation, it still matters which school you went to.' Another woman lawyer from Otago said: 'Socio-economic status, particularly the "right" school and the "right" contacts has a bearing on placement in firms in larger cities.' Men lawyers' comments were similar. One Wellington man said he 'felt a lack of opportunity for advancement through having the wrong school tie'.

The 'wrong' schools it seems are rural or small town high schools or city schools with 'bad' reputations. But this depends very much on the view and experience of the prospective employer. Many employers will have attended non-private, non-elite schools and may be aware of the negative perceptions by members of the profession about public schooling and the advantages of that type of school background.

Clearly, to the extent that schooling compatibility is an issue or a benefit, men will be the beneficiaries simply because there are more of them in employment decision-making roles. As such, men lawyers have greater possibilities for being favoured for having the same school tie.

Class consciousness seems to be heightened in the two larger metropolitan areas. Wellington and Auckland lawyers readily pointed to socio-economic discrimination while Hamilton, Canterbury and Otago lawyers did not find it widespread. Certainly, South Island lawyers were less likely to have personally experienced this type of discrimination.[44]

However, women lawyers in Canterbury commonly speak of the conservatism of the profession there and the effect this has on the opportunities for women lawyers.[45] A woman lawyer who moved south from Auckland commented: 'Christchurch especially has a cliquey "old boys' " network which makes it difficult for women graduates to get jobs.' The perception that such socio-economic preferences by employers were alive and well was confirmed by Anna Tutton, the branch director of the Canterbury IPLS. From her observations of law graduate employment in the Christchurch region it was apparent that the old boys' network was helping the men graduates obtain jobs, particularly those who had attended private schools and played rugby.[46]

Through these preferences or prejudices for and against certain types of school background, the segregation of classes through the school system is reproduced in the legal profession.

Competitive sports

When recruiting, law firms have been known to place some weight on a candidate's background in competitive sports. (It is preferable that this is in the past as the time commitment involved in competitive sports makes that pursuit incompatible with or at least difficult for those with a 'serious' professional career.) Some firms have reputations for recruiting those who played first fifteen rugby or first eleven cricket—historically male sports. National firm Bell Gully Buddle Weir, for example, had a recruitment policy which targeted those from 'a restricted group of boys' schools and especially applicants with a good sporting record'. Julia Millen wrote in her history of the firm: 'Even among current partners, typical answers to the question: "How did you happen to come to Bell Gully?" are: "My father played rugby with Wild", "Dad was with Simpson in the war", "I was captain of the First Xl at school".'[47]

Although initially criticised as a game for larrikins, from the early 1900s rugby was recognised in New Zealand as 'training in respectable manliness'.[48] Through this game, generation after generation of boys have learnt physical courage, team work, heroism, and controlled and sometimes violent combat. Today, success in sport is seen still as symbolic of strength and virility while rugby administrators are beginning to grapple with adverse public reaction to excessive displays of violence.

Law firms' emphasis on cricket and rugby has a distinct gender bias. While there is a long history of both sports in New Zealand, only recently have schools and clubs started to encourage girls and women to play them. Given the preference for femininity in women, however, it is unlikely that playing rugby would be regarded as a favourable item in a woman lawyer's curriculum vitae.

Compliance with the rules

At an organisational level, the fact that compatibility is important makes sense. Organisational success traditionally has been viewed as dependent on the workers accepting the organisational rules and culture. Efficient, productive functioning of an organisation is believed to be wholly related to compliance with the rules designed for that purpose. Those who reject the objectives or processes of an organisation are viewed as hostile, uncooperative or reluctant participants. They are likely to be viewed as counterproductive and therefore expendable in a business sense.

Women lawyers, more so than men lawyers, are inclined to question or challenge the rules.[49] The fact that so many women personally experience or see discrimination in the profession indicates that they doubt the legal system and its ability to be fair. This scepticism in turn provides a strong incentive to act. Just under 80 percent of women lawyers in the 1992 survey believed that action had to be taken to reduce discrimination, while just over 50 percent of men thought this.[50] The increasing number of initiatives by women lawyers and their associations demonstrates that they are prepared to challenge the status quo and initiate change.

The divergence of views between women and men in the profession is particularly marked when comparing the views of women lawyers and men partners. On nearly every issue relating to discrimination, opportunities and benefits in the 1992 national survey, men partners were more optimistic than women lawyers.[51] No wonder then that men partners, more so than any other group, disagreed that change was necessary to eliminate discrimination.[52] On this issue alone, conflict between women lawyers and men partners is inevitable.

At the 1993 Women's Law Conference, Jane Meares, a partner in the Wellington office of Bell Gully Buddle Weir, urged women lawyers to understand the rules and the culture of the firm they work in. She pointed out:

> The rules have to be accepted and I do not think that women do themselves justice by railing against them every time. Men seem to love to bait women and then, when women try to deal with it, they are accused of having no sense of humour. Irritating as that may be, it is sometimes best to swallow one's pride. It is important that women choose their moments.[53]

Meares pointed out that women aiming for partnership had to comply with the rules even where they realised the rules were outdated or unfair. The rationale is largely pragmatic. Meares described her own approach: 'I have no doubt that I have played by the rules to get to be a partner and I did that when I was irritated beyond belief. Until I became part of the club I did not feel I would ever have a chance of changing those rules.'[54]

However, for some women who do make partnership they have no intention to try to achieve change. In the 1992 survey it was evident that many women partners shared the views of men partners on questions of partnership criteria, women's opportunities, the prevalence of discrimination and the explanations given for women's position in the profession.[55] Women partners' views on these issues were often closer to the views of the men partners than to those of women lawyers in general. Therefore, 'compatibility' is likely to require a high degree of consensus on the interpretations of and explanations for workplace problems.

Ethical or moral positions

Men and women lawyers, according to academics and psychologists, tend towards different ethical or moral positions which will affect their work and their professional approaches. From childhood, girls development and socialisation is believed to lead to 'the morality of care' where harm is to be avoided and relationships preserved. By comparison, boys tend towards competitive, goal-focused activity with the result that men's identity is more 'rights based'.[56] Other research is reopening the debate about brain differences between women and men. The location of specific functions in a typical male brain is said to be more specialised while a typical female brain will be more diffuse. As a result, men are believed to tend toward sequential, logical, detailed, fact-based thinking while women are inclined to intuitive, empathetic, creative, 'big picture' thinking.[57]

Where these theorists diverge from those who expounded these views in the nineteenth and early twentieth centuries, is that they do not prescribe a negative value to women's morality and a positive value to men's. Instead, as Jack and Jack concluded:

> Each gender receives its own gifts, its own limitations, and its own ways of making sense of life. Experiences of most boys prepare them for a world of advocacy, stoic detachment, autonomy, and suspension of judgment. Girls' experiences usually instruct them for roles requiring sensitivity to others' feelings, cooperation, involvement, and contextual understanding.[58]

In practical terms, the ethical differences may mean that women lawyers are more likely to take cooperative or inclusive approaches in relation to decision making and dispute resolution. Men, on the other hand, are expected to argue in favour of the existing rules and practices.

This is certainly borne out in relation to women lawyers' disinclination to respect the organisational rules within law firms and by men lawyers' inclination to defend the status quo. As significantly however, women lawyers are more likely than men lawyers to doubt that the law itself and legal services operate in a neutral environment. For example, in a 1987 national survey, 61 percent of women lawyers believed that unequal access to the law was a major or serious problem. This view was shared by only 41 percent of men lawyers. Likewise, women lawyers were more concerned about the low level of community service provided by lawyers: 44 percent believed this was a major or serious problem compared with only 11 percent of men.[59]

In the 1990s, many women lawyers and judges continue to demonstrate their concerns about inequity in the law by being involved in a range of organisations and projects, in addition to developing alternative legal analyses under the umbrella of 'women's law'.[60] Whether politically or ethically motivated, women lawyers' high level of participation in challenges to the law and the legal system differentiates them from the majority of their male colleagues.

According to Jack and Jack, each type of morality 'potentially threatens the other, and each evolves its own strategy for self-perpetuation'.[61] Given that men in the legal profession have the tools to ensure survival largely in their control, women lawyers more frequently will be found to be ethically incompatible.

Conclusion

Although in the 1990s there is a veneer of inclusion, women lawyers remain social and professional 'misfits'. The 'old boys' network' may have changed its appearance but arguably it remains as powerful as it was in the early part of the nineteenth century. Equally, as in the past, it is most often men lawyers who decide the degree of women's inclusion—not clients as men lawyers have suggested.

'Compatibility' in legal profession decision making produces the same gendered outcome as is achieved by the notion of 'merit'. Women, by virtue of their backgrounds, experiences and perspectives, in general will not measure up. On most tests, the majority of women lawyers are simply incompatible. Again, this disadvantages women but it also disadvantages the profession and legal businesses.

Methods used by law firms to identify 'compatibility' are imprecise. Personality, for example, is commonly assessed during interviews and not by a purpose-designed personality test. Few decision makers in law offices have any training in determining which personality factors are job related and which are irrelevant to performance. Even human resource practitioners are cautioned to ensure this distinction is made and that personality tests are used in a disciplined manner.[62] If concerns about validity affect the assessments made by human resource practitioners, the concern must be at least doubled for the inexperienced decision maker. Human resource practitioners test; lawyers guess.

Most importantly, decision making in the legal profession proceeds on the assumption that something valuable is to be gained by looking for 'compatibility'. As the cornerstone of decisions relating to recruitment and partnership admissions, this criterion effectively screens out 'difference'. In this way, the predominantly male-defined value system remains intact in the legal profession and is reproduced largely without question.

Chapter Ten

A Question of Choice?

Alongside the belief that merit, not gender, determines opportunities in the legal profession, is the equally powerful notion of individual choice. Women lawyers, according to many, choose not to complain about discrimination because it is not that significant; they choose to leave the profession; they choose to work outside private practice; they choose their families over their careers; and they choose not to advance by not putting their names forward for positions in the law societies or other positions of authority.

Men lawyers too are widely thought to be expressing personal preferences or choices which have nothing to do with discrimination. Men prefer their careers over their families; they choose to work in private practice; they choose business models that suit them; they choose partners and employees who fit their idea of personal and professional compatibility; and they choose to engage in 'social banter' with women employees and colleagues. Of course, some women choose to be offended while others enjoy the attention.

Like the ideal of merit, the notion of choice provides a neat explanation for the gender difference in the career paths and career experiences of men and women lawyers. It is no one's fault and no one's responsibility. Many in the profession will state categorically that any individual, man or woman, can select from the range of opportunities and courses of action available.

How then, given all these personal preferences, can there be discrimination? Has it become an excuse for the fact that women lawyers are choosing not to run in the race? In reality, are women presented with the same choices as men and are they simply choosing to opt out?

This chapter examines two 'choices' women lawyers are said to exercise: the choice to place their families before their careers and the choice to work outside private practice.

Women's career commitments

Women lawyers, contrary to popular belief, are dedicated to their careers in law. In fact, when asked about their commitment to being in the legal profession, women in private practice have been consistently more committed than their male colleagues.

Hannah Sargisson's study in 1982, for example, found that 86 percent of women declared a long-term commitment to their careers compared with 80 percent of men, some of whom were equivocal in their answers.[1] In 1988, Stephanie Knight noted 'how seriously [women lawyers] take their commitment to their career'.[2] In 1992, women lawyers still expressed a high level of commitment to being in the legal profession; a commitment which in the short to medium term exceeded that of men lawyers.[3]

Women's aspirations

Women lawyers also report having high aspirations within the legal profession.

In the 1987 survey by the Auckland District Law Society, women lawyers employed in law firms were found to have equal aspirations with respect to achieving partnerships as their male colleagues. In the 1992 national survey, women lawyers' ambitions to achieve partnerships actually exceeded those of men. Of the 729 lawyers who are intending to reach partnership within the next two to ten years, 408 (56 percent) were women.[4]

Women lawyers also aspire to other positions in the profession particularly in the judiciary. In the 1992 national survey, women lawyers were more likely to aspire to be judges than men lawyers: 15 percent of women lawyers signalled their desire to be appointed to the Bench in the next two to ten years while only 9 percent of men lawyers had that goal. Despite the increased likelihood of obtaining District Court appointments (there being three times the number of positions than are available on the High Court Bench), women lawyers aspired to High Court appointments. Their ambitions to be appointed to either court exceeded those of their male colleagues.[5]

Despite their ambitions, women lawyers were quite realistic that their career paths would not be that straightforward. For example, while they aspired to High Court appointments, they had fairly low expectations of becoming Queen's Counsel (QCs). Not one of the 785 women lawyers in the 1992 national survey said they aspired to be a QC within the next two years. Only eight aspired to that position in five years while forty women were hoping to be appointed QCs by the year 2002.[6] Women judges were equally sceptical about women's chances of being appointed QCs. Over two-thirds of those surveyed in 1993 did not believe that women have the same opportunities to reach QC as men do.[7]

Women lawyers, more so than men lawyers, recognise they may need to make career moves to increase their opportunities. For example, women expect that to obtain a partnership they will need to look outside their current firm. In the 1992 survey, of the 233 lawyers who aspired to partnerships in firms other than their current one, 71 percent were women. This inclination to look to another firm demonstrates an acceptance by women lawyers that their prospects are otherwise limited. Men lawyers, on the other hand, are fairly confident about their prospects in the firm where they currently work.[8]

Going by the recent assessment of partnership decision makers, women's chances of making partners are still not good—regardless of where they work. Partners of both sexes rated women lawyers chances of making partnership poorly in the 1992 survey. Only 38 percent of existing partners thought women had the same opportunities to achieve partnership as men lawyers. This assessment by partners is three times more optimistic than that of women lawyers themselves.[9]

Families v careers

Women assumed to choose their families over their careers

One very powerful argument which has been advanced consistently over the past one hundred years is that women lawyers are more committed to their families than to their careers. Since the 1980s, women lawyers' 'choice' of families over careers has been a principal explanation for women's low status and poor prospects in the profession.[10] Women lawyers are believed to leave private practice or to make career changes to accommodate their family preferences. Discrimination is not the problem; it is a matter of choice.

In the 1990s, lawyers of both sexes still say that women's choice of families over careers is a primary explanation for women lawyers' position.[11] Of the men who believed that women's family commitments were the real problem, few connected this with discrimination. Instead they attributed the problem to women's choices and to the wider social convention which dictates that women should, or simply would, look after children. According to men lawyers, 'the firm' and the legal profession are under no legal, moral or commercial obligations to redress the wider social issue of child care.

In distinct contrast, some women lawyers suspect that the family versus career argument is in fact discrimination in another guise. Of the women lawyers who referred to this argument, several observed that their supposed preference was a perception and not a reality; that employers assumed all women would follow the one path—out; while others said that they had been openly discriminated against when pregnant or while on maternity leave.[12]

Why should family commitments hamper women lawyers' careers and not men lawyers' careers? Men lawyers are nearly twice as likely as women lawyers to be parents.[13] Women lawyers are twice as likely as men lawyers to be single—nearly 30 percent in the 1992 survey were unmarried and not living in de facto relationships. Despite these significant demographic differences, women lawyers, according to their male colleagues, are the ones who have problems with their family responsibilities.

Legal practice: a male model

Why is there such a difference in perception between men lawyers and women lawyers on this issue? The answer lies in some basic assumptions about the manner in which legal practice has been and therefore must continue to be conducted. A male-centred model is the predominant mode of legal practice.

Law is a jealous mistress

For many men in the legal profession 'the law' is much more than a nine to five job. The majority of men lawyers are principals and as a consequence have the added responsibility of running the business side of practices. Still others see 'the law' as a calling and are committed to serving clients' needs regardless of the hour and regardless of other commitments.

Men lawyers have long been aware of the impact of their work on their wives and families. At a 1954 Bar dinner speech, the speaker confided in the exclusively male audience:

> every one of us has good reason to know that the life of the wife of a lawyer is not always an easy one. It is an old and trite saying that the law is a jealous mistress. Whether that is correct I do not know, but it is true that our profession makes claims upon the life and time of a man which no wife and few children would dare to exercise. It makes us irritable, it makes us tired, but it rewards us with some triumphs and some intellectual compensations. Yet such is the nature of those triumphs and those intellectual compensations that our wives can share but partly in them.[14]

Forty years later, law was still consuming a large proportion of men lawyers' energy. In the 1992 national survey, 85 percent of men were working in excess of 40 hours per week. Half worked between 40 and 49 hours on average per week while the other half commonly worked in excess of 50 hours per week. Men partners and principals topped the scale with the majority working at least 50 hours per week on average.[15]

Lawyers specialising in court work also work long hours over sustained periods. When Deputy Solicitor-General Craig Thompson was appointed a District Court judge in 1992 he thanked his family to whom, he said, he owed his achievement. According to the *Dominion*, he also offered his apologies:

> He was sorry that, as was the case with the families of many litigators, too often they had been forced to put up with extended absences while he was at trial. And when he was at home he was often tired, distracted and irritable . . . The bad news is that going on what I've heard, probably not much will change.[16]

Families and careers must be separate

From the late 1970s, when women started to enter the law in relatively large numbers they met with a professional culture which unashamedly required families and careers to be separate and, where there were competing priorities, careers would come first. Men lawyers were firmly of the view there would be no concessions for family and personal lives. In a 1978 poll of lawyers over 80 percent of those surveyed 'disliked the idea that any concessions should be made to female lawyers which would allow them to have a family and to keep working'.[17]

According to many law firm employers surveyed in 1992, women lawyers' childbearing and childrearing roles make them uneconomic and inconvenient employees. The comment of one male sole practitioner was typical: 'Maternity leave, school holiday leave, part time, child care etc [are] incompatible with the nature of legal business particularly the demands of client development.' This perspective has resulted in limited opportunities for women with children to gain employment, advance within firms or be considered for partnership.

For some firms, as one man associate partner said, women are considered 'risky investments', particularly in the early years of their careers when they are likely to have children. This concern has prompted firms to screen out women lawyers who might have these intentions. Questions asked of women in recruitment interviews about plans to marry, to have children or even about the possibility of needing 'time-off during "the monthly"' were not asked to plan maternity leave or sick leave in advance; they were asked to exclude candidates from selection. In 1985, Auckland law graduate, Hanneke Morton described the screening process: 'Employers ask the most extraordinary questions when you apply for a job . . . They want to know what you'll do if you have a sick child . . . Most women lawyers with preschoolers are politely shown the door.'[18]

Within the workforce, women lawyers' potential or actual child-bearing and childrearing roles are used to explain why they have fewer opportunities than their male colleagues. As the 1989 Auckland working party explained: 'Often the decision to have children is seen as necessarily involving the sacrifice of the right to receive more interesting lucrative work and to gain advancement within the power structure.'[19]

Equally, many lawyers in the 1992 survey attributed women's poor prospects of partnership to the perceived likelihood that they would have children. As one barrister, a former partner of a large firm, said: 'There is apparently still resistance to admitting women to partnership as readily as men. I do not think ability is the issue. Generally it is due to the issues arising if the woman partner wishes to have/or does have family responsibilities.' A male partner in a large firm noted that any request for domestic related leave was enough: 'If women seek flexibility in the job their prospects for advancement are poor.'

Marriage is recommended

The separation of careers and families, in many cases, is accommodated by marriage. The pressures of men lawyers' jobs and the hours involved have meant that wives and families provide an essential domestic support network for the majority of men lawyers. An estimated 80 percent of men lawyers in New Zealand were either married or living in de facto relationships in 1992.[20] Likewise, the majority of male judges were married.[21] For most men working in the profession, their domestic partners enable them to have a home life without the responsibility of running the household and, importantly, caring for children.

Over half of the men in the national survey had domestic partners at home who took main responsibility for the household tasks of cooking, cleaning and shopping. Very few men had sole responsibility for these tasks and only one-quarter shared the tasks equally with their partner.[22] When it came to child care, 61 percent of men lawyers had domestic partners who had primary responsibility for looking after the children. For 69 percent of the lawyer-fathers, their domestic partners looked after the children when they were sick.[23]

These domestic arrangements mirror the arrangements in the households where many men lawyers grew up. In Georgina Murray's 1984 study of lawyers she found that the prevailing occupation of lawyers' mothers was that of housewife. Only one percent of men lawyers' mothers were in the highest socio-economic group, which would include, for example, those employed in professional occupations. By comparison, 10 percent of women lawyers' mothers were categorised as having the highest socio-economic status. Predicably, most lawyers' fathers were in full-time paid employment.[24]

While today's men lawyers are enjoying domestic support, the reality for women lawyers is vastly different. In many ways woman lawyers' experiences match more closely the model of the male lawyers' wives than the male lawyers. An estimated half of the women lawyers have primary responsibility for cleaning, cooking and shopping in their households. Where most men lawyers rely on their wives to perform these functions, less than 5 percent of women lawyers can rely on someone else to do so.

For those women in the profession who are parents, over half will have primary or sole responsibility for children. They are more likely to use paid childminders, friends or relatives and daycare centres than to rely on their domestic partner to care for children while they are at work. When their children are sick, women lawyers are five times more likely than their male colleagues to take unpaid leave to care for children.[25]

A 'wife' equivalent

To perform the job, women lawyers have often needed a 'wife' equivalent. Even the early women lawyers who remained unmarried had assistance on the domestic front so that they could meet their career commitments. Ellen Melville, for example, lived at home until her mother died and then her sister, May, gave up her small stationery shop business to return home. According to Melville's biographer: 'Living at home suited Ellen Melville's busy lifestyle. May ran the household, leaving her sister free to pursue her public career and attend to her business.'[26] Likewise, Dorothy Raymond's sister, a midwife, gave up her profession to keep house for her lawyer-sister.[27]

Women lawyers subsequently have emphasised the importance of domestic help. Often the person who provided this was their partner. Senior women lawyers refer to the extensive involvement of their husbands in preparing meals, caring for children after school and in managing the administration of their practices. Other women lawyers employ domestic workers.

For many, this assistance was essential to their success. Augusta Wallace, for example, on her appointment to the Bench in 1975, said: 'I've always had household help .. You can't have a full-time occupation and run a home and family. I know people who do and I think they are doing themselves a dis-service.'[28] Judge Carolyn Henwood has also said: 'The really important thing is having the support of your partner, not trying to do everything yourself.' After much soul searching, they decided to employ someone to clean the house once a week. One of the dangers Judge Henwood saw as women advanced into higher positions was that they would 'be perceived as superwomen, somehow more brilliant and better able to cope with balancing a family and a career than other women'.[29]

In 1993, Nadja Tollemache, lawyer and Insurance Ombudsman, recommended that women lawyers combined careers and families but cautioned 'clear priorities must be set. I think the "superwoman" complex

must be avoided at all costs and, for example, good household help not
considered a luxury but a basic essential'.[30]

Women lawyers make useful wives

In the debates on the entry of women into the profession, it was suggested
that women lawyers could be especially useful wives for men lawyers.
When Arabella Mansfield, one of the first American woman lawyers, was
admitted to the Bar in 1869 at the same time as her husband, the editor of
the *Canada Law Journal* wrote: 'I presume the "Professor" will secure the
services of his better half as a junior partner in a professional as well as a
domestic way.'[31] In 1893, a woman with 'legal proclivities and aspirations'
was advised to 'marry a lawyer'. Although they could study and practise
together it would be 'on the principle of both doing the loading and
letting him do the shooting'.[32]

Two of New Zealand's first women law graduates did marry legally
qualified men. Ethel Benjamin's husband, Alfred de Costa, was a
sharebroker and land agent and had also worked as a law clerk.[33]
Likewise, Stella Henderson's husband, Edwin Allan, had trained and
qualified in law in England. According to the *Freelance*, he would be a
'valuable aid in her practice'.[34]

Encouragement for women lawyers to marry their male colleagues
would later turn into criticism as more women entered the law schools.
Women, it was said, were going to law school for the primary reason of
finding husbands. However, a study in America in the 1970s found that
while some women students did marry men students, the women also
went on to practise law.[35] Significantly, the accusation of 'wife hunting'
was not levelled at the men who married their women classmates.

By the 1990s, many New Zealand lawyers were married to or living in
de facto relationships with other lawyers. In the 1992 national survey,
9 percent of women lawyers had spouses or partners who were currently
working in the profession.[36] As the survey did not include domestic
partners of men lawyers who were qualified but not working as lawyers,
it is likely that the total number of lawyers married to other lawyers is in
fact much higher.

Family firms provide some of the better prospects for women

Marriage to a lawyer has been said to increase a woman lawyer's career
prospects. As Shirley Parr (who qualified in 1953) recalled: 'We used to
say that women had to be born into partnership, marry it, or go out on
their own.'[37]

Working in family firms or family-friendly firms has also assisted
women lawyers to work and have children. Here, where the other lawyers
usually have a familial interest in the child, flexibility and time off are less

of a problem. Paddy Steele, for example, could take her sons with her to work and 'sit them on the counter'.[38] Likewise, Shirley Smith found a job with men lawyer friends where she 'was free to have time off if my small daughter were ill, or in school holidays ... an excellent arrangement for me'.[39] In the 1970s, another women lawyer, once becoming pregnant, rang up a firm she thought would be sympathetic to a woman lawyer with family responsibilities and started the next day.[40]

In 1981, the Auckland working party found that while family connections in the profession benefited men more so than women: 'family connections have been helpful to women who do have children and leave the law for a period. Of the women who worked part time because of family commitments, most worked in family firms or with their husbands.'[41]

Law firm policies on family and child care

Inevitably, the idea that careers override families has been translated into law firm policies and practices. Firms are quick to point out that policies on maternity, paternity and parental leave comply with statutory requirements. Many other firms claim they offer flexible hours, part-time work, job sharing, school holiday leave, and, to a lesser extent, childcare assistance. However, the practices show that these policies do not apply across the board and are taken up infrequently.

In 1980, the Maternity Leave and Employment Protection Act required that employers provide a total of six months' unpaid maternity leave for employees having children. That Act was replaced with the Parental Leave and Employment Protection Act 1987 which extended the leave available to twelve months and confirmed that an employee could not be dismissed by reason of pregnancy or by taking parental leave. New fathers were entitled to two weeks' paternity leave and could share the one year extended leave entitlement with their partner. A complaints procedure was provided for employees who were treated unfairly as a result of requiring maternity, paternity or parental leave.

Regardless of the law and law firms policies, there is a poor understanding of family-related leave entitlements among lawyers. In 1982, less than 10 percent of women lawyers in Wellington thought they could take parental leave. One-third of women lawyers were reasonably confident that they could arrange flexible work hours but far fewer thought they could get school holiday leave.[42] Ten years later, approximately 40 percent of lawyers confidently said that their firms provided part-time work and flexible hours; 30 percent thought that paid maternity and paternity leave were offered and another 24 percent said that school holiday leave was available. However, on closer examination it was clear that these benefits were not available to all staff—only select groups, predominantly partners, had access to these benefits.[43]

A 1993 *LawTalk* survey of nine large law firms, confirmed that flexible work policies and family leave policies were available but not to everyone. While the firms offered a range of flexible work options to support staff only half made these available to employed solicitors. Partners, again were found to be most likely to be offered flexible hours, but not in all firms.[44]

Despite the claims by 30 percent of lawyers in the 1992 national survey that paid maternity and paternity leave could be taken, the 1993 *LawTalk* survey revealed that few of the larger firms actually offered this benefit. Most offered the statutory minimum of one year unpaid parental leave (including fourteen weeks' unpaid maternity leave) under the Parental Leave and Employment Protection Act. Several firms would .make exceptions and negotiate arrangements with individual staff members or partners. Their inclination to do so varied depending on the seniority and perceived value of the staff member concerned.[45]

Men lawyers in the 1993 survey were half as likely to take leave as women lawyers and where they did they took paternity leave. Of the men partners, only two had taken family-related leave—in both cases paternity leave.[46]

Women partners' seniority does not necessarily make it easier to negotiate maternity leave. To the contrary, in the 1990s, maternity leave for partners in some firms is a particularly sore point. Typical comments by women partners in the 1992 survey included:

> Partners do not like the disruption or perceived disruption of maternity leave . . . Maternity leave is a major issue and one that partners would like to ignore.

> Time away from practise affects your client relationships, practical experience etc. Even if you don't take maternity leave, male partners will anticipate this happening and react accordingly.

According to a number of men partners however, women partners are unrealistic in wanting maternity leave. A male partner in a large national firm pointed out:

> The only problem is that partnerships are businesses. Partners must contribute equally. Maternity leave creates problems if one takes a purely business approach—that is the way fairness and equity amongst partners in a business demands.

Other lawyers disagree, believing maternity leave is no different to sabbatical leave. Many law firms willingly accommodate the 'entrenched practice' of sabbatical leave entitlement, allowing in some cases three months or more paid leave on a regular basis.[47]

The 1993 *LawTalk* survey found that the bulk of leave taken or flexible arrangements actually used was by women support staff. Over a two year period to September 1993, 245 support staff in the surveyed firms had taken some type of family-related leave compared with forty-two women solicitors and eleven women partners. Support staff made up 87 percent of those working part time, 75 percent of those taking parental leave and 100 percent of those using job sharing arrangements.[48]

Support staff in law firms have traditionally enjoyed greater flexibility and more certainty in relation to family-related leave than professional staff. In the 1982 Wellington survey, lawyers believed secretaries and support staff had better flexible employment options than professional staff.[49] Women support staff, unlike women lawyers, are comparatively well unionised but more importantly are not subject to the family versus career competition. Secretaries are generally expected to put their families first. In 1984, a woman lawyer observed: 'In my first job there was glide time for the secretaries but not for the lawyers. It was thought unprofessional. There is no physical problem to working at home. The problem is the professional image.'[50]

Extra burdens for women lawyers

It was marriage, now it's children

In the 1990s, the problem remains that taking family-related leave is considered an insult to the professional requirement that careers must come first. Women lawyers are expected to emulate, or even exceed, the career commitment demonstrated by men.

Originally, forgoing marriage was the primary statement of a woman's career commitment. While men lawyers could readily marry, marriage for women signalled the end of their careers. So, in the early years of women's involvement in the profession, some women demonstrated their commitment to their careers by remaining unmarried. In 1936, all seven of the women lawyers were unmarried while more than three-quarters of the men lawyers were married.[51] Even into the 1960s, women lawyers hesitated before getting married as it was assumed their careers would be interrupted if not ended altogether.[52] A significant number of the now 'senior' women in the profession are unmarried or have no children.

In the 1990s, as one woman lawyer said: 'Marital status often is not a "problem" unless a child is on the way!' Even, the presumption that children will follow marriage means that from the time of getting married, some women lawyers are treated differently. A woman with four years' experience described how, when she got married, she 'got a lot of flack from some of the partners' where she was working at the time and 'a sense that [she] was taken less seriously'. Another woman, an associate partner, observed:

> My status and occupation seemed inextricably linked with being someone's wife or mother—not the fact I was a solicitor. I was introduced to client's as 'Y's' mother and then they had to listen to the story about how I kept my name and so on! This would not happen to a male.

In 1989, a Canadian judge, Rosalie Abella, described in *LawTalk* the 'psychological contraceptive blackmail' of young women lawyers where it was acceptable for men to have children but not for women.[53] Women lawyers have clearly got the message that their progress may depend on them remaining childless or, at least, child free. In the 1981 Auckland study, of the twenty-eight women who had children, eleven had sought admission to the Bar after their children reached school age.[54] In 1987, men lawyers were more than twice as likely as women lawyers to be parents.[55] Where women lawyers did have children, they had fewer than men.

Women recently admitted to the profession have also received the message that children and partnerships do not mix. One woman working in a large national firm commented in the 1992 survey: 'As long as you are childless, you can progress and get the good work, but the commitment required is so high that its very hard to combine with other commitments.' Another woman, also in her first year of practice and working in a large firm observed: 'If you want to opt out for a while, for children, partnership is out. Our partners are all childless.' To the contrary, most partners in large firms do have children—they just do not have the responsibility for the primary care of those children.

Since the 1970s, the most common way in which women lawyers complied with the career primacy rule was by delaying having children or by taking very limited maternity leave. From this time, there were sufficient numbers of women entering from graduation that career breaks and maternity leave should have been on the rise. Instead, the 1981 working party found that a third of the women lawyers surveyed had returned to work shortly after having babies, taking no longer than the usual sabbatical term of three months.[56] The following year Hannah Sargisson found that the number or female employees and partners taking three months or more off work (for any reason) was significantly less than the number of male employees and partners. In addition, the length of time taken off by the women was significantly less than the time taken off by the men.[57]

Of the women surveyed in the 1987 Auckland study who had taken time out from law office employment, only 10 percent had taken any maternity leave while no men had taken paternity leave.[58] In 1992, 62 percent of women lawyers surveyed who had children had not taken any parental leave. Where they took maternity leave, only 37 percent had taken three months or more, meaning the majority had taken considerably less than the statutory minimum.[59]

Even then the minimal leave taken by women lawyers was still noticeable when compared with the leave taken by the men in the profession. In the 1982 Wellington survey, only one man had taken time out for family commitments.[60] Four years later in Auckland, none of the 238 men in the survey had taken time off for paternity leave or family commitments.[61] Again, in 1992, of the 198 men who had taken three months or more out of the profession since admission only one percent had done so for family related reasons while two-thirds had done so for holidays.[62] Of the very few men lawyers who did take parental leave, they usually took one to three days or a week at most.[63]

'Superwoman'

By the 1990s, the 'superwoman' woman lawyer had in fact become one of the primary models for women lawyers, particularly for those within mainstream legal practice. Women partners were taking barely any leave when their children were born and even when they did, they still kept files up to date.

Men lawyers, observing this phenomenon, in some cases expected the same behaviour from all women. As one male associate commented in 1992, there was no reason why firms found potential wives and mothers more problematic than potential husbands and fathers, 'a woman can get married or have a child on a Saturday and still perform the same job the following Monday'.

Burn-out

For women lawyers (including the 'superwomen'), managing children and careers in the 'no concessions' culture, is a major source of stress. In 1982, the pressure from other people's expectations and demands on their time, particularly husbands and children, was said by some women to be a factor inhibiting their chances in the profession.[64] In 1987, just over 70 percent of women lawyers with children were experiencing stress in relation to child care while only 14 percent of men had this problem. The stress resulted from concerns about the cost of child care, the ability to do well and to concentrate on the job, and the making of arrangements for after-school care and when children were ill.[65]

Women lawyers are much more likely to pay for child care than their male colleagues and to pay for it at a higher rate. In 1992, most women lawyers with children were paying between $100 to $200 per week for child care. One-third of the women paid in excess of $200 per week— mostly women in the higher income brackets.[66]

The hours of work required of professional women mean that the more affordable, government subsidised daycare centres and kindergartens are often not used. Instead, women lawyers draw on a range of childcare help—childminders for after-school care, nannies, friends and relatives. Outside these arrangements, when the children are sick, women lawyers rely on their domestic partners or take unpaid leave. Less than a third take paid leave to care for sick children and usually this comes out of their sick leave entitlement.[67] The loss of income coupled with the cost of child care can make staying in the workforce uneconomic for women.

For some women, the effort involved in juggling families and careers is too great. A 1991 survey of Christchurch and Auckland lawyers found a number of female practitioners who wanted to 'warn young female law students of the future difficulties that they might face in combining legal practice with motherhood'.[68] By 1992, 29 percent of women lawyers surveyed who had children had considered resigning from their jobs because of childcare difficulties. The source of stress was often related to their children's health, a breakdown in childcare arrangements or too few quality hours at home. One woman in a medium size firm said:

> I find myself becoming fearful for my future ... I feel my commitments as a mother limit my opportunity to put into the firm what I believe is necessary to achieve a partnership. Sometimes my life seems nothing more than a constant round of cooking, cleaning, legal work, children—with very little time for myself.

Ironically, women lawyers who contemplated resignation as a solution to their family and work stress were more likely than others in the profession to be working in organisations which supposedly offered part-time work, flexible work hours and school holiday leave.[69]

Despite their personal stress, these women lawyers will not necessarily leave the profession. To the contrary, they were just as likely as all other women to express commitment to their professional careers. The women who contemplated resignation as a solution to their family and career conflicts said they would still be in the profession in two, five or ten years time—a commitment that over the short to medium term exceeded that of the men lawyers.[70]

The culture and priorities of established law firms are not of women lawyers' making. Policies and practices, to a large extent, ensure the ideal of career primacy remains intact. Women must either emulate the male model or move on. For many, this does not mean they will end their careers. They will instead leave private practice or develop new practices outside the established, male dominated law firms.

Other career choices

Nearly all the women who have been successful on traditional terms within the legal profession have been exceptions to the rule. Many are exceptional professionally and personally. Their academic abilities, legal skills, hard work and sheer tenacity make them stand out in a profession which is otherwise inclined to overlook them because they are women.

Most women lawyers still have limited career choices compared with the choices enjoyed by men lawyers. Opportunities for employment, good work, promotions and partnerships are limited by assumptions about what women can do, might do or should do. Even where women lawyers are making positive steps, working outside private practice or outside the traditional firm structures, those steps can be traced back to the perception or knowledge that their opportunities were otherwise restricted.

Looking for jobs and promotions

Historically, legal employment for women lawyers was much easier to find outside a law firm. Women law graduates without family connections in the profession had little chance of obtaining a job inside a law firm. Instead they went out on their own 'devilling' for barristers or sole practitioners, or found employment in the law schools or in government departments.

Women lawyers have also avoided or left the firms because there were few if any prospects of promotion. When Shirley Smith was contemplating work options she intentionally 'avoided the discrimination ... of being overlooked for promotion or partnership, by never offering my services to a firm since my first employment'.[71] Olive Smuts-Kennedy also elected sole practice over a firm where she suspected she would 'end up in a backroom' and never be made partner.[72] Another woman lawyer who graduated in the 1950s recalled that it was 'impossible to obtain employment with prospects of partnership' so, along with many other women law graduates in this period she joined the public service.[73]

In surveys and studies since the 1970s, women lawyers have said repeatedly that their limited opportunities for promotion and partnership were instrumental to their decisions to leave employment in law firms. In 1975, Carolyn Henwood observed that: 'Many women have found it difficult to find partnerships and in the past have often been forced to become sole practitioners.'[74] In the 1981 Auckland study, seven of the fifteen women barristers and sole practitioners identified lack of partnership prospects as a reason for going into practice on their own account.[75] In 1982, women lawyers in Wellington were much more likely than men to mention lack of partnership prospects as the reason why they were in sole practice.[76] Fourteen women said their decision to go it alone was 'because they were women'. Another twenty-eight women thought they would have better opportunities as sole practitioners.[77] And still others decided to set up in practice in 'women's firms'.[78]

Women lawyers, like men lawyers, choose to leave private practice, make career changes or start their careers outside the traditional law firm path for a range of reasons. But, the one compelling factor that will influence women's decisions at some point in their careers and not men's will be gender related. When describing their career choices women lawyers and law graduates repeatedly refer to the lack of opportunities and the lack of prospects within mainstream law firms in particular. They look elsewhere because elsewhere offers the promise or at least the hope of equality.

Practising outside the traditional firms

In the 1990s, for women lawyers, the 'choice' to work outside the mainstream firms took on a restricted meaning. Of the 218 practitioners working outside a law firm in the 1992 national survey, men were more likely to be doing so than women: 75 percent of men working outside the firms had chosen this type of employment compared with 69 percent of the women.[79] Even then, women who said they had chosen their present type of employment, qualified their answer. One woman lawyer described her 'choice' in these terms: 'I left a large firm because I knew I'd never get any further. I'd started there as a Secretary. I was over qualified for the jobs then advertised so I decided to set up on my own. It was a choice in difficult circumstances.' A Wellington woman sole practitioner commented: 'It was a choice to become a sole practitioner but because no other partnerships in Wellington offered a way of practising law that I could create for myself—so not really a choice.'

Women lawyers' decisions to work outside the firms were influenced by their lack of prospects in the firms to a greater extent than men lawyers' decisions: 12 percent of women and 7 percent of men were working outside law firms because of lack of prospects.[80] At the same time, only 2 percent of the men barristers and sole practitioners attributed their decisions to go out on their own to poor partnership prospects.[81]

Greater risks in 'going it alone'

Some women lawyers leave firms and start out in practice on their own through no choice or from limited choices. These women are likely to be taking a greater risk than men lawyers who set up on their own 'when the time is right'. Women in this situation are more likely to forgo the 'right' amount of experience, the 'right' contacts in the profession, the 'right' reputation and the 'right' preparation. In effect, their decisions to set up in practice could start from negative rather a positive bases.

For this reason a number of women lawyers who branched out on their own at an early stage in their careers into sole practice or as barristers faced considerable difficulties getting clients and work. Their businesses built very slowly and not without some hardship to the women concerned. Their newness in the profession also meant they were easily isolated, knowing few practitioners and feeling unwelcome at law society functions and seminars. The experience of women in government and corporate work was similar. In 1989, the Auckland law society working party observed:

> There are an increasing number of women lawyers employed in both governmental and corporate areas of work. Many 'in-house' lawyers have

expressed a feeling of isolation from the profession and also within their own organisation.[82]

Being outside the firms did not necessarily mean an end to discrimination. Women sole practitioners and barristers have also experienced discrimination. In the 1981 Auckland law society survey, the perception of discrimination of women barristers and sole practitioners was higher than the average.[83] In the 1982 Wellington law society survey, many more women lawyers saw drawbacks in sole practice than in employment in law firms. Some thought client prejudice would work against them. Others saw a loss of work variety, support, income and the fewer chances of elevation to the Bench.[84] Women barristers and sole practitioners in the 1990s have difficulty securing good quality work outside the areas of law traditionally practised by women.[85]

Women wishing to set up their own firms or practices have also had to contend with discrimination from banks and other lending institutions. Women-only firms, for example, have encountered difficulties raising finance for their businesses. Law firm partners, Rowena Lewis and Sandy Callanan found the banks less than supportive when they approached them for a small business overdraft. Of the four banks they approached, only one took their application at face value. The others wanted to know their marital status and demanded guarantors.[86] The women-only accounting practice, Loudon Hough, several years later found their bank manager more supportive although he did ask if their husbands would be signatories on the practice bank account.[87] There is no reason to believe that this kind of discrimination has ceased. Research in 1991 found that New Zealand banks apply 'different and tougher criteria .. to the performance and potential of a woman as opposed to a man'. The researchers concluded that to obtain finance a woman 'has to be better to be equal'.[88]

Government: an obvious career move

Government departments have consistently employed women law graduates since the 1940s. For many women lawyers, government employment is an obvious career move.

The first woman lawyer admitted in Southland in 1942, Sheila Campbell Williams (née Macdonald), joined the Public Trust Office legal staff. Alison Pearce, admitted to the Bar in Wellington in 1951, joined the then Department of External Affairs.[89] The following year Alison Quentin-Baxter joined the Department of External Affairs after working as a law clerk at Hanna and Coates in Auckland.[90] Patricia Webb joined the legal section of the Department of Justice in 1951, ten years after her admission to the Bar.[91] Olive Smuts-Kennedy had a varied career, working as a law clerk in the Department of Maori Affairs, an editor at Butterworths, office solicitor in the Department of Health as well as several stints in sole practice.[92] Eileen O'Connor, who graduated with bachelors degrees in arts and law in 1953 and 1956 respectively, joined the Department of Justice as a legal officer in the Wellington Lands and Deeds Office in 1959.

When Margaret Vennell finished law school in 1958 she had considerably more difficulty getting a job in a law firm than her male colleagues did. She was told that she 'was too academic' and that there was no point in employing her because 'she would get married and leave'. When she did manage to find a job in a firm, she enrolled with one of the other staff solicitors for a masters degree. He was allowed time off to attend lectures but she was not. (He is now a Court of Appeal judge.) After one year in private practice, Vennell, with many women lawyers before her, joined the public service. She worked as a legal adviser in the Civil Aviation Department, the Ministry of Works and the Department of Justice until 1967 when she joined the staff at Auckland University.[93]

By 1964, when Judith Potter was finishing her law degree, women lawyers were expected to go into the public service. Potter recalls: 'I got a job in the Companies Office because I was told that if I wanted to practise law being a woman, I would almost certainly have to work for the Government. I accepted that because I knew no different.'[94] When Helen Melville began her job hunt in 1971 she did not apply to any law firms because she had no contacts in private practice nor was she aware that it was 'the done thing'. After being turned down for jobs by BP and New Zealand Steel, she tried 'the Government'. Without difficulty she was employed by the then State Advances Corporation.[95]

Even into the 1970s, Margaret Wilson explained: 'it was simply assumed that women law graduates would go into the government sector. It was clearly seen as second best.' But women lawyers at about this time, she said, started to expect the same opportunities as the men. In her year, none of the six women did in fact go into government.[96]

In the 1990s large numbers of women lawyers continue to work in government. Between 40 and 50 percent of legally qualified employees in government agencies in 1993 were women.[97]

Better prospects

Compared with the private sector, women lawyers employed in the public sector could do well. The majority obtained high positions several decades before women became partners in mainstream law firms or members of law society councils. Alison Pearce, for example, served as a New Zealand consul in San Francisco and Rome; Alison Quentin-Baxter headed the legal division of the Department of External Affairs, was First Secretary at the New Zealand Embassy in Washington DC, represented New Zealand at meetings of the United Nations General Assembly and was Director of the Law Commission from 1987 until her retirement in 1995.[98] Patricia

Webb was appointed the Chief Legal Officer in the Department of Justice and, like Quentin-Baxter, represented New Zealand at the United Nations. Janice Lowe and Margaret Nixon would also hold positions of authority in the Law Reform Division of the Department of Justice. Eileen O'Connor achieved a long string of firsts being appointed New Zealand's first woman district land registrar in Blenheim, assistant land registrar in Wellington, registrar in Nelson, registrar in Wellington and finally, district land registrar in Auckland in 1988.

In the 1960s, unlike law firms, the public sector was inclined to publicise promotions of women. When O'Connor was appointed district land registrar in Blenheim in 1962, the then Secretary of Justice, J L Robson, told a newspaper interviewer: 'I have always strongly maintained my policy of promotion on merit irrespective of sex.' Again, fifteen years later, on her appointment as the first woman district land registrar in Wellington, the Registrar General of Land L McClelland was quoted as saying he was 'pleased to see such occupations attracting women'.[99]

Discrimination in other quarters

While employment and promotions for women lawyers may have been more available outside the law firms, freedom from discrimination did not necessarily follow.

Before the late 1970s, the public service openly and legally discriminated against women employees.[100] Alison Quentin-Baxter's career, for example, was punctuated with advice that she would not be eligible for employment or considered for advancement because she was a woman. She recalls: 'I was told in 1952 at the outset of my foreign service career that, as a woman, I could not expect promotion beyond a certain point.' In fact this did not prove to be the case as she moved ahead of some of her male contemporaries, becoming head of the department's legal division. In 1961 on her marriage to a fellow foreign service officer, she was required to resign because the Department of External Affairs at that time would not grant leave to women wanting to accompany their husbands on overseas postings. One of her bosses mentioned, semi-jokingly, that she had got married just in time before she 'became a serious competitive threat to the men'.[101]

Discrimination also occurred in the corporate sector. In 1964, when Quentin-Baxter applied for a position at General Motors she was told that although she was 'obviously qualified for the job, as a woman [she] was not suitable'. The sad thing, she adds, was that at the time she was not even surprised.

The Department of Justice was also hesitant to give equal opportunities to women employees. Carolyn Henwood (later Judge Henwood) joined the department in 1965. Working in the High Court, Henwood recalled: 'we were not allowed to take the court—act as registrars—the men always did that, even though we were better qualified academically.'[102] After several years of working in the courts, Henwood applied for permission to study law at the university and to continue in her job. The department's response was 'no', without an explanation. Although the State Services Commission later reversed the decision, Henwood was 'disappointed and frustrated'. She successfully applied for a law clerk job with Wellington law firm Buddle Anderson Kent with the time off she needed to study law.[103]

Of the women lawyers in the state sector in 1982, Hannah Sargisson found that a small number were in top jobs. Nearly 90 percent of women legal officers had the lowest grading. A similar employment pattern was discovered in the English and Australian public services. Legally qualified women were disproportionately working for the government and were more likely than men to be employed in low status positions.[104]

Women lawyers also experienced discrimination while working in the law schools. In 1969, after four years' experience in law lecturing, Quentin-Baxter was turned down for a senior lectureship position at Victoria University: 'the reason being, I was told, that as my husband had just been appointed a Professor, I would stay anyway, and it was decided that the promotion should go to someone the University might otherwise lose.' She resigned the next day.[105]

Margaret Vennell, who joined the staff at the University of Auckland law school, was also treated as expendable. She was employed on an annual contract without tenure from 1967 to 1976 despite her extensive publishing record and recognised expertise in tort law and accident compensation law. Her contract status meant she did not qualify for study leave, the superannuation scheme or other benefits available to tenured staff. In 1977, she was finally appointed a senior lecturer in law, and in 1992 she was appointed the University of Auckland's first woman associate professor of law.[106]

Nadja Tollemache, who also lectured at the Auckland law school during this period, points out that women academics were overlooked for promotions. In her view, 'standards and expectations were notched up when women applied for positions, especially at the professorial level'.[107] Dr Julie Maxton was appointed the Auckland law school's first woman professor in August 1993. Professor Michael Taggart, then the dean, said that Maxton 'provided an excellent role model for other women teaching law and for the 55% of law students who are women'.[108]

Government addresses workplace discrimination

As an employer the government, has developed its workplace policies and has provided various legal frameworks to address discrimination against women and minority groups.

In 1962, a new State Services Act provided that appointments and promotions in the public service should be determined solely on merit. By 1965, equal pay was fully implemented in the state service. In 1973, flexible working hours were introduced on a trial basis. Finally in 1978, the public sector introduced a 'package of measures' to eliminate discrimination to promote equal employment opportunities (EEO) for women and men. Included in the package were provisions for maternity leave, re-entry after an absence due to child care, paternity leave, flexible working hours, part-time work, appointments and promotions on merit and sexual harassment procedures.[109]

In the 1982 Wellington survey, men and women lawyers perceived the government as a better employer for women. One lawyer observed: 'discrimination is not apparent in Government legal circles. Several senior positions are held by women except in the Crown Law Office.'[110]

Virtually all the Wellington lawyers who considered the government a better employer of women lawyers in the 1982 survey attributed this to the fact that government was required to adhere to a stated EEO programme and, in some cases, generous maternity leave and flexible work hours. One woman said that the public sector 'offers excellent prospects for women ... If private firms could follow Government's attitude in the employment of women, I believe women could achieve a great deal towards true equality.'[111]

The 1987 New Zealand Law Society survey found women in sole practice, corporations and government work were much more likely than their private sector colleagues to be in management roles.[112]

In 1988, the agreement by public sector employers to implement EEO was translated into law in the State Sector Act 1988. Under that Act, chief executives of government departments became personally responsible for the implementation of and compliance with employment equity objectives as agreed each year in consultation with staff and the State Services Commission's Equal Employment Opportunities Unit. State-owned enterprises likewise were required by law to be 'good employers' which meant they were required to operate EEO programmes.[113] By 1994 most laws relating to government bodies or agencies contained separate legislative requirements to implement employment equity programmes.[114]

In recognition of these advances since the 1980s, lawyers have continued to consider the government a 'better employer' for women lawyers.

In the 1992 survey, lawyers of both sexes said that the public sector EEO policies and practices were superior to those of law firms. One woman lawyer with three years' experience—two in a firm and one in a government department—observed: 'Government EEO provisions are a step ahead of the private sector.' Wellington lawyer Joy Liddicoat, when comparing her experiences in private practice and in government, observed: 'on the whole I found the government working environment much less *overtly* hostile to women, including feminist women.' The positive working environment was aided by the implementation of EEO and also the willingness of others to address women as 'Ms' rather than 'Miss' and to adopt gender-neutral language.[115]

To some extent, the rosy view of the public sector taken by private sector lawyers is exaggerated by the belief that law firms are such bad employers. Certainly, the EEO policies and practices in government agencies and state-owned enterprises are less than perfect. The 1992 annual report of the State Services Commission showed that a significant number of government departments were failing to meet their EEO objectives. While several departments had met all the requirements others showed 'non-compliance, incompetence in planning and reporting, and lack of commitment to EEO'.[116]

A different culture

While women lawyers have elected to leave mainstream private practice because of limited opportunities, they have also made more positive choices to work outside male dominated firms in search of a different culture. Women lawyers who have joined the public sector, academia, or set up in practice on their own or in firms with other women lawyers often refer to their desire to create a different culture to that prevailing in the traditional law firms. Equal employment opportunities and family-friendly policies and practices are commonly part of that new culture, which allows these women to develop new ways of practising law.

Designing new models for legal business

Women sole practitioners emphasise the shift from a male dominated culture. Kathryn Lucas, a Dunedin sole practitioner, set up on her own in 1991 'because [the] traditional model of partnership seemed to be limiting in the way a practice is set up and run and in the ways of dealing with clients and the value put on "people orientated" aspects of law'. Similarly, Anita Chan, who entered sole practice in 1990 has said that the 'male culture' which prevails in established firms does not provide an optimally stimulating and satisfying work environment or career base for her as a woman. Annis Cook described her decision in 1987 to become a sole practitioner as allowing her 'to gain control of own female environment without the restraint of traditional, established legal practices'. The advantages, according to Cook, include being able to work with women 'who understand team work' and to control the type of law practised.[117]

The physical environment of women lawyers' own businesses also express new styles. These women tend to choose their own decor rather than paying consultants and tend toward the unconventional as law firms go. Victoria Chambers, where Judith Medlicott, Kate Weatherall and Sue Bathgate practised in the 1980s, was painted shocking pink. Leigh Rodgers and Margaret Powell, based in Wellington, intentionally designed their offices to be informal and non-threatening.

Often situated outside the central business district in suburban shopping centres, women-only law practices are more accessible to the public than city firms. This suits many women only law firms as they do not target their services to large corporate clients based in the city centres. As Rodgers and Powell have observed, many people are turning away from the high fees and high overheads of the corporate law firms. As a result, businesses like theirs are prospering.[118]

Women-only firms make access by their clients a priority. Lewis and Callanan intentionally chose a ground floor office to ensure easy access for their elderly clients. Rodgers and Powell chose to be in the heart of the Wellington Cuba Street retail and business community so they were easily reached by clients. Hanley, Marks and Morton had a policy of being open on Saturday mornings with the supermarket. Hanneke Morton has said: 'The law is just a service like everything else . . . Over the years, it's been put into the realm of something else. We'd like to put it back to being a service.'[119]

Wider range of legal work

Women lawyers in their own practices can take on legal work they might not be offered in a traditional law firm. Lewis and Callanan, for example, could 'develop the business into areas that interested them' and that included doing commercial law and civil litigation.[120] This does not mean that women-only firms abandon family law and conveyancing or legal aid work. To the contrary, many of these firms specialise in the 'traditional' fields of women lawyers' work but, in their own firms, there is no problem with this work being treated and paid as second rate.[121]

Some women-only firms do work predominantly for women clients. Linda Kaye who practised in the Auckland suburb of Mount Eden from 1984 to 1993 and employed only women solicitors had predominantly women family law clients.[122] Wellington lawyers, Rodgers and Powell, do a lot of work with the local women's refuge and the community law centre and as a result have a large number of legally aided women clients. Their practice 'caters for people who probably wouldn't get their legal needs met elsewhere'.[123] The Rotorua firm run by partners Jan Walker and Claudia Elliot has mostly women clients and is also attracting an increasing number of lesbian and gay clients. Lesbian and gay clients may assume rightly that women lawyers will be more empathetic given their shared experience of being on the outside.

Although some women-only firms have large female client bases, they are also attracting an increasing number of men clients. The reason for this, according to the lawyers, is that women professionals are seen as less threatening to men clients. Deb Hurdle believes there are just as many men who like to have women solicitors as there are women. Hurdle and Nicola Mathers have a cross-section of both sexes in their client base.[124] Rodgers and Powell have observed that as with many women clients men are attracted by the less intimidating atmosphere provided in their offices. Others have pointed out that men clients feel they can ask questions of women professionals without being treated as ignorant or losing face.[125]

Women in sole practices, working as barristers and in their own firms commonly are involved in women's issues and women's groups. Lewis and Callanan, for example, take active roles in the Women in Management Network and the Auckland Chamber of Commerce Business Women's Network. They have actively lobbied government in relation to women's issues and have assisted with submissions on childcare policy. Partners at King Alofivae Malosi say they are 'EEO in practice' and are firmly committed to playing a part in issues concerning women and Maori and Pacific Islands people.[126]

Being different

How to position the firm—from the perspective of the profession and clients—has posed some difficulty for women-only firms. When Mathers and Hurdle set up the first women-only law firm in Wellington in 1989 they decided to market the firm using their full names and therefore to position themselves as an all-women team from the outset. Their intention was to notify all prospective clients that the partnership comprised two women but at the same time they were aware that 'a lot of people thought we were feminists chasing women clients'.[127] In 1993 in Auckland, Niamh McMahon and Sheila McCabe were equally conscious of the impression they had an aggressive lawyering style. McCabe pointed out: 'We may be perceived in legal circles as a couple of stroppy Irishwomen ... but that requires no apology. We simply give the best advice we can in a manner that is professional and in the best interests of our clients.'[128]

Women-only firms generally try to adopt client communication styles that set them apart from many old style legal practices. Lewis and Callanan, for example, say they 'put more emphasis on enlightening clients and including them in the decision-making process.'[129] Other women partners in these firms say they are keen to demystify the law—to make clients understand what is going on.[130]

McCabe believes that being '[f]reed from a traditional partnership structure' has allowed her and partner McMahon to 'develop a true team approach to providing the best possible counsel to our clients'.[131] Powell and Rodgers say that 'being an all-women firm probably makes them less adversarial and more willing to mediate'.[132]

In addition to choosing a partner for their complementary legal skills, most women who have started all-women firms have looked for someone with compatible lifestyle and work goals. When Callanan and Lewis were looking for a partner, neither intentionally considered that the partner had to be a woman. But as Callanan pointed out it may have been a subconscious factor. She 'was looking for someone in the same position as me and by default that would be a woman'.[133] Jan Walker who started the first women-only partnership in Rotorua said that partner Claudia Elliot was the obvious choice. They both did lots of family law work and shared the same philosophical views about women in the profession and women's issues. In addition, Elliot was one the few lawyers she could get hold of when working at night.[134]

This does not mean that women-only firms are full of clones. Irishwomen McMahon and McCabe point out that their backgrounds are very different. In fact they say that 'it is their differences that have bonded them together and provided strength to their legal practice'.[135] When they admitted their new partner, family lawyer Gabrielle Wagner, in 1996, they wrote to clients and friends saying: "We have asked Gabrielle to change her name. We believe McWagner or Murphy would be appropriate. Watch this space!"[136]

Combining families and careers

The one choice which women in the legal profession have been making consistently is to combine their family commitments and their careers. Tired of asking and waiting for change and tired of struggling with the limited models of working within established law firms, women have been carving out new paths and new ways of working.

Women have consistently questioned the culture which requires career primacy rather than career and family compatibility. In 1986, Helen Melrose described the culture as:

> a very structured set-up where the main goal is to be the best, meaning the hardest working, the highest fees, the most perfect law(yer), the longest hours—five twelve hour days and a day at the weekend . . . It's an outstanding example of what the maleness of it is all about.[137]

Similarly, in all the studies and surveys, women lawyers have repeatedly said that the requirement to sacrifice all for the firm or the job is unreasonable, unhealthy and unnecessary.

In the 1992 national survey, ninety-seven women described their desire to balance their careers and their family commitments.[138] Typical comments included:

> The reason most women don't progress to partnership is that career isn't central to their self-esteem the way it is for men—a job/career is not always the 'be-all-and-end-all' to their existence, so that the sacrifices to be a partner in a law firm often don't seem worth it for the reward.

> [W]omen, whether they have kids or not, generally don't want to commit their whole lives in that way. They want more balance.

> I feel to achieve the highest goals in the legal profession you must 'love' the law. I put my family priorities clearly before loving the law.

Just as Olive Smuts-Kennedy and Shirley Smith, among others, opted to set up in sole practices so that they could combine careers and families, women lawyers are continuing to do so in the 1990s.

In the 1992 survey, one Auckland woman who had been in sole practice for three years explained:

> I chose to set up sole practice because law firms could not/would not provide the flexibility required to meet the sometime uncertainties of family commitment. The 'down' side is isolation and the total weight of responsibility. But meeting family obligations is worth it.

In the 1993 survey of women sole practitioners in Dunedin, the majority mentioned the lure of greater flexibility as one of the main reasons for going out on their own. Seven of the ten women concerned had children and said flexibility was needed to enable them to meet their family commitments.[139] (Figure 11)

Lifestyle flexibility is also a primary motivation for women who set up their own firms. Lewis and Callanan point out that working with a woman partner makes it easier to balance family life and career because they are not made to feel guilty about spending time with their families. In their view:

> what counts is the quality of the work, not the hours. Focusing on results and having the flexibility to work at home when necessary removes the pressure to keep up appearances and makes it easier to keep the partnerships equal.[140]

The objective for most women sole practitioners and women-only law firms is to successfully juggle their families and careers. There are similarities in the strategies adopted to achieve this aim. The partners in these firms seem to work together in a more cooperative manner than partners in larger and traditional firms. They work from home as required and there is no compunction about taking a baby or pre-schooler into the office. At King Alofivae Malosi an extra office is set aside as a creche, with one of the two secretaries doubling as a nanny when required.[141]

Figure 11

Dunedin women sole practitioners and children, 1993

Adults back row from right: Kam Niak, Carla Papahadjis and Jane Wilson; front row from right: Annis Cook and Anita Chan.

This photograph of some Dunedin women sole practitioners and their children was previously published in *LawTalk*, no 402, October 1993, 37. It has been reproduced with the permission of the New Zealand Law Society.

Unlike many traditional law firms, Hurdle and Mathers prepared their budgets and time-recording estimates to accommodate what they considered to be acceptable levels of holidays and paid working hours. In the majority of law firms, holidays and hours of work are dictated by financial goals—not the other way around. 'Friends, families and other interests,' said Hurdle, 'are equally important and should not be neglected simply in search of the dollar.'[142]

Doing 'useful' work: government and academia

The EEO programmes adopted by government and academic employers also offer women lawyers a way of balancing families and careers. In addition, women lawyers who work in government or academia commonly refer to the desire to 'do something useful' when explaining their reasons for working outside the private sector. Government departments and universities, unlike law firms, are less driven by commercial imperatives. While cost-efficiency is encouraged, time sheets and client budgets are replaced with ministerial, Cabinet or teaching deadlines. For some women lawyers who were concerned with the quality of service they were able to provide to their women clients when in private practice, this less fee and time conscious environment can be more palatable. Abel and Lewis, in their international study of lawyers, noted: 'In both common and civil law worlds, women appear to prefer ... the public sector over the private (because of its greater universalism).'[143]

In many instances, women lawyers in the public sector and academia have applied their legal knowledge and skills to the benefit for women in general. Certainly, New Zealand women legal academics and law officers in government agencies have long traditions of working on laws and policies affecting women.

There is a tendency, particularly among lawyers, to perceive women's interest in public sector work and commitment to advancing the position of women as being motivated by altruism or high ideals. Employment in government agencies has traditionally been viewed as 'service to the nation' and, similarly, women's interest in concentrating on women's issues as being driven by empathy for the underdog. Instead, it may be more accurate to view this work as feminist work—deliberately undertaken in organisations such as government and academia where change is more likely—or as remunerated work which offers better prospects for career advancement.

Conclusion

Just as the methods used to define merit and allocate opportunities are gender biased, the notion of choice is equally gender skewed. Choice presupposes options and opportunities—things women lawyers are less likely to enjoy. Women lawyers not only have a narrower range of 'choices' than men lawyers; the quality of the choices they do have are also limited.

Women lawyers are voting with their feet; but this should not be confused with free choice. The idea that women lawyers have ultimate control over their career directions is not borne out by the evidence. To the contrary, only a minority of women lawyers will get what they choose, that is: to enjoy the same career opportunities as men.

With regard to partnerships and the judiciary, in particular, it is clear that women lawyers' career preferences are being frustrated. Some, however, are refusing to be beaten. Women lawyers are developing new models of legal business, finding innovative ways to balance family and career commitments, and using their skills to advance women's status in New Zealand society.

Chapter Eleven

Sexual Harassment

Although 'sexual harassment' did not exist as a concept before the early 1960s, women law students' and women lawyers' sexuality was certainly a subject of discussion. Male politicians and lawyers in the late 1800s expressed concerns that the entry of women into law offices would result in unnecessary 'flutter and flirtation'. They thought that women barristers would charm judges and juries with their physical presence. One solution proposed was for law firms to employ only plain and uninviting women lawyers. No one suggested that the men could change their behaviour.

In the 1950s, when more women were in practice, 'blue jokes' were being told at Bar dinners and law students' functions. Women present at these events generally considered the behaviour objectionable. However, the majority of women who practised law from the 1950s to the 1960s pointed out that they did not experience unwanted sexual attention during their careers. The few who said they did, added that it was nothing they could not cope with. One woman, for example, described an experience in her first job where one of her bosses chased her around a table a few times but, she pointed out, he did not resent the fact that she refused his overtures. She did not complain because she felt she could cope and, in any case, was moved to other duties eventually.

A number of women lawyers noted that they did receive compliments from colleagues. For example, Nadja Tollemache, who was admitted to the Bar in 1960, recalled that male colleagues were very gentlemanly—it was only 'the odd judge' at social parties who made comments which, she thought, were 'probably intended to be "gallant" '. In this context, there was no need to seek assistance in dealing with the attention. She simply handled it by herself.

However, since the 1970s, at the same time that more women entered the law schools and the workforce, social expectations about interactions between women and men changed. Women lawyers, exposed to the new ideas about women's rights to control their bodies and their sexuality, were more inclined to be suspicious of or object to behaviour that emphasised their physical attributes. They were more likely to pride themselves on their academic ability, professional skills and expertise than on their hairstyles or clothing. Compliments about beauty or clothing seemed inappropriate and irrelevant and raised concerns about the intentions of the person commenting.

Despite the changing social climate, harassment of women law students still occurred. At a law lecture at Canterbury University in the early 1970s, when one of the female students came in late, the lecturer stopped what he was doing, and very obviously drew the other students' attention to her. When she sat down with great embarrassment, he said with sexual overtones: 'Oh, I've lost my concentration now.' In response the male students began to call out: 'We lose our attention too when she comes into the room.' In reply, the lecturer invited the men students to 'Come and see me afterwards about a cold shower'. Another woman law student at Canterbury University was experiencing constant comments of a sexual nature in a tutorial where she was the only woman. One day a comment was made by a lecturer about what she was wearing and she was invited to get on to the table and parade in front of the men so they could eye her clothing.

Women appearing in court were also subjected to unwarranted sexual attention. When Silvia Cartwright made her first appearance as counsel in the High Court, she encountered the premeditated antics of the Crown Prosecutor who, she said:

> decided to make something of an occasion out of this particular event. There was a jury in the Court waiting for my appeal to finish so they could resume a jury trial. Within the sight of the jury, but so the Judge could not see, of course, the Crown Prosecutor drew this large picture out of his bar jacket and held it up ... It depicted a woman barrister with the correct wig and gown on, except the gown stopped at thigh level.[1]

In July 1985, sexual harassment in the male dominated legal system, possibly for the first time, was placed under scrutiny in the public arena. The year before, an Auckland woman lawyer seeking to interview a client at Christchurch Police Station had reluctantly agreed to be strip-searched. After the search she was shocked to find that a male police officer had been watching her undressing on a series of monitors in another room. On the advice of a senior colleague she 'let the whole thing drop and [did] not make a fuss about it'. Almost a year later, she was approached during a court recess by two prominent Auckland men lawyers who told her they had seen a video of her being strip-searched. They claimed that there were four copies of the video; the one they had watched was at the Crown Law Office premises in Auckland.[2]

The woman lawyer, despite her colleague's threats of adverse publicity, immediately complained to the Minister of Justice, the Minister of Police and to the New Zealand Law Society (NZLS). She demanded that the videos be located and destroyed. Although the Auckland lawyers' detailed account accurately described the Christchurch strip-search, the police denied there was any substance to the report. According to Deputy Assistant Commissioner of Police John Jamieson there was no capacity to videotape at the Christchurch Police Station: 'this was just a joke between two lawyers.' Presumably, he was referring to the men.[3]

Research reveals widespread problem

From 1981, research on the status of women in the legal profession demonstrated that sexual harassment was common. Where, previously, there had been only anecdotes of harassment, there was now evidence of it being widespread.[4]

The first study, by the Auckland District Law Society in 1981, found that 42 percent of women lawyers surveyed said they had been 'subjected to discrimination in the form of belittling or embarrassing talk or conduct'.[5] The Wellington District Law Society survey the following year found that 23 percent of women surveyed had experienced sexual harassment; 54 percent had experienced derogatory or belittling comments directed at them personally; and 70 percent had been subjected to belittling talk or derogatory remarks directed at women in general. In all types of harassment, colleagues and employers were the main culprits.[6]

In the 1987 Auckland study, over half the women practitioners surveyed had experienced some form of sex-related harassment in the course of their employment or practice. For example 54 percent of women had personally experienced derogatory remarks from partners and 51 percent had this experience from colleagues.[7] Over 10 percent of women said they were experiencing offensive sexual talk from clients and partners. Another 8 percent of women, mainly employed solicitors, were being subjected to unwanted sexual advances from clients at the time of the survey.[8]

During this time, sexism also occurred in social interactions between men and women lawyers. In Wellington in 1982, women lawyers referred to the 'maleness' of law society functions as a deterrent to them attending.[9] In Auckland in 1987, the law society working party reported that social interaction between the sexes was still occurring largely on male terms. Men gathered in clubs or bars where women could not attend or did not wish to attend. Social talk was considered 'exclusionary', centring on 'stereotypically male pursuits' such as rugby and cricket and involving coarse, sexist jokes. Women remained outside the social circle 'unless they participated as "one of the boys" '.[10]

In 1988, a similar conclusion was reached by Stephanie Knight in her research on the use of alcohol by Auckland women lawyers. She found that the women were cautious drinkers, constantly striking a balance between being accepted as 'one of the boys' and maintaining respect.

They had little scope for letting their guard down, particularly when drinking with colleagues.[11]

Sexual misconduct toward clients

Male lawyers have also sexually harassed women clients and other women. In 1985, a South Island practitioner sexually abused a teenage babysitter in his home. The parents of the complainant did not lay a complaint with the police, instead asking the local district law society to investigate. The district council referred the charges to the New Zealand Law Practitioners Disciplinary Tribunal which found the practitioner guilty of conduct unbecoming a barrister or solicitor.

Medical reports, which were 'not detailed', did 'indicate that [the practitioner] acted at a time when he was suffering a medical condition' which enabled the tribunal 'to accept the submission that [the practitioner] was not aware of what he did'. For this reason the tribunal determined it would be inappropriate to impose a censure or a fine. The practitioner instead was ordered to pay $5,506, being the costs and expenses incurred by the district law society and the NZLS in hearing the complaint.[12]

In January 1992, two Auckland women's health groups decided to make a video about sexual abuse by lawyers, doctors, counsellors, and clergymen. According to the groups' spokesperson, Jenny Chilcott, most unacceptable behaviour 'involved male professionals and women seeking help in difficult circumstances, such as marriage breakdown'. Professional organisations, she said, tended to ignore the ethical question of sexual relationships with clients: 'Someone in the Law Society said what a lawyer does in their own time is their own business . . . It's not seen as an issue at all.'[13]

Graham Weir, then executive director of the Auckland law society, was asked to respond. He said he was unaware of any complaints of sexual misconduct by lawyers nor had he considered whether it was unethical for a lawyer to continue acting for a client with whom he had a sexual relationship:

> I imagine a good many lawyers had met their future wives and husbands when they came through the door as clients and it would be a sorry state of affairs if we nipped off any burgeoning romance at the outside on the grounds it was unethical.

The society, however, would consider disciplinary action if the client could prove she or he had been disadvantaged in some way.[14]

According to the Human Rights Commission's proceedings commissioner, the commission had received an increasing number of inquiries about sexual misconduct by professionals (including lawyers) but had received few formal complaints. The commission could only act if the misconduct constituted sexual harassment.[15] The police response to client sexual abuse was also the subject of media attention. In September 1992, the *Dominion* reported that a Christchurch woman had been trying for almost seven years to lay a rape complaint against her lawyer. She approached the police who reportedly told her: 'You are not going to get anywhere with this.' She made three attempts to take the matter to the law society. Each one was turned down.[16]

In May 1992, the Human Rights Commission investigated six complaints by women who claimed sexual harassment by male professionals.[17] The New Zealand Medical Council decided to host an interdisciplinary seminar on the problem and, following the seminar, passed an ethical rule prohibiting sexual relations between practitioners and clients.[18] The NZLS Ethics Committee decided that a proactive approach was needed—although there was doubt as to whether client sexual harassment occurred in the legal profession, an ethical rule was appropriate.[19]

Finally, the NZLS council agreed to adopt a new commentary to the ethical rule 1.01, effective from 1 October 1993: 'The relationship of confidence and trust may be breached where a practitioner and client enter into a sexual relationship.' The explanatory notes from the Ethics Committee advise:

> It is fair to say that there have been no instances of sexual abuse in professional relationships within the profession in New Zealand that have come formally to the attention of the New Zealand Law Society. Nor have any disciplinary proceedings been based on instances of abuse.

It seems the committee considered that the media reports were not formal reports and was unaware of the 1985 case involving the babysitter. A member of the committee, however, was aware of instances of victimisation by practitioners in New Zealand, particularly in the family law area.[20]

Family law would provide the context for the first publicised case of client sexual abuse. In September 1995, the New Zealand Law Practitioners Disciplinary Tribunal met in Wellington to hear a charge of professional misconduct against a South Island family law practitioner who, over a period of weeks, had entered into a personal relationship with a client which included sexual contact at the practitioner's office and at the complainant's home. Although the contact was consensual, the tribunal said that this consent 'properly needed to be placed in the context of the matrimonial issues on which the practitioner was representing the complainant; the complainant was vulnerable and the practitioner abused his position of trust'. The practitioner pleaded guilty to the charge, was censured, fined $2,000, ordered to pay compensation of $1,938 to the complainant for her legal costs, and ordered to pay a total of $15,000 to the district and New Zealand law societies.[21]

Harassment of women lawyers

By the early 1990s, an estimated one-third of the women lawyers in practice and half the women judges have experienced some form of sexual harassment during their careers.[22]

Men lawyers have also been subjected to sexual harassment. Of the 685 men surveyed in 1992, 6 percent had experienced sexual remarks and sexual innuendo; 4 percent had experienced deliberate touching; 3 percent had experienced unwanted advances; and a striking 19 percent had experienced misuse of position or power.[23] However, women lawyers are much more likely to have personally experienced sexual harassment.

From the comments made by women lawyers, and especially younger women practitioners, harassment is very much a current reality.[24] The most common form of harassment recorded in the 1992 national survey were sexual remarks and sexual innuendo: 38 percent of women lawyers had personal experience of this type of harassment. Over a quarter had experiences where another person misused their position or power; 18 percent had experienced unwanted advances; 16 percent had experienced deliberate touching; and 5 percent had either received requests for sexual favours or been told that a promotion depended on a sexual favour.[25]

Sexual harassment in the early 1990s was experienced by women lawyers regardless of their position in the profession or type of workplace. Women lawyers were subjected to harassment regardless of their age and women partners were as likely as women employees to have been exposed to harassment.[26]

Status, however, may reduce exposure to harassment for women who are appointed to the Bench. Before appointment, six of the ten women judges surveyed in 1993 had been subjected to harassment in the form of misuse of position or power, sexual remarks or innuendoes, unwanted advances, or being deliberately touched or brushed up against. After appointment, only two women judges had experienced harassment—in the form of sexual remarks and innuendo.[27]

As in the 1980s, male lawyers were the group largely responsible for sexual harassment of women lawyers and women judges. Partners and employers were most likely to harass women lawyers, being mentioned by 49 percent of women lawyers surveyed in 1992. Second to bosses were other colleagues, mentioned by 29 percent of women, and then clients, mentioned by 17 percent of women. Staff solicitors, who are in most cases the workmates of women lawyers, were said to be responsible for only 14 percent of sexual harassment.[28] The pattern was the same for women judges. Harassment had been from partners or employers and from other colleagues, but also from other judges. In no instances had women judges been harassed by court staff, clients, offenders, witnesses, plaintiffs or defendants.[29]

Men lawyers and judges, it seems, do not inadvertently harass women lawyers and judges. Of the six women judges who had experienced sexual harassment none said that the behaviour was completely unintentional: three said there was a mixture of intentional and unintentional behaviours, while two said it was simply intentional.[30] This corresponded with women lawyers' experiences of discrimination in general.[31]

Sexism is not confined to the office or to social interaction between colleagues. According to women judges surveyed in 1993, it also features in courtrooms. Seven of the ten judges surveyed had experienced inappropriate or disrespectful comments or behaviour on account of their sex in the courtroom. For three of the judges this occurred while they were on the Bench. Another four judges had encountered inappropriate comment or behaviour towards women counsel, women victims and other women in the courtroom. One judge explained: 'Women counsel appear to attract more derogatory comments than men and more comments on appearance.' Another referred to 'deliberate sexist jokes or barbs about women'.[32]

Again those responsible for this behaviour were more likely to be lawyers than lay people. All seven of the judges who had experienced gender bias pointed to practitioners or counsel as those responsible. Four women judges referred to other judges as the source of inappropriate gender-related comments or behaviour toward either women counsel, women victims, women judges, or other women in the courtroom.[33]

Again, as with the sexual harassment, in no instance was the behaviour unintentional. All of those who behaved or commented negatively toward or about women did so with an element of intention.[34]

Appearance and body shape

In the 1992 national survey, 43 percent of women lawyers said that appearance and body shape discrimination occurred in the profession. Twenty-six percent of the men lawyers surveyed agreed. As with most types of discrimination, women lawyers were much more likely to experience 'appearance and body shape' discrimination than men. Just over one hundred women lawyers had personally experienced this compared with fourteen men lawyers.[35]

What is appearance and body shape discrimination? In terms of the law, there is no such category of discrimination. However, inappropriate comments or behaviour relating to physical appearance may constitute harassment (or even discrimination) if the emphasis is on race, disability or age.[36] When explaining what is *not* appearance discrimination, women and men lawyers say that lawyers need to conform to a professional dress standard. Employers are particularly quick to comment that good appearance generally, regardless of gender, is an important factor in employment. For this reason, standards of appearance and body shape are said to relate to professionalism rather than sex.

It is apparent, however, that for many women lawyers there is an emphasis on their appearance unrelated to any professional standard. 'Appearance and body shape' are in fact criteria applied to women lawyers in a way that differs considerably from the criteria applied to their male colleagues. In some cases, what may have been referred to or dismissed as 'a personal compliment' in the past is now considered a form of discrimination. Where a comment is unwelcome or offensive, and is either repeated or of such a significant nature that it has a detrimental effect on an employee, a 'compliment' will be considered unlawful sexual harassment.[37]

There is also a discernible link between appearance and sexuality or race. The resulting 'impression' clearly influences whether some women lawyers get jobs, promotions and unwanted sexual attention.

With regard to employment prospects, the comment of one newly-admitted woman solicitor working in a large Wellington law firm was typical of many: 'How one looks seems to play a huge part in job prospects—especially for women. Comparing young female solicitors to young male solicitors, looks seem to play quite a large part. I cannot think of one overweight woman lawyer.' The same double standard was referred to by a city based woman solicitor who pointed out: 'While it is acceptable for male lawyers to be balding, grey and pot bellied, women are not forgiven any flaws in their appearance.' Another newly-admitted woman lawyer put the problem this way: 'If you are not a white middle class male you have problems! A fat middle-aged Tongan lesbian is highly unlikely to be hired by a mainstream big firm.'

Comments by employers confirm that women's 'appearance and body shape' are relevant factors at entry, promotion and partnership levels. A man partner in a small Wellington firm said: 'I think that women, homosexuals, plain, fat and short people are discriminated against. A short, plain, fat lesbian would have no chance of employment or partnership.' For other employers, however, women's appearance can strengthen their preference to recruit women lawyers. One man partner with twenty-five years' experience in the law said: 'I would rather employ a woman because they are better workers in my experience—they are also visually more appealing most times.'

Just as Ethel Benjamin was expected to charm judges and juries with her sexuality,[38] some women lawyers today are still said to owe their successes to their looks or their sexuality. When a newly admitted woman lawyer reported her success in court to a male partner in a large Auckland firm, he winked and asked if she had smiled at the judge. A senior partner in a provincial law firm, when speaking with a client, observed how a newly-employed woman lawyer was 'a beautiful woman' and that this was 'advantageous to the firm in that it enhanced [her] ability to create a client base'. Silvia Cartwright (later Justice Dame Cartwright) had a similar experience after obtaining her first law position. She recalls her first employer telling everyone, in humour, that she got the job over the other contenders because of her legs.[39]

Women lawyers notice that the women partners fit a certain physical mould. An Auckland woman lawyer in a large firm observed: 'The women partners here are attractive—most of the women lawyers are too. Not so of the men.' There have even been instances where failing to have the right 'look' has been a factor in women losing their jobs. An Otago woman lawyer commented in the 1992 survey on two instances where women lawyers had lost their jobs partly as a result of their appearance and body shape not being considered 'partnership material'.

Stereotypically 'beautiful' women lawyers are frustrated by the fact they repeatedly receive unwanted comments and attention. One solicitor who describes herself as 'young, blonde and small in stature' was repeatedly told by colleagues that she appeared to be 'a blonde bimbo'— until she opened her mouth. An Otago woman lawyer observed: 'If you're "pretty" you are either dumb or there for another purpose.' That other purpose is sex, or at least sexual gratification.

Many women lawyers are offended by comments about their appearance where the same comments would not be made to men. As one woman lawyer put it: 'Other solicitors and police comment on my appearance—they would not do so if I were a male lawyer.' An Otago-based woman lawyer recalled her experience where a High Court judge approached her at a function, tipped her under the chin and said: 'Let me have a close look at you.' Her physical appearance was the first point of scrutiny and from this examination she could be summed up. It is difficult to imagine a male High Court judge measuring a male lawyer in this same way.

Understandably some women lawyers feel they have had no choice but to play the part. An Auckland associate partner described how the appearance and body criteria were 'particularly insidious' because 'young female solicitors fall for appearances at all costs—which in turn reinforces "empty-headed" stereotypes'. The American television show *LA Law* is blamed for perpetuating the 'model' image required of women lawyers. According to a Christchurch-based solicitor: 'in the *LA Law* mould a woman lawyer must look under 30 and dress impeccably.' Failing to do so means she does not meet the standard.

Age is another appearance-related factor that affects women and men lawyers differently. Social convention holds that women's beauty dissipates with youth, hence the mass of beauty products to disguise aging and the wide range of plastic surgery options aimed at women so they can regain youthful looks. By comparison, maturity in men is much admired—particularly where those men are dispensing wisdom as in the legal profession. But for women who have been valued at least in part for their appearance, aging is a scourge to be avoided.

For many women lawyers, unwanted and inappropriate comments about their appearance and body rankle and undermine confidence. The clear implication is that women do not succeed in the profession on their merits or, even worse, that their sexuality is part and parcel of their professional merit.

Prohibited behaviour

Sexual harassment is a form of discrimination which has been unlawful since 1981. Although the Human Rights Commission Act 1977 did not specifically mention 'sexual harassment', it was open to argument that sexual harassment was a form of sex discrimination. In a 1981 case, the Equal Opportunities Tribunal determined that sexual harassment was a form of sex discrimination and accordingly was prohibited by the 1977 Act.[40]

The Act at that time contained no definition of sexual harassment, so, following the 1981 decision, the Human Rights Commission issued a policy statement, which read:

sexual harassment in employment generally occurs when there is verbal or physical conduct of a sexual nature by one person toward another; and:

the conduct is unwelcome and offensive and might reasonably be perceived as unwelcome and offensive; and

the conduct is of a serious nature or is persistent to the extent that it has a detrimental effect on the condition of an individual's employment, job performance or opportunities.[41]

To assist employees and employers to recognise sexual harassment, the commission provided examples of workplace sexual harassment. Sexual harassment, according to the commission, would include personally offensive verbal comments, sexual or smutty jokes, repeated comments or teasing about a person's alleged sexual activities or private life, persistent and unwelcome social invitations, and physical contact such as patting, pinching, touching or putting an arm around another person's body at work.[42]

The Labour Relations Act 1987 provided the first statutory definition of sexual harassment and gave employees the option of taking a personal grievance for harassment. These provisions were carried over into the

Employment Contracts Act 1991. Where an employer or employee requested sexual intercourse, sexual contact or other forms of sexual activity (containing an implied or overt promise of preferential treatment, or an implied or overt threat of detrimental treatment), sexual harassment will have occurred. In addition, the 1991 Act defined sexual harassment as including the use of words (written or spoken) of a sexual nature, or physical behaviour of a sexual nature which is unwelcome or offensive to an employee and is repeated or of such a significant nature that it has a detrimental effect on that employee's employment, job performance or job satisfaction.[43] Sexual harassment by clients is also covered by the Act in certain circumstances.[44]

The Human Rights Act 1993 contains a similar two-tiered definition of sexual harassment. First, it is unlawful for any person to request any other person to perform sexual acts where that request contains an implied or overt promise of preferential treatment or an implied or overt threat of detrimental treatment. Secondly, it is unlawful for any person to use language, material or behaviour of a sexual nature that is unwelcome or offensive to another person and is either repeated or of such a significant nature that it has a detrimental effect on that person. To be covered by the Human Rights Act, both types of sexual harassment must occur in relation to employment (including applying for a job, doing unpaid work, and participating in a partnership) or in relation to access to such things as goods, services, places, education and unions.[45]

But women don't complain

From 1981, sexual harassment has been clearly defined and has been prohibited by law—a fact arguably better known to women lawyers than any other group of women in society. Yet, in over two-thirds of the cases of harassment reported by women lawyers in the 1992 national survey, no action was taken.[46]

The examples of harassment reported in the majority of cases would meet the legal tests. Women and men lawyers relay stories of men partners and of other employers—hugging women solicitors instead of giving handshakes after the women have insisted that 'hugs' were inappropriate; debating the merits of women staff members' bodies and what they would like to do with them; referring to women support staff repeatedly as 'fannies'; making repeated requests for sexual favours; and, of one partner 'causing sheer hell' for a woman lawyer over a period of six months.

In addition, women lawyers have not hesitated for lack of avenues for complaint, as three formal avenues exist. First, sexual harassment is grounds for a personal grievance complaint under the Employment Contracts Act. Secondly, they could have made a complaint to the Human Rights Commission, requesting an investigation or (failing settlement) initiating proceedings before the Equal Opportunities Tribunal (now the Complaints Review Tribunal). Thirdly, women lawyers could have made a complaint to their district law societies on the basis that sexual harassment would be covered by the ethical rule on discrimination.

A number of firms also offered an in-house alternative: 21 percent of those surveyed in 1992 worked in law firms which had formal written procedures for dealing with sexual harassment. Regardless, the existence of the procedure did not affect the likelihood of action being taken.[47]

So, why don't women lawyers complain? The answer is found in the stories men and women lawyers have told.

Men's view

The problem is exaggerated

According to a considerable number of men lawyers, the problem of sexual harassment is exaggerated. Men in the profession are more inclined to dispute the existence, the extent and the seriousness of sexual harassment than of discrimination generally.[48]

Typical comments by men lawyers in the 1992 survey included:

I believe the issue of sexual harassment is now over-exaggerated. A lot of situations can be taken out of context.

In spite of *LA Law* I do not believe that this happens as often as is reported or represented but who am I to comment?

I have yet to see sexual or other harassment in a legal office. Maybe I lack sensitivity! Or are others overly sensitive?

When commenting on in-house harassment procedures, one man, a partner in an Auckland firm, commented: 'None needed. It does not happen.' Harassment, according to another male partner, is 'an unlikely event'.

Even when some men partners accept that harassment has occurred they point out that it was of little importance—even where more serious and direct types of harassment were involved. A senior partner in one Christchurch firm, which had no written sexual harassment procedure and no women professional staff, commented that the cases of harassment which had occurred in the firm were 'minor incidents with no appreciable effects on anyone to my knowledge'. The 'minor' incidents were recorded as unwanted advances and deliberate touching of a sexual nature by partners to women in the firm. A partner in a Wellington firm referred to sexual innuendo and unwanted advances by clients to women in his firm by saying: 'All occurrences were of a minor nature—usually humour in poor taste.'

In categorising sexual harassment as inconsequential, men lawyers are reinforcing the idea that women fabricate or exaggerate the problem. This reaction is not unique to women lawyers' complaints but is also a tactic used by lawyers in the courtroom.

Women judges have observed for example that some prosecutors and defence counsel 'speak down to women witnesses and belittle their experiences and reactions'.[49] One judge described the inappropriate comments made by defence counsel when dealing with women victims as including 'put down comments or suggestions that no harm was done or that the parties were reconciled therefore she was not serious in making a complaint in the first place'.[50] In effect this strategy belittles the complaint and the complainant. It is also reminiscent of the historical argument used to keep women out of the legal profession: that women cannot be trusted to tell the truth.

'But some women like the attention'

Many of the men who doubt or minimise the existence of sexual harassment have been in practice for more than twenty years. The social conventions with which this generation were most familiar dictated that men should notice and compliment women on their appearance and that women would be flattered by this attention. As Auckland barrister Kevin Ryan observed: 'males of my generation often think women are fair game.'[51] Younger men in the profession are also aware that the attitudes of older men lawyers, often senior partners, are problems in their firms. As a Wellington-based partner in a national firm pointed out: 'In the case of unintentional innuendo (which happens all too often) older partners, in particular, simply refuse to acknowledge the reality of the situation.'

That women lawyers consider their colleague's sexual attention as harassment has been well documented in surveys and studies since the early 1980s. Arguably men lawyers—of any generation—have been on notice long enough that sexual innuendo is inappropriate in the work context.

It's just a joke

Regardless of age, men lawyers have frequently responded to suggestions or complaints of sexual harassment by saying: 'It was just a joke.' This was the response, in 1985, from the Deputy Assistant Commissioner of Police John Jamieson, when the Auckland woman lawyer lodged a complaint with the Minister of Police, the Minister of Justice and the NZLS about the video-taping of her being strip-searched.[52]

Likewise when a Maori woman lawyer complained of racism and sexual harassment in 1990, her concerns were 'treated as a joke'. A woman lawyer in the 1992 survey commented: 'In a semi-social business setting a client persistently tried to kiss me. I told one of the partners and he laughed about it.' Another woman who complained of harassment by a colleague brought this to a manager's attention—he thought she was joking.

Women's realities

It's not a joke

The reality for women in the legal profession is that very few think that sexual harassment is a joke. Of the women who commented in the 1992 survey on the nature of the harassment experienced, less than 20 percent said that incidents were of a humorous nature and were not intended to offend.[53] For the majority, the behaviour is offensive hence the use of negative descriptions such as 'unwanted advances' and 'misuse of position or power'.

Even women lawyers who thought that what looked like sexual harassment could sometimes be genuine attempts at 'humour' had their doubts. They still referred to feeling uncomfortable about the 'underlying innuendo' or the times when the humour was 'carried away beyond normal conversational banter'. Even the few who thought that women can and do 'exploit our femaleness' by using sexual remarks in fun recognised they, in turn, were being exploited also. As one Auckland woman lawyer in a large national firm explained: 'The difficulty is often that it is not a particular instance of harassment but the creation of an environment where you feel that you shouldn't take these things too seriously—if it happens, it should be laughed off.'

Failing to see the 'humour' in the harassment opens women lawyers to criticism from their male colleagues. The most common criticisms are that they take things too seriously, they are not 'good sports' or they are radical feminists. One woman associate partner in a national firm who complained of sexual harassment was told that she was 'an uptight frigid feminist' while others point out that they refrained from complaining for fear of attracting a negative label such as 'strident feminist'.[54]

The overwhelmingly reality of the joke is that it is on women. By failing to take complaints of sexual harassment seriously, employers and partners have effectively silenced the problem. In every case where the incident of harassment was treated as a joke by the employer or the firm, no action was taken.

Complaining is career suicide

Another way in which potential sexual harassment complaints have been silenced in the legal profession has been the ensuring that the repercussions of complaints are, or are perceived to be, so severe that women lawyers cannot afford to take action. Ironically, it is the women who are in line for punishment rather than the perpetrators or the firms.

The publicly reported experience of the Auckland woman lawyer in the 1985 strip-search video case was instructive. When she told the two 'prominent male lawyers' who had volunteered to her that they had seen the video that she intended to make a complaint, one was reported to respond: 'I wouldn't even think of laying a complaint if I were you, because *Truth* will get hold of this. They'll probably get hold of the video as well, and then you'll be splashed in your underwear right across the front page of that newspaper.'[55] Whether or not the advice was genuine, the message was clear: she would be the loser if she made a complaint.

In the 1990s, women lawyers have received the message loud and clear that speaking out about sexual harassment is a bad career move. A woman barrister who had received requests for sexual favours and been told that her opportunities in a firm would depend on her providing sexual favours said, quite simply: 'It would be suicidal to speak out—both career wise and personally.' Women fear they will be forced out of the firm as a result of the complaint and this message is learnt fast. One newly-admitted Wellington woman lawyer wryly observed: 'You can't take action against a partner in your firm—realistically, you'd probably be fired. In this economic climate that's not a good idea.'

Lawyers are also expected to be ferocious in their defence if personally 'accused' of harassment. Frances Joychild, a legal adviser at the Human Rights Commission, pointed out that for women who are sexually harassed in law firms:

> there is an extreme fear of making a complaint . . . because the person they are complaining against is a lawyer who they believe will 'know every trick in the book' and will pull out every legal defence and create every legal obstacle to make it very difficult to establish their case.

For this reason, one woman employed by a barrister who approached the commission for help concluded she had no option but to leave her job. The daily harassment was making her ill but the barrister concerned was so aggressive on behalf of his clients, she feared 'he would be even more so if he was the accused'.[56]

The worse cases of sexual harassment are veiled in secrecy. Women lawyers, from personal experience or otherwise, know of severe incidents of sexual harassment but are sworn to confidentiality. One women lawyer, for example, commented: 'I know of a "rumoured" case where a woman partner was raped by the Office Manager. Eventually he was dismissed. She was told (effectively) to shut up about it.' A first year lawyer noted: 'Rumours abound about women receiving requests for sexual favours and stories of promotions depending on sexual favours. I don't know if these are true.'

There is no doubt that news about sexual harassment travels. For every type of harassment, women and men lawyers were well aware of it happening to others in their firms and in the profession generally.

Women, in particular, were conscious of the incidents where a promotion had been predicated on a sexual favour being provided: thirty-nine women lawyers in the 1992 national survey knew that this had happened to others but only eight women acknowledged it had happened to them. As the survey canvassed only those still in private practice it is conceivable that other women lawyers who experienced this type of harassment are now employed elsewhere.[57]

On some occasions, the action taken by an employer in response to sexual harassment has the unintended effect of damaging the woman lawyer's career. Women who have suffered sexual advances from supervising partners are sometimes relocated in the firm to another department or team. The objective is to minimise their contact with the harasser but, particularly in small or medium sized firms this relocation will also mean the women lawyers are now working outside their areas of expertise. Not only do they need to deal with the personal effects of the harassment, professionally they have to start again.

A heavy burden of proof

Although ignoring harassment is a common response, at the other extreme some men lawyers claim that any incidents of sexual harassment warrant severe legal penalties. The emphasis on the legal consequences suggests that to some extent male lawyers, and employers in particular, are mindful of the legal implications and want to be seen to be taking harassment seriously or perhaps are simply concerned at the potential for bad press.

Some lawyers, partly as a result of their training, have an excessive fixation with the legal implications of sexual harassment complaints. They often talk in terms of the 'guilty party' and 'proving' the harassment occurred. This has a strong deterrent effect on women who have experienced harassment and are concerned at the effect on them and their careers. Women comment that 'it is virtually impossible to "prove" harassment . . . therefore nothing is done'.

Treating harassment in a strictly legal sense can also act as a deterrent to accepting the validity of complaints. Some employers jump the gun and assume that harassment, where proved, warrants severe penalties. Employers make comments like: 'If real sexual harassment is proved to have occurred I would support severe action to remedy it' and 'I would regard harassment of a sexual nature as being a fireable offence.'

Assuming that only the severest penalties would be warranted is an indication that there is little appreciation that sexual harassment occurs in degrees and that the penalty must be matched to the problem.

Ineffective procedures

Predictably, the negative stance on sexual harassment taken by men lawyers surfaces in the procedures implemented within law firms. Since the mid-1980s, women lawyers have been faced with non-existent or ineffective procedures for handling sexual harassment complaints.

In the 1987 Auckland survey, over half of the women employee solicitors were not aware of any avenue for dealing with sexual harassment problems or did not think those avenues were adequate. The size of the firm made no difference to the awareness of a sexual harassment procedure.[58]

At best, an estimated 20 percent of New Zealand law firms had sexual harassment procedures in 1992,[59] and even then 11 percent of lawyers in those firms are likely to believe the procedures are inadequate.[60]

Even more of a concern is the fact that in 1992, the existence of a written sexual harassment procedure in the workplace made no difference to whether any action had been taken in response to an incident of harassment.[61] Doubts about the efficacy of procedures were more likely to come from women than men and usually related to the attitudes of partners or their involvement in the complaints process.

Many law firms have no management structure and so partners are apparently considered the best people to receive and act on complaints of sexual harassment. Where firms employ management staff, they too are frequently involved in handling complaints.

With good reason, women lawyers express doubts that a partner-based complaints procedure will work impartially. Partners, according to women lawyers, are involved as the perpetrators in half of the cases of sexual harassment, so why would a victim of harassment seek assistance from the harasser? The same problem can arise where management staff are involved. In one firm where the office manager was sexually harassing women staff, he was a central figure in the proposed procedure to deal with the problem.

Even where the harassing partner is not the person receiving complaints, experience has taught women lawyers that partners will close ranks. A woman lawyer with three years' experience was 'stunned' when she received deliberate touching and unwanted advances from a partner in a large national firm. She immediately told her supervising partner who, she said, 'initially tried to "downplay" the incident'. Only when he saw how serious she was did he take 'the matter more seriously although he didn't do anything about it as far as [she knew]'. In a similar case of partner harassment, again involving a woman with three years' post-admission experience, the woman said: 'All the partners were aware of the behaviour (the partners were all men) and the behaviour was approved by all the partners.'

Women lawyers are well aware that employers and managers do not recognise sexual harassment and therefore are likely to dispute the fact that such behaviour has occurred. This knowledge acts as a clear deterrent for women to make complaints about sexual harassment. As a woman lawyer working in a large Auckland firm said: 'the harassers often have no idea at all of what they are doing and if it was brought to their attention they would be totally surprised and then disbelieving.' Within a year of joining the firm she had experienced deliberate touching by a partner but took no action. A solicitor in Wellington observed: 'We have no female partners in our office. The female solicitors believe that if there was harassment, the partnership would close rank and we would not be believed or taken seriously.'

The negative attitudes of some partners present real difficulties for those who advocate the introduction of procedures or harassment prevention education. Regardless of firm size and location, women lawyers relay similar experiences:

> We had completely inadequate procedures—it has taken a full year to get changes made—even after we showed the partners a survey taken of all female solicitors in the firm, which clearly demonstrated an urgent need for change. You would think the benefits would have been obvious to the partners but they preferred to deny that there was a problem.

A women lawyer in a provincial firm described the steps they had taken: 'Staff met about sexual harassment. A Memorandum set out the circumstances and the possible solutions. This was delivered to partners. No action was taken. Their comment was—"We don't deal with matters like this at this firm".' A woman in a large firm expressed doubts that the recently implemented procedure would work at all. She observed that from the outset: 'the procedure has been deliberately undermined by partners (including at a senior level). Efficacy diminished. Made a laughing matter.'

This negative approach is evident even when law firms discuss sexual harassment with consultants. Hamilton consultant psychologist, Ruth Arcus, observed in August 1995 that when her client firms are asked whether they have sexual harassment policies: 'Whilst there is some interest, responses generally have ranged from negative to flippant.' Her impression was that very few law firms had satisfactory sexual harassment policies.[62] This view was shared by consultants in Wellington and Auckland.

Only a minority of women lawyers described confidence in their firm's sexual harassment procedures. One Wellington woman lawyer commented that as a result of what she considered 'good procedures' in her current firm, 'the atmosphere is positive for women'. Another woman working in a large firm that has recently formulated a sexual harassment procedure said: 'I would feel confident that if I had a legitimate complaint about sexual harassment there are people I could go to and it would be dealt with.'

Small firms are less likely to have written procedures but that does not mean there is no process. Most small firm employers who commented said that they dealt with sexual harassment complaints—on a personal basis. A partner in a Hamilton firm explained: 'We are a small firm and issues which may arise are always fully discussed and resolved by consensus.' When they received a complaint that a staff member had received unwanted advances from an employed solicitor, two of the partners discussed the matter with the staff member concerned and gave him a written warning. Another employer in a small Wellington firm said: 'A frank and open discussion with staff and employer is the best way to deal with most problems in this area.'

In some firms, the partners believe that they will know when harassment is occurring. This was the view of a partner in a medium sized Auckland firm where a staff solicitor had made unwanted advances and requests for sexual favours of others in the firm. There was no sexual harassment procedure except, as the partner said: 'We are watchful and would act if aware [sexual harassment] occurred.'

While it may be reassuring to the staff members that the partners are on the look out for harassment, this alone is insufficient. Those who harass can be very clever and manipulative about disguising their behaviour, and those harassed, for the reasons mentioned above, are unlikely to disclose the harassment unless the workplace has an open attitude to dealing with incidents as they arise. The publication and implementation of a procedure is a significant statement that complaints will be taken seriously and dealt with properly.

Women's real choices

Given the inadequacies of the procedures within law firms and the very real disincentives to taking action via the available legal channels, women lawyers' real choices when faced with sexual harassment are limited. Their most common responses are to ignore, avoid, counter or deflect the behaviour, or to resign.

Ignore

Women lawyers' most common response to sexual harassment in 1992 was ignoring the behaviour.[63] The reasons for doing so included: not seeking to lower themselves to the level of the harasser; the firm belief that a complaint would not be believed or taken seriously; doubt that any positive action would result; or fear of even worse consequences such as being labelled a trouble-maker or being fired. In each case, women's collective experience confirmed that these were feasible and even probable outcomes when women complained about harassment.

None of these reasons for inaction are positive; all convey an element of fear and distrust.

Avoid

Since the 1980s, women lawyers have been quite open about the fact that they take steps to avoid being harassed by colleagues, partners and clients. Women lawyers in Wellington and Auckland in the early 1980s, for example, disclosed that they chose not to attend professional social functions where mixing with colleagues could lead to inappropriate behaviour.[64]

In the 1990s, some women lawyers still opt not to attend functions. As one Christchurch lawyer who had experienced unwanted sexual remarks from colleagues said: 'I avoid Law Society functions now—they are a joke.' Newly-admitted women lawyers comment that they will intentionally leave law firm social functions when they sense that professional barriers are breaking down. They suspect that, as the night goes on and the alcohol consumption increases, they will be perceived as 'fair game' for unwanted attention.

As in earlier decades, some women lawyers in the 1990s are limiting their professional interaction with men lawyers. Men lawyers are not noticeably modifying their behaviour, except that they no longer exclude their women colleagues overtly, as they did up to the 1970s. By excluding women from Bar dinners and law school functions, men lawyers were taking steps to remove their temptation to harass women. Likewise, in the 1970s, some Auckland firms would not allow women litigators to go with senior male partners to the Court of Appeal in Wellington because the obligatory overnight stay raised fears of potential sexual impropriety. At this time, the majority of women lawyers were young and unmarried. For a woman lawyer to go out of town overnight alone with a man was considered a risk apparently.[65]

Counter

A minority of women lawyers deal with unwanted sexual advances or comments on the spot. In approximately 18 percent of incidents of sexual harassment, women lawyers will have personally approached the person concerned and explained that the conduct was inappropriate and offensive.[66] A woman partner, after receiving sexual remarks from another partner in social situations, did just that. It was, she said, 'straightforward to deal with and certainly not a problem'. For another woman lawyer when sexual innuendoes start to cross the boundary of 'normal conversational banter' she 'immediately makes the point that it is not acceptable. It seems to work.'

The competence of some women lawyers in dealing with unwanted or offensive comments has led some employers to think that all women lawyers are equipped to resolve sexual harassment without the need for policies or procedures. The partner in one firm that had no procedure said: 'Our female staff are vocal enough to be able to make their complaints known in the unlikely event of sexual harassment.' Statistics on complaints made strongly suggest otherwise.

Deflect

In response to inappropriate comments, some women lawyers have been able to respond with witty replies that put the comments in context, convey the message that such comments are out of line and still maintain a cordial relationship. An example of one such come-back was used by a woman law student in the early 1970s. A lecturer observing her knitting in class remarked: 'I hope you realise that knitting is considered a form of masturbation.' She apparently replied: 'Fine—you masturbate in your way and I'll masturbate in mine.'[67]

Women lawyers in the 1992 survey commented that they had been able to defuse potentially out-of-hand exchanges in similar ways. In their view it was this intervention, in a humorous or non-confrontational manner, that stopped situations from escalating.

The difficulty for many women lawyers is that the witty response is not always appropriate or easy. The expectation that they will respond 'in kind' also places an unfair burden on them. Women usually have no warning that a conversation will turn to sexual remarks about their appearance or to requests for intimacy. Because harassment occurs at work, in court, with clients, or in social professional settings, women lawyers if they were expected to respond in 'good humour', would need to be continually on guard and ready with appropriate responses.

In addition, while women lawyers relay stories about quick one-liners like survival stories, for some men they are evidence of women's complicity with the 'joke'.

Resign

Where sexual harassment is serious enough and no action is taken, some lawyers have been left with no option but to resign. In the 1992 survey alone, eleven women and four men lawyers volunteered that they had left a job as a result of discrimination or harassment.[68] This is likely to represent the tip of the iceberg, as the 1992 survey respondents did not include those lawyers who were unemployed or working outside private practice.[69]

When people leave jobs as a consequence of harassment, their confidence, self-esteem, and sense of justice are undermined. Psychologists point out that the victim's distress is often compounded by the continued denial of a problem by the employer.

One woman in the 1992 survey who was both lucky and good enough to find another job commented: 'I left my first job without a reference because the senior partner took an "unprofessional" interest in me. It was easier to resign and not take a stand over the matter.' Likewise a woman lawyer who experienced sexual remarks, deliberate touching, and requests for sexual favours from a partner took no official action but said: 'The partner in question was a jerk. I left.' Another woman who had experienced unwanted advances, sexual comments, deliberate touching and being brushed against said: 'I took action but was told the partners would do nothing. I left because of the situation six months later.'

In the worst cases, after one victim leaves, the harasser will find someone else to take her place. As one woman lawyer with three years' experience said:

> I was sexually harassed by a partner, my employer at that time. I told him to stop. But the damage to my professional confidence had been done so I left . . . Other women victims also told him to stop. In each case they left soon after. One subsequent employee made an official complaint.

In another case relayed by a woman barrister, a woman who had experienced unwanted advances from one of the partners and from the office manager in a firm was fired after making a complaint. After further harassment, the partners later fired the office manager.

Why does harassment occur?

Women's perceived sexual availability

For men to harass women, they must believe that women are sexually available to them as of right. This belief enables harassers to persist with their behaviour even when women object. A person's right to say 'no' to unwanted sexual attention is overridden by the belief of the other person that he or she has a greater claim to impose his or her wishes.[70] The first person is most often a woman while the second person is most often a man.

Women's perceived sexual availability to men has a long history. It was only in 1985 that married women in New Zealand were legally granted the right to say 'no' to having sex with their husbands. Until then, a husband was entitled to force sex on his wife, without fear of recourse. This view of women as men's property can be traced back to the common law disabilities which limited women's economic and legal rights (including entry into the legal profession) until the 1890s.

In the 1990s wives, at least theoretically, enjoy the protection of their person, while women in the workforce, including women lawyers, are in practice fair game.

Putting women down

Sexual harassment also serves as a way for men to put women down, and according to researcher Jock Phillips putting women down is a time-honoured 'sport' in New Zealand male culture.[71]

The explanation for this behaviour apparently lies in the need for men to deny that they are in any way like women. Social scientists and researchers who have examined male behaviour believe that one of the ways in which boys and men affirm their masculinity (and hence their superiority) is by downplaying or denying any sign of femininity in themselves. So, for example, men who fail to comply with the expected masculine standard are also 'put down' by insults such as 'You're throwing like a girl.'[72]

Power and vulnerability

Regardless of the harasser's motives, sexual harassment is a misuse of power. The fact that those with relatively more power (law firm partners and other employers) harass those with relatively less power (employees) demonstrates that sexual harassment is as much a power issue as it is a gender issue.

For this reason, harassment of men does occur and will continue to occur. As more women achieve positions of status and authority on traditional 'male terms' sexual harassment of men employees can be expected to increase. Already, an estimated 20 percent of men in practice have had personal experiences of a partner, client or colleague misusing their position or power. Their vulnerability is no different to that of their women colleagues, as demonstrated by their reluctance to complain about harassment. Men lawyers who reported personal experience of harassment in the 1992 survey were less likely to have taken action than women lawyers.[73]

Other potential sexual harassment victims include people with disabilities, ethnic minorities, lesbians and gay men. In the present environment, these groups are already vulnerable.[74]

Not all people in positions of status and authority harass women, but those who do are likely to adhere to the beliefs that women are sexually available to them, as of right, and that sexual interaction is not incompatible with professional interaction. In addition, the workplace culture and environment, either overtly or covertly, will condone sexual harassment. Judging by the reports of women lawyers, this dangerous combination of power, vulnerability, and workplace acceptability of harassment is relatively common and is a major factor in the perpetuation of the problem.

Women and men who have been sexually harassed recognise that there is frequently a power imbalance that works in favour of the harasser. A woman who had received unwanted sexual advances from persons in positions of power referred to the difficulties this created when contemplating action. Another said: 'Being in a position of inferior power it takes an extremely strong woman to take positive steps—particularly if there is likely to be any scandal. In addition one is likely to be blamed for attracting the unwanted attention.' A woman lawyer with four years' experience agreed, saying: 'It is difficult to bring up matters of harassment when you are a junior solicitor and the perpetrator is a partner on whom you depend for work.'

The problem is similar where the harassment is by clients, as one newly-admitted man lawyer said: 'What action can you take, you've got no power to influence and if you have, ie over a client, you'll jeopardise your relationship.'

Will sexual harassment ever stop?

Over the past decade, the incidence of sexual harassment has changed little. What hope is there for the future?

In 1991, Waikato University lecturer Bill Rout studied sexual harassment in a boys' school and in a coeducational school. His results give little hope about changes in the attitudes of the next generation of New Zealand men.

Many previously boys-only schools are introducing girls into sixth and seventh form classes. The stated objective of this practice is to encourage competition and allow interaction similar to the university and work environments. But, as Rout's research found, the introduction of girls into a traditionally male school resulted in extensive harassment of the girls. The boys mimicked the girls, made sexist jokes, called the girls nicknames (such as 'Horse'), commented out loud on their physical attributes and stared (or ogled) at their bodies. While the girls said they objected to the behaviour, the boys did not perceive the environment as negative or detrimental. Few could explain why they harassed the girls. One boy commented that the harassment was 'part of the school tradition'.[75]

Rout concluded that boys in single-sex and coeducational schools 'learned to accept as "normal" the sexual harassment of girls and women'—including seeing girls and women as 'sexual objects'.[76]

Conclusion

Sexual harassment of women lawyers by men lawyers represents the tip of the iceberg.

If women lawyers are hesitant to complain, with all their knowledge about the law and their comparatively high status in the workforce, how do women support staff fare? An estimated seven thousand women work in the profession as secretaries, word processors, filing clerks, receptionists, librarians and legal executives.[77] If, as the evidence suggests the likelihood of sexual harassment increases as the vulnerability of the victim increases, these women are likely targets for harassment.

Lawyers have also been known to harass women clients. On several occasions in recent years, district law societies have received complaints involving sexual misconduct of male lawyers towards women. In response to these complaints, the law societies' disciplinary tribunals have censured the lawyers concerned, awarded payment of costs, and suppressed the lawyers' names. If these complaints were the subject of criminal proceedings, imprisonment would be expected.

The law societies' response to solicitor-client sexual harassment requires examination in future as does the non-response to the harassment of women lawyers.

While the New Zealand Law Practitioners Disciplinary Tribunal has recognised that sexual misconduct towards clients is an abuse of power, the district and national tribunals and the law societies need to appreciate that women clients face very similar barriers to making complaints as are faced by women lawyers. Like women lawyers, women clients will be reluctant to make allegations of misconduct against their lawyers who they would perceive as being inclined and well-equipped to deny, downplay or defend the accusations. The true extent of solicitor-client sexual abuse and harassment of women lawyers and women support staff, will not be known until there exists a 'woman-centred' complaints process.

Chapter Twelve

Judges: Getting to the Bench

Of all the law and gender related debates, the under-representation of women in the judiciary is often at the forefront. The visual absence of women from the Bench and the symbolism of that absence strikes a chord with those who have contemplated the issue. The debate has centred on the need for more women judges.

Why more women judges?

There are three main arguments for increasing the number of women judges. The first relates to representation. There is widespread agreement that for the justice system to maintain (or some say to obtain) credibility, the judiciary must become more representative of the population it serves.[1] The under-representation of women and Maori in particular throw up the challenge that justice in New Zealand is dispensed almost exclusively by white men.

A second argument in favour of appointing women judges is that women's judgments are different and will make a difference.

The third argument stems from the concern about gender bias within the existing judiciary and a belief that the appointment of women may go some way towards alleviating this.

It is important to examine these arguments briefly because they provide the rationale for the hesitant and undefined policy of appointing more women judges.

A representative Bench

While no one disagrees with the objective of having a 'representative' Bench, there is contention over how this goal should be achieved. Should women be appointed to the Bench because they are women? Have some of the appointments of women involved compromising the standards otherwise applied to men? Has the political imperative overridden the principle of merit?

During the mid-1980s, the third Labour Government introduced affirmative action in relation to the appointments of women to boards, committees, tribunals and the Bench. The then Minister of Justice, Geoffrey Palmer, accepted the argument that only by bolstering the number of women in positions of power according to a concerted plan would there be any real movement towards gender equality in representation and decision making. When adopting this strategy, the Labour Government recognised that the traditional criteria were not necessarily the only criteria, that people grow into jobs and that there had been appointments of men that involved a level of risk. Why not the same with women appointees?[2]

There was no secret about the affirmative action policy. After Margaret Lee's appointment to the District Court Bench in 1987, she observed: 'I think this Labour Government has been quite open about promoting women to positions of responsibility—I think they've been out looking.'[3]

This proactive policy attracted some criticism within the profession—mostly in private. But on occasion, the negative comments surfaced publicly. For instance, Auckland law firm partner Donald Dugdale wrote in *LawTalk*:

> District Court judges are more numerous [than High Court Judges] and tend to be obscure in their origins. Only the other week I spent a whole dinner party addressing with genial avuncularity an argumentative young woman as 'Lass' only to be told afterwards that she was one of Geoffrey Palmer's more bizarre pieces of reverse discrimination and was really Her Honour District Court Judge someone or other.[4]

Disaffection largely arises from the impression that initiatives to appoint women to the Bench, boards and committees disadvantage men. One male associate partner said in the 1992 survey: 'As the evening up process continues I believe it is an advantage to be a woman.' Another man lawyer stated: 'Positive discrimination [is] widely practised, [it is] an advantage to be a woman.'[5]

The view that being a woman is an advantage is held by very few women lawyers. None of the women surveyed in 1992 were of the view that their gender was an advantage.[6] However, a converse view has been expressed. For example, Christine French, a partner in her family firm in Invercargill, stated at the 1993 national law conference:

> when it comes to appointments to various committees and organisations, women (and women solicitors in particular) have the edge. Local authorities and Government agencies are increasingly conscious of the need to have female representation.[7]

Women judges are aware that their former colleagues may not have supported their appointments. For example, one women judge commented in a 1993 survey of women judges: 'I think Counsel, in particular, focus on women Judges with a view to highlighting personal attributes that are perhaps ignored or, at least accepted, in male Judges. There is, I think, a higher degree of scrutiny and criticism.'[8] In turn, some lawyers have commented that women judges tend to be overly sensitive.

Perhaps to silence the criticism, some politicians and law society presidents involved in appointments hasten to point out that women judges are appointed on their merits—not because they are women. Between the late 1980s and the early 1990s, gender was often expressly denied as a factor influencing appointments. Since that time, however, the official position on the relevance of 'gender' is less clear and varies depending on the judge, politician or law society president concerned.

Principal Family Court Judge Pat Mahony, for example, referred to Judge Jan Doogue's appointment to the Family Court in July 1994 as 'necessary to address the current imbalance of men and women judges as quickly as possible'.[9] Again, at the swearing in of Judge Jill Moss in June 1995, Judge Mahony emphasised the need to redress the imbalance between male and female judges in the Family Court. In his speech, the Wellington law society president, Gary Turkington, suggested otherwise, saying it was important to remember appointments to high office did not occur because the appointee was a woman: 'Rather, the particular qualities are such that the appointment is inevitable where being a woman is a coincidence, not a handicap.'[10]

Women judges it seems are caught in the cross-fire. On one hand they must confirm the view that they are selected on merit, while on the other they must acknowledge that they bring additional skills and views to the Bench because they are women.[11] At least one judge, Justice Elias, has publicly recognised that her appointment was a representative one.[12]

No doubt many women hold the view that women should be appointed to the Bench simply to redress the current situation: there is a clear gender imbalance on the Bench. New Zealand lawyers and politicians are quick to claim a superior system of appointment compared with that in the United States, but there are some similarities. In 1991, a United States commentator observed:

> Those who insist that race and gender should never be factors in Supreme Court appointments . . . fail to grasp that white males also have a race and sex, and that until recently being of that race and sex was the sine qua non for appointment to the Court.[13]

Are women's judgments different?

According to women judges surveyed between July and September 1993, women judges bring perspectives and experiences to their work which are different to those brought by men judges. All nine respondents who answered this survey believed that women judges bring different perspectives and experiences to their work but for a range of reasons. The following comments were made:

Most women have had a different upbringing to men—have not assumed that they are superior and have more understanding of victims and the fears of those of lesser physique.

We are different. We do think differently and see things from different viewpoints. On the question of compassion—I think there is no gender difference—there are some very compassionate male judges.

Given our ages and our backgrounds, the whole process of socialisation is likely to have been different from that of our male colleagues.

Women usually have direct experience of being treated as a minority. The legal profession is still run by men for male views but this is changing.

Because of greater involvement with everyday running of a household/children's activities—less status conscious. Generally I think women have a more low key, more flexible approach to their work.

Women are familiar with feeling vulnerable. Experiences of motherhood etc are valuable.

In addition, several women judges believed that their unique perspectives are an advantage to them in their judicial capacities. Comments by women judges in this regard included:

A different perspective and greater understanding of a woman's position in a stress situation—particularly as it affects actions as a victim.

Advantages—wider perspective in some areas, different life experience.

Being less confrontational as a rule, women tend to defuse rather than exacerbate tension.[14]

In recent times, women judges have not shied away from publicly stating their 'difference'. For example, on being appointed a District Court judge, Judge Jill Moss commented: 'I will approach this position as a woman and a mother. Without the latter qualification I would have been a great deal poorer in judgment and compassion.'[15]

Men judges have also referred to women's different perspectives and the need for them to be reflected on the Bench. The then president of the Court of Appeal, Justice Robin Cooke, made headlines in February 1993 when he suggested that justice would have been better served by the involvement of a woman judge in a de facto property case. He commented:

The six Judges who have sat on this case in the two Courts are all men, most of us of more than middle age. This is a type of case suggesting that a woman's insight would be helpful on at least one of the Benches in assessing the claims, personality, and situation of a litigant woman and arriving at justice between man and woman.[16]

Principal Family Court Judge Pat Mahony has said: 'Women members of the judiciary have a vital part to play in addressing gender issues and the substance and administration of the law by the Courts where they work to the detriment of fairness and equity.' Judge Mahony pointed out that New Zealand had the opportunity in conjunction with the judiciary in

Australia and Canada to 'better understand these issues and lead the process of change'.[17]

Not everyone considers that women's difference is positive. There are still people in the 1990s, for example, who believe that women's perceived propensity to emotion disqualifies them from appointment to the Bench.[18]

No detailed New Zealand research has been undertaken to compare women's judgments with those of men in terms of judicial style or legal outcome. One woman judge has suggested that while there might be inherent differences in the way women judges approach matters, 'the end result may not differ markedly'.[19] Only a clearly defined 'equity audit' of judgments would definitively answer this question. It is apparent that women judges, at least, believe their judgments bring different perspectives to the administration of justice in the courts.

Is there gender bias on the Bench?

Women's appointments to the Bench are also supported on the basis that they will help to remove or, at least, dilute gender bias within the judiciary.

New Zealand judges have been spared the intense scrutiny faced by their counterparts in the United States, Canada, the United Kingdom and Australia. In each jurisdiction problems of gender bias in the judiciary have been claimed, examined and confirmed.

Since the 1980s, numerous studies in the United States have uncovered judicial gender bias in the form of stereotyped myths, beliefs, and biases.[20] In 1991, the Ontario Law Reform Commission published a discussion paper proposing the appointment of women for the reason, in part, that women on the Bench might help to minimise the existence of gender bias in existing legal doctrine and judicial decisions.[21] In 1993, the Canadian Bar Association Task Force on Gender Equality found discrimination by men judges against women judges and women counsel.[22]

A United Kingdom study of equality at the Bar found that the reasons why women barristers were discouraged from applying for judicial appointment included the potential experience of discrimination and the patronising treatment from some male judges who will determine appointment.[23] In 1994, after intense media scrutiny of gender bias in the Australian judiciary, a Senate Committee found that the problem of gender bias was 'wider than a handful of isolated instances'. Reforms were considered essential.[24]

How different should we expect New Zealand's judges to be if subjected to the same intense examination? Across a range of topics, politicians, women's organisations, women academics and scholars have pointed to problems of gender bias in the New Zealand judiciary. Judges' attitudes to violence against women have frequently been the subject of adverse comment. The level of sentences for convicted rapists and judicial response to domestic violence in particular have prompted criticism. At the launch of the *Legal Guide for Rape Survivors* in July 1993, lawyer Dot Kettle observed that in New Zealand 'we are lucky to have Judges who are more aware of the issues than Judges in Australia . . . But, we still don't have the degree and level of understanding that women deserve.'[25]

Law lecturer Elisabeth McDonald (later employed by the Law Commission), in her 1993 law society seminar paper, recounted examples of judicial adherence to and application of the myths about rape: that men rape because they are unable to control their sexual urges; that women and girls fantasise about rape; and that women have a propensity to lie about rape. She concluded: 'The legislation is clear and its philosophy apparent. It is also apparent that the ability to hear women's stories in the courts is still limited by subscription to rape myths and stereotypical views about women's sexuality.' She proposed that judges were 'best placed to counter these myths by how they define what the jury may hear and what they say to the jury about the evidence before them.'[26]

In 1991, the Minister of Police, John Banks, criticised Justice Greig for imposing a seven-year sentence on a three-time gang rapist.[27] In a controversial 1992 report by Waikato University lecturers Ruth Busch and Neville Robertson, Family Court judges were said to be making decisions that effectively condoned the offender's actions in domestic violence cases.[28] A year later the leader of the Labour Opposition, Mike Moore, compared judges' leniency towards domestic crimes to the attitudes from last century that saw women as property.[29] In 1993, Minister of Women's Affairs Jenny Shipley criticised Justice Williams for sentencing a rapist to three years' jail and allowing the man's drunkenness to be a mitigating factor. She also criticised the judiciary generally for imposing only an average actual sentence of 5.9 years' jail for rape offenders where the maximum available penalty at that time was 14 years.[30]

In 1994, women's organisation Rape Crisis criticised Justice McGechan for his comments and decision in regard to the sentencing of a man who had raped his sister over many years. According to Rape Crisis, the sentence of four years' imprisonment and the judge's comments suggested there was no crime to be answered for.[31]

In response to these and other criticisms, judges claim that only those present in the court and privy to all the information can truly assess what is just in the circumstances of any given case. Some criticism, judges say, stems from a misunderstanding of judges' roles in the criminal justice system in particular. For example, in 1993, the Chief Justice pointed out in response to criticism from the Wellington Sexual Abuse Help Foundation that a judge had shown gender bias by saying: 'In summing up to the jury, the judge is required to be impartial and objective, and has to put both sides of the case to the jury, including matters which may assist an accused.'[32] Other judges point to the inadequacy of the options available to them when it comes to sentencing. Jail terms in particular are believed to be futile.

Judges' roles in the court system mean that they are sometimes seen by women as defenders of the justice system. By fervently asserting their roles as neutral agents in the system, some judges fail to hear and acknowledge the real concern underlying the criticism—that the justice system does not provide justice for women and that the design and practice of the system is biased against women, in every sense—procedurally, substantively and administratively. It is difficult for some women to accept that judges are neutral actors in this system. Certainly, on occasions some judges have taken positions defending what to women are obvious flaws in the system.

In addition, some judges have fallen into the trap of blaming women for the inadequacies of the law's response to women's needs. For example, in 1993, Judge Erber, presiding in the Christchurch District Court, was reported as saying that he and other judges were 'disturbed at the number of alleged domestic assaults in which women appeared to use the police as a safety valve.' Although he said he was aware of the pressures that compelled women not to proceed with their complaints in the court, Judge Erber believed 'in the long run it did not do the status of married women or de facto wives a great deal of good'. Women's reluctance to proceed with complaints led to scepticism about the degree of domestic assaults which, he believed, was not really justified.[33]

Women subjected to domestic violence are legally entitled to 'use the police as a safety valve' where their safety is at risk. Their reasons for not proceeding with the complaints in court often include the fact that the justice system can compound problems rather than provide solutions.[34] Comments by judges that discount this reality do nothing for women's confidence in the justice system or the judiciary. In the case mentioned above, the judge would have been more constructive had he vented his criticism toward the inadequate solutions offered by the justice system in response to domestic violence rather than criticising the victims of the violence.[35]

In a 1994 rape case, Justice McGechan justified a short term of imprisonment by reference to the inappropriateness of the punishment required by law. He said:

> The only purpose served by a sentence . . . is to satisfy a desire on the part of the New Zealand community to punish, to inflict retribution and, I am sad to say, in the eyes of many victims, to exact revenge. It is to me a primitive and unattractive justification for such sentences.[36]

Like Judge Erber's comments about women withdrawing their domestic assault complaints, Justice McGechan also partly blamed women (the victims of rape) for the inadequacies of the system. Many women are not solely, or even primarily, motivated by revenge when it comes to sentencing for rape. They are more often motivated by fears that they themselves will not be safe or that other women will be exposed to the same pain and injury they have suffered if the rapist is not removed from society. They, like the judges, are offered no alternative to prison. Retribution underpins a justice system into which women have had very little input. It is inappropriate for judges to chastise women for the imperfections of that system.

To a large extent the problems stem from a lack of understanding of or empathy with women's experiences. This affects seemingly insignificant decisions and decisions fundamental to the administration of justice. It affects women complainants, witnesses and lawyers. In 1994, for example, a High Court judge refused to allow Auckland barrister Deborah Hollings to wear a maternity dress during a three-week murder trial in the High Court. Although seven months pregnant she was still required to wear the traditional court garb of skirt, blouse, waistcoat, white bib and black gown.[37] While this was later explained by the Chief Justice as a misunderstanding, some women lawyers and the media saw it as further evidence that tradition continued to override women's realities.[38]

Again, in July 1996, a High Court judge revived concerns about the judiciary's adherence to rape myths. While summing up in a rape trial at the New Plymouth High Court, Justice Morris told the jury that if every man throughout history had stopped the first time a woman said 'no', the world would be a much less exciting place. Within 45 minutes, the jury acquitted the defendant. Toni Allwood, a spokeswoman for Rape Crisis immediately responded to the judge's direction, saying:

> Justice Morris's comment was unacceptable and offensive. I would like to ask in what way will the world be more exciting and for whom? . . . If every man stopped when a woman said 'no', the world would be a much safer place to live in.[39]

The Auckland Women Lawyers Association (AWLA) reported to its members:

> Perhaps what has incensed people the most, and particularly women and members of the legal profession is that this comment is not an isolated one. It is widely known that Justice Morris has made similar comments in numerous other sexual abuse and rape cases . . . Justice Morris' inappropriate way of referring to genitalia is also well known. He often unnecessarily uses words [like] 'cock' and 'cunt' in trials where these words have not even been used by the complainant or the accused.

The AWLA intended to register its protest with the Chief Justice and the Attorney-General.[40] The NZLS, possibly for the first time, reported that it had written to the Chief Justice and the Attorney-General 'expressing concern' about Justice Morris' 'well documented comments'.[41] As had occurred on other occasions of 'injudicious conduct' by judges, Justice

Morris' comments revived calls for reform of the process for judicial appointments. According to a commentator in the *Listener*: 'We do not need to put up with poor judicial behaviour. We could bring the judges to account ... as [in] Canada, New South Wales and many American states.'[42] The seriousness of the judge's words was perhaps best illustrated by the Chief Justice who took the 'unusual step' of publicly condemning the comments as inappropriate.[43]

Are women judges biased?

The allegation of gender bias is sometimes made in the reverse. In a famous and bitter 1976 American case involving a claim of sex discrimination against a New York law firm, the law firm challenged the right of the woman judge to hear the case. Judge Constance Baker Motley was the only woman among thirty-two judges then on the New York Federal Bench. She was also a celebrated black civil rights lawyer.

Assignment to the case had been done by random selection from names in a drum. The law firm asked that she excuse herself on the basis of her sex. They asserted that she could not decide the case because she was a woman. She refused to withdraw and commented:

> if background or sex or race of each judge were, by definition, sufficient grounds for removal, no judge on this court could hear this case, or many others, by virtue of the fact that all of them were attorneys, of a sex, often with distinguished law firm . . . backgrounds.

The firm appealed her decision but lost. The United States Circuit Court of Appeals agreed that Judge Motley was entitled to hear the case.[44]

A recent Australian example involved a Melbourne solicitor seeking judicial review of a planning tribunal decision, where the tribunal member was five months pregnant, on the ground that 'the tribunal was pregnant'. An affidavit in support was provided which contained 'expert medical opinion' that, when pregnant, women lost their previous clarity of mind and precision of thought. The application was withdrawn.[45]

Although no New Zealand litigant has gone to the extreme of challenging a women judge's ability to hear a case, there have been some rumbles of discontent. One New Zealand woman judge in the 1993 survey referred to her experience where the suggestion had been made by a party to a court action that as a woman judge she 'would be likely to favour a woman'. Another judge reported an occasion where: 'One man in the Family Court on being confronted by his former wife, a woman court clerk and me (a woman judge)—there were no counsel present—said "How can I expect justice here with all women dealing with the case!" '[46]

The appointment of women judges alone is unlikely to solve the problems of or the confusion surrounding gender bias. Increasing the number of women judges would increase the informal interaction between the sexes on the Bench, but the hierarchical nature of the judiciary may make it improbable that women judges could 'correct' their colleagues on gender issues. Few women have been appointed to the appellate courts and so have limited opportunities, at more formal levels, to review their fellow judges' decisions.

In recognition of the need to address the gender bias issue in New Zealand, the Courts Consultative Committee established a Judicial Working Group on Gender Equity in January 1995. This committee intends to provide education programmes for judges, to increase their awareness of systemic and personal gender bias within the judiciary.

In addition to educating judges, it must also be remembered that both men and women judges in many cases are dealing with flawed instruments—the law, the legal process and the views put forward by advocates appearing before them.[47] Judges themselves are acutely aware of this. Members of the judiciary at the March 1996 multidisciplinary conference on rape were reported to be unwilling to recommend to their wives and daughters that they pursue a rape complaint through the present system—a chilling vote of no confidence.[48]

Procedures for appointment

Whatever the motives for appointing women judges, it must be asked whether there is there anything within the decision-making process, the criteria for appointment or the job itself which disproportionately affects women's chances of success? Or, as within the profession itself, is 'merit', in relation to judicial selection and appointment, a selective and gendered concept?

A parliamentary question put to the Minister of Justice by Labour politician David Lange in December 1977 asked why no women had been appointed to the Bench since Judge Augusta Wallace two years before. The minister responded:

> The policy is that if any woman is proposed for appointment she is considered in exactly the same manner, and the same criteria are applied, as for men. I am anxious to see more women on the bench, and I would welcome hearing of any suitably qualified women who might be willing to accept appointment . . . [you] will appreciate, however, that the field is limited, because there are relatively few women in private legal practice.[49]

In the 1990s is the same criteria applied in the same manner to women as it is to men? Who are the decision makers and what influences their decisions?

Are appointments apolitical?

Although the Governor-General makes judicial appointments on behalf of the Queen, the true decision makers are politicians. The Attorney-General recommends to the Governor-General the appointment of High Court judges and the Minister of Justice recommends the appointment of District Court judges. There are no reports or even rumours of the Governor-General having ignored a recommendation.

The Attorney-General and the Minister of Justice are not accountable in any formal way for their choice of judges. This can be contrasted with other government appointments to boards, committees and so on, where, in the normal course, Ministers are accountable to Parliament through the convention of ministerial responsibility. Sir Geoffrey Palmer, Attorney-General during Labour's term in government, points out that these other appointments can be questioned and debated. The minister can be held to account for the choice, and scope exists for parliamentary select committee examination of appointments and appointment policies.[50]

According to the decision makers, judicial appointments fall outside this usual political procedure because the appointments themselves are not political. But history suggests the contrary. In 1978, when a National Government was in office, the Royal Commission on the Courts commented that appointments were open to Cabinet discussion.[51] In 1983, Kenneth Keith wrote in the *New Zealand Law Journal*: 'The recent debates about appointments to Courts and tribunals have made it clear that there is a political input, both through cabinet and caucus, into the appointment of tribunal members.'[52]

But, from July 1984 to October 1990, during Labour's two terms in government, there was no discussion in Cabinet on any judicial appointment.[53] In 1991 Paul East, the National Government Attorney-General, reported that his role in the appointments of High Court judges was 'something distinct from government decision making. In fact these matters are not discussed by the Cabinet, or by me with my ministerial colleagues.'[54] The Chief Justice, Sir Thomas Eichelbaum, confirmed in 1993 that he was:

> unaware of any example in New Zealand history where an appointment has been criticised as politically motivated. In the only case within memory where a person with a distinct political background was elevated to the bench, the appointment was by a Government of the opposite political persuasion to his.[55]

However, there is a wide discretion vested in the individual making the decision. As the Chief Justice observed: 'Having had some experience of the consultative process as President of the Law Society and Chief Justice, and with I think five different Attorneys, I will cause no surprise if I say that the nature of the process varies widely.'[56]

The selection and appointment process for judges rests solely on the integrity and acumen of the decision makers. It is possible to make an impact when exercising this power. As Sir Geoffrey Palmer said, he 'tried hard to put a stamp on the judiciary of New Zealand'. By this he meant he 'looked for qualities that went beyond the dry, technical legal qualities . . .

tried to find people who had a broad view of and interest in society as a whole. They needed to be good lawyers, but being a good lawyer was not enough.'[57] In Sir Geoffrey's case his influence was without doubt. He held, at one time, the positions of Minister of Justice and Attorney-General and was therefore solely responsible for all appointments at every level of the judiciary.

It seems improbable that such weighty decisions by politicians can be classified as 'apolitical'.

A secretive process of consultation

The decision makers are very concerned to ensure that the selection of judicial candidates is conducted in a confidential manner. The argument is that careers would be ruined if it was known that individuals were up for consideration but failed to get the job. This is surely a weak argument. It could equally be said of any higher office appointed by government including, for example, board members of state-owned enterprises and Crown Health Enterprises.

More importantly, what makes lawyers so special that their careers need protection? Most judges come from particular occupations (Queen's Counsel (QCs), law firm partners and barristers sole). In all these occupations there is an expectation that some will go on to become judges and some will aspire to be judges but will not achieve that goal. In fact failure to 'get the nod' is very much an occupational hazard, and no doubt is an experience shared by many in the profession today.

The method of selecting judges has developed through convention. The most simple description is that the selection of a potential judge is made after 'consultation'. This consultation process has varied depending on the government in power.

There is no guarantee that consultation on judicial appointments has occurred for our existing judges, and, if it has, that it was genuinely consultative. Wellington lawyer Tony Black observed in 1978 that informal consultation with the law society contained no guarantee that the 'exercise will prove more than "window-dressing" '. Experience at that point had shown that consultation ranged from 'an invitation to submit names followed by consultation before appointment, to "advice that certain appointments had been made".'[58]

Under the 1980s Labour Government, names of those who made up the 'pool of possibles' for District Court judges were provided by the Chief District Court Judge, the Principal Family Court Judge, other members of the judiciary, the presidents of the law societies and 'much less frequently, the candidates themselves'.[59]

In 1988, it was announced that consultation would be undertaken by the Secretary for Justice who would discuss the prospective appointment 'as appropriate' with the Chief District Court Judge, the Chief Justice and the Solicitor-General (the head of the Crown Law Office). A check would also be made with the president of the NZLS and the president of the district law society where the candidate practised. Judges who may have presided over cases in which the candidate appeared and 'fellow senior members of the Bar' might also have been asked to comment. No individual, however, had 'any right' to be consulted.[60]

In 1988, the Attorney-General also announced that the government wanted to take 'a direct approach to advertising'. By this he did not mean advertisements in the daily newspapers or recruitment through employment consultants—names would still come from the traditional law society and judicial sources. But, for the first time, the Attorney-General wanted to 'actively encourage direct approaches from interested people'.[61]

Since 1990, under the National Government, District Court selection passed from the Secretary for Justice to the Chief District Court Judge, then Dame Silvia Cartwright. Names were still provided from the same sources but Dame Silvia openly encouraged women lawyers to put their own names forward. At the 1993 New Zealand Law Conference session on women in the law, for example, Dame Silvia invited eligible candidates, and women in particular, to 'indicate their interest' in judicial appointment.

This invitation was repeated by her successor, Chief District Court Judge Ron Young. In October 1995, in an unprecedented move, *LawTalk* published an article titled 'Chief Judge seeks nominations for women's appointment to bench'. That article reported that the Chief District Court Judge had sought the assistance of the NZLS Women's Consultative Group and women lawyers' groups nationwide in nominating and regularly updating information on potential judicial candidates. He requested that they maintain a list of names of potential candidates, up to date curricula vitarum (CVs), and letters consenting to appointment if offered. For the information of interested women lawyers, Judge Young provided a half page description of the terms and conditions applying to District Court appointments.[62]

Until mid-1995, these invitations made the selection of District Court judges slightly more transparent than the selection of High Court judges. No statements had been issued to the profession inviting applications to these positions, nor were there any policies or statements indicating how names were selected.

For High Court and Court of Appeal appointments under the National Government, the Attorney-General, Paul East, had simply said he 'made a point of consulting widely before making those decisions'. The process involved consultation with '[t]he Chief Justice, the President of the Court of Appeal and the other members of the judiciary, the Law Society, and the Bar Association'.[63]

Presumably the law society referred to was the NZLS, but the reference may also have been intended to include the district law societies. Likewise it was unclear whether he meant the New Zealand Bar Association or the Criminal Bar Association or both.

In April 1995, the Attorney-General announced that he would in future consult with 'legal groups beyond the present "establishment" '.[64] He specified the Maori Law Association (presumably Te Hunga Roia Maori o Aotearoa (the Maori Law Society), the AWLA and 'other less formal women's lawyer groups', the National Council of Women and the Federation of University Women. (At least three of the other women lawyers' organisations in New Zealand at the time were incorporated societies, and therefore had the same formal status as the AWLA.) East said that the main reason more women and ethnic minorities had not been made judges 'was that there had not been many people from those groups experienced enough in law to be considered'. [65]

Names from non-traditional sources?

Consultation with these groups was said to be for the purpose of inviting potential High Court nominees rather than consulting on the merits of any proposed appointee. Although an improvement, the new process was no more systematic or transparent as a result. For example, in 1995 AWLA membership consisted of less than one-third of women lawyers in practice in Auckland. Although some members were students and from outside private practice, the membership did not include the significant number of qualified women working outside private practice. None of the women lawyers' groups maintain reliable databases on women, nor do they hold information relevant to appointments.

Understandably, some express concerns that recommendations from these groups will still be a result of 'who you know', with the 'old girls' network' replacing the 'old boys' club'. In response to these concerns, the AWLA executive proposed in November 1995 to establish a comprehensive database on all women lawyers in the Auckland region. Lack of resources prevented this going ahead and AWLA executive members continued to respond in an unsystematic manner to requests for input on judicial appointments.

Although not named by the Attorney-General in his April 1995 list, the NZLS Women's Consultative Group also received approaches from the Attorney-General and the Chief District Court Judge for names of suitable candidates for appointment to the High Court and District Courts. In relation to a request for names for consideration for appointment to the High Court the minutes of a meeting of the group in July 1995 recorded simply: 'The group members held a detailed discussion. It was agreed that the matter should not be recorded further.' Again, at the group's meeting on 10 November 1995, the minutes record that 'it was agreed that details of the discussion would be kept confidential'.[66] Although the rationale for confidentiality was said to be for the protection of the prospective appointee, it also meant that there was no transparency as to the policies and processes used by the NZLS Women's Consultative Group when it identified likely candidates. Like the Attorney-General, it is probable that the Women's Consultative Group has no guidelines on how to determine who is an eligible candidate.

At various times, women lawyers have been urged to register their CVs with the Nominations service of the Ministry of Women's Affairs (previously the Women's Appointments File).[67] Theoretically, the government consults this database when making appointments. This practice, however, has been ad hoc and usually at very short notice.[68] Some women lawyers suspect that there is little point in being included.

There has traditionally been a reluctance for interested lawyers to put their names forward as interested judicial appointees. There has been a notion that it is 'unseemly or immodest' to do so.[69] While some may be too modest to volunteer their interest, others are just as likely to be deterred by the lack of concrete information about what is required of judges and what the job entails. Where there is no information women lawyers are more likely to assume they are ineligible. They need only to look to those already holding these positions to see that they lack one fundamental qualification: male gender.

Who influences the decision?

To date in New Zealand, those involved in the selection and appointment of judges and QCs have been almost without exception men who have qualified as lawyers. The Attorney-General, the Minister of Justice, the Chief Justice, the Chief District Court Judge, and the Solicitor General are all trained lawyers. Justice Dame Silvia Cartwright, when Chief District Court Judge, and Judith Potter, when president of the NZLS, were probably the first (and only) women formally involved in the consultation process for judicial appointments. Since 1994, however, neither women has had a direct role.

The Attorney-General's description of the current consultation process as 'wide' involves a stretch of the imagination. The majority of the people consulted are either lawyers or judges. Through the law society and professional networks, they will be known to each other probably on a personal as well as a professional basis. Nowhere is there an indication that references are sought from work colleagues, mentors, clients or other 'non-legal' sources. Although a doctor's certificate is sought there appears to be no specific check on whether the appointee is physically and mentally capable of the task. No one checks whether the prospective appointee has widely held values or prejudices.

Some of those consulted during the selection and appointment processes have been, and may continue to be, influenced by negative or stereotyped views about women. With regard to the failure to appoint women justices of the peace (JPs) to sit on the District Court Bench, the 1975 Women's Rights Committee found evidence that this was partly due to the fact that 'male JPs prefer not to work with women'.[70] When Geoffrey Palmer as Attorney-General tried to appoint both a woman and a Maori to the High Court in the late 1980s, he said he was unsuccessful 'because of the adverse views of the judges as reported to me by the then Chief Justice'.[71]

In 1988, the New Zealand Criminal Bar Association and several senior members of the profession, including a retired High Court judge, publicly objected to the appointment of Josephine Bouchier as a District Court judge because she was married to a police officer.[72] If the appointment had been subject to the human rights laws this opposition may have amounted to discrimination on the grounds of marital status.

Lawyers and judges determine which lawyers will be judges. If the emphasis was solely on achieving 'sameness' and meeting the legal criteria then the views of these legally trained people may be enough. If a representative Bench is the goal then a representative process is required.

Conflicts of interest

By reason of their positions, some of those who are presently consulted have a possible conflict of interest regarding judicial appointments. The Solicitor-General is often consulted in relation to High Court appointments, yet the Solicitor-General's role is to represent the Crown in important cases. As Sir Geoffrey Palmer observed: 'It could be suggested he or she may wish to appoint judges who will favour the cause of the Crown, especially in the Court of Appeal.'[73] The same could be said of the Attorney-General and the Minister of Justice.

Law society presidents are themselves likely future candidates for High Court appointments, as is the Solicitor-General. To what extent might that affect their impartiality when commenting on the suitability of other prospective candidates?

In April 1995, Attorney-General Paul East proposed that the Crown Law Office would, in future, maintain records of factual biographical material on people who conceivably could be on the shortlist for appointment and would collate comments made during the consultation process. No details were provided on how this would be achieved.[74] It is questionable whether the Crown Law Office should be charged with compiling and maintaining a dossier of potential judges given that the Crown Law Office is the Crown's legal advocate and its staff appear before the judges on a daily basis.

These potential conflicts of interest are not necessarily by themselves a reason to disqualify these individuals and organisations from involvement in the process. They merely raise the question of whether they should be able to influence the decisions to select and appoint so exclusively.

Information about judges

In the same way that information about the job is largely gained by a combination of luck, favouritism and osmosis, the gathering of information about the applicants can be equally haphazard.

Senior members of the Bar, often next in line for appointment to the Bench, are of course well known to judges. Often they are the contemporaries or even one-time proteges of the judges. Even if they are not, their frequent appearances in the courts will make their name, talents, specialties and rates of success familiar. Palmer commented in 1988 that the 'closeness' of judges and front-rank barristers 'in a wide variety of situations—winning, losing, under stress, in combat, tired, impatient, or angry—gives both parties the chance to make a pretty accurate assessment of each other'.[75] This 'on the job' familiarity does not assist in any objective evaluation of candidates, nor is it information which is other than anecdotal.

Information on candidates for judicial appointment, at least according to one previous Attorney-General, was far short of rigorous. Palmer recalled with some frustration that when he acted as Attorney-General and Minister of Justice 'it was difficult to secure adequate systematic data on potential candidates'. The difficulty was not so much with regard to High Court appointees who were 'usually leading members of the legal profession who were nationally known and known to the Attorney'. The difficulty was with regard to District Court appointees who frequently had 'a more local reputation and were not as well known.' For Palmer, 'the absence of information was frequently exasperating'.[76]

He did try while in office to obtain and store information about potential candidates. The Secretary for Justice at the time accompanied Palmer to England where they examined the record system held by the Chancellor.[77] The profession was told that CVs and information would be stored with a formal report from the NZLS and relevant district law societies.[78] The Secretary for Justice would administer the proposed system.

However, the plan failed and responsibility for appointments moved outside the Department of Justice and into the Chief Judges' realm. It seems that the 1995 proposal by the Attorney-General, that the Crown Law Office collect dossiers on prospective judges, revived this idea—except the Crown Law Office would be responsible and not the Department for Courts or the Ministry of Justice (previously both part of the Department of Justice).[79]

At present, when judges are appointed, the *New Zealand Law Journal* and *LawTalk* contain short reports on the appointment and summarise the judges' backgrounds. Aside from this brief and often incomplete information, before April 1995, the Attorney-General nor the Crown Law Office nor the Chief Justice held additional biographical information on appointees.[80] Interestingly, it is commonly the appointments of women that attract in-depth media comment. Their credentials, personal and professional, are comparatively easy to find.

Overall, the dearth of quality information on judges is a product of the informal system where the assessment of candidates is based on personal knowledge and perceived reputation.

Old boys' network

Given the unsystematic approach to collating information about potential judicial candidates, it is little wonder that decision makers resort to appointing people they know. No one wants to be associated with the appointment of a judge who turns out to be wholly unsuited to judging; an old law school classmate, a colleague or a friend is understandably preferred to an unknown risk.

Sir Geoffrey Palmer has suggested that appointments occur according to the 'good mates club' rather than the 'old boys' network'. Through what he calls the 'exquisitely intricate personal networks' operating in New Zealand, it is 'likely that the Minister or Attorney will appoint people known to him or her because that way there can be confidence in their abilities'.[81]

Judges have inferred that selections tap into the old boys' networks. In 1993, President of the Court of Appeal Justice Robin Cooke likened New Zealand's appointment process to the English system which, he said, 'has been criticised for being secretive and likely to perpetuate old-boy networks'.[82]

Judges point the finger at politicians as having the most influence on who is selected, and vice versa. According to Justice Cooke: '[N]o government would lightly forgo the patronage of judicial appointments, particularly at the highest levels.'[83] On the other hand, politicians suggest that the patronage is that of the existing judges. In response to the proposal to establish a judicial commission as the appointing body, Paul East observed it would 'inevitably' be made up of judges. 'Why,' he asked, 'should it be sitting judges who should determine who was qualified to join their ranks?' They would, he warned, be 'more likely to continue to pick from the traditional pool rather than to strive to ensure the judiciary is representative of the whole cross section of society'.[84]

This tension between the key players in the judicial selection process has not lead to a wider pool from which judges are selected. Instead, we are left with a process which is difficult to pin down and with little confidence it will change.

Who are judges?

In 1974, Jack Hodder researched the composition of the judiciary and reported in the *New Zealand Law Journal*:

> the person appointed to be Judge in New Zealand in the years since the Second World War is a middle-aged Caucasian male; he is well-educated; and he is a successful and prominent member of the legal profession, and, as such, is almost certainly wealthy, a member of the upper-middle class, and lives in an urban environment.[85]

More than twenty years later have the characteristics of judges changed? Although the attributes required to become a judge are not readily known, the statutory criteria provide some information on who are judges.

Statutory criteria

Judges, in all the courts in New Zealand, are appointed under statute. The criteria and the process differ slightly depending on the level of the court.

At law, only lawyers are eligible for judicial appointment. This criteria was introduced in the late 1800s after the law societies protested at the appointment of non-lawyers as magistrates. From that time, New Zealand has followed most other English speaking nations in confining its judicial appointments to members of the legal profession.

Practising certificates

For District Court and High Court appointments, the prospective judge must have held a practising certificate for at least seven years. In the case of District Court appointments, the appointee can also be a person employed as 'an officer of the Department of Justice' for at least ten years of which a minimum of seven years must have been spent as a court clerk or court registrar. The clerk or registrar has to have been qualified for admission, or admitted, to the Bar, again for at least seven years.[86] For High Court appointments there is no option to appoint anyone other than a person who has held a practising certificate as a barrister or solicitor for at least seven years.[87]

The 1991 census definition of a judge's qualifications is confusing. The standard classifications guide states that a judge will have a '3–4 year university degree, professional examinations, practising certificate in law and up to 10 years' experience as a practising barrister and/or solicitor'.[88] By statute, only seven years' experience is required and, in practice, the years of experience are closer to twenty than to ten.

As it happens, a lawyer admitted to the Bar is eligible to hold a practising certificate and need not actually practice. Although it has never happened it is legally possible that a person who has purchased an annual practising certificate for at least seven years could be appointed to the Bench.

In terms of these criteria, a large number of women would appear to qualify. An estimated one-third of women lawyers in practice have more than seven years' experience—the statutory minimum period of experience required for judicial appointment.[89] Of those women who are law firm partners, an estimated 40 percent have between ten and twenty years' experience in the law—a proportion which closely matches that of men partners.[90]

Legal experience

For the most part, there is no statutory legal experience requirement for judicial appointment. The exceptions are in relation to Family Court and Youth Court appointments.

As the Family Court is a division of the District Court, a person appointed as a Family Court judge must meet the criteria for a District Court judge. In addition, they must be, by reason of 'training, experience, and personality, a suitable person to deal with matters of family law'.[91] These extra criteria were set in 1980 at the time the Family Courts were established. They gave statutory efficacy to the idea that these new courts required new philosophical and legal approaches. The adversarial judging and lawyering style typical of the other courts was inappropriate.

Similarly, Youth Court judges must qualify first as District Court judges but, in addition, they need to meet particular statutory criteria. The Children, Young Persons, and Their Families Act 1989 states that a person shall not be designated a Youth Court judge unless that person is a suitable person to deal with matters within the Youth Court by virtue of that person's training, experience and personality, and understanding of the significance and importance of different cultural perspectives and values.[92]

For Youth Court judges, the emphasis is on the prospective judge having an appreciation of cultural differences. Empathy and understanding are, of course, highly relevant when determining what is in the best interests of the children and young people coming before the Youth

Court. While an understanding of the significance and importance of cultural difference should be a factor in the administration of justice in all other courts, other judges do not have a statutory requirement to demonstrate such an understanding.

Age

There are lower and upper age limits for judges. By requiring that judges have a minimum of seven years in practice post-admission, they cannot be any younger than 28-years-old. Admission to the Bar cannot be attained until a law graduate is 21-years-old, so the two requirements combined create a lower age limit of 28 years.

Many women lawyers meet the statutory minimum age requirement. In the 1991 census, 56 percent of women lawyers (774) were aged over 29 years.[93]

At the upper age level, all District Court and High Court judges are required by statute to retire when they reach 68 years. There is, however, an age exception in both courts with regard to the appointments of temporary judges and acting judges. In the District Court, the age limit for an acting judge is 72 years. For former judges appointed as acting High Court judges, the age limit is extended to 73 years, while for temporary High Court judges, there is no upper age level prescribed by statute.[94]

The current practice of appointing acting judges (who are retired High Court judges) limits the number of new appointments and, by virtue of the present male-dominated Bench, effectively disadvantages women. While not disputing the value of utilising trained and experienced judges, this practice limits opportunities to increase or diversify the pool of judges.

Other personal attributes

The District Courts Act 1947 provides little guidance on the attributes of the person to be appointed. The Governor-General is required to appoint 'fit and proper persons' as District Court judges. For the High Court, there is no such reference.

The most qualitative statutory guideline to judicial criteria is found in the judicial oath. On appointment, all judges are required to swear to 'do right to all manner of people after the laws and usages of New Zealand without fear or favour, affection or ill will'.[95]

Practical criteria: characteristics common to judges

Aside from these minimal statutory guidelines, there is no job description in New Zealand for the job of judge. There are no advertisements seeking applications. There are no formal interview process, competency examinations or trial periods for judging. The appointment is for life and early resignations are not well received.

So, based on the current pool of judges, what are the criteria? Perhaps the best guidelines of the qualities and experience sought in judges are the criteria applied in practice. By examining the biographies of the existing judges some consistent professional and personal factors can be identified. These factors give a good indication of the historical criteria for judicial appointments. It is against these that women's eligibility can be measured.

For the purpose of this assessment, information was collated on the thirty-two judges on the High Court Bench as at 1 August 1993. Of the thirty-two judges, there was one woman, twenty-seven permanent appointees, and four acting High Court judges.[96] The High Court was selected because women are particularly underrepresented on that Bench. In 1996, women made up only 12 percent of High Court judges.[97]

School background

The vast majority of men High Court judges in the 1993 study attended secondary school in one of the four large metropolitan centres: 77 percent went to school in either Auckland, Wellington, Christchurch or Dunedin. The most common type of school attended by these judges was a single-sex secondary school. Eighty-one percent of these judges had attended boys' schools, the remaining 19 percent had attended coeducational schools.

Most of the schools attended by the judges were state-funded. Seventy-four percent of the judges went to State schools while 26 percent attended private fee-paying schools. The one woman High Court judge on the Bench in 1993 also attended a State-funded single-sex secondary school.[98]

Academic background

All judges have tertiary academic qualifications, the vast majority having LLBs: 97 percent. The one judge without such a degree qualified in Britain with an MA.

Just over 40 percent of the High Court judges have a qualification in addition to an LLB, most having LLMs or BAs. None of the judges hold bachelor of commerce degrees. Some of the judges have extensive academic qualifications. Examples include judges with the following combinations: LLB, LLM (Auckland) and LLM (Harvard); LLB, LLM and LLD (Victoria); LLB, MJurisprudence (Auckland) and LLM (Illinois); BA, LLB, LLM (Victoria) and LLM (Harvard); and BA, LLB, LLD (Otago) and LLM (Virginia). Almost one-third of the judges have one or two masters degrees.

Where second degrees are held, the judges have commonly studied overseas as students or practitioners, in five cases at American universities.

It seems the High Court judges are as well qualified in a formal sense as those in the legal profession. In the 1992 national survey of lawyers, 55 percent had academic qualifications in addition to LLB or LLB(Hons) degrees. However, on closer examination, it is apparent that men judges' academic backgrounds bear more similarity to the academic qualifications of men lawyers than women lawyers. Of the women lawyers surveyed in 1992, 60 percent had qualifications in addition to their LLBs. By comparison, 48 percent of men lawyers had more than LLBs.[99]

Age

The relative youth of women lawyers has consistently been referred to as a reason why they have been ineligible for judicial appointments. It is not the statutory requirement that works to women's disadvantage, it is the age limit which has been imposed by the decision makers.

The preference for older appointees, particularly in the High Court, has placed a significant limit on the number of eligible women. The average age on appointment of all High Court judges as at 1 August 1993 was 50 years.[100] Few women lawyers are over 50 years of age. In the 1991 census, 57 women lawyers were aged 50 years and over compared with 846 men lawyers.[101]

The average age of women appointed to the District Court is much lower than the average age of appointment to the High Court Bench. In 1993, the average age of women judges at the date of appointment to the District Court was 41 years.[102] This average therefore, is close to the historically lowest age of a High Court judge at appointment—42 years. There has been no suggestion that the younger age of women judges has worked to the detriment of thé District Court or to the women judges themselves.

With older age, it is thought, comes a certain wisdom and capacity to reflect with a host of life's experiences to draw on. However, older age does not necessarily bring the broadest minds to the job. Some have suggested to the contrary, that: 'the older a person becomes the less naturally receptive he [or she] becomes to new attitudes and ideas.'[103] This view is readily supported by reference to those presently most eligible for appointment—the older members of the legal profession. Lawyers, especially men lawyers aged over 50 years, were found in the 1992 national survey, to be more likely to take a conservative view of the importance of a social issue such as gender. Older lawyers were more inclined to believe discrimination, in its many forms, is largely a figment of the disaffected person's imagination.

There is little comprehensive information on the merits of youth compared with older age. In recognition that age can be just another irrelevant factor limiting employment opportunities, the Human Rights Act 1993 was extended in 1995 to include age as a prohibited ground of discrimination. However, this Act does not apply to judicial appointments.

The 1995 appointments to the High Court of Sian Elias and Lowell Goddard, who were both in their early forties, indicates that the age limit for High Court appointments may now be more flexible.

If 40 years and over was to be used as a judicial appointment benchmark, there would be a significant proportion of women lawyers eligible for appointments. In the 1991 census, 249 women lawyers were aged 40 years and over: 18 percent of women solicitors and barristers.[104] If the category of those eligible for appointments was extended to 'other legal professionals' another 342 women were over the effective average age in 1991, making a total of almost 600 women with legal qualifications and experience who were aged 40 years and over.

Experience required in the practice of law

Working in the profession as partners, senior barristers and QCs are standard pre-requisites for appointment to the High Court. Of the men judges on the High Court Bench in 1993, 83 percent had at some point in their careers been partners in private practice law firms, 57 percent had practised as barristers, and all the barristers had been appointed QCs.[105] Law firm appointees also predominate in District Court appointments.[106]

At the time of appointment, 53 percent of men High Court judges held the position of QCs, 19 percent were partners in private practice, and the remainder were appointed directly from their positions as Crown Solicitor, Solicitor-General or other judicial positions.[107]

Appointments to the Court of Appeal are usually from the High Court. Exceptions are made, for example, when Justice McKay was appointed directly to the Court of Appeal from a partnership at Kensington Swan.

Women lawyers have limited opportunities to satisfy the career criteria for judicial appointment. Nearly 80 percent of all High Court judges were partners or QCs at the time of appointment. By comparison, in 1995, 17 percent of women lawyers were principals (partners and sole practitioners) and in June 1996, the two women QCs represented less than 4 percent of all current QCs.[108]

The demonstrated obstacles to women obtaining partnerships leaves little confidence that there will be a mass of women candidates qualified for the Bench in the near future.[109] There is also little hope of many women advancing to the High Court from the ranks of QCs. Although women made up 22 percent of the barristers sole in 1995,[110] their experience at the Bar suggests they are some way off 'taking silk'.[111]

Queen's Counsel appointments

Given the large numbers of QCs who are appointed to the High Court, it is important to examine whether women face particular obstacles in obtaining these appointments. Of all the types of honours and promotions available to lawyers, women are least represented among QCs. As at July 1996, there had been only four women appointed QCs—two in 1988, one in 1995 and one in 1996.

There is no published information about the specific kind or length of experience required of a prospective QC only that a QC will be a barrister. The law is more concerned with what a QC can do after appointment than the qualifications required for appointment.[112] The uncertainty about the degree or type of knowledge required for QC appointment may have been the motivation behind the 'Queen's Counsel qualification quiz', published in the *New Zealand Law Journal* in 1982. The unnamed wit concluded the quiz with the question: 'What is the answer to life, the universe, and everything?' The answer was '42'. For those who wished to count their scores they were advised to 'add 10 points if you are male and have silver hair'![113]

By law, QCs are appointed by the Governor-General on the recommendation of the Attorney-General and with the concurrence of the Chief Justice.[114] Statements have been issued from time to time regarding the procedure to be followed when appointing QCs. In 1980, the then Chief Justice, Sir Ronald Davison, and the Minister of Justice, Jim McLay, published a procedure and in 1991, the Chief Justice and Attorney-General reviewed the procedure. Published in *LawTalk*, the new one page procedure was no more specific than its predecessor.[115]

The 1991 procedure required that applicants state their year of graduation in law, the date of their admission to the Bar and the date of commencement of practice as a barrister sole. No year limit was specified although the procedure noted that the 'normal requirement' will be that a barrister has spent 'a reasonable period of time in practice as an independent barrister before applying for silk'.[116]

A reasonable time at the Bar

What constitutes 'a reasonable period of time' in practice as a barrister varies widely and has certainly changed in the last sixty or so years. In 1929, a writer in the *New Zealand Law Journal* pointed out that while there was 'no immutable law or custom' on the number of years of practice required to qualify for a silk gown, it was the exception for a King's Counsel (KC) (who is appointed while the British monarch is a king) to be appointed with less than ten years standing as a barrister. Of the British and New Zealand appointments cited, only one, Francis North, had several years short of ten at the Bar but then his appointment, as the commentator pointed out, occurred in 1668 at the end of a sixty year period where there had been no KCs appointed at all.[117]

While nearly all the KCs up to the late 1920s were appointed on or about their ten-year anniversary at the Bar, the pattern in the 1990s is very different. John Wild's appointment as QC in 1992 followed seventeen years as a barrister sole while Graham Panckhurst's appointment in 1993 came after only two years at the independent Bar. Queen's Counsel appointed between 1993 and 1995 (excluding Judith Ablett-Kerr) had on average eight and a half years' experience at the Bar before appointment. Ablett-Kerr was a double exception, being the first woman appointed QC since 1988 (the third ever) and having practised as a barrister sole for twenty-five years before her appointment.[118]

Although there is no specific requirement, the career experience of those appointed as QCs involves a significant amount of court work, at a very senior level. Women barristers and litigators within law firms report that they have limited opportunities to receive this type of prestigious work.[119]

Consultation

When the QC appointment procedure was reviewed in 1991, the consultation process became less specific. Under the 1980 procedure, the Chief Justice was required to seek the views of judges of the High Court and the Court of Appeal 'as to the suitability of all applicants for appointment'. The Attorney-General was also required to consult with 'other persons as he thinks appropriate' which was specified as including 'consultation with appropriate judicial officers of any specialist jurisdiction in respect of which the applicant claims expertise; the law society or any other person'.[120] Eleven years later, the Chief Justice alone consulted with judges of the High Court and Court of Appeal. Gone was the specific reference to the Attorney-General consulting with other judges regarding expertise and with the law society. A general statement says: 'Consultations take place with such other persons as are thought appropriate.'[121]

The involvement of judges in the consultation process increases the need for women lawyers to be seen and heard in major litigation. On Lowell Goddard's admission to the inner Bar, President of the Court of Appeal Sir Robin Cooke referred to her conduct of difficult and serious criminal law cases before the Court of Appeal, saying: 'My colleagues and I in that Court have been impressed by her firmness yet sense of responsibility as an advocate.' Sian Elias likewise was counsel in *New Zealand Maori Council v Attorney-General*,[122] a case Sir Robin Cooke said:

'may come to be seen by future generations as marking a turning point in the history of New Zealand law, indeed of New Zealand itself.' She was also, at the time of the admission, 'in the midst of a big television case'.[123]

One woman judge observed in 1993 that the lack of 'high profile' work done by women barristers meant that they were 'not seen performing on the more important cases and so [did] not "catch the eye of the selectors".'[124]

A 'mysterious process'

Queen's Counsel positions are not advertised and, since 1980, aspiring QCs were advised to make applications directly to the Solicitor-General.[125] Before this time prospective QCs were meant to advise their peers that they sought to move to the 'inner Bar'. The 1991 procedure for appointments reiterated that the old practice of applicants giving 'informal notice to those their senior in call at the bar' was no longer required.[126]

The Attorney-General, a co-signatory to the 1991 appointment procedure, later expressed doubts about the method of selecting QCs. In 1993, he said: 'I think rather we should be asking whether we should have some mysterious process of selection whereby certain barristers are plucked from their ranks and bestowed with the appellation of Queen's Counsel.' He suggested that the profession must revisit this issue along with other anachronisms like wigs and gowns.[127]

In 1995, the Attorney-General himself was so bestowed. This was arranged in a hurry so that he had the appropriate status when representing New Zealand at the World Court in anti-nuclear litigation against France.

Government appointments

In addition to holding high positions in the profession, it is common for a High Court candidate to have had other government appointments. Many High Court judges had experience representing or advising the Government before their appointment to the High Court Bench. Of the men High Court judges in 1993, 33 percent were members of a government law reform committee, 13 percent had sat on a public committee of inquiry and 13 percent had been tribunal or commission members. It was also relatively common for judges to have been involved in the High Court Rules Committee, an involvement which continued after appointment.

In relation to this criteria, women in the 1990s were certainly better off than their counterparts in the 1980s. In 1982, Hannah Sargisson found that women made up less than 4 percent of those on tribunals, commissions, authorities and boards.[128] In 1993, women made up a total of 32 percent of those on tribunals, commissions, authorities and boards.[129] Of all new appointments made by the National Government in the year ending 31 December 1994, only 27 percent were women. Of those reappointed during that period, 39 percent were women.[130]

When making appointments to these bodies, ministers and government departments are given the names of possible women candidates through the Ministry of Women's Affairs' Nominations Service. As at 30 June 1995, 217 women lawyers and women with legal qualifications were listed on the database. By comparison, only 125 women with accountancy qualifications and experience were on the database. According to the Ministry of Women's Affairs: 'the range of skills, experience and qualifications held by women lawyers makes them ideal candidates for consideration for statutory boards and committees.'[131] Even so, the women lawyers and legal professionals listed on the database represented only 7 percent of the possible 2,919 women with legal skills and qualifications.[132]

Despite the overall advance in women's participation on these bodies, there are tell-tale signs of a gendered distribution. Women's representation on government-appointed bodies tends to be inflated by their larger numbers on the 'family-related' committees. For example, women make up the majority of members on the Complaints Review Tribunal (formerly the Equal Opportunities Tribunal), and the Abortion and Assisted Reproductive Technologies Committee. Censorship is another area where there have been significant numbers of appointments of women on to committees.

In contrast, women remain under-represented on important government-appointed commissions and tribunals. In 1993, women made up only 22 percent of the total commission members. There were no women on the Employment Court, the Maori Land Court or the Taxation Review Authority. Six of the eight-one coroners were women. There was only one woman member on each of the Employment Tribunal, the Land Valuation Tribunal and the Motor Vehicle Disputes Tribunal. One woman was a district land registrar and one was an investigating officer for the Police Complaints Authority. When compared with the type, status and number of government appointments received by men, women lawyers do not fare well.

New Zealand Law Society office

Law society involvement is another common feature in the CVs of High Court judges. In Jack Hodder's study in 1974, at least twenty High Court judges had served as district law society presidents.[133] In 1993, the majority of those on the High Court Bench, before their appointment, had had extensive involvement in the affairs of the NZLS and the district law societies, usually holding office as president, vice-president or treasurer.

Of the male High Court judges, 60 percent were at one time president of their district law society, and 70 percent had sat on the NZLS council, an NZLS committee or both. Just under one-third had held office as president or vice-president of the NZLS.[134]

Professional involvement for many of the judges also extended beyond the law societies but still emphasised law-related work. Several had been involved in the New Zealand Bar Association, the Medico Legal Society, the Council of Legal Education and the New Zealand Council of Law Reporting.[135]

Going by recent QC appointments, law society office will continue to feature. Of the QCs appointed from 1992 to mid-1994, all but one had sat on a law society committee or council. In the majority of cases, their involvement in law society affairs was extensive. So much so that in 1994, the NZLS specifically acknowledged 'the particular contribution to law society affairs' made by all four appointees.[136]

Women lawyers' involvement in the law societies is at a much lower level than the men lawyers and, again, much lower than their overall representation in the profession.

What is so special about professional association involvement? Certainly having working knowledge of the administration of the legal profession is valuable experience. Leadership of one's peers may also be one of the more challenging leadership roles. But can these skills and experiences be acquired through other avenues?

Community involvement

What of other more community-based involvement? In 1993, Sir Geoffrey Palmer commented that judges need 'solid first hand knowledge of the community. They need social awareness. If they move only in legal circles they will tend to have a narrow range of community knowledge.'[137]

The scant biographies of the present High Court judges give little indication of their community involvement outside professional associations. The fact that community work did not feature in the information published suggests that few of the High Court judges have done this work. Their high levels of law society and other professional association involvement, in addition to their positions as senior barristers, judges or law firm partners, makes it hard to envisage just how much time they would have had for obtaining 'solid first hand knowledge of the community'.

In 1992, an estimated 20 percent of lawyers did unpaid work for the law society, a law centre or a community group. Very few spent more than four hours per week on these activities. Overall, women lawyers were more likely to be doing unpaid law-related work for other than a law society than men lawyers: 20 percent of women did unpaid work for a law centre (compared with 13 percent of men); and 14 percent did unpaid work for a women's group (compared with one percent of men). Men outnumbered women only slightly with regard to unpaid work for other community groups (25 percent of men compared with 20 percent of women).[138]

If community involvement carried more weight in judicial appointments, women lawyers could be expected to do as well, if not better, than their male colleagues.

Geographical location

Judicial vacancies occur in various courts around New Zealand at unexpected times. Accepting an appointment therefore can involve relocating to a new city or town. This has influenced women's inclination to accept appointments. In 1995, for example, the Attorney-General indicated that some women lawyers were not contenders for District Court appointment due to an unwillingness to move to provincial centres. Women lawyers, however, explain that the remuneration for District Court judges may be insufficient to compensate a family moving to provincial centres particularly if a woman's domestic partner has to give up a career to do so.[139]

Women lawyers are much more likely than men lawyers to be concerned with the effects of judicial appointment on their partners' career opportunities as, unlike men lawyers, their partners are more likely to have careers. Similarly, in a two-career family, a change in children's schools cannot so readily be eased by a full-time domestic partner.

Conclusion

The system for appointing QCs and judges in New Zealand is a remarkable anachronism which is long overdue for reform. The process is insular. The result is a Bench which, rather than being representative of society, is representative of the law society.

Lack of numbers and lack of experience are the two most common explanations given for the small number of women judges. These reasons may have held true twenty years ago but they are substantially less valid today. There is a significant number of women lawyers who aspire to the Bench and have the requisite years of experience.

The truth is that women do not easily acquire the qualifications required in practical terms to be appointed as judges. In addition, these requirements are not easily found nor summarised. They are not publicly advertised and they are not easily scrutinised. Judges are identified and selected through reputation, personal contact, association, convention, and 'consultation'.

There is a total absence of transparency in the process of appointment. Justice can only be done, in this instance, if it is seen to be done.

Chapter Thirteen

Lots of Words but Little Action

On the whole, despite the laws providing otherwise, women lawyers in the 1990s remain under-employed, under-paid and limited in their opportunities. Despite all the surface changes, little in substance has changed except that the number of women in the legal profession now affected is greater than in the past.

In 1991 the national law society broke with tradition and for the first time had a woman president, Judith Potter. Six months into her term, Potter reported in *LawTalk* that she had attended a session on gender equality at a Canadian Bar Association conference. In her view, it was 'a matter of extreme urgency that lawyers recognise that we must provide sufficient flexibility to ensure that women remain within the profession as a vital part of its present impetus and future planning'.[1]

So, given the continuing problem of sex discrimination and gender bias in the 1990s, what have women lawyers, men lawyers, law societies and employers been doing? What steps have they taken (or not taken) to address the position of women lawyers? What is the pace of change?

Responses to the plight of women lawyers

Women lawyers

During the 1990s, women lawyers continued to seek education and training on career development. Conferences and seminars offering negotiation skills for women and 'breakthrough strategies' for women managers were direct-marketed to women lawyers.[2] Women lawyers' groups ran training workshops on career opportunities, how to obtain promotions and how to negotiate pay increases.

During this period, membership of the Auckland, Wellington and Otago women lawyers' groups grew and new groups formed. In 1990, after heated debate and opposition from women members of the Canterbury law society council, the Canterbury Women's Legal Association (CWLA) was formed. In a replay of the 1980s debates in Auckland and Wellington, some women lawyers opposed the establishment of a separate women's group, arguing instead that women's issues should be addressed within the law society. However, like the other women lawyers' associations the Canterbury group wished to address issues relevant to women in general, not simply those concerning women lawyers. They also suspected the law society was not willing to advance their interests.

Outside the main city centres, women lawyers continued to meet informally. In Invercargill, Nelson, Hamilton, Tauranga and Rotorua, for example, women lawyers met to socialise and to share information. Women lawyers also joined or formed new groups, such as the Feminist Lawyers' Group in Auckland and the Women's Legal Resource Project in Wellington. By the mid-1990s, the informal Hamilton women lawyers' group had evolved into the Waikato Women Lawyers' Consultative Group, drawing on the Waikato/Bay of Plenty District Law Society membership. The group met regularly and held panel discussions on topics such as career development.[3] In September 1993, Wellington lawyer Dot Kettle, assisted by others, launched New Zealand's first exclusively feminist law publication—the *Feminist Law Bulletin New Zealand Aotearoa*. The first issue announced that women often lacked information about legal development as well as analysis of what those changes meant for women. The *Bulletin* aimed to fill that gap.

According to women lawyers surveyed in 1992, the women lawyers' associations were widely appreciated as a useful way for women lawyers to network and to discuss gender issues. They also provided the opportunity for women to have social contact with other lawyers without 'people getting drunk and making unwanted advances'. Critics said the groups were elitist and insufficiently proactive. A minority saw the organisations as anachronistic and sexist and refused to join.[4]

Through the mid-1900s women lawyers' groups in Auckland, Wellington and Dunedin, at least, were challenged for being mono-cultural, liberal, ineffective, captured or irrelevant. Ironically, other criticisms levelled at the groups were that they were too political and too radical. For the women donating their time and energy to the groups it was sometimes hard to know if the effort was worth it.

Despite the divergent views, the women lawyers' organisations generally flourished and were active in the business of the group. Individual women lawyers, by comparison, were reluctant to take action when it came to their personal encounters with sex discrimination or harassment. Sixty-five percent of women lawyers in the 1992 national survey had experienced discrimination on the ground of sex, 13 percent on the ground of appearance, and another 13 percent on the ground of marital status. Only 18 percent had done something about it.[5]

Men lawyers

As in the past, many men lawyers in the 1990s disagreed with sex discrimination in principle but downplayed the amount or significance of the problem.[6] While an encouraging 52 percent of the men lawyers surveyed in 1992 said that action should be taken to reduce discrimination, these men were not the decision makers. The men in the profession with influence over employment opportunities and the priorities of the law societies (the partners, sole practitioners and predominantly older men) made up the remaining 48 percent who did not think any action was needed to reduce discrimination in the legal profession.[7] The majority of men partners were of the view that women lawyers already had the same opportunities as their male colleagues, except perhaps with regard to achieving partnerships.[8]

In the 1990s, there are still the men who openly state that change is necessary and that men in the profession needed to take some responsibility for solving the problem of sex discrimination. In 1993, for example, when Peter Salmon QC was president of the Auckland law society, he argued for a change in the male-oriented culture of the profession, saying: 'A bit of tinkering, a bit of adding and taking away, will not achieve the appropriate result.' While this would be 'a hard lesson' for the men of his generation, Salmon suggested that younger members of the profession would have less difficulty adjusting.[9] At the Auckland law society's annual church service in February 1994, Justice Robert Smellie told the predominantly male audience: 'it is time for male lawyers (and judges), especially those who profess themselves Christian, to do what we can to eliminate discrimination.'[10]

Initiatives of the law societies

The responses of the national law society and the fourteen district law societies to the problems experienced by women in the law have been mixed. Of the district societies, only those in Wellington and Auckland have purposefully addressed gender issues. Where action has been taken, it has consisted largely of consultation, encouraging women's participation in the law societies, and information gathering. Education and equal employment opportunities (EEO) initiatives outside Auckland have been limited.

Consultation

Law societies have changed their approach noticeably to consultation on issues of sex discrimination. Before the 1970s, where decisions were made affecting women members the law societies did what politicians and many other decision makers had always done: they made decisions without consulting women on an assumption that they knew what was best for women. However, from the early 1980s such paternalism was replaced with a desire to confer with women lawyers about the problems they were facing. Women were invited to law society council meetings and from the mid-1980s outstanding women were encouraged to stand for positions on the councils.

Men lawyers still retained control, however. When the Auckland and Wellington law societies established working parties to study the position of women in the law, women lawyers were made members of the groups, but the societies ensured they did not outnumber men and that men lawyers were in charge.[11]

Consultation with women practitioners on issues directly affecting them was also undertaken by other district law societies. The Canterbury and Otago law societies, for example, have said they do not make decisions on matters concerning women practitioners without first consulting the local women lawyers' group.[12] Outside these districts, where there are no formal women lawyers' groups, the task of advancing women lawyers' interests usually falls to women council members.

In recognition of the need for women's input into the national law society decision making, the creation of the New Zealand Law Society (NZLS) Women's Consultative Group (WCG) was proposed in 1993. On the initiative of outgoing National President Judith Potter a group of eleven women, representing women lawyers from Auckland, Hamilton, New Plymouth, Wellington, Blenheim, Nelson, Christchurch, Dunedin and Invercargill, met on 16 September 1993 to discuss forming a national consultative group. Potter explained that the proposal was aimed at providing 'a responsible women's voice on the appointment of women lawyers to the judiciary and to positions of responsibility/power in the profession and in society generally.' In addition, a national group could undertake research and coordinate activities being conducted at a local level. The representatives attending the meeting endorsed the proposal, putting forward a range of initiatives considered necessary.[13]

Although there was unanimous support for the establishment of a national consultative group, it was accepted that its objectives would be necessarily limited by the resources provided by the NZLS. Potter had suggested that the group apply for funding of $3,000 from NZLS plus 250 NZLS staff hours. The Wellington Women Lawyers Association (WWLA) and the CWLA, in submissions following the September meeting, argued that this was insufficient if the group was to achieve anything meaningful. The WWLA observed that the costs of flying members to meetings would quickly use up the funds.[14]

Despite these concerns, the proposal to establish the group with a budget of $3,000 was put to the NZLS board at its meeting on 4 March 1994. Members of the board expressed reservations about the need for a national women's group. One member queried whether the new group might 'hijack' decisions of the board. Another member wondered whether women lawyers 'remained as a sufficiently distinct group to justify the approach taken'. He was concerned about 'the potential problem of every decision of the Board having to be checked with the group'. Others recognised that the problem of discrimination had been well documented and ignoring it would not make it go away. The proposal to establish the WCG was approved on the basis that the role and future of the group would be reviewed after two years.[15]

In September 1994, following its inaugural meeting, the WCG reported in *LawTalk* that it had set its terms of reference and identified priority matters 'recognising that while there were a range of important issues it would like to address it was constrained by limitations on funding and other resources'. Even so, the range of issues to be tackled was extensive.[16] By February 1996, nearly two years after the group was formed, it had met only five times. The meetings mostly involved responding to requests for information and advice, discussing judicial appointments, and liaison visits from representatives from other agencies. Proactive initiatives were in the minority.[17]

In 1995, the NZLS increased the budget for the WCG to $5,000. This new budget represented approximately 4 percent of the $120,000 spent annually on NZLS committees (excluding the council and the board). When compared with other annual expenses (such as NZLS board expenses ($51,000), the president's honorarium and expenses ($123,000), public relations ($40,000) and 'international relations' ($63,000)), the WCG budget paled into insignificance.[18]

In June 1996, NZLS President Austin Forbes QC, reported that: 'the Board had no difficulty in unanimously approving the WCG's continued existence . . . The Board also agreed to increase substantially the funding for the WCG.'[19] The new budget was $15,000 plus some law society staff administration time. The president himself along with board member Christine Grice, would liaise between the WCG and the NZLS board. Despite the increase in the budget and the president's support, members of the WCG privately reported doubts that the group had the resources or ability to properly fulfil its terms of reference.

Women's participation in law societies

The underrepresentation of women on law society committees and councils in the 1990s has remained a sore point. One half of the women lawyers surveyed in 1992 did not believe the district law society committees fairly represented the profession, while two-thirds of men thought they did. A similar pattern was revealed regarding representation at the national law society level. Again, men lawyers had more positive views than women: 59 percent of men thought the NZLS represented the profession compared with 45 percent of women.[20]

Women lawyers have been quick to challenge the law societies for their 'maleness', while the law societies are equally quick to point out that women are welcome to put their names forward but rarely do so. Why is it that so few women put their names forward for law society committees and councils? As members they are entitled to take active roles in law society affairs—they only need to stand for election or volunteer for positions.

Cynics say that if women actually wanted to do something (rather than just complaining) about the position of women in the profession, they should volunteer for law society work and get on with the job. While the criticism is often borne of exasperation and may be well intentioned, it is misdirected.

Women lawyers looking at the profile of the law society councils could rightly assume that they lack one basic qualification—status. Many council members are law firm partners or high profile barristers and sole practitioners. Women lawyers are not only less likely to hold these positions in the profession, they are also less likely to have the profile which law society council members and committee members tend to have. Unless women lawyers are made aware of the criteria for these appointments, they will continue to doubt their eligibility.

Although the larger law societies openly seek nominations for councils and invite members to put their names forward for committees, the process in smaller district societies is less transparent. In some districts, nominees for law society council and for office are elected unopposed. In most districts, the position of law society president is reserved for the person who held the position of law society council secretary or treasurer in the previous year. Only very recently, in the larger centres, has the position of president been contested.

In 1995, for the first time, the NZLS advertised for nominations to NZLS special committees. Included in a *LawTalk* article was a statement that: 'The Board is committed to finding the best and most suitable people for each committee, and takes account of the need for balance in terms of seniority and youth, main centres and provincial centres, gender, and ethnicity.'[21] However, the board noted that it was not bound to appoint only from the nominations received. There was no provision for voting by members.

Although the time involved in law society work is a disincentive for lawyers regardless of sex, women lawyers are more likely to have added family responsibilities. Women lawyers with children say they do not have the time to go on law society committees. Judith Potter recognised that the huge amount of time involved in law society work was a disincentive to women lawyers. During most of her time on law society councils, Potter explained, she was single and 'always able to give the sort of time that the men were giving'. However, for many women lawyers she says that encouraging them to stand for law society committees and councils 'is asking an enormous amount of them'.

Women who would be sought out for law society work will also be women who are trying to succeed as lawyers. They will be juggling budgets, time-costing requirements, contributions to the firm and marketing and may also be running homes and caring for families. Expecting them to join a committee, Potter says, is almost tantamount to asking them to kill themselves.

Quite apart from women's eligibility and time restraints, some women lawyers are reluctant to become involved in the law societies. They have very real doubts that it would be possible to advance women's interests through the law society structure. Women lawyers have good reason to be critical of the law societies which historically have acted against the interests of their women members across a range of issues.[22] More recently, through their omission (or reluctance) to act on behalf of their women members, law societies have demonstrated their disinterest and ignorance of the inequities within the profession. Where they could be leading, the majority of law societies are ducking or reluctantly following. Women lawyers who wish to be effective in many cases have chosen not to expend their energy on behalf of the law societies.

Women lawyers suspect that on becoming involved in the law society structure, particularly where women are a minority, they would be forced into the roles of protagonists and educators on 'the women's perspective'. For many, these are roles they have had to assume at their place of work and the prospect of fighting more battles is a disincentive. As a minority, there are also concerns that the battles could ever be won and so the main purpose served by being involved is to lend credibility to the process because women's concerns were raised (although not implemented).[23]

For many women who seek to advance the position of women lawyers (or women in general), the law societies are poor mechanisms for achieving change. Law societies tend to place women's concerns very low on their agendas. Their reticence to confront the political issues underlying discrimination was one of the primary reasons for establishing the independent women lawyers' associations. For women lawyers who are primarily concerned with advancing women's status at law, they can be more effective in women's organisations or groups formed for that specific purpose.[24] Through these groups, women lawyers make submissions on bills, lobby decision makers, and provide help to individual women and to women's organisations without first having to argue the validity of their perspective with men.

Figure 12

Law Week 1989

Each year the New Zealand Law Society runs a community-based law awareness programme called Law Week. In 1989, the poster for Law Week indicated an awareness of gender issues although the actual content of the week's education programme did not highlight gender specifically. The poster is reproduced with the permission of the New Zealand Law Society.

By the mid-1990s, the NZLS and the district law societies had focused on the numbers of women elected to their councils. In April 1995, the new Wellington law society president, Gary Turkington, reported that the number of women elected to council had doubled (from two to four), one had become the treasurer, and that therefore this was a 'thoroughly healthy state of affairs'.[25] In the annual district law society presidents' letters to the profession in December 1995, three of the fourteen district law societies (Otago, Southland and Westland) referred to women's representation on their respective committees or in their membership. None of the fourteen referred to any initiatives to tackle the problem of discrimination.[26]

Ethical rules and procedure

In 1992, new ethical rules were published by the NZLS. Excluded from the new rules was the hard won explanatory note highlighting the problems being faced by women in the profession. When the NZLS Ethics Committee was considering the new ethical rules, it decided that the general discrimination rule was sufficient and so deleted the specific explanatory note.[27] In doing so, the committee unwittingly acted out the original suggestion made by the Auckland law society Committee on Women when the ethical rule and explanatory note were first proposed in 1982. The Auckland committee had expressed the hope that 'the need for such an explanation . . . will be entirely obviated within the next 5 to 10 years.'[28]

As at March 1994, of the four major law societies, only the Auckland law society had ever received complaints of sex discrimination under the ethical rule. In Auckland, according to then Executive Director Graham Wear the two complaints received did not go to the Disciplinary Tribunal.

Information gathering

On being approached, the Auckland, Wellington and New Zealand law societies agreed to sponsor the 1992 national survey of women and men lawyers as a 1993 Suffrage Year project. As with earlier surveys, the NZLS council did not debate or act on the survey's findings. The Auckland society assessed the findings to check and adjust the work already under way while the president of the Wellington law society, Peter Jenkin QC, referred to the report saying: 'It is disturbing reading for those (and I am one of them) who had thought that the law had made far more significant strides toward gender neutrality than this report would indicate.'[29]

At the request of the WWLA committee, the Wellington law society council discussed the report at a joint meeting of the two committees. According to the women at that meeting, very few of the council members had read even the executive summary of the report. Some still insisted that discrimination was not a problem, referring to anecdotal evidence that appeared to show women progressing. However, the council did invite the WWLA to put forward suggestions for action.

Two proposals were put forward. First, following the launch of the Auckland law society's EEO kit in 1993, the WWLA proposed that the Wellington law society promote the kit to Wellington law firms. Secondly, they proposed the Wellington law society undertake detailed research on the exit patterns of women and men lawyers. Although a scoping study for the research was commissioned, funding problems stalled the project.[30]

Outside Auckland and Wellington there was no publicised action to address discrimination against women lawyers or to implement EEO. Neither the Canterbury law society nor the Otago law society had given any specific consideration to the position of women in the profession in their own districts, aside from liaising with the local women lawyers' groups.[31]

Education

Law society-sponsored education about sex discrimination, gender bias and EEO within the New Zealand legal profession has been largely confined to the triennial national law conferences and to sporadic, poorly-attended seminars held in the major city centres. For example, from 1990 to 1995, the Wellington law society organised three seminars on gender issues. These resulted from the efforts of the WWLA, the women council members on the Wellington law society, and the society's then executive director, Colleen Singleton. Education on the problem was organised but the speakers were talking largely to the converted. For example, the two seminars on sexual harassment and EEO targeted specifically at employers were attended by mostly women employees. Professor Kathleen Mahoney, a Canadian expert on gender discrimination, presented the third seminar on gender bias, again attended almost exclusively by women lawyers.

Education in the Auckland profession consisted almost exclusively of articles in the *Northern Law News*. From January 1990 to December 1995, an estimated fifty articles about EEO were published. Topics addressed included the benefits or merits of EEO, the aims of EEO programmes, predicted demographic changes in society, and the business advantages of implementing EEO. A review of the Auckland law society's EEO publicity found that a high content of material in *Northern Law News* was repetitive and appeared to be 'justifying' EEO. Only a minority of articles had a more proactive educative focus. During this same period, the Auckland law society had held only a handful of seminars on EEO or sexual harassment. Again, they were attended predominantly by women lawyers or by members of other minority groups.[32]

Likewise, education organised by the NZLS has largely been comprised of articles in *LawTalk*, including two special supplements relating to women's concerns and EEO. In November 1993, the NZLS sponsored a travelling seminar (to the four main cities) on laws affecting women, but subsequently has not included gender issues or EEO in its continuing education programme.

Given that the law societies annually provide to their members a range of seminars on topics relating to law and to practice management, the nominal education provided on sex discrimination and EEO suggests a low priority is given to these issues.

Sponsoring education on gender issues was certainly a high priority for the New Zealand Law Foundation. The foundation, an independent charitable trust, provided funding for research for this book during 1993 and 1994, research and development of a two day seminar on gender equity issues for judges in 1995 and 1996, a visit by keynote speaker Helena Kennedy at the 1996 New Zealand Law Conference, and the Auckland Women Lawyers Association (AWLA) symposium celebrating the centenary of women's right to be admitted to the Bar in October 1996.[33]

Equal employment opportunities

As in the 1980s, the Auckland law society has remained ahead of the rest of the legal profession with regard to acting on the problems faced by women and other minority groups. In 1990, following the report of the second Auckland working party, the Auckland law society formed an EEO Committee for the specific purpose of designing and implementing policies that would eliminate discrimination against all minorities in the profession, including women. The next year, Lydia Smith was appointed the society's EEO coordinator and a detailed consultation programme with minority groups was undertaken.[34] Seminars on sexual harassment and EEO were held and law firms were invited to contribute. In August 1991, the Auckland society adopted an EEO policy which applied to its staff and was offered as a model for the profession to follow.[35]

The impetus behind the moves to introduce EEO into law firms came in part from legislation passed by the Labour Government in 1990. The Employment Equity Act, a long debated measure, provided for the staggered introduction of compulsory EEO into the private sector. Law firms with one hundred or more employees were under a statutory obligation to comply with employment equity principles from 31 January 1993.[36] However, only weeks after the Act came into effect, it was repealed by the newly-elected National Government. In its place the government set up a contestable fund of $300,000 for the promotion of EEO and research on discrimination in the labour market.

On behalf of the AWLA its president, Denese Bates, wrote to the Minister of Labour expressing disappointment with the government's decision to repeal the legislation. She pointed out that overseas experience with employment equity had shown that 'little real progress is made in the absence of legislation'.[37] The minister's response confirmed that the government supported 'a non legislative approach to EEO as it is less prescriptive and more reflective of the needs of employers'.[38]

Although the Auckland law society pressed on with its work, launching a comprehensive EEO kit in November 1993, none of the other district law societies was proactive in redressing sex discrimination until the 1993 Suffrage Centennial Year when there was a renewed focus on women's position in society in general, and in particular occupational groups.

Even then, only the Wellington law society, at the prompting of the WWLA, expressed an interest in EEO. In March 1994, the Wellington law society 'adopted the principles' of the Auckland society's EEO policy. Wellington law firms were encouraged in *Council Brief* to consider introducing programmes.[39] The Auckland law society EEO kit was not marketed in any way to the Wellington profession nor was any other information or advice offered.

In May 1995, the NZLS board agreed for the first time to an EEO 'initiative'. The substance of the initiative, as published in *LawTalk*, comprised:

Developing a programme of consultation with Maori lawyers.

Promoting the role and opportunities for women in the profession and providing resources and support to the Women's Consultative Group established in 1994.

Promoting an awareness of EEO within the profession through *LawTalk* articles or otherwise.[40]

By February 1996, three articles relating to EEO had been published in *LawTalk*. Like the articles in *Northern Law News*, these articles described EEO, listed the benefits to law firms and exhorted the profession to do something. Although it is important to raise the profile of EEO, this type of passive information provision is unlikely to achieve EEO implementation.

In his closing address at the 1996 national law conference, NZLS President Austin Forbes remarked that the legal profession was failing women and Maori. He said: 'We need to convince them that we value their contribution, and that we can adapt to make space for them and can value the different perspectives and new skills they may bring to the law.' He made no comment on the steps the NZLS would take to achieve this. Instead, he noted that the profession must be ready to accept and act on the recommendations of the Judicial Working Group on Gender Equity (relating to judges and gender bias) and the Law Commission's Women's

Access to Justice project (relating to substantive law and legal services).[41] In the May 1996 AWLA newsletter a conference participant reported that: 'the impression is that the Law Society as a whole has no real commitment to constructively seeking changes to address . . . inequality.'[42]

Family-friendly initiatives

Again, with regard to 'family-friendly' initiatives, the Auckland law society surpassed the other districts and the NZLS.

In 1990, following the 1989 report of the second working party, the Auckland law society established a childcare centre appropriately named 'Minor Proceedings'. Although the centre receives government early childcare funding and is operated on a cost recovery basis (twelve full-time childcare places at an approximate cost of $165 each per week), the law society and AWLA organise regular fundraising events to assist with finances. The Auckland law society guarantees the lease and provides administrative and financial assistance. Eight large Auckland law firms underwrite the centre to an amount of $10,000 each.[43]

Law firms

In general, New Zealand law firms have made little progress in ensuring equal opportunities for women lawyers. Predictably, those firms that have made efforts to introduce EEO are located in the Auckland region. Even then, their progress is slow and in some cases their efforts are misdirected.

Women partners

As in the 1980s, medium and large sized law firms still tend to focus on the numbers of women becoming partners as evidence that they provide equal opportunities for all women lawyers. Colin Beyer, senior partner at Simpson Grierson Butler White, reported in the firm's March 1993 client newsletter:

> Something we cannot forget is that 1993 is the centenary of women's suffrage in New Zealand. Simpson Grierson Butler White is proud to say we have the most women partners of any law firm in New Zealand—currently six, and we also employ almost sixty women lawyers.[44]

Unfortunately this claim backfired, particularly within the firm, because Simpson Grierson did not in fact have the most women partners at the time. Six months later, Auckland firm Glaister Ennor made headlines in the *National Business Review* when three women were made partners, although it was acknowledged by senior partner Robert Narev that: 'The only reason why we did not appoint lady partners before, has been up till this stage we did not have anybody that was suitable partnership material.'[45]

In June 1996, the *Sunday Star-Times* reported that of the 435 partners in the ten largest national firms, only forty-seven (11 percent) were women. Russell McVeagh, which had the second lowest proportion of women partners, was invited to comment. The practice manager at the firm, Lois Dickinson, said she had tracked the path of women lawyers at the firm and had found that 'a high percentage' had used their experience as a springboard to other careers while men at the firm took 'a much narrower track'. While all large law firms should be worried, she noted, hers 'has a well-defined equal opportunities policy'.[46] (Table 22)

Table 22

Partners in large law firms, 1996

Law firm	Number		Women %
	Total	Women	
Bell Gully Buddle Weir	60	6	10.0
Brookfields	25	5	20.0
Buddle Findlay	53	5	9.4
Chapman Tripp	47	4	8.5
Hesketh Henry	21	1	4.8
Kensington Swan	45	4	8.9
Phillips Fox	37	4	10.8
Rudd Watts	45	8	17.8
Russell McVeagh	52	3	5.8
Simpson Grierson	50	7	14.0
Total	435	47	10.8

Source: *Sunday Star-Times* 16 June 1996, C5.

Brookfields, the firm with the highest proportion of women partners, also featured in the survey. Each of the women partners interviewed emphasised work and family flexibility and paid maternity leave for partners as important reasons why the firm attracted and kept senior women lawyers.[47]

Equal employment opportunities

Contrary to the National Government's policy, employers of lawyers across the country certainly did not rush to introduce EEO policies and procedures voluntarily. Exactly one year after the decision to repeal the Employment Equity Act 1990 which required employment equity in the private sector, 45 percent of the lawyers surveyed in 1992 were aware of EEO policies in their workplaces. Employers were more likely to offer carparks to staff than to have in-house EEO policies.[48] Only 21 percent of lawyers knew that their firms had written procedures for dealing with sexual harassment, while another 20 percent were unsure.[49]

Even where EEO policies and sexual harassment procedures were in place, their effectiveness was in doubt. The existence of in-house procedures made little or no difference to the likelihood that action was being taken to redress problems of discrimination.[50]

In 1994, a year after the Wellington law society adopted the Auckland EEO kit and recommended it to the Wellington profession, apparently little had changed. Penny Webb-Smart, on behalf of the WWLA, surveyed thirteen law firms including some of the large national firms and six medium sized firms on their progress with implementing EEO.

Of the firms contacted, three avoided her calls, four were 'actively committed' to implementing EEO, and five 'smugly described themselves as having an EEO policy which, on further investigation, was discovered to consist merely of a statement that they were an equal employment opportunities employer in some larger staff manual'. Given that one of the firms surveyed was the Crown Law Office, which as a public sector employer is required by law to have an EEO policy and procedure, only three firms were voluntarily implementing full EEO procedures.[51]

A 1995 survey of EEO implementation in Auckland law firms commissioned by the Auckland District Law Society showed little progress. Although nearly 43 percent of the 995 lawyers surveyed said that their workplaces had EEO policies, only 20 percent actually had programmes or plans of action for implementing EEO. In other words, EEO (where it existed) was no more than an informal understanding. Very few lawyers had copies of their workplace policies, and support staff were commonly not involved in or informed of the policies. Only 194 of the lawyers surveyed worked in workplaces that had sexual harassment procedures. Fewer than 150 of those surveyed had attended workshops or seminars on EEO in the previous two years.[52]

Family-friendly initiatives

The 1995 Auckland law society EEO survey also found that very few law firms or other employers of lawyers provided 'family-friendly' initiatives. While the statutory requirements for maternity, paternity and parental leave were included in firms' EEO policies, firms were less likely to cover flexible work options, part-time work and childcare assistance.

Of the few workplaces in the Auckland legal profession with EEO programmes, a minority included specific initiatives for people with family commitments. Only 15 percent of lawyers working in firms or workplaces which had EEO programmes said that consideration had been given to the needs of staff with children or other dependants.[53]

It is unlikely that firms in other regions would deviate from this pattern. If anything, Auckland law firms, given their greater exposure to EEO-related information and ideas, would be more advanced than those in other district law society regions.

Conclusion

Up to the mid-1990s, the response of law firms and law societies to the well-documented problem of unequal opportunities has been half-hearted or nonexistent. In contrast, women lawyers' groups and women's committees within the law societies have continued to develop solutions. Information has been made available to law firms and law societies, particularly on EEO and how to implement it, but very few law firms and law societies have shown interest.

Overall, there have been lots of words but little action.

Chapter Fourteen

Obstacles to Change

T he legal profession has reached an impasse in understanding and solving the gender problem. Explanations, experiences and perceptions diverge and philosophical and practical differences between the players compound the problem.

Misunderstandings over achievements and the reasons for them have led to a high level of complacency among decision makers. For many, more time and greater numbers of women are the commonly offered solutions to the gender problem. Others, keen to advance solutions, suspect the problem rests largely in the attitudes of the people involved.

Attitudes

While many lawyers accept that there has been a shift in attitudes since the 1970s, the majority of women and men lawyers still believe that negative attitudes provide the greatest barriers to women's advancement in the law.[1] Whether women have the same opportunities as men in a workplace is said to depend on the attitudes of partners or employers; whether women will be successful barristers depends on the attitudes of clients and briefing solicitors; whether women are disadvantaged by the old boys' network depends on the attitudes of those already in the network; and whether women are appointed judges depends on the attitudes of existing judges, politicians and law society presidents. In nearly every instance, the attitudes which affect the outcome for women are those of men. But where women hold power or authority in the profession, their attitudes will influence the results for other less powerful women.

Age and attitudes

Older men lawyers in particular are thought to be those holding the most outdated attitudes about women lawyers. In the 1992 survey, older members of the profession were more likely to think that there was no discrimination in the legal profession.[2] The comment of one male barrister with twenty years' experience was typical: 'Older male partners are not as adaptable to the changes in thinking necessary to enable women to assume their rightful place in the profession, including partnership.'

It is important to recognise that older members of the profession have been held responsible for old-fashioned attitudes about women lawyers for at least the last two decades. It is comforting to attribute the problem to the older generation of lawyers because it can be assumed that when they retire, so will the problem. But if age alone was the explanation for the under-representation of women in the profession, we would expect to have seen marked changes already as older lawyers have retired and new 'enlightened' lawyers have entered the profession. Instead, we find prejudice against women has remained.

Nor should it be presumed that discrimination is entrenched only among the older generation of lawyers. Some of the older, senior members of the profession have been among those articulating more modern ideas on gender issues. In many cases, the leading advocates of change over the past one hundred years have been older men practitioners and judges, while some of the more vociferous or uninformed objection has come from younger men lawyers.

New family dynamics

Family connections have meant also that some older men lawyers have a greater awareness of the gender problem. As in the past, many of the new women entrants into the profession have lawyer fathers and other male relatives who appear to be among the greatest advocates of redressing sex discrimination. These men, as Judith Potter has observed, do not want their daughters to encounter the career opposition that women lawyers faced in the past. Some of these very same men, she points out, were once firm opponents of women advancing in the law.

Unlike the previous generation, younger men lawyers are likely to be married to or living with career women, some of whom will be women lawyers.[3] Gender bias operates in most New Zealand industries and professions, and it is conceivable that many of the women who are married to or live with men lawyers will face the same career blocks experienced by women in the law, especially those with future or present childcare commitments.[4] Therefore, women lawyers' domestic partners may be more aware of the barriers to women's advancement in the profession and in the workforce generally, and possibly may be willing to assist in the removal of those barriers.

From a different perspective, however, these men lawyers may also find that discrimination (where it affects their domestic partners) can ultimately narrow their own opportunities. As women's careers stumble or as women move out of the workforce to raise children, the careers of their domestic partners take on increased importance. Men in this situation become the sole income providers in households with previously high levels of income expectation. Their inclination to agitate for change in the workplace or even to make their own career changes may be inhibited by the overriding need to ensure income security.

Certainly, a large number of men lawyers are expressing dissatisfaction with the culture of the profession and its effect on their personal lives. Just over half of the men in the 1992 national survey wanted more flexibility in the hours they worked or in the way in which they worked. The main reason given was to improve their quality of life, although a desire to spend more time with their children and domestic partner also rated highly.[5]

While half the men lawyers in practice may be unhappy about their personal, family, and career conflicts, they are largely happy about their career rewards and prospects.[6] The current system works to their advantage and promotions go to those who fit in. Their inclination to make changes is more likely to be designed to meet their personal lifestyle objectives than to bring about any greater change for women lawyers.

Interaction

The increasing number of women entering the profession has meant that men lawyers have had no choice but to interact with women in a professional capacity. Men who have studied law since the early 1970s have shared lecture theatres, tutorials and study groups with women students. Many of these younger men lawyers have watched their female classmates fail to make partnership or 'drop out' of the profession despite their exceptional abilities.

Gendered experiences and perceptions

While the views of women and men lawyers are influenced and shaped by their age, family connections, race, politics, religion and class, there is one other fundamental difference that has always divided women and men in the profession: personal experience of discrimination. Ever since surveys or studies of the New Zealand legal profession have been undertaken, it has been found that the personal experiences of women and men in the legal profession have been vastly different.

Most women lawyers share the common experience of discrimination during their careers while most men lawyers share the common experience of discrimination-free careers.[7]

Given the gender gulf in experiences, it is no wonder that there has been a parallel gender gap when it comes to perceptions of discrimination and gender bias. Men lawyers, unlike women lawyers, are inclined to doubt that discrimination in the legal profession in fact exists or, if they think it does, they tend to believe that women exaggerate its effects. Men lawyers are three times more likely than women lawyers to say: 'The sexes are equal. Progress depends on ability.'[8] When looking at career opportunities, men lawyers on average are three times more confident than women lawyers that women have the same opportunities to progress in organisations or to achieve partnership as men do. Men were also, on average, twice as confident that women had the same opportunities as men to get 'good' work and 'good' training and supervision.[9]

The difference in perceptions extends beyond sex discrimination. Women lawyers are more likely to believe there is discrimination in the profession on the grounds of race, ethnicity, age, marital status, appearance, disability, socio-economic status and political views. Discrimination on the ground of sexual orientation is the only type of discrimination of which men and women have similar perceptions and discrimination on the grounds of religion is the only area where men lawyers perceive more discrimination occurring than women lawyers.[10]

Given the predominantly rosy view taken by men lawyers, it is no wonder that much of the action in response to the problem to date has been hesitant and largely reactive.

Power and perception

There is a correlation between power and an individual's perception of the gender problem. For this reason, women lawyers occupying positions of status and authority are more likely to share the views of the men in those same positions. As a result in the 1990s there is a discernible level of distrust between women and men lawyers and between women lawyers and senior women in the profession.

While women lawyers expect opposition to come from men lawyers, and partners in particular, they also believe that some women who have 'made it' to the top of the profession do not help other women climb to the top but actively stand in the way of any initiatives to assist women.

The perception, especially among younger women lawyers, that senior women lawyers are self-interested has led to considerable resentment. Some suspect that women judges and senior women practitioners, having had the advantage of being novelties among men and having enjoyed the support of the women lawyers' groups, have then lost interest and left these groups once they have cemented their careers. One woman in the 1992 survey referred to a 'suspicion' that senior women leave the organisations 'because they want to disassociate themselves from such bodies . . . and/or they do not perceive such bodies as being of any use to them in furthering their careers"

Women come in for particular criticism. Numerous comments by women lawyers in the 1992 survey referred to women partners as part of the problem, not the solution. One woman sole practitioner commented: 'The women partners I know who have gained seniority in partnerships jealously guard their patch and resent female intruders. I've experienced very little support from female partners in large firms—in fact quite the opposite.' A woman lawyer in a large Auckland firm commented: 'Many women who have "succeeded" do not promote/support other women beneath them ... The least encouraging comments I have had in my career have been from other women. The most encouraging, from men.' A first year solicitor in a large firm observed: 'In our firm there are very few women partners. Those who are work unbelievably hard—more so than their male counterparts. I do not see them doing anything to further women's cause within the firm. The 'boys' network feels very strong.'

However, from women partners' points of view the situation is not quite so simple. Women partners interviewed in 1993 and 1994 confirmed that the findings of the 1989 Auckland working party remained relevant. The working party reported that:

> [women partners] often experience a sense of isolation from being one woman in an often large group of men. As the new partner they often feel forced to compromise/modify their views on women's issues or even refrain from expressing them at all. They also feel unable to have much influence in the decision-making process because of their newly admitted, junior status.[11]

The distrust between women employees and women partners is complicated when the partner is delegated the task of resolving gender-related problems in the firm. She is placed in the role of go-between but her status as a partner makes it difficult for her to perform this function. Non-partner women are in a double bind. If they confide in the partner, will their concerns be relayed to the partnership in a manner that protects them from those who are the subject of their concerns or from those who may be hostile? If they say nothing, will the partnership retrench to its 'we're all right mate' position and no change occur?

Communication problems

Communication difficulties also impede the profession's ability to openly address the gender problem. Since the 1970s and 1980s, when men and women lawyers first clashed in relation to sexist language, discussions on gender became vexed. Some men, who were not conversant with the new language of neutrality, became hesitant to broach gender related subjects for fear of affronting women or attracting criticism. For many women, their greater knowledge and understanding of discrimination has meant they often talk at cross purposes with men on the subject.

The 1980s attack on sexist language, where successful, lessened women's day-to-day confrontations with sex discrimination but it also provided a useful disguise for decisions or actions that discriminate against women. Gender-neutral language lent the veneer of neutrality and objectivity to visual and spoken language but did not mean that the person concerned had altered their views or changed their practices. The willingness with which the profession adopted gender-neutral language was in fact entirely consistent with the profession's general inclination to neutralise forms of expression—hence phrases such as 'one thinks' and 'one feels'. Gender neutrality, like the third person tense, is part and parcel of the mantle of authority and impartiality which lawyers assume as part of their role as advocates. The downside, for the discrimination debate, has been that eliminating the visible and the audible signs of discrimination, effectively drove discrimination underground.

'Language discrimination' still surfaces, however, where gendered assumptions are made about lawyers or lawyers' roles. For example, in November 1995, Peter Williams QC wrote in *LawTalk* thanking 'lawyers, judicial officers, lawyers' wives, legal executives and title searchers' who generously donated funding to an anti-nuclear protest at Mururoa. The reference to lawyers' wives caused an immediate written response from women lawyers in Whangarei, Auckland and Wellington—all making the point that many lawyers have husbands.[12]

As a result of the overall poor communication on the subject of discrimination, there is an increasing frustration at the continuation of the problem and the inaction by the law firms, employers and the law societies. Women lawyers' failure to be heard on the issue of gender bias may be even more debilitating as it effectively undermines their professional skills as well as their personal positions. Women lawyers are trained to be articulate. Presentation of arguments is the essence of their work. The 'discrimination case' is one they very rarely win.

Paternalism

Although in the 1990s there is a much greater readiness to consult with women lawyers, particularly by the law societies, a degree of paternalism remains. Some decision makers remain as convinced that they are acting in the best interests of women lawyers as the decision makers of the 1890s. Women are still thought to be unaware of the full picture within which decisions must be made and men are more likely to assume they have a greater understanding of the problems and the solutions for the simple reason that as decision makers they supposedly have access to all relevant information.

Obstacles to change

The overall low or inhibited understanding and interest in gender issues translates into a lack of commitment by employers, partners and other decision makers, and ultimately affects the efforts made to achieve change.

Impetus remains on the fringe

Within the judiciary, the law societies, the law firms and the wider profession, women are creating the impetus for change. While this is inevitable given the divergence of perceptions between the sexes, it is in fact part of the problem. While the men lawyers and judges and the male dominated law societies see women lawyers taking responsibility for gender problems, the wider problem remains on the fringe; a minority problem—a women's problem.

Likewise, the problem is seen to involve only a minority. Women make up just over a quarter of the profession nationally and in some areas are only 20 percent of the lawyers. For the law firms, as long as there are enough qualified people who want jobs, the problems of women are of little moment. There are usually bigger problems believed to affect more people and having a bigger impact on profitability.

For the law societies, over-emphasising the problems of a minority can also be difficult to justify when there are other pressing demands on resources. The comment of one senior Wellington lawyer in the 1992 national survey reflected the views of other senior practitioners:

> Too much time is spent pandering to small groups. The Law Society needs to spend more time promoting the Profession as a whole ie. United. No group of people or system is perfect but today the Profession is quite well established and fair minded. We should concentrate on trying to improve our image without all these splinter groups moaning about little problems here and there.

Presenting a united front is considered crucial for a number of reasons. The legal profession retains the right to regulate and control its members within reasonably liberal statutory parameters as long as ethical standards are maintained and discipline is dispensed. The internal disciplinary system, which relies heavily on the recognition and acceptance of censure by senior lawyers, would soon crumble in a profession characterised by dissension in the 'lower ranks'. Therefore, the 'splinter groups' pose a problem to the security of those who benefit under the present system. Discrimination has to date brought only bad press to a profession already labouring under a poor public image.

Ignorance of and opposition to the law

For some lawyers, the legal notion of discrimination can be conceptually difficult and the suggestion that it exists in the profession even more difficult to grapple with. Asserting that there is discrimination among the 'advocates of justice' deeply offends a primary tenet of legal thinking—that all people irrespective of colour, creed, sex or status are equal before the law and within the legal system. It is critical to the rule of law that the law is seen as impartial and of equal application to all. The impartiality by necessity must extend to the actors in the system; the judges and the lawyers. If the law or those who are responsible for its application are found to be biased then the legitimacy of the law is stripped away.

In addition to this philosophical opposition, there is, within the legal profession, a poor understanding of the anti-discrimination laws. Lawyers regularly ignore and breach the laws against discrimination. In interviews with senior partners, comments were made to the effect that the Human Rights Act 1993 was toothless and so there was no point complying with it anyway. Some have even contested the existence of illegal discrimination, for example, lawyers in the 1992 survey commented: 'Discrimination is entirely natural'; 'I have no objection to discrimination. I consider it natural and healthy'; and 'The legal profession is made up of thousands of individuals. Each one has personal likes/dislikes and prejudices. A perfectly normal person will discriminate on some ground or another.'

Stating that discrimination is normal and healthy confuses unlawful discrimination (behaviour which disadvantages an individual or group by reason of personal characteristics) with preferences (neutral choices with no adverse effect on others). By merging all likes and dislikes into preferences, these lawyers are denying that discrimination by some people negatively impacts on other people.

Another example of poor understanding of the law is the view taken by some women and men lawyers that women lawyers' organisations discriminate against men. In fact, the 1993 Act exempts clubs.[13] In the 1992 survey men lawyers referred to women lawyers' associations as 'sexist groups' which encouraged women lawyers to discriminate against their male colleagues. Others referred to 'feminism' as a type of discrimination.

In a similar vein, Australian lawyer Peter Furness responded to the formation of 'another exclusive club dominated by feminists', the Australian Association of Nurse Lawyers, by proposing the formation of an Australian Gentlemen's Lawyers' Club. He observed: 'There is hardly a decent club left where a chap can have a quiet drink and smoke which has not had to admit feminists.' He proposed that the gentlemen lawyers' club should apply for a $100,000 grant to educate feminists against gender bias.[14]

In June 1993, when an advertisement appeared in *LawTalk* for expressions of interest in forming a women's law practice in Wellington,[15] a practitioner complained to the editor that 'the advertisement and the proposition is detrimental to women's interest'. According to the correspondent, the proposal for a women-only firm would breach the Human Rights Commission Act if there were six or more partners and, in any case, it discriminated against men and invited discrimination against women in established practices. In his view, a women-only firm would 'hamper the progression of the profession towards the situation where admission to partnership and appointment to office is not influenced by the sex of the individual, but only by ability to perform'.[16]

These allegations of discrimination are misguided. The Human Rights Act 1993 (as from 1 February 1994) specifically contemplates such measures being taken for the purposes of advancing the position of minority groups, such as women in the law.[17] Measures to ensure equality that would otherwise be a breach of the law are exempted, although two tests need to be met. First, it must be demonstrated that the proposal to set up an association or firm comprising solely of women is done in good faith for the purpose of assisting or advancing women lawyers. The second test requires that women lawyers 'need or may reasonably be supposed to need assistance or advancement to achieve an equal place with other members of the community', in this case the legal profession.

All research supports the conclusion that women lawyers do not enjoy equality in the legal community in general and in partnerships in particular. If the decision to form a women-only association or firm is to remedy the first act of sex discrimination then it cannot itself be discriminatory. The motive is the important consideration.

Frequently underlying the opposition to the discrimination laws is the belief that discrimination is not really about legal rights but is about politics. This view was particularly evident in the 1995 Auckland law society equal employment opportunities (EEO) survey. A small but vocal minority claimed that equal opportunities programmes were a political ploy, designed to indoctrinate people with ideas that benefit minority groups. Efforts to implement change were said to be 'political correctness' gone wrong.[18]

Opposition to EEO based on the fact that EEO is political, ignores the fact that the status quo is also political. All instances of discrimination can be traced back to personal political views relating, for example, to the perceived proper role for women or the perceived intelligence of Pacific Islands peoples. Harassment of lesbians and gay men, for instance, stems from a political perspective that individuals from these groups are lesser human beings and can therefore be put down. Although not always overt, discrimination is an expression of a political perspective.

For some, EEO is seen as a threat to the status quo. Labelling it as 'politically correct' (and the status quo therefore as politically neutral), makes EEO unacceptable. However, the evidence suggests strongly that it is the status quo which is unacceptable. The dismissal of EEO as political nonsense, the notion that discrimination is natural or that initiatives designed to redress sex discrimination discriminate against men, demonstrate just how ineffective the discrimination laws have been. That the law fails to work within one context where it should be best understood is possibly the greatest indicator that the problem will survive this and further generations.

An impossible burden of proof

Part of the problem when talking even informally about discrimination with lawyers relates to the legal inclination to apply a burden of proof. Conclusive evidence is demanded. Personal reports of career discrimination or sexual harassment are said to be insufficient; sceptics or protagonists want facts and figures, reasons and answers. Individuals are singled out. The woman raising a gender-related problem is told that other women have no problem—so it is clearly just her problem. Her ability, skill or personality are brought into issue.

What is little understood by those who have had no personal experience of discrimination is that it is a very emotional and difficult thing to describe. Discrimination affects women lawyers as women, not as lawyers. Men lawyers and law firm partners have misread emotion-laden explanations from women solicitors as 'outbursts' because they expected clinical blow by blow relays of the evidence. Women who have experienced sexual harassment or discrimination are inclined to speak about how the behaviour made them feel, while the employer or manager wants to know the facts. Demonstrating or explaining the personal effects can be seen as weakness.

The pre-occupation with 'hard evidence' and the ever-increasing standard of proof has resulted in the devaluing of women's personal experiences.

In other situations, instead of listening, partners and senior managers, sensing a potential litigant, have immediately denied or downplayed the complaint. This initial reaction creates an adversarial environment and precludes any neutral or fair inquiry by the firm into that incident or the problem generally. In informal discussions between the sexes, women lawyers risk being labelled as having no sense of humour or of being complainers or problem makers. They risk having their professional skills questioned in retaliation—turning their supposed lack of ability into the issue in dispute.

Women also predict the firm will react this way where there is no procedure setting out how complaints and concerns will be handled.

The demand to satisfy a high standard of proof has resulted in research on discrimination becoming increasingly sophisticated. Women lawyers and researchers now point to national evidence while those in decision-making positions employ anecdotes and their own personal experience to counter the claims. They conduct straw polls of women colleagues or employees to disprove discrimination or revert to their own experience that discrimination does not exist.[19] Where this double standard occurs there is no level playing field on which to conduct the debate. The burden of proof becomes impossible to displace.

Because the onus has fallen on women to prove there is a problem not of their own making, the failure to meet the burden of proof is theirs. This becomes self-fulfilling because women's lack of success then remains a result of their personal choices. The following comment of an Auckland woman lawyer is a classic illustration. She asked the partners in her firm why eight younger female lawyers 'who appear talented and able to do the job' had departed since she had joined the firm in 1989: 'There is no reason,' they said, 'they just leave.'

Everyone agrees that discrimination complaints are difficult, hard to prove and very sensitive but little effort has been made to design procedures for handling complaints. The law societies' efforts have been unsystematic. The solution adopted by the Wellington law society in 1983 was to appoint a women lawyer to the Amicus Panel which dealt with complaints.[20] The Otago law society procedure in the 1990s involves referring informal complaints to council members and consulting with the Otago Women Lawyers' Society (OWLS).[21] While it is admirable that law societies recognise that discrimination requires special treatment, these efforts are unlikely to produce consistent and fair outcomes for all.

Complaints stemming from a breach of the ethical rules (prohibiting discrimination) in future also may be subject to a further evidentiary hurdle. Ethical rules by their nature prohibit conduct considered unacceptable by the majority in a profession. When answering an allegation of breach of the ethical rule on discrimination, a practitioner could conceivably introduce evidence showing a division of opinion within the profession as to whether discrimination is acceptable, and whether the law society has an appropriate role in determining the matter. In the context of the New Zealand Medical Council's policy prohibiting sexual activity between doctors and patients, research has demonstrated that doctors were divided on the policy. As a result it was argued that 'If an offender can demonstrate that a majority of their colleagues do not regard their behaviour as an offence, it is not one.'[22]

Eliminating the competition

In the legal profession there are high levels of disinterest in the gender problem and self-interest in its continuation.

It cannot be forgotten that discrimination is an effective means of eliminating or, at least, controlling competition. In the hard and fast world of business, gender niceties tend to become drowned out by greater imperatives—money and power being the most seductive. Some men lawyers are not immune to using discriminatory tactics to their advantage in this contest.

For example, the arguments that men are better at commercial work and that clients prefer it this way are particularly self-serving for men lawyers. Commercial work offers the best prospects for advancement followed by banking and finance. In addition, these areas of work pay very well.

The fact that men lawyers dominate the lucrative areas of work is not lost on women lawyers. Some women lawyers point out that their exclusion from the profitable commercial work is not by accident. According to one women in a small firm: 'Women are denied quality work at the risk of allowing women to compete with the partner delegating work or with other men.' Another woman observed: 'Men will ensure they get the best paid most interesting work, women get what is left.'

Other women lawyers believe that the predominance of women lawyers in criminal and family law work is tolerated for the simple reason it is work most men do not want. The pay and prospects are not attractive enough.

Changes in the economic fortunes of the profession still dispro-portionately affect women's prospects. For example, before the 1987 share-market crash when there was an explosion in commercial law work and too few commercial lawyers, women lawyers moved into commercial work. During this period, employers' previous preoccupations with client opposition to women lawyers was overlooked in the scramble to service client demand. In the early 1990s however, after the recession hit, women lawyers again found their commercial law prospects limited and the barriers reinstated.[23]

Conversely, the economic downturn of the early 1990s encouraged some men lawyers, particularly in the provinces, to pursue opportunities in family law work (on the basis that when work is scarce any work is attractive). An inter-disciplinary committee examining problems in the family law area reported to the Principal Family Court Judge on the 'observable trend' in some centres where 'relatively senior practitioners' with no previous family law experience were taking up practising in the Family Courts.[24] By virtue of 'seniority' many of these lawyers would have been men.

Sexual harassment and sexist put-downs are other powerful tools to disable competition. While the power imbalance between women and men lawyers remains, and while women are perceived as even a mild threat, women will continue to be put in their place—as women—by behaviours such as sexual harassment. Career blackmail, such as the extraction of sexual favours in return for work opportunities, is one of the more insidious ways of disempowering women lawyers.

Denial and personal interest

Partners have more investment in there not being a problem with discrimination than with there being a problem. They are named as the primary group who discriminate against women lawyers and who sexually harass women lawyers and, as such, face liability under the law. Even where partners are not the ones discriminating against or sexually harassing women lawyers, they remain liable as employers for the actions of their employees and clients. In addition, many partners believe that they would face extensive costs if they were to take action to remedy the situation. It is no wonder then that partners deny discrimination exists or, if it does, they do not think any action should be taken.[25]

Men lawyers too have more of an investment in the family/career conflict culture because without it they seem less superhuman. If women lawyers can successfully juggle families and careers then men lawyers may appear inadequate, given the high levels of domestic support which they enjoy.

On a more personal level, many decision makers in the profession have difficulty accepting that the system of determining merit is other than neutral and fair. Today's decision makers were promoted in the legal hierarchy under a system which valued their skills, accepted their culture, and assumed their abilities. Questioning the legitimacy of the system is tantamount to questioning the legitimacy of their own success.

Conformity encouraged

For those who might be inclined to support change in the legal profession and the legal system, there are some major disincentives.

Because so much rests on the impartiality of the law, the legal system and the actors within it, challenges are not taken lightly. A complex, informal system of rules ensures that the notion of impartiality is upheld or at the very least is difficult to displace. Lawyers who openly criticise the workings of the profession open themselves to censure. The effectiveness of the response to criticism is so good that dissension is usually contained and largely eradicated.

The tradition of conformity, the convention of neutrality and the swift response to those who question it silences most criticism—no matter how sincere or constructive its intent. Speaking out about incidents of discrimination, particularly those involving more senior members of the profession or the law societies, is a bold act. One quarter of the lawyers who volunteered or agreed to be interviewed for this project did so only on the promise of anonymity. They feared being labelled 'feminists', rebels or complainers. They feared reprisal from employers, colleagues, or from the profession generally.

Feminist women lawyers certainly attract criticism from senior members of the profession. Usually this is confined to private conversations although it has on occasion extended into the professional journals and newspapers. For example, Donald Dugdale, a partner at the national firm Kensington Swan and 'a well known wit in legal circles',[26] is equally famous for his criticism of women and women's organisations. In 1989, he likened the decision to seek advice from the Ministry of Women's Affairs on changes to the matrimonial property laws as being 'about as sensible as commissioning a draft for a new Criminal Justice Act from the Mongrel Mob'.[27] Again in 1993, in relation to the appointment of censors under the Films, Videos, and Publications Classification Bill he proposed that 'there would be more confidence that we will be spared zealots if the Ministry of Women's Affairs were left out of the appointment process'. In his view: 'The very words of the Bill betray an origin in feminist propaganda.'[28]

In 1993, William Johnstone, a retired Christchurch solicitor, responded in *LawTalk* to comments on interspousal rape made by Sally McMillan, the convenor of the OWLS, with the retort:

> Perhaps the correspondent has been brainwashed by the so-called 'feminist-liberationist' movement (which of course is neither). One assumes her 'experience' . . . has been narrow and unbalanced—eg from acting only for women.[29]

In a similar vein, women lawyers meeting together has drawn negative comments—usually from men lawyers. Helen Melrose recalled the reaction to women lawyers going out to dinner together in 1985: 'This caused a bit of controversy with the men, who felt we were getting together and that wasn't on. A few of them were quite hostile.'[30] In 1992 a first year woman lawyer working in Auckland noted that women lawyers sometimes received 'ribbing . . . about being females'. Her membership of AWLA was referred to as her belonging to 'the sisters'. These comments were, she said: 'All on a joking level but you can tell there's a serious undercurrent.' Another woman lawyer in Dunedin experienced the same kind of 'ribbing' every time her supervising partner put her copy of the OWLS newsletter in her in-tray.

Women lawyers' groups are seen by some as fringe organisations with little credibility. Comments by men partners in the 1992 survey included that: 'Women lawyers associations are absolutely irrelevant and useless' and that they give 'the apprehension of the "Female Mafia" at work'. In some firms the opportunity for women to meet with each other has been hard won and while supported or simply tolerated by the majority, a minority continues to oppose or ridicule the initiative.

While 'speaking out' is discouraged, there is, for women as for men, one other major incentive to 'play by the rules': the potential rewards. Employers want employees who will 'fit in'. Partners want partners who meet the compatibility test. Judges become judges by first being partners and Queen's Counsel. Being known and accepted in mainstream professional networks is the only way to 'succeed' in traditional terms, and in some cases, it is essential just to survive.

For the many women lawyers who aspire to partnerships, this is a very powerful disincentive to take action on discrimination at a broader level. The predominantly male partnerships are more inclined to promote women who ascribe to the 'there is no problem' view than ones who are demanding change. For this reason, women who make partnership are less likely than women non-partners to say they have had personal experience of discrimination during their legal careers.[31] Nearly one half have 'made it' unscathed.

Minority rules

The legal profession has a long history of denouncing discrimination and declaring that change must happen and doing nothing. As it is the majority who usually say that change is required, it can only be assumed that the minority is ruling or is, at least, overriding the stated good intentions of the majority. Or it may simply be easier to say something should happen rather than to do anything.

In discussions on discrimination, fervent or even casual opposition from a few or in some cases only one participant has persistently introduced enough doubt to swing the balance back to inertia or the 'lets wait and see' approach. In part, this readiness to give weight to minority views is fuelled by a lack of understanding about the issues. An articulate view against a proposal can outweigh a majority view where the arguments are being advanced on what appears to be emotional, 'warm, fuzzy' grounds. Lawyers pride themselves on their ability to follow reason—tackling discrimination with gut reactions is seen as weakness or simply poor decision making. References to perceived 'costs' and 'business' and 'economic realities' frequently re-introduce doubt and inertia even though these arguments may be equally unsubstantiated.

No clear strategy and objectives

Overall the legal profession has lacked a clear strategy and specific objectives in relation to solving the gender problem. From the 1970s, decision makers and leaders within the profession have treated the achievements of individual women as being achievements made on behalf of all women. In his speech at Justice Elias' swearing in at the Auckland High Court in September 1995, the Attorney-General, Paul East QC, said to the new judge:

> you stand apart as a great role model for women, both those entering the profession and those within it. This is important because there is a need for the profession to *appear* to encourage all practitioners of ability to enter it and to have realistic opportunities for attaining high office. (Emphasis added.)[32]

Keeping up the 'appearances' of promoting equality has in fact been the profession's predominant response to the problems of inequality.

The advancement of some exceptional women within partnerships, the law societies, at the Bar and within the judiciary has given some degree of representation for women among decision makers, but has not translated into structural change. In effect, highlighting the achievements of individual women is no more than window dressing; little more than rhetoric has been aimed at the causes of the problem.

As in the 1970s, lawyers in the 1990s remain largely uninformed about how to tackle the gender problem. Equal employment opportunities (EEO) programmes are relatively new in New Zealand and little specific thought has been given to other possible solutions. Even so, lawyers reluctantly take advice. By comparison, they willingly acknowledge the need to obtain expert management assistance, financial advice or marketing advice. Discrimination and EEO advice, for the most part, is not sought, is ignored or is half heartedly applied as lawyers muddle along.

Advances for women are reactive not proactive

Nearly every 'advance' for women in the legal profession has been made in response to broader social and political change occurring outside the profession rather than from any widespread movement within the profession. Educational developments from the 1870s made it possible for women to obtain the knowledge and qualifications required for entry into the profession. Legal and political developments in the United States and the United Kingdom prompted the change of law in New Zealand. Economic and social changes from the 1920s to the 1950s provided opportunities for women in the profession. The beginning of full-time legal study (rather than part-time study with part-time law clerking) in the late 1960s, the move to academic entry requirements, the high demand for legal services, and the feminist movement, made it possible for women to take up careers in law in the 1970s. In none of these advances did the law societies or law firms take the lead. Each advance was piggybacked on wider change.

Even where more obvious milestones have been achieved, the reasons are more frequently related to political or business expediency than to any concerted plan or commitment to justice and equality. It is no accident that progress has usually followed centenaries or periods of intense activity by women.

'Special' years in women's history, for example, have heralded important milestones for women in the law. In the 1975 International Women's Year, Carolyn Henwood observed that it was 'suddenly fashionable to have women in your firm'.[33] During that year, the first woman judge, Augusta Wallace, was appointed to the District Court Bench. In 1993, Suffrage Centennial Year, law firms boasted about numbers of women partners or employees and law societies highlighted the numbers of women on their committees and councils. Again, a woman was appointed to high office in the legal system; Silvia Cartwright (later Dame Silvia) became the first woman High Court judge. (Figure 13)

Figure 13

Justice Silvia Cartwright, 1993

From left: Justices Doogue, Gallen and Hardie-Boys, Chief Justice Sir Thomas Eichelbaum and Justice Cartwright.

Photograph taken by Anthony Phelps at Justice Cartwright's swearing in as New Zealand's first woman High Court Judge on 28 July 1993. Photograph first published in the *Dominion*, 29 July 1993, and is reproduced with the permission of the *Dominion* and *New Zealand Times*, Wellington, New Zealand.

Outside the Auckland law society, there has been no deliberate plan of action to tackle the problem of discrimination in the profession. Instead, the emphasis on inequality during these celebratory years or in other periods of heightened activity by women lawyers has pricked the consciences of the predominantly male decision makers. The response in this regard differs little to the profession's reaction to change in general.

Lawyers are well known for their resistance to change and tendency towards 'paralysis by analysis'.[34]

Despite the generally ad hoc and reactive responses to gender bias and sex discrimination, many see the advances made as indicative of the inevitable shift toward equality. For them, these advances become living proof that more time and more numbers is all that is needed.

More time and more numbers are old arguments

Since at least 1980, government and law society working parties, and senior members of the profession have resorted to the time and numbers solutions to women's unequal position in the profession. In 1980, in response to the few women employed in Wellington law firms, the Government Advisory Committee on Women concluded: 'Time may be all that is needed to increase this to 50 percent, as more and more women become qualified.'[35] In 1988, on her appointment as president of the New Zealand Law Society, Judith Potter predicted that the 'process of time' would ensure equality for women in the profession. She said:

> with the numbers of women now coming into the profession and the quality of those women, my guess would be that in five to seven years time the sort of questions you and I are discussing now will not even arise. Women will be represented throughout the legal system.[36]

On 15 April 1988, when Sian Elias and Lowell Goddard became New Zealand's first two women Queen's Counsel, they were said to be part of 'the first wave of a tide of women' coming into prominence. Women lawyers, it seemed, were now well on their way to the Benches of the High Court and the Court of Appeal. All that was needed was the passage of time.[37] It was another five years before Justice Silvia Cartwright was appointed to the High Court, and of the twenty-four QCs appointed in the following six years, none were women. The third woman QC was appointed in 1995 and the fourth in 1996. As at August 1996 there were no women on the Court of Appeal.

In 1993, the Minister of Justice, Doug Graham, told the International Women Judges' Conference that he was committed to seeing more women on the Bench. He said:

> In New Zealand, women graduates in law now outnumber their male counterparts. This trend has not yet been reflected in the number of women partners in the country's legal practices nor the number of women judges but I believe that will come in time.[38]

Reliance on false assumptions

The 'time and numbers' solution is built on several false assumptions. First, it is assumed that numbers alone will be enough. For women, numbers have never brought equality. In New Zealand society, where women make up 51 percent of the population, women do not enjoy equality.[39] If equal numbers amounted to equality there would be no need for sex discrimination laws.

Even where women numerically dominate a profession, as in primary and secondary teaching, they are still over-represented in the lower paid, lower status positions.[40] Numbers can give the impression of equality but change in the balance of opportunities, rewards and power does not naturally occur as of right by numbers alone.

Secondly, relying on more time and more numbers falsely assumes that the profession offers a level playing field where the new women entrants have equal access to the opportunities that are available to the men. However, all evidence points to an extremely tilted playing field—only exceptional women are able to defy gravity and succeed. The remainder leave or carve out other opportunities in the profession.

The incidence of discrimination in the legal profession over the past decade remains unchanged. For example, in 1982, 60 percent of Wellington women lawyers said they had received 'adverse reaction[s]' from partners and colleagues and, ten years later 59 percent of Wellington women lawyers had experienced discrimination from partners and solicitors. Since the 1980s, the incidence of sexual harassment and/or the willingness to report it has increased.[41]

Likewise, pay inequity remains in the profession (Figure 11). In the ten years between the 1982 Wellington survey and the 1992 national survey, very little changed. The gender pay gap closed marginally at the lower income levels but increased at the higher income levels. The pay gap in the Wellington region itself was significantly higher than the national average with men lawyers being nearly six times as likely to earn over $95,000 per year than women lawyers.[42]

In the 1990s, the gender income disparity exists in all sectors of legal employment and remains when comparing those with the same years of experience in the same position doing similar work.[43]

It is absurd to think new women graduates entering a hierarchical profession could mitigate the effects of a century of gender bias. New graduates, of either sex, do not have access to the information, resources, status or power that would allow them to negotiate with and influence decision makers in law firms or law societies. They may not agree with the gender imbalance or gender stereotyping and may expect better opportunities, but they are hardly in a position to argue for substantive change.

Figure 14

Pay inequity in the legal profession

An insightful 'cartoon' about women's unequal pay situation in the legal profession from the cover of *LawTalk*, no 431, April 1995. Cover reproduced with the permission of the New Zealand Law Society.

Yet, the hope that women will eventually be equally represented throughout the profession, particularly in partnerships and the judiciary, rests on these keen new graduates. Why should new women graduates fare any differently than existing women lawyers? These women are as privileged, as bright and as competent as their predecessors. What assurances are there that action is being taken to keep them in the profession? There needs to be something fundamentally different about these women graduates and the profession they enter to determine for them a course different to that of their predecessors.

The 'drop-out' rates

The more time and more numbers answer ignores the ever present 'drop-out' rate of women from the legal profession. Consistently over the one hundred years of women's participation in the legal profession women have left the profession at a higher rate than men. Of the women lawyers admitted to the Bar between 1897 and 1959 an estimated 44 percent of never practised or practised for fewer than nine years. Not all gave up their careers to raise families. A significant number of these women left the law for careers in teaching, office work or journalism.[44] By comparison, the men who qualified over this period more commonly had life-long careers in practice—usually as partners in their own firms, as sole practitioners or as barristers.[45]

Before the 1960s, it was common that women would not complete their law degrees, or where they did it was not unusual for them to not seek admission to the Bar or to not enter the profession. From 1936 to 1970, ninety women graduated with LLBs but very few were in practice over that period. However, over that same time, the numbers of men in the profession increased in proportion to the numbers graduating.[46]

Since 1979, most women who have graduated in law have sought admission to the Bar—the numbers of women and men graduates over the years 1979 to 1990 fairly accurately match the numbers of women and men new admissions. In 1993 for the first time, new admissions of women exceeded admissions of men—266 of the 515 new admissions were women.[47] Therefore, it is not at the admission stage that women lawyers fare differently to men lawyers. The drop-out rate soars post-admission.

From 1980 to 1992, qualified women lawyers left the profession at nearly three times the rate of men lawyers. Over that period an average 10 percent of women lawyers dropped out each year compared with only 4 percent of men lawyers.[48] While retirement after a long career in the law accounts for the majority of men who have left, it does not explain the high exit rate of women. In the 1991 census only twenty-four women lawyers were aged 55 years or older compared with 558 men lawyers.[49]

Certainly, the reasons for women dropping out of the profession have changed. It was originally marriage and has progressively shifted to pregnancy, to childbearing and to childrearing. Other reasons include the consistent lack of work opportunities, client contact, pay equity and partnership opportunities. Likewise, harassment has also forced some women to leave. Regardless of the reason, the resulting exit rate means that the new women graduates, as in the past, are still replacing the experienced women who leave. While the rate remains high, it seems improbable that women lawyers will ever make up 50 percent of the profession's membership.

A false sense of security

Predictions that more time and greater numbers are all that is needed to solve the gender problem have helped lull the profession into a false sense of security. Placing faith in the passage of time has excused many from taking action and has allowed the profession to abdicate responsibility for the position women lawyers are in today and to enable it to overlook the basic obstacles to change.

Likewise, averring to the bigger social problem of discrimination or gender bias excuses individuals and organisations from identifying the ways in which they contribute to the problem and from playing their part in eliminating the problem. In effect, the more time and more numbers option are 'do nothing' options.

The emphasis on time and numbers ensures that the onus to achieve change remains on women's shoulders. Despite their minority numbers, their low status in the profession and the silent opposition to their advancement, women lawyers are expected to miraculously make it to the top. When the majority of women are unsuccessful, as they predictably will be, women themselves can again be blamed. It is then women who fail—not the profession.

The turnover of women lawyers in the 'struggle' against discrimination has been extremely high. Fighting for change while trying to counteract the personal and largely imperceptible impact of discrimination has left many women lawyers worn out and disaffected. Some have realised that being in the fight has worked against their own career opportunities while others have been exhausted by the need to constantly repeat the same arguments. Certainly, more women lawyers mean that there will be more replacements at the frontline. The question is when will the solutions be the focus rather than the struggle.

History shows that intervention is inevitable and essential to break the discrimination cycle. The legal profession's choice is clear—will that intervention be controlled and planned, or ad hoc and reactive?

Chapter Fifteen

Women: Enforcing the Law on Equality

W omen lawyers have in their grasp one of the most empowering tools available in western democratic societies: the law. In the same way that the law was used to keep women out of the profession over one hundred years ago, now it can be utilised to keep them in and to deliver equality of opportunity. Causes of action and remedies exist across a range of employment and constitutional issues. Wielding these tools will enable women to demand equality and expand the boundaries in the workplace, in the profession and in the legal system.

Women lawyers, of all groups of women in society, are best equipped to enforce the law on equality. That law is of direct relevance to the legal profession and the legal system. Lawyers, more than most, appreciate the consequences of breaching or ignoring the law; they recognise and respect it as a benchmark and a guide to standards.

Women lawyers historically litigation shy

Unlike their counterparts in the United States, Canada, Scotland and the United Kingdom, New Zealand women lawyers have been litigation shy historically. As a consequence, the New Zealand legal profession has been spared the legal spotlight on sex discrimination.

While the nineteenth century New Zealand debate about women's access to the profession took place rather sedately in Parliament and in law society council rooms, women in other jurisdictions took direct legal action. In America, women law graduates sued the Bar associations and professional examining bodies for declining their applications to join the profession.[1] In Canada, Clara Brett Martin engaged in a six-year battle with the Law Society of Upper Canada and was finally admitted as a barrister and solicitor on 2 February 1897, only months before Ethel Benjamin was admitted in New Zealand.[2] In three other Canadian provinces, women law graduates and law clerks took legal action against the law societies who opposed their admission. Newfoundland was the last Canadian province to admit women lawyers, in 1933.[3]

In Scotland in 1901 a woman sued the Incorporated Society of Law Agents for denying her application to practise as a law agent.[4] In England in 1903 Bertha Cave appealed the refusal of Gray's Inn to call her as a barrister. A special tribunal involving the Lord Chancellor, the Lord Chief Justice and five other judges confirmed the decision.[5] Ten years later, Mrs Bebb also appealed the English law society decision which prevented her admission as a solicitor and the Court of Chancery agreed she was ineligible.[6] In 1909 and 1912, women in South Africa took legal action against the law societies.[7] In all these cases, among the legal points argued was the question of whether women were persons at law.

In the late 1960s, American women took legal action to improve the position of women in law firms. Aware that the firms were preferring the recruitment of their lesser qualified male colleagues, graduates from New York, Columbia and Berkley law schools filed complaints with law school deans, the school placement offices and the Human Rights Commission. Investigations revealed a pervasive pattern of discrimination not just in hiring but in promotion, partnership and equal pay.

The resulting complaints, heard by the New York Human Rights Commission and the federal Equal Employment Opportunities Commission during the late 1960s and the early 1970s, created a wave of sensitivity in the predominantly male American profession. Settlements in these cases involved undertakings to correct interview procedures, agreements not to hold firm-sponsored events in clubs that barred women, and in one case, a guarantee that the firm would offer over 25 percent of its positions each year to women graduates. In a number of cases, the women graduates involved in the complaints were offered and accepted positions with the firms. For the first time, American women law graduates and lawyers were being actively sought and recruited by firms.[8]

From 1977, New Zealand had human rights laws providing remedies for discrimination but women lawyers have been reluctant to seek those remedies. As Frances Joychild, a legal adviser at the Human Rights Commission since 1983, noted, it was ironic that women working in the law perceived themselves as having less protection from the operation of anti-discrimination laws than women who worked in other occupations.[9]

In the 1990s, discrimination litigation is back in the courts in the United States, Canada and England. Since the early 1990s, major American law firms have faced an increasing number of discrimination-related complaints, with one commentator describing the legal profession's exposure to sexual harassment law suits in particular as being 'treacherous'.[10] As more and more women were turned down for partnerships, *Law Practice Management* warned that claims were likely to increase. Women lawyers 'may no longer have an interest in remaining quiet'.[11] By 1993, a United States list of new 'hot' practice areas included the employment law areas of harassment and discrimination.[12]

Will the New Zealand legal profession face the same scrutiny? What are the incentives for women lawyers to take more confident approaches towards their legal rights? Have women lawyers' expectations and attitudes altered so that now they may be more inclined to enforce their rights?

Women's career expectations

As a group, women lawyers' attitudes and expectations have changed significantly over the past one hundred years—turning full circle.

The very first group of women to qualify in law—Ethel Benjamin, Stella Henderson, Ellen Melville, Geraldine Hemus and Annie Lee Rees—were, in today's terms, leading feminists. Unusual for their times, they all had life-long careers (although not necessarily in law) and spoke out strongly on behalf of women's rights to education, employment, equal pay and equal opportunity. While they did not take action through the courts they frequently addressed public meetings and wrote papers and newspaper articles.

The second group who entered the law from 1915 through to the second World War took a different tack. The majority of these early women lawyers accepted their backroom roles and their limited prospects. Even in interviews relating to this research, some of these women did not wish to be identified nor to seem ungrateful for the, albeit limited, opportunities that they did have. Discrimination, as a legal concept, simply did not exist. Modesty, femininity and hard work were the professional qualities most admired in these women, a combination which effectively kept them 'in their place'.

The third group of women to enter the profession—from the second World War to the early 1960s—were more inclined to notice that they enjoyed fewer opportunities than their male counterparts. Complaining was still considered unladylike although several women lawyers in this group were prepared to speak out. By and large, these women accepted the convention that careers and marriages were incompatible or would limit their career prospects and range of employment options. Many 'retired' on marriage or pregnancy but re-entered the workforce when later social or economic changes made it possible.

The fourth group of women lawyers who studied law and entered the profession during the heydays of the women's liberation movement were more likely to seek equality. They made submissions and lobbied for laws outlawing discrimination and improving women's legal position. From the 1970s, women lawyers were asking for partnerships, maternity leave and equal pay. In the 1980s, judicial appointments, affirmative action and childcare assistance were added to the list. At the same time there were many women who ascribed to the view that if they worked hard enough for long enough, they must succeed despite the odds. These women were the beneficiaries of the first efforts to appoint women to boards, committees and the Bench. As a result, this group produced many of those who are known as 'exceptional' women lawyers—pioneers who made inroads into higher levels of the profession.

Today's recently admitted women lawyers want and expect equality. They aspire to partnerships, the judiciary and other positions in the legal system but not as rewards for being the same as men lawyers. Many of these women lawyers recognise the double standard inherent in the 'be the same' requirement because even when they are the same (in terms of abilities, skills and aspirations) they are still treated differently.

Many women lawyers now want the opportunity to be different—to practise law differently and to bring different qualities to the law. They talk often of 'balance; between families and careers and, unlike their counterparts in the previous decades, do not expect that they must relinquish their ambitions if they marry or have children. These women lawyers are inclined to say that the profession needs to change to accommodate women rather than the other way around. They make positive choices to do something else once they have tried and failed to succeed on the profession's terms.

A more confident approach

In the 1990s, there are signs that New Zealand women lawyers are taking a more confident approach in acting on discrimination. Awareness of the problem of discrimination is high but women lawyers are also more inclined to believe that action is necessary to eliminate the problem. In the 1992 national survey, 78 percent of women lawyers said that action was needed. Although these women looked to the law societies, the firms and other employers, and their colleagues to take action they also considered that they needed to take action themselves.[13]

Women lawyers' increasing inclination to look to legal remedies has been demonstrated by their desire that women lawyers' groups support their members' complaints. In the 1992 survey, women recognised the important role that these organisations could or did play in proactively tackling incidents of discrimination.[14] A newly-admitted lawyer in Christchurch proposed that a support group be established 'where complaints can be made and handled confidentially'. A woman partner in a provincial firm suggested that the reluctance to complain could be eased if other women could offer job security.

In a similar vein, women lawyers in Canada have provided support to women taking legal action through the Women's Legal Education and Action Fund, a government-sponsored initiative providing funding and support for complainants who might otherwise be unable to take human rights cases.[15] The Women Solicitors Association in the United Kingdom has also recently taken the initiative, announcing that it will not hesitate to support any solicitor who has 'a good case' of sex discrimination.[16]

There is no reason to believe that with the right support, women lawyers will deviate from the general trend of making complaints about discrimination and sexual harassment. Since the late 1980s, the Human Rights Commission and the employment courts and tribunals have seen a huge increase in the number of complaints involving sex discrimination and sexual harassment.[17] Likewise, the law societies are likely to face an increasing number of complaints of sex discrimination. While there were no complaints during the 1980s, the Auckland District Law Society received the first complaint in 1992 and the second in 1994. As in America, discrimination is a new area of legal practice. In February 1996, Auckland lawyer Brett McGuire described sexual harassment as 'the personal grievance of the year'. Employers, he cautioned, could not afford to be ignorant of the law.[18]

Economic reality may mean that women lawyers simply have no choice but to take a more confident approach toward enforcing their legal rights in employment. Unlike earlier generations of women, women lawyers entering the profession since the 1980s are less likely to have the 'fall-back' position of 'retirement' into marriage. They are more likely to expect the benefits and opportunities afforded to their male counterparts and, assuming present single-parent family trends continue, they may have the sole responsibility for supporting children and dependent adults.

From the early 1990s, law students have paid an estimated $10,200 to enrol in the four-year degree course plus an additional $2,450 for the professional legal studies course. In addition, students living away from home may have taken out loans of up to $34,000 to fund their legal education under the user-pays university education system. It remains to be seen how these women will respond to their comparatively limited ability to repay these loans and to enjoy the financial rewards of their studies.

Individual actions

Choice of procedures

In New Zealand a person may take civil legal action for discrimination under the Human Rights Act 1993 or the Employment Contracts Act 1991. While both laws provide similar legal protection from discrimination, the processes differ. Under the Human Rights Act, the complaint is handled by the Human Rights Commission which investigates the complaint on a confidential basis and attempts to conciliate between the parties. Failing conciliation, the Proceedings Commissioner may refer the complaint to the Complaints Review Tribunal (previously the Equal Opportunities Tribunal) which functions more like a court. Questions of law may be referred to the High Court which also hears appeals on decisions of the Complaints Review Tribunal.

The alternative procedure open to employees only is to take a personal grievance to the Employment Tribunal or the Employment Court. Although mediation may be pursued, it is optional. In the first years of the Act's operation most harassment cases have proceeded to adjudication following unsuccessful attempts at mediation.[19]

Some incidents of sexual harassment also warrant criminal sanctions. The Crimes Act 1961 and Summary Offences Act 1981 cover offences involving indecent acts, sexual violation, indecent assault, intimidation, offensive behaviour or language, and peeping or peering into a dwelling house. Although initially reluctant to take action, the police have more recently changed their approach, and have successfully prosecuted a sexual harasser where the behaviour occurred in a work environment. The judge in that case ordered a compensation payment to the woman concerned.[20]

In addition to these legal remedies, lawyers who experience discrimination from other lawyers may also rely on the professional ethical rules. The basic rule, rule 6.01, provides that a lawyer 'must promote and maintain proper standards of professionalism in relations with other practitioners'. The commentary to the rule states: 'No practitioner shall discriminate against or treat unfairly any other practitioner by reason of the colour, race, ethnic or national origin, sex, marital status or religious or ethical belief of that other practitioner.'[21]

Lawyers may make a complaint to any of the local district law societies, each of which have a disciplinary tribunal made up of eight lawyers and two lay people. The district law society has a discretion to refer a complaint to the New Zealand Law Society Disciplinary Tribunal. Alternatively, most district law societies operate a Friends Panel where council members or other senior practitioners are available to advise on personal and professional matters such as drug and alcohol addiction. Although office management and staff relations are usually covered, advice on discrimination and sexual harassment are not offered specifically.

Lawyers who work in government agencies where equal employment opportunities (EEO) programmes are in place may use the in-house procedures for complaints relating to discrimination and sexual harassment. These procedures are available to few private sector lawyers as only an estimated 20 percent of firms have sexual harassment procedures.[22]

Direct and indirect discrimination

Discrimination and sexual harassment need not be intentional to be unlawful. In proceedings under the Human Rights Act it is not a defence that the breach of the Act was unintentional or without negligence.[23] In the case of an employer's liability for an employee's actions, the employer need not be aware that harassment or discrimination has occurred.[24]

The Human Rights Act is specifically concerned with prohibiting behaviour and practices that have the effect of discriminating against a person or group on one of the prohibited grounds. Any conduct, practice, requirement or condition that at face value may not appear to contravene the Act but 'has the effect of treating a person or group of persons differently on one of the prohibited grounds of discrimination' will be unlawful unless the person responsible for the act or practice 'establishes good reason for it'.[25]

What constitutes 'good reason' is undefined. In a recruitment or promotion context, it has been suggested that the 'good reason' test should only be satisfied where a qualification is necessary for performing a job.[26] On any rational interpretation of this test, many instances of indirect discrimination in the context of the legal profession would be found unlawful.

Employees

At law, individual employees have rights in relation to recruitment, pay, terms of employment, conditions of work, training, supervision, promotions and benefits, termination, sexual harassment, maternity leave, paternity leave and parental leave. For protection under the Human Rights Act 1993 complainants need not be in permanent paid employment—the Act covers job applicants, independent contractors and unpaid workers.[27]

Recruitment and termination

Asking questions in interviews of women lawyers relating to family status, intentions to marry, plans to have children, or arrangements for the care of children will amount to discrimination if those questions indicate or 'could reasonably be understood as indicating' an intention to discriminate against that applicant.[28] Even a discriminatory line of questioning by one interviewer in an interviewing panel may taint the entire process. Interviews by law firms in the United States have been found to breach discrimination law where other interviewers have acquiesced to a discriminatory line of questioning by one member of the interviewing panel.[29]

Taking New Zealand job applicants to a strip-show as part of their recruitment interview may also amount to a 'form of application for employment' which indicates an intention to discriminate. Although the show itself is not illegal, the mode of interviewing could reasonably be expected to deter women lawyers from applying.[30]

Employers will unlawfully discriminate where they refuse or omit to employ a person for a job by reason of their sex. Therefore, recruitment policies aimed at achieving a 'balance' of men and women will infringe the law.[31] If the sex of an applicant is a reason affecting the recruitment decision (which is not otherwise authorised under section 73 of the Human Rights Act) it amounts to sex discrimination, be it against women or men.[32] Likewise, employment agents asked by firms to exclude women candidates will infringe the law which states that it is unlawful for any person concerned with procuring employment for other persons to treat any applicant differently by reason of their sex.[33]

Where financial difficulties necessitate the retrenchment of employees, employers need to take care that the method of selection does not discriminate against women lawyers.[34] A recent Australian case held that the 'last on first off' policy of retrenchment, used also in New Zealand, indirectly discriminated against women employees.[35] Likewise, termination of employment must be conducted in a way that is not by reason of any of the prohibited grounds of discrimination.[36]

Refusing or omitting to employ a person as a result of her or his family commitments also breaches the Act. In a 1993 case before the Equal Opportunities Tribunal, the receiver of an employer company told the complainant that while she had the experience and the ability to do the job, he had 'one major reservation'—the fact that she had a young child. Although the receiver argued it was parenthood discrimination not sex discrimination, the tribunal found that 'the relevant factor was that she was a woman with a child'. The receiver employed a man to do the job—he also had children but that had not disqualified him.[37]

The Human Rights Act 1993 removed any doubt that parenthood was a ground of discrimination. From 1 February 1994, 'family status' was specifically included as a prohibited ground of discrimination. Since that time, employers and service providers legally cannot offer less favourable opportunities, treatment or benefits to people with responsibility for the part-time or full-time care of children or other dependants.[38] Of direct relevance to the legal profession, is that the law applies if an employer has simply 'assumed' or 'suspected' that the person has responsibility for children.[39]

Opportunities and benefits

The majority of women lawyers consider that they do not have the same opportunities to get 'good' work or 'good training' as their male colleagues.[40] This amounts to discrimination where better quality work or training is available to male employees of similar abilities.[41]

The Human Rights Act 1993 and the Employment Contracts Act 1991 provide slightly different tests as to ability and as to the work involved. 'Ability' is measured under the human rights legislation by comparing the complainant with other employees 'of the same or substantially similar capabilities', while the employment law test compares the complainant with other employees 'of the same or substantially similar qualifications, experience, or skills'. To satisfy the Human Rights Act, the other employee also needs to have been employed 'in the same or substantially similar circumstances *on work of that description*' (emphasis added) while, for the purposes of the Employment Contracts Act 1991, they need only be 'employed in the same or substantially similar circumstances'.[42]

Under the Human Rights Act then, for women lawyers to suffer sex discrimination, there needs to be a male lawyer of the same or similar capability in the workplace who has been employed to do the same work. Whether the Complaints Review Tribunal will apply this narrow test remains to be seen. Neither that tribunal nor its predecessor have deliberated on the meaning of this provision.[43] However, in practice the Human Rights Commission has found substance where there has not been an absolute comparator. The commission looks beyond the actual work done and examines the circumstances or status of the type of work involved or the position held when determining unlawful discrimination.[44]

Under the Employment Contracts Act 1991 the statutory test is wider and a court is likely to decide that it covers situations where the same opportunities were not offered to both men and women lawyers of similar or same abilities employed in similar circumstances although not to do the same type of legal work specifically. This may be relevant, for example, in a case of law clerk recruitment where clerks are employed to do general legal work but after a short period of employment, men clerks are allocated good fee earning commercial files while the women are given low fee-earning family law files.

The gender stereotyping of women lawyers into family law work and out of commercial work may also expose law firms to claims of discrimination if commercial work is available to a male lawyer of the same or similar capabilities employed in similar circumstances. So, for example, a firm that employs two law clerks to do general law clerk jobs across the firm will discriminate against the woman clerk if she alone is allocated family law work and family law work in that firm is 'less favourable' work.[45]

Where the allocation of work to women lawyers results in less favourable opportunities for promotions, a law firm is also discriminating. In the *Air New Zealand* case, men flight attendants were afforded a definite career path while women flight attendants were 'locked in' to a limited career path.[46] The Equal Opportunities Tribunal concluded that no woman attendant could actually achieve a truly comparable position with her male counterparts despite her individual merits. If, in the allocation of work and opportunities, law firms lock women lawyers into a limited career path, they will also infringe the Human Rights Act. This argument could have particular relevance in firms where associate partnership is the highest level women do in fact reach.

Denial of promotion opportunities in general will contravene the Human Rights Act. In 1995, the Human Rights Commission settled a case where a woman senior executive had been denied overseas business trips and promotion opportunities because of her sex. The company's chief executive had also sexually harassed the employee. The company agreed to pay the senior executive $37,600 which included her legal fees, $10,000 for humiliation and $20,000 for a university course.[47]

Law firms will be unable to hide behind their informal decision-making processes. In 1995, the Human Rights Commission upheld a complaint of promotion discrimination made by a senior woman manager in a commercial organisation. Her performance had been rated above average consistently and she had the qualifications and experience for the position but the company promoted a male manager. The commission found 'a high level of subjectivity in the respondent's appointment process. No interviews were conducted, nor was there a job description at the time of the appointment.' The company had made no efforts to properly consider the woman applicant and had no checks and balances to address the possibility of discrimination 'apart from a general statement in the Equal Employment Opportunity policy to the effect that there should not be any discrimination'. In addition, the commission's findings were supported by the experiences of other women in the organisation's management.[48]

Admission to partnership

Partnership discrimination is one of the prime areas for sex discrimination litigation involving the legal profession. At best women make up at best 12 percent of the partners in private practice and both men and women lawyers agree that women do not have equal partnership opportunities.[49] Nearly 90 percent of women lawyers are of the view that women do not have the same opportunity to achieve partnerships as their male counterparts. Of all the types of discrimination experienced by women in the legal profession, men lawyers agree that discrimination in partnerships is the worst.[50]

From 1 February 1994 the prohibition against discrimination in admission to partnerships applied to all firms regardless of size. From that time, under the Human Rights Act 1993, it was unlawful for persons promoting the formation of a firm or making partnership admission decisions to exclude a person by reason of their sex. There is no need to compare the ability of a woman candidate with that of a male candidate as there is for other types of promotions—it need only be proved that the refusal was by reason of sex, family status or any other prohibited ground of discrimination. In addition, firms cannot offer or afford 'less favourable terms and conditions' to one partner than are offered to other members of the firm by reason of that partner's sex. In this instance, the discrimination is ascertained by comparing the aggrieved partner's total remuneration and other benefits with those of other partners, of non-partners or of prospective members of the firm.[51]

Where access to partnership is in issue, other practices and policies may be relevant as evidence of discrimination in the partnership decision. In *Seitz v Peat Marwick Maine & Co* the plaintiff showed that accounting firm Peat Marwick had a policy of limiting the number of women law graduates recruited from university and that the intention of that policy was to avoid 'a large number of women coming up for partnership in later years'. Although Peat Marwick argued that its recruitment policy was irrelevant to its partnership decisions, the court took a different view and found a 'direct relationship' between the hiring policies and the partnership admission decisions.[52]

In the case of *Price Waterhouse v Hopkins*, which involved the multi-national accounting firm Price Waterhouse, it was claimed that the board in turning down a woman candidate had relied on evaluations from partners which had contained sex-stereotyped comments. After a long legal battle, the United States Supreme Court ruled in 1989 that the refusal to admit the woman to partnership was discriminatory because the board had 'generally relied very heavily on such evaluations in making its decision' and had failed to disclaim reliance on the negative stereotyped comments.[53] Where unanimous decisions on admissions to the partnership are required, as in most New Zealand law firms, the discrimination-based objection of only one partner, if instrumental to the decision not to admit a woman lawyer, can expose the entire firm to liability.

In a sex discrimination case involving a Philadelphia law firm, aside comments by partners amounted to evidence of discrimination when it came to partnership. At the time Nancy Ezold was hired, one partner told her, she 'would have a hard time because she was a woman, because she hadn't graduated from an Ivy League school and because she hadn't been on law review'. Partners steered complex matters away from Ezold, instead allocating to her routine 'pink ghetto' work. Combined, these events were accepted by the court as proof of discrimination by the firm.[54]

American women partners have also sued their firms for discrimination. In 1992, Baker McKenzie a multi-national law firm, faced a suit for sex and age discrimination filed by Ingrid Beall, a partner in its

Chicago office. Beall, who in 1961 had been made the firm's first woman partner, claimed that she had been criticised by partners in the firm for not being 'one of the boys'. Her efforts on behalf of other women in the firm 'drew hostile reactions and derogatory remarks from her peers'. The response was so negative that she had decided that her efforts were more of a hindrance than a help to other women in the firm.[55]

New Zealand courts are as likely as American courts to recognise the importance of partnership to professional employees. Where partnership opportunities have been used as a recruitment device, the later omission to admit eligible women candidates to partnerships may amount to discrimination—especially if equally or less qualified men are made partners. In light of New Zealand women lawyers clearly stated preference for achieving partnerships, it is conceivable that they will not allow their sex to stand in the way.

Political opinion

Since 1 February 1994, political opinion has been included in the prohibited grounds of discrimination covered by New Zealand human rights law.[56] Defined as 'any political opinion including the lack of a particular political opinion', this ground will be of direct relevance to feminist women lawyers. Women and men observed in the 1992 national survey that discrimination against feminists or women perceived to be feminists was a type of political discrimination in the profession and comments made indicated that women lawyers had been denied opportunities or had been subjected to harassment as a result of their politics.[57]

New Zealand law firms may find that partners' or employers' offhand comments about feminism or feminists come back to haunt them. In a 1990 United States case involving a woman lawyer employed in a corporate's legal department, evidence that the woman attorney was 'warned not to let woman's issues "get in the way" [and] told to read a book about women's supposed fear of success' was sufficient evidence to shift the burden of proof to her employer to prove it did not discriminate.[58] Likewise in the case involving Baker McKenzie, the hostile reaction to the discussion of women's issues within the firm formed part of the discrimination claim.

Sexual harassment

Following Anita Hill's disclosure of sexual harassment during the Clarence Thomas United States Senate confirmation hearings in November 1991, sexual harassment awareness around the English speaking world soared.[59] Harassment charges received by the United States Equal Employment Opportunities Commission increased by

71 percent. At the same time, the number of discrimination lawsuits filed by American women lawyers increased noticeably.[60]

The situation in New Zealand was no different. In the year to 30 June 1991, the Human Rights Commission had received 204 inquiries and 26 complaints relating to sexual harassment. Two years later the tally was 507 inquiries and 73 complaints.[61] By March 1994, the commission was 'deluged' with complaints, many of which related to sexual harassment.[62] Complaints relating to sexual harassment unexpectedly dropped in 1995, prompting the Chief Human Rights Commissioner to ask if this was due to the success of larger corporates introducing sexual harassment programmes or whether it was just a temporary change.[63] In the case of the legal profession the former explanation is unlikely. In any event, the number of inquiries and informal complaints about sexual harassment have continued to rise.[64]

Women's increasing awareness that sexual harassment is illegal, coupled with improvements in legal remedies and processes are no doubt helping to overcome women's reluctance to take legal action. Of the complaints investigated by the Human Rights Commission, the majority are found to have substance and those that are discontinued are usually done so on the basis of a successful settlement.[65] The Employment Tribunal and the Employment Court have taken more adversarial approaches which have recently attracted criticism from women lawyers, but the majority of cases claiming sexual harassment have been found to have substance.[66]

Overseas, the complainant success rate for sexual harassment cases is also high. Over half the cases taken in the United Kingdom between 1986 and 1990 were found to have substance, nearly double the success rate of cases of work-related discrimination in general.[67] Likewise the success rate of litigation taken in America is increasing. A 1991 Chicago study found that of the women who filed charges of workplace harassment, a large majority won their cases or settled out of court with their employers. In a survey by the American Management Association, 52 percent of its 524 member companies had dealt with sexual harassment claims in the last five years. Sixty percent of those claims resulted in disciplinary action against the harasser while only 17 percent were dismissed without action.[68]

As in the partnership discrimination area, New Zealand lawyers and employers in the profession have a huge risk of exposure to sexual harassment lawsuits by women lawyers.

In the 1992 national survey, as in previous district surveys, women lawyers reported incidents of harassment involving requests for sexual favours or advice that a promotion or career opportunity depended on a sexual favour.[69] Under the Human Rights Act 1993 and the Employment

Contracts Act 1991, requests for any form of sexual activity involving an implied or overt promise of preferential treatment or threat of detrimental treatment are unlawful.[70] In addition, this type of harassment would attract criminal sanctions under the Crimes Act 1961 or the Summary Offences Act 1981.

Other forms of harassment mentioned by women lawyers but by very few men lawyers were unwanted advances, sexual remarks or innuendo, deliberate touching or being brushed against, and misuse of position and power. Where the behaviour or comment is unwelcome or offensive and is either repeated or is so significant that it has a detrimental effect on the woman concerned, it will amount to sexual harassment.[71]

The inclusion of client sexual harassment in the Human Rights Act has also opened a new course of action for self-employed women lawyers (namely partners, barristers and sole practitioners). Before 1 February 1994, these women lawyers had no remedy outside the criminal law for sexual harassment by clients. Now they may make a complaint to the Human Rights Commission.

The 'laid back' approach?

Law firm partners and other employers would be wise to take complaints of sexual harassment seriously. Employers are principally liable for sexual harassment which occurs in the workplace—whether it involves employees, clients, customers or, more commonly in the legal profession, themselves.[72] The Employment Contracts Act and the Human Rights Act anticipate that (where the employer is not the harasser) the employer will do something to prevent harassment. For example, where an employee complains of client harassment in writing to an employer, the employer is required to investigate the facts and, if satisfied the behaviour occurred, is obliged to take 'whatever steps are practicable to prevent any repetition' of the behaviour. Where the behaviour continues and the employer had not taken preventative action, the employer will be in breach of the law.[73] The employee will have the option of making a complaint to the Human Rights Commission or pursuing a personal grievance under the Employment Contracts Act.

In 1992, a Houston firm was sued for ignoring staff complaints of sexual misconduct by one of its partners.[74] Multinational law firm Baker McKenzie found that within a year of filing, two sexual harassment suits had snowballed into nine complaints—all involving the same partner and most having been brought to the attention of management. In each case the firm had turned a blind eye, had downplayed the problem or had taken ineffective action to stop the discrimination, prompting the *American Lawyer* headline, 'Too little, too late'.[75] In September 1994 the first claim involving a legal secretary was successful. She was awarded US$7.1 million in punitive damages. The firm said it would appeal.[76]

Under the Human Rights Act, where New Zealand employees discriminate against or sexually harass other employees, employers are liable regardless of whether they knew of the behaviour or action. Unlike client sexual harassment, the employer does not have a second chance to take action to stop the harassment. The statutory defence simply requires that he or she 'took such steps as were reasonably practicable to prevent the employee from doing that act'.[77] The employer is expected to act *before* the harassment occurs.

What constitutes 'reasonably practicable steps' or just 'practicable steps' is not defined in the statutes. In practice, the Human Rights Commission has interpreted this to mean that an employer should have 'an active, up-to-date sexual harassment policy and programme in the workplace before they can avail themselves of the defence'.[78] The NZLS, in its submission on the Human Rights Bill, interpreted this clause to mean that 'employers who do not have in place anti-harassment programmes will be strictly liable'.[79] The steps required to prevent a reported incident of harassment recurring under the Employment Contracts Act is to a different standard. In 1989, the Employment Tribunal found that an employer having acted on a complaint of harassment by warning employees not to repeat the behaviour was sufficient to activate the defence.[80] More recently, however, an employer who issued a written warning to an employee for sexual harassment took 'an approach that was so laid back and ineffective' that it fell short of the defence.[81]

Two potential plaintiffs

A law firm's response to complaints of discrimination and sexual harassment must be on the basis that there are two potential plaintiffs. Where a complaint is false or not honestly made, has exposed a person to ridicule or contempt, and has injured their reputation, that person can sue for defamation. The alleged harasser or discriminator may also be aggrieved by the process if the principles of natural justice are ignored. This occurred in 1995 when Taranaki Health Care Ltd dismissed an employee following a complaint of sexual harassment. The Employment Court found that the employer had given insufficient notice of the specific allegations to the employee and had not afforded a real opportunity for explanation. These shortcomings amounted to procedural unfairness.[82]

A well-designed EEO or sexual harassment procedure should set out the basic steps for handling discrimination and sexual harassment complaints. This will ensure defamation does not occur and that principles of natural justice are complied with. Requirements will include: providing notice to the alleged harasser that a complaint has been received and that an investigation is to be held, allowing the alleged harasser an adequate opportunity to respond, investigating without undue delay, interviewing witnesses and recording their comments, reporting back to the alleged harasser and to the victim, complying with the Privacy Act 1993, and maintaining confidentiality.[83]

Appropriate action against the harasser where sexual harassment has been found to have occurred will depend on the degree and seriousness of the harassment. In the case of inappropriate sexual comments, an apology and sexual harassment training may be all that is required. In more serious cases, suspension followed by dismissal may be warranted. It is not necessary for an employer to have advised staff that harassment may amount to serious misconduct justifying dismissal. In a 1994 decision by the Employment Tribunal, the dismissal of an employee was upheld even though there was no written sexual harassment policy statement that sexual touching and sexual remarks were serious misconduct. The employer had properly investigated the complaint and complied with the principles of natural justice, and was entitled to dismiss summarily.[84]

Damages

Where a complaint of discrimination or sexual harassment is not settled and the Complaints Review Tribunal is satisfied that there was a breach of the Act, damages or remedies may be awarded. From 1 February 1994 the maximum damages payable was raised to $200,000, the same as the limit in the District Court.[85] Damages may be awarded for pecuniary loss suffered as a result of the action or behaviour, loss of any benefits, whether monetary or otherwise, and damages for humiliation, loss of dignity and injury to the complainant's feelings.[86] Although a lack of knowledge or intention will not provide a defence, the conduct of the defendant will be taken into account in the tribunal's decision on remedies to be granted.[87]

Persisting with denials or downplaying discrimination and sexual harassment could make matters worse. One United Kingdom law firm which 'felt it important to fight' a case of employee sexual harassment 'as a matter of principle' derived no favourable publicity from taking that stance.[88] In another discrimination case, the award of damages was increased where an employer which 'prides itself on being an equal opportunities employer' chose to attack the employee and continue the discriminatory behaviour after the complaint. The tribunal in that case made the maximum award against the respondent.[89]

Settlements negotiated by the Human Rights Commission may include a payment of compensation.[90] Before 1 February 1994, these sums infrequently exceeded $5,000, although in a case in 1993 two women who claimed age discrimination received compensation totalling $26,000 for the loss of their jobs and for distress. The employer also gave an assurance of future compliance with the Act.[91] In 1995, the commission negotiated a settlement involving the payment of $37,600 to a woman senior executive who had been denied promotion opportunities and subjected to sexual harassment.[92] In 1996, the commission reported it had achieved a settlement of $90,000 for a woman employee who had been harassed by three managers in the same company.[93]

Compensation negotiated or damages awarded under human rights legislation appears to be at a higher average rate than that awarded by the Employment Tribunal or the Employment Court—at least with regard to complaints of sexual harassment. The highest award relating to sexual harassment was made in 1991 by the Employment Court's predecessor, the Labour Court, when it awarded $95,000 to a male employee who had been unjustifiably dismissed for sexually harassing a co-worker.[94] In no known case had a woman complainant received compensation or damages anywhere close to that level.[95] However, by 1994 cases of sexual harassment taken under the Employment Contracts Act were resulting in employers paying compensation of up to $32,000.[96]

Compensation or damages for loss of wages sought by women lawyers could easily exceed the amounts awarded or settled in discrimination cases to date. Highly paid professional women who are able to prove discrimination in say admission to partnership may be able to claim up to the maximum of $200,000 placing them in a similar league to women lawyers in the United States. Although the compensation for injury to feelings and for legal fees would be no different to that sought by women in any other occupational group, the wages component in the legal profession context makes discrimination that much more expensive.

It would also be within the court's jurisdiction to consider making an order that a woman lawyer be made a partner by a firm which had discriminated against her in relation to partnership.[97] As in United States discrimination cases the focus is on placing the victim of discrimination in the position she or he would have been in but for the unlawful discrimination. In the *Price Waterhouse v Hopkins* case, this meant making the plaintiff a partner, awarding her US$371,175 back pay plus interest and US$422,460 attorney's fees. The court in that case noted that the size of firm involved would be a factor in the decision to award partnership but the larger the firm the more likely that partnership would be part of the award made.[98]

If international trends are any indication, awards of damages for discrimination and sexual harassment in New Zealand may increase. Following the American lead, the limit on compensation able to be awarded by United Kingdom industrial tribunals was removed in November 1993.[99] Indicative of the new legal standard, Gillian Wood, a salaried partner in a Leicester law firm, received £17,000 in an out of court settlement of her claim for equal pay and unfair dismissal. In addition, the firm agreed to implement an EEO policy.[100] High awards of damages have also been made in Australia. For example, in 1985 the New South Wales Anti Discrimination Tribunal awarded almost A$35,000 to a woman who suffered sexual harassment at her work. Nearly A\$27,000 was for pain and suffering, loss of enjoyment of life and injury to feelings.[101]

Implementing a sexual harassment programme

Although the Human Rights Commission can negotiate the implementation of a harassment prevention programme in the settlement of complaints, a 1994 High Court decision has cast doubt on the Complaints Review Tribunal's jurisdiction to order employers to do the same.

Before the 1994 *New Zealand Van Lines Ltd* case, the Equal Opportunities Tribunal (the predecessor to the Complaints Review Tribunal) had assumed it had jurisdiction to order defendants to take positive steps to prevent repetition of harassment or discrimination. As a result, the tribunal had ordered that defendants obtain educational material from the Human Rights Commission, attend education sessions approved by the commission, or implement a three year EEO programme.[102] In June 1993, the tribunal had made a similar order when, having found that a complaint of sexual harassment had substance, it ordered New Zealand Van Lines Ltd to implement, in consultation with the Human Rights Commission, an anti sexual harassment policy and programme at its Mount Maunganui branch. The order also required that the company meet the commission's normal consultancy charges in respect of implementing this change.[103]

On appeal to the High Court, Justice Smellie ruled that this and earlier decisions by the Complaints Review Tribunal were wrongly decided. While the tribunal was entitled to make restraining orders that prohibited harassment from occurring again according to Justice Smellie, it did not have jurisdiction under the Human Rights Commission Act to make orders requiring positive action. In legal terms, the legislation fell short of the power to grant mandatory injunctions.[104]

Although the decision turned on the interpretation of the law, it was also influenced by three other factors. First, the content of the order was problematic. The tribunal had required that the company use and pay for the consultancy services of the Human Rights Commission. Although encouraging and assisting with implementing programmes is one of the commission's statutory functions, Justice Smellie pointed out that, the Act indicated that 'this area of the Commission's work should be voluntary in nature, and [sexual harassment] programmes should be implemented as part of negotiated settlements'. In addition, the order was 'open-ended'. The tribunal had not set any parameters on the extent of the programme or the level of consultancy fees that would be charged. Yet, the level of damages that could be awarded was otherwise clearly fixed in the Human Rights Commission Act.[105] Although Justice Smellie refrained from comment, the inference was that the order was imprecise and potentially unjustifiably onerous.

Secondly, the order was sought and made under the incorrect provision in the Act. The order to implement a sexual harassment programme was requested on the basis that it would redress any loss or damage suffered by the complainant, but the complainant had left her employment with the company more than four years before the tribunal's order.[106] Justice Smellie could not see what benefit the programme would have to this complainant.[107] She was, in addition, the only female employee at the company's Mount Maunganui branch. In the alternative, the judge considered whether the order to implement a programme was allowed under the provision enabling the tribunal to grant '[s]uch other relief as [it] thinks fit'. But, even taking a 'liberal and enabling interpretation', he found that the tribunal was not authorised to impose remedies which 'the parties might well agree to as a term of a negotiated settlement'.[108]

Finally, Justice Smellie viewed the order to implement a sexual harassment prevention programme as coercive and therefore outside the legislative intent of the Human Rights Commission Act. He acknowledged that if the legislation was to achieve its purpose, the tribunal must be empowered to 'strike at the heart of the problem' preventing its recurrence and requiring that steps be taken to enhance the work environment. He added:

> But the enactment of anti-discrimination legislation is a delicate political exercise, in which it is essentially for the elected representatives of the community to decide what objectives are best accomplished by education, encouragement and negotiation, and which in the end must be enforced by coercion. [It was not for the tribunal or the High Court to] usurp the function of the legislators ... however beneficial such extended powers might appear to those working in the human rights field.[109]

The implications of the *New Zealand Van Lines Ltd* decision are far-reaching. Although the decision related to an order requiring implementation of a sexual harassment policy and programme, the decision would equally apply to implementation of other EEO policies and programmes. Short of a legislative amendment or a successful appeal of the decision, the Complaints Review Tribunal cannot now compel an employer to take positive action, although it can make an order restraining employers from repeating the unlawful behaviour. At a practical level, such an order is likely to be ineffective with regard to those employers who will not take tangible steps (such as sexual harassment and EEO programmes) to remedy the causes of the problems. Undoubtedly, prudent employers will continue to implement sexual harassment policies and procedures to avoid liability under the Human Rights Act and the Employment Contracts Act. But, for those who continue to ignore their responsibility in this area, the courts, as a result of the *New Zealand Van Lines Ltd* decision, cannot compel them to do the same.

Following that decision, the Human Rights Commission has continued to conciliate complaints and effect settlements on the basis that the company or firm implements new policies and procedures, provides training sessions on sexual harassment to employees or undertakes training in pre-employment procedures. All these steps are voluntary but will ensure that those employers, at least, are less likely to be the subject of complaints to the Complaints Review Tribunal. In 1996, the commission's harassment prevention coordinator reported that most Human Rights Commission settlements were against organisations which did not have prevention policies in place.[110]

People or profit?

Law firms tempted to argue that implementing EEO programmes or sexual harassment prevention procedures are too costly, might find the courts unsympathetic.

In 1993, the Privy Council determined, in the context of the statutory requirement that New Zealand state-owned enterprises operate as successful businesses, that 'the creation of profit is of no greater importance than the other objectives identified in [the State-Owned Enterprises Act 1986]'.[111] The other objectives referred to included being 'a good employer' (which expressly includes providing an EEO programme) and exhibiting 'a sense of social responsibility by having regard to the interests of the community in which it operates'.[112]

The court decision carries an important policy direction that profitability should not override other fundamental responsibilities such as providing EEO. Although the Privy Council decision applies only to state-owned enterprises, it provides an indication of how the highest New Zealand court may interpret human rights related legislation when that legislation appears to cut across business imperatives.

Collective action

Women lawyers also have access to a range of collective actions which could be used to enforce their legal rights. These include 'class' actions, Human Rights Commission investigations, actions under the New Zealand Bill of Rights Act 1990 or claims at international law.

'Class' actions

A mechanism which may 'spread the risk' for women lawyers seeking redress for discrimination is to use 'class' or representative actions. The Human Rights Commission Proceedings Commissioner is able to bring proceedings on behalf of a class of persons seeking remedies against a person or business carrying on a discriminatory practice.[113]

Where there is more than one aggrieved person involved in proceedings before the Complaints Review Tribunal, the total amount of damages that may be awarded is multiplied by that number.[114] For example, in a case involving five women lawyers claiming discrimination against their employer, the total liability exposure could be $1 million— more than most law firms face in client negligence claims.

The Human Rights Act does not limit a person's right to bring any proceedings in any other court, leaving open the option of taking action directly in the High Court.[115] Class or representative actions may be taken in the High Court where two or more persons have 'the same interest in the subject matter' of the proceeding, and the consent of others with like interest is available or at the direction of the court.[116] Women lawyers, for example, could sue firms for breach of contract or seek exemplary damages in cases of prolonged harassment or particularly serious discrimination.

Human Rights Commission investigations

The Human Rights Commission is specifically empowered to initiate an investigation into any act, omission, practice, requirement or condition which is or appears to be direct or indirect discrimination of a group covered by the Act.[117] Following complaints of recruitment discrimination against Westpac Bank and the Bank of New Zealand in the early 1980s, the commission decided to examine the employment policies of all trading banks in New Zealand. This investigation resulted in a recommendation that the trading banks prepare special plans to assist women to advance in all areas of the banks' activities.[118] In June 1986, the commission reported that, as a result of action taken, 'a number of positive changes in employment practices and structures have been made in the banking industry'.[119]

Likewise in Australia, the federal Human Rights Commission has elevated awareness of the rights of minority groups through public inquiries. In turn, the heightened public interest has forced the government to direct resources towards redressing the problem.[120]

Investigations by the commission are certainly consistent with the notion that the victims of discrimination or harassment should be protected from the revictimisation that can occur when complaints are pursued. Whether the commission will be able to dedicate the necessary resources toward wide scale investigations is a different matter.[121]

New Zealand Bill of Rights Act 1990

In addition to challenges using the Human Rights Act 1993, there is scope for legal action under the New Zealand Bill of Rights Act 1990. This law protects the right to freedom from discrimination on the grounds of sex, marital status, race, ethnic or national origins or religious or ethical belief. Acts by the legislative, executive and judicial branches of government must comply with this right. Failing to do so will give rise to remedies by an aggrieved person or class of persons.[122] The protection offered by this law also extends to the district and national law societies, being organisations which perform public functions, powers or duties conferred by law.[123]

Law society leaders, judges and politicians frequently point to the legal profession's special position in the legal system. Most lawyers appreciate that the law society is not simply a club or a union which exists to advance the interests of its members. The Law Practitioners Act 1982 provides that the national and district law societies exist for a dual purpose—to promote the interests of the legal profession and to promote the interests of the public in relation to legal matters. As Judith Potter has commented, the legal profession is charged with 'protecting and maintaining an independent profession and an independent judicial system'.[124] The extent of sex discrimination in the profession certainly brings into question the law societies' abilities to perform their statutory duties.

International human rights laws

New Zealand is a party to several international covenants affecting women's rights—among them the Convention on the Elimination of Discrimination Against Women (CEDAW) and the International Covenant on Civil and Political Rights. In relation to CEDAW, New Zealand is obliged to report annually to the United Nations on its compliance with the convention.

In August 1995, Justice Dame Silvia Cartwright, at a speech to the AWLA, suggested that New Zealand lawyers should become more familiar with CEDAW. The United Nations CEDAW committee, of which Justice Cartwright was a member, was fighting to implement a system which would enable complaints on the failure to implement CEDAW to be heard by the committee. Without the system there was no formal opportunity for women to air their complaints outside New Zealand.[125]

There is, however, the possibility of petitioning the New Zealand Parliament. In New Zealand, as in many jurisdictions, there is an increasing awareness that sex inequality detracts from the legitimacy of the law and of democracy. In November 1994, a group of women led by ex-member of Parliament Marilyn Waring launched a challenge to the unequal representation of women in Parliament. As a State party to international human rights laws, their petition claimed that the New Zealand Government was obliged to ensure equal representation to women in the government of the nation. By 1993, one hundred years after women had won the vote, only 36 of the total 1,163 members of Parliament had been women. Further changes to the system of representation, the petition claimed, must now redress that inequality.[126]

Lending force to the petition was a 1989 Supreme Court of Canada decision, *Law Society of British Columbia v Andrews*. In that case, three of the five justices ruled that the determination of rights was 'not to be made only in the context of the law which is subject to challenge but rather in the context of the place of the group in the entire social, political and legal fabric of our society.' Distinctions between groups and individuals by the Legislatures 'should not bring about or reinforce the disadvantage of certain groups and individuals by denying them rights freely accorded to others'.[127] Although the decision of that court is not binding in New Zealand, the analysis of how to assess inequality and rights is relevant to the interpretation of the international laws protecting those rights.

The under-representation of women and ethnic minorities in the judicial branches of government is open to the same challenge. The exposure to this challenge will increase as the evidence of gender bias within the judiciary increases.[128] Men and women lawyers, and judges themselves, are questioning how justice can be dispensed properly when there are so few women involved in its administration.[129]

Conclusion

Legal remedies provide a potent tool which women lawyers and other women are increasingly willing to use in achieving equality. The targets of this action could include law firms, the judiciary, law societies and other decision makers in the legal system. Under civil, criminal and constitutional laws, their exposure to liability is extensive.

Women lawyers, from the late 1990's may be more inclined to take discrimination and equal rights litigation. Their career expectations and economic realities may leave them with little choice.

Business: Benefits of Diversity

While the legal remedies available to women lawyers may force a reappraisal of the profession's response to gender issues, there are other compelling business and professional reasons for change. The legal profession, like other professions, has yet to appreciate fully the costs of discrimination and gender bias and the benefits which can be gained from eliminating those problems.

Gender bias is a form of cultural bias where one 'norm' is preferred over another. In the case of the legal profession that norm is the male model where family and paid work are kept largely separate and women's and men's roles are defined accordingly. However, this is not the only form of cultural bias which exists within the profession. According to lawyers, other types of bias are also evident, particularly in the areas of race, ethnicity, age, sexual orientation, disability and class.[1]

Eliminating all types of discrimination and cultural bias is a business and professional imperative. The ever increasing diversity of the New Zealand population and workforce provides an opportunity for business success. In other words, workplaces with staff of diverse sexes, races, ethnicities, ages, sexual orientations and disabilities will no longer be seen as problem workplaces but ones with potential strategic advantages.

Although the predominant culture in the New Zealand legal profession has developed to accommodate men's traditional lifestyle, a range of social and political changes have made those practices irrelevant and burdensome for men as well as for women. As law firms and other employers approach the twenty-first century, those that adopt a new inclusive culture will not only survive but will thrive.

Putting the problem in perspective

In the past, the costs and inconveniences flowing from sex discrimination and gender bias, where recognised, were attributed to women. This was all part and parcel of the 'woman problem' experienced by law firms and the profession. The solution for some firms was not to employ women lawyers or to underemploy them so that they made less impact when they left or when their 'special needs' had to be accommodated. Alternatively, some firms simply overlooked women when it came to promotions or partnerships.

As the profession enters the next century, these 'solutions' will continue to recreate the problem. Workforce demographics and population trends mean that it will not be feasible to overlook women and ethnic minorities or to continue to ignore the family needs of all employees and partners. Clients, in an increasingly discrimination-conscious world, will expect the legal profession to provide a relevant and modern service—including having women lawyers and ethnic minority lawyers represented at all levels of the profession and the legal system. Developments in business and management know-how will also prompt a reassessment of gender bias and discrimination.

It is legal business that must change—not women.

Costs of discrimination

The hidden costs

When talking about the costs of discrimination with lawyers, the conversation generally turns to the costs of taking steps to eliminate the problem: the expenses and headaches involved in providing family leave, childcare assistance, pay equity and equal opportunities. Employers are quick to assert that they are running businesses, not charities. The costs are perceived to be prohibitive and when weighed against the need to stay in business, few are convinced that it is feasible to make changes.

While lawyers are reasonably up front about the costs of change, few openly acknowledge that discrimination and gender bias can and have returned a tidy profit. Using women lawyers as a largely lowly paid expendable workforce has been to the profession's advantage. When labour shortages have occurred, women have been brought in as semi-skilled labour or recruited by law firms on temporary bases. Alternatively, in times of recession, fewer women have been employed or promoted—an effective way of ensuring they would eventually leave. The fact that discrimination and gender bias are perceived to pay, for some firms, is a disincentive to change the status quo or is even an incentive to retain it. What is little appreciated is that there are also costs associated with discrimination and in the final analysis there may well be a net loss rather than a perceived profit.

Whether intentional or unintentional, discrimination and gender bias extract a very high and largely hidden price from women, the businesses they work in, the profession and New Zealand society. The nature of New Zealand's accounting and fiscal systems, at government and organisational levels, means that these costs are rarely quantified. Part of the reason for this is that discrimination and gender bias are difficult to define in monetary terms and so tend to be omitted from the economic ledger. However, another reason has been the lack of interest in or necessity to include these costs because the system appears to have largely worked without doing so.

Because discrimination and gender bias are built into the economic framework of legal business, they must be addressed within that context. To do so, law firms and other employers must consider all aspects of the equation when declining to take action about discrimination. The actual costs involved will vary in each organisation but, regardless of size, the costs provide a compelling reason to take action to eliminate discrimination and gender bias.

Legal liability

As demonstrated in chapter fifteen, New Zealand law firms and other employers in the profession have a potentially huge exposure to liability from discrimination law suits. The Human Rights Act 1993 in particular impacts on the legal profession by expanding partnership discrimination and employer liability for sexual harassment.

Before 1994, the damages exposure was in the tens of thousands of dollars, at most; law firms and other employers now face maximum penalties of $200,000. Prudent employers may seek to obtain insurance cover for this contingency, while others might request that partners or employees indemnify the partnership for any discrimination or sexual harassment litigation. Where insurance is sought, a firm's potential exposure to litigation is likely to be of interest to the insurance company when fixing the premium.

Reputation

While difficult to quantify in dollar terms, discrimination complaints or a history of discrimination will affect a law firm's reputation. Information about a firm's discriminatory practices or about sexual harassment within a firm travels quickly through professional networks. With regard to sexual harassment, both men and women lawyers in the 1992 national survey were well aware of the frequency with which it had been experienced by others. In 1992, approximately one-quarter of the male lawyers surveyed said that sexual remarks, sexual innuendo, misuse of positions of power and unwanted advances had occurred in their workplaces. For each type of harassment, women lawyers were much more aware than men that it had happened.[2]

Firms with 'bad reputations' are avoided by women, Maori and ethnic minority lawyers. While this may be an outcome that the firm is happy with in the short term, it is not advantageous in the long term as the workforce demographics change. In addition, firms with this kind of reputation will be well known outside the profession. Clients who prefer to instruct EEO employers will not hesitate to go elsewhere.

The present nature of partnership liability also means that the antics or misbehaviour of one partner within a firm taints the entire firm. On top of the legal liability, the effect on the reputations of individual partners could be devastating. New Zealand law firm partners frequently hold public offices or positions on public or professional committees and boards. Their association with a high profile discrimination case could be devastating. In an American case, where a partner of the president of the local state Bar was accused of sexually harassing a number of women employees, counsel for the women publicly called for the president to step down until the allegations were resolved. His leadership of the Bar was said to be 'an affront to its female membership'.[3] This kind of adverse publicity could be hard to live down.

Reputation, for individual lawyers and for law firms, can be determinative of success or failure within the profession and in business. Association with discrimination, no matter how widespread it may be in the community, the profession or in business is unlikely to be condoned when publicly aired.

Low productivity

Discrimination erodes employees' commitments to their jobs. For some women lawyers it can seem that no matter how hard they work they are never going to earn the recognition earned by their male colleagues. They see few women doing well in their workplaces, few prospects for their own advancement and no genuine hope that this will change. As a last ditch means of self-empowerment, the only strategy open to some women is to do the bare minimum required by the job. Sadly, this becomes a self-fulfilling prophecy as it feeds employer assumptions that women lawyers are not serious about their careers and will not rise to the challenges presented by legal practice.

Sexual harassment has an even more marked effect on the productivity of women lawyers. Where the problem continues unresolved, the effects multiply. In a case of harassment by a colleague in the same workplace for example, the woman lawyer will be constantly reminded of the harassment and conscious of her potential exposure to further harassment. Where the harassment involves a partner, the effects will be worse, particularly if the partner takes the stance that sexual harassment has not occurred.

Continued problems of sexual harassment result in high absenteeism or the adoption of strategies such as the victim avoiding work assignments where contact with the harasser is involved. It is not unusual for women subjected to sustained harassment to become physically ill. They may need time off from work to get help, including counselling or psychiatric help.

Where sexual harassment or discrimination are also affecting others in the same workplace, the resulting productivity problems are multiplied. Employee focus will turn to the experiences of discrimination or harassment rather than to work-related or positive exchanges. The poor response rate by law firms to complaints of discrimination and sexual harassment to date does not augur well for cost effectiveness and productivity.

Retention problems

Many people leave their workplace when it is not possible to resolve discrimination. Although the question was not specifically asked in the 1992 national survey, eleven women and four men lawyers volunteered that they had left their jobs because of discrimination or sexual harassment.[4] This survey also canvassed only lawyers in practice, so these fifteen lawyers are likely to represent the tip of the iceberg.

According to the Human Rights Commission, in approximately 80 percent of the cases of sexual harassment which come before it, the women complainants have already left their jobs.[5] High staff turnover within a firm is one of the clearest signs that sexual harassment is occurring. In the legal profession, it is also one of the clearest indicators that women lawyers' career paths are blocked. 'Moving on' is frequently mentioned by women lawyers as a solution to their lack of prospects.

Even where 'disaffected' employees leave, it would be thoughtless of employers to assume that they have taken the problem with them.[6] More often than not the problem is within the organisation itself, and it will resurface and affect others who remain in the firm. This is particularly so in the case of sexual harassment and other forms of discrimination. As executive director of the Equal Employment Opportunities Trust, Trudie McNaughton has pointed out the work environment itself is toxic, so even where employers recruit a replacement who has the desired qualities, the likely outcome is that the person will under-achieve or leave.[7]

Other costs

The attrition of women due to discrimination means that the investment in their legal education and their training in law firms is wasted—at least from the profession's perspective. For every trained lawyer who leaves a firm, the firm incurs the costs of advertising, recruiting and training. As women gain experience, there is also the increasing possibility that they will take their clients with them when they set up on their own or join another more EEO conscious firm. Even where the clients remain, the firm suffers the down time while the new lawyer becomes familiar with the client's work.

In the United States, businesses have become acutely conscious of these otherwise unquantified discrimination-related costs. A 1988 survey of Fortune 500 companies showed that the average company could expect to loose US$6.7 million a year from lost productivity, absenteeism and employee turnover in addition to damages, attorneys' fees and costs of litigated lawsuits.[8] More recently, United States recruitment consultants estimated that replacement costs usually amount to 90 percent of the departing employee's annual salary.[9]

New Zealand organisations are also beginning to quantify the expense involved in ignoring gender bias and discrimination. The Treasury and the Inland Revenue Department, for example, have estimated it costs $18,000 to replace a senior policy analyst.[10] The Police Association has estimated that it costs $45,000 to train one officer. In response to the high exit rate of trained personnel, the association introduced flexible policies with the expectation that $1 million will be saved each year.[11]

Costs of work and family separation

Legal practice, as presently organised, extracts a high personal price from an increasing number of lawyers. Hours of work, practice methods, management systems and family leave policies and practices simultaneously create and reinforce a culture which dictates the separation of work and family. The impact of this has fallen most heavily on women lawyers but increasingly it is affecting men lawyers.

Unbalanced lives

Contrary to predictions, technology has not freed professionals from working long hours in the office or at home. In fact, facsimile machines, electronic mail and mobile telephones have made lawyers more available to clients and to the firm for more hours. Where only 25 percent of lawyers in Auckland in 1987 were working more than 50 hours per week, that proportion had increased to 31 percent five years later.[12]

City-based lawyers work longer hours than their colleagues in the smaller centres and provinces. Lawyers in Auckland and Wellington, for example, tend to work longer hours than their colleagues in the Hamilton and Otago regions, and as a result are more likely to express a desire for greater work flexibility. Even so, an estimated one-quarter of lawyers in other centres were working in excess of 50 hours per week on average in 1992; very few worked less than 30 hours per week.[13]

Part-time work is rarely available. In 1992, an estimated 10 percent of women lawyers and 4 percent of men lawyers were working part time in private practices. Only a few of these lawyers were partners and most were working up to 30 hours per week.[14]

The long hours worked, particularly by men lawyers, mean lawyers are working outside usual business hours. While this will cut into their time with their families and friends, it also means they have less time to themselves.

Stress of the job

Stress levels among New Zealand lawyers are high and appear to be on the increase.[15] John Caldwell, in his 1991 survey of one hundred experienced practitioners from Auckland and Christchurch, found that 67 percent regarded their stress levels as high or very high. Another 26 percent described their stress levels as moderate, leaving only 7 percent who considered they experienced low levels of stress. Contrary to the 1992 national survey, Caldwell found that stress levels were marginally higher in Christchurch than they were in Auckland.[16]

As in legal practice, being a judge is very stressful. A survey of women judges by psychologists Kaye Allen and David Winsborough during the 1993 International Conference of Women Judges in Wellington found 66 percent of the judges mentioned judicial duties as a source of stress. On the scale of occupational stressors, judicial work surpassed all other sources of stress. Women judges reported feelings of tiredness, tension and emotional strain caused by their jobs.[17]

Of course, not all stress is bad. Respondents in Caldwell's survey pointed out that the stress added to the excitement and challenge of legal practice and so was not 'an entirely negative feature'. Over 70 percent of the lawyers surveyed rated their job satisfaction as high or very high.[18] While this is encouraging, it must be remembered that the survey canvassed only lawyers who were self-employed as partners, sole practitioners or barristers.[19] As the 1992 national survey discovered, it is these lawyers who generally enjoy greater flexibility and a sense of control over their work, their finances and their lifestyles.[20] They were more likely than others to have greater work benefits, many of which could lead to decreased stress: gym memberships, club memberships, flexible hours, medical insurance and car parking.[21]

The type of legal work being undertaken will also effect the likelihood of stress. Psychologists rate family and criminal law as areas involving high levels of emotion and stress.[22] Practice management consultant Doug Arcus and psychologist Ruth Arcus have encountered women lawyers working in family law who after three to four years are experiencing severe stress. In some instances, these lawyers have symptoms of burn-out and may be suffering from depression. Their advice to firms is 'do not feed young women lawyers a constant diet of family law work'.[23]

In addition to the stress faced by women lawyers as a result of the types of work they perform, they will experience stress as a result of discrimination and sexual harassment. If they complain about discrimination they may be criticised or subjected to scrutiny for their own supposed lack of performance. Demonstrating emotion or indecision may be read as weakness. They may feel they need to be twice as good to get half as much. These stress factors affect women lawyers and judges. The Winsborough and Allen survey of women judges found that in some cases women judges were reluctant to consult on decisions because they feared consultation would be interpreted as an inability to make decisions and therefore a weakness.[24]

For some lawyers, balancing parenting with their careers is a major source of stress. Personal, home and work conflicts are common for mothers as well as for fathers working in the legal profession. While child-rearing books exhort fathers to spend time with their newborn babies, for many, work demands mean they cannot.

For many lawyers there is usually no warning that extended hours will be required, making it even more difficult to make family and personal arrangements with any certainty. Domestic partners of lawyers know well the six o'clock telephoned apology from their partner that they cannot make it home for a dinner engagement, school parent-teacher interview or other commitment. In a similar way, holidays are often subject to last minute changes or the threat of change or involve the lawyer-partner being available to the firm or clients while on holiday.

At the end of the day, work stress ends up in the bedroom. Men and women lawyers, like other work-stressed professionals, suffer problems with unsatisfactory sex lives. Psychologist Yvonne Edwards explained that the problems arise in a couple when the women are trying to do three different jobs: trying to be a successful parent; trying to be a professional; and trying to be a partner. Their male partners are also working in excess of 40 hours per week and 'when they should be at their most virile, [they] are putting a lot of that virility into work'. The extension of the working week, and the invasion of new technology into what would otherwise be 'quality time' can mean that sex for professionals becomes just another performance stress.[25]

Handling stress

Lawyers as a group are not well known for their ability to deal with stress. While the effect of stress on each individual will vary significantly depending on the method of stress management, Winsborough observed that lawyers tend to use 'repressive coping styles'. When it comes to work-related stress, they are inclined to intellectualise to cope with the stress—a coping mechanism, he suggests, which fits neatly with the ideals of objectivity and independence instilled through legal training. There is usually little opportunity for debriefing or workplace support and as a result the lawyer is left carrying the emotional burden.[26]

Several studies suggest that women lawyers and men lawyers will take different paths in handling stress. A 1988 study of Auckland women lawyers found that alcohol played a significant role in their workplaces and there was little or no pressure to limit the amount of alcohol consumed. Women lawyers in the study placed their own restraints on their drinking and intentionally reduced their alcohol intake when under pressure. Male colleagues, in contrast, were believed to be more inclined to drink to relieve stress and to rely more heavily on alcohol as a pressure release.[27] This may be the case even where they might not have initially turned to that form of stress release. As one recent law graduate observed in the 1992 survey, he 'was alarmed by the amount of alcohol consumed and the pressure on [him] to drink also'. Another respondent described alcohol as 'an occupational hazard'.

However, Winsborough and Allen note that the stress levels shown in the survey of women judges are no different from those found in men judges. A study of Canadian male judges showed that they too experienced high levels of stress. The important difference between the women and men judges was that the women judges adopted more effective coping strategies. Strategies most frequently used by women judges when faced with job stress were planning, positive reframing, taking action, acceptance and restraint. Strategies least used were alcohol, denial and behavioural and mental disengagement. 'Less positive' coping styles were more frequently adopted by the men judges.[28]

Although a specifically New Zealand based study has not been done, this research suggests that New Zealand men and women judges may be affected differently by job-related stress. As a group, judges, of course, are not immune from usual human problems. As Sir Geoffrey Palmer has pointed out, judges have 'personal and matrimonial difficulties. Health problems can beset them. Some suffer from depression. Alcoholism and drinking problems can afflict them.'[29]

While women in the legal profession may use more constructive coping styles than men, women lawyers may still be more inclined to abuse alcohol than non-professional women. A wider study conducted at the same time as the 1988 Auckland women lawyers' study found when comparing groups of women and their use of alcohol that business and professional women were inclined to heavier drinking compared with women in other occupations.[30]

The hazard of alcohol and drug abuse has hit home in the Canadian and United States legal professions. According to a 1993 Washington study, 18 percent of lawyers surveyed were said to be addicted to alcohol—8 percentage points higher than the rate in the general population. Another one percent abused cocaine. Fourteen percent were estimated to suffer from severe depression.[31] Russ McKay, the coordinator of the British Columbia Law Society programme designed to assist lawyers with drug problems, estimated that one-third of the profession 'is probably in trouble'. The numbers of lawyers seeking help for substance abuse, relationship problems, depression and anxiety was increasing every year.[32]

The problem of gambling addictions have certainly confronted the New Zealand legal profession. In 1993, an Upper Hutt lawyer's gambling addiction, along with other defalcations by lawyers, cost every principal in practice $10,000 to cover the fidelity fund shortfall used to repay client's money stolen to service the addiction. The time and energy required to clean up the resulting public relations disaster also meant that the Wellington and New Zealand law societies diverted valuable resources away from other more constructive initiatives.

The larger district law societies and the national law society operate Friends Panels or similar services where senior practitioners are available to assist with professional, financial and personal difficulties. These schemes, while designed to operate on confidential bases, are little-used, as lawyers fear they will open themselves up to professional scrutiny and possibly censure. In addition, they rely on volunteer lawyers who have personal and professional experience but, for the most part, have had no training in crisis counselling.[33] Many lawyers do not know that the schemes exist, as they are rarely advertised in the professional newsletters and magazines.

Stressed lawyers make bad decisions not only for clients but which are potentially devastating for firms. Lawyers operating under sustained high stress levels are at best inefficient and at worst completely unproductive. According to at least one insurance broker, 90 percent of the claims made by lawyers on income protection policies related to stress associated illnesses which prevented them from working.[34] Firms which remain oblivious to impaired staff performance may find that their revenue is down and that their exposure to negligence liability is wide open.

Without proper intervention and management, work-related stress will continue to impact on family lives as well as productivity. A 1993 report by the International Labour Organisation concluded that job stress had become a 'global phenomenon' and was 'one of the most serious health issues of the 20th century'.[35] Another international study has suggested that New Zealand may be badly hit by the stress epidemic.[36]

Inflexibility and productivity

There has been little change in the inflexible approach of law firms and other employers in the profession. In 1987, 31 percent of Auckland lawyers wanted more flexibility in their work, while another 30 percent wanted more flexibility in their hours. Five years later, over half the lawyers surveyed in 1992 wanted more flexibility in the hours or the way that they worked—60 percent of women lawyers said so compared with 51 percent of men. The reasons given by both sexes for wanting more flexibility included improving their quality of life, improving their health and decreasing stress, and being able to spend more time on outside interests, leisure and family.[37]

The desire to spend more time with family was felt particularly by men lawyers. In the 1992 survey, 67 percent of men wanted more flexibility so they could spend more time with their family compared with 57 percent of women. Conversely, more women than men wanted flexibility so they could fulfil family obligations: 27 percent of women compared with 17 percent of men. Another significant issue for lawyers was a desire to spend more time in education. More women than men wanted time to further their education.[38]

For whatever reasons flexibility is needed, the effects of inflexibility are ultimately borne by businesses. Research by the New York-based Families and Work Institute has identified the productivity effects of work-family concerns:

- Twenty-five percent of United States employees with children under 12 years of age had between two and five childcare arrangement breakdowns within a three-month period. These breakdowns were found to correlate directly to higher absenteeism and lower concentration at work.

- One-third of employees with children spent time regularly worrying about childcare—a stress which detracted from concentration and productivity.

- In a one-month period, one-third of mothers in the United States with children under 12 years of age had a sick child. Fifty-one percent of those women stayed home with the child while the remaining 49 percent went to work and spent the day feeling distracted and guilty.[39]

These findings are equally relevant to the experiences of lawyer-parents in New Zealand law firms. The uncertainty of childcare arrangements experienced by some lawyer-parents means that they may be physically at work but psychologically elsewhere. When children were ill, or usual childcare arrangements broke down, 33 percent of women lawyers took unpaid leave and 30 percent took paid leave. In the minority of instances firms allowed lawyer-parents to take their children to work when care arrangements broke down at short notice. Otherwise, parents looked to relatives and friends to fill the gap.[40]

Retention problems

Economists point out that women's labour force participation is more wage sensitive than men's participation because women most commonly bear the burden and the costs of child care.[41] Women lawyers certainly agree that the high cost of child care is a disincentive to continuing in the workforce, especially where the time-management balance between home and paid work adds to the pressure. As one woman observed in the 1992 national survey: 'When you weigh up that you have to pay for quality childcare and what you are earning, you have to be on a pretty good salary to make returning to work worthwhile.'[42]

Childcare difficulties have prompted nearly 30 percent of women lawyers with children and 4 percent of men lawyers with children to contemplate resigning from their jobs. Costs of child care weighed heavily on women lawyers as did the sheer energy and effort required in working and having children. Some of the men who have considered resigning say they were influenced by the memories of their own unavailable fathers. One male lawyer described his preference as: 'I would rather be a father than a lawyer.'[43]

Workforce demographics

Women lawyers

Women lawyers make up a significant proportion of the workers in the profession. Although only 27 percent of total practitioners, they make up more than one-third of the employees in law firms and approximately 80 percent of legally trained employees in government agencies and corporates. In the Wellington region alone, women lawyers make up 38 percent of total employee lawyers, a proportion which has been increasing over the past three years. While the exit rate of these women may cause no problem to firms during economic recessions, this is unlikely to be the case in an expanding economy. As in the past, professional skill shortages may arise with little notice.

Overall, the exit rate of women lawyers from private practice, if unabated, will result in a skills drain which the profession can ill-afford. On current figures, by the year 2004, more than three hundred men lawyers will be over 60 years of age while only twelve women lawyers will be facing retirement.[44] Assuming there is no change in the exit rate of women, the profession will simply replace the skill and expertise held by that large group of men with that of the next generation of men lawyers.

Short of substantive change in the prospects offered by private practice, the profession simply may be unable to attract qualified women back into the law.

The exit rate of women lawyers also raises the wider professional problem of the specific type of skills drain which is occurring. Women lawyers' predominance in family law and criminal law means that their departure signals the loss of expertise in those particular areas. This is of concern not only to clients and firms but ultimately to the legal system itself which relies on a depth of skill and experience within the profession in order to function efficiently.

Family and domestic arrangements

National trends relating to family and domestic affairs will impact on the profession as on other types of business.[45]

Compared with previous generations, New Zealand women on average are having fewer children, and having them later in life. Women lawyers, like women in the population generally, are now less likely to marry and more likely to be single parents than women in previous generations. Divorce statistics continue to rise and 'reconstituted' families are becoming more common.

For the legal profession this means that the problems flowing from work-family stress, inflexible policies and high staff turnover will increase as more women lawyers reach the later average childbearing age. The question of family leave for women partners will become more central, and the need for family leave for senior women staff will become more acute.

Another significant issue facing New Zealand businesses is the aging of the population and the consequent increase in elder-care. Changes in the health system and national superannuation mean that the burden of elder-care will fall more heavily on family members. While lawyers in paid employment may be well placed to meet financial costs, they will be less able to provide the time and energy needed.

These and other trends will also affect men lawyers. Women married to or living with men lawyers who graduated since the late 1970s commonly have their own careers. Their desire to remain within the workforce or to return to it shortly after having children will have a direct impact on the domestic arrangements of many men lawyers. In future, assuming employment opportunities increase for women returning to the workforce, large numbers of male lawyers will be unable to rely on the domestic support of women working in the home. Unless professionals obtain home help, not as a back-up but to take primary responsibility for social, family and household affairs, there will need to be a change in the roles that men presently play in legal practice.

Ethnic diversity

The future generation of workers will be more ethnically diverse than ever before. In 1991, in the New Zealand population there were twice as many Maori and Pacific Islands children under 15 years of age as there were European/Pakeha children. Estimates show that of the 400,000 children expected to be born between 1981 and 2011, almost half will be of Maori descent.[46] Asian population growth is also phenomenal. Since 1986, the number of Chinese in New Zealand increased by 88 percent. That increase was surpassed only by the increase in the Indian population.[47]

These trends are not promising in light of the evidence of race and ethnicity discrimination in the legal profession. According to 35 percent of lawyers surveyed in 1992, discrimination on the grounds of race or ethnicity occurs in the profession. Women lawyers were more perceptive of this type of discrimination than men lawyers.[48]

Asian, Pacific Islands and Maori lawyers are more likely than European/Pakeha lawyers to experience discrimination on all grounds. Nearly 60 percent of non-European lawyers in the 1992 national survey had experienced some form of discrimination compared with 45 percent of European/Pakeha lawyers. Predictably, racial discrimination was the most prevalent, with 35 percent of non-European lawyers having personally suffered from it compared with only 4 percent of European/ Pakeha lawyers.[49]

Some law firms and employers advertise specifically for the employment of ethnic minority lawyers, while others refuse to hire non-European lawyers.[50] Several Malaysian women law graduates who were unable to find employment in law firms in 1993 were told in interviews: 'We don't think you will fit the New Zealand corporate culture' and 'We would prefer to take on a Kiwi guy.'

While law firms appear keen to employ Maori law graduates for work involving Treaty of Waitangi issues, they will need to revisit their career advancement prospects as these lawyers become better qualified. Treaty of Waitangi legal work, which was performed by more than half the Maori lawyers in the 1992 survey, was rated as offering the lowest prospects for advancement.[51] So, despite firms' desire to employ Maori lawyers to do Treaty work, it seems at least from the profession's perspective that this may not translate into partnership or promotion prospects. It must also be examined whether these rewards are relevant to Maori lawyers in light of what, for many, is an overriding obligation to advance the position of their iwi (tribe).[52] According to Maori, Pacific Islands and other ethnic minority lawyers surveyed in Auckland in 1995, discrimination remains a pressing problem. Race and ethnicity affected opportunities to obtain work and promotions. Mainstream law firms were said to be providing little or no cultural support.[53]

It appears that some ethnic minorities' groups, like women lawyers, are creating their own work opportunities outside mainstream legal practice. In the 1995 Auckland survey, several small law firms and one barristers' chambers were identified as consisting solely of Pacific Islands lawyers and support staff. Outside those workplaces, very few Pacific Islands lawyers were known to be principals.[54] One Otahuhu, Auckland firm, King Alofivae Malosi, consisted of three women partners (La-Verne King, Sandra Alofivae and Ida Malosi)—one Maori partner and two Samoan partners. Of the four staff members in that firm three were Maori and one Pakeha/European. Other firms (for example Rangitauira & Co in Rotorua, Kumar & Co in Hamilton, and Loo & Koo and Tunnicliffe Williams in Auckland) are known to consist either solely or pre-dominantly of partners and legal staff who are from the same ethnic minority group. While European/Pakeha law practices have traditionally comprised employees and staff of European ethnicity, these lawyers have not consistently reported experiences of career discrimination on the grounds of race or ethnicity. Therefore, it must be asked whether disproportionate numbers of ethnic minority lawyers are working outside established firms because they have unequal opportunities within them.

Further research is needed to ascertain the full extent of race and ethnicity discrimination in the profession and to assess the effects of multiple or compound discrimination. As with the Malaysian women, comments by the nineteen Maori women lawyers who responded to the 1992 survey indicated that race and sex discrimination had occurred during their careers in the profession.[55] How this impacts on their opportunities and career paths must be ascertained as a human rights and professional imperative.

Changing client culture and client base

Clients have wised up

Clients in general have wised up about what they expect from lawyers. The increase in information about the law and legal services, and the shift toward 'plain legal language', has made clients better informed about how to get quality service and value for money.

Since the mid-1980s, it has became apparent that the client/professional relationship is undergoing significant change.[56] City clients no longer give life-long loyalty to the local family lawyer, while in smaller towns and communities clients will travel more readily to a larger centre to increase their choice of representation. Communication and technology advances such as electronic mail and facsimile machines have also enabled clients to use lawyers outside their immediate locality.

Women

There is no doubt that the New Zealand client base is changing both in regard to the number of women in decision-making positions and to the anti-discrimination consciousness.

Large New Zealand companies are adopting equal opportunity initiatives in relation to their staff and to their client development. Fletcher Challenge, ASB Bank, Nissan New Zealand, Telecom, Electricorp and Foodtown are among the companies leading in this area.[57] Westpac Banking Corporation sponsored the 1993 Unifem Suffrage Conference, pointing out in the conference marketing material that Westpac had 'won awards in the past for its progressive EEO policies' and that it was 'working to ensure that . . . delivery of services and . . . communication include [its] women customers'. Another business targeting women is Price Waterhouse, which recently advertised itself as being, 'Committed to understanding and meeting the needs of women in management'. A specially formed Women In Business focus group within Price Waterhouse works actively with women decision makers in companies.[58]

A similar pattern is occurring in Australia, where the Affirmative Action Agency compiles a list of initiatives undertaken by businesses. Examples include the Women's Career Network of Westpac Banking Corporation's Victoria division which has developed to increase the number of women returning after maternity leave. AMP Australia is implementing a similar network.[59] Seminars and businesses target the growing number of women with independent incomes and wealth.[60]

As more women move into higher management positions and into business generally, there is likely to be a correspondingly heightened understanding that sex discrimination is unacceptable.[61]

Not only are the numbers of women managers and directors increasing, there is also a growing number of women lawyers who work as in-house counsel for corporates and local government and in the public sector. Under the state sector EEO programmes it is expected that women will feature more often as senior managers and decision makers within the public sector. When choosing which law firm or barrister to brief, these decision makers may be influenced by the firm's or barrister's attitudes to working with women professionals. In this way, market knowledge that a firm is hostile towards women lawyers could be a liability to the firm.

Individual women clients also clearly require a change in the service traditionally provided by law firms. At the 1993 Women's Law Conference, women consumers reported that they found the profession to be impersonal and inaccessible. They pointed out that legal services needed to be more readily available for women and asked for a rethinking of the traditional hours that lawyers are available for routine legal matters. Preliminary reports from the Law Commission's Women's Access to Justice project confirm that women clients want changes.[62]

Ethnic minorities

Ethnic minorities, consistent with their demographic profile, will increasingly require legal services and may legitimately expect that there will be trained lawyers within the profession who are multi-lingual and have cross-cultural skills. Regional differences will affect employers response to increasing ethnic diversity. Auckland, for example, remains the largest Pacific Island city in the world while South Island cities have fewer Maori and Pacific Islands people.

Asian investment in New Zealand along with the growth in Maori business initiatives will affect firms right across the country. Firms or individual lawyers who discriminate on the grounds of race or ethnicity are unlikely to attract or to retain this work.

International standards

International business standards and expectations with regard to equality and discrimination will increasingly impact on the New Zealand legal profession.

Corporate lawyers will need to be more conversant with human rights and discrimination laws and practices as clients from other jurisdictions will want to assess their liability within New Zealand. Already United States corporates and multi-nationals seeking to invest in New Zealand businesses are querying the efficacy of employment equity programmes in those organisations. Overseas law firms, having experienced the legal downside of discrimination, have a heightened appreciation and interest in New Zealand law firms' records on that front. Within the more enlightened overseas firms, they may also wonder why so few women lawyers front deals or grace the letterhead of the local firms and may read that as a lack of innovation in the new business environment.[63]

Law firms looking to measure their practices against those in overseas law firms will increasingly look at EEO programmes and expectations. Developments in human rights laws in Australia will have an increasing effect on the New Zealand profession as the Closer Economic Relations programme is completed.[64] International legal networks may conceivably demand EEO compliance by all members in light of legislative or quality management standards in some member countries.

Strategic advantage and equal employment opportunities

For those lawyers and law firms who are business-minded, the increasing diversity of the population and the workforce provides opportunities for gaining strategic business advantages. The advantages will be achieved by an EEO view on basic business management.

Business or profession?

The legal profession is going through perhaps a final phase of professionalisation—the transformation from profession to business. Close on the heels of the early 1990s run on the Solicitors' Fidelity Fund, lawyers and their clients called for a rethink of the profession's organisation and the conduct of business within the profession. Large law firms and members of law society councils have lobbied for the abolition of the fidelity fund and for the corporatisation of firms. The New Zealand Law Society (NZLS), in conjunction with the New Zealand Society of Accountants has raised the possibility of partnerships incorporating.[65] While the primary focus of these proposals is to limit principals' liabilities, the ramifications of a new approach to legal business are much broader.

Quality management

Consistent with the move towards corporatisation of the profession is the adoption of new management ideas. 'Quality management', encompassing total quality management, quality assurance, quality improvement and re-engineering, is the catch-cry of the 1990s. New Zealand law firms need to recognise the need to adopt quality management systems to gain competitive advantages.

In adopting quality management systems, firms may need to undergo 'substantial cultural change at all levels to achieve success'.[66] Although the New Zealand quality management movement has largely overlooked gender issues, these clearly need to be addressed within the cultural overhaul. The United Kingdom Law Society has recognised this by incorporating, within their Practice Management Standards, a specific clause on employment equity. The standard requires that firms have regard to the EEO policies and procedures published by the law society.[67] Moves are afoot for a similar set of quality management guidelines issued by the NZLS. The national law society board included the proposal to develop these guidelines among the society's major objectives in 1994.[68]

Although the New Zealand guidelines, like the United Kingdom standards, are unlikely to be mandatory, law firms may be compelled to comply with them when contracting for services as has occurred in the United Kingdom. As a result of the United Kingdom Legal Services Board decision to accredit for legal aid only those firms which implement the law society's standards, many firms have no choice but to implement EEO programmes.

Another alternative is that government contracts will be available only to those firms which prove they meet either legal or quality management standards regarding discrimination or employment equity, as has occurred in Australia. There is already a precedent for this kind of requirement in New Zealand where funding bodies, such as New Zealand on Air, require applicants to demonstrate that they operate appropriate EEO programmes. Funding may be declined or withdrawn if the EEO requirement is not met.[69]

People management

Introducing quality management requires a review of personnel management. Management of women lawyers within law firms, for example, is done to a different, lower standard than the management of men lawyers.[70] On the training aspect alone, women lawyers believe they are given less training or training of a poorer quality than their male counterparts.

Where management of women staff is second rate, productivity and profitability will suffer. Following the 1992 law firm practice comparison survey, Doug Arcus, consultant and member of the NZLS Practice Management Committee, noted that 'a significant part of the success of the top performing firms, [was] the ability to recruit, train, manage and motivate professional staff'.[71] This formula alone should prompt firms to reconsider their approach to the management of women lawyers.

Larger New Zealand law firms are following the Australian lead in shifting from the single managing partner model to management teams or boards which in some cases involve non-lawyer professionals.[72] Kensington Swan, one of the larger national firms, appointed two prominent businessmen to its board in 1993, breaking the New Zealand profession's tradition of all board members being partners within the firm.[73] Other larger firms have followed suit, appointing executive managers or chief executives who are full-time managers.[74]

Smaller law firms are recognising the need to free professional staff from administrative and management responsibilities, but this seems to be occurring mostly at partner level. Only a minority of these firms are recognising that personnel management requires expertise and even then they usually confine this to recruitment assistance.[75] For most, the perceived costs are considered prohibitive.

Management expertise has particular relevance when dealing with gender bias and discrimination. Larger firms are employing personnel managers, while some smaller law firms are calling in the services of external consultants. Where these people are delegated the task of implementing EEO, it is important to ensure they have appropriate training and the mandate to achieve the task.

There has been a tendency within New Zealand law firms to dump EEO at the door of the human resources manager. Where there is no commitment or at best an equivocal commitment from partners and employers, the human resources manager has little chance of success, despite any personal commitment to implementing EEO. Where EEO is delegated to employees the scenario is the same as they also have little influence over resource and policy implementation decision making.[76]

Systems assessment and gender bias

Quality management involves assessing and improving existing workplace systems involved in the creation and delivery of legal services. On the road to achieving quality management, experts warn partners and employers not to overlook their staff—both professional and support staff. Their input into the planning process is essential, and consultants advise: 'It is from these same people that many of the best ideas for improvement will also arise.'[77]

To enable employee participation in the quality management process, it may be necessary to undertake 'substantial cultural work and education' first. The amount required will depend on the existing culture within the firm and, it is suggested, also on the extent of gender bias and discrimination.[78]

It is probable that where gender bias and discrimination are operating, the input of women lawyers and support staff into the quality management process will be impeded. For example, the discriminatory allocation of workplace information means that women are unlikely to know about existing systems in the same way that men do. Take, for instance, information relating to the track to partnership—the input of men lawyers into any discussions on career tracks will be better informed than that of women lawyers. This does not mean that women are unable to form views on the value of processes, rather that they are not working from the same level of knowledge as men.

An 'outsider's' view is often the most insightful and innovative but, where women are coming from this perspective, their contribution may be received as ill-informed or commercially naive. For example, assumptions about women's lesser knowledge of 'things commercial', their lower status in the workplace or doubts about their long-term commitment to the firm could cloud their roles in the quality management process. Even where not explicit, gender-biased assumptions will work as psychological inhibitors in terms of women's contributions and the firms' valuations of those contributions.

In the most subtle ways then, gender bias presents a significant barrier in the quality management process. Before that process can commence, this barrier must be eliminated.

Diversity and adaptability

New business management models emphasise the need to identify and maximise strategic differences. In this way, law firms and businesses are able to differentiate theirs service from those offered by competitors, perhaps by targeting certain clients and building client loyalty rather than offering general legal services.[79] Strategic planning is needed if only to accommodate the predicted revolutionary changes in the role of the lawyer in the twenty-first century.

Within the law itself, new developments are reflecting a more diverse and holistic style of social thinking. Biculturalism in the legal system is increasingly under discussion. Alternative dispute resolution is now used in family law, employment law, small claims, civil disputes, human rights law, youth justice and in some lesser criminal cases. Criminal justice models are moving away from retributive justice to restorative justice. Victims' rights are likely to form part of the new legal framework.

Consistent with these changes, legal education is moving away from the study of black letter law toward a form that is more 'conceptual, contextual and critical'.[80] Law students are being encouraged to obtain degrees that are 'valuable in social equity terms'.[81] Lawyers are being urged to become more involved in what the law should be, not only what it is. In the new environment of mixed member proportional (MMP) representative government, lobbying by lawyers is likely to become more prevalent as interest groups vie for input and influence.[82]

Finally, another fundamental change is the increasing interest in access to justice for women and minority groups. In 1995 the Law Commission commenced its research on women's access to justice and the Courts Consultative Committee announced a project on gender equity and the judiciary. Included in the Law Commission's terms of reference was an examination of the legal services provided to women, particularly to Maori women and ethnic minority women. As barriers to justice are removed piece by piece for women, Maori and other minority groups in New Zealand, the profession needs to adapt or it risks becoming irrelevant.

As these changes impact on the profession, lawyers increasingly will need to fulfil functions outside the traditional legal role. While special- isation was the catch-cry of the 1980s, multi-skilling is now being widely introduced, and transferable skills will be a professional necessity in 2000 and beyond.[83] Diversity and adaptability are the way of the future.[84]

Decision makers planning for the future and law firms seeking strategic advantages would do well in this context to re-examine the skills, experiences and expertise offered by women in the law.

Women lawyers' skills

On a number of levels, women in the law have the skills, experiences and expertise which will assist the profession to meet the challenges presented by this new legal environment

Women lawyers' career paths alone mean that they are more likely to have diverse experiences within the law itself. In particular, the large number of women lawyers entering the public sector means that law making and law reform may become another female dominated area of legal work. As MMP representation is introduced, women's experiences in these fields is likely to make women lawyers more attractive to private practice. Whether they will seek to work in that environment will depend on the opportunities which are available there.

While women lawyers are as likely as their male colleagues to have accounting or business work experience, they are more likely to have other work experience outside the law, particularly in teaching and secretarial work. Teaching skills will be particularly valuable as in-house legal training increases in importance. A background in teaching will also assist in team building and the motivation of junior staff. Secretarial skills ensure that women lawyers are well equipped to understand the job performed by support staff but in addition they also mean women lawyers have a higher level of computer literacy. Approximately 10 percent of women lawyers have secretarial skills compared with one percent of men lawyers.[85] Familiarity with computers will increasingly become an essential skill across all types of legal work.

The communication and problem-solving skills with which women lawyers are frequently accredited are particularly well suited to the new environment which is the result of a philosophical shift within the legal system and consequently in legal practice. Auckland University law lecturer Bernard Brown has observed that women students have greater interest in contextual matters (including a deeper experience of 'equity') and demonstrate versatility and flexibility when practising or teaching law.[86] The juggling of roles and responsibilities, particularly motherhood and paid work, is also believed to make women more adept at handling multiple tasks simultaneously. Women lawyers' experiences as household managers and primary caregivers likewise broaden the skills and experience base of the profession.

While more men than women lawyers are parents, few men lawyers have the major responsibility for the care of children.[87] It is through caring for children that women interact with and rely on a range of people, service providers and sectors. Adults without children are less likely to come into contact with these aspects of society.[88] These individuals and groups interact and rely on the legal profession and the legal system in some way, making women lawyers' experiences that much more valuable.

The value in difference

Sex, race, class, sexual orientation, religion and disability, among other personal characteristics, affect an individual's ability to perceive the actual position and needs of others. Lawyers from minority groups within the profession are likely to be more aware of these issues and as a consequence are more likely to be willing to respond to them.

Angela Muir Van Etten, for example, a New Zealand trained lawyer now working in the United States, advises on legal issues relating to the disabled. As a Little Person, Van Etten encountered prejudice and ignorance from the minute she entered the New Zealand profession.[90] Her 'difference' enabled her to understand the position of others coming into contact with the legal system, and encouraged her to take action to remove barriers. Similar stories are told by members of the Auckland Lesbian and Gay Lawyers' Group and other 'EEO designated groups'.

The benefits of balance

Research by the Ministry of Women's Affairs in 1993 found that employers and employees benefited from policies that enabled workers to lead balanced lives.[91] In United States businesses, where family-friendly policies have been implemented since the mid to late 1980s, evaluations reveal significant benefits. One firm in Minneapolis saved US$65,000 in the first nine months after introducing a 'sick childcare programme'. Staff turnover reduction studies also demonstrate large savings. Aetna Insurance, for example, was having difficulty retaining high performing senior women who left on maternity leave and did not return or returned only for short periods. After modifying its parental leave policy to extend the period of maternity leave and provide the option of part-time work, they cut their staff turnover by 50 percent for three years running. Aetna calculated that in the first year alone it had saved $1 million in turnover costs.[92]

Other studies in United States firms have showed dramatic improvements in staff productivity and business culture. One medium sized business, when evaluating its work-family programmes, found that the people using the programmes 'had the highest job performance evaluations, the lowest intentions of leaving the company, and the lowest record of disciplinary actions'. Of direct relevance in the quality management context, employees who used the work-family benefits showed more initiative and contributed more ideas to the quality improvement teams.[93]

An innovative New Zealand project, Work and Family Directions, which involves fifty-five private and public sector organisations, found that work and family strategies provided a range of business benefits. Participating organisations, which each implemented a family-friendly initiative, reported that employees and managers were positive and enthusiastic about the initiatives; employees were better able to balance work and family responsibilities; employee satisfaction and staff morale improved; commitment to the job by employees increased; leave usage reduced; staff returned from parental leave; and the organisation's profile as a 'good employer' was raised. Manukau City Council observed that an outcome of their new flexible annual leave policy was that managers were spending less time managing staff time because staff were now empowered to manage their own time.[94]

With the exception of childcare centres, none of the organisations participating in this scheme said the costs of introducing work-family policies were prohibitive. In addition, although the programmes were relatively new, organisations expected future benefits in recruitment and retention, decreased absenteeism, and a better ability to attract skilled staff into the organisation. New Zealand Post Ltd, which introduced a Shiftwork Lifestyle Programme, estimated that every one percent improvement in absenteeism was equivalent to a saving of $112,000 per year.[95]

Ensuring the productivity and loyalty of staff is essential to business success. As Rae Torrie, EEO adviser at the State Services Commission points out: 'Greater productivity is achieved by people who lead balanced lives, who are not overstressed, and who are valued and recognised in their workplace.'[96] Balanced work and family practices are good for people and good for business.

Conclusion

If change is to occur in the New Zealand legal profession, a fundamental starting point must be the acceptance that gender bias and discrimination is the profession's problem and not women's problem.

Then it must be accepted that action to eliminate this problem is a business and professional imperative. Lawyers, law firms, professional groups and associations, and the judiciary need to design rational responses to eliminate existing problems and to meet the needs of a changing environment. Women need to stop apologising when they ask that action be taken. Change cannot be left to chance.

The legal profession must situate itself within the new paradigm where the public and private domains are no longer separate spheres. In doing so, the profession, law firms, the judiciary and others involved in the legal system will be putting into effect a new culture where difference does not preclude participation or reward but adds something of significance and value.

Chapter Seventeen

Equity at Work

To eliminate sex discrimination and harness the benefits of diversity, law firms, professional groups and decision makers must reassess and redesign the systems within which discrimination and gender bias operate. There is no point redefining the culture of the profession or an organisation if the structural aspects remain unchanged. In other words, if the current policies and practices in law firms and other workplaces are not redesigned, they will simply reproduce the status quo.

Of course it is not possible to overhaul all workplace and professional systems overnight and so there needs to be a transition phase. In each organisation and for each process that transition phase will differ. Realistic goals must be set and the change process properly managed.

This process is relevant to the judiciary, the law societies, other professional organisations, law firms of all sizes, barristers and sole practitioners. It is relevant to all decision making affecting appointments to the judiciary, the inner Bar, law society committees and to any other offices or positions held by lawyers. It is relevant to the criteria and processes involved in recruitment, work allocation, remuneration, promotions and partnership admissions.

Structural redesign need not be onerous or costly. In most cases, the tools for achieving change are already on hand and simply need to be applied. Virtually every law firm, employer and decision maker has access to technology, training, human resources, management skills and management systems. Each of these will play a role in the process of achieving equity at work.

New goals

Profession-wide goals

On a profession-wide basis, the overall goal should be to ensure that basic human rights are protected within the profession. In practical terms this requires the provision of equal opportunities for all.

In relation to women lawyers, strategies need to be designed that enable:

- Women lawyers to stay in or re-enter the profession;
- Women lawyers to have equal career opportunities with men; and
- The allocation of opportunities and benefits on the basis of merit.

These objectives are interrelated. For example, for women to be able to stay in the profession they need to have equal career opportunities with men. Equal career opportunities require a definition of merit which does not overlook or undervalue women's skills and experiences. Ensuring that all appointments and opportunities are allocated on the basis of merit will also ensure that women advance within the profession and hence are more likely to stay in the profession.

Equality through equity

In aiming for equal employment opportunities (EEO) lawyers must be careful not to apply a limited concept of equality.

For over one hundred years, New Zealand women have argued for sex equality and on paper they have been largely successful. Laws such as the Equal Pay Act 1972 and the Human Rights Commission Act 1977 aimed to deliver equality by providing recourse where individual women received unequal treatment; but the reality is different. As the experience of many women in the legal profession demonstrates, 'equality' is no more than an ideal—an empty promise. Even worse, the goal of 'equality' has become part of the problem.

The goal of equality has presented a catch-22 situation for women in the law because from the outset 'equality' has been synonymous with 'sameness'. In theory, the terms on which women were allowed to participate and advance in the profession were the same as those applied to men. In practice the terms were quite different, but the myth has remained that if women are to succeed in the law, they must do so according to the same criteria and using the same processes as apply to men.

The truth has been that for women to succeed in the profession, women lawyers simply have had to be better than men to be noticed or have had to compromise their personal and family lives in ways not expected of men. 'Being one of the boys' has meant losing respect as a woman or being marginalised and isolated as 'one of the few or only girls'. For many, attempting to conform to the traditional mould has meant too great a personal or even a professional sacrifice. Many women simply did not fit in.

Where women and other minority groups in the profession are preoccupied with trying to fit in, difference and diversity are squashed. The result can only be bad for the individual and for business.

The profession needs to accept that eliminating discrimination and gender bias is not the same as achieving 'sameness'. Women lawyers no longer want the right to be 'equal' with men lawyers if it means the continuation of the present cultural framework where they are expected to be like men. The standard against which people are measured must shift from a male-focused standard to a human standard. 'Humanising' equality can be achieved by applying the principles of equity.

Equity has historically provided a pathway to justice. As in the law, equity in employment strives to correct the inflexibility of existing rules where they have resulted in injustice. So, for example, current promotion practices which work well for men but not for women can be re-examined and reshaped to produce fair results. Doing this does not disadvantage men or business. It means that irrelevant criteria are eliminated and inefficient processes are remedied. Competent people will be recruited, rewarded and promoted on merit. This benefits all.

In this way, employment equity is a valuable business tool. It is not static but is forward looking. It is not concerned solely with numbers and appearances but with the quality of outcomes.

As importantly, employment equity enables workplaces to recognise, value and encourage difference and diversity. Properly utilised, human capital is as important as economic capital to business growth.

Treaty of Waitangi

At least concurrently with any redesign of professional and organisational culture to eliminate gender bias, the profession must consider its obligations under the Treaty of Waitangi in relation to the delivery of legal services and in relation to the Maori members of the profession. An increasing body of research is demonstrating the ways in which the law and the legal profession have acted against the interests of Maori, in contravention of the Treaty of Waitangi.[1] Others are considering the impact of the Treaty of Waitangi on the development and delivery of equal opportunities for Maori in the workplace.[2]

No specific studies have examined the progress of Maori in the legal profession but, in the context of research on women and EEO issues, some information has been gathered. In 1989, the second working party of the Auckland District Law Society reported on a submission received from the Auckland Women Lawyers Association (AWLA) which set out specific problems which were being experienced by Maori women lawyers. First, there was a 'major financial prohibition' on Maori women obtaining law degrees. The AWLA warned that this would become a greater problem with the trend towards user-pays education.[3] The trend for Maori women lawyers to go into the public sector was noted, as was the 'conflict' which Maori women experienced in relation to the monocultural values within the legal system.[4]

In the 1990s, Maori women lawyers have taken a lead in placing Maori lawyers in the public and profession's consciousness.[5] Annette Sykes spoke on Maori women's position at law and in the profession at the 1993 New Zealand Law Conference, as did Anne Phillips at the Women's Law Conference three months later. Articles profiling or written by Maori women lawyers have been published in professional magazines and community newspapers.[6] In addition, women have a high profile in Te Hunga Roia Maori o Aotearoa (the Maori Law Society), with Gina Rudland as president and Marama Henare as secretary in 1993 and 1994.

In the context of EEO implementation, some Maori lawyers have been consulted. Maori lawyers in the Auckland area, for example, were invited to participate in the development of the Auckland law society EEO programmes in the early 1990s. As Prue Kapua, partner at Brookfields and one of the authors of the EEO kit, explained: 'It is essential that this consultation and participation occurs. Without it the product will not work.'[7]

Aside from initiatives in Auckland, professional associations have largely failed to acknowledge the unique role of Maori in the profession and the legal system. In 1993, the New Zealand Law Society (NZLS) did not even have contact details for Te Hunga Roia Maori o Aotearoa. In February 1993, Annette Sykes criticised the NZLS at the national conference for failing to accord special status to Te Hunga Roia Maori o Aotearoa or to establish a standing committee to represent the legal needs of indigenous peoples.[8] The NZLS did not rush to rectify the situation. Four months later, the NZLS still had no contact details for Te Hunga Roia Maori o Aotearoa.[9]

However, improved recognition of Maori lawyers did take place in the context of action on sex discrimination. In mid-1994, in the establishment of the NZLS Women's Consultative Group an unprecedented decision was made to allocate a position specifically for a representative of Te Hunga Roia Maori o Aotearoa. As a result, Wellington lawyer Caren Wickliffe became a member of the committee in 1994, followed by Kathy Ertel in 1995. Representation for Maori women was expanded to two positions in 1996. In 1995, the national law society also employed Maori lawyer Anne Phillips as Director of Legal Affairs and resolved, for the first time, to consult with Te Hunga Roia Maori o Aotearoa generally with regard to professional issues.

While the professional associations have dragged their feet when it comes to recognising the Treaty of Waitangi, law firms have acted on the commercial benefit to be gained from employing Maori lawyers, particularly to work on land and asset claims. From the early 1990s, most of the large law firms established special Maori law commercial and litigation teams offering specialist services to Treaty of Waitangi claimants. However, one law firm which trumpeted its new Maori Services Department in 1993 was criticised by the media for having a short memory. Principals in that same law firm more than one hundred years before had been heavily involved with 'grabbing as much [Maori land] as they could, by fair means or foul—mostly foul'.[10]

If the legal profession is to maintain (or perhaps obtain) credibility and address issues of equal opportunities for Maori lawyers, it must also consider its obligations under the Treaty of Waitangi. This process should be led by Te Hunga Roia Maori o Aotearoa and the NZLS in discussion with members of the profession. Members of the Auckland Maori lawyers group, Te Runanga Roia Maori o Tamaki Makaurau, observed in 1996 that the treaty is central to Maori lawyers. It cannot be separated from EEO and other employment issues.[11]

New ways of decision making

Decision making in the legal profession will change in an equal opportunity environment. Equal opportunity decision making involves accountability, consultation, and transparency. It also requires a re-thinking of the role of discretion.

The role of discretion

Discretion in decision making goes with positions of power—the more power, the greater the discretion.

The concept of equal opportunities directly confronts the exercise of discretion, which is why decision makers tend to distrust equal opportunity initiatives and may resist attempts to implement them. What these decision makers fail to appreciate is that equal opportunity processes offer safeguards for decision makers. Where there is a clear and just process for decision making, the outcome can be justified in terms of that process and not on any political or personal favour or disfavour of the decision maker.

Equal opportunity initiatives do not eliminate the role or importance of decision makers. Law society presidents, politicians, judges and senior members of the profession will still need to make decisions. The difference will be that with explicit EEO procedures they will not be making ad hoc and possibly semi-informed decisions—their jobs will simply be easier.

Consultation

To build on the past achievements of women in the law, further change will be achieved by both sexes working together. Employers and employees also need to share responsibility for designing solutions for their workplaces. Finding constructive ways of working together is the first step in redressing discrimination and gender bias.

Consultation is the process of seeking, valuing and incorporating input from all relevant parties when developing action plans to eliminate discrimination and gender bias. This process requires an open environment and a new language for it to be effective, whether it occurs within a law firm, the law societies, the women lawyers' groups or any other organisation involved with the profession.

Trust is the most important ingredient missing in many gender-related discussions and debates. To create trust there needs to be a recognition of the gender power imbalance and an agreement that that power will not be misused. Until this occurs, doubt and mistrust will continue to prevail.

Generalisations and negative stereotypes also need to be eliminated. Author Naomi Wolf has pointed out: 'Never choose to widen the rift between the sexes when we can narrow it without censoring the truth.'[12] As experience holds the key to understanding the problem, women lawyers must be heard first. The purpose is not to emphasise the problem but to explore its resolution. A shift from a preoccupation with the evidence to examining the solutions will ensure the profession is better able to achieve solutions.

Accountability

Equal opportunity decision making involves decision-maker accountability. Where decisions affect others in the profession, a workplace or a law society, the person or group making the final decision needs to account for the decision. In a law firm, for example, a supervising partner could report to the partners and to the individual staff member affected by the decision. Too often this step is missed out and confusion occurs where none is warranted.

Likewise, when implementing EEO initiatives and involving staff in planning the change process there is an obligation to report back regularly to those who have participated. A project's success may depend on this. For example, the majority of businesses participating in the 1995 Work and Family Directions project attributed the success of their projects to regular liaison with and feedback from staff involved. Ultimately, it is the people in a workplace or an organisation who are most affected by the implementation of equal opportunities. It therefore makes sense to involve them and keep them well informed of the direction a project is taking.

Accountability also needs to be introduced into decision making by the district and national law societies. While they regularly report to members on law reform work, management of the fidelity fund and disciplinary matters, the law societies' involvement in judicial appointments, for example, is kept silent. Minutes of meetings of the NZLS Women's Consultative Group even record that there is to be no report on comments made at its meetings about potential judicial appointments. Confidentiality is claimed on the ground that careers might be ruined if it was known that individuals were up for consideration for an appointment but failed to get it. While it is arguable that there is no real reason for this,[13] the law society should still be accountable to the profession for the process used, the criteria applied and the reasons for the decision made. Even where motives are genuine, confidentiality can seem like an excuse to maintain secrecy.

Transparency

Equal opportunity decision making requires visible, known criteria and processes. All persons and organisations affected by particular decisions should have access to information about the criteria and procedures used in the decision making and the reasons for the decision made. The principles in the Official Information Act 1982 and the Privacy Act 1993 provide useful guidelines—particularly for official decision making by the law societies, for example, in relation to recommending particular lawyers for appointments.

In the case of employment decision making, employees need to know what decisions affect them and their work, the criteria and processes to be applied and the reasons for decisions. This applies in relation to work allocation, promotion, pay reviews, partnership admissions, leave allocation and training opportunities. Although transparency enables equal opportunities, it also makes good business sense. When people understand the reasons for decisions, they are likely to perform better, know where improvement is needed, and accept decisions more readily.

Information is particularly important to individuals who belong to a group that is under-represented because they are more likely to question their eligibility for a position than those who belong to the group that dominates the position. To redress this, women must be able to accurately assess their eligibility for appointments. For example, in the appointment of Queen's Counsel, information about criteria and the appointment process must be published and be available to women. Information, coupled with actual appointments of women, will help to alleviate the impression that gender is a criteria for appointment and that the correct gender in nine out of ten cases is male.

Transparency in the decision-making process will also assist those making decisions. The close-knit nature of the New Zealand legal profession and the interconnectedness of networks can make decision making more difficult than in other overseas jurisdictions where there are tens of thousands of lawyers and potentially hundreds of eligible applicants. Sir Geoffrey Palmer recalled his dilemma when considering the judicial appointment of a particular lawyer who had opposed him in the parliamentary elections in the electorate he represented. The candidate, according to Palmer, was 'highly qualified' for the District Court but he feared the press could charge him with getting rid of a political opponent by appointment to the Bench. Palmer decided to go on with the appointment.[14] If the decision rested on clearly set out criteria and not on the shoulders of one person these potential conflicts would be minimised.

Transparency in decision making is essential to remedy the lack of trust which is presently common between women and men, and employees and employers. It will also ensure that progress, where made, is visible and appreciated.

Responsibility

In designing strategies to ensure equal opportunities in the legal profession, responsibility rests with employers, employees, law societies, the judiciary and government.[15] Individuals also have important roles to play.

Examining the role which each group can play ensures the best use of resources and the least risk that the ad hoc, reactive approach taken to date will not be continued.

Individuals

On an individual level, every lawyer, judge and decision maker needs to re-examine their own position on discrimination and gender bias by challenging their own attitudes, thoughts and conditioning. Individuals could consider questions such as: How do I behave in the workplace around women/men? Am I interested in others and pleased when they succeed? Am I open, professional and courteous, or protective, competitive and distrusting? How much does my job stress affect my relations with others? How do I behave at home? Do I take responsibility for my own emotions, health and well-being? Am I prepared to participate in and support efforts to achieve equal opportunities for all people?

Individuals are often quick to suggest others should do something rather than taking personal responsibility and acting in their own spheres of influence.

Men and women

The responsibility for eliminating sex discrimination and gender bias must not be left to women lawyers. If that approach is taken then men are assuming no responsibility for the problem and the current inaction will continue. Women lawyers confronted with this response need to make it clear that discrimination is not their problem alone nor is it their job to resolve it alone. Sex discrimination is a gender problem—it belongs to both sexes.

Women lawyers' groups and committees will continue to provide a conduit through which women lawyers can make their input into the change process. These groups also need to develop their own goals and prioritise them. In doing so, they need to avoid taking victim-based approaches where half-hearted responses from other organisations are accepted as sufficient and move to empowerment models where nothing short of positive change is accepted.

Employers

All employers, including law societies, law firms, sole practitioners and barristers, need to take responsibility for implementing EEO. In all workplaces this should consist of an EEO plan, a harassment procedure, and flexible work-family practices.

An equal employment opportunities plan

Every workplace would benefit from an EEO plan. Developing and implementing an EEO plan involves securing employer commitment, allocating resources, setting specific objectives, undertaking an EEO audit, reviewing and revising existing policies and practices, and implementing any special measures.[16]

Employer commitment

Employer commitment to the goal of equal opportunities and to the process of achieving that goal is essential. Without this commitment, efforts to achieve change will fail. Lack of decision-maker commitment has impeded EEO success in the legal profession as it has in every other industry, occupation and sector.[17]

Employer commitment in the legal profession cannot be confidently predicted because employers are unlikely to consider EEO is needed. In the 1992 national survey, women lawyers were more likely than men lawyers to think that firms and employers must take action to reduce discrimination: 64 percent of women said this compared with 40 percent of men.[18] Again, in the 1995 Auckland law society's EEO survey, women were more likely than men to say that their workplace would benefit from the implementation of policies on EEO, harassment or work-family relations.[19] As men are the predominant employers this difference is fundamental.

Law firms and other employers should have greater motivation to implement change because they presently have a high exposure to discrimination litigation,[20] and stand to benefit from the business advantages of managing diversity.[21] There may need to be further incentives offered by the law societies or by government.

Resources

To develop and implement an EEO plan, employers must allocate resources to the task. It is usually recommended that a budget is allocated which will enable each workplace to achieve its specific EEO objectives. However, it seems that few employers in the legal profession have taken this step. In the Auckland EEO survey, only 8 percent of lawyers surveyed knew that a budget had been allocated to EEO.[22] A budget for EEO is as important as a budget for technology or marketing. Few law firms would manage these aspects of their businesses on no budget.

Some staff time will also be needed. Where a staff member or an EEO group has been delegated the job of overseeing the development and implementation process, the time involved should be taken into account when setting those individuals' fees targets. Although EEO implementation can be conducted in an efficient and timely manner, it is very important that the people responsible are not penalised for doing this non fee-earning work. It is also important to signal to others in the workplace that the EEO plan is a valuable, strategic part of the business. Valuing the time spent on this work confirms that message.

Each employer in the profession need not bear the full cost of implementing change. Where initiatives can be developed that are of benefit to other employers, those workplaces should consider joining forces and sharing costs. This will be particularly relevant to small workplaces, such as sole practitioners' and barristers' offices, where there are relatively few employees. Employers could also look to the law societies to coordinate and/or resource some of the core aspects of implementing equal opportunities.

Specific objectives

Because each workplace differs in terms of its staff profile, business objectives and management systems each EEO plan will be different. For that reason, specific objectives in each workplace need to be developed. Consultation with staff and others will assist in determining EEO goals.

The objectives of the EEO plan must be developed in conjunction with and as a fundamental part of a business' strategic plan. Where EEO is a separate or add-on initiative, it will become sidelined and irrelevant. Thorough business planning inevitably involves giving consideration to the staff, the management and the client base. As outlined in chapter 16, the profession is undergoing a revolution in each of these areas. Equal employment opportunities strategies are tools which will enable law firms and other legal businesses to maximise the benefits of these changes.

Specific EEO objectives might relate to the advancement or retention of women in a firm, the development of a minority ethnic group client base, the development of teams made up of individuals from diverse backgrounds, or the provision of flexible work-family policies. The options are endless and the specific objectives in each workplace will reflect the direction in which that workplace seeks to go.

Audits of equal employment opportunities

An EEO audit serves two purposes. First, the audit canvasses the staff and partner profile in the workplace. This is to compile an accurate database on all employees and partners (where relevant) which will form the primary source of information about a range of EEO-related issues: recruitment patterns; positions held by different groups within the organisation; the level and type of work performed by different groups; career development; performance reviews; pay rates and pay increases; seminars attended; leave taken; work-family needs; promotions; and partnership admissions.

Secondly, existing policies and practices must be documented (if not already) and reviewed to assess whether equal opportunities are being achieved. The Auckland law society's EEO kit contains examples of policies and practices which are relevant to law firms. For example, with regard to access to partnership, the kit recommends that training and development policies are reviewed to ensure equity of access for all employees, that partnership criteria are communicated to all potential candidates, and that feedback is given to each candidate regarding their path to partnership. With regard to pay and other entitlements, the kit proposes that the law firm's pay structure be examined to identify discrimination. This review would include assessing the benefits attaching to permanent part-time work, other leave entitlements (for example parental leave and conference leave) and a review of overtime payments and bonuses.[23]

From the audit, the firm or organisation will be well placed to make an assessment of the position of men, women and other groups, the contributions made by each group, staff development and likely future requirements, the staff pay profile and the distribution of other benefits and rewards.

Once this organisational information is collated into a database, the next stage is to examine that profile against the goal of equal opportunities. Relevant questions to be asked at this stage include: Where are women and ethnic minorities positioned in the workplace? On historic information, has this profile changed at all? What are the recruitment patterns in terms of sex, ethnicity, race, disability, sexual orientation? Are staff members doing similar work being paid similar salaries? Are leave entitlements conveyed to all staff? Is information about promotion and partnership criteria available to everyone? Are work-family needs being obstructed or met? Have complaints of harassment or discrimination been resolved to the satisfaction of all parties? What policies, practices or strategies are already in place which produce equal opportunities? Could these be applied in other areas?

An EEO audit need not be a difficult task. In fact, the staff profile aspect of an EEO audit can be easily incorporated into a spreadsheet on the firm's word processing computer using readily available software. In the 1990s, computers are becoming an integral part of the time and office management systems in the offices of nearly every law firm, sole practitioner and barrister. State of the art law practices are also using computer email and similar tools for product delivery. As a means of storing, updating and analysing EEO information, they are also an important equal opportunity tool.

As for the policy and practices aspect of the audit, most firms have staff manuals or partners manuals. If not, the process of documenting employment and partnership policies and practices can be done with equal opportunity outcomes in mind. For those firms pursuing International Standards Organisation (ISO) accreditation or implementing total quality management methods, they will have documented and reviewed their various policies and practices already.[24] The EEO audit follows from this.

Once the audit has been conducted, the information learnt will form the core of the workplace's EEO strategy. The information should be updated annually in smaller firms and more frequently in larger workplaces. The EEO group or coordinator can then prepare an annual or six-monthly report to assess progress towards the workplace's EEO objectives and will reveal any 'hot' or problem areas.

Revision of policies and practices

As a result of the audit, it may be necessary to revise certain policies and practices to eliminate discrimination and bias. The objective will be to ensure that equal opportunities are available in practice and not just in theory. Two examples of what may need to be revised as part of this process are the definition of merit and the setting of fee targets.

Merit

The concept of merit is one of the cornerstones of EEO. From an employer's perspective it means identifying the qualities required in a potential employee applying for a particular position. It also means ascertaining and comparing the merits of candidates for pay rises, training opportunities, promotions and so on. An EEO-based definition of merit will assist the employer to appoint the best person for the job and to reward them accordingly.

Unlike in the public sector, in the private sector there is no statutory guidance on how to employ or appoint on merit. In government agencies covered by the State Sector Act 1988, chief executives and other persons delegated the task of appointing staff are under a mandatory obligation to 'give preference to the person who is best suited to the position'.[25] 'Best suited' has been construed to mean best suited at the time the appointment is made, having regard to the information available.[26] The employer does not have a subjective discretion to determine who is best suited for the position, but must determine objectively the best applicant and then appoint that person.[27] A person aggrieved by a recruitment decision can appeal to the Public Services Appeal Board or initiate judicial review proceedings.

In the private sector, although the law does not define 'merit' it does offer some clues on what it means, at least from the perspective of assessing when equal opportunities have been denied. In the Human Rights Commission Act 1977 'merit' related to an employee's 'qualifications' for the work.[28] However, from 1 February 1994, the Human Rights Act 1993 focused on an employee's 'capabilities'.[29] This changes the emphasis from the possession of formal qualifications to having the ability to do the job. Measuring ability is more likely to include looking at a broader range of skills and experience than the formal qualifications of an employee.

Another legal guideline on what constitutes 'merit' is found in statutory exemptions to the prohibition against age discrimination. Sections 27(1) and 30(1) of the Human Rights Act 1993 enable employers to discriminate according to sex or age where being of a particular sex or age is a 'genuine occupational qualification' for a particular position. A genuine occupational qualification is not defined or considered in any New Zealand case law but guidance on what it means can be found in overseas law. Attempts to use this exception as a justification to discriminate for stereotyped or sexist reasons have failed in the United States, Canada and Australia. The cases show that an employer must take into account each individual employee's ability to perform the job regardless of stereotyped assumptions about physical, intellectual or emotional attributes.[30]

The Australian Public Service Reform Act 1984 states that where an appointment to the public service is to be made, it is to be made on the basis of:

an assessment of the relative suitability of the applicants for the appointment, having regard to:

(i) the nature of the duties to be performed by the person appointed; and

(ii) the abilities, qualifications, experience and other attributes of each applicant that are relevant to the performance of those duties.[31]

As this definition shows, the key to defining merit is in identifying the tasks of the job first and then assessing each applicant against those tasks. In many law firms, the job is not adequately defined and value judgments, stereotypes and assumptions can easily cloud the employer's judgment about a particular applicant's abilities, experiences and qualifications for that job.[32] To counter the myth that historically employment decisions have been based on merit, employers must be certain to eliminate any irrelevant factors and to properly define all relevant factors. A practical way of achieving this is to prepare job descriptions for all positions within a workplace.

Fee targets

To ensure fee targets do not present barriers to women lawyers' progress within workplaces, firms' fee setting policies and practices must be assessed for systemic bias. If the type of work generally performed by women lawyers makes it impossible for them to compete on the same basis as their male colleagues—in relation to salary increases or promotion prospects—then the targets may need to be reassessed. For example, a woman lawyer doing predominantly family law or legal aid work should not be penalised if she is as capable, qualified, and experienced as another lawyer doing non-family law or non-legal aid work.

Where a firm undertakes to do legally aided work it must be careful to ensure that the person performing the work is not automatically placed on a slower and lower paid career track. Measurements of the value of that work should take into consideration other factors, such as the certainty of the work flow and hence the certainty of income to the firm, or the recommendations from legally aided clients that other potential clients use the firm's services. When looked at in this broader framework, the lawyer doing legal aid work in fact may be making a contribution to the firm equivalent to that of other lawyers. This may be overlooked if fee targets are the only or the main measure.

Firms that compare the fees of lawyers who act solely for individuals with the fees of lawyers acting for corporates may also need to adjust fee targets and budgets to reflect the viability of the different types of work.

In some firms, family lawyers are expected to match the same targets as commercial or conveyancing lawyers. Again, the firm must identify and value the benefits of providing a family law service to clients and not penalise the lawyer who is employed to do that work.

Audits should monitor the allocation of pro bono work and write-offs of time and fees. Women lawyers who refer to their poor performance will frequently mention that their time is written off, that they have a disproportionate share of pro bono work referred to them by other staff and partners, or that their supervising partner is frequently taking a 'cut' of their fees. These practices are entirely consistent with the assumption that women lawyers are not there for the long haul, so they receive little assistance to ensure they meet targets, get quality work and compete fairly against others.

Special measures

Once policies and practices have been reviewed and revised to eliminate gender bias and discrimination, there still may be specific initiatives that a workplace seeks to implement to achieve its EEO objectives. Measures to ensure equality are authorised by law where they are done in good faith for the purpose of assisting or advancing persons or groups which may need assistance or advancement to achieve an equal place with other members of the community.[33]

Under this provision, measures developed to advance women, Maori, ethnic minority groups, people with disabilities and other minority groups in the profession would be justified. These initiatives are not intended to elevate these minority group members over others in the workplace but to enable them to achieve equality.

Harassment procedures

A harassment procedure should cover all types of harassment (including sexual, racial, ethnic, political, lesbian and gay, and age-related harassment) and should be implemented in every workplace.

Although separate and distinct from the EEO plan, similar steps are involved in designing a harassment procedure. The Human Rights Commission recommends that a sexual harassment prevention programme follows these steps:

1. Appointment of a coordinator who is properly resourced and supported.

2. Formulation of a policy statement describing the firm's 'no tolerance' position on sexual harassment.

3. Development of a complaints procedure.

4. Selection and training of contact people within the organisation and identification of resources available outside the organisation.

5. Promotion of the policy and the procedures and education on sexual harassment (for existing and new employees).

6. Monitoring and evaluation of the policy and the procedures.[34]

The Auckland law society's EEO kit sets out a purpose designed procedure for developing law firm sexual harassment procedures. The kit advises that partners and supervisors be appraised of their responsibilities to eliminate sexual harassment; that firms distribute their sexual harassment policies widely; that firms provide awareness training for all staff as part of induction and staff development courses; and that firms take speedy and effective action on complaints.[35]

Because harassment other than sexual harassment (for example, racial harassment) occurs, it is important to extend the harassment procedure beyond sexual harassment. This will ensure that there is recognition that all types of harassment are inappropriate and unacceptable, and provides an avenue for discussion and resolution of all harassment concerns.

There is simply no good reason for a firm not to have a harassment policy and procedure.

Flexible work-family policies

The 1990s heralded the advent of 'work-family' or 'family-friendly' awareness. Where media coverage of individual women (and sometimes, but rarely, men) had previously turned the spotlight on childcare difficulties the focus has now widened. Business and glossy magazines have reported that business generally was having a family crisis. United States corporate leaders were one step ahead—by 1996 they were already talking about 'life-work'—the happy co-existence of lifestyle, personal and work goals.

Innovation

The Ministry of Women's Affairs suggested in 1993 that the number and types of family-friendly policies was 'limited only by the imagination of those in the company involved'.[36] The best sources of innovative ideas are the employers, solicitors and support staff in each workplace. The unique combination of people in every organisation will produce equally unique solutions for the work-family needs of that organisation. Firm size and budget need not limit the imagination applied to the task and may lend greater creativity to it.

Programmes which have been successful in New Zealand include: 'warm-lines' where school-aged children are able to telephone for advice or homework assistance; short-term or emergency childcare programmes;

school holiday activities and field trips; provision of space for breast-feeding mothers; flexible lunch hours; and the supply of 'beepers' to expectant fathers. Another successful initiative implemented by a small Auckland employer was to provide a minibus to collect school children after 3 pm so that the employees could continue to work effectively instead of worrying about their children.[37]

In Australia, family-friendly businesses have introduced schemes including: career break schemes allowing employees unpaid time off for family reasons, travel or study; a gymnasium at work for employees to use during lunch hours or before and after work; work experience for employees' children; provision of health and dental insurance; family days where employees' families are invited to attend the workplace and are shown around; a six weeks' free nappy washing service for employees on parental leave; family oriented Christmas parties; provision of counselling for employees facing family or marital problems; and financial assistance in special circumstances, for example to help meet the funeral costs of employees' relatives.[38]

Work flexibility

Types of work 'flexibility' are also unlimited. The EEO Trust defines flexible work conditions as including: flexitime; a compressed work week, for example four 10-hour days instead of five 8-hour days; part-time work at all levels within the firm; term-time working, where a parent stops work during school holidays; job-sharing, where two or more employees share one job; job-splitting, where one job is split into two or more part-time positions; flexible leave provisions, including career break schemes and domestic leave; and flexible workplaces, for example employees telecommuting from home.[39]

Telecommuting is becoming increasingly popular in Australia.[40] Telecommuters spend the greater part of their working weeks at home but have full technological links to the office using facsimile machines, computers, modems and couriers. Lawyer Kathleen Clothier convinced McCullough and Robertson, an old established Brisbane law firm, that she needed to telecommute so that she could raise her child and remain in paid work. She works in the office from 9 am to 3 pm two days each week, and works from home three days each week using electronic mail and a courier service to receive and send information and documents. The success of the arrangement prompted McCullough and Robertson to form a telecommuting committee to explore expanding the home-work options to other legal and managerial staff.[41]

Out-sourcing provides a flexible work option for women lawyers who seek to work part time. An estimated 40 percent of United States law firms are out-sourcing at least some of their functions—communications, maintenance, management, accounting, administration, information technology and legal services.[42] Out-sourcing is beneficial to law firms, barristers and sole practitioners as they can obtain services as required at hourly rates or contract prices. Coupled with technology compatibility, out-sourcing offers women lawyers a viable option for retaining an involvement in legal work while raising children or as a way for women lawyers to gain confidence and skills when seeking to re-enter practice.

Part-time work may be made available on a permanent or a temporary basis. Permanent part-time work could be linked with job-sharing arrangements in addition to being available to parents in paid work, those undertaking further education or study, or those who are coming back to paid work after a period away. Part-time employees under an EEO programme have access to all the benefits and responsibilities available to full-time employees on a pro-rata basis. For example, they should have access to identified career paths including promotion and partnership tracks.[43]

The United Kingdom Association of Women Solicitors has prepared a useful set of guidelines for part-time work. The guidelines recommend that employers develop thorough part-time work policies and procedures which identify the criteria for part-time work, legal considerations (for example employment protection, employee status and entitlements such as sick leave), advertising, interviewing and practical aspects such as secretarial support.[44]

Common mistakes

Experiences of firms and other employers implementing EEO have revealed some common pitfalls. One of the most common mistakes is the belief that an EEO policy amounts to EEO implementation. A policy is usually a statement that equal opportunities are desirable. Policies rarely explain how this will actually occur. Equal employment opportunities plans or programmes translate the policies into practices, setting out the tangible steps which will be taken to ensure EEO human resource decision making and outcomes. Best practice EEO involves a policy and a plan.

In some law firms work-family initiatives have been half-heartedly or ineffectively introduced. In 1992, for example, an estimated 40 percent of lawyers believed that their workplaces offered flexibility but for the vast majority of lawyers with children the flexibility offered made no difference to the stress involved in parenting.[45] New Zealand lawyers are familiar with part-time arrangements which in effect amount to full-time work. In the United States 'part-time' in large firms commonly equates to 40 hours per week.[46] Employers also need to avoid providing work-family schemes to some groups of workers and not to everyone in the firm.

Employers must also be careful not to treat the employees who take parental leave or use family-friendly programmes as second-class employees.[47] It may be advisable to ensure that all workers understand that in some cases these are legal entitlements, and in other cases are otherwise business-driven initiatives. In some workplaces this message can be delivered by renaming work options and avoiding potentially negative descriptions such as 'part-time'. In any case, information and consultation will ensure employees know that family-friendly policies are for the benefit of the firm and all individuals within the firm.

In relation to EEO plans and harassment procedures, law firms must be careful to avoid inadvertently rendering new policies and procedures ineffective. Common mistakes include appointing supervising partners as the sole sexual harassment coordinators (research indicates that partners are the most likely harassers); preparing harassment policies but not procedures for implementation; having policies and procedures but keeping them in the managing partner's top drawer; or confining EEO to women and overlooking Maori, other ethnic minorities, employees with disabilities, lesbians, gay men and other groups.

Unrealistic expectations placed on in-house EEO coordinators or committees or by co-workers can also jeopardise EEO and harassment procedures. These are not quick fix solutions. They are paths towards eliminating discrimination and bias.

Law societies

According to many women lawyers, law societies have the main responsibility for taking action to redress discrimination and gender bias. In the 1992 national survey, 55 percent of women lawyers and only 29 percent of men lawyers said that the NZLS should take action, and only slightly smaller proportions were of the view that the district law societies should also play a role.[48]

Of the 130 specific comments on that question, not one respondent suggested that the law societies should establish a committee—which is what the national society subsequently did by forming the Women's Consultative Group. Instead, seventy women and sixty men were of the view that the law societies, alone or in conjunction with employers, should develop employment equity policies and take active roles in educating the profession about gender and discrimination issues. Some were of the view that these policies should be more than just pieces of paper, and should be 'enforceable' or take the form of 'practice codes' or 'minimum standards'.[49]

With the exception of the Auckland law society, the NZLS and the other thirteen district law societies are inclined to the view that EEO is not law society business. In 1996, the NZLS board confirmed this position but agreed to promote EEO in *LawTalk* articles and to support in principle the work of the Auckland law society.[50] Even in the Auckland society, where efforts to implement EEO have been under way since 1990, some practitioners still insist that the society should not interfere.[51]

However, there are several compelling reasons why EEO implementation is law society business. These arguments are summarised in the Auckland law society's EEO management plan and include:

- National and district law societies are required by law to: promote the interests of the legal profession in relation to legal matters; promote and encourage proper conduct among members of the profession; suppress illegal, dishonourable and improper practice; and maintain the integrity and status of the profession.[52] Implementation of EEO falls within these statutory objectives because EEO redresses the practice of discrimination.

- Major changes to New Zealand's population and workforce demographics require consideration by the law societies. Individual firms and employers should take steps to harness the business opportunities resulting from these demographic changes but overall direction and planning are required from the law societies.

- As the predicted demographic changes occur, concerns about the profession's ability to meet the needs and interests of certain communities will increase. To provide relevant and comprehensive services to the public the profession must ensure that lawyers and employees from new and increasingly diverse backgrounds are afforded equal opportunities. The task of managing this profession-wide process of change is one appropriately undertaken by the law societies.[53]

Coordination

As the statutory bodies charged with looking after the interests of lawyers, the law societies should be the central focus for the coordination and resourcing action on discrimination and gender bias. These organisations already have in place many of the tools needed to administer the change process.

District law societies are particularly well placed to coordinate the initiatives of regional groups and employers, while the national law society should provide support to the district societies and take an overall coordination role. In other countries, where national action on gender bias has been taken by the legal profession (such as in Canada and the United States) the local and national professional associations have set the direction, provided resources and coordinated the work. In this way, law firms do not bear the sole responsibility, and progress and quality can be monitored.

Other voluntary professional associations are also well placed for co-ordinating change among their membership groups. Their administrative, management and networking systems provide an existing framework within which change can be planned, developed and promoted. In 1993, the New Zealand Bar Association, for example, decided to assess the applicability of the United Kingdom Bar policies on equal opportunities for local barristers' chambers. Although the clerking system of allocating briefs does not apply in New Zealand, the policy, as Secretary to the New Zealand Bar Association Sonja Clapham, observed, would still be relevant to the selection of new members of chambers, the monitoring and distribution of work in chambers, equality targets and complaints procedures.[54] The New Zealand Bar Association, like the law societies, would be well placed to develop these policies and practices for adoption by their members.

Programme budgets

Within the law societies' budgets, EEO programmes must be allocated high priority and incorporated into five and ten year plans. In the case of the national law society, funds could be redirected readily from other budgets, for example from the annual public relations budget, which is often not fully used.

If some law societies are unwilling to take responsibility for resourcing and supporting initiatives in any particular regions, it could be argued justifiably that a proportion of the practising certificate fees collected by the societies should be redirected to those groups or firms that will act to redress discrimination on behalf of the local profession. If a law society still considers that discrimination and gender bias are minor problems which do not justify society resources, lawyers in that region may consider withholding a proportion of their practising fees on the basis that the law society is not acting in accordance with its statutory duty to further the interests of the members. The other option is to elect a new and representative council.

Given the significance of introducing equal opportunities in the profession, the law societies may consider it appropriate to approach the government for assistance.

Closing the information gap

What is not known about the membership of the legal profession probably outweighs what is known and gender issues are no exception. Even where obvious official opportunities for collecting data have arisen, gender has been overlooked or forgotten.[55]

The structure and organisation of the New Zealand legal profession has not lent itself easily to the development of a national professional database. The fourteen district societies collect a range of information by various methods, depending on their size, their budgets and their administration. Some societies, for example, were unable to produce lists of women lawyers for the 1992 national survey and had to manually identify women practitioners from their full membership list. However, other societies have sophisticated databases and are able to identify the gender of their members easily. Each year, each district law society forwards to the NZLS basic information about numbers of principals, employees and barristers. This information plus names and addresses of practitioners is the extent of the national database.

A proposal to develop a comprehensive national database has been under discussion since at least the early 1990s. In November 1994, the district law societies and the national law society were still debating whether this would go ahead in the context of wider reforms to centralise law society functions. In December 1995, it was decided that the national database could proceed as an initiative separate to the structural reforms, but by July 1996 there was no reported evidence of progress.

If the national database is to assist in meeting the profession-wide goal of ensuring equal opportunities for all, it will need to record information by sex, race, ethnicity, age, sexual orientation, disability, family status and marital status.[56] It would also track career progression, and entry into and exit from the profession. The exit of practitioners from the profession should be monitored to determine whether they leave private practice to enter other employment in the public or corporate sectors, academia or voluntary organisations. Tracking the entry or re-entry of practitioners would also identify changes in legal sectors. A significant amount of information about each practitioner will be required for this database. Although it would take some time to establish the database, the annual practising certificate form provides a useful opportunity for collecting relevant information and enabling regular updating of the database.

If, as it has been suggested, the new national database is also used to identify eligible candidates for judicial and other appointments it will need to hold further information about practitioners. To satisfy the current judicial appointment criteria, information would be needed on years of experience, expertise (types of law and types of practice), community involvement and law society involvement. If the criteria were to be reviewed to ensure equal opportunities, other details about practitioners would be required.[57] If the database was to be used for the purpose of judicial appointment, it is probable that practitioners would need to signal their interest when completing the annual practising certificate form.

Another information gap which the law societies could address is the monitoring of district law society programmes which link prospective employees with employers. At present, to identify nationally the numbers of women and men using the programmes and their success rates, each district has to manually review its files. There is also no monitoring of the scheme run by the Institute of Professional Legal Studies (IPLS), where graduates are taken on by barristers as unpaid observers. Annual reports on the EEO outcomes of services such as these need to be prepared as a matter of course.

Resources and research

The law societies, on behalf of the profession, could develop EEO resources and undertake research. Services should be provided to firms and to smaller workplaces in particular to assist them in implementing EEO.

The national law society could, for example, usefully develop human resources and EEO software specifically for law offices of varying sizes. This would enable firms to undertake regular EEO audits without each workplace spending time developing a staff database. Other projects could involve developing model part-time policies and procedures for law firms or compiling family-friendly project kits summarising a range of options and how to implement them.

The primary focus of law society research and resource development would be to establish good EEO business practices. These, in turn, could be translated into professional standards.

Members of the profession and others who are inclined to argue that EEO is not law society business should examine other services provided by the law societies. In 1995, for example, the NZLS Practice Management Committee assisted in the development of guidelines for law firms seeking ISO 9000 accreditation. In addition, it was recommended that the Continuing Education Committee organise a further seminar on ISO 9000 for law firms.[58] These services, provided by the NZLS, could equally relate to EEO. Like ISO accreditation, EEO implementation is good practice management.

Professional standards and monitoring

As it is likely that many employers in the legal profession will continue to ignore and downplay discrimination and gender bias, the law societies may need to consider introducing EEO standards. These standards could describe the policies and practices which should be adopted and used in workplaces. The EEO plan, harassment procedure, and work-family policies and practices could form the basis of the standards. Obviously, a time frame would be needed to enable employers to develop and implement these initiatives. Likewise, different targets would be required for different sizes and types of workplaces.

Like the auditing of law firm trust accounts, the district and national law societies could monitor firms' EEO plan compliance. The obvious way to achieve this would be to require all principals to provide an annual report on their EEO plans, harassment procedures and work-family policies and practices.[59] To assist the process, a standardised EEO audit tool would be advisable.

Law societies' monitoring of workplace EEO audits would provide a check against half-hearted implementation and abuse. There is no point in undertaking an audit, for example, of the childcare needs of staff in a law firm if the wrong questions are asked or if the questions are framed to elicit only that information the employer or decision maker wants to hear. Review of audit procedures could be provided as a law society service which would eliminate incomplete or self-serving audits by employers.

The professional EEO standards requirement need not be draconian in purpose. Like the public sector reports to the State Services Commission's EEO Unit, regular reporting reveals which organisations are making progress and which require assistance. Standardised reporting enables assessments to be made of areas of common difficulty where further resources may be required or of new areas where new solutions are needed. These annual reports from employers could readily form the substance of a profession-wide annual report which would save the time and expense of further surveys of the profession.

If standards were introduced, employers could claim that they have a certified EEO workplace. This certainly would assist in defending claims of harassment and discrimination as well as ensuring the business benefits of best practice EEO.[60]

Education and training

To date lawyers have relied heavily on education as a solution to gender problems but have done little to effect it. In every study and survey since the early 1980s, education has been seen as the key. Aside from saying that education was essential, however, few outside the women lawyers' groups or women's committees within the law societies have actually made change happen. To the men who propound the education solution, few have actually taken their own advice.[61]

Education and training are essential to the successful implementation of EEO policies and programmes. The district and national law societies are particularly well placed to coordinate the provision of education and training on EEO programme implementation. The NZLS and larger district law societies have education departments where seminar planning and organisation is done.

New lawyers entering the profession may have no knowledge that they may face discrimination or systemic bias. Within the law school environment, the impression of equality prevails, at least among the student body. Some will encounter discrimination when seeking employment but many more will experience discrimination or gender bias in career opportunities and rewards. For some women lawyers, discrimination or gender bias can come as something of a shock and few are aware of how to respond.

Women lawyers and other minority groups in the profession need to be informed about discrimination and gender bias before entering the profession. The IPLS makes passing reference to the ethical obligation of an employer not to discriminate but, unless a particular tutor is aware of the wider equal opportunity issues in the profession, there is no further discussion or information. As Richard Moss National Director of the IPLS commented in 1992, discrimination was a low priority for the profession, and as a result could not be made a priority within the course. As it was, the IPLS was constantly battling for credibility, especially in the eyes of the larger law firms which have questioned the value of the thirteen-week course.[62]

The IPLS is well placed to include a module on discrimination, sexual harassment and equal opportunities in the course. For women and other minority groups entering the profession, these are very real professional issues. Their ability to cope with these issues as they arise would be greatly enhanced if the issues were discussed in the IPLS course.

The compulsory law society Flying Start programme for lawyers seeking to become principals should also be expanded to cover EEO and harassment. At present the course is completed in less than six hours (plus a take home exam) and the focus is on trust accounting and the financial and practical basics of business. Although passing reference is made to practice management, there is no comprehensive coverage of how to be a good employer.[63] Most lawyers becoming principals in law firms or sole practice have no experience of being on the other side of the employment relationship.

New principals need to be informed about how to implement EEO and harassment policies; and more specifically about how to translate those policies into practice when recruiting, interviewing, supervising staff, managing teams, mentoring and undertaking performance reviews. As employers they will become liable at law for discrimination and sexual harassment in their workplace. They will also have a business interest in maximising the human resources for which they now have responsibility.

In the same way, existing principals need to be educated about their obligations at law and the solutions to discrimination and harassment problems. Specific courses should be designed for partners and other employers. Targets could be set to ensure that representative numbers of principals from the large and medium sized firms attended courses. For smaller firms, the courses could be purpose-designed to reflect smaller staff numbers. To ensure attendance, the NZLS could consider implementing compulsory continuing education programmes as do the accountancy and medical professions.

The most successful education strategy relating to discrimination and gender bias in the profession has been where those who have had little or no exposure to such problems have listened to others who have experience and understanding. Dame Augusta Wallace pointed out that until she 'listened' to other women lawyers' and judges' stories of discrimination, she had not appreciated the problem.[64] Wellington District Law Society President Wayne Chapman commented that listening to Kathleen Mahoney, a Canadian law professor, speaking on gender bias had expanded his horizons. He recommended that others seek out education which was outside their usual 'sphere of interest'.[65]

'Talking heads' education on discrimination in general is not as effective as workshop style training. Within a less formal, smaller group environment, individuals can engage in debate about discrimination and equal opportunities without the barriers which are often present in larger groups. Because EEO solutions are workplace based, training also needs to be provided within that forum. Contextual learning is one of the best forms of education. To accommodate these factors, when providing EEO education the law societies would need to deviate from their usual style of education.[66]

Firms and law societies should also offer information and seminars on career planning, career opportunities and partnership tracks. Specific law society seminars need to be targeted at lawyers who have left private practice or the workforce generally to encourage or assist their re-entry.[67] In many cases, these will be women lawyers who left as a result of unfriendly work-family policies and a lack of other work options.

In the wider role of educators on legal issues, the law societies could also provide information on discrimination to the public. Particular groups which have demonstrated a low level of understanding of human rights laws, such as employment consultants and banking and finance sector clients could be targeted. Doing so would serve a dual purpose— women lawyers would see the societies taking tangible steps to eliminate discrimination and the public would see the profession promoting the law.

Complaints

The present mechanisms for dealing with discrimination complaints in the profession need to be reviewed. In particular, it is important to determine whether the disciplinary procedures and the informal advice options are appropriate for women and others affected by discrimination. Are they accessible, understandable, effective, culturally appropriate, efficient, safe and fair?[68]

A review of these aspects of the complaints processes is warranted given the low numbers of people using existing procedures and the high numbers of people experiencing discrimination.[69]

Conclusion

For EEO and true equity to be achieved in the New Zealand legal profession, there needs to be concerted efforts made by individual members of the profession, employers, employees and law societies. New goals will give direction, and new ways of decision making will ensure an inclusive process, but, to a large extent the tools of change are already on hand. From here, what is most needed is the commitment to change.

Chapter Eighteen

Judges: A Representative Bench

To date, most discussion on the need for reform of the judicial appointment process has focussed on the proposal to establish a judicial commission. First recommended in 1978 by the Beattie Royal Commission on the Courts, a judicial commission would act as an independent board to oversee judicial appointments.[1] Although there are differences of opinion between politicians, judges and other commentators as to its makeup, it is generally agreed that a judicial commission would consist of those already involved in the judicial appointment process plus perhaps one or two government appointees.

The major change from the present appointment process would be that everyone would know the process, not just the politicians and senior judges. A commission would consult all interested parties and recommend candidates for appointment to the Minister of Justice and the Attorney-General.[2] Although these politicians would retain the final say on who was appointed, the processes of selection and recommendation by a commission would be more visible, systematic, and accountable than the current process.

Calls for establishing an appointment commission or board have increased since 1993, sometimes being raised in the context of discussion about the number of women judges.[3] In February 1996, the Auckland District Law Society Courts Committee recommended that a judicial commission be established and, in the interim, a formal process of consultation be developed. In particular, the committee argued that the process undertaken by the law society president when giving an opinion on a proposed appointment needed analysis. The Auckland law society council decided that a detailed report should be presented to the New Zealand Law Society (NZLS).[4]

Those in support of a judicial commission or similar appointments board have usually been members of the profession and since 1993 the judiciary, while those opposing the idea are usually politicians. According to Attorney-General Paul East QC, a judicial commission would not bring about an improvement in the quality of judicial appointments. There would be a danger that a commission would restrict the potential candidates and 'would allow incumbent judges to choose who will join them on the bench'.[5]

Increasing the accountability of judges is also a hotly debated topic. Currently, an incompetent judge can be fired only by the Governor-General at the request of the Minister of Justice or Parliament.[6] To date, this has not occurred in New Zealand. Some proponents of a judicial commission consider it should review judicial performance and if necessary fire poorly performing judges. In August 1996, the New Zealand Medical Association added its voice to the debate by calling for a peer review system to make judges more accountable. This unprecedented step was prompted by the association's belief that doctors were more accountable than judges and treated more harshly when they made errors in professional judgment.[7]

While the debate about a judicial commission is important because it focuses attention on the method of decision-making, what is more important is ensuring more women, Maori and people from other ethnic minorities are appointed. Regardless of whether decisions are made by a commission or made under the present system, it is necessary to develop new criteria and processes for the selection of candidates, and to examine the job itself. The objective is to ensure equal opportunity appointments.

New criteria and appointment process

If a representative Bench is to be achieved, new rules which govern selection and appointment are needed. Particularly needed are:

- Criteria which directly relate to job performance.
- Selection from the widest possible pool of suitable candidates.
- Objective methods for assessing candidates' suitability for the job.
- Job flexibility and support mechanisms (such as education) to ensure judges are able to do the job to best of their ability.

It is helpful to examine overseas judicial appointment processes and other New Zealand quasi-judicial processes, particularly those which aim to achieve a high representation of women. In New Zealand, the processes used to select and appoint Tenancy Tribunal adjudicators and Disputes Tribunal referees are particularly instructive.

Tenancy Tribunal adjudicators

According to the Residential Tenancies Act 1986, adjudicators like District Court judges are appointed by the Governor-General on the recommendation of the Minister of Justice. But there the similarity ends. The appointment of the people who preside over Tenancy Tribunal hearings in District Courts is governed by a distinct procedure outlined in a five-page, nine-annexure circular to Tenancy Tribunal registrars and court managers from the Principal Tenancy Adjudicator.[8]

The step-by-step guide to the process of appointing Tenancy Tribunal adjudicators begins with a statement of the aims of the procedure:

> to: recruit as diverse a field of applicants as possible in terms of backgrounds, ethnicity, age and sex; base appointment as objectively as possible on the criteria deemed critical to effectiveness as a Tenancy Adjudicator; and arrange publicity which attracts appropriate candidates without embarrassing present appointees.

From the outset of the process, proactive recruitment of prospective candidates is undertaken. The District Court registrar, who doubles as the Tenancy Tribunal registrar, invites local groups to inform their members that an adjudicator position has arisen and encourages them to submit nominations and applications. The groups specified are: the district law society, the Justices of the Peace Association, the Ministry of Women's Affairs' Nominations Service (previously the Appointments File) for information on local women, the National Council of Women, Maatua Whangai (the Maori Women's Welfare League), the local Maori council, the Maori Affairs Department (now Te Puni Kokiri/Ministry of Maori Development), local Pacific Islands organisations, and 'other appropriate local organisations'.[9] Cultural advisory officers are available to assist in the contacting of Maori and Pacific Islands organisations. 'Suitable individuals' are also contacted and invited to apply.

Each applicant must provide a detailed appointments curriculum vitae using the standard form of the Department for Courts and answer a set of questions about why she or he wishes to be appointed a Tenancy Tribunal adjudicator.

The position is widely advertised in local media, and direct contact may be made with other organisations and individuals. The procedure specifies that publicity should be obtained through news items on commercial radio, in radio talkback sessions and in press releases and notices in local newspapers, especially in 'give away' papers. The timetable allows just over one month from the commencement of advertising to the application deadline.

All applicants are provided with written material on the 'person specifications', 'duties' and 'principal working relationships' involved in the job. The 'person specifications' include:

> 2   Qualifications: Barristers and/or solicitors, or persons who by reason of 'special knowledge or experience' are considered capable of performing and exercising the duties, functions and powers of a Tenancy Adjudicator.
>
> . . . . .
>
> 4   Attributes:
>
>   i) In summary, proven commonsense with a practical and fairminded approach to situations; tolerance, self awareness, flexibility, assertiveness—an impartial approach is essential.

    ii) Ability to listen constructively and deal tactfully but firmly with people in a public hearing.

    iii) Ability to achieve quick rapport with a wide variety of people.

    iv) An interest in assisting people to settle their differences.

    v) Awareness of cultural differences and issues.

    vi) Ability to apply the provisions of the Residential Tenancies Act to cases before the Tenancy Tribunal.[10]

The adjudicator's job is to:

> determine expeditiously, and in accordance with the provisions of the Residential Tenancies Act, and with any directions ... made by the Principal Tenancy Adjudicator, all disputes arising between landlords and tenants which are referred to the Tenancy Tribunal.

Selection of an adjudicator is done by a selection panel convened by the Principal Tenancy Adjudicator and the Regional Courts Manager in conjunction with the local registrar. Membership of that panel comprises a registrar or deputy registrar (from outside the region where the adjudicator will sit) and two other people appointed by the Regional Courts Manager for 'their expertise, training and/or experience'. The selection procedure involves a one hour interview of which half an hour is spent role playing (where the applicant takes the part of an adjudicator), and a one hour group discussion.

Assessment of candidates is formal. Panellists complete assessment sheets on each applicant, and a report and recommendation is sent to the Principal Tenancy Adjudicator who advises the Minister of Justice. The Minister of Justice is required by law to consult with the Minister of Housing.[11]

What is it about this position and this process that meant, in 1993, women comprised 48 percent of the Tenancy Tribunal adjudicators? While not all the adjudicators held legal qualifications, women made up the majority of those who did.[12]

The relatively equitable representation of women has been achieved as a direct result of the appointment procedure. First, a concerted effort is made to contact women's groups and to obtain names of local women with the necessary qualifications and skills. Secondly, the short-listing criteria require the selection panel to have regard to the 'desirability of a diverse group of applicants' going through the selection procedure. In other words, the range of interviewees should represent the community. Thirdly, each selection panel includes a woman member, selected for her 'expertise, training and/or experience'. Last, and certainly not least, the objectives of the appointment procedure include recruiting as diverse a field of applicants as possible in terms of backgrounds, ethnicity, age and sex.

In addition, the structure of the job 'attracts' women. Tenancy Tribunal adjudicators work part time—the usual commitment ranges from one half day to two days each week. As such, the job is ideally suited for lawyers with family responsibilities and for lawyers who have rejected private practice culture. Women lawyers are more likely to be in these categories than men lawyers.

Disputes Tribunal referees

The Disputes Tribunal is another example of a legal forum where women are well represented. Of the fifty-four Disputes Tribunal referees in 1993, thirty-one (57 percent) were women

The Disputes Tribunal (which replaced the Small Claims Tribunal in 1989) is for many citizens the first (and only) port of call for the resolution of civil disputes. Disputes Tribunals hear claims up to the value of $5,000. Submissions are confined largely to facts and are made by the individuals concerned and not by lawyers. Like the Family Court, the Disputes Tribunal is a division of the District Court.

As with District Court judges, Disputes Tribunal referees are appointed by the Governor-General on the advice of the Minister of Justice.[13] But, unlike appointments of judges and Tenancy Tribunal adjudicators, the selection and appointment process is set out in legislation. The task of organising and overseeing the process falls to the Secretary of Justice. In practice, the Department for Courts has hands-on responsibility.

Publication of a vacancy in the area served by the Disputes Tribunal is required by law. The Department for Courts is to invite 'members of the public to submit . . . names of any people whom they consider would be suitable for appointment as Referees'. The Secretary of Justice is also required to appoint an assessment panel which is to consist of a District Court registrar, a referee and two other people chosen for 'their expertise, training and experience'.[14]

Rules made under the Disputes Tribunals Act 1988 set out the criteria and procedures for appointment and reappointment of referees. As with Tenancy Tribunal adjudicators, there is a short-listing process and an assessment panel which conducts the interview which includes role playing and group discussion. Formal assessments are undertaken and a likely appointee is subjected to 'an intensive and scrupulous reference check'.[15]

Referees need not be legally qualified but, under the Act, have to be 'capable, by reason of . . . personal attributes, knowledge, and experience, of performing the functions of a Referee'.[16] The Disputes Tribunals Rules 1989 are specific as to the qualities required in referees. When assessing personal attributes, the assessment panel is directed to look at the ability of the applicant to: listen; assess information and make decisions; relate to and communicate with a variety of people; respond sensitively and appropriately to cultural differences; express himself or herself clearly; engage in alternative ways of resolving disputes; and have the ability to assess when alternatives are appropriate. Additional personal attributes of the applicant include: maturity and self-awareness; use of common sense and practical judgment; fairmindedness and impartiality; attitude towards or suitability for training in the work of a referee; and any other personal attributes the panel considers relevant.[17]

In assessing knowledge and experience, the rules are quite specific. The panel is to consider the applicant's knowledge of or experience in: the work of a referee; the law and the legal system generally; mediation, arbitration and conflict management; language and customs of any ethnic group; any profession, business, trade or other occupation whether paid or otherwise; any skill or interest, any community organisation or voluntary organisation; and any other matter the panel considers relevant.[18]

As with Tenancy Tribunal adjudicator appointments, there are specific aspects of the job and the procedure which should ensure an equitable representation of all groups in society on Disputes Tribunals. Most referees work three days each week which suits those with childcare or other dependant-care responsibilities. Recognition of unpaid work and reference to participation in voluntary organisations takes into account women's wider experiences. Organisations contacted for nominees include the Maori Women's Welfare League, the National Council of Women, Zonta International and the Ministry of Women's Affairs' Nominations Service. Assessment panel members are advised that during the process they are 'expected to act in a manner which is consistent with Human Rights and Race Relations Legislation, [and] not discriminate as to sex, marital status, religious or ethical belief'.[19]

The interviewing process for Disputes Tribunal referees is also designed to highlight any conscious or subconscious culturally or gender biased attitudes held by the prospective appointees. Questions at selection interviews aim to ascertain the applicant's sensitivity to client needs and in particular whether applicants are aware of and sensitive to the needs of Maori, Pacific Islands peoples, and women. Gender issues also arise in the course of the role-play scenarios, enabling the assessment panel to determine whether sex stereotyping would influence the applicant's judgment.[20]

Equal opportunity judicial appointments

The combination of criteria and processes used in the appointments of Tenancy Tribunal adjudicators and Disputes Tribunal referees are systematic and transparent. These processes have resulted and will continue to result in equal opportunity appointments for women.[21]

Adjudicators and referees are not judges. In fact, any aspirations to be judges are noted in the appointment procedure guidelines for adjudicators as indicating unrealistic expectations or inappropriate motivations on the part of the applicants. Regardless of their judicial status, the majority of members of the public who are involved in civil disputes will take recourse in one of these two tribunals. Many will consider the adjudicators and referees to be judges. The importance of the roles of these tribunals is reflected in the care taken to select and appoint the right people to adjudicator and referee positions.

There is no valid reason why the same precision should not apply to the appointments of District Court and High Court judges. To do so would involve reassessing the criteria and procedures presently used with the objective of achieving equal opportunity judicial appointments.

Relevant experience

The barriers women face in obtaining what is currently required as 'relevant career experience' must be countered if equal opportunity judicial appointments are to be achieved.[22] This may require a reassessment of what comprises relevant experience, and an acceptance that women's career experiences may not be the same as men's career experiences. Until women lawyers have equal opportunities to achieve partnerships, prominence at the Bar, and appointments as Queen's Counsel, the judicial appointment process will continue to be tainted by the inequity in the legal profession.

From an equal opportunity perspective it is essential that the experience criterion is fully described and not simply assumed by virtue of a position already held. For example, if litigation experience in jury trials is relevant, this needs to be specified with other court work experience. Breaking 'relevant experience' into its component parts may reveal, for example, that litigators working in firms are as well qualified as barristers at the independent Bar.

Job and person descriptions

Apart from the brief description of the terms and conditions of a District Court judge published in 1995 there are no job or person descriptions available for District Court or High Court positions.[23] Defining the judge's job is possible—as demonstrated by the job descriptions compiled by the Law Society of England and Wales in 1993, for example. As for any position of employment, the description sets out the responsibilities, knowledge, skills, special aptitudes and disposition of the person required for the job. Among the reasons behind the initiative was the belief that clear information about the judge's job would encourage applications from under-represented groups such as women and ethnic minorities.[24]

Various New Zealand commentators have listed the personal and professional qualities they consider should be sought in a judge.[25] On occasion, judges have also described the content of the job.[26] The personal specifications required of Tenancy Tribunal adjudicators and Disputes Tribunal referees may also be relevant to the position of judge. This information could readily be translated into person and job descriptions for District Court and High Court positions.

In formulating the person and job descriptions, the fundamental concern must be with identifying the criteria that relate to the performance of the job. The qualities sought must be described in specific terms so that irrelevant criteria are not used. For example it may be necessary for the applicant to be mature in their handling of difficult situations so this should be clearly stated rather than requiring the applicant to be over 40 years of age and using age as a proxy for maturity.

Sex itself should not be a criterion; rather, the particular qualities and knowledge referred to by women judges need to be described as relevant factors in the job description.[27] In performing their jobs, judges may need skills, knowledge or experiences relating to children, parenting, domestic work and the status of women and minority groups in New Zealand society. These should be standard criteria for District Court and High Court appointments. At present, the gendered experiences of women and men would mean that women were more likely to meet these criteria but it is incorrect to assume that only women have this knowledge and these experiences.

The basic judicial qualities sought in District Court and High Court judges should be recorded in statute as is the case with Family Court and Youth Court judges. These statutory guidelines give a higher degree of certainty that the right people are being sought for jobs. Where that is not the case, a wrong appointment could be lawfully challenged.

Advertising

If the intention is to widen the pool of judicial candidates, there is no reason why High Court and District Court positions should not be advertised. At present, although names of interested candidates are sought for District Court appointments, there is no specific notification that a particular position is available. Circumstances and career preferences change, and the current method does not enable all who might be interested and eligible at the particular time to apply. The advertising of specific vacancies would also enable those interested in a particular location to choose to apply for that position, therefore overcoming the problem faced by women who, because of their partners' careers or family considerations, have tended to be less mobile than men.

The advertisement of judicial openings occurs in other jurisdictions. In July 1993, the English Lord Chancellor announced a series of measures to improve the judicial appointment system, including the 'progressive introduction of open advertisements for some judicial vacancies'.[28] In February 1995, the Kingdom of Tonga advertised the position of Chief Justice in *LawTalk*. Expressions of interest were sought from qualified New Zealand senior judicial personnel. A description of the position, responsibilities, terms and conditions was provided with a promise of confidentiality.[29] A New Zealand candidate was successful and there was no adverse publicity about the unsuccessful applicants.

Perhaps encouraged by the success of that process, the judicial position of master of the Auckland High Court was advertised in 1996, being possibly the first advertisement for any judicial vacancy in New Zealand. The advertisement described the skills and experience required for the position and the basic conditions of employment. Applicants were invited to forward their CVs to the Attorney-General.[30] Overall, these judicial advertisements remain unique. Throughout 1996, judges were appointed by the Attorney-General and the Minister of Justice to the Court of Appeal, the High Court, and the District Courts under the old system.

Application forms

Application forms would allow decision makers to obtain all the relevant personal and professional information from different candidates and to properly compare their applications. At present, lawyers provide their curricula vitarum (CVs) in whatever form they think best. There is no uniformity as to the content or the presentation style, no doubt making it difficult for decision makers to assess and compare applicants.

Some jurisdictions do have purpose-designed application forms so that aspiring judges can provide the right information to the selectors. England leads the way having had a judicial application form since 1990. To ensure that appointment of members of ethnic minorities are properly monitored, the forms were amended in 1991 to ask applicants to identify their ethnic origin.[31]

Consultation

Whose opinions are sought and the weight given to those opinions during the judicial consultation process must be explicit if the appointment system is to have credibility. Consultation on other appointments is set out in statute and there is no convincing reason why this cannot be done for judicial appointments. As Sir Geoffrey Palmer has argued, judicial consultation should be mandatory and statutory.[32]

Consultation at all levels by all involved (including, for example, district and national law society presidents, the Solicitor-General, the Chief District Court Judge and the Chief Justice) needs to be specified. At the very least these should be recorded in policies but preferably also in regulations under the relevant statute. If, within the processes used by any of these individuals when gathering information or consulting others, there is an element of gender bias, then the judicial appointment process is similarly tainted. In other words, equal opportunity appointments depend on unbiased information and advice on which a decision is based.

The weighing of views is vitally important. In doing this, the influence of status held, if any, must be determined. The English Lord Chancellor, has stated as the number one precept guiding all appointments, that 'no one person's view of a candidate in the round of consultations is decisive in itself, no matter how important or eminent the person expressing that view'.[33]

The job itself

Although improving the selection process and criteria will ensure more women and ethnic minorities are appointed to the Bench, it is also necessary to re-examine the job itself. Women and men have expressed concerns about the structure of the job but because women generally have greater responsibilities for children and other dependants, the nature of the job is more likely to affect women negatively than men.

Training

Because judges are appointed for life, there is no formal reassessment of their competency and no mandatory retraining. Judges attend conferences and seminars and each year hold their own conferences, but nothing obliges a judge to review his or her perspective on important social and political issues such as gender and race discrimination. In other words, even a judge who is unbending in the face of changing social values (even as interpreted in law) is likely to remain a judge until retirement.

Job training for new District Court judges involves the opportunity to meet with other judges informally and a one week training course held once a year which may coincide with the time of appointment. High Court judges receive no formal training and learn instead from their colleagues. According to a committee of senior judges which examined judicial education in 1995: 'A High Court judge by tradition starts sitting with no prior instruction and without any formal orientation programme.' Learning how to judge is basically done on-the-job. The committee recommended the creation of a New Zealand Judicial Studies Institute which would provide education, information and research services to the judiciary.[34]

As a result of the minimal training received, some judges have recalled their first few months on the Bench with horror. The horror is doubled for those who are appointed to sit in courts in which they have no practical experience. Judges, it seems, are meant to be versatile enough to start their judging career in fora completely foreign to them, dealing with procedural rules and law they know little of. No doubt judges are allocated to tasks and courts according to the needs of the justice system, but are the needs of justice served by throwing judges in at the deep end?

By comparison with the training of judges, the training provided to other judicial-type appointees is systematic and occurs before the commencement of the job. Disputes Tribunal referees are given training in the skills of mediation, arbitration and conflict management. Appointees not qualified in law are also required to complete training in the relevant law.[35] Equally, Tenancy Tribunal adjudicators are required to undertake training before their appointments. For these positions training is easier. The fixed term appointment of adjudicators and referees means that significant numbers come up for review at the same time. Training programmes can be scheduled accordingly.

Since the early 1990s, New Zealand's District Court judges have been provided some information and training in gender issues. In 1991, for example, the National Collective of Women's Refuges was invited to present a paper on domestic violence at the annual conference of District Court judges. In 1993, Professor Kathleen Mahoney addressed the annual conference on gender bias in the judiciary. Sessions on gender bias and strategies for coping with the role of judging were also held at the International Women Judges' Conference but these were attended by women only. In 1995, Judge Marion Frater held a seminar and a video workshop for District Court judges on identifying gender bias. For the first time this session was attended by a newly-appointed High Court judge. In May 1996 the District Court judges organised the orientation week for all New Zealand judges, Australian Family Court judges and judges from Papua New Guinea and Samoa. Half a day was devoted to gender issues.[36]

Attendance at these sessions has been voluntary and the reception has not always been positive. As with many lawyers, opponents of judicial education on gender issues claim it is yet another type of 'politically correct' thinking.[37] They argue that it is feminist brainwashing, and is in conflict with the impartiality required in judging and the objectivity of the law. Therefore, this is not education but indoctrination.

'Political correctness' has also been raised by judges in relation to Maori legal issues. According to former judge Peter Trapski, a member of the Waitangi Tribunal, when the Maori Language Act was passed in 1987 (recognising the Maori language and entitling people to speak it in the courts) 'some judges saw it as political humbug'. On investigation he found that the Act resulted from a Waitangi Tribunal report detailing the injustices that had occurred when Maori had spoken in their own language. He duly distributed copies of the report to other judges: 'Some of them were fairly conservative, but it made a big impression ... they were put on the road to Damascus by reading it.' [38]

This one-off type of education offered to judges, like that offered to lawyers, although commendable, cannot be said to comprise a needs-driven, systematic programme of education. In taking this approach, New Zealand has followed the path taken by United States judges with an ad hoc approach to education on gender issues. According to Professor Norma Wikler, an American sociologist and expert in the judicial education field, only a few states in the United States have mandatory training for judges and then it is largely confined to judges working in family law. She pointed out that this 'haphazard approach' was in part the reason why gender bias remained in the judiciary. [39]

In recognition of the difficulties in educating New Zealand judges about gender and the law, Justice Dame Silvia Cartwright and Chief Justice Thomas Eichelbaum formed a Judicial Working Group in 1995. One of the primary tasks of the group is to identify New Zealand based information about gender and the law so that judges might be convinced of the need for such education. Sessions on gender equity are planned for the judicial conference to be held in September 1996.

Monitoring performance

Regular training and retraining of judges provides an opportunity for their performances to be monitored. Other assessments of ability and competence could be made by regular annual reviews of courtroom performance, case management, judgment writing, and the education and training completed. The purpose of judicial monitoring is not for 'big brother' (or 'big sister') surveillance but to provide constructive feedback to judges, guidance on areas needing improvement and opportunities to learn new skills or knowledge. This role could be performed by a judicial commission or an institute of judicial studies.

Where a judge's performance is persistently poor, there need to be some mechanism to revoke an appointment. But if judges are carefully selected, properly trained and well aware of their performance criteria, this step would be rare.

Flexibility

In the same way that lawyers' jobs have been defined in nineteenth century terms, so have those of judges. Now that notions of the nuclear family with a male breadwinner who is a workaholic, career-focused professional are losing favour, the judge's job is as open to review and reform as any other job. Women are the catalyst for this change but women and men, and ultimately those affected by the justice system, will be the beneficiaries.

Introducing flexibility into judging does not mean compromising the independence of the judiciary. Appointments should still be for life so that the Executive is not able to rid the Bench of judges who do not adjudicate in favour of the government of the day. However, the term of the appointment needs to be at the option of the appointee with certain restraints on activities after judging. For example, a former judge should not act as advocate on the appeal of a case she or he presided over. Any restraint on activities would need to be reasonable and limited to a fixed period.

A judicial career path should be developed to provide more flexibility. At present, judges can and do take sabbaticals and study leave. In 1993, for example, Judge Anand Satyanand took three months' sabbatical leave from his 'day-to-day diet of criminal and civil cases' to work on a book at the University of Auckland law school. The judge commented that it was 'lovely to be removed from the constraints of a tightly structured job that a Judge has, and to remain within the legal community but in a different part of it'.[40]

Apart from sabbaticals and study leave, there is very little job flexibility. The hours are dictated by current court hours (usually 9 am to 4 pm) although some evening fixtures are arranged. However, the actual time spent on-the-job by most judges exceeds actual court hours. For judges on circuit to provincial courts, additional time is sent travelling away from home during weekdays. When Judge Jill Moss was appointed in late 1995 she was required to sit outside Wellington where she lives with her young daughter and partner. She was fortunate that her partner was able to take responsibility for the care of their child.

As in other areas of the legal profession, it is possible to introduce 'family-friendly' options, including part-time work and job sharing, into the judiciary.

Increase statutory limit on the number of judges

To introduce job flexibility, the statutory limit on the number of judges would need to be increased. Traditionally, the limit has been imposed so that a particular government is not able to stack the Bench with judges who might support the government's position on legal matters. However, if the criteria and the process used in judicial appointments was transparent and based on merit, there would be less need for a check on the appointments made by any particular government.

Certainly, a larger pool of judges would help to prevent the backlogs of cases which frequently occur. Easing the workload placed on judges would also enable them to maintain contact with the wider community and to pursue their own research and writing.

Quite apart from gender and work-family considerations, it is conceivable that New Zealand will need more judges in the future for the simple reason that judges are having an increased input into law making. As Sir Geoffrey Palmer has noted, judges in New Zealand have new powers as a result of wider scope for statutory interpretation, increased powers of judicial review of administrative action, the advent of Treaty of Waitangi litigation, the passage of the New Zealand Bill of Rights Act 1990, and the restructuring of the State. Mixed member proportional representation may also require an increase in judicial power.[41]

Part-time judging

In 1978, the Royal Commission on the Courts rejected the idea of introducing part-time judges drawn from the Bar. Leading the opposition was the NZLS which submitted that:

> [the proposal would] have the disadvantages of being detrimental to the image and standing of the magistracy and of creating potential embarrassment at the bar because a lawyer might not feel comfortable pressing an issue with a colleague knowing that he could shortly be in a position of judicial influence over him.

The society also thought the proposal would 'downgrade the administration of the criminal law' and be undesirable and impracticable in the New Zealand context.[42]

Other jurisdictions have introduced part-time or contract judges with some success. In Germany, probationary lawyers work as judges before qualifying to practise law. Although Australia does not have part-time judges, the Australian Law Reform Commission has recently suggested that among the advantages of part-time judicial appointments is that they would be attractive to many women (and men).[43]

In Britain there are as many categories of part-time judges as there are full-time judges. Part-time appointments include: deputy High Court judges, recorders, assistant recorders, deputy district judges, deputy Supreme Court masters and registrars, and acting stipendiary magistrates.[44] Subject to performance and availability, these part-time positions can be direct routes to full-time appointments. Part-time judging is considered as relevant experience when full-time judges are selected.

Expatriate barrister John McLinden pointed out that it had been the practice in England for many years 'that if one has aspirations to any form of judicial appointment, one must first sit as a recorder'. In 1992, over 1,200 barristers were employed as part-time 'recorders' or 'assistant recorders'. The advantages of part-time judges, says McLinden, include: having an available pool of trained judges; having fewer delays in hearing cases; better assessment of the performance of part-time judges and their suitability for permanent appointment; and the opportunity for judicial aspirants to ascertain whether judging suits them. It is even accepted among the English Bar that the performance of the part-time judge barrister generally improves as a result of the judicial experience. [45]

Part-time judicial experience is now a fundamental precept underpinning the English judicial appointment system. According to the Lord Chancellor: 'before being considered for a full-time post a candidate must have served in a part-time capacity for long enough to establish his or her competence and suitability.'[46]

Based on the success of the English model, Justice Wallace, a law commissioner and High Court judge, revived the proposal that New Zealand should follow suit. He argued that, contrary to common belief that conflicts could arise where part-time judges also practise at the Bar, the English experience showed that: 'there was no problem with part-time Judges sitting in quite small cities, even though they practise there as barristers and solicitors or are teaching at a university.' Justice Wallace observed that this was also the experience in New Zealand in relation to part-time appointments to tribunals.[47]

Specifically in relation to increasing the pool of women available for appointments, Justice Wallace pointed out that:

> [part-time judicial work] would be attractive to many women with family commitments, and for that matter to many men also. It would help alleviate the problem of women saying that judging is simply not a job they wish to undertake.

As in England, he suggested that full-time appointments could follow in due course.[48] No doubt, it would also be desirable to have permanent part-time judges or full-time judges on fixed term contracts where requested by the appointee.

The English practice of using of part-time judges has not harmed the principle of judicial impartiality.[49] The English equivalent of the New Zealand Department for Courts, the Lord Chancellor's Department, monitors the performance of recorders and there are provisions for part-time judges' terms not to be renewed. For example, reports on the progress of deputy district judges are obtained and only where progress is satisfactory is the appointment extended. Likewise, if an acting metropolitan stipendiary magistrate's performance over a two year period is 'not up to standard', the magistrate will be 'given guidance and if necessary may no longer be invited to sit'. The review procedure is undertaken by a team of officials in the Lord Chancellor's Department after consultation with judges and senior members of the profession as appropriate.[50]

Another argument against having part-time judges is the possibility that there would be conflicts of interest with their other work.[51] As in any other combination of roles (for example, law firm partner and corporate board member or law society office holder) potential and actual conflict can be recognised and managed. Legislation could easily limit the other roles or duties of part-time judges, as presently occurs with Tenancy Tribunal adjudicators and Dispute Tribunal referees.[52] It would be fairly simple to determine whether any other office and employment would impair the proper discharge of judicial duties.

It has also been assumed that part-time judges would necessarily practise law also. Part-time judges of course could do non-legal work or simply be in part-time employment as judges.

Job sharing

Given proper training, judicial positions could be shared by two or more appointees. Job sharing would be particularly useful in provincial areas where there are only one or two positions. The judge's job lends itself well to such an arrangement. Particular judicial duties (such as interlocutory hearings) could be the responsibility of one judge with rotation on a regular basis. Each judge could oversee the conduct and completion of individual cases.

With proper management, job sharing has been very successful in other occupations.[53]

Flexibility in the job of judging may overcome some of the problems identified in the present system, for example isolation would be lessened.[54] There could be greater opportunities for judges to be involved in the communities in which they are called on to judge. Job stress would be reduced. The expertise of different judges could be better utilised, with judges presiding over cases where they have specialist knowledge. Those who prefer the 'general practice' system could of course maintain a diverse case load. The job itself could be more attractive to those averse to the present 'life sentence' of judging. Of particular relevance to women, the job could enable women judges to more easily meet their family commitments.

Lay judges and amicus curiae

While judges are receiving training in gender issues and while the appointment process is under debate, there are alternative means of ensuring that knowledge, skills and experiences relating to the impact of gender on the law are available in the courts. For example, lay judges and amici curiae (independent expert advisers to the court) could be appointed.[55]

High Court appointments for non-lawyers are being made to bring expertise to certain cases.[56] Why should this mechanism be confined to commercial areas? Senior members of the judiciary, such as Sir Robin Cooke (later Lord Cooke of Thorndon) have recognised the need for 'a woman's perspective' to be brought to court cases to achieve justice.[57] This indicates that at least some judges realise that the requirements of justice are not always being met. As an interim measure, until more women lawyers are appointed to the High Court and Court of Appeal, lay appointments of those with knowledge and understanding of gender issues could be considered.

As an alternative to lay judicial appointments, New Zealand could adapt the Canadian Women's Legal Education and Action Fund programme of bringing women's expertise to the court by appointing them amici curiae. In cases involving gender issues, judges could take advice from independent experts other than experts presenting evidence on behalf of one of the parties. Although expert opinion can always be contested, the court could appropriately seek its own advice on the balance of opinion. In addition, due to limited resources, women before the courts are less likely to be able to afford to present expert opinions. An amicus curiae would ensure this was available.[58]

In adopting either of these strategies, decision makers must be careful not to inadvertently introduce a second-class judicial or legal role for women while men continue to preside on the Bench. Doing so would certainly not advance the credibility of the judiciary nor demonstrate any genuine commitment by decision makers to achieving equity.

Widening the pool

Any genuine attempt to ensure the widest possible range of women lawyers are considered for judicial appointment would certainly include consideration of the many women working outside private practice and those who are otherwise qualified but not presently in paid employment.

It is estimated that there are as many women qualified in law working outside private practice as in private practice. Take for example those women with legal skills who are not barristers or solicitors. In 1991, there were 1,044 people in the 'other legal professionals' census category. Of those professionals, 843 (81 percent) were women.[59] From the description of the tasks performed, these people have skills which may be consistent with those required of judges. They draft new laws and advise on legal aspects of legislation, conduct legal research and write comparative analyses and legal codes, provide advice to organisations on legal matters, study jurisprudence, and perform other legal tasks. All these 'other legal professionals' had university degrees.[60]

Also eligible for consideration are the many women who have taken a break from practice to raise children. In addition to their legal skills, many are actively involved in the running of schools, kindergartens and childcare centres or are involved in other community-based initiatives. Many of these women will have had at least the required seven years' legal experience and because the profession provides limited career options will not have re-entered mainstream practice. With training, their experiences and knowledge would be great assets to the judiciary.

The English Lord Chancellor's guidelines for the appointment of assistant recorders specifically recognise that appointments may occur outside the usual age group (35 to 50 years), 'for example when a woman has returned to practice after a break in her career to have a family'.[61]

Removing the effective age criterion and focusing instead on the actual qualifications needed to do the job will also significantly increase the pool of eligible women. In New Zealand, a large number of women lawyers are 30 years or over (56 percent) but a smaller proportion are aged 50 years and over (4 percent).[62]

Broadening the range of eligible candidates outside the ranks of Queen's Counsel and partnerships to those practising as sole practitioners and barristers would also significantly increase the number of eligible women. It is arguable that job-related experience is as readily obtained by sole practitioners and barristers as by law firm partners and Queen's Counsel. In any case, the demonstrated barriers to women obtaining those positions supports the widening of the type of legal experience expected in judicial candidates.

The many women who at present occupy quasi-judicial positions should also be included in the pool of potential applicants. Following the British system, their experience and performance as part-time or full-time tribunal, committee or commission members would assist in assessing their suitability as judges.

Finally, it must be asked whether only lawyers should be eligible for judicial appointments.[63] The appointment of lay members to the High Court demonstrates that justice can be achieved when a person with non-legal knowledge and skills works alongside a judge with legal training and skills. Women in the wider community have valuable experiences and training which would be of great benefit to the administration of justice.

For too long decision makers have complained about the shortage of women eligible for judicial appointments. The point is that there are many eligible women who should be considered for appointments—it is all a question of how the net is cast.

Conclusion

To achieve a truly representative judiciary, equal opportunity appointments and flexibility in the job of judges must be introduced. As with introducing EEO and balanced work-family practices into the legal profession, this involves the introduction of a systematic, equitable and accountable process into the judicial system. Ascertaining relevant criteria for the person and the job would ensure that all appointments were made on merit. These changes would assist the decision makers in their task of appointing judges and enable them to claim, with certainty, that the best candidates have been appointed.

Making judging a more attractive career will increase the calibre of the Bench and the quality of judgments dispensed from it. As importantly, it would open the possibility of a judicial career to those for whom it would be otherwise impossible, such as those with family commitments and those who presently cannot acquire the 'right' experience.

Recognising the value of experiences, skills and knowledge relating to women, children and the family, when appointing judges will also mean that New Zealand women may more confidently expect to receive justice in the courts. This is not a complete solution. Justice for all will only be achieved when all ethnic minority groups are fairly represented on the Bench and throughout the legal system, and solutions are found for race discrimination, other forms of discrimination and cultural bias.

Government Action and Law Reform

If law businesses and law societies do not adopt measurable, proactive, and positive approaches to implementing equal employment opportunities (EEO), it is arguable that the government should intervene. Political scrutiny of the profession and its non-response to discrimination and gender bias is justified and some would argue long overdue. However, if this were to occur, politicians may be forced to reassess their stance on human rights and equal opportunity laws, and on childcare policies and funding.

Policy inconsistencies between the public and private sectors, and between human rights laws and employment-related laws, raise questions about the political position taken to date on private sector equal opportunities. The law making and law enforcement processes inadvertently perpetuate the problems.

The challenge faced by legislators at the end of the twentieth century may be how best to define and secure human rights in employment in the twenty-first century.

Political scrutiny

In New Zealand, there is already a precedent for government regulation of professions. In 1987, the Economic Development Commission reviewed the occupations subject to statutory control. Lawyers were included in the occupations considered appropriate for statutory registration but others, such as dentists and pharmacists, were found appropriate for restructuring. Justice McKay, a Court of Appeal judge, criticised the report and warned the profession that it could be the subject of reform which he considered to be based on 'naive and simplistic advice'. In his view, members of the profession needed to 'ensure that integrity and service [were] the hallmarks of our own professional lives, and that we [were] worthy of the respect which our professions have traditionally enjoyed'.[1]

Reforms affecting other professions have taken place in the 1990s. The accountancy profession was the subject of a restructuring proposal in

1995. Among the legislative reforms was the proposal that the new Institute of Chartered Accountants register a code of ethics with the Registrar of Companies.[2] Plans to restructure the medical profession in the mid-1990s also involved new legislation. The resulting Medical Practitioners Act 1995 changed the requirements for: registration, competence to practise, quality assurance, practitioner disability, discipline, complaints, laying of charges, structure of the Medical Council, membership of the disciplinary committees and powers of the Disciplinary Tribunal.[3]

Under the Act, no practising certificate is issued if a practitioner has at any time failed to maintain a reasonable standard of professional competence.[4] Lianne Dalziel, the Labour Opposition's health spokes-woman, commented that: 'this is appropriate not just for the medical profession, but also for the legal profession and for a number of other professions as well.' In her view the issuing of practising certificates should be based on principals of competence and not merely the payment of annual fees.[5]

Despite moves to restructure and regulate the accountancy and medical professions, the legal profession has remained largely untouched. During the late 1980s and early 1990s, the New Zealand Law Society (NZLS) reassessed various aspects of law society business, but progress was slow. Then in late 1995, perhaps to pre-empt political intervention, the NZLS announced plans to review comprehensively the purpose, functions and structure of the law societies. The consultants undertaking the review said in their proposal: 'A new look is called for, to prepare the law societies in New Zealand to serve their members in the most effective and efficient way as we enter the 21st century.'

An extensive plan of consultation and a list of issues to be explored omitted any reference to women lawyers' groups, women lawyers' concerns or the concerns of any other minority group in the profession.[6] The Auckland District Law Society did in any event arrange for the consultants to meet with 'EEO groups' as one of the practitioner interest groups. Similarly a meeting was arranged with women lawyers in Wellington in response to concerns that few women had taken part in the review.[7]

New Zealand politicians have been quick to criticise the New Zealand legal profession for failing on nearly every issue except gender. For example, David Lange, Labour Party politician and ex-Prime Minister, said: 'the legal profession needn't be run on principles disturbingly evocative of the arrangements of some of the more influential Italian families.' He urged the National Government to restructure the legal profession.[8] Hamish Hancock criticised the lobbying skills, or lack thereof, in the profession.[9] Attorney-General Paul East QC accused lawyers of 'being retained to . . . evade the major legal rules of our society rather than simply to address them'. In the struggle to satisfy clients the Attorney-General said legal ethics were becoming 'something of an inconvenience'.[10]

Other occupational groups have suffered political scrutiny for their poor gender record. In 1994, the Opposition police spokesperson, George Hawkins, called for more senior policewomen. Although the number of women being recruited into the police had increased in recent years, few women were working as commissioned officers. Hawkins observed that there needed to be 'more balance to reflect their overall numbers in the police force ... Women are often the victims of crime and victims, historically, have received very little from the police force or justice system.'[11] The same criticisms could well be levelled at the legal profession.

In a more direct manner, the State Enterprises Select Committee has shown a keen interest in the gender record of state-owned enterprises. Under the State-Owned Enterprises Act 1986, these corporations and businesses are required to be 'good employers' which involves meeting EEO standards. The select committee is responsible for assessing compliance, and in 1994 it roundly criticised Electricity Corporation New Zealand (ECNZ) for its failure to be a good employer, particularly in the employment equity area. According to the committee, ECNZ had policies that were no more than 'broad statements of principle' and there was no specific plan of action or targets. The corporation had 'demonstrated inadequate commitment to EEO programmes' and 'could do a lot more'.[12] In congratulating another state-owned enterprise, Government Computer Services Ltd, on its EEO progress, the select committee observed that it would continue to take an interest in the issue 'as it intends to do in respect of other State enterprises'.[13]

Political ultimatums have certainly been issued to legal professions elsewhere. The Canadian legal profession recently got the message that it needed to correct its poor record of response to gender bias and sex discrimination. According to Professor Kathleen Mahoney, the Canadian Bar Association was 'served notice' in the early 1990s by the Minister of Justice, Kim Campbell, that if they failed to do something about the gender problem she would initiate a review. Mahoney observed that the motivation for the Canadian Bar Association's substantial research on sex discrimination was self-survival.[14]

Public scrutiny

Public approbation toward the legal profession's attitude on gender issues is also gathering momentum. Generally, lawyers are not held in high esteem—often being ranked lower than accountants, engineers, dentists, doctors and bank managers in public popularity polls—and their response to gender-related matters is only compounding the problem.

In 1992, a letter to the editor of the *Sunday Times* complained that a junior prosecutor during a court adjournment had 'offered a paper tissue to another person and then laughed and rather scornfully said "we keep these handy for rape cases" '. The writer noted that the lawyer thought he was being funny but 'should have been rebuked for his crass remarks'.[15] Two months later in Wellington, a letter to the editor of the *Dominion* complained about a defence lawyer in a rape case who said 'the accused's position as a baby sitter did not involve as great a breach of trust as it would had he been a caregiver'. The accused in the case concerned had raped his seven-year-old niece over several years. The author of the letter pointed out that any sexual abuse was an unforgivable breach of trust and noted: 'is it any wonder that the legal fraternity is now held in such low esteem?'[16]

Again, in 1994 when a High Court judge declined a request by Auckland barrister Deborah Hollings that she be permitted to wear maternity clothing in court, he opened the judiciary to media and public scrutiny. The *Dominion* editorial reported:

> strange as it may seem to lawyers, the public does not see any deep or direct link between the quality of justice and counsel sporting medieval gowns and crowning themselves with horsehair. Nor will it easily be persuaded that justice is served by insisting that a pregnant lawyer must be more uncomfortable in court than she needs to be.[17]

By 1996, the Law Commission had reached the preliminary view that inadequate legal services were a significant barrier to women's access to justice. Among the matters raised by the women consulted were concerns about lawyers' attitudes, the lack of choice in terms of lawyers' ethnicity, lawyers' stereotyped views of how women should or will act, and the lack of control women felt they had over legal matters once lawyers become involved. According to the Law Commission in January 1996, the problems that women experience at the 'service end' of the legal system posed such fundamental barriers that the commission decided to give priority to those issues by concentrating its research in that area.[18]

At a more practical level, the profession opens itself to criticism from all quarters for the waste of taxpayer funds resulting from discrimination. Women lawyers enter the profession after a minimum of four years' university study and a further thirteen weeks' professional training. Even with the trend towards greater user-pays tertiary education, their education has been largely subsidised by the state.

It is the taxpayer who bears much of the financial cost of discrimination. Having paid once through the taxation system for women lawyers to receive a tertiary education (with no guarantees that they will be allowed to reach full or long-term productivity), taxpayers pay again through high legal fees charged by firms trying to cover costs incurred as a result of retention and productivity problems. To add insult to injury, taxpayers also fund the organisations and courts that clean up when discrimination is identified and challenged. On this count alone, members of the public may be inclined to ask why the government has not intervened.

Policy and law making

Gender inequity within the government policy making process itself must be rectified before any effective legislative action seeking to achieve equality within the legal profession or any other occupation can be taken. Women's access to policy development and law making processes and their opportunities to be heard within them are typically overshadowed by an imbalance of power fundamental to politics. Failing to recognise this barrier to women's full participation ignores the fact that the resulting policies or laws themselves will be created within a flawed framework.

Political power

In law making and negotiation, decision makers need to recognise and compensate for the political gender power imbalance. As in the legal profession, men retain majority control over the process of law making and government while many women are marginalised. Women politicians report experiences of masculine cultural biases similar to those evident in the legal profession.[19] As in the practice of law, these biases are not simply one-off individual prejudices but are systemic, translating into policy and legislation. It is this gender power imbalance that is central to the existence and perpetuation of inequality in the political institutions and governance of New Zealand.

At present, the law-making process itself often defeats the struggle for equality. Women battle to have their concerns included in the agendas of political parties, governments and Parliaments. Reliance is placed on a relatively small group of women who have influence within government, Parliament, the judiciary, academia and bureaucracies. Years of energy and effort are required to place and then keep women's issues on the political agendas, let alone to then translate them into legislative proposals.[20]

Even when a law relating to discrimination and equality is passed, it commonly represents a compromise by women in the face of opposition from men or, more particularly, between the interests of the 'personal' private sphere and those of the 'public' corporate sphere.[21] Compromise is inevitable in laws where competing interests are involved, but it is an important question whether those who benefit from discrimination should shape the laws which protect the right to freedom from discrimination.

Personal power

When designing and administering laws and processes, law makers must also have regard to the imbalance of personal power which exists between women and men. A good example of procedures and laws which strive to recognise this imbalance is found in the domestic violence area. Outside that sphere, efforts to redress the power imbalance are often secondary 'add on' considerations when it is in fact central to the problem.

This personal power imbalance affects women's abilities to take legal action against men, be they husbands, employers, colleagues or strangers. Even where the legal burden of proof does not rest on women's shoulders, the psychological cost of participating in a male-biased legal system can be enough to keep women silent and therefore compliant. For others, the barriers are economic or career-related. That so many women lawyers baulk at the personal cost of seeking legal remedies is a sure sign that for the majority of women in New Zealand obtaining justice must be beyond contemplation.

When designing laws or policies that aim to redress sex discrimination and gender bias, the onus of proof needs to be shifted to those who have the power to shape and allocate opportunities and rewards. For example, under the Human Rights Act 1993 the person experiencing discrimination is required to prove that actions or behaviours, or the criteria or processes, were biased. Instead the onus should rest on the decision makers to prove that they were neutral. Although an employer would seek to do this when defending a claim of discrimination, the employee first must assert the nature of the discrimination. From a practical perspective this is difficult as few employees have access to all relevant information. Mechanisms for collecting that information are also time-consuming, technical and costly.[22] As a result, the process itself can become a barrier preventing access to justice.

Economic power

New Zealand women, in general, have less economic clout than men.[23] Pay inequity, unequal career opportunities, lower status work, the unequal distribution of unpaid work and other forms of discrimination operate to keep women economically disempowered. Even among a predominantly middle-class employed group such as private practice women lawyers, there is a sense of economic insecurity. Yet supposedly these are some of the most powerful women in our society.

The pattern is replicated within organisations involved in law making and government. Women-dominated organisations are more likely to rely on voluntary labour while male-dominated organisations are more likely to have administrative staff, buildings and membership fees.[24] The same economic power disparity exists between government bureaucracies—

those aimed at eliminating inequalities have far fewer resources than those focused on economic affairs. For example, in 1994 the Human Rights Commission had a budget of $3.7 million, while the 1993 Commerce Commission budget was approximately $5 million. Similarly, the 1994 budget of the Ministry of Women's Affairs was $3.4 million while that of the Ministry of Commerce was $29.4 million.

The EEO Trust is also under-funded. Established in December 1991 to encourage the development of equal opportunities in paid employment with a particular emphasis on the private sector, the trust is funded by a combination of members' donations, grants, sales of resources and government funding. In the year ended 30 June 1995, government contribution to the trust was $83,177. In total, the trust had a budget of $444,348.[25]

A review of the EEO Trust in March 1995 concluded that: '[it] is too small to be effective in the longer term and in the broader community. It is under-resourced and under-staffed. Its achievements are commendable given its limited resources but they cannot have wide enough impact.'[26]

According to the review team, improved funding of the trust was essential: 'Inadequate funding in the short term would result in many of the benefits achieved by the Trust being lost.' This plea was answered in the 1996 budget when the government increased its contribution to $445,000. However, whether the trust actually receives this funding depends on the financial contributions made by the employer members of the trust. Government financing of the trust is provided on a 'dollar-for-dollar' basis—for every dollar raised from members the government contributes a dollar. So, rather than simply spending this increased funding on promoting and developing EEO resources, the EEO Trust instead needed to embark on a major membership drive.[27]

Economic power disparity is also supported by the law. For example, costs involved in defending actions of discrimination are tax deductible for law firms and other businesses but not for individual complainants.[28] For the individual it is likely that an act of discrimination or harassment will affect their ability to earn an income, and taking action to redress the discrimination will be, therefore, an action to regain or protect their income earning ability. The individual is in that sense equivalent to a business entity but for tax purposes this analogy is not recognised.

In addition, a business found liable for a personal grievance or complaint of discrimination or harassment may claim the damages award as a tax deduction. For the individual, any compensation received as a result of a successful complaint (excluding compensation for humiliation, loss of dignity or injury to feelings) will be treated as assessable income and therefore is subject to tax.[29]

These distinctions in the tax treatment of individuals and businesses in relation to defending employment rights are unjustified and inequitable.

Policy inconsistencies

The influence of economic power in the process of law making is perhaps best illustrated by the policy inconsistencies between the human rights standards expected of the private and the public sectors. Private sector lobby groups effectively quashed moves to implement EEO programmes in the private sector on the grounds that they were unnecessary impositions on business. Yet governments have acquiesced to some public sector employers implementing such programmes voluntarily since the early 1980s and then, bit by bit, have required all public sector employers to do so by law since the late 1980s.[30]

In the 1990s, while the public sector and state-owned enterprises are required to comply with laws on employment equity, the private sector still is expected to introduce employment equity on a voluntary basis. The public sector is required to appoint on merit while private sector employers may appoint staff according to whatever principles they choose (within the constraints of the human rights legislation).[31] Public sector standards are set and compliance is tested by agencies such as the State Services Commission and the State Enterprises Committee while the private sector, which employs most paid workers, is not monitored or assisted in meeting basic human rights standards. As a result, an estimated 76 percent of the workforce is not covered by EEO legislation and is subject to the whims of private sector compliance.[32]

The legal profession is by no means unique in taking a casual approach to human rights laws. In 1993, the EEO Trust reported very low levels of interest in and understanding of EEO among members of the trust (which include private sector employers that have joined the trust and supposedly use its services).[33] Even family-friendly initiatives, which are generally more popular than broader EEO policies, had found favour with only a few private sector companies as at June 1994.[34] A March 1996 Auckland EEO conference, specifically aimed at private sector chief executives and senior managers, attracted very few enrolments from the private sector. Over fifty enrolments were received from public sector managers, whose interest at a minimum is required by law.

What is the rationale for this double standard? Why should state sector employers be required to be better employers than private sector employers? Are human rights of less value in the private sector? Does the double standard reflect a view that discrimination is necessary for the profitability of private sector businesses? If so, how is it that 'formerly lethargic government departments' with their EEO obligations are now out-performing the profitability of private sector corporates?[35]

Private sector flexibility with regard to human rights legislation compliance is one of the reasons why the status quo will remain. The laws on equality relating to the public sector are better designed for tackling systemic discrimination, while the remedies in the private sector rely predominantly on individuals being prepared and able to act on their own. As seen in the legal profession, this is a rare occurrence compared with the actual incidence of discrimination. The private sector law on equality offers solutions to aggrieved individuals predominantly and does little to address the more serious and bigger problem of systemic discrimination.[36]

Systemic sex discrimination—gender bias

As demonstrated in the context of the legal profession, systemic sex discrimination—or, as it is more commonly known, gender bias—exists within the policies and practices which inform decision making at all levels and in all businesses and institutions. Consciously or sub-consciously, decision makers apply prejudices, assumptions and stereo-types about women and men and their respective roles in society and the workforce. The effect for women lawyers is a distinct narrowing of opportunities and rewards. The more informal the policy or practice, the more likely it will contain elements of systemic bias.

Current legislation attempts to address systemic discrimination by incorporating concepts such as 'indirect discrimination', 'unintentional discrimination' and 'assumptions' or 'suspicions' which might inform decision making.[37] While these are dimensions of systemic discrimination, they, like other legal initiatives affecting gender relations, are 'add ons' and not part of the central framework of the law. They are concepts which will assist in the identification of systemic discrimination but the act of identification will only occur where an individual or the Human Rights Commission Proceedings Commissioner is aware that discrimination is happening *and* has the resources or power to respond.

In a similar way, the Employment Contracts Act 1991 and the Human Rights Act 1993 recognise that programmes of action are needed within organisations and workplaces but provide no statutory guidance on what that action should be. In relation to sexual harassment, 'practicable steps' must be taken by employers but there is no statutory direction as to what constitutes these steps even between similar sizes or types of employers.[38]

The Human Rights Act provides that 'measures to ensure equality' or 'special measures' will not breach the law where they are designed 'in good faith for the purpose of assisting or advancing persons or groups of persons' against whom discrimination is unlawful. These groups must 'need or may reasonably be supposed to need assistance or advancement in order to achieve an equal place with other members of the community'.[39] Again, the law alludes to the strategies needed to address systemic discrimination but does no more than say they are not unlawful. There is no reference to the content or quality of the assistance only that it be assistance in 'good faith'.

In its approach to systemic discrimination, the law is essentially passive and prohibitive where it ought to be active and educative. For example, at present 'practicable steps' are required in some circumstances only *after* sexual harassment has occurred and 'special measures', whatever the quality, may be lawful. As we have seen in the case of the legal profession, the impetus for these initiatives relies heavily on the very groups who are least likely to have sufficient power to act. While individual and group legal actions are the predominant means of recourse provided, systemic discrimination will remain intact. The legal framework should arguably be more constructive and aimed instead at assisting private sector employers and employees to address the causes as well as the effects of discrimination.

There are some very simple and practical ways in which systemic discrimination could be addressed within the existing legal framework. Three examples are the introduction of compliance standards, the development and enforcement of special measures, and the introduction of a sunset clause.

Compliance standards

What constitutes compliance with the discrimination and sexual harassment laws in the Human Rights Act 1993 and the Employment Contracts Act 1991 needs to be defined. Under the Human Rights Act, the Human Rights Commission is empowered to publish guidelines for the avoidance of acts or practices that may be inconsistent with or contrary to the Act.[40] In 1995, guidelines were published on advertising and pre-employment. The commission's 1996 work programme includes the production of guidelines for the insurance industry, the education sector (on sexual harassment), the finance sector (on the provision of credit) and for employers generally (on sexual harassment).[41]

While those guidelines will usefully assist private sector employers, including law firms, to understand some aspects of the law on discrimination, there is no legal requirement for such employers to take any notice of the guidelines.[42] Certainly the availability of this information is important but the incentive to observe the guidelines is lacking— particularly where complaints are assumed to be unlikely.

In other legislation, the standards expected of employers are more stringent. For example, under the Health and Safety in Employment Act 1992, employers are required to 'take all practicable steps' to ensure that employees and contractors are not harmed while doing any work. The 'practicable steps' obligation is similar to that required of employers in relation to sexual harassment in the Human Rights Act and Employment Contracts Act contexts but the health and safety law goes further and specifies the standards to be met. Under the Health and Safety in Employment Act, the Secretary of Labour can publish codes of practice which will be considered by the court in determining whether a person charged with failing to comply with the Act has done so.[43]

In contrast to human rights legislation, employers have been quick to comply with the Health and Safety in Employment Act. That Act clearly places the onus on the employer and sets out a procedural framework for enforcing liability. The reality of potential prosecution under the Act is motivating employers to comply voluntarily.[44] In contrast, if the legal profession is any indication, enforcement of the Human Rights Act is piecemeal and of little consequence to most employers.

Codes of practice in the employment sphere could canvass how to comply with the human rights laws in relation to recruitment procedures, advertising, defining merit, promotions, pay equity, training, work opportunities, family-related leave and retrenchment. Different sizes and types of workplaces could be considered but the main focus of the standards would be to achieve consistency in the quality of outcomes from employment policies and practices across the private sector.

Setting standards is a practical and efficient way of enforcing the law. It removes the doubt about what is required and most importantly ensures that the intention of the law is translated into practice. Penalties can be tagged to levels of non-compliance so that the worst offenders receive the greatest sanctions. Flexibility to accommodate changes beyond the contemplation of the legislature can be achieved through changes to the codes of practice.

Special measures

Although the law permits 'measures to ensure equality', it provides no incentive to initiate or support such measures. Again, the law is passive where it needs to be active in enabling otherwise disadvantaged groups to 'achieve an equal place' with other members of the community. It is widely accepted in the public sector that special measures may include employment equity and work-family policies and practices. Translating these into meaningful projects is required and could be the subject of direction from and monitoring by the Human Rights Commission or the EEO Trust.

Special measures in the context of the legal profession, like the compliance standards, should be designed to measure and improve the quality of processes and outcomes. For example, special measures to ensure women's access to partnerships might involve providing training and advice to all law firm partnerships about the barriers women currently face and the legal requirement to address these. Audits of law firms' recruitment and promotion practices could be directed, and appointments to the judiciary could be reviewed to ensure compliance with EEO standards. In any 'special measures' project the objectives must be specifically identified, the work properly resourced and the outcomes monitored.

Projects should not focus on fulfilling quotas of women or minority groups in particular positions. The number of minority group members is only one indication of equity. Targets (which may involve measuring changes in numbers of certain groups of employees) are helpful, but aiming solely at achieving equal numbers tends to divert people from the tasks of ensuring equality of access and opportunity to all.

A sunset clause

The government, in repealing the Employment Equity Act 1990, did not deny that there were considerable economic benefits to be gained from the introduction of equity initiatives into the workplace. These economic benefits are now being demonstrated in New Zealand and overseas.[45] That being the case, there is no sustainable policy objection to requiring legislative compliance, especially in light of the practical advantages referred to above. At the very least a sunset clause is warranted where private sector organisations would meet specified anti-discrimination and equality goals by the early twenty-first century.

To achieve this, the EEO Trust or the Human Rights Commission must be sufficiently resourced to provide the information, advice and monitoring required to assist businesses in meeting this target.

New law: compulsory equal employment opportunities

There is no logical reason for a distinction in the approach to EEO between the public and private sectors. While the changes referred to above will go some way to assisting private sector employers, it is arguable that only compulsory EEO will deliver compliance in all sectors. Administrative and resource practicalities may dictate this approach. Certainly, the 'dollar-for-dollar' approach taken by the government has not prompted high levels of interest. Six of the EEO Trust's private sector foundation members failed to renew their membership in 1996, which at a maximum cost of $2,000 (tax deductible) could hardly be called expensive. As at March 1996, only 178 organisations had joined the EEO Trust, prompting the new chairperson, David Patten, to ask 'but how many private sector employers are there in New Zealand?' He warned employers: 'If the membership does not increase significantly, and employers do not become more publicly involved and committed to EEO action, then it is likely that legislation will be introduced.'[46]

A change of government may also see a shift from the voluntary free market approach to a more regulated employment market. The Leader of the Labour Party, Helen Clarke, has already signalled that a Labour Government would support laws on employment equity.[47] Other Labour members of Parliament have introduced proposals to improve the position of parents in paid work and in particular to introduce paid parental leave.[48] The Alliance Party has also expressed support for compulsory private sector EEO. Even without a change in government, the change to mixed member proportional representation in 1996 is likely to mean that equity-based laws will receive better hearings than previously.

Childcare expenses

Revisiting the laws on equal opportunities will only go some way to producing equality between women and men. New approaches to parental leave, childcare funding and tax deductibility are required if women and men are to be equal in the workplace.

Parental leave

Despite the provisions for child-related leave provided in the Parental Leave and Employment Protection Act 1987 few lawyers avail themselves of their entitlements. While, for some women, taking limited leave is a choice, many others do so as a result of financial necessity (parental leave being unpaid), work pressures or the need to appear committed to the job. It is generally understood that women's career prospects are negatively affected by taking maternity or parental leave, despite the protection against this supposedly offered by the Parental Leave and Employment Protection Act and the Human Rights Act (in relation to family status).[49]

Government policies on parental leave require reassessment in light of this evidence and changing family and workforce demographics. Career barriers, at least in the legal profession, clearly limit access to parental leave. To the extent that financial necessity is making maternity, paternity and parental leave impractical the current unpaid leave policies and laws are not working.

Paid parental leave has been recommended many times, for example in 1986 by the Working Party on Payment for Parental Leave, in 1988 by the Royal Commission on Social Policy, and in 1990 by a Research Advisory Group for the National Advisory Council on the Employment of Women. Despite these recommendations, New Zealand has continued to reserve its position on paid maternity leave, although it is a party to the Convention on the Elimination of Discrimination Against Women which requires that member States 'take appropriate measures ... to introduce maternity leave with pay or with comparable social benefits without loss of former employment seniority'.[50]

Paid parental leave is now available in most western European countries, where up to sixteen weeks' leave is available with payment of up to 70 percent of salary. Most paid maternity leave schemes are part of social insurance schemes which involve contributions from employers and employees, with the government underwriting the scheme. In some countries, a compulsory paid month's leave for fathers is available.[51]

The limited leave taken by women in the legal profession also cuts across the public health policy of promoting the practice of breastfeeding. The Public Health Commission has set breastfeeding targets which aim to increase the numbers of mothers breastfeeding at three months from 60 percent in 1991 to 70 percent in 1997.[52] Judging by the small number of women lawyers who take three or more months' leave and the even smaller number who work part time, only a minority would be breast-feeding for three months or more. As one commentator has pointed out: 'it appears, particularly in light of recent labour market changes, that government needs to gives more consideration to whether it can continue to simply promote breastfeeding without actively protecting it.'[53]

Likewise, the limited role played by men lawyers in the care of children raises questions about public policy on men and child care. As with women lawyers, the negative career stigma attaching to 'excessive' childcare involvement or commitment acts as a disincentive to men. Equally, pressures on time and energy prevent men lawyers from being involved in child care. Yet, according to psychologists and researchers, men gain emotionally from a greater involvement in their children's upbringing, benefits which may translate into their better decision making in the public sphere.[54] As the government has become increasingly concerned with men's role in families, through child support laws, domestic violence laws, and child sexual abuse issues, it may also need to reconsider men's roles in child care.[55]

Employer-provided child care

In 1990, the Minister of Women's Affairs observed that the new 'universal' childcare system, which funded childcare providers not users, might alleviate some of the problems. That system, introduced in 1989, was to be fully implemented by 1994. Consistent with the focus on funding the service providers, the Ministry of Women's Affairs was directed to explore methods to encourage employers to provide childcare assistance as another option for expanding the amount of affordable and quality child care.[56]

While Fletcher Challenge, the Reserve Bank of New Zealand, and the Inland Revenue Department, for example, successfully operate childcare centres for their employees, few if any law firms do so. Childcare assistance from law firms, in the form of facilities or support, was available to only 6 percent of women lawyers and 4 percent of men lawyers in the 1992 survey.[57] Even then, that assistance did little to alleviate the pressure of child care.[58] The Auckland law society provides twelve places in the Minor Proceedings childcare centre, but no other law society offers such a service.

The costs of establishing a childcare centre are enormous and include management time, the identification and possible purchase or lease of land and buildings, the modification of buildings to meet the stringent regulatory requirements, purchasing of equipment and furnishings and the ongoing running expenses.[59] For law firms located in city centres the option of locating the centre within their premises usually will be eliminated by the regulatory requirement that there be adequate outdoor facilities. The cost of floor space alone makes the establishment of childcare facilities prohibitive for many firms.

Offsetting these costs are government subsidies of up to $8 per child per week and fees paid by parents. The majority of centres are operated on user-pays bases. Businesses providing childcare centres have exemptions from fringe benefit tax and can of course deduct the expenses involved in setting up the centre. Depreciation is also available on buildings, land and furnishings. It is possible to operate a childcare centre on a cost recovery basis or even profit basis.

Perhaps the greatest problem with this 'solution' to child care for parents in paid work is not the financial cost but employers' general disinclination to accept any responsibility for providing assistance. In the context of the legal profession, decision makers believe that women's primary commitment should either be their firms or their families. There is little middle ground and many proceed on the assumption that family and children is the 'choice' women ultimately will make. Providing childcare assistance is not seen to be the employers' obligation—babies have no place in business.

Until economic reality (with or without legal backing) forces employers to take positive roles in providing childcare assistance, responsibility will continue to fall on the parents in paid work.

History of tax deductibility proposals

Following the recommendations of the second Auckland working party in 1989, the Auckland Women in Law Committee proposed the tax deductibility of childcare expenses as a partial solution to the economic barriers preventing the full participation of women in the workforce.[60] Tax relief, it was argued, would give greater choice to parents in paid work, would reduce the cost of child care which fell largely on women, and would help ensure that a range of women could take up other positions of responsibility in society. In this way, tax relief would go some way toward promoting the equality of women.[61] The Auckland law society endorsed the submission and asked that it be forwarded to the government with the support of the NZLS.

As the Women in Law Committee appreciated, the implications of the proposal were immense.[62] Members of the NZLS Executive Committee queried whether the law society should be supporting 'political moves of this nature' and noted that the logical extension was the suggestion that unpaid child care in the home should also attract 'notional deductibility'. As a member of the Executive Committee, Judith Potter pointed out, the unpaid labour aspect 'would create all sorts of problems which were incapable of being answered because society had not yet dealt with them'. There were also concerns that the proposition of tax deductibility would be seen as benefiting the 'elite' even though it was proposed that it would cover all parents in paid work.[63]

In the end, the national law society advised the Minister of Finance and the Minister of Women's Affairs that it would support a concept of childcare deductibility 'across the board'. Women in other fields of work, it was suggested, would also be experiencing difficulties similar to those of women lawyers.[64]

Government support for the proposal was not forthcoming. Even before the submission had been considered by the national law society, the Deputy Prime Minister had indicated to women lawyers in Auckland that it would not be well received.[65] The Minister of Women's Affairs, in her reply to the law society, set out seven reasons why the tax deductibility proposal was inadequate: existing subsidies were available regardless of the reason for the parent needing child care; tax deductions assumed the parent could afford to pay for child care in the first place; deductions would not ensure that childcare services were available; funds should be directed to quality early childhood care so that benefits accrued to a wider group; deductions would not be equitable across different income groups; the tax system was not a good funding mechanism; and tax reforms generally were moving away from deductions for work-related expenses. In relation to this last reason the minister said: 'any proposals to reverse this trend will . . . require substantial evidence to support them..[66]

Despite women lawyers' groups and Auckland law society and NZLS support for the proposal, tax deductibility for childcare expenses remained off the government's agenda.

A *new approach to tax deductibility*

For tax purposes there is a distinction between taxpayers who are employees and self-employed taxpayers. In general, employees are unable to deduct expenses, including childcare costs. Even when the law previously allowed certain types of employment-related expenses to be deducted, the courts held that child care was a private or domestic expense. This was the case even where it was incurred to enable the parent to undertake paid work.[67]

Self-employed taxpayers can benefit from tax deductions for certain kinds of expenses but they too are unable to deduct childcare expenses. This is because the courts have traditionally been of the view that childcare expenses are domestic or personal costs and are not sufficiently connected to the production of income.

These outdated policies penalise care providers in paid work. Expenses relating to the education and transportation of taxpayers can be structured to be deductible, as can the costs of home offices. In all cases these costs are incurred to enable the taxpayer to undertake paid work; as such they are little different from childcare costs. This connection is recognised in Canada where deductions are granted for childcare costs. The Canadian legislature has specifically recognised that such costs permit the taxpayer to pursue employment, business, training or research activities.[68]

A policy shift is required at governmental level to reverse the prohibition on deductions for child care. This can easily be achieved, using models from countries such as Canada.

The simple approach would be to allow deductibility for self-employed taxpayers by making a small amendment to the Income Tax Act 1994. However, if this was the only change it would confer an unfair advantage on the self-employed, particularly as most taxpayers are employees who are unable to benefit from deductions. A simple mechanism is also needed to deliver the same type of benefits to employees.

One mechanism is already available. Under current law, employees can receive certain tax free or tax exempt allowances from their employer. To qualify, the type of allowance must be approved by the Inland Revenue Department in advance of payment. Certain additional transport allowances are one example of this type of exempt allowance. If approved, the allowance is tax free to the employee and deductible to the employer.[69] Fringe benefit tax would not apply.

This tax free or tax exempt allowance provides to employees the same benefit that deductibility confers on self-employed taxpayers. A simple amendment would be required to the Income Tax Act recognising child-care allowances as exempt. In light of increasing dependant care responsibilities falling on individual tax payers, it will also need to be determined whether the costs of this care will attract tax benefits.

These suggestions are in no way exhaustive—a number of other methods could be pursued by government to achieve deductibility or its equivalent for all taxpayers. Providing tax benefits for parents paying childcare costs could be an incentive for those parents to pay fair market wages to childcare providers, be they individuals or organisations. At present, many childcare workers working outside childcare centres are believed to be paid 'under the table'. The reasons for this include the fact that some parents in paid work simply cannot afford to pay fair market rates. Therefore, these childcare workers do not pay tax.

The cost of child care is a barrier for women entering or remaining in the legal profession and in other spheres of employment. It has also been a primary factor in the creation of a 'childcare black market'. While this issue may not have been a priority for past generations it is an impediment which will continue to impact on women into the 1990s and beyond. It is time for a change.

The 'persons' law

The current Acts Interpretation Act 1924 still contains the rule of statutory interpretation that 'words importing the masculine gender include females' if not inconsistent with the context.[70] Although in the current political climate it is inconceivable that a court or Parliament might again rely on this provision to render women invisible or outside the law as was done one hundred years ago, the fact it remains on the statute books keeps the possibility alive.

This definition has certainly remained in the consciousness of lawyers, going by the references to this legal rule as the justification for the use of masculine pronouns to include females.[71] In 1990, the Law Commission recommended that the provision be replaced with a new rule: 'words denoting a gender include each other gender.' According to the commission the current rule: 'is objectionable in that it can be seen as supporting an aspect of the subordination of women.'[72] However, six years later, it remains on the statute books.

Conclusion

It is time that the legislature demonstrated that it is serious about the implementation of EEO in the private sector. The rationale for the double standard between the private and public sectors is less justifiable as government agencies are corporatised and generally become more service-orientated and cost-conscious. It could be argued that in enforcing equal opportunities in the public sector, but not in the private sector, the government has given the public sector a strategic business advantage.

Certainly with the recent out-performance by corporatised state bodies over traditional public companies and the flood of women lawyers into government agencies, private sector law firms are being lulled into a false sense of security.

Experience shows that the private sector does not follow the public sector heedlessly. In equal pay, this has not been the case. In employment equity, more than ten years since the introduction of EEO into the state sector, only an estimated 20 percent of law firms have policies and even then they do not necessarily have procedures. Nor is there any quality control. Before relying further on voluntary EEO implementation, the government must be certain of its success to date. Full consideration needs to be given to mandatory equal opportunity standards which will translate EEO policies into more meaningful practices.

Perhaps more importantly is the question of how human rights laws are developed. In developing strategies and laws, successive governments and lobbyists have interpreted questions relating to human rights as employment issues or access to service issues. By taking this interpretation, competition between the interests of employers and employees has been invited and the State has retreated to the relatively safe middle ground. It must be asked whether this is the correct formula for defining and protecting human rights.

These are not solely employment issues. The human rights infringements which occur at the transaction levels of employment, education, health, housing and so on, influence the ultimate position of groups in society. So, for example, unequal opportunities and pay inequity ensure that women remain with less economic power and hence less access to other opportunities in society. All social, political and economic rights hinge on the basic human right to be free from discrimination.

Governments must not only recognise but must regulate for the economic impact of discrimination and gender bias on women's workforce participation. It is generally accepted that women's participation in the workforce is affected by the costs of childbearing and child caring. At present, economic recessions and booms affect women lawyers more significantly than men lawyers, in terms of numbers employed or promoted. Policy development must focus on alleviating the inequitable effects of economic cycles on women's employment prospects vis-à-vis men.

If the government is to be serious about protecting human rights it needs to reconsider the priority given to this function of government. Redressing human rights cannot be done as an 'add-on'. This issue is central to the role and the legitimacy of the state and of democracy.

In light of the persistent problem of discrimination, legislators need to provide meaning to the otherwise empty promise of the law.

Conclusion

One hundred years have passed since women were granted the legal right to enter the New Zealand legal profession. Over that time, hundreds of women have taken up this opportunity and after only a brief stay many have left. Despite this pattern, women are now clearly a part of the profession. In 1996, the centenary of women in the law, there are an estimated two thousand women lawyers working in paid employment and in each following year, about another three hundred women will enter the profession.

What does the future hold for these women and for the legal profession? Progress to date suggests more of the same . . . slowly. Sex discrimination and gender bias certainly remain as constants. Other forms of discrimination and cultural bias are coming to light and when fully explored may outweigh the problem of sex discrimination. There seems to be little hope that the future for women in the law will be fundamentally different.

However, some glimmers of hope do exist. The prospect of positive change can be seen in the efforts of those within the profession and judiciary to 're-gender' justice. The Law Commission's Women's Access to Justice project is due to be reported on in 1997 and undoubtedly will recommend that the legal profession and the judiciary take significant roles in ensuring justice for women. The Judicial Working Group on Gender Equity will also have commenced judicial education on gender issues. The October 1996 Auckland Women Lawyers Association symposium celebrating the centenary of women in the law is likely to reinforce to law societies, law firms and government the need to implement equal employment opportunities (EEO).

These and other initiatives will create a broader understanding of gender bias and will build a framework for change. To succeed, these new initiatives will need to examine how 'justice' is defined. If the present concept of justice is retained, it will continue to overlook differences (of status, power, access and opportunity) between individuals and groups. A new definition needs to recognise and accommodate the social, political and economic realities of all people. To achieve this, laws and legal processes would be redesigned to ensure equity in access and outcomes. Outcomes simply can not be assumed but need to be enforced and monitored. The actual achievement of justice will be the measurement of justice.

Prejudice against women and other groups in New Zealand has been under similar scrutiny by other commissions, government committees and independent groups in the past. It is unlikely that radical action will occur as a result of these new initiatives alone. Change will also be driven by the actions of women and men lawyers where that action has a direct impact on the business of legal practices.

Action by women and men is conceivable. For example, top women law graduates in future could consistently refuse employment offers from traditional legal practices, choosing instead to work outside private practice or in other occupations. Large law firms may face class actions for career discrimination or harassment taken by employees who are tired of waiting for change. Men lawyers, faced with childcare responsibilities, may have no choice but to demand and take paternity and parental leave. Excessive work-related stress may force lawyers to seek other careers. Women clients, having acquired greater power in business decision making, may elect to use only women lawyers or lawyers who have adopted equal opportunities thinking. New Zealand may face its own version of the Anita Hill revelations, throwing the judicial selection process and the legal system under intense scrutiny.

Broader business changes will also leave the legal profession and legal practices with no choice but to rethink their approaches to management and EEO. In the information age, technical competence will no longer be a distinguishing factor. Instead, innovation, adaptability and flexibility will differentiate lawyers in the market. These attributes are contained in many women lawyers survival kits and have been demonstrated in relation to law, social policy, legal practice and business. Employers who overlook this do so at their own risk.

Fundamental changes to the demographic make-up of New Zealand will pressure legal business to change. Business in the twenty-first century is predicted to involve completely new markets which require an understanding of gender, ethnicity, family status, sexual orientation, disability and age. These same factors will inform policy making and make 'managing diversity' a touchstone for all forms of decision making.

Competition may also influence the legal profession to review its response to managing diversity. Accountancy firms and an increasing number of businesses run by legally trained consultants may take work from traditional legal practices. Established, traditional client-firm relationships will lessen in importance. Price, not quality, is already driving client preferences in some instances.

Boutique legal businesses, with lower overheads and unique expertise, could well be the way of the future. If so, law firms and practices which are adept at managing diversity and providing equal opportunities are more likely to thrive. Firms adopting these management strategies will have highly skilled, happy workforces and will achieve higher profits at lower costs. Among these boutique firms will be those run and staffed by women lawyers. Women have already formed practices along these lines and in an expanding economy may be expected to compete for the business presently going to traditional law firms.

As previously, much of the pressure for change is external to the profession and the practice of law. But, business pressure coupled with a new, inclusive concept of justice may provide the right formula for positive change. Re-engineering on both fronts is essential if women in the law are to progress without prejudice.

Table A1

Law students and law graduates, 1874–1990

Year	Law students[a]				Law graduates[b]						Total	Women %
					Bachelors		Honours		Masters & PhDs			
	Women	Men	Total	Women %	Women	Men	Women	Men	Women	Men		
1874	0	17	17	0.0	-	-	-	-	-	-	-	-
1878	0	16	16	0.0	-	-	-	-	-	-	-	-
1881	0	89	89	0.0	-	-	-	-	-	-	-	-
1886	0	60	60	0.0	-	-	-	-	-	-	-	-
1891	0	44	44	0.0	-	-	-	-	-	-	-	-
1896	0	34	34	0.0	-	-	-	-	-	-	-	-
1901[c]	1	94	95	1.1	-	-	-	-	-	-	-	-
1906[c]	1	83	84	1.2	-	-	-	-	-	-	-	-
1908	-	-	-	-	0	7	0	1	0	0	8	0.0
1909	0	47	47	0.0	0	9	0	0	0	1	10	0.0
1911	1	227	228	0.4	0	23	0	0	0	1	24	0.0
1912	0	236	236	0.0	1	30	0	2	0	1	34	2.9
1913	1	238	239	0.4	0	20	0	4	0	1	25	0.0
1914	1	207	208	0.5	0	21	1	2	0	2	26	3.8
1915	1	161	162	0.6	0	10	0	1	0	3	14	0.0
1916	1	183	184	0.5	0	15	0	4	0	2	21	0.0
1917	4	153	157	2.5	1	8	0	0	0	1	10	10.0
1918	7	195	202	3.5	-	-	-	-	-	-	-	-
1919	7	402	409	1.7	0	24	0	0	0	0	24	0.0
1920	0	49	49	0.0	1	38	0	3	0	2	44	2.3
1921	8	535	543	1.5	0	49	0	2	0	3	54	0.0
1922	-	-	-	-	0	46	0	10	0	13	69	0.0
1923	12	541	553	2.2	0	53	0	6	0	8	67	0.0
1924	8	578	586	1.4	0	37	0	9	0	13	59	0.0
1925	9	512	521	1.7	0	30	0	10	0	16	56	0.0
1926	13	479	492	2.6	1	26	0	5	0	9	41	2.4
1927	12	553	565	2.1	2	37	0	4	0	3	46	4.3
1928	12	492	504	2.4	1	40	0	4	0	7	52	1.9
1929	12	453	465	2.6	0	45	0	5	0	10	60	0.0
1930	18	444	462	3.9	0	43	0	9	0	7	59	0.0
1931	18	410	428	4.2	3	57	0	6	0	5	71	4.2
1932	22	412	434	5.1	2	45	0	9	1	3	60	5.0
1933	19	374	393	4.8	0	48	0	10	0	7	65	0.0
1934	16	359	375	4.3	0	37	0	4	1	8	50	2.0
1935	19	325	344	5.5	2	38	0	4	0	4	48	4.2
1936	16	307	323	5.0	2	38	0	5	0	7	52	3.8
1937	12	343	355	3.4	2	44	0	5	0	9	60	3.3
1938	13	350	363	3.6	6	38	0	6	0	7	57	10.5
1939	10	359	369	2.7	2	26	0	6	0	5	39	5.1
1940	7	288	295	2.4	1	25	0	0	0	2	28	3.6
1941	7	246	253	2.8	1	17	0	1	0	0	19	5.3
1942	12	124	136	8.8	1	2	0	1	0	0	4	25.0
1943	8	156	164	4.9	0	7	0	0	0	1	8	0.0
1944	13	254	267	4.9	1	10	0	1	0	1	13	7.7
1945	15	302	317	4.7	1	21	0	1	0	2	25	4.0
1946	17	566	583	2.9	1	47	0	4	2	0	54	5.6
1947	17	625	642	2.6	0	60	0	2	0	5	67	0.0
1948	17	604	621	2.7	1	69	0	3	0	5	78	1.3
1949	20	542	562	3.6	0	62	0	1	0	5	68	0.0
1950	22	488	510	4.3	2	46	0	3	0	4	55	3.6
1951	14	440	454	3.1	1	50	0	1	0	3	55	1.8
1952	19	525	544	3.5	1	64	0	4	0	3	72	1.4
1953	26	617	643	4.0	1	49	0	4	0	2	56	1.8
1954	29	718	747	3.9	1	53	0	1	0	4	59	1.7
1955	29	757	786	3.7	0	57	3	1	0	3	64	4.7

continued...

Table A1—*continued*

Law students and law graduates, 1874–1990—continued

Year	Law students[a]				Law graduates[b]						Total	Women
					Bachelors		Honours		Masters & PhDs			
	Women	Men	Total	Women %	Women	Men	Women	Men	Women	Men		%
1956	32	818	850	3.8	3	69	0	1	0	2	75	4.0
1957	33	876	909	3.6	0	72	0	2	0	2	76	0.0
1958	37	896	933	4.0	3	86	0	0	0	2	91	3.3
1959	38	914	952	4.0	3	98	0	2	0	0	103	2.9
1960	43	1,039	1,082	4.0	3	110	0	3	0	0	116	2.6
1961	66	1,040	1,106	6.0	2	84	0	4	0	2	92	2.2
1962	58	1,009	1,067	5.4	2	98	0	4	0	2	106	1.9
1963	51	1,100	1,151	4.4	1	100	0	6	0	1	108	0.9
1964	66	1,222	1,288	5.1	5	129	0	7	0	1	142	3.5
1965	59	1,278	1,337	4.4	5	128	0	0	0	10	143	3.5
1966	84	1,456	1,540	5.5	2	133	0	0	0	14	149	1.3
1967	100	1,612	1,712	5.8	12	140	0	4	0	25	181	6.6
1968	133	1,739	1,872	7.1	6	142	0	7	4	19	178	5.6
1969	181	1,880	2,061	8.8	4	157	2	18	1	18	200	3.5
1970	207	1,925	2,132	9.7	14	219	1	27	0	15	276	5.4
1971	-	-	-	-	-	-	-	-	-	-	-	-
1972	367	1,931	2,298	16.0	11	225	6	53	0	14	309	5.5
1973	391	1,726	2,117	18.5	25	222	6	49	1	27	330	9.7
1974	477	1,823	2,300	20.7	19	252	6	59	1	13	350	7.4
1975	587	1,756	2,343	25.1	44	223	10	58	1	13	349	15.8
1976	644	1,707	2,351	27.4	64	235	7	45	2	19	372	19.6
1977	786	1,825	2,611	30.1	56	240	21	41	1	14	373	20.9
1978	792	1,754	2,546	31.1	55	301	12	39	1	13	421	16.2
1979[d]	871	1,817	2,688	32.4	104	265	-	-	1	12	382	27.5
1980[d]	821	1,536	2,357	34.8	94	276	13	31	1	9	424	25.5
1981[d]	1,021	1,708	2,729	37.4	115	235	15	33	3	12	413	32.2
1982[d]	1,185	1,721	2,906	40.8	101	227	20	32	2	11	393	31.3
1983[d]	1,354	1,788	3,142	43.1	115	213	26	39	6	9	408	36.0
1984[d]	1,511	1,832	3,343	45.2	103	196	8	23	6	10	229	51.1
1985[d,e]	1,322	1,543	2,865	46.1	134	202	20	33	1	17	407	38.1
1986[d,e]	1,379	1,644	3,023	45.6	142	195	21	42	3	14	417	39.8
1987[d,e]	1,498	1,605	3,103	48.3	157	195	30	30	5	15	432	44.4
1988[d,e]	1,721	1,748	3,469	49.6	177	245	34	37	4	6	503	42.7
1989	2,317	2,276	4,593	50.4	207	182	32	33	2	9	465	51.8
1990	1,571	1,556	3,127	50.2	185	207	33	41	2	5	473	46.5

[a] Law students are the students attending lectures for that course for that year.

[b] Law graduates are the successful candidates for the degree examination of that year.

[c] Law students include articled clerks.

[d] Law students include law intermediate students.

[e] Law students include external students.

Note: Data post-1990 is not published and would need to be collated from each university.

Source: *New Zealand Census of Population and Dwellings*, 1874–1906; *Appendices to the Journals of the House of Representatives*, 1908–1944; and *Education Statistics New Zealand*, 1945–1990.

Table A2

Typists in the legal profession, 1901–1921

Census year	Number			Women %
	Women	Men	Total	
1901	1	10	11	9.1
1906	3	4	7	42.9
1911	57	4	61	93.4
1916	616	0	616	100.0
1921	481	1	482	99.8

Source: *New Zealand Census of Population and Dwellings*, 1901–1921.

Table A3

Articled and non-articled law clerks, 1901–1916

Census year	Articled law clerks			Women %	Non-articled law clerks			Women %
	Women	Men	Total		Women	Men	Total	
1901	1	94	95	1.1	28	672	700	4.0
1906	1	83	84	1.2	111	737	848	13.1
1911	1	108	109	0.9	201	982	1183	17.0
1916	0	79	79	0.0	485	649	1134	42.8

Source: *New Zealand Census of Population and Dwellings*, 1901–1916.

Table A4

Law clerks, 1874–1986

Census year	Number			Women %
	Women	Men	Total	
1874	0	194	194	0.0
1878	0	267	267	0.0
1881	0	320	320	0.0
1886	-	-	-	-
1891	1	490	491	0.2
1896	14	577	591	2.4
1901	29	766	795	3.6
1906	112	820	932	12.0
1911	202	1,090	1,292	15.6
1916	485	728	1,213	40.0
1921	707	1,079	1,786	39.6
1926	610	990	1,600	38.1
1936	500	666	1,166	42.9
1945	515	305	820	62.8
1951	-	-	451	-
1956	401	407	808	49.6
1961	604	531	1,135	53.2
1966	473	454	927	51.0
1971	988	703	1,691	58.4
1976	1,758	620	2,378	73.9
1981	2,175	477	2,652	82.0
1986	3,525	576	4,101	86.0

Note: The category of 'law clerk' does not exist in any census after 1986.

Source: *New Zealand Census of Population and Dwellings*, 1874–1986.

Table A5

Women barristers and solicitors, 1897–1959

Name[a]	Year of Admission
Ethel Benjamin (de Costa)	1897
Eliza Ellen Melville	1906
Geraldine Marian Hemus	1907
Annie Lee Rees	1910
Harriet Joanna Vine	1915
Lyra Veronica E Taylor	1918
Rebecca Macky (Pallot)	1921
Esther Ellen Ongley	1921
Prudence Rose Collier	1926
Margaret Smith Mackay	1929
Mary Catherine Enright	1931
Olive Virginia Nelson	1931 (barrister 1936)
Julia Dunn	1932
Marion van Beeresteyn Hollway (Kirk)	1933
Marjorie Taylor (Feist)	1936 (barrister 1942)
Isobel Wright (Matson)	1938
Margaret Rutherford Kennedy	1938
Alison Christobel Carey	1938
Dorothy Archdall Raymond	1938
Elisabeth Marjorie Urquhart	1939
Audrey Ngaire Gale	1939
Valerie Yvonne Anderson	1939
Ellen Evans	1939
Dorothy Simes (Thompson)	1939
Jocelyn Margaret Miller (Gregory)	1940
Patricia Mary Webb	1941
Sheila Campbell Macdonald	1942
Betty Webster (Thorpe)	1943
Mary Moir Hussey	1947
Pamela Montague (Mitchell)	1947
Audrey Langley (Ricketts)	1948
Isabella C C Gordon	1949
Alison Pearce	1950 (barrister 1951)
Fay Estelle Matson (Wellwood)	1952
Alison Burns Souter (Quentin-Baxter)	1952
G C P Augusta Dunlop (Wallace)	1953
Shirley Anne Parr	1953
Olive E Smuts-Kennedy	1955
Paddy West-Walker (Steele)	1955
Eileen Patricia O'Connor	1955 (barrister 1957)
Shirley Smith	1956 (barrister 1957)
Anne Shorland (Gambrill)	1958 (barrister 1960)
Ann Elizabeth Kearsley	1958
Margaret Louise Smith	1959

[a] The women's married surnames, where known, are in parentheses.

Source: District law societies' new admissions and practising certificate records.

Table A6

The Legal Profession and Lawyers, 1851–1991

Census year	Women	Men	Total	Women %
		Legal profession		
1851	0	14	14	0.0
1853	-	-	-	-
1855	0	12	12	0.0
1858	0	74	74	0.0
1860	0	4	4	0.0
1861	0	94	94	0.0
1864	0	153	153	0.0
1867	0	161	161	0.0
1871	0	229	229	0.0
		Lawyers		
1874	0	230	230	0.0
1878	0	285	285	0.0
1881	0	362	362	0.0
1886	0	511	511	0.0
1891	0	571	571	0.0
1896	0	604	604	0.0
1901	1	635	636	0.2
1906	2	783	785	0.3
1911	3	947	950	0.3
1916	3	1,122	1,125	0.3
1921	4	1,230	1,234	0.3
1926	4	1,631	1,635	0.2
1936	7	1,755	1,762	0.4
1945	19	1,436	1,455	1.3
1951	-	-	1,641	-
1956	28	1,917	1,945	1.4
1961	33	2,058	2,091	1.6
1966	31	2,335	2,366	1.3
1971	47	2,587	2,634	1.8
1976	142	3,306	3,448	4.1
1981	348	3,570	3,918	8.9
1986	759	4,011	4,770	15.9
1991	1,377	4,413	5,790	23.8

Source: Census of New Ulster, 1851; regional census, 1853; Auckland census, 1855; Hawkes Bay census, 1858; and *New Zealand Census of Population and Dwellings*, 1860–1991.

Table A7

Practising certificates, 1977–1995

Year	Women	Men	Total	Women %
1977	168	3,512	3,680	4.6
1978	215	3,556	3,771	5.7
1979	241	3,630	3,871	6.2
1980	279	3,737	4,016	6.9
1981	342	3,982	4,324	7.9
1982	459	3,961	4,420	10.4
1983	483	4,031	4,514	10.7
1984	548	4,086	4,634	11.8
1985	613	4,367	4,980	12.3
1986	746	4,329	5,075	14.7
1987	859	4,393	5,252	16.4
1988	1,045	4,472	5,517	18.9
1989	1,231	4,473	5,704	21.6
1990	1,225	4,479	5,704	21.5
1991	1,345	4,724	6,069	22.2
1992	1,383	4,860	6,243	22.2
1993	1,548	4,902	6,450	24.0
1994	1,686	5,059	6,745	25.0
1995	1,940	5,055	6,995	27.7

Source: Annual New Zealand Law Society practising certificate data.

Table A8

New admissions to the Bar, 1979-1995

Year	Women	Men	Total	Women %
1979	82	233	315	26.0
1980	102	286	388	26.3
1981	108	246	354	30.5
1982	103	240	343	30.0
1983	119	229	348	34.2
1984	131	265	396	33.1
1985	170	234	404	42.1
1986	134	161	295	45.4
1987	186	216	402	46.3
1988	303	356	659	46.0
1989	226	243	469	48.2
1990	225	266	491	45.8
1991	245	275	520	47.1
1992	263	296	559	47.0
1993	266	245	515	51.6
1994	347	295	642	54.0
1995	361	349	710	50.8

Source: District law societies' new admissions records.

Table A9

Women judges

Name	Jurisdiction	Year (month) of appointment
Augusta Wallace	District Court	1975 (September)
Silvia Cartwright	District Court	1981 (September)
Carolyn Henwood	District Court	1985 (November)
Heather Simpson	District Court	1987 (January)
Margaret Lee	District Court	1987 (May)
Cecile Rushton	District Court	1987 (June)
Anne Gambrill	High Court (Master)	1987 (August)
Josephine Bouchier	District Court	1988 (July)
Patricia Costigan	District Court	1989 (January)
Anne Gaskell	District Court	1989 (August)
Dale Green	District Court	1989 (September)
Shonagh Kenderdine	District Court	1990 (September)
Marion Frater	District Court	1990 (October)
Coral Shaw	District Court	1992 (June)
Silvia Cartwright	High Court	1993 (July)
Jane Lovell-Smith	District Court	1994 (March)
Jan Doogue	District Court	1994 (July)
Sharon McAuslan	District Court	1995 (April)
Jill Moss	District Court	1995 (June)
Sian Elias	High Court	1995 (November)
Lowell Goddard	High Court	1995 (November)

Source: Announcements of appointments made in law society newsletters and in the national media.

S hort titles have been used when citing some works in the notes; for full references see the bibliography. The following abbreviations have been used in the notes.

ADLS	Auckland District Law Society	L Ed 2d	Lawyers edition, *United States*
AJHR	*Appendices to the Journal of the House of Representatives*		*Supreme Court Reports*, second series
AWLA	Auckland Women Lawyers Association	LR CP	*Law Reports, Common Pleas* (England)
CDLS	Canterbury District Law Society	NW	*North Western Reporter* (United States)
CWLA	Canterbury Women's Legal Association	NZ	New Zealand
DLR (4th)	*Dominion Law Reports* (Canada)	NZAR	*New Zealand Administrative Reports*
EEO	equal employment opportunities	NZLS	New Zealand Law Society
EOC	*Australian and New Zealand Equal Opportunity Cases*	NZLJ	*New Zealand Law Journal*
ERNZ	*Employment Reports of New Zealand*	NZLR	*New Zealand Law Reports*
F Supp	*Federal Supplement* (United States)	NZPD	*New Zealand Parliamentary Debates*
FRNZ	*Family Reports of New Zealand*	ODLS	Otago District Law Society
GDLS	Gisborne District Law Society	OWLS	Otago Women Lawyers Society
IPLS	Institute of Professional Legal Studies	TCL	*The Capital Letter*
		WCG	Women's Consultative Group
		WDLS	Wellington District Law Society
		WWLA	Wellington Women Lawyers Association

The Research

1 'Gender' refers to the assumptions about men and women (about their behaviours, their natures and their roles) which underpin family, work and social arrangements.
2 Gatfield and Gray, *Women Lawyers*.
3 After the survey was completed there was some criticism of the response rate:

Collins, 4; Gatfield, 'Don't shoot 1469 messengers.'
4 Gatfield, 'Discrimination in the legal profession'; Gatfield, 'Maori women lawyers.'
5 Gatfield, *Women Judges*.
6 Gatfield, *Early Women Lawyers*.
7 Gatfield, *Biographies of New Zealand's High Court Judges*.

Chapter One

1 Coke, para 128a.
2 Blackstone, para 442.
3 Ibid.
4 Stephen, 'Book III,' 409–410.
5 Blackstone, para 442.
6 Stephen, 'Book III,' 412.
7 Blackstone, paras 444 and 445.
8 Stephen, 'Book III,' 413.
9 Blackstone, para 442.
10 Stephen, 'Book IV,' 494.

11　Ford, 6.

12　The Married Women's Property Act 1884 gave to married women the legal rights of a *feme sole*, or unmarried woman, in relation to property, taking court action, entering into contracts (repealed in 1894), bankruptcy (repealed in 1892) and trade.

13　Stephen, 'Book III,' 406.

14　In 1878, of the population aged at least 15 years there were 2.5 unmarried men to every one unmarried woman: 1878 census, 'Conjugal condition of the people,' Part VI, table III, 178. See also Charlotte Macdonald, *Woman of Good Character*, 140.

15　For introductory commentary on the status of Maori customary law, see Chen and Palmer, *Public Law*, 302.

16　Sykes, 162; Szaszy. It has been suggested that there would have been more women of rangatira status signing the Treaty of Waitangi had the missionaries encouraged them to sign: Anne Phillips, presentation to the Women's Law Conference, 22–23 May 1993.

17　Tui MacDonald, 179.

18　Parliamentary Disabilities of Women Abolition Bill, NZPD, 18 July 1894, 570.

19　McHugh, 90, 94.

20　Waterhouse, NZPD, 33, 1881, 137.

21　*Rira Peti v Ngaraihi Te Paku* (1888) 7 NZLR 235.

22　Sachs and Hoff Wilson, 77.

23　Stephen, 'Book III,' 307–308.

24　Bishop, 519.

25　Stephen, 'Book V,' 348.

26　Stephen, 'Book III,' 414–415.

27　Stephen, 'Book V,' 348.

28　Raewyn Dalziel, 'Colonial helpmeet,' 59.

29　1878 census, 'Occupations of the people,' Part VII, tables I and VII.

30　Charlotte Macdonald, *Woman of Good Character*, 152–153.

31　Graham, 137.

32　Married Women's Property Protection Act 1860, sections 2 and 7.

33　Raewyn Dalziel, 'Colonial helpmeet,' 152; Tennant, 108; NZPD, 9, 1870, 338.

34　The Married Women's Property Protection Act 1870 extended the rights of a *feme sole* to a wife who was 'subjected by her husband to cruelty without adultery'; where he was 'guilty of living in open adultery'; 'guilty of habitual drunkenness'; or, generally, failing to maintain his wife and children without unavoidable cause. In addition, the Act enabled a woman who could prove that her earnings were insufficient to support her children to seek maintenance from her husband.

35　NZPD, 9, 1870, 338.

36　Muller, 462; Grimshaw, 14–15.

37　Tulloch, 105.

38　Sachs and Hoff Wilson, 23.

39　*Chorlton v Lings* (1868) LR 4 CP 374.

40　Ibid, 374 and 377. It was also argued that there were legal precedents for women's vote.

41　Ibid, 379.

42　Ibid, 387 per Chief Justice Bovill, 388 per Justice Willes, 394 per Justice Byles and 395 per Justice Keating.

43　Ibid, 386 per Chief Justice Bovill.

44　Ibid, 383.

45　Interpretation Act 1858

46　Interpretation Act 1868, section 12.

47　How the NZ amendment came about appears to be lost to history. The parliamentary debates did not record any comment on the inclusion of the proviso in the Interpretation Bill, and no records are held in the NZ Archives which shed light on the amendment.

48　NZPD, 29, 1878, 211; NZPD, 33, 1879, 173, 182. Despite many politicians being in favour of women's suffrage, opinion was divided on whether it should be restricted to propertied women or be universal: Grimshaw, 18 and 19.

49　NZPD, 36, 1880, 399–404.

50　For example, changes to the licensing laws, the Employment of Females and Others Bill and the Deceased Husbands' Brother's Marriage Bill.

51　Sachs and Hoff Wilson, 85–90.

52　Berger Morello, 43-44.

53　*Bradwell v The State* [1872] 16 Wall 130; *Matter of Goodell* [1875] 20 Am Rep 42 and *In re Goodell* (1879) 81 NW 551.

54　*Albany Law Journal*, 11, 1875, 277.

55　*Bradwell v The State* [1872] 16 Wall 130, 141 per Justice Bradley.

56 *Matter of Goodell* (1875) 20 Am Rep 42, 47.

57 *Bradwell v The State* [1872] 16 Wall 130, 141–142 per Justice Bradley.

58 Berger Morello, 21.

59 *In re Goodell* (1879) 81 NW 551.

60 Berger Morello, 34.

61 'Current topics,' *Solicitors' Journal,* 20 December 1879, 139.

62 Ibid.

63 Ibid, 143.

64 *Solicitors' Journal,* 17 April 1880, 470.

65 Waterhouse, NZPD, 33, 1881, 135.

66 Married Women's Property Bill 1881. This bill did not become law until 1884.

67 Henry Scotland, NZPD, 33, 1881, 136.

68 1881 census, 'Occupations of the people,' Part VII, table 1, 244.

69 Kate Milligan Edger (1877), Anne Jane Bolton (1880) and Helen Connon (1880). See Gardner, *Colonial Cap and Gown,* 89.

70 Law Practitioners Act 1861. It was also possible to qualify for entry via a number of routes which did not involve obtaining a university degree: Cullen, 113–115.

71 Law Practitioners Bill 1881, clause 2. Unlike in England, there had never been a strict separation between the two branches of the profession in NZ— a lawyer could practise as a barrister and as a solicitor if qualified to do so: Cooke, *Portrait of a Profession,* 138–141; Cullen, 113. However, as the profession grew barristers specialised in court work while solicitors concentrated on conveyancing, wills and estates, family law and business transactions.

72 NZPD, 39, 1881, 425.

73 Ibid.

74 Law Practitioners Act 1861, Part I, section V and Part II, section XV. William Downie Stewart had been involved in the drafting of previous legislation relating to the legal profession: Cullen, 40.

75 CDLS council minutes 13 July 1881; ODLS council minutes, 15 July 1881;

ADLS council minutes, 21 July 1881 and 29 July 1881. The WDLS minute books for 1881–1885 have been lost.

76 Law Practitioners Bill 1881, NZPD, 38, 1881, 424.

77 *Dictionary of New Zealand Biography,* 160–164.

78 Sir George Grey introduced at least 11 bills to reform entry into the legal profession over 1880–1892.

79 NZPD, 38, 1881, 429.

80 Ibid.

81 Law Practitioners Bill 1881.

82 Fluency in Latin 'helped the lawyer to feel at home in a world in which the nature of a man's craft could be deduced even from his mode of dress': Birks, 161.

83 Kirk, ch 11.

84 Sinclair, *History of New Zealand.* See Kirk, 109; Birks, 210–212.

85 *Law Times,* no 38, 7 February 1863, 189–190, in Greenaway, 7–8.

86 Cullen, 35–37; Cooke, *Portrait of a Profession,* 142.

87 In 1878 there were 16 law students, by 1881 there were 89. See the appendix, table A1, 449–450.

88 *New Zealand Jurist (NS),* 1, Part V, 1876, 40–41.

89 Raewyn Dalziel, 'Politics of settlement,' 97.

90 *New Zealand Jurist (NS),* 1, Part X, 1876, 82.

91 The number of lawyer-politicians was never less than 10% of the total over 1896–1949: Milne, table 11. Of the 13 ministries in power since 1856, 10 were led by lawyers: Gore, 10.

92 ADLS council minutes, 16 January 1891.

93 NZPD, 39, 1881, 428.

94 Ibid.

95 25:24.

96 26:17.

97 NZPD, 39, 1881, 430.

98 Berger Morello, table, 37–38.

99 Law Advocates Bill 1881 and Law Practitioners Bill 1882.

Chapter Two

1 Sir William Fox, Law Advocates Bill 1881, NZPD, 40, 1881, 437–438; Sir George Whitmore, Law Practitioners Bill (No 3) 1882, NZPD, 42, 1882, 528.

2   William Speight, Law Advocates Bill 1881, NZPD, 40, 1881, 437.

3   Colonel Trimble, Law Practitioners Bill 1884, NZPD, 42, 1884, 246–247.

4   Gardner, 'Colonial economy,' 75–76.

5   Stone, 'Anatomy of the practice of law,' 423–424; Stone, *Making of Russell McVeagh*, 44–51; Millen, 78–79; Gore, 29 and 74.

6   Gore, 21; Stone, *Making of Russell McVeagh*, 27.

7   The bankruptcy rate ran at its highest in the period 1879–1888: Gardner, 'Colonial economy,' 76.

8   In 1891, William Reynolds, an Otago politician, said that lawyers were 'so numerous that they cannot make a living unless they make business for themselves by getting up cases to fleece their clients': Law Practitioners Bill 1891, NZPD, 72, 1891, 476.

9   Dr John M Brown, 'Otago University: presentation of diplomas,' *Otago Daily Times*, 28 August 1885, 3.

10   Mill, *Collected Works*, 403.

11   Equal pay for women and men was included in the objectives of the National Council of Women when it was formed in 1896: Hill, 89–90.

12   The Arbitration Court incorporated different rates of pay for women and men in its first award in 1903: Commission of Inquiry into Equal Pay, 14. Those different rates only confirmed what had been the practice in NZ already.

13   Bunkle, 52.

14   Raewyn Dalziel, 'Colonial helpmeet,' 64.

15   Grimshaw, 67.

16   Law Practitioners Bill 1891, NZPD, 73, 1891, 435.

17   Grimshaw, 67–68.

18   Law Practitioners Bill 1891, NZPD, 73, 1891, 435.

19   Ibid.

20   'Miscellaneous,' *Otago Daily Times*, 25 August 1891.

21   'The Ladies Gallery and female suffrage,' *Otago Daily Times*, 25 August 1891.

22   [1891] AJHR 204–205 (20 August).

23   'Proposed admission of lady lawyers,' *Press*, 21 August 1891.

24   NZPD, 72, 1891, 436.

25   'Proposed admission of lady lawyers,' *Press*, 21 August 1891; 'Proposed admission of lady lawyers,' *Otago Daily Times*, 21 August 1891.

26   'Women as barristers,' *New Zealand Herald*, 22 August 1891. That member was William Lee Rees whose daughter Annie would later become NZ's fourth woman lawyer.

27   *Press*, 24 August 1891.

28   *Otago Daily Times*, 22 August 1891.

29   'Women as barristers,' *New Zealand Herald*, 22 August 1891.

30   ODLS council minutes, 7 August 1891.

31   Raewyn Dalziel, 'Politics of settlement,' 98.

32   'Women as barristers,' *New Zealand Herald*, 22 August 1891.

33   *Press*, 24 August 1891. The Legislative Council's power to reject legislation, in theory, was to be exercised for the 'good of the people.' See Jackson, 25.

34   'Parliamentary jottings,' *Evening Post*, 21 August 1891.

35   'Sir George Grey's Bills,' *New Zealand Herald*, 22 August 1891.

36   NZPD, 74, 1891, 472.

37   Life tenure would be replaced with 7-year (renewable) terms in 1892. See Jackson, 25.

38   Grimshaw, 93–94.

39   As with the 1891 bill, the primary objective of the Law Practitioners Act 1882 Amendment Bill 1894 was to compel the judges to examine law candidates in English not Latin.

40   Law Practitioners Act 1882 Amendment Bill 1894, clause 6.

41   CDLS council minutes, 14 August 1894.

42   Ibid.

43   Law Practitioners Act 1882 Amendment Bill 1894, NZPD, 84, 1894, 632.

44   Letter to John Joyce, Member of the House of Representatives, 20 August 1894, recorded in CDLS council minutes, 25 September 1894.

45   'Schedule of public bills' [1894] AJHR xlix.

46   William Izard was appointed the sole law lecturer at Canterbury University College in 1883, a post he held until 1902: 'William Izard,' in *MacDonald*

Dictionary of Biographies; Cooke, *Portrait of a Profession*, 257–258.

47 'Stella M Allan recalls many happy days with: my finest teachers,' 26 August 1958, biographies off-print articles, Alexander Turnbull Library; 'Miss Stella Henderson,' *White Ribbon*, 3(36), 1898, 1.

48 Carol Brown, ch 2.

49 Vindex, 120–121.

50 'Miss Stella Henderson,' *White Ribbon*, 3(36), 1898, 1.

51 'George Warren Russell,' in *MacDonald Dictionary of Biographies*.

52 NZPD, 84, 1894, 635–636.

53 [1895] AJHR 64 (12 July).

54 Dr John M Brown, 'Otago University: presentation of diplomas,' *Otago Daily Times*, 28 August 1885, 3.

55 ODLS council minutes, 19 April 1895.

56 CDLS, *Annual Report 1894-1895*.

57 'Schedule of public bills' [1895] AJHR xli.

58 'Of interest to the ladies,' *Evening Post*, 18 June 1896.

59 'Women's societies,' *White Ribbon*, 2(13), July 1896, 3.

60 'Women's Political League,' *Press*, 4 September 1896.

61 Removal of Women's Disabilities Bill 1896, NZPD, 92, 1896, 337.

62 Ibid, 338.

63 Ibid.

64 Ibid, 339.

65 Dr Pollen, Chinese Immigrants Bill 1881, NZPD, 38, 1881, 211. European fears of a 'Chinese invasion' had prompted specific policies and legislation to control the Chinese population: Ng, 272.

66 Law Practitioners and New Zealand Law Society Bill, NZPD, 94, 1896, 368. A 'Tom Tiddler's ground' is a place where it is easy to pick up a fortune or make a place in the world for oneself: *Brewer's Dictionary of Phrase & Fable*, 14th ed, London, Ivor H Evans.

67 'Removal of women's disabilities,' *Evening Post*, 3 July 1896.

68 'In Parliament,' *White Ribbon*, 2(15), September 1896, 8.

69 NZPD, 92, 1896, 584.

70 Ibid.

71 'Women as legal practitioners,' *Evening Post*, 3 July 1896.

72 NZPD, 94, 1896, 273–274.

73 Ibid, 274.

74 The House of Representatives had rejected the Admission of Women to Parliament Bill a month before: NZPD, 92, 1896, 50–60. Premier John Seddon noted that opposition to the measure also came from the Legislative Council.

75 NZPD, 94, 1896, 274.

76 Grimshaw, 89.

77 'Fooling the women,' *Press*, 5 September 1896. However, Seddon did support the 1896 Admission of Women to Parliament Bill, although it may have been convenient for him to do so at the time.

78 'Notes and comments,' *White Ribbon*, 1(4), October 1895, 2; 'Women's societies: Malvern Women's Institute,' *White Ribbon*, 2(13), July 1896, 3.

79 'Not worth the candle,' *White Ribbon*, 2(13), July 1896, 7.

80 The fact that all the bills on the parliamentary agenda relating to women's rights were private members' bills was pointed out: 'Of interest to the ladies,' *Evening Post*, 18 June 1896.

81 New Zealand Law Society Act 1869.

82 Cooke, *Portrait of a Profession*, 147–149; Cullen, 36.

83 *New Zealand Jurist (NS)*, 1(Part X), August 1876, 82.

84 Sir George Whitmore, Law Practitioners and New Zealand Law Society Bill 1896, NZPD, 94, 1896, 369.

85 Bowie, 238-280.

86 WDLS, *Annual Report For the Year Ending 20 March 1895*, 2.

87 WDLS council minutes, 6 July 1896.

88 Sir Robert Stout had an illustrious legal and political career as a law lecturer, Minister of Education, member of the House of Representatives, Attorney-General, Premier, Chancellor of the University of New Zealand and Chief Justice: Sir Ivor Richardson, 'Sir Robert Stout,' 44–46.

89 Grimshaw, 15; Stella M Allan, '*Lyttelton Times* engaged Dominion's first woman parliamentary reporter,' 1954 article in the private collection of Mrs Moira Henderson.

90 Francis Henry Dillon Bell, like Sir Robert Stout, had an outstanding legal and political career. He was a founder of the law firm Bell Gully, Mayor of Wellington, Attorney-General and Prime Minister: Millen, 100, 148 and 151–155.
91 Ibid, 102. Although Bell supported women lawyers in 1894, his views on other areas of women's legal rights were later criticised: *White Ribbon*, 2(14), August 1896, 8.
92 William Walker, when moving the second reading of the Law Practitioners and New Zealand Law Society Bill 1896, said that a national society would provide 'a more effectual means of giving expression to the views of the united Law Societies of the colony': NZPD, 94, 1896, 369.
93 WDLS council minutes, 3 August 1896.
94 William Bolt, NZPD, 94, 1896, 567.
95 George McLean, NZPD, 94, 1896, 367; Sir George Whitmore, NZPD, 94, 1896, 366; Henry Scotland, NZPD, 94, 1896, 567.
96 Law Practitioners and New Zealand Law Society Bill 1896, NZPD, 94, 1896, 525.
97 William Bolt, NZPD, 94, 1896, 525 and see Thomas Kelly, NZPD, 94, 1896, 524.
98 Female Law Practitioners Bill 1896, NZPD, 94, 1896, 565.

99 Ibid.
100 Charles Bowen, NZPD, 94, 1896, 565; James Bonar, NZPD, 94, 1896, 566.
101 William Bolt, NZPD, 94, 1896, 567.
102 Law Practitioners and New Zealand Law Society Bill 1896, NZPD, 94, 1896, 92.
103 Ibid.
104 Ibid, 93.
105 NZPD, 95, 1896, 180.
106 Ibid; James Bonar, NZPD, 94, 1896, 566.
107 NZPD, 95, 1896, 180.
108 George McLean, Female Law Practitioners Bill 1896, NZPD, 95, 1896, 346; George McLean, Law Practitioners and New Zealand Law Society Bill, NZPD, 95, 1896, 351.
109 William Downie Stewart, Female Law Practitioners Bill 1896, NZPD, 95, 1896, 346; Charles Bowen, NZPD, 95, 1896, 346.
110 Thomas Kelly, Law Practitioners and New Zealand Law Society Bill, NZPD, 95, 1896, 349.
111 William Walker, NZPD, 95, 1896, 350.
112 NZPD, 96, 1896, 234.
113 'Female law practitioners,' *Press*, 5 September 1896.
114 WDLS, *Annual Report For the Year Ending 20th March 1897*, 4.
115 ODLS council minutes, 9 October 1896.
116 'In Parliament,' *White Ribbon*, 2(15), September 1896, 8.

Chapter Three

1 See Dr Newman, Removal of Women's Disabilities Bill 1896, NZPD, 92, 1896, 339; Downie Stewart, Law Practitioners and New Zealand Law Society Bill 1896, NZPD, 94, 1896, 372; George Jones, Law Practitioners and New Zealand Law Society Bill 1896, NZPD, 94, 1896, 525.
2 William Walker, Female Law Practitioners Bill 1896, NZPD, 94, 1896, 367.
3 Sachs and Hoff Wilson, 172.
4 Stone, *Making of Russell McVeagh*, 72; Wiren. The employment of women as law copyists in England had already drawn objections from the editors of the *Solicitors' Journal*. They could not see 'why these poor people should be thrown out of work to provide for female copyists': *Solicitors' Journal*, 9 October 1880, 884.
5 Stone, 'Anatomy of the practice of law,' 421.
6 Commission of Inquiry into Equal Pay, 14.
7 See the appendix, table A2, 451.
8 See the appendix, table A3, 451.
9 Kirk, 122.
10 Millen, 102; Wiren. The exact date Barnicoat commenced work is not known although it was from about the mid-1890s that half the firm's letters were typed.
11 Millen, 141.
12 Stone, *Making of Russell McVeagh*, 95.

13 C J Parr was later a Member of Parliament and the New Zealand High Commissioner in London.

14 Geraldine Hemus, letter to Mrs Roberts, 22 December 1956, Auckland Institute and Museum Library.

15 Albert Devore was prominent in Auckland local body politics, being Mayor of Auckland 1886–1889. James Martin had been a magistrate in Wellington and was appointed the President of the Court of Arbitration in 1900. See Carol Brown, 20–21, 24; Cooke, *Portrait of a Profession*, 270.

16 See the appendix, table A4, 452.

17 See the appendix, table A3, 451.

18 See the appendix, table A1, 449–450.

19 See also the appendix, table A5, 453.

20 Rosemary Rees, letter to Mrs Roberts, 7 June (year illegible), Women's Archives, Auckland Institute and Museum Library. Obituaries refer to Annie Lee Rees as a barrister but the GDLS has no record of her ever holding a practising certificate.

21 It is conceivable that Annie Lee Rees qualified specifically for the purpose of assisting her then aging father. Father and daughter had worked closely together on a number of literary and political projects. (In 1888, Annie had assisted her father in the publication of an economic essay, *From Poverty to Plenty. The Life and Times of Sir George Grey*, 1892, was co-authored by Annie Lee Rees and William Lee Rees.) In this period, some American women were said to have taken up legal studies for the purpose of working in their fathers' legal offices: Berger Morello, 54.

22 Harriet Vine's obituary in the *New Zealand Herald* claims that she worked at Treadwell and Gordon for more than 60 years but this seems unlikely. She studied law at Victoria University College until at least 1912 (probably being the only women in her graduation class) and was admitted to the Bar in Wellington in 1915. She died in 1962 in her late 80s: 'Woman lawyer killed in road accident,' *New Zealand Herald*, 4 September 1962; Beagley, 41; Gordon Swan, interview.

23 The ODLS, for example, immediately advanced £100 to the Empire Defence Fund, a sum it could ill-afford, and recommended that the NZLS create a fund based on subscriptions from the Bench and the Bar: Cullen, 83.

24 Stone, *Making of Russell McVeagh*, 95. The ODLS instituted a scheme where men of non-military age looked after the practices of lawyers on active service—a scheme which served in several instances to pressure eligible lawyers to join up: Cullen, 83.

25 See the appendix, table A4, 452.

26 The 1,104 women employed in law offices in 1916 were 616 typists (appendix, table A2, 451), 485 clerks (appendix, table A4, 452) and 3 lawyers (appendix, table A6, 454).

27 In 1913, there were 238 men students enrolled in law, in 1917 this had dropped to 153: appendix, table A1, 449–450.

28 See the appendix, table A1, 449–450.

29 Pallot family papers, August 1993.

30 Anderson, 43–46; Preston, 10.

31 *New Zealand Herald*, 25 June 1919, 8.

32 *White Ribbon*, 19 April 1919, 1. However, this advance was hampered by women 'doing the same work, for less wages than men'.

33 See the appendix, table A6, 454.

34 See the appendix, table A1, 449–450 and table A3, 451. The number of women medical students also declined: Anderson, 46.

35 There were 195 men law students in 1918 and 402 in 1919: appendix, table A6, 454.

36 Sinclair, *University of Auckland*, 124; Stone, *Making of Russell McVeagh*, 103.

37 Stone, *Making of Russell McVeagh*, 157; Gardner, *History of the University of Canterbury*, 274.

38 Cullen, 84.

39 Sinclair, *University of Auckland*, 124; Gardner, *History of the University of Canterbury*, 274.

40 Cullen, 88.

41 Gore, 112.

42 See the appendix, table A1, 449–450.

43   *New Zealand Tablet*, 25 February 1925. Even so, Mary Hussey did not enrol in law until the end of World War II: *Otago Daily Times*, 25 January 1993.

44   Koopman-Boyden, 118–119.

45   Hill, 91.

46   Sir W Fraser, Justices of the Peace Amendment Bill, NZPD, 196, 1922, 1122.

47   'Rachael Ngeungeu Beamish Zister,' biography held by the Dictionary of NZ Biography, record 5623.

48   Ellen Melville, letter to Lady Aberdeen, 17 February 1925, Alexander Turnbull Library, MS papers 3969. In 1918, Lyra Veronica Taylor was the first woman admitted to the Bar in Wellington, although she was not the first woman to practise in Wellington. Ethel Benjamin practised in Wellington about 1907–1910. Lyra Taylor ceased practising in 1926 on emigration to the US: WDLS practising certificate records.

49   Gordon Swan, interview. In fact, Harriet Vine was engaged to be married but her fiance was killed in the Boer War: 'Harriet Vine,' biography held by the Dictionary of New Zealand Biography, record 5228.

50   'Report of the Royal Commission on University Education,' 55.

51   Ibid, 102.

52   Beagley, 49–51.

53   Ibid, 45–46.

54   Cullen, 88.

55   Gore, 112.

56   Ibid.

57   Beagley, 42.

58   See the appendix, table A1, 449–450.

59   Elisabeth Urquhart, interview; ADLS practising certificate records.

60   *New Zealand Herald*, 4 July 1985, section 2, 2.

61   'Nothing else I wanted to do,' *Christchurch Star*, 2 July 1977, 5; Dorothy Raymond, interview.

62   Elisabeth Urquhart, interview.

63   May, *Minding Children*, 26.

64   Ellen Melville was a member of the Auckland City Council 1913–1946: Kuitert, 39, 63–69, 72.

65   Dooley, 3, in Beagley, 51.

66   Hyman, 'Equal pay for women,' 65; Commission of Inquiry into Equal Pay, 14.

67   May, *Minding Children*, 26.

68   Beagley, 49–51; 'New Zealand free lance,' *National Pictorial Weekly*, 26 May 1937, 8, in Beagley, 51.

69   In 1939, 44 Auckland practitioners and a smaller number of clerks enlisted. By 1942, 174 solicitors and clerks were on active service: Stone, *Making of Russell McVeagh*, 133.

70   Cullen, 109.

71   Millen, 172; Cullen, 108.

72   Stone, *Making of Russell McVeagh*, 133.

73   Cullen, 108.

74   At the outbreak of war, there were 78 men clerks and 46 women clerks. By September 1942, the number of men clerks had fallen to 23 while the number of women clerks had increased to 57: Cullen, table 4.2, 108.

75   May, *Minding Children*, 41.

76   Millen, 164.

77   Stone, *Making of Russell McVeagh*, 133.

78   Millen, 171.

79   Betty Thorpe, interview.

80   'Mrs Feist active in Hutt circles,' *Evening Post*, 4 October 1980.

81   Beagley, 45–46. See also Cullen, 206.

82   *CWLA Newsletter*, June 1993, 1.

83   Betty Thorpe, interview.

84   Elisabeth Urquhart, interview; 'Elisabeth Marjorie Urquhart,' *Rotorua Post*, 1993, in Elisabeth Urquhart's papers.

85   Taylor, 1075.

86   See the appendix, table A1, 449–450 and table A6, 454.

87   Occupational Re-establishment Emergency Regulations 1939 and Occupational Re-establishment Emer-gency Regulations 1940, in Taylor, 1275.

88   Millen, 165.

89   Taylor, 1076.

90   See the appendix, table A4, 452.

91   Cooke, *Portrait of a Profession*, 131 and 229.

92   Taylor, 1177–1178.

93   Ibid. Shirley Parr, Wellington's seventh woman lawyer, who studied at Victoria University College around this time,

recalls that the concession passes allowed 'rehabs' to obtain 40% to pass examinations: Shirley Parr, interview.

94   Stone, *Making of Russell McVeagh*, 133.

95   Taylor, 1282.

96   Fay Wellwood, interview.

97   'Mary Hussey,' 8; Beagley, 59–60; Murray Cochrane, letter, 26 August 1993.

98   Commission of Inquiry into Equal Pay, 15.

99   Stone, *Making of Russell McVeagh*, 157–158. Unfortunately the ADLS is unable to locate any references to the secondary schools targeted during this campaign.

100   Alison Quentin-Baxter, interview. In 1961, she was 'obliged' to resign from the Department of External Affairs because the department would not grant leave to women married to fellow foreign service officials so that they could accompany their partners on overseas postings: 'New stage in distinguished legal career,' 3.

101   Beagley, 55.

102   Fay Wellwood, interview. Fay Matson was the first woman to be capped LLB from Canterbury University College for nearly 12 years following the war.

103   Betty Thorpe, interview and correspondence, 7 September 1993.

104   See the appendix, table A1, 449–450.

105   See the appendix, table A4, 452.

106   *New Zealand Women's Weekly*, 7 June 1956, in May, 'Motherhood in the 1950s,' 65–66.

107   May, 'Motherhood in the 1950s,' 67.

108   'Paddy Steele: "a wonderful time in law",' *Council Brief*, September 1991.

109   Shirley Parr, interview.

110   Fay Wellwood, letter, 15 October 1993. Fay Wellwood recalled that Joan Thacker worked at Cuningham Taylor but the firm has no record of her employment. The first female law clerk in the firm was Judith Arnott in 1959, she was followed by Carolyn Withers in 1964: Neil Thomson, letter, 2 December 1994.

111   Koopman-Boyden and Scott, 125–126.

112   Beagley, 51–53.

113   Ibid, 54–55.

114   Other women would not return to legal work until the 1970s; Betty Thorpe, for example, returned to law part time in 1976 when her children had grown up.

115   Patricia Lee was admitted as a barrister at the same time.

116   Elisabeth Urquhart, interview; 'Elisabeth Marjorie Urquhart,' *Rotorua Post*, 1993, in Elisabeth Urquhart's papers.

117   Northey, 13; Stone, *Making of Russell McVeagh*, 158.

118   Sinclair, *History of the University of Auckland*, 258.

119   Bell Gully Buddle Weir, for example, did not employ its first woman law clerk, Geraldine Conway, until 1968. Her arrival coincided with the departure of Sir Denis Blundell who had always called each law clerk 'boy': Millen, 186.

120   Stone, *Making of Russell McVeagh*, 158.

121   *A Profile: Legal Executives and Their Institute*, brochure of the NZ Institute of Legal Executives. A few very senior legal executives have been made partners in NZ law firms but partnerships are predominantly reserved for lawyers.

122   Stone, *Making of Russell McVeagh*, 159.

123   ADLS, *Report of the Working Party*, para 2.4.

124   WDLS, *Full Report*, para 3.1. Women were also more likely to hold second degrees: para 3.2.

125   See the appendix, table A1, 449–450. In 1977, women made up 19% of the graduating class but were 33% of those graduating with LLB(Hons). With the exception of 1981, when the same proportion of women obtained honours as graduated, this pattern continued until 1983.

126   See the appendix, table A1, 449–450.

127   Murray, 'New Zealand lawyers,' 336.

128   See the appendix, table A6, 454.

129   See the appendix, table A7, 455.

Chapter Four

1   Gatfield, *Early Women Lawyers*, table 3.1.

2   Early women lawyers with male relatives in the profession included: Ellen Melville, Annie Lee Rees, Rebecca Pallot, Esther Ongley, Margaret Mackay, Julia Dunn, Isobel Wright, Dorothy Raymond, Elisabeth Urquhart, Patricia Webb, Sheila Macdonald, Betty Thorpe, Paddy Steele, Eileen O'Connor and Shirley Smith.

3   Cullen, 143, table 5.11. Between 1897 and 1961, only 4 women had been admitted to the Bar and practised in the Otago region: ODLS practising certificate records.

4   Aspiring lawyers faced law lecture fees (up to £16 in the 1890s), legal examination and admission fees (set at £23.2s for solicitors with a further 5 guineas for barristers under the Law Practitioners Act 1882 and remaining unaltered for 70 years despite several recessions) and annual practising certificate fees ranging between £3 and £9 depending on the district and year.

5   Dorothy Raymond, interview.

6   Although the rudiments of law schools did exist at the Canterbury and Otago university colleges from 1879, they were periodically closed due to lack of numbers or lack of finance. Otago law school, for example, was closed 1902–1904 and again during World War I. In 1925, the Royal Commission on University Education remarked that there was no law school in NZ at all.

7   'Report of the Royal Commission into the University of New Zealand,' 95; 'Report of the Royal Commission on University Educaation', 47.

8   Gatfield, *Early Women Lawyers*, table 3.1.

9   *Gisborne Herald*, 20 August 1949, in *New Zealand Obituaries*, 35, 141–142.

10   'Lady barrister admitted,' *New Zealand Graphic and Weekly News*, 28 September 1910.

11   McIntyre, 302.

12   'Women as barristers,' *New Zealand Herald*, 22 August 1891.

13   *Gisborne Herald*, 20 August 1949, in *New Zealand Obituaries*, 35, 141–142.

14   Hughes, 'Women and the professions,' 123–127.

15   *New Zealand Biographies 1976*, vol 1, 1.

16   Beagley, 45.

17   Dorothy Raymond, interview.

18   Confidential interview.

19   Pallot family papers.

20   Stone, *Making of Russell McVeagh*, 41.

21   J B R Russell, a founder of the national firm Russell McVeagh, was anxious to secure a place in the firm for his only son, while his daughter, 'the intelligent Martha Agnes' nursed the 'impossible hope' of studying law: Stone, *Making of Russell McVeagh*, 42.

22   For example, see Cullen, appendix 2.

23   Millen, 186.

24   Edwards, 11.

25   'Miss Stella Henderson,' *White Ribbon*, 3(36), 1898, 1–2.

26   Ibid.

27   'Stella M Allan recalls many happy days with: my finest teachers,' 26 August 1958, biographies off-print, Alexander Turnbull Library. Stella Henderson sacrificed her career in law to accompany her husband to Australia in 1903 so that he could take up a position as editor of the *Argus*. As Stella Henderson would have been aware, women were unable to practise law in Australia at that time. However, she did have a long and successful career in journalism: papers in private collection of Mrs Moira Henderson.

28   C J Parr was later a member of Parliament and the New Zealand High Commissioner in London. Geraldine Hemus, letter to Mrs Roberts, 22 December 1956, Auckland Institute and Museum Library.

29   Albert Devore was prominent in Auckland local body politics, being mayor 1886–1889. James Martin had been a magistrate in Wellington and was appointed President of the Court of Arbitration in 1900. See Kuitert, 20–21, 24; Cooke, *Portrait of a Profession*, 270.

30   Cooke, *Portrait of a Profession*, 337, 339. J M Gallaway, like Saul Solomon, founded one of Dunedin's long-standing legal firms: Cullen, 193. In 1898, he was elected president of the ODLS: Cullen, 185. Saul Solomon started practising in Dunedin in 1884. That practice can be traced to the firm of Quelch, McKewen, Fogarty and Tohill (now known as Solomons): Cullen, 198. See also Carol Brown, 33, footnote 15.

31   Cooke, *Portrait of a Profession*, 57.

32   'Lady barrister admitted,' *New Zealand Graphic and Weekly News*, 28 September 1910.

33   'Mrs Feist active in Hutt circles,' *Evening Post*, 4 October 1980. After Haldane's death in 1943, Marjorie Feist practised on her own account under her maiden name, M A Taylor.

34   Beagley, 49–50.

35   Ibid, 51.

36   Ibid, 54–55.

37   Raewyn Dalziel, 'Colonial helpmeet,' 63.

38   *Chorlton v Lings* (1868) LR 4 CP 374, 391 per Justice Willes.

39   Removal of Women's Disabilities Bill, NZPD, 92, 1896, 341.

40   Blackstone, 445.

41   Sachs and Hoff Wilson, 77.

42   *Matter of Goodell* [1875] 20 Am Rep 42, 47, 48.

43   Phillips, 232; Fry, 'Curriculum and girls' secondary schooling,' 33–36; Dale, 188.

44   Geraldine Hemus, letter to Mrs Roberts, 22 December 1956.

45   Dorothy Raymond, interview.

46   Edwards, 11.

47   Cullen, 52.

48   Edwards, 11.

49   Dorothy Raymond, interview; Edwards, 11.

50   Dorothy Raymond, interview.

51   *First Lady in Law*, TVNZ documentary, Marion Thomson interview, 19 January 1988.

52   Edwards, 11.

53   Ibid, 12.

54   Hon T B Mooney, in Beagley, 54.

55   Alison Quentin-Baxter, interview.

56   'Paddy Steele: "A wonderful time in law",' *Council Brief*, September 1991.

57   Confidential interview.

58   Shirley Parr, interview.

59   *Matter of Goodell* [1875] 20 Am Rep 42, 47.

60   Removal of Women's Disabilities Bill, NZPD, 92, 1896, 341.

61   Dorothy Raymond, interview.

62   *First Lady in Law*, TVNZ documentary, Marion Thomson interview, 19 January 1988.

63   Beagley, 50.

64   Fay Wellwood, interview.

65   There is evidence that women medical students were told to leave lectures. In a class on public health and medical jurisprudence, the lecturer announced that the women present had to withdraw before he would proceed. The women medical students 'complied, blushing and confused, to the sound of jeers and stampings from the men': Hughes, 'Women and the professions,' 130.

66   'Shirley Parr recalls her early days,' *Council Brief*, September 1991.

67   Smith, 1.

68   *First Lady in Law*, TVNZ documentary, Silvia Cartwright interview, 19 January 1988.

69   Edwards, 12.

70   Shirley Smith is the only one to mention an intention to object to her exclusion in the 1950s. Others, like Marion Thomson, did not regard their exclusion as discrimination: Beagley, 50. Judge Rushton ranked her exclusion as insignificant in the context of her wider experience.

71   Edwards, 11.

72   Judith Potter, interview; 'Helen Melrose,' 77.

73   McMullin, 10–11.

74   'Miss Stella Henderson,' *White Ribbon*, 3(36), 1898, 2.

75   Carol Brown, 35, 78–89.

76   Banwell, 175.

77   Ibid, 176; Millen, 167.

78   Stone, 'Anatomy of the practice of law,' 420.

79   This was the experience of Geraldine Conway when she joined Bell Gully in 1968. Her problem was resolved when the firm moved the law clerks into a new building: Millen, 187. See also Shirley Parr, interview.

80   One respondent was told she was turned down for a job because the firm did not know who she would have morning tea with: 'I couldn't have it with the secretaries and I couldn't have it with them!': Murray, 'Sharing in the "shingles"?' 188.

81   Benjamin to Stilling, letter, 1 May 1899, ODLS correspondence.

82   Benjamin to Stilling,' letter, 2 March 1898, ODLS correspondence.

83   Benjamin to Stilling, letter, 1 May 1899, ODLS correspondence.

84   Betty Thorpe, interview.

85   Shirley Parr, interview.

86   Shirley Smith gives a full and fascinating account of the tactics used by the WDLS and the Wellington Law Faculty Club to keep women out of social functions: Smith, 6.

87   Edwards, 11.

88   *First Lady in Law,* TVNZ documentary, Judith Mayhew interview, 19 January 1988.

89   Shirley Parr, interview.

90   Smith, 2, 6.

91   Ibid, 1–2 and Shirley Parr, interview.

92   In 1961, when the WDLS planned a dinner at the Wellington Club, Shirley Smith learned through the grapevine that 'any applications from women were to be set aside until the complement was full, and then they were to be told, "Sorry, there was no room for you." ': Smith, 6.

93   *Dominion,* 25 March 1993, 11. Katherine Dolby, while executive director of the ODLS, also observed that some male lawyers were 'horrified' when women were invited to the society's informal cocktail parties.

94   Smith, 2. She did in fact persevere and attended further dinners.

95   Shirley Parr, interview.

96   Such 'jokes' are still in circulation within the profession: Foster, 22, 116, 132.

97   'Conference dinner,' 156.

98   Ibid, 156–157.

99   Lundy, 4.

100   Justice Bucknell, in Fenn, 100.

101   Ibid, 102.

102   *Solicitors' Journal,* 40, 10 October 1896, 795.

103   Sir William Fox, Law Practitioners Bill 1881, NZPD, 38, 1881, 437–438.

104   Civis, 'Passing notes,' *Otago Daily Times,* 24 April 1897, 2.

105   *Otago University Students' Review,* 11(3), August 1897, 83, in Carol Brown, 25.

106   *Solicitors' Journal,* 21 November 1896, 58.

107   Backhouse, 29–30.

108   Cooke, *Portrait of a Profession,* 337.

109   'Women barristers' dress' (1961) 37 NZLJ 77.

110   Cullen, 67.

111   McIntyre, 302.

112   Victoria Thorpe, letter, 20 May 1993.

113   'Shirley Parr recalls her early days,' *Council Brief,* September 1991.

114   Prue Kapua, interview.

115   Confidential interview.

116   *First Lady in Law,* TVNZ documentary, Silvia Cartwright interview, 19 January 1988.

Chapter Five

1   William Walker, Female Law Practitioners Bill 1896, NZPD, 94, 1896, 273.

2   Thomas Kelly, Female Law Practitioners Bill 1896, NZPD, 95, 1896, 180. See Gardner, *Colonial Cap and Gown,* 83; Grimshaw, 18.

3   'Political notes,' *Otago Daily Times,* 22 August 1986.

4   Mr C H Benjamin, letter to Alexander Turnbull Library, 17 April 1967, T/L 3/1/2.

5 *Otago Daily Times*, 24 April 1897, 2; *Otago Daily Times*, 18 September 1897, 4; *Freelance*, 14 July 1900, 3a.

6 *Freelance*, 14 July 1900, 3a; *Freelance*, 7 December 1901, 4c; *Freelance*, 6 September 1902.

7 Ethel Benjamin, 'Women and the study and practice of the law,' *Press*, 13 September 1897, 5.

8 Greig, 149.

9 Ethel Benjamin, 'Women and the study and practice of the law,' *Press*, 13 September 1897, 5.

10 Greig, 145.

11 Ethel Benjamin, 'Women and the study and practice of the law,' *Press*, 13 September 1897, 5.

12 Ibid.

13 See Ritchie, 50.

14 *Canadian Legal Scrap Book*, 16 April 1892, 205, in Backhouse, 9. See also the view expressed by the Chief Justice of Georgia: *Albany Law Journal*, 48, 1893, 103, 104; Darwin, 858.

15 Fenn, 136.

16 Alpers, 217.

17 Removal of Women's Disabilities Bill, NZPD, 92, 1896, 366–367.

18 Darwin, 860–861.

19 For example, see Russell, NZPD, 92, 1896, 341.

20 Sutch, 76.

21 Fry, *Different for Daughters*, 29–30; 'Report of the Royal Commission into the University of New Zealand,' 13.

22 Fry, *Different for Daughters*, 39; and 'Report of the Royal Commission into the University of New Zealand,' 103.

23 Fry, *Different for Daughters*, 29; Gardner, *Colonial Cap and Gown*, 97; Fry, 'Curriculum and girls' secondary schooling,' 33.

24 Fry, *Different for Daughters*, 39.

25 Herbert Spencer, *Principles of Biology*, vol 2, London, 1867, 512–513, in Backhouse, 3–4.

26 Fry, 'Curriculum and girls' secondary schooling,' 33–34; Ritchie, 53.

27 Edward Clarke, *Sex in Education*, Boston, 1873, 40, in Ritchie, 53.

28 Female Law Practitioners Bill, NZPD, 94, 1896, 366.

29 NZPD, 94, 1896, 567.

30 Phillips, 227.

31 'The vitality of the race,' *Otago Witness*, addresses by Drs Batchelor and King, 26 May 1909, 70.

32 Ibid.

33 Penelope, 'New Zealand's first lady lawyer,' *White Ribbon*, 3(26), August 1897, 1; 'Miss Stella Henderson,' *White Ribbon*, June 1898, 2.

34 *Evening Star*, 28 May 1909.

35 Sutch, 80–81, 84.

36 [1914] AJHR E7, table MB, 5. A total of 16 women were attending medical lectures, but 7 were studying massage. See also the appendix, table A1, 449–450.

37 In her first year, Ethel Benjamin took first place in the first class division in jurisprudence and in constitutional history and law. In her second year she came first in the colony in Roman law, and in her third and final year, took first place in equity and evidence and first equal in criminal law and in real and personal property. See Penelope, 'New Zealand's first lady lawyer,' *White Ribbon*, 3(26), August 1897, 1.

38 'Law notes,' *Otago University Review*, 8(1), May 1895, 20.

39 'Our lady students,' *Otago University Review*, 10(5), October 1896, 145, 146.

40 Ibid, 147.

41 'Miss Stella Henderson,' *White Ribbon*, 3(36), 1898, 1.

42 Papers in the private collection of Mrs Moira Henderson: H H Loughnan testimonial, 12 January 1900; J McMillan Brown testimonial, 3 January 1900.

43 *Gisborne Herald*, 20 August 1949, in *New Zealand Obituaries*, 35, 141–142.

44 Gatfield, *Early Women Lawyers*, tables 2.1 and 2.2.

45 Regional Women's Decade Committee, 100.

46 'Woman barrister,' *New Zealand Herald*, 22 June 1943, 5.

47 Betty Thorpe, interview.

48 Darwin, 856–858.

49   *Bradwell v The State* [1872] 16 Wall 130, 142 per Justice Bradley.

50   Darwin, 857.

51   Herbert Spencer, *Principles of Biology*, London, 1867 and *Principles of Sociology*, London, 1876, in Bunkle and Hughs, 175. See also Backhouse, 3–4; Jack and Jack, 5 and 130–131.

52   Mill, *Subjection of Women*, 112.

53   Ibid, 113.

54   Removal of Women's Disabilities Bill, NZPD, 92, 1896, 339.

55   George Russell, NZPD, 92, 1896, 341.

56   NZPD, 39, 1881, 428.

57   Ibid.

58   Hall-Jones, Removal of Women's Disabilities Bill, NZPD, 92, 1896, 340.

59   Ibid, 341.

60   Ethel Benjamin, 'Women and the study and practice of the law,' *Press*, 13 September 1897, 5.

61   Briant, 5; Anderson, 7 and 67.

62   Newman, 101.

63   Ethel Benjamin, 'Women and the study and practice of the law,' *Press*, 13 September 1897, 5.

64   Greig, 150–154.

65   Carol Brown, 35.

66   Kuitert, 30, 119, 124.

67   Confidential interview.

68   *Canada Law Journal*, 16, 1880, 161, in Backhouse, 14.

69   *Canadian Law Times*, 12, 1892, in Backhouse, 21.

70   P M MacCallum, correspondence, 15 September 1993.

71   Royden Somerville in 'Mary Hussey,' 8.

72   Murray Cochrane, letter, 26 August 1993.

73   Papers in private collection of Mrs Moira Henderson: William Izard, letter to Victoria College, 4 January 1900; H H Loughnan testimonial, 12 January 1900; S Saunders, testimonial, 10 January 1900; J McMillan Brown, testimonial, 3 January 1900. There is no record of Stella Henderson being conferred her LLB but her references and other papers confirm she had completed the degree requirements.

74   Ibid.

75   Smith, 3.

76   Regional Women's Decade Committee, 100; Edwards, 11; Liz Velde, Staffing Office, University of Canterbury, letter, 8 December 1994.

77   Lawyer and Auckland City councillor, Ellen Melville, was an exception. In 1913, she was reported as being 'not afraid to raise her voice when seated at the Council table. Moreover, she seems quite capable of holding her own in discussion': *New Zealand Freelance*, 13 September 1913, 4a.

78   Williams, 191.

79   Civis, 'Passing notes,' *Otago Daily Times*, 24 April 1897, 2.

80   Penelope, 'New Zealand's first lady lawyer,' *White Ribbon*, 3(26), August 1897, 1.

81   Ethel de Costa, letter to J Harrison, secretary of the WDLS, 19 September 1907.

82   Edwards, 11.

83   Sir Francis H D Bell, letter to Francis Rolleston, Attorney-General, 28 May 1926, Sir Francis H D Bell papers, Alexander Turnbull Library (researched by Daniel R Ernst, Fulbright Fellow, Alexander Turnbull Library, June 1996).

84   Sir Francis H D Bell, letter to Arthur Fair, Solicitor-General, 28 May 1926, Sir Francis H D Bell papers, Alexander Turnbull Library (researched by Daniel R Ernst, Fulbright Fellow, Alexander Turnbull Library, June 1996).

85   'Devilling' involved research and opinion writing and was usually undertaken for barristers on a freelance basis by law students, law graduates or newly admitted lawyers.

86   Olive Smuts-Kennedy, letter, 18 October, 1993. Smuts-Kennedy notes that the then secretary of the ADLS, Mr Good, was also very supportive of her during her early years in practice.

87   Fay Wellwood, letter, 15 October 1993.

88   Smith, 3–4 and 5–6. Shirley Smith recalled that the magistrates were tactfully helpful and no practitioner took advantage of her inexperience.

89   Judith Potter, interview.

90 Betty Thorpe, interview.
91 Findlay, 178. Cecile Rushton, of course, overcame her nervousness, specialising in litigation and by 1982 became a barrister sole doing mostly criminal law work in the High Court. She was appointed a District Court judge in 1987.
92 November, 89.
93 'Auckland's first woman barrister' (1933) 5 NZLJ 92. The ADLS records of persons admitted as barristers and solicitors do not record Hollway on the barristers' roll. Olive Virginia Nelson signed the roll as the first woman barrister 3 years later on 18 June 1936.
94 ADLS records.
95 'Christchurch's first lady barrister' (1938) 14 NZLJ 179.
96 Smith, 3.
97 Booth, 70. At the time, Patricia Costigan ignored the advice, but ironically several years later she specialised in family law work.
98 'Capital's first lady prosecutor,' *Evening Post*, 8 June 1982.
99 Justices of the Peace Amendment Bill 1922, NZPD, 196, 1922, 1111, 1121.
100 'NZ Listener 50 years ago,' *Listener*, article 17 from April 1942, 20 April 1992.
101 The Society for the Protection of Women and Children was formed to tackle what is now known as domestic violence and sexual abuse. The society: initiated proceedings in cases of cruelty, seduction, outrage or excessive violence to women and children; gave advice and aid to women who had been cruelly treated; provided neglected children with homes; and agitated for improvements in the law in respect to the protection of women and children. Although largely conservative in its membership, the society at times was linked with the women's movement—a connection that was not particularly favourable: MacCuish, 9–10, 18 and 35.
102 Penelope, 'New Zealand's first lady lawyer,' *White Ribbon*, 3(26), August 1897, 1–2; *Otago Daily Times*, 3 February 1899, 4; Carol Brown, chs 3

and 4. At the same time women doctors were also offering their services free of charge. Dr Emily Siedeberg, for example, volunteered to be the first honorary medical officer of the Society for the Protection of Women and Children: Carol Brown, 40.
103 'Miss Stella Henderson,' *White Ribbon*, June 1898, 1, 2.
104 *Freelance*, 30 March 1901, 4a.
105 *Freelance*, 7 December 1901, 4c; Wilson and Labrum, 286–287; papers in private collection of Mrs Moira Henderson.
106 *Press*, 6 March 1963.
107 *New Zealand Herald*, 26 June 1919, 8; *New Zealand Herald*, 13 October 1919, 9.
108 *Parliamentary Star* article, undated, in Ellen Melville's papers, Auckland Institute and Museum Library.
109 Kuitert, 118 and 119.
110 Geraldine Hemus, letter to Mrs Roberts, 22 December 1956, Women's Archives, Auckland Institute and Museum Library.
111 Kuitert, 30, 64, 118–119, 131. See also Else.
112 Sandra Coney, 'Ellen Melville,' 442.
113 Rosemary Rees, letter to Mrs Roberts, 7 June (no year), Annie Lee Rees' papers, Auckland Institute and Museum Library.
114 *Gisborne Herald*, 20 August 1949.
115 'Woman lawyer killed in road accident,' *New Zealand Herald*, 4 September 1962; Beagley, 41.
116 Ellen Melville, letter to Lady Aberdeen, president of the International Council of Women, 17 February 1925, Alexander Turnbull Library, MS Papers 3969.
117 John Pallot, biography of Rebecca Pallot, August 1993, held in Pallot family papers.
118 *Hutt News*, 28 September 1976; *New Zealand Biographies*, 2, 1976, 182; 'Mrs Feist active in Hutt circles,' *Evening Post*, 4 October 1980. Marjorie Taylor was also actively involved in the National Party, was honorary solicitor to the Hutt Valley Table Tennis Association and the Women's Bowling Club, and a representative on the

Board of Governors of Hutt Valley High School.

119 Dorothy Raymond, interview; 'Second language needed when visiting continent,' *New Zealand Herald*, 6 February 1968; 'Retiring woman barrister recommends law career,' 1968, unsourced, in Dorothy Raymond's papers; 'A background of varied interests,' *Auckland Star*, 9 June 1971; 'Dorothy Raymond legal pioneer,' *Timaru Herald*, 12 March 1977; 'Nothing else I wanted to do,' *Christchurch Star*, 2 July 1977; *CWLA Newsletter*, 1993.

120 Elisabeth Urquhart, interview; 'Elisabeth Marjorie Urquhart,' *Rotorua Post*, 1993, in Elisabeth Urquhart's papers.

121 Alexander Turnbull Library Biographies.

122 Patricia Webb, interview; 'Could well be a modern Portia,' *Weekly News*, 24 January 1962, 72.

123 Sheila Campbell Williams' papers, Auckland Institute and Museum Library.

124 Olive Smuts-Kennedy, interview.

Chapter Six

1 Charlotte Macdonald, *Vote, the Pill, and the Demon Drink*, 161–162.

2 Commission of Inquiry into Equal Pay, 15 and 17.

3 Wilson, 'Areas of discrimination,' 177.

4 Henwood, 1–2.

5 Henwood, 1; 'Mary Hussey: dedicated to the service of others,' *LawTalk*, no 389, April 1993, 8.

6 'Women lawyers unite,' 612.

7 Turner and Vaver; Tapp and Wilson. (Pauline Vaver reverted to her earlier name, Tapp.)

8 Pope, 620.

9 Margaret Wilson and Pauline Tapp started teaching the optional women and the law course at the University of Auckland law school in 1976.

10 'Interfectus observes conference,' *Northern News Review*, May 1975.

11 E W Thomas, memorandum to the ADLS council, no 13, 9 June 1975.

12 Ibid, 2–3.

13 Lundy, 5.

14 Ibid.

15 *Dominion*, 25 March 1993, 11.

16 Henwood, 1.

17 Ibid.

18 *Women's Rights Committee*, 1975, 40.

19 See the 1971 survey of employers' attitudes conducted by the Society for Research on Women and the National Advisory Council on the Employment of Women, in *Women's Rights Committee*, 14–15.

20 Ibid, 15.

21 Secretary for Justice, letter to Chief Parliamentary Counsel, 23 September 1976. Other prohibited grounds of discrimination included race, colour, ethnic or national origins, marital status, and religious or ethical belief.

22 NZLS, *Submission on the Human Rights Commission Bill*, 1. The NZLS was unable to locate any files on the bill. As a result, copies of NZLS papers relating to the bill were provided by the Department of Justice.

23 Human Rights Commission Bill 1977, clause 16.

24 NZLS, *Submission on the Human Rights Commission Bill*, 3.

25 Ibid.

26 NZ Society of Accountants, *Submission on the Human Rights Commission Bill*, 24 March 1977.

27 Department of Justice, *Human Rights Commission Bill*.

28 Wilson, *Submission on the Human Rights Bill*.

29 Department of Justice, *Human Rights Commission Bill*, 16.

30 Government Research Unit, *Submission on the Human Rights Commission Bill*, 10.

31 Human Rights Commission Act 1977, section 15.

32 Deirdre Milne, vice-president of the Women and the Law Research Foundation, letter to members, 9 November 1978.

33   Women and the Law Research Foundation pamphlet; Margaret Robins, 'The origins of the association: an interview with Margaret Wilson,' *AWLA Newsletter*, June 1985, 3.

34   'Justice Minister explains Human Rights Commission,' *Northern News Review*, October 1977, 11.

35   *LawTalk*, no 61, 11 August 1977.

36   'Briefly,' *LawTalk*, no 74, 27 April 1978.

37   'Lecture on a Sunday,' *Northern News*, 40, 1978, 1.

38   See discussion of the 1978 Heylen Poll in ADLS, *Report of the Working Group*, para 4.5.1. A copy of the original survey report could not be located by the NZLS or the Heylen Research Centre.

39   Ibid.

40   Megan Richardson, 10.

41   Committee on Women, covering letter sent to law firms (undated).

42   Committee on Women, 3.

43   Ibid, 6.

44   Ibid.

45   *LawTalk*, no 110, 14 July 1980. The NZLS files and minutes of council and Executive Committee meetings contain no references to the Committee on Women's findings.

46   'Women lawyers encouraged says council,' *Council Brief*, no 62, May 1980, 7.

47   Justice Thomas, speech to ADLS launch of the EEO Implementation Project, 27 July 1995.

48   The 1981 working party members were Rod Hansen (convenor), Denese Bates, Sian Elias, Norman Elliott, Rodney Harrison, Deirdre Milne, John Phillips, John Sheppard, Briar Wilson and Pam Mitchell (who was replaced by Hannah Sargisson in August 1981).

49   ADLS, *Report of the Working Party*, paras 4.4.2 and 4.4.3.

50   Ibid, para 4.5.8.

51   Ibid, paras 4.4.2 and 4.5.2.

52   Ibid, para 4.4.3.

53   Ibid, paras 5.1 and 5.2.

54   Ibid, paras 5.3–5.6.

55   Ibid, paras 2.4 and 4.2.

56   Ibid, para 5.3.1.

57   Ibid, paras 5.3.3 and 5.3.4.

58   Ibid, paras 6.1–6.4 and 7.1–7.4.

59   'There's sex discrimination within the legal profession,' 5.

60   'No resentment,' *Northern News Review*, 7(1), February 1982, 11.

61   Members of the committee (Sian Elias, Rob Hansen, Helen Melrose, Hannah Sargisson, John Sheppard and Ted Thomas) languished under a workload that was 'unduly burdensome' so its early demise was not unexpected: Cockayne, para 8.6, 103.

62   Ibid, 95.

63   Ibid, Part 8.

64   Sargisson.

65   Ibid, 47–48.

66   Ibid, 56.

67   Ibid, 59.

68   NZLS Code of Ethics, rule 3.1.2 (as at 1 July 1980).

69   ADLS, letter to the NZLS Ethics Committee, in 'Ethics Committee: Women in the Profession,' Supplementary Order Paper Item no 15, NZLS council meeting, 26 November 1982, paras 1 and 2.

70   Ibid, paras 4 and 5.

71   Sian Elias, letter to Bruce Slane, president of the NZLS, 15 September 1982 (confirming points discussed at the meeting).

72   Ibid.

73   NZLS council minutes, 26 November 1982.

74   Ibid, item 13, 17.

75   Ibid; 'Women in the profession,' 1982.

76   NZLS Code of Ethics, rule 3.1.2 and the statement which follows.

77   Megan Richardson, 10.

78   Ibid, table 2 and 9. For details of estimated drop-out rates for the years 1980–1992, see ch 7, table 21, 157.

79   'Proper research, not "throw away lines", wanted on women in law,' *Council Brief*, April 1982, 3.

80   Ibid.

81   Ibid.

82   Ibid.

83   Members of the Wellington working party were Mike Antunovic, Helen Cull, John Gibson, Linda Howes, Graeme MacKay, Sandra Moran, Chris Pottinger (convener), and subsequently, Keith Matthews.

84   WDLS, *Full Report*, paras 5.6, 6.3, 6.5 and 8.6. See also 'Reader survey results,' 3.

85   Ibid, paras 5.1–5.3.

86   Ibid, paras 4.4.4, 5.2 and 5.2.2.

87   Ibid, appendix, 3.

88   Ibid, para 8.6 and appendix, 10.

89   Ibid, 17 and appendix, 8.

90   Ibid, para 9.2 and appendix, 17.

91   Ibid, para 7.1 and appendix, 18.

92   'There's sex discrimination within the legal profession,' 5.

93   WDLS, *Full Report*, para 10.4.

94   Ibid, 'Conclusions and recommendations,' 17 and 'XI Conclusion.'

95   Ibid, 18.

96   One had been set up in Auckland. However, the existence of any other district law society committee has not been traced.

97   WDLS, *Full Report*.

98   'Comment on the WDLS study,' *Morning Report*, Radio NZ, 1 December 1983.

99   'Rural ramblings,' *Council Brief*, June 1984.

100 'Comments on women rebutted,' *Council Brief*, 120, August 1984, 8.

101 Colleen Singleton, interview; WDLS council minutes, 22 March 1982, 22 September 1982, 15 December 1982, 11 February 1984 and 7 March 1984.

102 'Study confirms prejudice,' 1–2.

103 'Discrimination moves under scrutiny,' 1.

104 Ibid and see Commonwealth Secretariat Legal Division, 316–317.

105 'Discrimination moves under scrutiny,' 1.

106 Ibid.

107 Margaret Wilson, interview; inaugural meeting planning notes, Margaret Wilson's personal papers; Margaret Robins, 'The origins of the association:

108 AWLA minutes, 28 May 1984, 27 August 1984, 6 May 1987; Kate Davenport, letter, 10 September 1993.

109 Margaret Wilson, introductory speech, inaugural meeting, 16 April 1984.

110 AWLA minutes, 16 April 1984.

111 Hannah Sargisson, interview.

112 'Women lawyers band together,' *National Business Review*, 23 April 1984.

113 Ibid.

114 AWLA minutes, 28 May 1984.

115 AWLA minutes, 27 August 1984. Secondary schools visited by AWLA representatives in 1985 included Edgewater College, Auckland Girls' Grammar School, Green Bay High School and Kelston Girls' High School.

116 *AWLA Newsletter*, October 1984.

117 Ibid, 3.

118 Ibid, 2. At that time, the first name on a title was allocated a vote on local body matters.

119 'Women's subcommittee,' *AWLA Newsletter*, August 1985, 9.

120 *AWLA Newsletter*, September 1986, 9.

121 For example, see 'More ways to write sex-neutral language,' 6; 'How to avoid sexist language,' *Just News*, March 1987; *AWLA Newsletter*, April 1987, 15.

122 Patricia Vene, interview. In 1994, that policy was still being adhered to by all judges and their associates in the Wellington High Court.

123 Members of the 1983 committee were Helen Cull, Carolyn Henwood, Linda Howes, Clara Matthews, Sandra Moran (convenor) and Shirley Parr, .

124 Colleen Singleton, interview; WDLS, *Annual Report 1983*.

125 WDLS, *Annual Report 1984*.

126 WDLS, *Annual Report 1985*.

127 'Women lawyers form independent group to represent their views,' *Council Brief*, no 120, August 1985, 3.

128 'WWLA: EEO, sexual harassment,' 40; *Wellington Women Lawyers Association Constitution*, 1985, clause 2; Christine O'Brien, letter, 17 September 1993.

129 The organisers of the 1984 conference lunch were Christine Grice, Heather McColl and Marilyn Waring. Catherine Wilson, letter, 15 September 1993.

130 Meeting with executive of OWLS, 24 March 1993; Claire Elder, secretary of OWLS, letter, 22 December 1993.

131 *Otago Women Lawyers' Society Constitution*, 1986.

132 'Report of the annual general meeting of the Auckland District Law Society, 7 March 1985,' *AWLA Newsletter*, April 1985, 2.

133 The members of the Partnership Support Group were Helen Melrose, Susan Rhodes and Hannah Sargisson: *AWLA Newsletter*, April 1985, 7.

134 'May interviewing programme,' *AWLA Newsletter*, August 1985, 5.

135 Leigh Simpkin, *May Interview Results*, Auckland University Law Students' Society, 1986.

136 Ibid, 6 and 16.

137 A 1984 national survey found that practitioners were 'most likely to agree' that women solicitors were less likely to become partners than men solicitors: Heylen Research Centre, *Executive Summary*, vol 1 of *Legal Profession: Practitioners' and General Public's Perceptions*, 23.

138 *AWLA Newsletter*, September 1986.

139 Isabel Mitchell, convener of the Women Practitioners' Committee, letter to women practitioners, *AWLA Newsletter*, September 1986.

140 WDLS, *Annual Report 1988*.

141 Colleen Singleton, interview.

142 Murray, 'Sharing in the "shingles"?'; Murray, 'Women lawyers in New Zealand,' 439–457; Murray, 'New Zealand lawyers,' 318–347.

143 *AWLA Newsletter*, December 1986. Mary O'Regan gave similar speeches (at a December 1985 lunchtime seminar organised by the WDLS Women in Law Committee and at the 1987 New Zealand Law Conference). See 'Eliminating discrimination will benefit all'; 'Affirmative action for women,' *New Zealand Law Conference 1987 Conference Papers*, 294.

144 NZLS, *Polls of the Profession and Public*, 6.

145 McInman and Associates, table 281.

146 Ibid, 8.

147 Ibid, 53.

148 Ibid, 8; NZLS, *Polls of the Profession and Public*, 20.

149 NZLS, *Polls of the Profession and Public*, 20.

150 *Female Lawyers Lack Opportunities Says Survey*, NZLS press release, 6 October 1987. Even the 'aggressive public relations programme' aimed at addressing the public 'stereotyping' of women lawyers recommended in the report did not eventuate: Ibid, 19 and 30.

151 O'Regan, 295.

152 'Women in the law (II), '148.

153 Downey, 1.

154 This view was shared by a number of men lawyers including Ted Thomas who also lobbied for the law society to appoint a woman as convener.

155 Members of the 1989 working party were Andrew Becroft, Gerard Curry, Patrick Gibson, Helen Graham, Margaret Jensen, Deirdre Milne, Elizabeth Minogue, Michael Ruffin, Norman Shieff and Nadja Tollemache.

156 Cockayne, 41.

157 Ibid, 40–43.

158 Ibid, 60–61.

159 Ibid, 60.

160 Knight, 21–23.

161 Cockayne, 54.

162 Ibid, 4.

163 Ibid, 91.

164 Ibid, 92–94.

165 'Equality now women lawyers say,' *New Zealand Herald*, 11 September 1989.

166 'Where men still rule,' *Dominion*, 13 September 1989, 16.

167 'Feedback on women lawyers problems sought,' 1.

168 Ibid.

169 Ibid.

170 Judith Potter, interview.

171 Confidential interview.

172 Cushla McGillivray, letter, 11 April 1994.

173 Katherine Dolby, letter, 28 March 1994.

174 Rae Mazengarb, interview.

Chapter Seven

1   Gatfield and Gray, table 25. The survey was undertaken in September 1992 and sampled 1,469 practitioners (784 women and 685 men) in numbers proportionate to the distribution of practitioners within the fourteen district law society regions.

2   Gatfield, *Women Judges*, para 1.2.

3   Gatfield and Gray, table 26.

4   Gatfield, *Women Judges*, table 4.

5   In 1991, of all employed barristers, solicitors and lawyers 4% were Maori women. The total number of women lawyers was 1,377, giving a total of 2 Maori women lawyers: correspondence with Statistics New Zealand, 12 October 1993. Note that there is a difference of 32 between the numbers of women lawyers holding practising certificates in 1991 (1,345) (appendix, table A7, 455) and the number counted in the census (1,377).

6   'We need more,' *New Zealand Herald*, 30 August 1982.

7   See also the appendix, table A7, 455.

8   Doug Arcus, Arcus Consulting Ltd, 9 February 1995, December 1994 provisional figures.

9   Jenny Stenning, secretary of the NZ Institute of Legal Executives.

10   Statistics New Zealand, *All About Women*, 92.

11   Doug Arcus, Arcus Consulting Ltd, figures as at December 1994.

12   Auckland data from the ADLS. Wellington data from David Clarke, the WDLS executive director.

13   Theft of client money by lawyers in the late 1980s and early 1990s resulted in a run on the Solicitors' Fidelity Fund. To meet the claims, a $10,000 levy was imposed on every principal in practice in 1993.

14   Gatfield, *Wellington District Law Society Scoping Study*, table 4.

15   NZLS membership data, 1993; 'Women go solo in Dunedin,' 37.

16   Of the 279 Auckland barristers sole, 78 were women: ADLS membership data, as at 28 July 1995.

17   *New Zealand Barristers and Solicitors Directory*, Auckland, ADLS, November 1995. The Attorney-General, Paul East, was not included in the list of barristers and so has been added to the 54 QCs listed.

18   NZ Standard Classification of Occupations, code 24231.

19   *NZLS Annual Report to Year Ended 30 November 1995*, 7.

20   Sargisson, 16.

21   Gatfield and Gray, table 10. Of the 113 lawyers employed in government departments, 78 were women and 35 were men.

22   These figures were obtained from the Corporate Lawyers' Association's mailing list, as at August 1993. When the association became a section of the NZLS at the end of 1993 there were approximately 750 corporate lawyers the list but their gender could not be identified.

23   ADLS membership data, as at 28 July 1995.

24   WDLS, *Full Report*, 1983, para 6.4; McInman and Associates, 8; Cockayne, 13.

25   Gatfield and Gray, table 20.

26   McInman and Associates, 14–15; Gatfield and Gray, table 21.

27   Research undertaken by Sue Brown for Equity Works Ltd involved the review of nearly 250 unreported Wellington High Court judgments issued January–August 1993.

28   'No women's robing room,' *Council Brief*, September 1993, 4.

29   'Waikato University,' *AWLA Monthly Update*, May 1996, 2, 3.

30   Gatfield and Gray, table 23.

31   Ibid, tables 20, 21 and 23. Career issues relevant to women commercial lawyers comprised nearly half the programme

in the Inaugural Women Business Lawyers in Asia and the Pacific Conference held by the Inter-Pacific Bar Association in Singapore, December 1995.

32 Ibid, tables 20, 21 and 23.

33 Ibid, table 21.

34 Ibid, table 20.

35 Gatfield and Gray, para 7.1 and table 23.

36 Ibid, para 6.5 and table 21.

37 Ibid, tables 20, 21 and 23.

38 'Public lack understanding,' 5.

39 Research by Cedric Hunt, law tutor at Wellington Open Polytechnic, found that law firms were more likely to employ legal executives than law graduates: 'Legal executive certificate now well established,' 8.

40 Gatfield and Gray, table 24. Only 11% of women lawyers considered that women had the same opportunities as men to reach partnership.

41 Ibid, para 7.5.

42 Ibid, para 6.7.

43 Ibid, table 9.

44 Ibid, table 8.

45 Ibid, para 7.3.

46 Burke-Kennedy, 68.

47 Millen, 173; Stone, 200–203 and 131.

48 Gatfield and Gray, para 4.6.

49 *Business Law Today*, May/June 1993, 22.

50 Nicola Schaab, secretary, NZLS WCG, letter, 30 November 1994.

51 State Services Commission statistics: 'Women in only 18pc of top jobs,' *Dominion*, 15 July 1993, 7.

52 Gatfield and Gray, table 12.

53 Ibid, table 14.

54 Information was provided by the Department of Justice, the Ministry of Foreign Affairs and Trade, the Inland Revenue Department, the Department of Labour and the Treasury.

55 Gatfield and Gray, table 13.

56 Ibid, para 5.1. Only 10% of women lawyers surveyed in 1992 were working part time (less than 30 hours per week on average) and those working part time had a varying amount of post-admission experience.

57 Ibid, para 4.10.

58 Cockayne, 11.

59 Gatfield and Gray, table 14.

60 'Judges receive pay increase,' 2.

61 WDLS special general meeting minutes, 7 May 1992

62 Council members include elected councillors, office holders and immediate past presidents who remain on the council.

63 'Women on NZ Law Society committees,' *Council Brief*, November 1994, 3.

64 Milroy, 36.

65 'What it means to be a JP,' *Dominion*, 20 September 1994.

66 Neither the Department for Courts nor the Ministry of Justice have information about how many women JPs sit in the District Courts. To obtain this information each regional Justices of the Peace Association would have to search its membership list manually.

67 Statistics provided by the University of Auckland Registry, as at 2 October 1995.

68 Statistics provided by the Waikato University law school, as at 3 April 1996.

69 See the appendix, table A8, 455.

70 NZ Vice-Chancellors' Committee, 1994, 51.

71 National censuses and labour force participation surveys do not measure law graduate unemployment. Relevant information is collected by the NZ Vice-Chancellors' Committee and the IPLS but the statistics on those who are unemployed and actively looking for work are not broken down by sex.

72 NZ Vice Chancellors' Committee, table C, 1990 and 1994.

73 Ibid, 1992–1994.

74 Ibid, 1994, 45.

75 The IPLS runs 13-week courses which must be attended by law graduates before they seek admission to the Bar. The courses cover the practical skills needed in the practice of law, such as conveyancing settlements, interviewing techniques, professional ethics and negotiation.

76   Robin Fuller, Wellington branch director, IPLS, interview, 19 May 1994.

77   Data includes intakes 1–3 of 1993 and intake 1 of 1994. Note that not all jobs are in law: IPLS, Otago branch.

78   Anna Tutton, Canterbury branch director, IPLS, interview, 26 May 1994.

79   Mark Mason, Auckland branch director, IPLS, interview, 26 May 1994.

80   Data from the Victoria University of Wellington Career's Advisory Service, 1993 and 1994 law recruitment programmes.

81   ADLS, *Report of the Working Party*, para 4.5.2; WDLS, *Full Report*, paras 5.1, 5.2 and 5.2.2.

82   Gatfield and Gray, tables 24 and 25.

Chapter Eight

1   Fifty-seven percent of the men lawyers who commented on gender differences in legal work in the 1992 survey said that the sexes were equal and that progress depended on ability. Only 16% of women lawyers agreed: 'Questionnaire comments summary paper,' Gatfield and Gray, question 29.

2   Gatfield and Gray.

3   Melrose, 86.

4   Sargisson, 14–15; ADLS, *Report of the Working Party*, para 2.4.

5   Statistics on 1995 student grades was provided by Alison Roberton, School of Law, University of Auckland, as at 14 May 1996. To obtain comparative data, this information was also requested from the Waikato University School of Law, but data on student grades by gender could not be extracted from its database. It is understood that this is the case in the other law schools also.

6   Examination results of first year students at Victoria University of Wellington 1989–1990 showed that the women students performed better than the men students: Sturrock, 75.

7   Caldwell, 'Graduate employment.' See also ch 9.

8   See ch 7, 152–153.

9   Michele Slatter, interview.

10   Gatfield and Gray, paras 5.2 and 5.2.2.

11   Cockayne, 25.

12   Elizabeth Medford, interview.

13   Caldwell, 'Graduate employment,' 163.

14   See ch 7, 137–138.

15   John Laurent, interview.

16   Human Rights Act 1993, sections 22(1) and (2), and 65 (previously the Human Rights Commission Act 1977, sections 15(1) and (2), and 27).

17   Gatfield and Gray, table 27.

18   Jessica Percy, 'It's an appealing career,' *Dominion*, 2 August 1994, 5.

19   Alison Fulcher, interview; Anna Tutton, interview.

20   Elizabeth Medford, interview.

21   Gatfield and Gray, para 8.3.

22   Caldwell, 'Graduate employment,' 163.

23   Information on performance appraisal procedures was obtained in interviews with 26 lawyers (14 women and 12 men) from a range of firms and locations in NZ in 1993 and 1994. The lawyers concerned requested that their identities be protected.

24   Gatfield and Gray, table 18.

25   Ibid, para 6.7.

26   Ibid, para 6.1.

27   Ibid.

28   Ibid, para 5.3.

29   Byrne, 20, 26; 'Warning over false harassment cases,' *Dominion*, 24 August 1994, 3.

30   Gatfield and Gray, para 5.2. The majority of partners work more than 40 hours per week. An estimated 44% of partners work more than 50 hours per week compared with 28% of non-partners.

31   Ibid, para 7.2.

32   Ibid, tables 24 and 25.

33   Ibid, para 5.3.

34   *Report for the Principal Family Court Judge*, a review of the Family Court, April 1993, 96–98.

35   See note 23.

36   Cockayne, 14; Gatfield and Gray, table 21.

37   Gatfield and Gray, para 6.5.
38   In the 1987 survey, company law was the only non-conveyancing commercial-type category: Cockayne, *Tabulations*, vol 2, 101.
39   Gatfield and Gray, table 20.
40   Ibid, para 7.1.
41   Ibid, table 21 and para 6.5.
42   Ibid, table 23.
43   Family Proceedings Act 1980, sections 8 and 19.
44   Twenty-seven percent of women practised in criminal law compared with 21% of men: Gatfield and Gray.
45   Ibid, table 21 and para 6.5.
46   Ibid, table 20.
47   For women's scholarship in this area, see McDonald and Austin; 'Symposium: issues relating to women and the law'; *NZLS Seminar: Challenging Law and Legal Processes; Women's Law Conference Papers.*
48   See also ch 6, 112; ch 14, 312 and 317–318; ch 15, 340; ch 18, 415–416.
49   Heylen Research Centre, *Findings*, vol 1 of *Women in the Legal Profession*, para 2.3.3, 28.
50   'Questionnaire comments summary paper,' Gatfield and Gray.
51   Shreves, 123.
52   Sonja Clapham, secretary of the NZ Bar Association, letter 22 September 1993.
53   Burns and Coleman, 8.
54   Ibid, appendix I.
55   The tendency of employers to describe female work attributes as 'natural' rather than as 'skills' is one of the

56   reasons why women do not have pay equity: Burton, 26.
      Ibid, 4–7; McLennan et al, 225–226 and 239–241.
57   Gatfield and Gray, para 3.5.
58   Dale, ch 12.
59   Dale, 241–242 and 244–245.
60   Dale, 183, 245.
61   Only 5% of men and 4% of women rated length of experience as an important partnership criterion: Gatfield and Gray, table 22.
62   Ibid, para 4.12.
63   Sonja Clapham, secretary of the NZ Bar Association, letter, 22 September 1993.
64   Dyhrberg, 17.
65   Sonja Clapham, secretary of the NZ Bar Association, letter, 22 September 1993.
66   Coleman, 12.
67   Ibid, 10.
68   'Queen's Counsel: recent appointments' [1981] NZLJ 114.
69   The other counsel were Susan Bambury and Christine French. Denese Bates was later appointed Queen's Counsel.
70   Cockayne, 24.
71   Gatfield and Gray, table 22.
72   Ibid, para 6.6.
73   Only 1% of lawyers of both sexes referred to hours worked as a partnership criterion: ibid, table 22.
74   Ibid, para 5.2.
75   Ibid, para 10.1 and table 32.
76   Quinn, 159.
77   Meares, 'Woman and issues in commercial law,' 27.
78   Dakin and Smith, 131.

Chapter Nine

1   Gatfield and Gray, para 7.2.
2   Murray, 'Women lawyers in New Zealand,' 441; Abel and Lewis, *Civil Law World*, 37.
3   Murray, 'New Zealand woman lawyer,' 145; Gatfield and Gray, para 3.6.
4   Eighty men lawyers and 125 women lawyers voluntarily attributed women lawyers' lack of progress to the fact

      that the legal profession remained an 'old boys' club': Gatfield and Gray.
5   Gatfield, *Women Judges*, para 2.6.
6   Dyhrberg, 17.
7   The Northern Club 'admitted women to its ranks' in 1990: 'Le Petard's without a word of a lie,' *National Business Review*, 4 December 1992, 12. The Auckland Club included women in its membership in April 1993: 'Women for club,' *New Zealand Herald*, 8 August

1993, 3. The Wellington Club allowed women members in August 1993: Anamika Vasil, 'Men-only club throws open doors to women,' *Dominion*, 11 August 1993, 1 and 3. The Wellesley Club voted to allow women in December 1993: 'Women join Wellesley Club,' *Evening Post*, 7 February 1994, 19.

8   'Another woman presents poser for boys-only club,' *Dominion*, 3 August 1993; 'Club in dark on admitting Dame,' *Dominion*, 4 August 1993; 'Club's honorary male suggestion "offensive",' *Dominion*, 5 August 1993, 3; Anamika Vasil, 'Men-only club throws open doors to women,' *Dominion*, 11 August 1993, 1 and 3; 'Women welcome men's club move,' *Dominion*, 12 August 1993, 4.

9   Letter to women practitioners from Colleen Singleton, member and Stuart Brooker, committee member, 2 May 1994.

10 *Evening Post*, 2 July 1994, 19.

11 Falling membership was also said to be behind the decision of the London men's club to open to women.

12 Burton, 5.

13 Gatfield and Gray, table 28.

14 Ibid, para 8.2.

15 Shreves, 124.

16 Epstein, 199, footnote.

17 Confidential interview.

18 NZLS, *Lawyers: An Image Study*, 19.

19 Ibid.

20 Ibid, 20.

21 Henwood, 2.

22 ADLS, *Report of the Working Party*, para 5.5.2.

23 Sargisson, 54

24 WDLS, *Full Report*, paras 8.1–8.3.

25 Ibid, table 8.2. ADLS, *Report of the Working Party*, para 5.5.2; Sargisson 54.

26 ADLS, *Report of the Working Party*, para 5.5.5.

27 Sargisson, 54.

28 ADLS, *Report of the Working Party*, para 5.5.4.

29 Ibid, para 5.5.6.

30 Sargisson, 54–55.

31 Shreves, 124.

32 WDLS, *Full Report*, para 6.5.2.

33 ADLS, *Report of the Working Party*, 1989, 30.

34 Heylen Research Centre, *Findings*, vol 1 of *Women in the Legal Profession*, para 2.3.3, 28.

35 Caldwell, 'Graduate employment,' 162. Seventy-seven percent of the 62 law firms surveyed ranked personal attributes as the most important factor when recruiting.

36 Dakin and Smith, 131.

37 Ibid, 163.

38 'Procedures for appointment of Queen's Counsel,' 9.

39 Gatfield and Gray, para 6.6, 24.

40 Dyhrberg, 17.

41 Humphries and Grice, 210–212; Ellis and Wheeler, 33.

42 Murray, 'Sharing in the "shingles"?' 123.

43 Gatfield and Gray, para 3.5.

44 Ibid, para 8.6.

45 Numerous comments were made on the conservative nature of the Christchurch profession during a meeting with members of the CWLA on 26 March 1993.

46 Anna Tutton, Canterbury branch director, IPLS, interview.

47 Millen, 186.

48 Phillips, 230–231.

49 See also ch 8, note 47.

50 Gatfield and Gray, para 8.5.

51 Gatfield, 'How are women doing 100 years later?' 145.

52 Gatfield and Gray, para 8.5.

53 Meares, 'Women and issues in commercial law,' 29.

54 Ibid.

55 Gatfield and Gray, paras 7.2 and 8.1–8.5.

56 For example, see Gilligan; Jack and Jack.

57 Chater and Gaster, 52–56 and 88–99; 'Sizing up the sexes,' *Time*, 20 January 1992, 36.

58 Jack and Jack, 131–132.

59 McInman and Associates, tables 49 and 57.

60 See ch 8, 176 and note 47.

61 Jack and Jack, 7.

Chapter Ten

1 Sargisson, 52.

2 Knight, 14.

3 Gatfield and Gray, table 19.

4 Cockayne, 21; Gatfield and Gray, table 18.

5 Gatfield and Gray, table 18.

6 Ibid.

7 Gatfield, *Women Judges*, table 1 and para 1.1.

8 Gatfield and Gray, table 18.

9 Ibid, tables 24 and 25.

10 ADLS, *Report of the Working Party*, para 5.2; WDLS, *Full Report*, para 8.6.

11 Ninety-seven women lawyers and 67 men lawyers explained that the main problem was the belief that women would choose their families over their careers: Gatfield and Gray, 'Questionnaire comments summary paper,' question 30. See also Davenport, 'Part-time lawyering,' 23–25.

12 Gatfield and Gray, 'Questionnaire comments summary paper,' question 30.

13 Sixty-nine percent of the men surveyed in 1992 had children compared with 36% of the women: ibid, para 10.1.

14 'Conference dinner,' 157.

15 Gatfield and Gray, para 5.2.

16 *Dominion*, 27 June 1992.

17 Heylen Research Centre, *The Legal Profession: A Survey of Lawyers and Members of the Public*, 3, in Murray, 'Women lawyers in New Zealand,' 453.

18 Helen Brown, 'Dream comes true: women lawyers make a go of it,' *Auckland Star*, 14 May 1986, B5.

19 Cockayne, 54–55.

20 Gatfield and Gray, para 3.3.

21 For example, of the men High Court judges in 1993, 96% were married: Gatfield, *Women Judges*, para 3.1.

22 Gatfield and Gray, para 3.4.

23 Ibid, tables 32 and 33.

24 Murray 'Sharing in the "shingles"?' 111–112.

25 Gatfield and Gray, paras 3.4 and 10.1–10.3.

26 Kuitert, ch 6.

27 Dorothy Raymond, interview.

28 *New Zealand Woman's Weekly*, 6 October 1975, 4, 5.

29 Varnham, 23. See also *New Zealand Listener*, 27 March 1993.

30 Nadja Tollemache, interview.

31 *Canada Law Journal*, November 1869, 307, in Backhouse, 13.

32 *Albany Law Journal*, 48, 1893, 103.

33 TVNZ documentary, 19 January 1988.

34 *Freelance*, 14 July 1900, 3a.

35 Epstein, 38, footnote.

36 Gatfield and Gray, para 3.6.

37 'Shirley Parr recalls her early days,' *Council Brief*, September 1991.

38 *Council Brief*, September 1991.

39 Smith, 3.

40 Confidential interview.

41 ADLS, *Report of the Working Party*, para 5.7.2.

42 WDLS, *Final Report*, para 5.4.

43 Gatfield and Gray, table 17 and para 5.7.

44 Gatfield, *LawTalk Survey*, tables 1.1 and 1.2. See also *LawTalk*, no 402, October 1993, 23–24.

45 Gatfield, *LawTalk Survey*, para 5.

46 Ibid, table 2.1.

47 For example, see Meares, 'Maternity leave for partners.'

48 Gatfield, *LawTalk Survey*, tables 2.2 and 2.3.

49 WDLS, *Full Report*, para 5.4.1.

50 Murray, 'New Zealand woman lawyer,' 198.

51 Department of Statistics, 1936 census.

52 Judith Potter, interview.

53 Abella, 35.

54 ADLS, *Report of the Working Party*, para 5.3.2.

55 Cockayne, 33.

56   ADLS, *Report of the Working Party*, para 5.3.3.

57   Sargisson, 45.

58   Heylen Research Centre, *Findings*, vol 1 of *Women and the Legal Profession*, para 2.5.5.

59   Gatfield and Gray, tables 16 and 33.

60   WDLS, *Full Report*, para 5.5.

61   Cockayne, para 2.1.5.

62   Gatfield and Gray, table 16.

63   Ibid, para 10.5.

64   WDLS, *Full Report*, para 6.5.2.

65   Cockayne, 36 and 69.

66   Gatfield and Gray, para 10.4. See also Cockayne, 34–35.

67   Gatfield and Gray, table 33; Gatfield and Gray, 'Questionnaire comments summary paper,' question 42.

68   Caldwell, 'Practice survey,' 255.

69   Gatfield and Gray, para 10.6.

70   Ibid.

71   Ibid.

72   Olive Smuts-Kennedy, interview.

73   Confidential interview.

74   Henwood, 1.

75   ADLS, *Report of the Working Party*, para 4.4.4.

76   WDLS, *Full Report*, paras 4.1 and 4.3.

77   Ibid, para 4.5.2.

78   Helen Brown, 'Dream comes true: women lawyers make a go of it,' *Auckland Star*, 14 May 1986, B5; Frances Martin, 'The professions: why women go into partnership,' *National Business Review*, 1 June 1991.

79   Gatfield and Gray, para 4.9 and table 11.

80   Ibid, para 4.9 and table 11.

81   Ibid, para 4.8.

82   Cockayne, 64.

83   ADLS, *Report of the Working Party*, para 4.4.4.

84   WDLS, *Full Report*, para 4.5.2.

85   See ch 8.

86   Frances Martin, 'The professions: why women go into partnership,' *National Business Review*, 1 June 1991.

87   Ibid.

88   Gray Matter Research Ltd and Rivers Buchan and Associates, 6, referring to research by Michael Fay and Leslie Williams in 1991.

89   *Counsel Brief*, September 1991.

90   'Queen's Service Award for public services to Law Commission director,' *Council Brief*, July 1993, 4.

91   'Could well be a modern Portia,' *Weekly News*, 24 January 1962. Patricia Webb retired as chief legal officer in 1976.

92   Olive Smuts-Kennedy, interview.

93   Margaret Vennell, interview.

94   'Interview with Judith Potter,' 151.

95   'Helen Melrose,' 78.

96   Margaret Wilson, interview.

97   See also ch 7.

98   'Queen's Service Award for public services to Law Commission director,' *Council Brief*, July 1993, 4.

99   *New Zealand Biographies 1980*, vol 2, 1, EP21.12.79; 'Blenheim's land registrar is unique in New Zealand,' 1960 and 'District land registrar,' 1979: unsourced newspaper clippings from Eileen O'Connor's private collection.

100 Hughes, 132.

101 Alison Quentin-Baxter, interview. See also 'New stage in distinguished legal career,' 3.

102 McLeod, 16.

103 Varnham, 23.

104 Sargisson, 17.

105 Alison Quentin-Baxter, interview.

106 Margaret Vennell, interview.

107 Nadja Tollemache, interview.

108 'First woman law professor,' 3.

109 Statement by Government Employing Authorities on EEO, 1984, 9–12.

110 WDLS, *Full Report*, appendix, 1.

111 Ibid, appendix, 11, 16.

112 Heylen Research Centre, *Women in the Legal Profession*, 8.

113 State-Owned Enterprises Act 1986.

114 For example the Broadcasting Act 1989, the Education Act 1989, the Defence Act 1990, the Accident Rehabilitation and Compensation Insurance Act 1992, the Health and Disability Services Act 1993, and the Health Reforms (Transitional Provisions) Act 1993.

115 Liddicoat, 83.

116 Alastair Morrison, 'So chins up, girls; things have never been better . . .,' *Dominion*, 11 December 1992, 11. See also Crossan, 'Equal employment opportunity in the public sector,' 249; Ministry of Women's Affairs, *Summary of Paper*, 10–13.

117 Cook, 37–38.

118 Frances Martin, 'Partners want to offer value,' *Evening Post*, 12 August 1992.

119 Helen Brown, 'Dream comes true: women lawyers make a go of it,' *Auckland Star*, 14 May 1986, B5.

120 Frances Martin, 'The professions: why women go into partnership,' *National Business Review*, 1 June 1991.

121 For example, see 'All women team,' 47.

122 Bernadette Little, 'Going solo is a hard struggle,' *New Zealand Herald*, 29 July 1986, section 2, 1. Linda Kaye, interview. The women solicitors employed were Liz Riddiford, Jo Rice, Kate McBreen and Angela Corry

123 Frances Martin, 'Partners want to offer value,' *Evening Post*, 12 August 1992.

124 All women team, 47.

125 Frances Martin, 'The professions: why women go into partnership,' *National Business Review*, 1 June 1991.

126 Wear, 7.

127 'All women team,' 47.

128 David Peach, 'Irish at law,' *Sunday Star-Times*, 1993, 6.

129 Frances Martin, 'The professions: why women go into partnership,' *National Business Review*, 21 June 1991; 'Women lawyers on television,' 1.

130 Helen Brown, 'Dream comes true: women lawyers make a go of it,' *Auckland Star*, 14 May 1986, B5;.

131 David Peach, 'Irish at law,' *Sunday Star-Times*, 1993, 6.

132 Frances Martin, 'Partners want to offer value,' *Evening Post*, 12 August 1992.

133 Frances Martin, 'The professions: why women go into partnership,' *National Business Review*, 21 June 1991.

134 Jan Walker, interview.

135 David Peach, 'Irish at law,' *Sunday Star-Times*, 1993, 6.

136 McCabe McMahon, letter, 12 June 1996.

137 'Helen Melrose,' 91.

138 Gatfield and Gray, 'Questionnaire comments summary paper,' questions 30, 32, 33 and 45.

139 Cook, 37–38.

140 Frances Martin, 'The professions: why women go into partnership,' *National Business Review*, 21 June 1991. Davenport, 'All women firm provides flexible work environment,' 46.

141 Wear, 7.

142 'All women team,' 47.

143 Abel and Lewis, *Civil Law World*, 36.

Chapter Eleven

1 *First Lady in Law*, TVNZ documentary, Silvia Cartwright interview, 19 January 1988.

2 'Report of the strip-search . . .,' *Morning Report*, 12 July 1985, Radio NZ Sound Archives.

3 'Police response to the report,' *Midday Report*, 12 July 1985, Radio NZ Sound Archives.

4 Frances Joychild, legal adviser, Human Rights Commission, letter, 2 September 1993.

5 ADLS, *Report of the Working Party*, para 4.4.3.

6 WDLS, *Full Report*, paras 10.1–10.4.

7 Heylen Research Centre, *Tabulations*, vol 3 of *Women in the Legal Profession*, 211.

8 Ibid, 54 and 212; Cockayne, 32.

9 WDLS, *Full Report*, paras 7.1 and 7.2.

10 Cockayne, 60.

11 Knight, 21–23.

12 NZ Law Practitioners Disciplinary Tribunal decision, 30 June 1986 and order, 30 June 1986. The tribunal, 'having regard to the interests of the persons concerned and to the public interest', also ordered that publication be prohibited of the name of the practitioner, the name of the complainant, the name of the district

law society and the district disciplinary tribunal, and any facts or material that might lead to the identification of those listed.

13 'Video to fight sex abuse in professions,' *Dominion*, 28 January 1992.

14 Ibid.

15 Ibid.

16 'Rape complaint "turned down",' *Dominion*, 23 September 1992.

17 'Professionals crack down on sex misconduct,' *Dominion Sunday Times*, 17 May 1992, 11.

18 'Sexual abuse in doctor-patient relationship,' seminar sponsored by the NZ Medical Council, 20 May 1992.

19 NZLS Ethics Committee, minutes, 27 February 1992 and 28 May 1992. See also Kristy McDonald, 13.

20 NZLS Ethics Committee, minutes, 27 February 1992 and 28 May 1992.

21 'NZ Law Practitioners Disciplinary Tribunal,' 7. Abuse of a woman client was also addressed in a High Court property case: 'Lawyer to pay former lover $135,000,' *Dominion*, 14 June 1994, 3.

22 Gatfield and Gray, table 29; Gatfield, *Women Judges*, table 17.

23 Gatfield and Gray, table 29.

24 In 1996, EEO and sexual harassment consultants in Auckland and Wellington confirmed that they are aware of current sexual harassment incidents in law firms. See also Ruth Arcus, 16.

25 Gatfield and Gray, table 29.

26 Ibid, para 8.3.

27 Gatfield, *Women Judges*, para 4.1.

28 Gatfield and Gray, table 30.

29 Gatfield, *Women Judges*, table 18.

30 Ibid, table 19. The sixth judge did not answer that part of the question.

31 Gatfield and Gray, para 8.2.

32 Gatfield, *Women Judges*, table 22 and para 5.1.

33 Ibid, para 5.2.

34 Ibid, para 5.3.

35 Gatfield and Gray, table 27.

36 Human Rights Act 1993, sections 21, 22 and 62.

37 Ibid, section 62; Employment Contracts Act 1991, section 29.

38 See ch 4

39 'Work,' Part 3 of *Standing in the Sunshine*, TV3 documentary series, Silvia Cartwright interview, 25 November 1993.

40 Joychild, 43–44.

41 Ibid, 47.

42 Human Rights Commission, *Sexual Harassment in the Workplace*, 6–7.

43 Employment Contracts Act 1991, section 29.

44 Ibid, section 36.

45 Human Rights Act 1993, section 62(1)–(3).

46 Gatfield and Gray, para 8.3.

47 Ibid, para 8.4.

48 One-third of the men who commented on sexual harassment downplayed the seriousness or the existence of the problem: ibid, 'Questionnaire comments summary paper,' question 36.

49 Gatfield, *Women Judges*, para 5.1.

50 Ibid.

51 Radio NZ, 12 August 1993.

52 'Police response to the report,' *Midday Report*, 12 July 1985, Radio NZ Sound Archives.

53 Of 94 voluntary comments on the type of sexual harassment, 17 women referred to the humorous nature of the incident: Gatfield and Gray, 'Questionnaire comments summary paper,' question 36.

54 These labels were also referred to by 5 women lawyers surveyed in Auckland in 1987. Assertive women were labelled 'aggressive', 'feminist', 'radical' and 'stroppy', while assertive men were referred to as 'strong-minded', 'firm' or simply 'assertive': Cockayne, 59.

55 'Report of the strip-search . . .,' *Morning Report*, 12 July 1985, Radio NZ Sound Archives.

56 Frances Joychild, legal adviser, Human Rights Commission, letter 2 September 1993.

57 Gatfield and Gray, para 8.3.

58 Cockayne, 33.

59 Twenty-one percent of lawyers surveyed knew that their firms had formal written procedures for sexual harassment complaints, 20% were unsure and 50% said their firms did not. Some of those who definitely knew of procedures would be working in the same firms so it is likely that the proportion of firms having procedures would be less than 21%: Gatfield and Gray, para 8.4.

60 Ibid.

61 Ibid.

62 Ruth Arcus, 16.

63 Gatfield and Gray, para 8.3. Twenty-three percent of women lawyers who commented on sexual harassment said it was best to ignore the conduct: Gatfield and Gray, 'Questionnaire comments summary paper,' question 36.

64 See ch 6.

65 Margaret Wilson, interview.

66 Seventeen of the 94 women who commented on sexual harassment said they personally spoke to the person involved: Gatfield and Gray, 'Questionnaire comments summary paper,' question 36.

67 Crossan, presentation at WDLS seminar on EEO, 4 August 1993.

68 Gatfield and Gray, para 8.3.

69 According to a survey of former police-women, sexual harassment by male colleagues was a reason why 20% of women surveyed had left the police force: 'Sex harassment "driving women out of police",' *Sunday Star-Times*, 21 July 1996, A5.

70 For a general discussion on New Zealand rape laws, see Elisabeth McDonald, 'An(other) explanation,' 43–67.

71 Phillips, 236.

72 Rout, 174, footnote 6. See also Burton, 1991, ch 1; King.

73 Gatfield and Gray, para 8.3 and table 29. Sexual harassment of a male employee by a woman manager was highlighted in a bestselling 1994 novel, *Disclosure*, by US author Michael Chrichton.

74 Gatfield, *Report*, vol 2 of *Towards 2000*, paras 9.2–9.7.

75 Rout, 176–177.

76 Ibid, 179.

77 This estimate is based on the average of one support staff member for every professional staff member. In larger law firms the ratio is lower, while in smaller practices the ratio is usually higher.

Chapter Twelve

1 See 'Dame Silvia fears for women in legal careers,' *Evening Post*, 5 March 1993; 'Law careers "tenuous" for women,' *New Zealand Herald*, 6 March 1993; Wilson, 'An introduction and an overview,' 5–6. For a list of NZ women judges see the appendix, table A9, 456.

2 Margaret Wilson, interview; Hannah Sargisson, interview.

3 Findlay, 182.

4 Dugdale, 'Due deference,' 9.

5 Gatfield and Gray, para 8.1.

6 Ibid.

7 French, 150.

8 Gatfield, *Women Judges*, para 6.1.

9 'Judge calls for limited public scrutiny of Family Courts,' 2.

10 'Comments at Judge Moss's swearing in,' *Council Brief*, July 1995, 4.

11 Gatfield, *Women Judges*, para 6.3. See also comments by Judge Moss: New judge ponders judicial role,' 5; *Dominion*, 3 June 1995, l; *Evening Post*, 3 June 1995, 10.

12 Justice Elias' speech at the annual general meeting of the AWLA, December 1995.

13 Schafran, 'Supreme Court nominees,' 38.

14 Gatfield, *Women Judges*, para 6.1.

15 'New judge ponders judicial role,' *Council Brief*, July 1995, 5.

16 *Phillips v Phillips* [1993] 3 NZLR 159, 172; (1993) 10 FRNZ 110, 124.

17 'Judge calls for limited public scrutiny of Family Courts,' 2.

18 Sharon Crosbie interview with Peter Williams QC, *Nine to Noon*, Radio 2YA, 25 August 1992.

19 Gatfield, *Women Judges*, para 6.2. See also Bernard Brown, 22.

20 Wickler. Note also that evidence has been documented of discrimination by judges toward women lawyers: American Bar Association Commission on Women in the Profession, *Summary of Hearings*, 2–3.

21 Grant and Smith, 76.

22 Canadian Bar Association, 192–196.

23 United Kingdom General Council of the Bar, *Without Prejudice?* 24.

24 Parliament of the Commonwealth of Australia, xiv and chs 3 and 4.

25 *Launch of Legal Guide for Rape Survivors*, National Radio, 20 July 1993.

26 Elisabeth McDonald, 'An(other) explanation,' 43–68.

27 'Minister caned over rape views,' *National Business Review*, 16 July 1991. See also *National Business Review*, 22 July 1991; *Dominion Sunday Times*, 21 July 1991.

28 *Hamilton Abuse Intervention Pilot Project: Six Month Report*, February 1992, 35. As a result of this criticism, the report was subsequently edited in the Department of Justice to remove the names of the judges.

29 'Moore steps up criticism of judges,' *Dominion*, 25 October 1993, 1 and 3.

30 'Shipley chides judge,' *Dominion*, 28 June 1993, 1.

31 'Judge "out of touch" on rape,' *Sunday Star-Times*, 22 May 1994, A2; 'Judge scorns traditional rape terms,' *New Zealand Herald*, 21 May 1994, 1. See also Radford, 4.

32 'Letters to the editor,' *Dominion*, 26 June 1993, 14.

33 'Dropped complaints concern,' *Dominion*, 28 January 1993.

34 For example, see Synergy Applied Research and Hinematu McNeill, 46; Family Violence Prevention Co-ordinating Committee. 'Family violence prevention in the 1990s,' in *Conference Proceedings*, vol 1, 78–79 and vol 2, 86, 280.

35 The Domestic Violence Act 1995, effective from 1 July 1996, increases the protection available to victims of domestic violence. The Act was developed over 8 years in consultation with Women's Refuge, lawyers and judges.

36 'Judge "out of touch" on rape,' *Sunday Star-Times*, 22 May 1994, A2.

37 'Judge refuses to loosen rules for pregnant lawyer,' *Dominion*, 27 May 1994, 1.

38 Ibid; 'Judging the judges,' *Dominion*, 27 May 1994, 6.

39 'Judge's comments at trial offensive, says Rape Crisis,' *Dominion*, 4 July 1996, 1. See also 'Mixed signals received from "no",' *New Zealand Herald*, 6 July 1996, 24.

40 'Justice Morris' remarks,' *AWLA Monthly Update*, July 1996, 1. WWLA also wrote to the Attorney-General protesting 'in the strongest possible terms': *WWLA Newsletter*, July 1996.

41 'July board briefs,' 6.

42 Hubbard, 7.

43 'Judge rebuked for comments,' *New Zealand Herald*, 5 July 1996.

44 Berger Morello, 212–213; Epstein, 186.

45 Graycar, 'The gender of judgments,' 266, footnote 12, Graycar cites Naylor Bronwyn, 'Pregnant tribunals,' *Legal Services Bulletin*, 14, 1989, 41.

46 Gatfield, *Women Judges*, para 5.1.

47 Ibid, paras 3.3 and 5.1; 'Women lawyers urged to speak up,' 3.

48 'Rape reforms: ten year report,' 19 TCL 11/1.

49 'Women SM's,' 7.

50 Palmer, 'Judicial selection and accountability,' 33.

51 'Report of the Royal Commission on the Courts,' para 118.

52 Keith, 241.

53 Palmer, 'Judicial selection and accountability,' 34.

54 'Attorney-General,' 112.

55 Eichelbaum, 122.

56 Ibid.

57 Palmer, 'Judicial selection and accountability,' 38.
58 Black.
59 Palmer, 'Judicial appointments,' 2.
60 Ibid.
61 Ibid, 3 and 4.
62 'Chief Judge seeks nominations for women's appointment to Bench,' 4.
63 'Attorney-General,' 113.
64 'Wider consultation promised,' 2.
65 'Changes in line for judicial appointments,' *Dominion*, 20 March 1995, 2.
66 NZLS WCG minutes, 28 July 1995 and 10 November 1995.
67 This has occurred at least since 1984. For example, see WDLS, *Annual Report 1985*.
68 'Notes of the meeting with Judy Lawrence (Chief Executive, Ministry of Women's Affairs),' NZLS WCG minutes, 28 July 1995 7; Judy Lawrence, speech at AWLA meeting, 12 October 1995.
69 Palmer, 'Judicial selection and accountability,' 4.
70 *Women's Rights Committee*, 40.
71 Palmer, 'Judicial selection and accountability,' 32.
72 Leary, 196–197.
73 Palmer, 'Judicial selection and accountability,' 43. However, Palmer concluded that despite the apparent conflict of interest he considered the Solicitor-General should administer the appointment process.
74 'Wider consultation promised,' 2.
75 Palmer, 'Judicial appointments,' 3.
76 Palmer, 'Judicial selection and accountability,' 37.
77 Ibid, 37–38.
78 Palmer, 'Judicial appointments,' 3.
79 In 1995, the Department of Justice was restructured into three agencies: the Ministry of Justice (responsible for policy); the Department for Courts (responsible for courts' administration); and the Department of Corrections (responsible for criminal justice and administration of prisons).
80 Howard Davies, senior private secretary to the Attorney-General,

letter, 26 August 1993; Elizabeth Woolcott, executive assistant to the Chief Justice, letter, 5 August 1993.
81 Palmer, 'Judicial selection and accountability,' 36.
82 'Top judge puts case for judicial appointment reform,' *Dominion*, 12 July 1993, 1.
83 Ibid.
84 Hon Paul East, speech notes, LawLink Conference, 19 March 1993, 8–9, reproduced in *Council Brief*, no 205, May 1993, 8. No other commentator has assumed that judges would dominate a judicial commission although Sir Geoffrey Palmer has suggested that the views of the judges on any such commission may hold considerable sway with lay members.
85 Hodder, 85.
86 District Courts Act 1947, section 5.
87 Judicature Act 1908, section 6.
88 NZ Standard Classification of Occupations, 1990, Unit Group 2422, 67. However, the general description and tasks of judges is possibly one of the better summaries of the judge's job.
89 Twenty-four percent of women lawyers had more than 10 years' experience and a further 28% had 5–10 years' experience: Gatfield and Gray, table 4.
90 Forty-two percent of men partners had 10–20 years' experience: ibid, para 4.5.
91 Family Courts Act 1980, section 5.
92 Children, Young Persons, and Their Families Act 1989, section 435(3).
93 See ch 7, table 2, 131.
94 District Courts Act 1947, sections 7, 10 and 10A; Judicature Act 1908, sections 11, 11A and 13.
95 Oaths and Declaration Act 1957, section 18.
96 The biographical information on which this data is based was obtained from the Alexander Turnbull Library. Sources included the *New Zealand's Who's Who*, the National Library newspaper collection, the NZLJ and *LawTalk*. Some biographical data was obtained directly from the judges themselves. For the full report, see

Gatfield, *Biographies of New Zealand's High Court Judges*, table 1.1.

97   See ch 7, table 16, 151.

98   Gatfield, *Biographies of New Zealand's High Court Judges*, tables 2.1–2.3.

99   Gatfield and Gray, para 4.2, table 5.

100   Gatfield, *Biographies of New Zealand's High Court Judges*, table 1.1.

101   see ch 7, table 2, 131.

102   The average age of women District Court judges at date of appointment was obtained from biographical information on the women judges on the Bench as at August 1993.

103   *The Judiciary*, the report of a justice subcommittee, chaired by Peter Webster QC, London, 1972, 63, in Hodder, 87. See also Pannick, 526.

104   There were fewer than 100 women barristers and solicitors in that age group in 1986 and less than half that again in 1981.

105   Gatfield, *Biographies of New Zealand's High Court Judges*, table 4.1. Only one High Court judge had practised as a sole practitioner.

106   Palmer, 'Judicial selection and accountability,' 40.

107   Gatfield, *Biographies of New Zealand's High Court Judges*, table 4.3.

108   See ch 7, table 4, 132 and 136.

109   See chs 8–10

110   See ch 7, table 7, 135.

111   See chs 7–9. See also comments by Judge Carolyn Henwood, in Ruth Nichol, 'Legal eagle at work in the wings,' *Dominion*, 16 August 1993, 11.

112   Law Practitioners Act 1982, section 62(2). This Act specifically prohibits law societies issuing to QCs practising certificates that would enable them to practise as solicitors, alone or in partnership with other lawyers.

113   'Being learned in law,' 288.

114   Law Practitioners Act 1982, section 62(1); Queen's Counsel Regulations 1987, regulation 3.

115   'Practice note: procedure for the appointment of Queen's Counsel,' 476; 'Procedures for the appointment of Queen's Counsel,' 9.

116   Ibid.

117   'King's Counsel,' 240.

118   'People,' *LawTalk*, no 395, 28 June 1993, 2; 'People,' *LawTalk*, no 417, 11 July 1994, 2; 'People,' *LawTalk*, no 434, 15 May 1995, 4–5.

119   See ch 8.

120   'Practice note: procedure for the appointment of Queen's Counsel,' paras 4 and 5.

121   'Procedures for the appointment of Queen's Counsel,' 9.

122   *NZ Maori Council v Attorney-General* [1992] 2 NZLR 576 (CA).

123   President of the Court of Appeal Sir Robin Cooke, remarks on the admission to the inner Bar of Sian Elias and Lowell Goddard: Cooke, 'Women in the law (I),' 147.

124   Gatfield, *Women Judges*, table 1 and para 1.1.

125   'Practice note: procedure for the appointment of Queen's Counsel,' para 9(b).

126   'Procedures for appointment of Queen's Counsel,' 9.

127   Hon Paul East, speech notes, LawLink Conference, 19 March 1993, 8, reproduced in *Council Brief*, no 205, May 1993, 8.

128   Sargisson, 21.

129   Information provided by: the Tribunals Division, Department of Justice, (as at 7 October 1993); the Broadcasting Standards Authority, the Police Complaints Authority, the Video Recordings Authority, and the Legal Services Board (all as at 20 October 1993); and the Lands and Deeds Registry, the Commerce Commission, the Law Commission, the Securities Commission and the Ombudsman's Office (all as at September 1993).

130   Cabinet Office statistics provided by the Ministry of Women's Affairs, letter, 12 March 1996.

131   Ministry of Women's Affairs, letter, 12 March 1996. Women lawyers' popularity for appointments is aided by statutory criteria for some positions which require that appointees hold a practising certificate or, as for judicial

appointments, have 7 years' legal experience.

132 The estimated number of legally qualified women includes 1,940 in private practice (1995), 136 barristers (1995) and 843 'other legal professionals' (1991).

133 Hodder, 85, note x.

134 Gatfield, *Biographies of New Zealand's High Court Judges*, table 5.1.

Chapter Thirteen

1 Potter, 34.

2 'Breakthrough strategies for women managers,' 'Challenges of the nineties,' paper presented at the Institute for International Research conference, April 1995, Auckland.

3 'Waikato University,' *AWLA Monthly Update*, May 1996, 2–3.

4 Gatfield and Gray, para 9.3.

5 Ibid, table 27 and para 8.2.

6 Ibid, para 8.1.

7 Ibid, para 8.5.

8 Ibid, table 25.

9 'Women in the profession,' 1993; McManus, 30.

10 'More scope urged for women lawyers,' 1.

11 See ch 6.

12 CDLS, letter, 11 April 1994; ODLS, letter, 28 March 1994.

13 NZLS meeting of the conveners of women lawyers' groups, minutes, 16 September 1993.

14 'Women in law: proposed consultative group: summary of comments,' WWLA, distributed to group representatives 15 February 1994; letter to NZLS, 23 February 1994

15 NZLS board minutes, 4 March 1994. The inaugural members of the WCG were Ema Aitken, Kate Davenport, Brenda Heather, Shuna Lennon, Linda Penno, Anne Todd and Karen Wickliffe.

16 'Women's Consultative Group meets,' 1.

17 NZLS WCG minutes, 29 July 1994, 16 November 1994, 24 February 1995, 28 July 1995, 10 November 1995

135 Ibid.

136 'People,' *LawTalk*, no 417, 11 July 1994, 2.

137 Palmer, 'Judicial selection and accountability,' 41–42.

138 Gatfield and Gray, para 5.4.

139 NZLS WCG minutes, 10 November 1995, 4.

18 'New Zealand Law Society 98th annual report.'

19 *LawTalk*, no 458, 24 June 1996, 1.

20 Gatfield and Gray, para 9.2.

21 'NZLS committee nominations for 1995,' 6.

22 See chs 4 and 6 for discussion about the exclusion of women from Bar dinners and functions, opposition to inclusion of partnership discrimination in human rights legislation, and reluctance to act in response to findings of discrimination.

23 These views were expressed at the 1993 NZ Law Conference Open Forum and at the Suffrage Centennial Women's Law Conference Women Lawyers' Forum; Charters, 4.

24 Fourteen percent of individual women lawyers worked an average 4 hours per week for women's groups and another 20% were involved in community law centres: Gatfield and Gray, para 5.4.

25 'Women candidates succeed in council election,' *Council Brief*, April 1995.

26 'From the districts,' 14–18. See also 'New Zealand Practitioners Disciplinary Tribunal, Chairman's Report 1995–96,' in *NZLS Annual Report to Year Ended 30 November 1995*, 22.

27 Secretary, NZLS Ethics Committee, memorandum, 2 September 1993, NZLS files.

28 Sian Elias, letter to Bruce Slane, president of the NZLS, 15 September 1982.

29 *Council Brief*, July 1993, 3.

30 Gatfield, *Wellington District Law Society Scoping Study*.

31   CDLS, letter, 11 April 1994; ODLS, letter, 28 March 1994.

32   Gatfield, *Report,* vol 2 of *Towards 2000,* paras 8.2 and 8.3, and appendix 6.

33   NZ Law Foundation, *Annual Report and Statement of Accounts for the year ended 31 December 1995;* 'Law Foundation assists gender projects,' 5.

34   *Northern Law News,* 25 January 1991, 7 June 1991 and 6 September 1991.

35   ADLS, 'EEO policy,' 1991; 'Society adopts equal employment opportunities policy.'

36   Employment Equity Act 1990.

37   'Denese Bates reads Bill Birch an EEO lecture.'

38   'Minister keeps open option on EEO law.'

39   'Society adopts EEO principles,' *Council Brief,* March 1994, 1.

40   'NZLS board business review,' 5.

41   Forbes, 13.

42   'A view from the NZ Law Conference,' *AWLA Monthly Update,* May 1996, 1.

43   Fisher.

44   Simpson Grierson Butler White, *Summing Up,* March 1993, 1.

45   'Glaister Ennor breaks partnership tradition,' *National Business Review,* 10 September 1993, 24.

46   'Bars remain for women lawyers,' *Sunday Star Times,* 16 June 1996, C5.

47   Ibid.

48   Gatfield and Gray, table 17.

49   Ibid, para 8.4.

50   Ibid, paras 8.2 and 8.3.

51   'Patchy EEO take-up among Wellington firms,' *Council Brief,* December 1994, 5.

52   Gatfield, *Report,* vol 2 of *Towards 2000,* paras 5.0–8.0.

53   Ibid, para 9.8.

Chapter Fourteen

1   'Attitudes' were the main reason volunteered by both sexes (125 women and 80 men) as to why women lawyers did not have the same opportunities as men lawyers: Gatfield and Gray, 'Questionnaire comments summary paper,' question 30.

2   Twelve percent of women and 35% of men thought discrimination was not a problem. Those women lawyers were more likely to be over 30 years of age than women in the sample as a whole and the men lawyers holding that view were more likely to be over 40 years than men in the sample as a whole: Gatfield and Gray, para 8.1.

3   In the 1991 census, 55% of married women were in the labour force part time or full time.

4   For example, see National Advisory Council on the Employment of Women; Olsson; Sayers and Tremaine; Durham, Salmond and Eberly; C M Research (NZ) Ltd.

5   Gatfield and Gray, table 15.

6   Ibid, para 6.2.

7   Sex discrimination is not the only problem. Except in relation to religious discrimination, women lawyers are more likely than men lawyers to say they have experienced discrimination: ibid, table 27.

8   Ibid, para 7.1.

9   Ibid, para 7 2.

10   Ibid, table 26.

11   Cockayne, 62. Helen Melrose's story about being a partner in a large firm is typical. She recounted: 'As a partner I'm isolated just by being a woman as well as by having ideas which aren't very compatible with male ideas. It's not easy to discuss some things with women who were partners because of my loyalty to the firm. I'm also cut off from other staff because of my status': 'Helen Melrose,' 91.

12   'Letters,' *LawTalk,* no 446, 6 November 1995, 2; 'Letters,' *LawTalk,* no 448, December 1995, 4.

13   Clubs were exempt from the provisions of the Human Rights Commission Act 1977 by section 24 and from the Human Rights Act 1993 by section

14 Furness, 793; Hughes-Pollock, 1015; Dawson, 127.

15 Classified advertisements, *LawTalk*, no 395, 28 June 1993, 8.

16 D J Lyon, letter to editor, *LawTalk*, no 398, 9 August 1993, 3. In the Human Rights Act 1993, as from 1 February 1994, the 6-partner discrimination threshold was removed.

17 Human Rights Act 1993, section 73; Human Rights Commission Act 1977, section 29.

18 Gatfield, *Report*, vol 2 of *Towards 2000*, para 10.9.

19 This is not unique to NZ. Critics of the 2-year national study on gender equality in the legal profession by the Canadian Bar Association included those who claimed, despite the evidence, that discrimination simply did not exist: Johnstone, 21.

20 WDLS council minutes, 7 December 1983 and 7 March 1984.

21 ODLS, letter, 28 March 1994.

22 'Survey findings consistent,' *GP Weekly*, 19 July 1995.

23 See also chs 7–9.

24 *Report for the Principal Family Court Judge*, a review of the Family Court, April 1993.

25 Forty-nine percent of the men who said no action should be taken were partners: Gatfield and Gray, paras 8.1 and 8.5, and table 25.

26 McLauchlan, 86.

27 Dugdale, 'Some polite observations on law reform,' 93.

28 Dugdale, 'Films Videos and Publications Classification Bill,' 17; Ursula Cheer, 'Correspondence: letter to editor' [1993] NZLJ 103.

Chapter Fifteen

1 See ch 1.

2 Backhouse, 1–31.

The first note continues:
44(4). In any case, these organisations are formed for the purpose of advancing women's position in the law and would be exempt under section 29 of the 1977 Act and section 73 of the 1993 Act.

29 William Johnston, letter to editor, *LawTalk*, no 390, 19 April 1993, 4.

30 Helen Melrose, 95.

31 ADLS, *Report of the Working Party*, para 4.4.4. In 1992, 55% of women partners had personal experience of discrimination compared with 69% of women non-partners: Gatfield and Gray, para 8.2.

32 Hon Paul East, Attorney-General, speech at the swearing in of Justice Sian Elias, 29 September 1995, 7.

33 *New Zealand Listener*, 16 January 1988.

34 Powell, 13; 'President's column,' *Canterbury Tales*, July 1994, 2.

35 Committee on Women, 5.

36 'Women in the law (II),' 150.

37 Ibid; Cooke, 'Women in the law (I),' 147; Downey, 1.

38 'Graham proposes integrated justice,' *Dominion*, 15 September 1993, 2; French, 151.

39 A 1990 study of women's position in NZ society came to the 'inescapable conclusion' that 'women still do not enjoy the same range of opportunities and life chances as men': Department of Statistics and Ministry of Women's Affairs, 10.

40 Statistics New Zealand, *All About Women in New Zealand*, 73.

41 Gatfield and Gray, para 8.7.

42 Ibid, para 4.12, 14.

43 See ch 7.

44 Gatfield, *Early Women Lawyers*.

45 1991 census data indicated that the majority of men lawyers continued in the profession until their retirement at age 60 years or older and were employers or self-employed.

46 See the appendix, table A1, 449–450 and table A6, 454.

47 See the appendix, table A1, 449–450 and table A8, 455.

48 See ch 7, table 21, 157.

49 See ch 7, table 2, 131.

3 Mossman, 'Women lawyers in twentieth century Canada,' 81.

4   *Hall v Incorporated Society of Law Agents,*
    1901, in Sachs and Wilson, 27–28.

5   *The Times,* 3 December 1903, in Sachs
    and Wilson, 28.

6   *Bebb v Law Society* [1914] 1 Ch 286.

7   *Schlesin v Incorporated Law Society,* 1909
    and *Incorporated Law Society v Wookey,*
    1912, in Sachs and Wilson, 36–38.

8   Epstein, 184–188; Berger Morello, 209–
    213.

9   Frances Joychild, legal adviser, Human
    Rights Commission, letter, 2 September
    1993.

10 Curtin, 18.

11 *Law Practice Management,* March 1992,
    31.

12 Ibid, March/April 1993, 12.

13 Gatfield and Gray, para 8.5.

14 Ibid, para 9.3.

15 Professor Kathleen Mahoney, WDLS
    meeting, 11 April 1994.

16 Willis, 3.

17 Discrimination complaints double,'
    Dominion, 4 April 1995, 8. In the year
    to 30 June 1995, the Human Rights
    Commission received 257 complaints,
    of which sex discrimination com-
    plaints made up 18% and sexual
    harassment complaints made up 12%:
    Tirohia, Human Rights Commission
    newsletter, December 1995, 10.

18 McGuire, 12.

19 Joychild, 54–59.

20 Ibid, 51–52.

21 NZLS, *Rules of Professional Conduct
    for Barristers and Solicitors,* 2nd ed,
    Wellington, 1993.

22 Gatfield and Gray, para 8.4.

23 Human Rights Act 1993, section 86(3).

24 Ibid, section 68(1).

25 Ibid, section 65.

26 Chen, 'Inadequacies of New Zealand's
    discrimination law,' 140.

27 Human Rights Act 1993, section 2
    (definition of 'employer').

28 Ibid, section 23. See also *Tirohia,*
    Human Rights Commission newsletter,
    July 1995, 7, and December 1995, 6.

29 *Law Practice Management,* March 1992,
    27. See also Human Rights Com-
    mission, *Pre-employment Guidelines.*

30 *Law Practice Management,* March 1992,
    27.

31 This recruitment strategy is apparently
    used by many law firms: Caldwell,
    'Graduate employment,' 162. See also
    ch 8.

32 In 1987, the Equal Opportunities
    Tribunal pointed out that the Act does
    not permit the selection of applicants
    to achieve a balance of the sexes: *Parr
    v Broadcasting Corp of NZ* (1987) EOC
    92-205.

33 Human Rights Act 1993, section 22(2).

34 Human Rights Act 1993, section
    22(1)(c); Employment Contracts Act
    1991, section 28(1)(b).

35 *Australian Iron & Steel Pty Ltd v Banovic*
    (1989) 168 CLR 165; EOC 92-271.

36 Human Rights Act 1993, section
    22(1)(c); Employment Contracts Act
    1991, section 28(1)(b).

37 *Proceedings Commissioner v Howell*
    [1993] 2 ERNZ 130.

38 Human Rights Act 1993, section
    21(1)(l)(i).

39 Ibid, section 21(2)(b).

40 Gatfield and Gray, table 24.

41 *Human Rights Commission v Ocean Beach
    Freezing Co Ltd* (1984) EOC 92-004.

42 Human Rights Act 1993, section
    22(1)(b); Employment Contracts Act
    1991, section 28(1)(a).

43 *Employment Contracts,* para HR22.10.

44 Richard Bennett, legal adviser, Human
    Rights Commission, interview, 5
    August 1996.

45 Human Rights Act 1993, section
    22(1)(b).

46 *Proceedings Commission v Air NZ Ltd*
    (1989) 2 NZELC 96,614; EOC 92-258.

47 *Tirohia,* Human Rights Commission
    newsletter, December 1995, 6.

48 Ibid, July 1995, 7.

49 See ch 7, table 6, 135.

50 Gatfield and Gray, table 25.

51 Human Rights Act 1993, section 36;
    Gatfield, 'New laws on discrimination,'
    9–10.

52 *Seitz v Peat Marwick Maine & Co* 704 F
    Supp 157 (ND III 1989), in *Law Practice
    Management,* March 1992, 30.

53 *Price Waterhouse v Hopkins*, 104 L Ed 2d 268 (1989), in *Law Practice Management*, March 1992, 27.

54 Presser, 24.

55 Hansen, 'Partner in name only,' 26–27.

56 For example, see *O'Dea v Transportation Auckland Corp* (1995) EOC 92-719.

57 See chs 11 and 14.

58 *Halbrook v Reichhold Chemicals Inc* 735 F Supp 121 (SDNY 1990), in *Law Practice Management*, March 1992, 31.

59 Morrison. Anita Hill, a law professor, testified at the confirmation hearings for Supreme Court nominees that Clarence Thomas had sexually harassed her when she worked for him in the early 1980s.

60 McPherson, 1.

61 *Report of the Human Rights Commission and the Office of the Race Relations Conciliator*, 30 June 1991 and 10 June 1993.

62 'Flood of human rights complaints,' *Sunday Star-Times*, 13 March 1994, A6.

63 Jefferies, 6.

64 *Tirohia*, Human Rights Commission newsletter, October 1995, 8. The Human Rights Commission received 631 inquiries and informal sexual harassment complaints in the year to June 1995.

65 *Report of the Human Rights Commission and the Office of the Race Relations Conciliator*, 10 June 1993; Joychild, 59.

66 See Wendy Davis, Wellington Working Women's Week paper, in 'Inequity seen in harassment rulings,' *Dominion*, 16 March 1994, 19; Joychild, 58–59 and 69.

67 *New Law Journal*, 8 November 1991, 1514.

68 McPherson, 1.

69 Gatfield and Gray, table 29 and appendix II, question 35.

70 Human Rights Act 1993, section 62(1); Employment Contracts Act 1991, section 29(1).

71 Human Rights Act 1993, section 62(2); Employment Contracts Act 1991, section 29(1)(b).

72 Women lawyers referred to clients, other colleagues and staff solicitors as the people responsible for sexual harassment, but most of all they mentioned partners and employers: Gatfield and Gray, table 30.

73 Human Rights Act 1993, section 69(2); Employment Contracts Act 1991, section 36 (also covers co-workers).

74 *American Bar Association Journal*, January 1992, 26.

75 'Too little, too late,' 5.

76 '$11.9 m award over sex harassment,' *Dominion*, 3 September 1994, 5.

77 Human Rights Act 1993, section 68(1) and (3).

78 Joychild, 50.

79 NZLS, *Submission on the Human Rights Bill*, 10.

80 *Fulton v Chiat Day Mojo Ltd* [1992] 2 ERNZ 38.

81 *NZ Van Lines Ltd v Proceedings Commissioner* [1995] 1 NZLR 100, 102; [1994] 2 ERNZ 140, 142.

82 *Sloggett v Taranaki Health Care Ltd* [1995] 1 ERNZ 553; (1995) 4 NZELC 98,335 (Digest).

83 Human Rights Commission, *Sexual Harassment in the Workplace*, 20–41.

84 *X v AB Co Ltd* [1994] 2 ERNZ 419.

85 Human Rights Act 1993, section 89(1).

86 Ibid, section 88.

87 Ibid, section 86(3).

88 *Gazette*, 20 May 1992.

89 *Wagstaff v Elida Gibbs Ltd*, in *New Law Journal*, 141, 8 November 1991, 1516.

90 Human Rights Act 1993, section 81(5).

91 *Tirohia*, Human Rights Commission newsletter, May 1994, 7.

92 Ibid, December 1995, 6.

93 *EEO Trust News*, no 14, June 1996, 1

94 *NZ Association of Polytechnic Teachers v Nelson Polytechnic* [1991] 1 ERNZ 662.

95 Joychild, 76.

96 *L v M Ltd* [1994] 1 ERNZ 123; (1994) 4 NZELC 98,260 (Digest).

97 For example, the Complaints Review Tribunal may grant an order that the defendant perform any act with a view to redressing any loss or damage suffered: Human Rights Act 1993, section 86(2)(d).

98 *Price Waterhouse v Hopkins* 104 L Ed 2d 268 (1989), in *Law Practice Management*, March 1992, 32–33.

99 *Gazette*, 9 February 1994, 3.

100 'Lawyer wins sex bias case,' *Solicitors' Journal*, 4 March 1994.

101 *Hill v Water Resources Commission of NSW* (1985) EOC 92-127, in *Law Institute Journal*, June 1992, 502.

102 *Proceedings Commissioner v S* (1990) 3 NZELC 97,684; [1990] NZAR 333; *Proceedings Commissioner v Pryor* [1993] 1 ERNZ 358; (1993) 4 NZELC 98,215 (Digest); *Proceedings Commissioner v Armourguard Security Ltd* (1992) EOC 92-412.

103 *NZ Van Lines Ltd v Proceedings Commissioner* [1995] 1 NZLR 100, 102; [1994] 2 ERNZ 140, 142.

104 Ibid, 107–108; 147–148.

105 Ibid, 106; 146

106 Human Rights Commission Act 1977, section 38(6)(d); Human Rights Act 1993, section 86(2)(d).

107 *NZ Van Lines Ltd v Proceedings Commissioner* [1995] 1 NZLR 100, 105, 109; [1994] 2 ERNZ 140, 146, 150.

108 Ibid, 109; 149.

109 Ibid, 108; 148–149.

110 *EEO Trust News*, no 14, June 1996, 1.

111 *NZ Maori Council v Attorney-General* [1994] 1 NZLR 513 (PC).

112 State-Owned Enterprises Act 1986, section 4.

113 Human Rights Act 1993, section 83(2).

114 Ibid, section 89(2).

115 Ibid, section 153(1). An employee, however, must choose the personal grievance procedure under the Employment Contracts Act 1991 or the complaints process under the Human Rights Act 1993 for harassment and discrimination complaints: Human Rights Act 1993, section 64 and Employment Contracts Act 1991, section 39.

116 High Court Rules, rule 78.

117 Human Rights Act 1993, section 75(d) and (e).

118 Human Rights Commission, *Women in Banking*, conclusion.

119 Human Rights Commission, *Progress Report*, 18.

120 'Protecting rights through public inquiries,' *Tirohia*, Human Rights Commission newsletter, August 1994, 6.

121 In 1994, the Human Rights Commission declined a request by the NZ Council of Trade Unions that it investigate sex discrimination in job evaluation schemes. Apparently, the reason given for declining the request was a lack of resources.

122 New Zealand Bill of Rights Act 1990, sections 19 and 3(a).

123 Ibid, section 3(b).

124 Potter, 'Collective responsibility,' 13.

125 'Pro-women convention under-used,' 3.

126 'Case for women MPs may be taken to United Nations,' *Dominion*, 24 November 1994, 2.

127 *Law Society of British Columbia v Andrews* 56 DLR (4th) 1, 32–33.

128 Cartwright, 'Violence and water,' 2; Parliament of the Commonwealth of Australia; Canadian Bar Association, *Touchstones for Change*, ch 10.

129 See ch 12. 'Male dominance in the judiciary detracts from its independence': Adama Deing, Secretary-General of the International Commission of Jurists, WDLS meeting, 4 May 1994.

Chapter Sixteen

1 Gatfield and Gray, table 26.

2 Ibid, table 29.

3 Hansen, 'Texas firm sued.'

4 Gatfield and Gray, para 8.3.

5 Joychild.

6 The tendency for lawyers to blame the person rather than the system is relevant also in the implementation of quality management: L'Estrange and Vicig.

7   McNaughton, 7.

8   McPherson, 5.

9   Stuart, 80.

10   Catherine Ashley-Jones, Treasury economist, WWLA meeting on tax and childcare issues, 23 March 1994.

11   *Contact*, 3 February 1994, 1.

12   Gatfield and Gray, para 5.9.

13   Ibid, para 5.8.

14   Ibid, paras 5.1 and 5.2.

15   This observation was made by a number of psychologists who have counselled lawyers over the past 5–10 years. See also Mary Stevens, Stress Management, WWLA, 25 May 1994; 'Work stress affects families' health,' 2.

16   Caldwell, 'Practice survey,' 254.

17   Winsborough and Allen; Kay Allen and David Winsborough, interview, 10 February 1994.

18   Caldwell, 'Practice survey,' 255.

19   As some of the principals pointed out, recent graduates 'were likely to be ill-prepared for the commercial realities and competition of modern legal practice' and so might experience 'particularly severe stress': Caldwell, 'Practice survey,' 254–255.

20   Gatfield and Gray, para 4.8.

21   Ibid, para 5.7.

22   Kaye Allen and David Winsborough, interview, 10 February 1994.

23   Doug Arcus, interview.

24   Winsborough and Allen.

25   'Job stress cools Kiwi love life,' *Sunday Star-Times*, 4 September 1994, A3; 'No sex please, we're too busy,' *Dominion*, 2 August 1994, 1.

26   David Winsborough, interview. See also Nefertari, 46.

27   Knight, 4–6, 12 and 19–20.

28   Winsborough and Allen.

29   Palmer, 'Judicial selection and accountability,' 74.

30   Banwell, 205.

31   Mucalov, 18.

32   Ibid, 19–20.

33   An exception to this is the ADLS Friends Panel which met with grief and trauma consultant John McEwan in August 1995 to obtain advice on how

to identify work, family and health stress: 'Work stress affects families, health,' 2.

34   Davenport, 24.

35   Mucalov, 18.

36   'Kiwis among most stressed workers, says world survey,' *Dominion*, 14 November 1994, 3.

37   Gatfield and Gray, paras 5.5 and 5.9. See also Davenport, 23.

38   Gatfield and Gray, para 5.5 and table 15.

39   Johnson, 5; Galinsky, Johnson and Friedman.

40   Gatfield and Gray, para 10.3.

41   Catherine Ashley-Jones, Treasury economist, WWLA tax and childcare meeting, 23 March 1994; Horsfield, chs 1 and 2.

42   Gatfield and Gray, para 10.6.

43   Ibid, para 10.6.

44   See ch 7, table 2, 131.

45   Statistics New Zealand, *New Zealand Now: Families*; Statistics New Zealand, *New Zealand Now: 65 Plus*; Statistics New Zealand, *Demographic Trends*. See also Koreman, 3; McNaughton.

46   McNaughton, 5.

47   Ibid.

48   Gatfield and Gray, table 26.

49   Ibid, para 8.2.

50   For example, see two advertisements for Asian lawyers in *Northern Law News*, December 1994.

51   Gatfield and Gray, para 6.5.

52   Sykes, 369–370; Gatfield, *Report*, vol 2 of *Towards 2000*, para 9.3.5.

53   Gatfield, *Report*, vol 2 of *Towards 2000*, paras 9.2–9.5.

54   Ibid, paras 9.4.3–9.4.5.

55   Gatfield, *Discrimination in the Legal Profession*.

56   Burke-Kennedy, 64.

57   EEO Trust, *EEO Success Stories*.

58   *The Independent*, 25 June, 1993, 16.

59   Law Society of New South Wales, *Equal Opportunity Task Force Report*, 14–15.

60   See *Creating Wealth: Women*, Creating Wealth Ltd brochure, 1994; Sharyn Cederman, 'How to target a powerful

market,' Women's Entrepreneur Network, 17 November 1994.

61 'Breaking down the boardroom door,' *Dominion* 27 April 1994, 23; 'Time for courage in the boardroom,' *Dominion*, 25 May 1994, 21; 'Evidence of bank discrimination,' *Dominion*, 14 November 1994, 11.

62 Law Commission, *Women's Access to Justice: He Putanga Mo Nga Wahine Ki Te Tika*, newsletters, January 1996 and June 1996; Morris, 'Women's access to justice.'

63 Rosener.

64 Amendments to human rights law have been proposed in Australia: Australian Law Commission.

65 *LawTalk*, no 410, 13.

66 'New Zealand Law Society Practice Management Committee,' 9.

67 Doug Arcus, NZLS Practice Management Committee, interview.

68 *LawTalk*, no 414, 30 May 1994, 3.

69 Broadcasting Act 1989, section 41.

70 See ch 8.

71 Doug Arcus, 16.

72 Bradley, 13.

73 *National Business Review*, 23 April 1993, 18.

74 'New management style for large law firms,' 5; 'Management task to build on partners' skills,' 3.

75 A telephone survey of six medium to large sized human resources and personnel consultancy companies in Auckland in September 1995 revealed that while larger law firms used their services on a regular basis, none had small or medium sized law firms as clients.

76 Gatfield, *Report*, vol 2 of *Towards 2000*, paras 4.0 and 10.0.

77 L'Estrange and Vicig, 9.

78 Ibid; 'Quality management,' 9.

79 For example, see Howell.

80 Margaret Wilson, Waikato University law school paper, 1994, 14.

81 Professor Tony Angelo, dean of the Victoria University of Wellington law school, *Council Brief*, September 1992. Compare with Gatfield, *Report*, vol 2 of *Towards 2000*, para 9.9.1.

82 Palmer, 'Lawyer as lobbyist'; Chen and Palmer, 'Practical issues for lawyers.'

83 *Fortune*, 11 April 1994, 2–7.

84 An ability to manage diversity has been included as one of eight key business skills considered essential to career advancement: *Fortune*, 15 January 1996, 26–27.

85 Gatfield and Gray, para 4.3.

86 Bernard Brown, 21.

87 Nine percent of men lawyer-parents surveyed had the sole or main responsibility for the care of children compared with 54% of women lawyer-parents: Gatfield and Gray, para 10.2.

88 For example, Joanne Morris, a law commissioner, described as a parent how she was required to participate in a wider range of societal institutions, for example, education, recreation and health and was more vulnerable to a wider range of social problems affecting her children, such as child abuse and sexism, than non-parents. In her view, these experiences added an extra dimension to the skills and knowledge she brought to her paid work, including making her more efficient: Morris, 155.

89 Gatfield, *Report*, vol 2 of *Towards 2000*, paras 9.1–9.8 and 12.2–12.5.

90 Van Etten. See John Nothdurf's comments about the Australian profession: *Northern Law News*, no 30, 21 August 1992, 1.

91 Heather McDonald, 28–30.

92 Johnson, 7.

93 Ibid, 8–9.

94 Families At Work and Top Drawer Consultants.

95 Ibid, 20.

96 Torrie, 208.

Chapter Seventeen

1 Orange; McHugh; Sharp.

2 Tremaine, 72–86; Spoonley, 87–98; Doherty, 257–264; May Paki-Slater,

address to Auckland EEO Interest Group, 18 April 1996.

3   The issue of the difficult access to the profession for Maori was raised, possibly for the first time, by Major Te Wheoro, a member of the House of Representatives, during the debates on the 1882 Law Practitioners Bill: NZPD, 41, 390.

4   Cockayne, para 3.5.2, 10.

5   In 1996, Georgina Te Heuheu, a member of the Waitangi Tribunal, is possibly the first Maori woman law graduate to stand for Parliament.

6   For example, see Milroy, 35–36; 'Celebrating wahine,' *City Voice*, 2 December 1993, 9; Henare, 13–14; Archie, 62.

7   Prue Kapua, interview.

8   Sykes, 164.

9   The author discovered this when asking the NZLS for contact details for Te Hunga Roia Maori o Aotearoa (the Maori Law Society) in July 1993.

10   'Bragging ad raises nasty old skeletons,' *Sunday Star*, 6 June 1993.

11   Gatfield, *Report*, vol 2 of *Towards 2000*, para 9.3.5.

12   Wolf, 332.

13   See ch 18.

14   Palmer, 'Judicial selection and account-ability,' 35.

15   See chs 18 and 19.

16   Two valuable guides to implementing an EEO plan are: Human Rights Commission, *Manual on Equal Employment Opportunities* and ADLS, *Equal Employment Opportunities Kit.*

17   Gatfield, *Report*, vol 2 of *Towards 2000*, para 4.0. In relation to local government, see Kolhase, 270. In relation to education, see Court, 230. In relation to the private sector, see McNaughton, 305–310. In general, see Ellis, 290–294.

18   Gatfield and Gray, table 31 and para 8.5.

19   Gatfield, *Report*, vol 2 of *Towards 2000*, para 12.2.

20   See ch 15.

21   See ch 16.

22   Gatfield, *Report*, vol 2 of *Towards 2000*, table 20.

23   ADLS, *Equal Employment Opportunities Kit*, 1993, appendix E.

24   The ISO has developed a series of internationally uniform quality assurance standards relating to the delivery of services.

25   State Sector Act 1988, section 60. Other public sector employers, such as those in the education service, are also required by law to appoint the person best suited to the position.

26   *Sewell v Sandle* [1973] 2 NZLR 584 (CA).

27   *Mansell v Commissioner of Police* [1993] 2 ERNZ 646.

28   Human Rights Commission Act 1977, section 15(1).

29   Human Rights Act 1993, section 22(1).

30   *Employment Contracts*, para HR27.04.

31   Public Service Reform Act 1984, section 33(1)(b), in Burton, 24.

32   See ch 8.

33   Human Rights Act 1993, section 73. See also ch 14.

34   Human Rights Commission, *Sexual Harassment in the Workplace*, 12–19.

35   ADLS, *Equal Employment Opportunities Kit*, 57–59.

36   *Make Your Workplace 'Family-Friendly,'* 11.

37   McNaughton, 9; Families at Work and Top Drawer Consultants.

38   *Work and Family Responsibilities*, 53–54.

39   EEO Trust, *Making the Most of a Diverse Workforce*, 22–23.

40   'Will we all work at home?' 16.

41   Ibid, 17.

42   'More and more firms outsourcing,' 9.

43   *Work and Family Responsibilities*, 38–42.

44   Association of Women Solicitors.

45   Gatfield and Gray, paras 5.7 and 10.6.

46   Altman Weil Pensa, letter to *LawTalk*, 21 September 1993.

47   Human Rights Act 1993, section 21(1)(i): discrimination on the grounds of family status (which includes having responsibility for the part-time or full-time care of children or other dependants) is unlawful. See also the Parental Leave and Employment Protection Act 1987, section 49.

48   Gatfield and Gray.

49   Ibid, 'Respondent questionnaire summary,' question 33. Similar comments were made in the 1995 ADLS survey: Gatfield, *Report*, vol 2 of *Towards 2000*, para 13.10. See also 'E-DEC consultation meeting with women lawyers,' *WWLA Newsletter*, July 1996.

50   Interview with Rae Mazengarb, editor, *LawTalk*, 8 May 1996. See also chs 13 and 14.

51   Gatfield, *Report*, vol 2 of *Towards 2000*, vol 2, para 10.8.

52   Law Practitioners Act 1982, sections 4 and 26.

53   Gatfield, *Report*, vol 2 of *Towards 2000*, vol 2, 1996, para 10.8.

54   Sonja Chapham, secretary of the NZ Bar Association, 22 September 1993.

55   Information which is collected but which · does not identify gender includes: law school student grades; IPLS student employment status information; NZ Vice-Chancellors' Committee data on unemployed law graduates; information about the appointment to law society committees and councils; and district law society associate membership data.

56   For an explanation of the arguments in support of a comprehensive EEO database and the Privacy Act 1993

57   considerations, see Gatfield, *Report*, vol 2 of *Towards 2000*, para 10.5.

57   See ch 18. See also note 24.

58   'Guidelines to ISO 9000,' *NZLS Annual Report For Year Ended 30 November 1995*, 18.

59   In July 1996, the Law Society of Upper Canada reported its intention to invite the managing partners of the 50 largest law firms to submit their firm's equity programmes to the law society: *Lawyers Weekly*, 16(11), 19 July 1996, 2.

60   See chs 15 and 16.

61   See ch 13.

62   Richard Moss, interview, 5 May 1992.

63   WDLS Flying Start Programme, 18 February 1995.

64   *More*, October 1989, 173.

65   'President's column,' *Council Brief*, May 1994, 3.

66   Gatfield, *Report*, vol 2 of *Towards 2000*, para 14.4.

67   Ibid, para 14.4.5.

68   These criteria were listed in the *Feminist Law Bulletin New Zealand Aotearoa*, no 3, February 1994, 2.

69   For a detailed analysis of law society and law office EEO complaints, procedures and recommendations, see Gatfield, *Report*, vol 2 of *Towards 2000*, para 14.6.

Chapter Eighteen

1   In its submission to the Royal Commission, the NZLS recommended the establishment of this type of body, calling it an Appointments Advisory Committee: Black. It is not known whether this proposal was supported in other submissions.

2   However it has been queried whether different people from those presently consulted would be consulted under a commission process: Keith, 241.

3   'Top judge puts case for judicial appointment reform,' *Dominion*, 12 July 1993, 1 and 12; Eichelbaum, 123; 'Remarks by the Rt Hon Sir Thomas Eichelbaum on the occasion of the swearing in of Dame Silvia Cartwright,'

28 July 1993, 3–4; 'Making of a judge,' 3. See also the appendix, table A9, 456.

4   'Commission supported for judicial appointments,' 1.

5   'East against judicial commission,' *Dominion*, 13 July 1993, 2. See also 'Attorney-General on future of legal profession,' Hon Paul East, speech notes, LawLink Conference, 19 March 1993, reproduced in *Council Brief*, no 205, May 1993, 8; 'No to judicial commission,' 7. Sir Geoffrey Palmer, the previous Attorney-General, agrees that a judicial commission is not appropriate because judges would 'drive the process': Palmer, 'Judicial selection and account-ability,' 71;

'Sitting in judgment on our judiciary,' *Sunday Star-Times*, 11 August 1996, C6.

In 1996, the Chief Justice, Sir Thomas Eichelbaum, also opposed the idea of a judicial commission, not because it would empower judges, but because it would be government-driven and therefore 'a very severe intrusion on the concept of judicial independence': 'View from the Bench,' 34.

6   'Sitting in judgment on our judiciary,' *Sunday Star Times*, 11 August 1996, C6.

7   'Doctors want judges watchdog,' *Sunday Star-Times*, 11 August 1996, A5.

8   Principal Tenancy Adjudicator circular to registrars of Tenancy Tribunals, 10 August 1992.

9   Ibid, annex A.

10   Ibid, annex D1.

11   Residential Tenancies Act 1986, section 67(3).

12   In 1993, 26 tenancy adjudicators (65%) were legally qualified, with women making up 54% of that group. An adjudicator is required to hold a practising certificate or 'an equivalent qualification issued or recognised' overseas, or, in the opinion of the Minister of Justice, is otherwise capable by reason of special knowledge or experience of performing the functions of a Tenancy Tribunal adjudicator: Residential Tenancies Act 1986, section 67(9).

13   Disputes Tribunals Act 1988, section 7(1). Although the Act does not specify that the appointment is on the recommendation of the Minister of Justice, this is implicit from section 8(3).

14   Ibid, section 8.

15   *Disputes Tribunals Referees Appointment Process*, information for panel, 1331R.

16   Disputes Tribunals Act 1988, section 7.

17   Disputes Tribunals Rules 1989, rule 38(2).

18   Ibid, rule 38(3).

19   *Disputes Tribunals Referees Appointment Process*, information for panel, 1331R.

20   'Disputes Tribunal referees selection,' (draft).

21   An EEO audit would reveal whether there are equal opportunities for other groups and whether the terms and conditions of work meet EEO standards. See ch 17.

22   See ch 12.

23   Ibid.

24   'Job description for judges,' 9.

25   See, for example, John McGrath QC, 'Speeches delivered at swearing in of Judge Craig Thompson,' *Council Brief*, August 1992, 6; Palmer, 'Judicial selection and accountability,' 40–42; Hon Paul East, 'Speech for the swearing in of Dame Silvia Cartwright,' 28 July 1993, 2–3.

26   See ch 12.

27   Ibid.

28   Lord Chancellor's Department, *Improvements in the Judicial Appointments System*, press notice, 7 July 1993.

29   *LawTalk*, no 429, 20 February 1995, 19.

30   'Situations vacant,' *LawTalk*, no 451, 4 March 1996, 21; 'Situations vacant,' *LawTalk*, no 452, April 1996, 43. In a similarly unprecedented move, membership of various appeal authorities was advertised in the situations vacant of *LawTalk*, no 451, 4 March 1996, 23.

31   Lord Chancellor's Department, press notice, 18 September 1991.

32   Palmer, 'Judicial selection and accountability,' 43.

33   Lord Chancellor's Department, *Lord Chancellor Urges More Women to Apply for Judicial Appointment: Speech to the Association of Women Solicitors*, press notice, 21 April 1993.

34   'School for judges needed,' *Dominion*, 10 September 1995.

35   *Person Specification*, Disputes Tribunal referee, 844R.

36   Joanne Morris, a law commissioner, ran a session based on the responses the Law Commission had received in its judges and lawyers' project, Elisabeth McDonald, an employee of the Law Commission, ran a session on syllogistic reasoning and evidence of prior sexual conduct, and there was a videotape on domestic violence. Half a day was also spent on cultural

issues: Joanne Morris, correspondence, 23 August 1996.

37   See ch 14.

38   'Tribunal "teaches" ex-judge,' *Evening Post*, 25 June 1991.

39   Wikler.

40   'Judge swaps Bench for books.'

41   Palmer, 'Judicial selection and accountability,' 12–13, 30 and 72.

42   'Report of Royal Commission on the Courts,' para 340.

43   Law Reform Commission, *Equality Before the Law: Law Reform Commission*, para 7.34.

44   Lord Chancellor's Department, 4.

45   McLinden, 7.

46   Lord Chancellor's Department, *Lord Chancellor Urges More · Women to Apply for Judicial Appointment: Speech to the Association of Women Solicitors*, press notice, 21 April 1993. However, two and a half months later, the chancellor modified this comment, saying: 'save only in the most exceptional circumstances, before being considered for a full-time post, a candidate must have served part time in a relevant judicial capacity': Lord Chancellor's Department, *Improvements in the Judicial Appointments System*, press notice, 7 July 1993.

47   Wallace, 34. In February 1996, the Department for Courts and the Ministry of Justice included having 'part-time lawyer-magistrates' among the options for dealing with minor matters in the District Courts: 'Lay magistrates: more efficient courts?' 4.

48   Wallace, 34.

49   It has been noted that no harm seems to have resulted from the Lord Chancellor's Department scrutiny of part-time judges: McLinden, 7.

50   Lord Chancellor's Department, 6–13.

51   For example, see 'Lay magistrates: more efficient courts?' 4.

52   Residential Tenancies Act 1986, section 67(7); Disputes Tribunals Act 1988, section 7(5).

53   *Work and Family Responsibilities*, para 1003; Families at Work and Top Drawer Consultants.

54   Off the record, judges in the District Courts and the High Court have referred to the sense of isolation they experience, especially in relation to having little contact with colleagues and friends in the profession, and working alone.

55   The Department for Courts and the Ministry of Justice have recently suggested the appointment of lay magistrates: 'Lay magistrates: more efficient courts?' 4. Historically, proposals to appoint non-lawyers have met with little support from the legal profession. This occasion is unlikely to be an exception. For example, see 'Fair trials compromised by lay magistrates plan,' 1.

56   Lay members are appointed under section 77 of the Commerce Act 1986. They sit with High Court judges and assist at hearings and in the preparation of judgments.

57   See ch 12.

58   In February 1996, the AWLA was invited to appear as amicus curiae in an appeal relating to 'battered women's syndrome' and leave to appear was sought in April 1996: *AWLA Monthly Update*, February/March 1996, 5 and April 1996, 6.

59   See ch 7, table 8, 137.

60   NZ Standard Classification of Occupations 1990, Unit Group 2423, 67.

61   Lord Chancellor's Department, 10.

62   See ch 7, table 1, 130 and table 2, 131 and ch 12.

63   The appointments of lay members has recently been considered in Australia: Parliament of the Commonwealth of Australia, 100–105.

Chapter Nineteen

1   McKay, 108.

2   Institute of Chartered Accountants of New Zealand Bill 1995, 18 TCL 31/9.

3   *New Zealand Medical Journal*, December 1994, 2–5 and February 1995, 3–6; Medical Practitioners Act 1995.

4   Medical Practitioners Act 1995, section 52.

5   Lianne Dalziel, 'A better bill to swallow.'

6   'Future of law societies in New Zealand,' 12–13.

7   'E-DEC consultation meeting with women lawyers,' *WWLA Newsletter*, July 1996.

8   David Lange, 'Lawyer mafia strung up in a dead tree,' *Dominion*, 27 July 1992, 10.

9   Hancock, 9; 'Banks rounds on lawyers,' *New Zealand Herald*, 13 April 1993, 1.

10 Paul East, 'Attorney-General on future of legal profession,' *Council Brief*, May 1993, 8.

11 'MP calls for more senior police-women,' *Evening Post*, 24 January 1994, 17.

12 State Enterprises Select Committee, *Report of the State Enterprises Committee on the 1992/1993 Review of Electricity Corporation of New Zealand Ltd*, Wellington.

13 State Enterprises Select Committee, *Report of the State Enterprises Committee on the 1992/1993 Review of GCS Ltd*, Wellington.

14 Professor Kathleen Mahoney, WDLS meeting, 11 April 1994.

15 I Y Applegren, 'Lawyers' manners,' *Sunday Times*, 20 December 1992, 8.

16 Mark Holland, 'Degrees of child abuse,' *Dominion*, 25 May 1993, 8.

17 'Judging the judges,' *Dominion*, 27 May 1994, 6. Similar reaction followed Justice Morris' inappropriate comments in a 1996 rape trial, see ch 12, 264–265.

18 Law Commission, *Women's Access to Justice: He Putanga Mo Nga Wahine Ki Te Tika*, newsletter, January 1996; Morris, 'Women's access to justice.'

19 'Street's ahead,' 88; *Votes for the Girls*, TVNZ, 8 June 1994; 'Parliament hostile to women—lobby,' *Dominion*, 9 August 1994, 10; 'Party lists an avenue for women,' *Dominion*, 30 March 1995, 8; Davies.

20 Three examples of this are pornography law reform, domestic violence law reform and tax deduct-ibility for childcare costs.

21 This is evident when reading the many submissions made by women and women's organisations on the 1977 Human Rights Commission Bill. See also Margaret Wilson, 'Making and repeal of the Employment Equity Act,' 79; Law Reform Commission, *Equality Before the Law: Justice for Women*, 69.

22 Official Information Act 1982; Privacy Act 1993; Human Rights Act 1993, Part V and sections 109–114.

23 Hyman; Scott; Waring.

24 For example, the law societies and the women lawyer's organisations. See also Else.

25 *1995 Annual Report of the EEO Trust: Year Ended 30 June 1995*.

26 *Report of the Review Team: Equal Employment Opportunities Trust*, 31 March 1995, 1–2.

27 EEO Trust, press release, May 1996.

28 This is particularly relevant where the complaint is taken under the Employment Contracts Act 1991. Under the Human Rights Act 1993, the Human Rights Commission takes the proceedings and therefore bears the costs, although some complainants also seek independent legal advice.

29 A draft ruling from the Commissioner of Inland Revenue in 1995 stated that all compensation payments received by employees under the Employment Contracts Act 1991 for personal grievances (such as sexual harassment and discrimination) would be treated as taxable income: 19 TCL 2/5. How-ever, this was not implemented and compensation for humiliation, loss of dignity and injury to feelings is not taxable.

30 See chs 10 and 13.

31 State Sector Act 1988, section 60.

32 Ministry of Women's Affairs, *Summary of Paper*, 8.

33 EEO Trust, *EEO Success Stories*, 11.

34 Ministry of Women's Affairs, *Summary of Paper*, 14.

35 Macalister, 68–70. See ch 16 for a summary of some of the reasons why

employers benefit from EEO implementation.

36   Chen, 'Reforming New Zealand's anti-discrimination law,' 179; 'Margaret Mulgan speech at launch of Human Rights Act 1993,' *Tirohia*, Human Rights Commission newsletter, May 1994, 4. This view of the law was reinforced by the decision of Justice Smelly in *NZ Van Lines Ltd v Proceedings Commissioner* [1995] 1 NZLR 100; [1994] 2 ERNZ 140.

37   Human Rights Act 1993, sections 65, 86(3) and 21(2)(b).

38   See ch 15.

39   Human Rights Act 1993, section 73(1).

40   Ibid, section 5(1)(d).

41   Jefferies.

42   Chief Human Rights Commissioner Pamela Jefferies has argued to the contrary that the 'advisory and educative' approach taken to date in NZ is appropriate: ibid.

43   Health and Safety in Employment Act 1992, section 20(1) and (9).

44   For example, see Shand. Fitzgibbon, 23; 'Health and Safety in Employment Act 1992,' NZLS seminar, May 1996.

45   See ch 16.

46   'EEO legislation a possibility: private sector must choose, and act,' *IPM News*, February/March 1996.

47   *Independent*, June 1994, 29.

48   Tennet.

49   See chs 10 and 15.

50   Tennet, 3.

51   Ibid, 1–2.

52   Galtry, 12.

53   Ibid.

54   Callister, 57.

55   Ibid, 53–54.

56   Jensen.

57   Gatfield and Gray, table 17.

58   Ibid, para 10.6.

59   Education (Early Childhood Centres) Regulations 1990.

60   ADLS, *Proposed Taxation Reform*. This submission was prepared with the assistance of the AWLA which also actively lobbied in support of the proposal. See 'Tax changes sought by women lawyers,' *New Zealand Herald*, 19 June 1989.

61   ADLS, *Proposed Taxation Reform*, 6–10.

62   Even at the stage of the 1989 working party there had been a dissenting view that tax relief would discriminate against unpaid childcarers in the home: Cockayne, 77.

63   NZLS Executive Committee, minutes, 2 March 1990, item 2.

64   Alan Ritchie, letter to the Minister of Finance, 1990.

65   Judith Potter advised the NZLS Executive Committee of this at the meeting on 2 March 1990.

66   Minister of Women's Affairs, letter to Alan Ritchie, 14 September 1990. See Ministry of Women's Affairs, *Government Funding Options For Early Childhood Care and Education*.

67   Pallot, 32.

68   *Canadian Master Tax Guide 1994*, 61, para 1350.

69   Income Tax Act 1994, section CB 12; Income Tax Act 1976, section 73.

70   Acts Interpretation Act 1924, section 4.

71   For example, see Liddicoat, 83.

72   Law Commission, 151–152.

Abel, Richard, and Phillip Lewis (eds). *The Civil Law World*. Vol 2 of *Lawyers in Society*. Berkeley: University of California Press, 1988.

———. *The Common Law World*. Vol 1 of *Lawyers in Society*. Berkeley: University of California Press, 1988.

Abella, Rosalie. 'Women in the profession: pain and frustration will be worthwhile.' *LawTalk*, no 316, 26 October 1989, 35.

ADLS *see* Auckland District Law Society

'All women team opts for lifestyle.' *LawTalk*, no 382, November 1992, 47.

Alpers, O T J. *Cheerful Yesterdays*. London: John Murray, 1928.

American Bar Association Commission on Women in the Profession. *Lawyers and Balanced Lives: A Guide to Drafting and Implementing Workplace Policies for Lawyers*. Chicago: American Bar Association, 1990.

———. *Lawyers and Balanced Lives: A Guide to Drafting and Implementing Sexual Harassment Policies for Lawyers*. Chicago: American Bar Association, 1992.

———. *Summary of Hearings*. Philadelphia: American Bar Association, 1988.

Anderson, Kathleen. 'Beyond the pioneer woman doctor: a study of women doctors in Auckland 1900–1960.' MA thesis, University of Auckland, 1992.

Archie, Carol. 'Denese Henare: not only looking the part.' *Mana*, no 13, Winter 1996, 62.

Arcus, Doug. 'Increasing variability in performance of law firms: results of the New Zealand Law Society Practice Comparison 1992.' *LawTalk*, no 387, 22 February 1993, 16.

Arcus, Ruth. 'Sexual harassment in the workplace: the responsibilities of law firm partnerships.' *LawTalk*, no 440, 7 August 1995, 16.

Association of Women Solicitors. *Guidelines for Part-time Working*. London: Law Society, 1992.

'Attorney-General: interview with Hon Paul East Attorney-General of New Zealand and Leader of the House of Representatives' [1991] NZLJ 109.

Auckland District Law Society. *Equal Employment Opportunities Kit for Law Firms*. Auckland: Auckland District Law Society, 1993.

———. 'Proposed Taxation Reform: Deductibility of Childcare Expenses.' Submission prepared with the assistance of the Auckland Women Lawyers' Association, Auckland: Auckland District Law Society, 1990.

———. *Report of the Working Party on Women in the Legal Profession*. Auckland: Auckland District Law Society, 1981.

Auckland Star, 9 June 1971–14 May 1986.

'Auckland's first woman barrister.' (1933) 5 NZLJ 92.

Backhouse, Constance. ' "To open the way for others of my sex": Clara Brett Martin's career as Canada's first woman lawyer.' *Canadian Journal of Women and the Law*, 1, 1985, 1.

Banwell, Cathy. 'I'm not a drinker really: women and alcohol.' In Julie Park (ed), *Ladies a Plate: Change and Continuity in the Lives of New Zealand Women*. Auckland: Auckland University Press, 1991, 173.

Beagley, Angela. 'Ladies at law.' BA(Hons) thesis, Otago University, 1993.

'Being learned in law: the QC qualification quiz.' [1982] NZLJ 287.

Berger Morello, Karen. *The Invisible Bar: The Woman Lawyer in America: 1638 to Present*. New York: Random House, 1986.

Birks, Michael. *Gentlemen of the Law*. London: Stevens, 1960.

Bishop, Joel Prentice. *Commentaries on the Law of Married Women under the Statutes of the Several States and at Common Law and Equity.* Vol 2. Boston: Little Brown, 1873–1875.

Black, Tony. 'Judicial appointments: time for a change.' [1978] NZLJ 41.

Blackstone, Sir William. *Commentaries on the Laws of England,* 19th ed. Vol 1. 1836.

Booth, Pat. 'Sisters in law: when will a woman's face fill this space?' *North and South,* June 1988, 65.

Bowie QC, E S. 'Canterbury.' In Sir Robin Cooke (ed), *Portrait of a Profession: The Centennial Book of the New Zealand Law Society.* Wellington: A H and A W Reed, 1969, 238.

Boxall, Peter, (ed). *The Challenge of Human Resource Management: Directions and Debates in New Zealand.* Auckland: Longman Paul, 1995.

Bradley, Graham. 'The shape of the 2000 law firm.' *Australian Lawyer,* May 1993, 10.

Briant, Robin. 'Where have all the women gone? 150 years of women in medicine.' Lecture, University of Auckland Winter Lecture Series, Auckland, 1993.

Briar, Celia, Robyn Munford and Mary Nash (eds). *Superwoman Where are You? Social Policy and Women's Experience.* Palmerston North: Dunmore Press, 1992.

Brookes, Barbara, Charlotte Macdonald and Margaret Tennant (eds). *Women in History: Essays on European Women in New Zealand.* Wellington: Allen and Unwin/Port Nicholson Press, 1986.

Brophy, J, and C Smart. *Women in Law: Explorations in Law, Family and Sexuality.* London: Routledge and Kegan Paul, 1985.

Brown, Bernard. 'Portia faces life.' *Quote Unquote,* no 35, May 1996, 21.

Brown, Carol. 'Ethel Benjamin: New Zealand's first woman lawyer.' BA(Hons) research essay, Otago University, 1985.

Bunkle, Phillida. 'The origins of the women's movement in New Zealand: the Women's Christian Temperance Union 1885–1895.' In Barbara Brookes, Charlotte Macdonald and Margaret Tennant (eds), *Women in History: Essays on European Women in New Zealand.* Auckland: Allen and Unwin, 1986, 52.

Bunkle, Phillida, and Beryl Hughes (eds). *Women in New Zealand Society.* Auckland: George Allen and Unwin, 1980.

Burke-Kennedy, David. 'Auckland's lawyers battle it out for your business.' *Metro,* August 1985, 64.

Burns, Janice, and Martha Coleman. *A Gender Neutral Approach to Designing a Generic Job Evaluation Scheme: The Development of Equity at Work: The New Zealand Experience.* July 1992.

Burton, Clare. *The Promise and the Price: The Struggle for Equal Opportunity in Women's Employment.* North Sydney: Allen and Unwin, 1991.

Byrne, Eileen. 'Women, science and the snark syndrome: myths out, policy strategies.' Shortened version of a paper presented at the Women's Suffrage Centennial Science Conference, Australia, 1993.

C M Research (NZ) Ltd. *Equal Employment Opportunities Within the NZSA.* Summary report. New Zealand Society of Accountants, 13 June 1995.

Caldwell, John L. 'Graduate employment survey.' [1990] NZLJ 162.

———. 'Practice survey: job satisfaction and attitudes.' [1991] NZLJ 254.

Callister, Paul. 'Men and childcare: an issue for public policy?' *Social Policy Journal of New Zealand,* no 5, December 1995, 53.

Canadian Bar Association Task Force on Gender Equality on the Legal Profession. *Touchstones for Change: Equality, Diversity and Accountability: Report of the Canadian Bar Association Task Force on Gender Equality in the Legal Profession.* Ottawa: Canadian Bar Association, 1993.

Cartwright, Dame Silvia. 'How are women doing 100 years later? Where are all the women in law?' In vol 1 of *The Law and Politics: 1993 New Zealand Law Conference: Conference Papers.* Wellington, 1993, 359.

———. 'Violence and water: women's issues, and the law.' *Otago Law Review,* 8(1), 1993, 1.

Charters, Ruth. 'Feminist/lawyer: an impossible dream?' *LawTalk,* no 137, 16 October 1981, 4.

Chater, Kerry, and Roma Gaster. *The Equality Myth: A Guide for Women Who Want to Make a Difference in the World of Business and for Men Who are Ready for Change.* St Leonards, New South Wales: Allen and Unwin, 1995.

Chen, Mai. 'Discrimination, law, and being a Chinese woman immigrant in New Zealand.' *Women Studies Journal,* 9(2), September 1993.

———. 'The inadequacies of New Zealand's discrimination law.' [1992] NZLJ 137.

———. 'Reforming New Zealand's anti-discrimination law.' [1992] NZLJ 172.

Chen, Mai, and Geoffrey Palmer. 'Practical issues for lawyers arising from MMP.' Paper presented at a New Zealand Law Society seminar, August 1995.

———. *Public Law in New Zealand: Cases, Materials, Commentary and Questions.* Auckland: Oxford University Press, 1993.

'Chief Judge seeks nominations for women's appointment to Bench.' *LawTalk,* no 445, 24 October 1995, 4.

'Christchurch's first lady barrister.' (1938) 14 NZLJ 179.

City Voice, 2 December 1993.

Collins, Judith. 'Women lawyers' survey lets profession "off the hook".' *Northern Law News,* 30 April 1993, 4.

Cockayne, Jeannine, (ed). *Women in the Legal Profession: The Report of the Second Working Party on Women in the Legal Profession.* Auckland: Public Relations Department of the Auckland District Law Society, 1989.

Coke, Sir Edward, Sir Thomas Littleton and Francis Hargrave. *The First Part of the Institutes of the Laws of England,* 19th ed. Vol 1. London: Clarke, Saunders and Benning, Maxwell, Sweet, Butterworth, Stevens, Pheney, and Richards, 1832.

Coleman, Martha. *Merit or Performance Related Pay.* Oxford: Trade Union Research Unit, 1993.

Collins, Judith. 'Women lawyer's survey lets profession "off the hook".' *Northern Law News,* 30 April 1993, 4.

Commission of Inquiry into Equal Pay. *Equal Pay in New Zealand: Report of the Commission of Inquiry into Equal Pay.* Wellington: Government Print, 1971.

'Commission supported for judicial appointments.' *Northern Law News,* 2 February 1996, 1.

Committee on Women. *Employment of Women in Legal Firms.* Wellington: Committee on Women, 1980.

Commonwealth Secretariat Legal Division. *A Decade of Women and the Law in the Commonwealth.* Australia: Commonwealth Secretariat Legal Division, 1985.

Coney, Sandra. 'Ellen Melville.' In Charlotte Macdonald, Merimeri Penfold and Bridget Williams (eds), *The Book of New Zealand Women: Ko Kui Ma Te Kaupapa.* Wellington: Bridget Williams Books, 1991, 442.

'The conference dinner.' (1954) 30 NZLJ 156.

Cook, Annis. 'Women go solo in Dunedin.' *LawTalk,* no 402, October 1993, 37.

Cooke, Sir Robin. 'The New Zealand national legal identity.' *Canterbury Law Review,* 3, 1987, 171.

———. 'Women in the law (I).' [1988] NZLJ 147.

Cooke, Sir Robin, (ed). *Portrait of a Profession: The Centennial Book of the New Zealand Law Society.* Wellington: A H and A W Reed, 1969.

Crossan, Diana. 'Equal employment opportunity in the public sector.' In Janet Sayers and Marianne Tremaine (eds), *The Vision and the Reality: Equal Employment Opportunities in the New Zealand Workplace*. Palmerston North: Dunmore Press, 1994, 249.

———. Presentation at a Wellington District Law Society seminar on Equal Employment Opportunities, 4 August 1993.

Cullen, Michael J. *Lawfully Occupied: The Centennial History of the Otago District Law Society*. Dunedin: Otago District Law Society, 1979.

Curtin Jr, John J. 'Combating gender bias.' *American Bar Association Journal*, April 1991.

Dakin, Stephen, and Mike Smith. 'Staffing.' In Peter Boxall (ed), *The Challenge of Human Resource Management: Directions and Debates in New Zealand*. Auckland: Longman Paul, 1995, 131.

Dale, R R. *Some Social Aspects*. Vol 2 of *Mixed or Single-Sex School?* London: Routlege and Kegan Paul, 1971.

Dalziel, Lianne. 'A better Bill to swallow.' *GP Weekly*, 13 December 1995, 9.

Dalziel, Raewyn. 'The colonial helpmeet: women's role and the vote in nineteenth century New Zealand.' In Barbara Brookes, Charlotte Macdonald and Margaret Tennant (eds), *Women in History: Essays on European Women in New Zealand*. Wellington: Allen and Unwin/Port Nicholson Press, 1986, 55.

———. 'The politics of settlement.' In Geoffrey W Rice (ed), *The Oxford History of New Zealand*, 2nd ed. Auckland: Oxford University Press, 1992.

Darwin, Charles. *The Descent of Man and Selection in Relation to Sex*, 2nd ed. London: John Murray, 1906.

Davenport, Kate. 'All women firm provides flexible work environment.' *Law Talk*, no 423, October 1994, 46.

———. 'Part time lawyering: career killer or life-saver?' *LawTalk*, no 431, April 1995, 23.

Davies, Sonja. *Bread and Roses*. Auckland: Penguin Books, 1984.

Dawson, Geoff. 'Cry freedom!' *Law Institute Journal*, 1, December 1993, 127.

'Denese Bates reads Bill Birch an EEO lecture.' *Northern Law News*, no 38, 18 October 1991.

Department of Justice. *Human Rights Commission Bill: Report of the Department of Justice to the Committee on the Human Rights Bill*. Wellington, 10 May 1977.

Department of Statistics. *New Zealand Census of Population and Dwellings, 1981-1991*. Wellington: Department of Statistics, 1982–1992.

Department of Statistics and Ministry of Women's Affairs. *Women in New Zealand*. Wellington: Department of Statistics/Ministry of Women's Affairs, 1990.

The Dictionary of New Zealand Biography: 1769–1869. Vol 1. Wellington: Allen and Unwin/Department of Internal Affairs, 1990.

'Discrimination moves under scrutiny.' *LawTalk*, no 181, 21 September 1983, 1.

Dixon and Davies. *Career Patterns in the Legal Profession and Career Expectations of Male and Female Law Students in Western Australia: A Comparative Study*. University of Western Australia Law School, 1985.

Doherty, Joe. 'EEO: the Maori perspective.' In Janet Sayers and Marianne Tremaine (eds), *The Vision and the Reality: Equal Employment Opportunities in the New Zealand Workplace*. Palmerston North: Dunmore Press, 1994.

Dominion, 13 September 1989–4 July 1996.

Dominion Sunday Times, 17 May 1992–21 July 1991.

Dooley, Sharon. 'Ivory tower idyll.' BA (Hons) thesis, Otago University, 1983.

Downey, P J. 'Women in law.' [1989] NZLJ 1.

Drachman, Virginia. 'The equity club: women lawyers and the quest for professional identity in late nineteenth century America.' *Michigan Law Review*, 88, August 1990, 2414.

Du Plessis, Rosemary, (ed). *Feminist Voices: Women's Studies Texts for Aotearoa/ New Zealand*. Auckland: Oxford University Press, 1992.

Dugdale, Donald. 'Due deference.' *LawTalk*, no 418, 25 July 1994, 9.

————. 'Films Videos and Publications Classification Bill.' [1993] NZLJ 16.

————. *Lawful Occasions: Notes on the History of the Auckland District Law Society, 1879–1979*. Auckland: Auckland District Law Society, 1979.

————. 'Some polite observations on law reform.' [1989] NZLJ 93.

Durham, Gillian, Clare Salmond and Julie Eberly. *Women and Men in Medicine: The Career Experiences*. Wellington: Health Services Research and Development Unit, Department of Health, 1989.

Dyhrberg, Marie. Review of *Eve Was Framed: Women and British Justice* by Helena Kennedy QC. *LawTalk*, no 413, 16 May 1994, 16.

Edwards, Adrienne. 'The fairer sex.' *Canterbury Tales*, October 1993, 11.

EEO Trust *see* Equal Opportunities Trust

Eichelbaum, Sir Thomas. 'Political influences in the legal profession: judicial independence: fact or fiction?' In vol 2 of *The Law and Politics: 1993 New Zealand Law Conference: Conference Papers*. Wellington, 1993, 120.

'Eliminating discrimination will benefit all: O'Regan says.' *Council Brief*, no 124, December 1985.

Ellis, Gill, and Jenny Wheeler. *Women Managers: Success on Our Own Terms: Career Strategies for New Zealand Women*. Auckland: Penguin Books, 1991.

Else, Anne, (ed). *Women Together: A History of Women's Organisations in New Zealand: Nga Ropu Wahine o te Motu*. Wellington: Historical Branch, Department of Internal Affairs/ Daphne Brasell Associates Press, 1993.

Employment Contracts. Wellington: Brooker's, 1991.

Epstein, Cynthia Fuchs. *Women in Law*. New York: Basic Books, 1981.

Equal Employment Opportunities Trust. *EEO Success Stories*. Auckland: Equal Employment Opportunities Trust, 1993.

————. *Making the Most of a Diverse Workforce: An Employer's Guide to EEO*. Auckland: Equal Employment Opportunities Trust, 1992.

Equal Opportunities Commission. *Women in the Legal Services: Evidence Submitted by the Equal Opportunities Commission to the Royal Commission on Legal Services*. London: Equal Opportunities Commission, 1978.

Evening Post, 21 August 1891–3 June 1995.

'Fair trials compromised by lay magistrates plan.' *Northern Law News*, 16 February 1996, 1.

Families At Work and Top Drawer Consultants. *Work and Family Directions: What New Zealand Champions are Doing/Te Whakapakari i ite Mahi me Te Whanau: Nga Mahi Kei te Mahia e Nga Toa o Aotearoa*. Wellington: Ministry of Women's Affairs/New Zealand Employers' Federation/Equal Employment Opportunities Trust, 1995.

'Feature: the lawyer as employer.' *LawTalk*, no 431, April 1995, 13.

'Feature: women and the law.' *LawTalk*, no 402, October 1993, 9.

'Feedback on women lawyers problems sought from all firms.' *Northern Law News*, no 37, 16 October 1989, 1.

Fenn, Henry Edwin. *Thirty-Five Years in the Divorce Court*, (colonial ed). London: T Werner Laurie.

Findlay, Katherine. 'On her honour: women on the Bench.' *More*, no 52, October 1987, 178.

First Lady in the Law. Television New Zealand documentary, 1987.

'First woman law professor.' *LawTalk*, no 399, 23 August, 1993, 3.

Fisher, Antonia. ' "Minor Proceedings": one childcare option.' *LawTalk*, no 402, October 1993, 22.

Fitzgibbon, Anna. 'Grace period gone.' *Employment Today*, March 1996, 23.

Forbes, Austin. ' "Profession in crisis": NZLS President Austin Forbes' closing address to the law conference.' *LawTalk*, no 454, 29 April 1996, 12.

Ford, H A J. *Principles of Company Law*, 2nd ed. Sydney: Butterworths, 1978.

Foster, Timothy. *Foster Harrington Book of Humorous Legal Anecdotes*. Ascot, Berkshire: Springwood Books Ltd, 1988.

French, Christine. 'How are women doing 100 years later? Balancing or juggling our private and public lives?' In vol 2 of *The Law and Politics: 1993 New Zealand Law Conference: Conference Papers*. Wellington, 1993, 149.

'From the districts.' *LawTalk*, no 448, December 1995, 14.

Fry, Ruth. 'The curriculum and girls' secondary schooling 1880–1925.' In Sue Middleton (ed), *Women and Education in Aotearoa*. Wellington: Allen and Unwin/Port Nicholson Press, 1988, 31.

———. *It's Different for Daughters: A History of the Curriculum for Girls in New Zealand Schools 1900–1975*. Wellington: New Zealand Council for Educational Research, 1985.

Furness, Peter. 'Gentlemen lawyers, where are you?' *Law Institute Journal*, September 1993, 793.

'The future of law societies in New Zealand: purpose, functions and structure.' *LawTalk*, no 448, December 1995, 12.

Galinksky, Ellen, Arlene Johnson and Dana Friedman. 'The work-life business case: an outline of a work-in-progress.' Draft paper distributed at the launch of the Equal Employment Opportunities Trust Work and Family Network, Auckland, 15 July 1996.

Galtry, Judith. 'Breastfeeding, labour market changes and public policy in New Zealand: is promotion of breastfeeding enough?' *Social Policy Journal of New Zealand*, no 5, December 1995, 2.

Gardner, W J. *Colonial Cap and Gown: Studies in the Mid-Victorian Universities of Australasia*. Christchurch: University of Canterbury, 1979.

———. 'A colonial economy.' In Geoffrey W Rice (ed), *The Oxford History of New Zealand*, 2nd ed. Auckland: Oxford University Press, 1992, 57.

———. *The History of the University of Canterbury 1873-1973*. Christchurch: University of Canterbury, 1973.

Gatfield, Gill. *Biographies of New Zealand's High Court Judges: A Statistical Picture*. Auckland: Equity Works, 1996.

———. 'Discrimination in the legal profession: Maori women lawyers.' Paper to the Maori Law Society and Maori Women Lawyers' Working Group, Auckland, 18 June 1993.

———. 'Don't shoot 1469 messengers.' *Northern Law News*, no 28, May 1993, 3.

———. *Early Women Lawyers: Careers of Women Admitted as Barristers and Solicitors in New Zealand, 1897-1959*. Auckland: Equity Works, 1996.

———. 'How are women doing 100 years later? Chalk and cheese: women and men in the law.' In vol 2 of *The Law and Politics: 1993 New Zealand Law Conference: Conference Papers*. Wellington, 1993, 140.

———. *LawTalk, Survey: Law Firm Policies on Family and Childcare Issues*. Auckland: Equity Works, 1993.

———. 'Maori women lawyers: research plan.' Paper prepared for discussion with Nga Wahine Ma Roopu, Auckland, 27 October 1993.

———. 'New laws on discrimination: lawyers face liability.' *LawTalk*, no 402, October 1993, 9.

———. *Report*. Vol 2 of *Towards 2000: Implementing EEO: Auckland District Law Society EEO Management Plan*. Auckland: Equity Works, 1996.

———. *Wellington District Law Society and Wellington Women Lawyer's Association Scoping Study: Why Women Leave the Legal Profession*. Auckland: Equity Works, 1994.

———. *Women Judges in New Zealand: A Survey*. Auckland: Equity Works, 1996.

Gatfield, Gill, and Alison Gray. *Women Lawyers in New Zealand: A Survey of the Legal Profession*. Wellington: Equity Works, 1993.

Gilligan, Carol. *In a Different Voice: Psychological Theory and Women's Development*. Cambridge: Harvard University Press, 1982.

Gore, Ross. *Chapman Tripp and Co: The First 100 Years*. Wellington: Chapman Tripp, 1975.

Graham, Jeanine. 'Settler society.' In Geoffrey W Rice (ed), *The Oxford History of New Zealand*, 2nd ed. Auckland: Oxford University Press, 1992.

Grainger, Jocelyn. 'The path to the organisation: some factors which influence women's career choices.' In Suzann Olsson (ed), *The Gender Factor: Women in New Zealand Organisations*. Palmerston North: Dunmore Press, 1992, 46.

Grant, Isabel, and Lynn Smith. 'Gender representation in the Canadian judiciary.' In Ontario Law Reform Commission, *Appointing Judges: Philosophy, Politics and Practice*. Ontario: Ontario Law Reform Commission, 1991, 57.

Grant, S W. *The Law Society of the District of Hawke's Bay*. Hawke's Bay: Law Society of the District of Hawke's Bay, 1986.

Gray Matter Research Ltd and Rivers Buchan and Associates. *Te Wahine Hanga Mahi: Women and Self Employment*. Wellington: National Advisory Council on the Employment of Women, 1993.

Graycar, Regina. 'The gender of judgments: an introduction.' In Margaret Thornton (ed), *Public and Private: Feminist Legal Debates*. Oxford University Press, 1995.

Graycar, Regina, (ed). *Dissenting Opinions Feminist Explorations in Law and Society*. Sydney: Allen and Unwin, 1990.

Graycar, Regina, and Jenny Morgan. *The Hidden Gender of Law*. Leichhardt, New South Wales: Federation Press, 1990.

Greenaway, Juliet. 'History of the New Zealand legal profession.' LLB (Hons) dissertation, University of Auckland, 1988.

Greig, G Flos. 'The law as a profession for women.' *Commonwealth Law Review*, 6, March–April 1909, 145.

Grimshaw, Patricia. *Women's Suffrage in New Zealand*. Auckland: Auckland University Press/Oxford University Press, 1972.

Gunew, Sneja, and Anna Yeatman (eds). *Feminism and the Politics of Difference*. Wellington: Bridget Williams Books, 1993.

Hagan, John, and Fiona Kay (eds). *Gender in Practice: A Study of Lawyers' Lives*. New York: Oxford University Press, 1995.

Hancock, Hamish. 'MP is disappointed in legal profession.' *Conferentia*, 5 March 1993, 9.

Hansen, Mark. 'Partner in name only.' *American Bar Association Journal*, January 1992, 26.

———. 'Texas firm sued.' *American Bar Association Journal*, January 1992, 26.

Harrington, Mona. *Women Lawyers: Rewriting the Rules*. New York: Penguin Books, 1995.

'Helen Melrose: lawyer.' In Virginia Myers (ed), *Head and Shoulders: Successful New Zealand Women Talk to Virginia Myers*. Auckland: Penguin Books, 1986, 72.

Henare, Marama. 'Maori women in the law: demands not restricted to professional pressures.' *LawTalk*, no 426, 21 November 1994, 13.

Henwood, Carolyn. 'Women lawyers and the profession.' Paper to the United Women's Convention, Wellington, 1975.

Heylen Research Centre. *The Legal Profession: A Survey of Lawyers and Members of the Public*. Auckland: New Zealand Law Society, 1978.

———. *The Legal Profession: Practitioners' and General Public's Perceptions*. Prepared for the New Zealand Law Society, 1984.

———. *Women in the Legal Profession*. 3 vols. Auckland: Heylen Research Centre, 1987.

Hill, Linda. '100 years of the vote: 80 percent of the pay: the politics of pay equity.' *Women's Studies Journal*, 9(2), September 1993. PAGE

Hodder, J E. 'Judicial appointments in New Zealand.' [1974] NZLJ 80.

Horsfield, Anne. *Women in the Economy: A Research report on the Economic Position of Women in New Zealand*. Wellington: Ministry of Women's Affairs, 1988.

'How to avoid sexist language.' *Just News*, March 1987.

Howell, Rosemary. 'Succeeding in the 90's: issues for legal partnerships.' New Zealand Law Society seminar, October 1994.

Hubbard, Anthony. 'Sitting in judgment.' *Listener*, 27 July 1996, 7.

Hughes, Beryl. 'Early professional women.' In *Women's Studies Conference Papers*. Wellington: Women's Studies Association New Zealand, 1981.

———.'Women and the professions in New Zealand.' In Phillida Bunkle and Beryl Hughes (eds), *Women in New Zealand Society*. Auckland: George Allen and Unwin, 1980, 118.

Hughes-Pollock, Kate. 'Gentlemen lawyers: who needs them?' *Law Institute Journal*, November 1993, 1015.

Human Rights Commission. *Advertising Guidelines*. Auckland: Human Rights Commission, 1995.

———. *A Manual on Equal Employment Opportunities*. Auckland: Human Rights Commission, 1989.

———. *Pre-employment Guidelines No 2*. Auckland: Human Rights Commission, 1995.

———. *Progress Report on the Implementation of Equal Employment Opportunity Programmes in New Zealand Trading Banks*. Auckland: Human Rights Commission, 1986.

———. *Sexual Harassment in the Workplace*. Auckland: Human Rights Commission, 1991.

———. *Women in Banking: A Report on Complaints of Sex Discrimination in the Employment of Women in the New Zealand Banking System*. Auckland: Human Rights Commission, 1984.

Human Rights Commission and the Office of the Race Relations Conciliator. *Report of the Human Rights Commission and the Office of the Race Relations Conciliator*. 30 June 1991.

———. *Report of the Human Rights Commission and the Office of the Race Relations Conciliator*. 10 June 1993.

Humphries, Maria, and Shayne Grice. 'Equal employment opportunity and the management of diversity.' In Peter Boxall (ed), *The Challenge of Human Resource Management: Directions and Debates in New Zealand*. Auckland: Longman Paul, 1995, 210.

Hyman, Prue. 'Equal pay for women in New Zealand: history and evaluation.' *Victoria Economic Commentaries*, 1(1), March 1993.

———. *Women and Economics: A New Zealand Feminist Perspective*. Wellington: Bridget Williams Books, 1994.

'Interview with Judith Potter, President of the New Zealand Law Society, 1991.' [1991] NZLJ 151.

Jack, Rand, and Dana Crowley Jack. *Moral Vision and Professional Decisions: The Changing Values of Women and Men Lawyers*. Cambridge, United Kingdom: Cambridge University Press, 1989.

Jackson. 'The failure and abolition of the New Zealand Legislative Council.' (1973) 54 Parl 17.

Jefferies, Pamela. 'Fence building for 1996.' *Employment Today*, February 1996, 6.

Jensen, Benedikte. *Employer Assisted Childcare: A Discussion Paper*. Prepared for the Ministry of Women's Affairs, Wellington: Business and Economic Research Ltd, 16 April 1991.

'Job description for judges.' *LawTalk*, no 398, 9 August 1993, 9.

Johnson, Arlene. 'Keynote address: work-family issues in the United States 1993.' In *Make Your Workplace 'Family-Friendly': Seminar Proceedings*. Wellington: Ministry of Women's Affairs, 1993.

Johnstone, Cecilia. 'Engendering respect.' *National*, January-February 1994, 8.

Joychild, Frances. 'A critique of the law of sexual harassment in Aotearoa/New Zealand.' In *Women's Law Conference Papers: 1993 New Zealand Suffrage Centennial.* Wellington: Women's Legal Group, Faculty of Law, Victoria University of Wellington, 1993, 43.

'Judge calls for limited public scrutiny of Family Courts.' *LawTalk*, no 419, 8 August 1994, 2.

'Judge swaps Bench for books.' *Northern Law News*, no 24, 9 July 1993.

'Judges receive pay increase.' *Northern Law News*, 4 March 1994, 2.

'July board briefs.' *LawTalk*, no 461, 5 August 1996, 5.

Kaye, Judith. 'Women lawyers in big firms: a study in progress toward gender equality.' *Fordham Law Review*, 57(1), 1988, 111.

Keith, K J. 'A judicial commission? Some comments on the independence of the judiciary.' [1983] NZLJ 239.

Kennedy, Helena. *Eve Was Framed: Women and British Justice.* London: Chatto and Windus, 1992.

King, Michael, (ed). *One of the Boys? Changing Views of Masculinity in New Zealand.* Auckland: Heinemann, 1988.

'King's Counsel.' [1929] NZLJ 240.

Kirk, Harry. *Portrait of a Profession: A History of the Solicitors' Profession, 1100 to the Present Day.* London: Oyez, 1977.

Knight, Stephanie. 'The place of alcohol in the lives of women in the legal profession living in Auckland.' BA(Hons) thesis, University of Auckland, 1988.

Koopman-Boyden, Peggy, and Claudia Scott. *The Family and Government Policy in New Zealand.* Sydney: George Allen and Unwin, 1984.

Koreman, Marie. 'Demographics: melting pot mix.' *Employment Today*, September/October 1995, 3.

Kuitert, V. 'Ellen Melville 1882-1946.' MA research essay, University of Auckland, 1986.

Law Commission. *A New Interpretation Act: To Avoid 'Prolixity and Tautology.* Report no 17. Wellington: Law Commission, 1990.

'Law Foundation assists gender projects.' *LawTalk*, no 459, 8 July 1996, 5.

Law Institute of Victoria. *Career Patterns of Law Graduates.* Australia: Law Institute of Victoria, 1990.

'Law notes.' *Otago University Review*, 7(4), September 1894, 120.

Law Reform Commission. *Equality Before the Law, Law Reform Commission of Australia.* Discussion paper no 54. Sydney: Law Reform Commission, 1993.

————. *Equality Before the Law: Justice for Women.* Part 1. Report no 69. Sydney: Law Reform Commission, 1994.

Law Society of British Columbia. *Gender Equality in the Justice System: A Report of the Law Society of British Columbia Gender Bias Committee.* 2 vols. Law Society of British Columbia, 1992.

————. *Women in the Legal Profession, Report of the Women in the Legal Profession Subcommittee.* Law Society of British Columbia, 1991.

Law Society of England and Wales. *Equal in the Law.* London: Law Society of England and Wales, 1988.

————. *Judicial Appointments.* London: Law Society of England and Wales, 1991.

Law Society of New South Wales. *Getting Through the Door is Not Enough: An Examination of the Equal Employment Opportunity Response of the Legal Profession in the 1990's.* Law Society of New South Wales, 1993.

————. *Equal Opportunity Task Force Report.* Law Society of New South Wales, 1992.

————. *Policy: Equal Employment and Promotion.* Law Society of New South Wales, 1993.

————. *Trends in the Profession.* Research and Policy Planning Unit, Law Society of New South Wales 1991.

Law Society of Upper Canada. *Transitions in the Ontario Legal Profession: A Survey of Lawyers Called to the Bar Between 1975 and 1990*. Toronto: Law Society of Upper Canada, 1991.

———. *A Recommended Personnel Policy Regarding Employment-Related Sexual Harassment*. Toronto: Law Society of Upper Canada, 1992.

Law Society of Western Australia. *A Report into Career Opportunities and Patterns of Legal Practitioners on Behalf of the Equal Opportunity Committee of the Law Society of Western Australia*. Reark Research, 1990.

'Lay magistrates: more efficient courts but lower standards of justice?' *Northern Law News*, 23 February 1996, 4.

Leary, Eb. 'My town: cadit quaestio.' *Metro*, June 1988, 196.

'Legal executive certificate now well established: survey.' *LawTalk*, no 408, 21 February 1994, 8.

L'Estrange, Noela, and Wally Vicig. 'Quality management.' New Zealand Law Society seminar, September 1994.

Liddicoat, Joy. 'Notes from a woman lawyer in government.' In Elisabeth McDonald and Graeme Austin (eds), *Claiming the Law: Essays by New Zealand Women in Celebration of the 1993 Suffrage Centennial*. Wellington: Victoria University of Wellington Law Review/Victoria University Press, 1993, 77.

Lord Chancellor's Department. *Judicial Appointments: The Lord Chancellor's Policies and Procedures*. London: Lord Chancellor's Department, 1990.

Lundy, Lesley. 'First woman on Bench likes sewing, cooking and gardening.' *New Zealand Woman's Weekly*, 6 October 1975, 4.

Macalister, Philip. '1994 top 200 companies.' *Management*, December 1994, 68.

MacCuish, F J. 'The Society for the Protection of Women and Children 1893-1916.' MA research essay, University of Auckland, 1983.

Macdonald, Charlotte. *The Vote, The Pill and the Demon Drink: A History of Feminist Writing in New Zealand 1869-1993*. Wellington: Bridget Williams Books, 1993.

———. *A Woman of Good Character: Single Women as Immigrant Settlers in Nineteenth-Century New Zealand*. Wellington: Allen and Unwin/Historical Branch of the Department of Internal Affairs, 1990.

Macdonald, Charlotte, Merimeri Penfold and Bridget Williams (eds). *The Book of New Zealand Women: Ko Kui Ma Te Kaupapa*. Wellington: Bridget Williams Books, 1991.

McDonald, Elisabeth. 'An(other) explanation: the exclusion of women's stories in sexual offence trials.' In *New Zealand Law Society Seminar: Challenging the Law and Legal Processes: The Development of a Feminist Legal Analysis*. Wellington: New Zealand Law Society, 1993, 43.

McDonald, Elisabeth, and Graeme Austin (eds). *Claiming the Law: Essays by New Zealand Women in Celebration of the 1993 Suffrage Centennial*. Wellington: Victoria University of Wellington Law Review/Victoria University Press, 1993.

McDonald, Heather. 'Combining employment and family: how are we doing in New Zealand?' In *Make Your Workplace 'Family-Friendly': Seminar Proceedings*. Wellington: Ministry of Women's Affairs, 1993.

McDonald, Kristy. 'Sex and the professional relationship.' *LawTalk*, November 1992, 13.

MacDonald, Tui. 'Airini Tonore.' In Charlotte Macdonald, Merimeri Penfold and Bridget Williams (eds), *The Book of New Zealand Women: Ko Kui Ma Te Kaupapa*. Wellington: Bridget Williams Books, 1991, 178.

MacDonald Dictionary of Biographies, Christchurch: Canterbury Museum Library, 1970.

McGuire, Brett. 'Annus horribilis: the nightmare continues.' *Employment Today*, February 1996, 12.

McHugh, Paul. *The Maori Magna Carta: New Zealand Law and the Treaty of Waitangi*. Auckland: Oxford University Press, 1991.

McInman and Associates. *New Zealand Law Society Poll of the Profession.* McInman and Associates, 1987.

McIntyre, M F. 'The East Coast enclave.' In Sir Robin Cooke (ed), *Portrait of a Profession: The Centennial Book of the New Zealand Law Society.* Wellington: A H and A W Reed, 1969, 299.

McKay, Justice Ian. 'Professions at risk.' [1993] NZLJ 104.

MacKinnon, Catherine. *Feminism Unmodified: Discourses on Life and Law.* Cambridge, Massachusetts: Harvard University Press, 1987.

Mackinolty, J, and H Radi. *In Pursuit of Justice: Australian Women and the Law 1788-1979.* Sydney: Hale and Iremonger, 1979.

McLauchlan, Mark. 'The new anatomy of power.' *Metro,* October 1991, 86.

McLennan, Roy, Kerr Inkson, Stephen Dakin, Philip Dewe and Graham Elkin (eds). *People and Enterprises: Human Behaviour in New Zealand Organizations.* Sydney: Holt, Rhinehart and Winston, 1987.

McLeod, Marion. 'Women at law.' *New Zealand Listener,* 16 January 1988, 16.

McLinden, John. 'The case for the Bar aiding the Bench.' *LawTalk,* no 377, 17 August 1992, 7.

McManus, Jenni. 'If attitudes won't change, then laws needed.' *Independent,* 1 July 1994, 28.

McMullin, Duncan Wallace. *The Law: A Career for You?* Wellington: Council of Legal Education and New Zealand Law Society, 1967.

McNaughton, Trudie. 'What are the benefits of diversity in the workforce.' Paper presented to the Equal Employment Opportunities Conference, Wellington, 23 February 1993.

McPherson, Marena L. 'Sexual harassment after Anita Hill.' *Perspectives,* 1(2), Spring 1992, 1.

Make Your Workplace 'Family-Friendly': Seminar Proceedings. Wellington: Ministry of Women's Affairs, 1993.

'The making of a judge.' *Feminist Law Bulletin New Zealand Aotearoa,* no 3, February 1994, 3.

'Management task to build on partners' skills.' *Northern Law News,* 6 October 1995, 3.

'Marketing of the profession: workshop II.' New Zealand Law Society paper presented at the 1984 New Zealand Law Conference, Rotorua, 27 April, 1984.

'Mary Hussey: dedicated to the service of others.' *LawTalk,* no 389, April 1993, 8.

May, Helen. *Minding Children, Managing Men: Conflict and Compromise in the Lives of Postwar Pakeha Women.* Wellington: Bridget Williams Books, 1992.

——. 'Motherhood in the 1950s: an experience of contradiction.' In Sue Middleton (ed), *Women and Education in Aotearoa,* Wellington: Allen and Unwin/Port Nicholson Press, 1988.

Mayhew, Judith. 'Woman at law.' [1992] NZLJ 85.

Mazengarb, Rae. 'The work-family dilemma: the secret lives of women lawyers.' *LawTalk,* no 402, October 1993, 16.

Meares, Jane. 'Maternity leave for partners: still an issue?' *LawTalk,* no 431, April 1995, 27.

——. 'Woman and issues in commercial law.' In *Women's Law Conference Papers: 1993 New Zealand Suffrage Centennial.* Wellington: Women's Legal Group, Faculty of Law, Victoria University of Wellington, 1993, 27.

Menkel-Meadow, C. 'The comparative sociology of women lawyers: the "feminisation" of the legal profession.' *Osgoode Hall Law Journal,* 24, 1986, 897.

——. 'Exploring a research agenda of the feminisation of the legal profession: theories of gender and social change.' *Law and Social Enquiry,* 1989, 289.

——. 'Portia in a different voice: speculations on a women's lawyering process.' *Berkeley Women's Law Journal,* 1, 1987, 44.

Middleton, Sue, (ed). *Women and Education in Aotearoa.* Wellington: Allen and Unwin/Port Nicholson Press, 1988.

Middleton, Sue, and Alison Jones (eds). *Women and Education in Aotearoa*. 2. Wellington: Bridget Williams Books, 1992.

Mill, John Stuart. *The Collected Works*. Toronto: University of Toronto Press, 1984.

———. *On the Subjection of Women*, 4th ed. London: Longmans, Green, Reader and Dyer, 1878.

Millen, Julia. *The Story of Bell Gully Buddle Weir 1840–1990*. Wellington: Bell Gully Buddle Weir, 1990.

Milne, R S. *Political Parties in New Zealand*. Oxford: Oxford University Press, 1966.

Milroy, Stephanie. 'Maori women lawyers: little profile in profession.' *LawTalk*, no 402, October 1993, 35.

'Minister keeps open option on EEO law.' *Northern Law News*, no 44, 29 November 1991.

Ministry of Women's Affairs. *Government Funding Options for Early Childhood Care and Education*. Wellington: Ministry of Women's Affairs, October 1990.

———. *Summary of Paper on Equal Employment Opportunities (EEO): 'Stocktake' on Implementation*. Wellington, 1995.

'More and more firms outsourcing.' *Legal Management*, March/April 1993, 9.

'More scope urged for women lawyers.' *Northern Law News*, no 5, 18 February 1994, l.

'More ways to write sex-neutral language.' *LawTalk*, no 240, 6;

Morris, Joanne. 'How are women doing 100 years later? Balancing or juggling our private and public lives.' In vol 3 of *The Law and Politics: 1993 New Zealand Law Conference: Conference Papers*. Wellington, 1993, 152.

———. 'Women's access to justice: He putanga mo nga wahine ki te tika: justice is not blind to the effects of gender.' In vol 1 of *1996 New Zealand Law Conference: Conference Papers*. Dunedin, 1996, 9.

Morrison, Tony, (ed). *Race-ing Justice, En-gendering Power: Essays on Anita Hill, Clarence Thomas, and the Construction of Social Reality*. London: Chatto and Windus, 1993.

Mossman, Mary Jane. 'Feminism and legal method: the difference it makes.' *Australian Journal of Law and Society*, 3, 1986, 30.

———. 'Women lawyers in twentieth century Canada: rethinking the image of "Portia". In Regina Graycar (ed), *Dissenting Opinions: Feminist Explorations in Law and Society*. Sydney: Allen and Unwin, 1990.

Mucalov, Janice. 'The stress epidemic.' *Canadian Lawyer*, May 1993, 18.

Muller, Mary. 'An appeal to the men of New Zealand, 1869.' In Charlotte Macdonald, Merimeri Penfold and Bridget Williams (eds), *The Book of New Zealand Women: Ko Kui Ma Te Kaupapa*. Wellington: Bridget Williams Books, 1991.

Murray, Georgina. 'New Zealand lawyers: from colonial GPs to the servants of capital.' In Richard Abel and Phillip Lewis (eds), *The Common Law World*. Vol 1 of *Lawyers in Society*. Berkeley: University of California Press, 1988.

———. 'The New Zealand woman lawyer: the invisible lawyer.' *International Journal of Sociology of Law*, 15 December 1984, 439.

———. 'Sharing in the "shingles"? Women, class and ethnicity: the generation and distribution of rewards in the New Zealand legal profession.' MA thesis, University of Auckland, 1984.

———. 'Women lawyers in New Zealand: some questions about the politics of equality.' *International Journal of the Sociology of Law*, 15, 1987, 439.

Myers, Virginia, (ed). *Head and Shoulders: Successful New Zealand Women Talk to Virginia Myers*. Auckland: Penguin Books, 1986.

Naffine, Ngaire. *Law and the Sexes: Explorations in Feminist Jurisprudence*. Sydney: Allen and Unwin, 1990.

Napoli, Joan. *Work and Family Responsibilities: Adjusting the Balance*. Sydney: CCH Australia, 1994.

National Advisory Council on the Employment of Women. *Beyond the Barriers: The State, the Economy and Women's Employment 1984–1990*. Wellington: National Advisory Council on the Employment of Women, 1990.

National Business Review, 23 April 1984–10 September 1993.

Nefertari, Nomalanga. 'Dysfunction in a law office (Do you recognize anyone here?).' *Law Practice Management*, 1994, 46.

'New judge ponders judicial role.' *Council Brief*, July 1995, 5.

'New management style for large law firms.' *Northern Law News*, 22 September 1995, 5.

'New stage in distinguished legal career.' *Council Brief*, March 1995, 3.

New Zealand Biographies 1976. Vol 1. Wellington: Alexander Turnbull Library.

New Zealand Herald, 22 August 1891–6 July 1996.

New Zealand Law Society. *Lawyers: An Image Study: Executive Summary*. New Zealand Law Society, 1987.

————. *Polls of the Profession and Public: Summary*. New Zealand Law Society, 1987.

————. *Rules of Professional Conduct for Barristers and Solicitors*, 2nd ed. Wellington, 1993.

————. *Submission by the Legislation Committee on the Human Rights Commission Bill*. Wellington, 19 April 1977.

————. *Submission on the Human Rights Bill*, 16 March 1993, 10.

'New Zealand Law Society 98th annual report: statement of accounts and balance sheet, for the year ended 30 November 1994.' *LawTalk*, no 431, April 1995.

'New Zealand Law Society Practice Management Committee.' *LawTalk*, no 414, 9.

New Zealand Law Society Seminar: Challenging Law and Legal Processes: The Development of a Feminist Legal Analysis. Wellington: New Zealand Law Society, 1993.

New Zealand Parliamentary Debates. 1870-1896.

New Zealand Society of Accountants. *Submission to the Parliamentary Select Committee on the Human Rights Commission Bill*. 24 March 1977.

New Zealand Vice-Chancellors' Committee. *Graduate Employment in New Zealand: A Summary of the Destinations of University Graduates, 1989–1994*. Wellington: New Zealand Vice-Chancellors' Committee, 1990–1995.

Newman, Corallyn, (ed). *Canterbury Women Since 1893*. Christchurch: Pegasus Press, 1979.

Ng, James. *How the Cantonese Gold Seekers and Their Heirs Settled in New Zealand*. Vol 1 of *Windows on a Chinese Past*. Dunedin: Otago Heritage Books, 1993.

'No to judicial commission: Attorney-General.' *Law-Talk*, no 398, 9 August 1993, 7.

Northey, J F. 'Legal education and the universities.' [1962] NZLJ 9.

November, Janet. 'A woman's place is . . . on the Bench.' In Elisabeth McDonald and Graeme Austin (eds), *Claiming the Law: Essays by New Zealand Women in Celebration of the 1993 Suffrage Centennial*. Wellington: Victoria University of Wellington Law Review/Victoria University Press, 1993, 85.

'NZ Law Practitioners Disciplinary Tribunal: personal relationship with client leads to professional misconduct charge.' *LawTalk*, no 445, 24 October 1995, 7.

'NZ Listener 50 years ago.' *Listener*, article 17 from April 1942, 20 April 1992.

NZLS *see also* New Zealand Law Society

'NZLS board business review.' *LawTalk*, no 435, 29 May 1995, 5.

'NZLS committee nominations for 1995.' *LawTalk*, no 428, 6.

O'Donovan, Katherine. *Sexual Divisions in Law*. London: Weidenfeld and Nicolson, 1985.

Olssen, Erik. 'Women, work and family: 1880-1926.' In Phillida Bunkle and Beryl Hughes (eds), *Women in New Zealand Society*. Auckland: George Allen and Unwin, 1980, 159.

Olsson, Suzann, (ed). *The Gender Factor: Women in New Zealand Organisations*. Palmerston North: Dunmore Press, 1992.

Ontario Law Reform Commission. *Appointing Judges: Philosophy, Politics and Practice.* Ontario Law Reform Commission, 1991.

Orange, Claudia. *The Treaty of Waitangi.* Wellington: Allen and Unwin/Port Nicholson Press, 1987.

O'Regan, Mary. 'Affirmative action for women.' In *New Zealand Law Conference: Conference Papers.* Christchurch, 1987, 294.

Otago Daily Times, 28 August 1885–25 July 1993.

'Our lady students.' *Otago University Review,* 10(5), October 1896, 145.

Page, Dorothy. 'The first lady graduates: women with degrees from Otago University, 1885–1900.' In Barbara Brookes, Charlotte Macdonald and Margaret Tennant (eds), *Women in History 2.* Wellington: Bridget Williams Books, 1992, 120.

Pallot, Marie. 'Tax relief for child-care expenses: issues and law reform proposals.' In *Women's Law Conference Papers: 1993 New Zealand Suffrage Centennial.* Wellington: Women's Legal Group, Faculty of Law, Victoria University of Wellington, 1993, 31.

Palmer, Geoffrey. 'Judicial appointments.' *LawTalk,* no 288, 3 August 1988, 3.

———.'Judicial selection and accountability: can the New Zealand system survive?' Paper prepared for the Legal Research Foundation seminar, Courts and Policy: Checking the Balance, Auckland, 5–6 August 1993.

———. 'Lawyer as lobbyist: the role of lawyers in influencing and managing change.' In vol 1 of *The Law and Politics: New Zealand Law Conference: Conference Papers.* Wellington, 1993, 279.

Pannick, David. 'Judging judges.' In *9th Commonwealth Law Conference: Conference Papers.* Auckland: Commerce Clearing House New Zealand, 1990, 526.

Park, Julie, (ed). *Ladies a Plate: Change and Continuity in the Lives of New Zealand Women.* Auckland: Auckland University Press, 1991.

Parliament of the Commonwealth of Australia. *Report of the Senate Standing Committee on Legal and Constitutional Affairs: Gender Bias and the Judiciary.* Canberra: Parliament of the Commonwealth of Australia, 1994.

Phillips, Jock. 'Mummy's boys: pakeha men and male culture in New Zealand.' In Phillida Bunkle and Beryl Hughes (eds), *Women in New Zealand Society.* Auckland: George Allen and Unwin, 1980, 217.

Pope, Jeremy. Review of *Women and the Law* by Kaye Turner and Pauline Vaver (eds). [1975] NZLJ 620.

Potter, Judith. 'Challenges of the nineties: access to justice, equality, communication.' *LawTalk,* no 360, November 1991, 33.

———. 'Collective responsibility is the foundation of an independent legal profession.' *LawTalk,* no 385, December 1992, 11.

Powell, Dr Michael. 'Partnership decision making.' *LawTalk,* no 378, 31 August 1992, 13.

'Practice note: procedure for the appointment of Queen's Counsel.' [1980] NZLJ 476.

Press, 21 August 1891–6 March 1963.

Presser, ArLynn Leiber. 'Law firm liable for sex bias.' *American Bar Association Journal,* March 1991, 24.

Preston, Frances. *Lady Doctor: Vintage Model.* Wellington: A H and A W Reed, 1974.

'Pro-women convention under-used.' *Northern Law News,* 4 August 1995, 3.

'Procedures for the appointment of Queen's Counsel.' *LawTalk,* no 356, 2 September 1991, 9.

'Public lack understanding of complaints procedures: lay observers.' *LawTalk,* no 423, October 1994, 5.

'Quality management: timely challenge for lawyers.' *LawTalk,* no 414, 30 May 1994, 9.

'Queen's Counsel: recent appointments.' [1981] NZLJ 114.

Quinn, Cathy. 'Where are all the women in law?' In vol 2 of *The Law and Politics: 1993 New Zealand Law Conference: Conference Papers.* Wellington, 1993.

Radford, Anna. 'Letters: Drunkenness as a mitigating factor in criminal cases.' *LawTalk*, no 428, 7 February 1995, 4.

'Reader survey results.' *Council Brief*, no 96, June 1983, 3.

Regional Women's Decade Committee. *Canterbury Women Since 1893*. 1979.

'Report of the Royal Commission on the Courts.' [1978] AJHR H2.

'Report of the Royal Commission on University Education in New Zealand 1925.' [1925] 2 AJHR E7A.

'Report of the Royal Commission to Inquire into and Report upon the Operations of the University of New Zealand and its Relations to the Secondary Schools of the Colony 1880.' [1880] 2 AJHR H1 (session 1).

Rice, Geoffrey W, (ed). *The Oxford History of New Zealand*, 2nd ed. Auckland: Oxford University Press, 1992.

Richardson, Megan. 'Women in law in New Zealand today.' *Council Brief*, no 80, December 1981, 8.

Richardson, Sir Ivor. 'Educating lawyers for the 21st century.' [1989] NZLJ 86.

———. 'Sir Robert Stout.' In Sir Robin Cooke (ed), *Portrait of a Profession: The Centennial Book of the New Zealand Law Society*. Wellington: A H and A W Reed, 1969, 44.

Ritchie, Jane. 'Psychology: the sexual politics of an academic discipline in the early twentieth century.' In Sue Middleton (ed), *Women and Education in Aotearoa*. Wellington: Allen and Unwin/Port Nicholson Press, 1988.

Rosener, Judy. *America's Competitive Secret: Utilizing Women as a Management Strategy*. Oxford: Oxford University Press, 1995.

Rout, Bill. 'Being "staunch": boys hassling girls.' In Sue Middleton and Alison Jones (eds), *Women and Education in Aotearoa. 2*. Wellington: Bridget Williams Books, 1992.

Sachs, Albie and Joan Hoff Wilson. *Sexism and the Law: A Study of Male Beliefs and Legal Bias in Britain and the United States*. New York: Free Press, 1978.

Sargisson, Hannah. 'Women in the legal profession: a discussion of their changing profile.' LLB(Hons) dissertation, Auckland University, 1982.

Sayers, Janet, and Marianne Tremaine (eds). *The Vision and the Reality: Equal Employment Opportunities in the New Zealand Workplace*. Palmerston North: Dunmore Press, 1994.

Schafran, Lynn. 'Gender and justice: Florida and the nation.' *Florida Law Review*, 42, 1990, 181.

———. 'Supreme Court nominees: should race and gender be factors in choosing justices? Yes: "more than a symbol".' *American Bar Association Journal*, September 1991, 38.

Scott, Claudia, (ed). *Women and Taxation*. Wellington: Institute of Policy Studies, 1993.

Scutt, Jocelynne. *Women and the Law: Commentary and Materials*. Sydney: Law Book Co, 1990.

Shand, Maria. 'OOS sufferers in litigation lineup.' *LawTalk*, no 431, April 1995, 29.

Sharp, A. *Justice and the Maori: Maori Claims in New Zealand Political Argument in the 1980s*. Auckland: Oxford University Press, 1990.

Shreves, Teresa. 'One woman's experience of commercial practice.' In Elisabeth McDonald and Graeme Austin (eds), *Claiming the Law: Essays by New Zealand Women in Celebration of the 1993 Suffrage Centennial*. Wellington: Victoria University of Wellington Law Review/Victoria University Press, 1993, 121.

Sinclair, Keith. *A History of New Zealand*, 4th revised ed. Auckland: Penguin Books, 1991.

———. *A History of the University of Auckland, 1883–1983*. Auckland: Auckland University Press/Oxford University Press, 1983.

Smart, Carol. *Feminism and the Power of Law*. London: Routledge, 1989.

———. 'Legal subjects and sexual objects: ideology, law and female sexuality.' In J Brophy and C Smart (eds), *Women in Law: Explorations in Law, Family and Sexuality*. London: Routledge and Kegan Paul, 1985.

————. *The Ties That Bind: Law, Marriage and the Reproduction of Patriarchal Relations.* London: Routledge and Kegan Paul, 1984.

Smith, Shirley. 'My life in the law.' In Elisabeth McDonald and Graeme Austin (eds), *Claiming the Law: Essays by New Zealand Women in Celebration of the 1993 Suffrage Centennial.* Wellington: Victoria University of Wellington Law Review/Victoria University Press, 1993.

'Society adopts equal employment opportunities policy.' *Northern Law News*, no 30, 23 August 1991.

Spoonley, Paul. 'Ambivalence and autonomy: the tension between biculturalism and EEO.' In Janet Sayers and Marianne Tremaine (eds), *The Vision and the Reality: Equal Employment Opportunities in the New Zealand Workplace.* Palmerston North: Dunmore Press, 1994, 87.

Statistics New Zealand. *All About Women in New Zealand.* Wellington: Statistics New Zealand, 1993.

————. *Demographic Trends 1995.* Wellington: Statistics New Zealand, 1995.

————. *New Zealand Now: 65 Plus.* Wellington: Statistics New Zealand, 1995.

————. *New Zealand Now: Families.* Wellington: Statistics New Zealand, 1995.

Stephen, Sir James. 'Book III: of rights in private relations.' In *Commentaries on the Laws of England,* 16th ed. London: Edward Jenks, 1914.

————. 'Book IV: of public rights.' In *Commentaries on the Laws of England,* 16th ed. London: Edward Jenks, 1914.

————. 'Book V: of civil injuries.' In *Commentaries on the Laws of England,* 16th ed. London: Edward Jenks, 1914.

Stone, Russell. 'Anatomy of the practice of law in 19th century Auckland.' [1988] NZLJ 419.

————. *The Making of Russell McVeagh: The First 125 Years of the Practice of Russell McVeagh McKenzie Bartleet & Co, 1863-1988.* Auckland: Auckland University Press, 1991.

'Street's ahead.' *Metro*, April 1994, 88;

Stuart, Peggy. 'What does the glass ceiling cost you?' *Personnel Journal*, November 1992.

'Study confirms distinct measure of prejudice.' *LawTalk*, no 187, 14 December 1983, 1.

Sturrock, Fiona. *The Status of Girls and Women in New Zealand Education and Training.* Wellington: Learning Media, Ministry of Education, 1993.

Sunday Star-Times, 1993–11 August 1996.

Sutch, W B. *Women with a Cause*, 2nd ed. Wellington: New Zealand University Press, 1974.

Sykes, Annette. 'How are women doing 100 years later? The implications of our tangata whenua status for Maori women in the law.' In vol 2 of *The Law and Politics: 1993 New Zealand Law Conference: Conference Papers.* Wellington, 1993, 161.

'Symposium: Issues relating to women and the law.' *Auckland University Law Review*, 7(2), 1993.

Synergy Applied Research and Hinematu McNeill. *Attitudes to Family Violence: A Study Across Cultures.* Wellington: Family Violence Prevention Co-ordinating Committee, Department of Social Welfare, 1988.

Szaszy, Dame Mira. 'The Treaty of Waitangi: a personal perspective.' Paper presented to the International Conference of Women Judges, 14 September 1993.

Tapp, Pauline, and Margaret Wilson. *Women and the Law in New Zealand*, rev ed. Methuen, 1982.

Taylor, Nancy M. *Official History of New Zealand in the Second World War 1939-1945.* Vol 2. Wellington: Government Printing Office, 1986.

Tennant, Margaret. *Paupers and Providers: Charitable Aid in New Zealand.* Wellington: Allen and Unwin/Historical Branch of the Department of Internal Affairs, 1989.

Tennet, Elizabeth. *Paid Parental Leave: A Discussion Paper.* 1994.

'There's sex discrimination within the legal profession: law society study reveals what women have known all along.' *New Zealand Woman's Weekly,* 12 April 1982, 5.

Thornton, Margaret, (ed). *Public and Private: Feminist Legal Debates.* Melbourne: Oxford University Press, 1995.

Tilson, Ross S. 'Tokenism within the legal profession.' Advanced business programme, University of Otago, September 1990.

Tirohia, May 1994–December 1995.

'Too little, too late.' *American Lawyer,* May 1994, 5.

Torrie, Rae. 'A reasonable request? A reasonable response? EEO and cost benefit analysis.' In Janet Sayers and Marianne Tremaine (eds), *The Vision and the Reality: Equal Employment Opportunities in the New Zealand Workplace.* Palmerston North: Dunmore Press, 1994.

Tremaine, Marianne. 'Different ways of making a difference: EEO Maori and tino rangatiratanga in public sector organisations.' In Janet Sayers and Marianne Tremaine (eds), *The Vision and the Reality: Equal Employment Opportunities in the New Zealand Workplace.* Palmerston North: Dunmore Press, 1994, 72.

Tulloch, Gail. *Mill and Sexual Equality.* Hertfordshire, England: Harvester Wheatsheaf, 1989.

Turner, Kaye, and Pauline Vaver (eds). *Women and the Law in New Zealand.* Wellington: Hicks Smith in association with Sweet and Maxwell, 1975.

United Kingdom General Council of the Bar. *Bar Race Equality Policy.* London: United Kingdom General Council of the Bar, 1991.

———. *Without Prejudice? Sex Equality at the Bar and in the Judiciary.* London: TMS Consultants Ltd, 1992.

Van Etten, Angela. *Dwarfs Don't Live in Doll Houses.* New York: Adaptive Living, 1988.

Varnham, Mary. 'Carolyn Henwood: "I'm no superwoman".' *New Zealand Women's Weekly,* 23 December 1985, 23.

'A view from the Bench.' *New Zealand Listener,* 4 May 1996, 33.

Wallace, Justice John. 'Women and the judiciary: where to from here?' *LawTalk,* no 402, October 1993, 33.

Waring, Marilyn. *Counting for Nothing: What Men Value and What Women are Worth.* Wellington: Allen and Unwin/Port Nicholson Press, 1988.

WDLS *see* Wellington District Law Society

Wear, Graham. ' "Team" approach in family-friendly firms." *Northern Law News,* no 29, 9 August 1996, 6

Weisbrot, David. *Australian Lawyers.* Melbourne: Longman Cheshire, 1990.

Wellington District Law Society. *Full Report: Women in the Legal Profession.* Wellington: Wellington District Law Society, 1983.

White Ribbon, October 1895–19 April 1919.

Wickler, Professor Norma. Presentation on Gender and the Law presented at the 1993 Suffrage Centennial Seminar sponsored by the Ministry of Women's Affairs and the Department of Justice, Wellington, 16 September 1993.

'Wider consultation promised in judicial appointments procedure.' *LawTalk,* no 432, 19 April 1995, 2.

'Will we all work at home?' *Golden Wing,* August 1992, 16.

Williams, Glanville. *Learning the Law.* London: Stevens, 1973.

Willis, Judith. 'Defeating discrimination.' *Gazette,* 9 February 1994, 3.

Wilson, Bertha. 'Will women judges really make a difference?' *Osgoode Hall Law Journal,* 28, 1990, 507.

Wilson, Margaret. 'An introduction and an overview.' In *New Zealand Law Society Seminar: Challenging the Law and Legal Processes: The Development of a Feminist Legal Analysis.* Wellington: New Zealand Law Society, 1993, 1.

————. 'Areas of discrimination.' In Sandra Coney (ed), *United Women's Convention Report*, 1973, 18–20. In Charlotte Macdonald, *The Vote, The Pill and the Demon Drink: A History of Feminist Writing in New Zealand 1869-1993*. Wellington: Bridget Williams Books, 1993, 176.

————. 'The making and repeal of the Employment Equity Act: what next?' *Women Studies Journal*, 9(2), September 1993.

————. 'The relationship between the law and equal opportunity for women in employment.' Paper presented at the Women Studies Conference, 29-31 August 1980.

————. *Submission on the Human Rights Bill*. February 1977.

————. 'Towards a feminist jurisprudence in Aotearoa.' In Rosemary Du Plessis (ed), *Feminist Voices: Women's Studies Texts for Aotearoa/New Zealand*. Auckland: Oxford University Press, 1992, 266.

Wilson, Margaret, and Bronwyn Labrum. 'Stella Henderson.' In Charlotte Macdonald, Merimeri Penfold and Bridget Williams (eds), *The Book of New Zealand Women: Ko Kui Ma Te Kaupapa*. Wellington: Bridget Williams Books, 1991, 285.

Winsborough, David, and Kaye Allen. 'Report on stress.' Paper presented at the International Conference of Women Judges, Wellington, February 1994.

Wiren, A F. 'Some experiences of an old legal accountant.' (1942) 18 NZLJ 21.

Wolf, Naomi. *The Beauty Myth: How Images of Beauty are Used Against Women*. London: Vintage, 1991.

————. *Fire with Fire: The New Female Power and How it Will Change the 21st Century*. London: Chatto and Windus, 1993.

Women and the Vote. Dunedin: Hocken Library, 1986.

'Women barristers' dress.' (1961) 37 NZLJ 77.

'Women go solo in Dunedin.' *LawTalk*, no 402, October 1993, 37.

'Women in the law (II): an interview with Judith Potter.' [1988] NZLJ 148.

'Women in the profession.' *LawTalk*, no 164, 15 December 1982.

'Women in the profession.' *Northern Law News*, no 25, 16 July 1993.

'Women lawyers on television.' *Northern Law News*, 11 June 1993, 1.

'Women lawyers unite.' [1975] NZLJ 612.

'Women lawyers urged to speak up on gender issues.' *Northern Law News*, 23 June 1995, 3.

'Women SM's.' *Northern Law News*, December 1977, 7.

'Women's Consultative Group meets.' *LawTalk*, no 421, September 1994, 1.

Women's Law Conference Papers: 1993 New Zealand Suffrage Centennial. Wellington: Women's Legal Group, Faculty of Law, Victoria University of Wellington, 1993.

Women's Rights Committee: The Role of Women in New Zealand Society: Report of the Select Committee on Women's Rights. Wellington: Government Printer, 1975.

'Work stress affects families' health.' *Northern Law News*, 11 August 1995, 2.

Working Group on Equal Employment Opportunities and Equal Pay. *Towards Employment Equity: Report of the Working Group on Equal Employment Opportunities and Equal Pay*. Wellington: Working Group on Equal Employment Opportunities and Equal Pay, 1988.

'WWLA: EEO, sexual harassment head priorities.' *LawTalk*, no 403, 26 October 1993, 40.

assertiveness training, 116
Auckland Boys' Grammar School, 197
Auckland Chamber of Commerce
  Business Women's Network, 226
Auckland Club, 69
Auckland District Law Society (ADLS),
    19
  career aspirations, 204
  discrimination, 233
  EEO management plan, 396
  EEO programmes, 298–301, 380
    coordination role, 395
    kit, 298, 300, 303, 387, 392
    survey, xi–xii, 204, 223, 297–298, 307,
      313
  family-friendly initiatives, 301, 304
  recruitment campaign, 55
  research, xi–xii, 104–113
  working party, 105, 122
    report, 192
Auckland Implementation Committee,
    105
Auckland Law Students' Society, 71
Auckland Lesbian and Gay Lawyers'
    Group, 375
Auckland University College *see*
    University of Auckland
Auckland Women Lawyers Association
    (AWLA)
  criticism of judiciary, 264
  Maori women lawyers, 379–381
  role of, 115–117
Australia
  AMP Australia, 368
  Association of Nurse Lawyers, 312
  family-friendly businesses, 393
  first woman lawyer, 80, 86
  flexible work options, 393
  Gentlemen's Lawyers' Club, 312
  judicial appointments, 418
  judiciary and gender bias, 261, 262
  Law Reform Commission, 418
  law students, 116
  Public Service Reform Act 1984, 390
  sex discrimination, 101
  sexual harassment, 345
  staff supervision, 171
AWLA *see* Auckland Women Lawyers
    Association (AWLA)

B

Baker McKenzie, 340
bankruptcies
  Long Depression, 24
Banks, John MP, 262
Bar admission, 91
Bar dinners, 69–73, 112
  alcohol consumption, 69–70, 72
  'blue jokes', 70, 72, 231
  exclusion from, 69–70, 100
  sexual harassment, 231
Barcham, Anne *see* McAloon, Ann
Barnicoat, Miss, 42
barristers, 217
  application for silk, 281
  appointment to Bench *see* judiciary
  comparative tables, 132, 135, 153
  court attire, 74–76
    maternity wear, 264
  obtaining work, 218, 129, 180, 283, 305,
  remuneration, 145, 181
  stereotyped skills, 178
Batchelor, Dr, 82
Bates, Denese, 136, 182, 300
Bathgate, Sue, 225
Beall, Ingrid, 339–340
Beattie Royal Commission on the Courts
    see Royal Commission on the Courts
Bell, Ernest, 34
Bell, Sir Francis, 34, 90
Bell Gully, 52, 61
Bell Gully and Izard, 42
Bell Gully Bell and Myers, 42
Bell Gully Buddle Weir
  competitive sports, 198
  hours worked, 184
  number of partners, 133
  women partners, 302
Bench *see* judiciary
Benjamin (later de Costa), Ethel, 28, 29,
    45, 50, 453
  academic achievement, 32, 83
  advertising for business, 89
  alcohol industry connection, 69
  Bar dinners, 71
  career as barrister sole, 42
    litigation and commercial work, 87
    paternalism, 62–63
    referral of work, 89–90